American Opera

Music in American Life

A list of books in the series appears at the end of this book.

American Opera

Elise K. Kirk

UNIVERSITY OF ILLINOIS PRESS

URBANA AND CHICAGO

Publication of this book was supported by a grant from the
Henry and Edna Binkele Classical Music Fund.

Library of Congress Cataloging-in-Publication Data
Kirk, Elise K. (Elise Kuhl), 1932–
American opera / Elise K. Kirk.
p.   cm. — (Music in American life)
Includes bibliographical references and index.
ISBN 0-252-02623-3
1. Opera—United States. I. Title. II. Series.
ML1711.K56   2001
782.1'0973—dc21   00-009959

C 5 4 3 2 1

To Harris, Colleen, and Karen

Contents

Preface   ix

Introduction: Opera—Lyric Barometer of American Life   1

Part 1: The Voyage, 1730 to 1915
1. The British Connection   11
2. The Earliest American Operas   23
3. National Themes and the American Image   36
4. Mime, Melodrama, and Song   58
5. Grand Opera—the American Way   78
6. In the Spirit of Comedy   99

Part 2: The Signposts, 1880 to 1960
7. Wagnerism and the American Muse   121
8. Native Americans through Symbolism and Song   139
9. American Opera at the Met: The Gatti-Casazza Story   160
10. From the Black Perspective   184
11. Innovators and Iconoclasts; or, Is It Opera?   206
12. The Impact of Mass Media   233

Part 3: The Discoveries, 1945 to the Turn of the Century
13. The New American Verismo   253
14. New York City Opera's "American Plan"   272
15. Dreamers of Decadence   292
16. Bold Turns on Familiar Paths   315
17. Heroes for Our Time   335
18. Toward the New Millennium and Beyond   359
Epilogue: American Opera at the Crossroads   383

Appendix: Milestones in American Opera   385
Acknowledgments   391
Notes   395
Index   437

Preface

ACCORDING TO A RECENT Opera America report, attendance at opera by Americans has been rising steadily since 1982. Between the decade of 1982 and 1992 alone, the American opera audience had grown by almost 25 percent, and the number of eighteen to twenty-four-year-olds attending opera in that period had increased by 18 percent. It is significant within the broad spectrum of American culture that this trend has continued through 1997, when opera's share of the total arts audience grew by 12.5 percent, more than any other art form. In 1997, the National Endowment for the Arts reported that attendance at opera in the United States totaled an impressive 9.2 million adults.

Along with this ever-growing interest in the art of opera, more operas composed by Americans are being commissioned, produced, published, and recorded now than ever before. The great success of John Corigliano's *Ghosts of Versailles* in 1991, moreover, and the millennium that seems to be encouraging nations to celebrate their cultures have spawned a new wave of operas and audiences. Still, when I told my opera-loving friend that I was completing a book on American opera, he said, "Oh, that will be a short one. There will be at least two, *Porgy and Bess* and *Nixon in China*." Indeed, the repertoires of opera companies continue to be dominated by Verdi, Mozart, Puccini, and Wagner. But lesser-known works are filling out the expanding seasons with increasing frequency as attendance at opera grows by leaps and bounds.

I was impressed by the fact that Edith Borroff discovered nearly four thousand operas composed by Americans over two centuries in her comprehensive *Checklist* (1992). If only a minutely small percentage of these operas are still performed, we have only to note how very few of the thousands of operas composed by Europeans over four centuries ever reach the stage. How many of Donizetti's some sixty-four operas are in the standard repertoires—six? How many Italian opera composers from the time of Verdi through Puccini, almost a century, can one name—eight, ten? History has shown that it takes years and decades to create true genius. If the quest for enduring American operas appears a fantastic voyage, it is a mission the composers, opera companies, and audiences of a still relatively young country must—and will—continue to explore.

Some argue that American opera is derivative. But isn't all art? As Robert T. Jones observes, "There are no virgin births in the realm of ideas. Everything is connected to something else." And how can a critic call Menotti—or anyone else for that matter—"dated"? Is Schubert dated? Mahler? Handel? We need to stand back and look at American opera as a special product of American culture—an operatic culture just as indigenous as jazz, Duncan Phyfe furniture, and apple pie. It should receive the same loving care in history books as European opera. Why should European music receive all the adjectives and verbs, asks Borroff, while American music is limited to nouns? European opera is studied and afforded lively discussion, whereas American opera is relegated to the "list." And if, once performed, American operas do not remain in the repertoire, perhaps we should reexamine just what it is we have created for the fickle American public whose obsession with the latest movie has the life expectancy of an ice sculpture.

For those who claim opera is "elitist" (that miserable cliché), let them follow the twists and turns of American opera as it journeyed across the wide landscapes of American theatrical history. American opera tells more about Americans and their nation than any other art form—how they viewed women and perceived race, sexuality, jazz, social issues, family life, and politics. Who were the nation's heroes? it asks. Whom and what did Americans admire? Where did they find spirituality? What moved them? Who were those who struggled to create these operas? What shaped their thoughts? What informed their creations?

Paul Henry Lang once said that opera is not a play with music but a play in music. I take the position that opera is a dramatic art form—a theater work whose story is told in music, text, and staging. Although the tale itself may at times be nebulous, its characters are invariably strong, interacting with true human feelings expressed through dramatic pacing and song. The term *opera,* from the Latin meaning 'work,' can imply a variety of music theater forms. In America, the term was used variously to describe masque, ballad opera, harlequinade, pantomime, melodrama, and music theater. In examining these early forms, I was interested not so much in *what* music appeared but *how* it was used, for it is music's vital role in heightening the drama that defines the true character of these works and unites them in a common aesthetic bond that extends to modern times.

Theater historians, often the only source for musicologists interested in this field, rarely mention, let alone discuss, the music that appears in nineteenth-century American plays and melodramas, yet many were infused with arias, choruses, and dramatic orchestral underpinning that bring them well into the realm of opera. The harlequinade (English pantomime) also played an important role in American operatic history through its vocal interludes, characteristic instrumental underscoring of action and mood, and spectacular stage effects. I felt it was important to examine these forms not only as forerunners of American grand opera but also because they tell much about how Americans combined music and drama. Even in the early ballad opera and pastiche forms, composers and compilers found expressive ways for music to serve the drama, and the importance Americans placed on music as a dramatic tool escalated as technology developed and the film industry flourished.

In selecting operas to discuss in my book, I chose those I found most interesting from the standpoint of artistic merit, popularity, historic importance, and cultural expression. I also chose works whose scores, librettos, and audiovisual sources are for the most part available in order to ease and encourage further investigation. Because many early opera scores have been lost, the corresponding extant librettos and promptbooks were invaluable because they usually indicated where, how, and what music was used and provided informative stage directions. I also investigated composers and librettists' manuscripts, archival recordings, radio broadcasts, television programs, and live performances. In most of my discussions of scenes from the operas, I have chosen to document my source for the entire opera rather than annotate individual lines.

For purposes of this study, "American composers" are those either born in the United States or immigrants who created a representative percentage of their major works in the United States and contributed to its cultural growth. American operas, because they are in the English language and represent the many moods, tales, and regions of the nation, provide an excellent basis for the study of American culture. Their dramaturgical and musical ties with nineteenth-century American melodrama—little studied until now—make this book valuable for understanding the nature of opera itself.

How librettists often adapted texts for operas from American plays is also a particularly fascinating study that enlarges understanding of both American literature and the process of creating opera. The style of the American libretto varied immensely not only from period to period but also from composer to composer. In Marvin David Levy's *Mourning Becomes Electra* (1967, rev. 1998), for example, Henry Butler retains only twenty lines of Eugene O'Neill's prose, and Philip Littell's libretto for Andre Previn's *A Streetcar Named Desire* (1998) is a much more literal version of Tennessee Williams's original play. The two approaches to their literary sources create very different musical works with varying levels of dramatic impact. American opera librettos, therefore, offer students and aficionados of the nation's cultural life many provocative paths for exploration.

I view this book as an introduction, a starting point in an area never before investigated from a wide historical perspective and a particular dramatic focus. Although the work is not a textbook, scholarly thesis, or production guide, it opens the door to all three possibilities. My aim is to present American opera within its historical and social context, leaving room for others to explore the myriad of related details such as literary history, revisions, prosody, aria forms, harmonic language, and many other areas I touch upon. My concern is not with defining American opera by its "American" attributes or with demonstrating an overall "American operatic style." Rather, I have tried to capture the flavor of American opera—to see how the nation combines music and drama and to explore the forces that shaped this most characteristic and vital of American arts. Having excavated this fertile ground, I leave it to others for building upon in the future.

American Opera

INTRODUCTION

Opera—Lyric Barometer of American Life

STORYTELLING THROUGH MUSIC is as old as humanity itself. From the mystical messages in the song of the wind to the spiritual terror of the ancient "Dies Irae," from the images of love in the French chanson to the lively wit of the English madrigal—tales are told through music in a manner like no other. Opera—that powerful melding of music and drama—is the ultimate musical tale. Through poetry, singing, acting, costumes, lighting, scenery, and instrumental color, personalities assume a stronger identity, emotions are validated, and the message of the theater, whether symbol or story, is intensified unlike any other artistic expression. Opera, moreover, opens not only eyes and ears but also minds and hearts, and it draws us irresistibly into a world of conflict and resolution, ritual, and reflection. Opera, then, is not only an art form. It is a unique mode of communication whose persuasive powers are derived from the creative melding of many varied elements of the theater.

Just as European opera tells much about a nation's surrounding culture, American opera reflects the life and times of its people. Its origins and early history, however, differed from those of Europe. Opera was born in Italy, where in 1597 Jacopo Peri's *Dafne* was given its premiere at the Palazzo Corsi in Florence. Three years later, at the Palazzo Pitti, Peri's *Euridice* and Giulio Caccini's *Il rapimento di Cefalo* were performed for the royal wedding of Henry IV of France and Marie de Medici. American opera began some 150 years later, not in a sumptuous palace but in a plain college hall where an audience from all levels of society attended the staged production of *Alfred* in 1757. The most popular theatrical forms in early America, however, were lighter, more accessible comic operas. They were often adaptations from the English and were usually performed in taverns, inns, and small theaters that had wooden benches and simple stages. America's first operas were born into a democracy that influenced both their creative development and the ways they were absorbed and perceived. America was a young nation of explorers, a gutsy, hardy breed—seeking adventure and craving surprises with a curiosity that kept expanding, Barnum-style, like a genie out of a bottle. In some respects, Americans are still like that. "We must always allow for, and welcome, the unexpected and improbable in any art and certainly in opera," Carlisle Floyd observes.[1]

During the nineteenth and early twentieth centuries, American operas of a more ambitious, serious nature spread across the nation. From East Coast cities to the plains of the Midwest, and from Vernal, Utah, to San Francisco, these productions played to a wide variety of audiences that numbered from fifty at a Chicago music club to twenty-two thousand at the Hollywood Bowl. Drawing first upon English and French models and then mainly upon Italian and German, American opera has always managed to bring something of its own to its scores, creating—through jazz, popular song, folk music, American Indian motifs, Hollywood cinematic techniques, minimalism, or all of the above—an energy of its own, a spirit of its own.

American operas have been composed by women, blacks, film writers, teachers, politicians, poets, and philanthropists during wars, prosperity, social crises, feminist unrest, racial tension, and political change. Its subjects have ranged from American history to Indian legend and from folklore to current news. Its characters—from Rip van Winkle and Porgy to Treemonisha and Harvey Milk—have been strong, provocative, and telling, revealing not only their souls but also something of our own as well.

With such a diversity of influences and impulses, is it any wonder that America has produced no "school" of opera composition, no one central style? American opera is a true celebration of diversity. Its eclecticism—its panorama of styles, subjects, and moods that seems to know no boundaries—both reflects and defines its people. With the possible exception of Gian Carlo Menotti in the 1940s and 1950s, there has been no one leader or enduring teacher. Whether William Henry Fry or Walter Damrosch in the nineteenth century or Deems Taylor, Virgil Thomson, George Gershwin, Douglas Moore, or Philip Glass in the twentieth, each composer, each opera, is distinctive and offers an element of surprise along the path to discovery that lies at the heart of American artistic expression.

Although the United States cannot claim a clearly defined "American" style of opera, as one speaks of an "Italian" style or "German" or "French," one can determine an approach to opera that seems especially characteristic of the modern American sensibility—a penchant for realism, or "American verismo." Made popular first by Gian Carlo Menotti with *The Medium* and *The Consul* and developed further by Lee Hoiby, Robert Ward, Stephen Paulus, Carlisle Floyd, and others, American verismo concerns everyday people caught in passionate crises underscored by a highly cinematic and expressive orchestral score. The dramatic impetus comes mainly from modern American literature and motion pictures. The musical realization of verismo, however, reflects each American composer's steadfast individuality in working with a particular melodic, tonal, and instrumental pallet. Through these means, composers create a wide variety of operatic idioms and styles true to the American creative spirit.

If that tells us, however simplistically, what is *American* about American opera, then what is *operatic* about it? That is a harder question to answer but no less exciting and challenging. To discover just what ties together all these styles and operatic modes of utterance is to discover an important element that defines the art of opera. It is commonly held that unless a theater work retains a narrative rise and fall of tension—or a plot—it is not opera. Yet there are many instances in opera, especially in American works, where symbolism, parody, ritual, spectacle, movement, and pageantry are not only part of opera but also the entire point. This book is not only about operatic functions—about Americanisms, social patterns, or even about history—but also about the powerful role that music plays in bringing characters, symbol, and drama to life. That vital role made explorers of composers and brought wonders to audiences.

The expressive powers of music have been well understood by American opera composers from James Ralph to Carlisle Floyd, providing a long continuum of dramaturgical thought that allows understanding their varied creative processes with greater clarity and interest. In general, from colonial times to the present, a progressively closer alliance between music and text has brought about a romanticizing—indeed, intensification—of American opera characters within their theatrical environments. As early as the first American comic opera, *The Disappointment* (1767), creative delineation of character was achieved through clever dialogue, progression of plot, and appropriate borrowed tunes. The sense of tragic loss in the heroic opera (or masque) *Alfred* was profoundly realized through the interpolation of dramatic arias from Handel and Terradellas.

The most expressive early form of American opera was the provocative harlequinade as interpolated by American-born James Ralph into his ballad opera *The Fashionable Lady,* first performed in London in 1730. In the harlequinade's alliance of music with gesture, action, and mood, many aspects of later American opera can be noted: a penchant for fantasy, passion, excess, and spectacle; varied musical idioms that express and motivate the drama; clearly delineated characters who define the action; and an orchestral fabric as vital to the finished product as thread to a tapestry.

Derived from the commedia dell'arte, the harlequinade as performed in America into the early nineteenth century pointed the way to the more serious pantomime, with its continuous background music reflecting character and action. That tradition in turn evolved into the melodrama, which had arias, choruses, and stronger orchestral underpinning, to form American grand opera.

Techniques of musical dramaturgy in nineteenth-century American melodrama, which underscored dialogue with music, became especially important in the all-sung operas of the later nineteenth and early twentieth centuries. In many American operas that were sung throughout, the recitative took over from what would have been dialogue in portraying rapid action and conflict. Highly charged recitative became increasingly dramatic and was often reserved for intensely aggravated moments, as in comparable scenes in the melodrama. The recitative in William Henry Fry's *Leonora* (1845), for example, bears expressive markings similar to those of concurrent melodramas—"stormy," "agitated," and the like.

In the early twentieth century, Kurt Weill and Mark Blitzstein used a collage of recitative, spoken dialogue, aria, and melodramatic techniques (music under dialogue) to propel the drama forward and enlarge characterization. In so doing they formed a new vernacular musical idiom that provided American opera with an important fresh dimension. Some composers used variants of recitative to shape the entire structure of their operas, as Bernard Herrmann's use of "parlando" (heightened lyrical speech) in *Wuthering Heights* or Louis Gruenberg's *sprechgesang* (a form of singing somewhere between dialogue and recitative) in *The Emperor Jones.* Others—William Grant Still (*Troubled Island*), Carlisle Floyd (*Susannah*), Robert Ward (*The Crucible*), and many more—forged well ahead of the old melodrama in exploring new dramatic paths through varied approaches to recitative. George Gershwin's compelling recitatives in *Porgy and Bess,* for example, not only illuminate the raw emotions of the characters but also the dramatic associative powers of the orchestra. Realistic dialogue stemming from the melodrama and realized musically through operatic recitative or lyric declamation has long been a characteristic strength of American opera composers.

Perhaps the most powerful influence on modern American opera is a form one step removed from melodrama: the motion picture. American opera came of age in the twentieth century, and although influences emanated from Europe (Wagner, Strauss, Puccini, and Berg) and from Broadway, American motion pictures with their pictorially evocative orchestral scores ultimately shaped the sound and temper of contemporary American opera. Early motion pictures contained orchestral scores with continuous music following the mercurial needs of the drama so closely that film composer Erich Korngold called them operas without singing.[2] Yet many opera composers, notably Samuel Barber in *Vanessa,* treat the orchestra as in a film—another character whose motifs, themes, and colors often reveal more about the drama than do the singers onstage.

Writing for both opera and film has enlarged the dramatic perspectives of several important American composers, such as George Antheil, Bernard Herrmann, William Grant Still, Aaron Copland, and Andre Previn, composer of *A Streetcar Named Desire* (1998). Previn claims that he learned from Hollywood what an orchestra was capable of doing. The scores of younger contemporary opera composers—Jake Heggie, Tobias Picker, Lowell Liebermann, and others—also reflect growing up with America's number one theatrical force: movies. Even audiences, maintains composer Libby Larsen, are so preconditioned by movies and television that their perception of how human emotions unfold has changed.[3]

As Mozart, Verdi, and many others drew inspiration from plays, composers now have at their disposal both plays and motion pictures to provide a rich font of dramatic, character-driven material for their operas. What gives American opera dramatic life? Lotfi Mansouri, general director of San Francisco Opera, which commissioned three new American operas for the early millennium years, claims "opera, like motion pictures, must have strong characters, a good central conflict and—most importantly— a subject the audience cares about."[4] Indeed, history has demonstrated that a successful subject for an American opera lies not only in its "American" framework but also in a composer's skills in realizing a subject as musical drama.

American opera fell under the spell of the ideology, dramaturgy, visual techniques, and musical approaches of motion pictures as early as the silent film era. John Philip Sousa used actual motion picture clips in *The American Maid* (1909, formerly *The Glass Blowers*) about the same time Scott Joplin was embellishing his score for *Treemonisha* with musical figurations of silent film pianists. In 1929 Joseph Breil wrote an opera with the fast action and "rapid outlines of a motion picture."[5] Large screens with projections, moreover, formed the stage designs of George Antheil's *Transatlantic* and Frederick Keisler's conceptions at the Metropolitan Opera during the 1930s.

It is no small coincidence that the American verismo style in opera should develop early in the twentieth century at about the same time as the motion picture. As the rich, romantic cinema scores of the 1930s, 1940s, and beyond developed—with their explicit associative themes and motifs—composers such as Blitzstein, Weill, Herrmann, Hoiby, Paulus, and many others wrote operas following along the lines and subjects of these popular films.

Motion picture directors have also played an important role in opera, often adding intensity to the characterization through effective movement and acting. Much of the success of Marvin David Levy's *Mourning Becomes Electra,* produced by the Metropolitan Opera in 1967, can be attributed to the high level of acting and passionate interaction of the characters as conceived by theater and movie director Michael Cacoyannis. And Washington Opera's powerful realization of Ward's *The Crucible* in 1999 owes much to Bruce Beresford's engrossing body-language approach.

The influence of film and television is also apparent in numerous American operas, from those of Dominick Argento and Philip Glass to the works of Libby Larsen and William Bolcom. Enormous demands have been placed on the role of directors or stage designers, now stars in their own rights. Resembling techniques of the modern film, rapid, short changes of scene are especially challenging—a kind of "constantly rolling from one world into another" in the words of Colin Graham, who has directed more than fifty premiere productions, including John Corigliano's grand opera buffa spectacle *The Ghosts of Versailles.*[6] Perhaps we are not as far removed from the old American harlequinade, with its spectacular staging and visual thrills, as we might think.

Undoubtedly the greatest bonus American opera now enjoys is the interest in the form shown by world-renowned singers such as Renée Fleming, Thomas Hampson, Susan Graham, Frederica von Stade, Samuel Ramey, Dawn Upshaw, Jerry Hadley, and many others. Some opera companies hire the singers before commissioning the operas, and composers often consult singers before even writing scores. In the early days of American grand opera, most of the best singers were foreign-born and did not know English, making it very difficult for American opera composers to see their works performed well or performed at all. The Metropolitan Opera's manager, Gatti-Casazza, remedied that by hiring a roster of fine American-born singers during the 1920s and 1930s, thus drawing attention to the beauties of the American voice and contributing to the success of many premieres.

To project their characters within the drama, singers now must use body language as well as voice, and their English diction must have passion as well as purity. Unlike the fluid warmth of Italian, the English language is replete with consonants that can often hinder the production of a beautiful tone. Some American composers prefer to set the most important lines of a passage in the lower or middle registers of the voice, knowing that offers better clarity in communicating the text than the higher registers.

Others use vowels and consonants for dramatic, expressive power, as Robert Ward does with short consonants or Jack Beeson with longer vowels. Ward also takes musical cues from the pitch inflections and rhythmic patterns of the English text, a practice he feels gives singers melodic lines with a natural-sounding dramatic flow.

For the Metropolitan Opera Auditions held across the United States, all singers are required to include at least one piece originally composed in the English language. Many young artists, though, are delighted to do so because they believe that modern operas connect to their own lives. "They feel they are part of something new," says composer Michael Daugherty.[7] American opera gives them a sense of bravery, a feeling they can become a whole singing actor by communicating with audiences more intimately and directly than through a foreign tongue.

Audiences for new opera must also have a sense of bravery. Although opera may be written in one's native language and have themes that relate to familiar experiences, American opera for most people is still "Opera"—an esoteric art form that requires stepping into a strange, larger-than-life world of imagination, passion, and overstatement. Still, more people than ever—whether young, old, prosperous, or of humble means—are packing opera houses to capacity. Opera has been produced and marketed as a democratic form of entertainment from the earliest days of the nation, but for many it is not perceived that way. For them, "elitism" and "opera" are synonymous. The reasons are complex and must be pursued with diligence. But one answer might be found in the cultural hierarchy set up during the later nineteenth century as wealthy power bases were needed to support the increasingly expensive and elaborate productions of opera. As the century turned, moreover, the commercial music industry separated pop from classical into vernacular and cultivated, manifest even in record bins and catalogs. The question is whether opera is destined to be not only about art and quality but also about class.

Hegel once observed that music expressed the ohs and ahs of the soul. "The human voice expresses a rich inner life," he said, "from which the soul breaks into utterance."[8] American opera composers from the earliest days have found many ways to meld music and drama into fine opera. From them we have learned some enduring lessons: The lines of demarcation between the various forms and styles of opera are transparent and pliable, and all share a common bond. Vernacular and cultivated, comic and serious, pageant and narrative—all reach out to the soul as well as to the eye and ear. How composers, librettists, performers, and entrepreneurs achieved this in a young nation that spread its wings and soared to amazing heights is a true adventure story—and the story of this book.

PART I

The Voyage, 1730 to 1915

I hear the chorus, it is a grand opera,
Ah this indeed is music—this suits me,

A tenor large and fresh as the creation fills me,
The orbic flex of his mouth is pouring and filling me full.

I hear the train'd soprano (what work with hers is this?)
The orchestra whirls me wider than Uranus flies,
It wrenches such ardors from me I did not know I possess'd them,
It sails me, I dab with bare feet, they are lick'd by the indolent waves,
I am cut by bitter and angry hail, I lose my breath,
Steep'd amid honey'd morphine, my windpipe throttled in fakes of death,
At length let up again to feel the puzzle of puzzles,
And that we call Being.
—Walt Whitman, "Song of Myself" from *Leaves of Grass,* 1855

1

The British Connection

When farce and when Musick can eke out a Play
Can write for the Stage, and contend for the Bay,
Hang Graces, and Muses, we need not their Aid,
'Tis our tunes that we trust, and our Tunes are all made.
  —James Ralph, *The Fashionable Lady; or, Harlequin's Opera,* 1730

NO ART FORM REFLECTS the moods, dreams, and passions of its people quite as powerfully as opera. The history of American opera is a history of the American people—how they felt about their country and expressed themselves in song and drama. The first settlers brought with them the diverse styles and forms of musical storytelling that were familiar to them and provided diversion. The earliest recorded theatrical performance presented in North America is believed to have been a Spanish *comedia* staged in 1598 near what is today El Paso, Texas.

In the seventeenth century, records indicate that religious plays with music were produced in Spanish missions in what is now Florida, and the many secular plays presented in eastern seaboard cities throughout the eighteenth century almost always contained music. The English colonists literally transplanted to American soil their lighthearted ballad operas, pasticcios, and the like—operatic forms that were satiric, political, and a bit bawdy at times but always entertaining. The new Americans drew from what they knew and shaped it toward the aesthetic and entertainment needs of their young nation. Within their attitudes was a rugged independence—a no-nonsense philosophy that believed the best living did not necessarily have to be founded on the most sophisticated thinking.

Unlike Mozart, Verdi, Wagner, and other European composers born into already rich national cultural legacies, American composers had a far different story to tell—a story all the more remarkable considering that their nation's operatic tradition began as settlers were discovering strange shores, plowing new lands, and fighting for freedom. Daniel Boorstin notes that "one of the contrasts between the culture of Europe and that of the United

States is that the older culture traditionally depended on the monumental accomplishments of the few, while the newer culture—diffused, elusive, process-oriented—depended more on the novel, accreting ways of
the many. . . . It was not the system of a few great American Thinkers, but
the mood of Americans thinking."[1] Crèvecoeur put it another way:"There
is room for everybody in America; has he any particular talent, or industry? He exerts it in order to procure a livelihood, and it succeeds."[2]

For the new nation, the term *opera* had many meanings. Far from Italian opera, which was sung throughout and considered esoteric in England,
American settlers enjoyed operas that were more in the nature of musical
shows, both with and without spoken dialogue or central plot. Ballad
operas, a type of light, satiric play interspersed with strophic songs set to
traditional or popular tunes, were especially enjoyed. But "pure" ballad
opera was a short-lived form. By the time John Gay and Johann Pepusch's
Beggar's Opera (1728) was first performed in America nearly a quarter of a
century after its London premiere, tunes from more serious dramatic works
were included in ballad operas and sometimes even newly composed for
them. In both England and America by 1800, "opera" could mean ballad
opera, now shortened to an "afterpiece"; comic opera, composed largely
by one person; pantomime, using dance and more elaborate staging; or even
melodrama, a play with background music to underpin the plot and height-
en emotions.

This admixture of terms and crossover of styles can be seen especially
in the subtitles of individual works: pasticcio, burletta, dramatic fable, farce,
extravaganza, opera-ballet, comic masque, interlude, afterpiece, and olla
podrida (hodgepodge). It was common to see a music theater piece advertised as "tragi-comi-pastoral farcical opera" or a "histori-tragi-comi-
ballad opera"; there was something for everyone it seems. There were also
melodramas and masques, which were often far more operatic in style and
scope than many works called operas. Plays, too, regularly contained songs,
marches, and choruses. For the audiences of the day, the word *opera* bore
a mantle of many hues. What was important about the early operatic works,
however, is not what they were called but what they expressed and not
what music was used but how it was used. The close alliance of music,
drama, and character now associated with the art form of opera developed
with more intensity as the century turned and Romanticism gained momentum.

As modern Americans do with movies and television, eighteenth-century Americans devoured musical entertainments. Whether in 1718 in
Williamsburg's proud new little theater with its five windows or New York's

more spacious Nassau Street Theatre in the 1750s, audiences cheered, hissed, visited with friends, and called out for their favorite songs. Many early productions were modestly staged in taverns, inns, or wherever appropriate space could be found. In Charleston, South Carolina, the first recorded performance of a ballad opera in America took place in a courtroom, where *Flora; or, Hob in the Well* by Colley Cibber and John Hippesley was performed on February 18, 1735, only six years after its London premiere. Unlike *The Beggar's Opera,* which is set in London, *Flora* takes place in a country village. Its frothy antics—a mother pulls her son out of a well and mistakes him for a monster (a "hob" is hobgoblin or elf)—seemed to appeal to America's more rustic sensibilities than *The Beggar's Opera* with its thieves and whores.[3]

Although New Orleans opened its first opera house in 1791, the main centers for ballad opera and its derivatives during the eighteenth century were Philadelphia, New York, Boston, Baltimore, and Charleston. It was Philadelphia, however, that became the springboard for the nation's earliest attempts at opera. But when James Ralph, America's adventurous opera composer, began his career early in the eighteenth century, Philadelphia was a city not quite born. Slightly larger than Boston, it had a population of ten thousand, and artistic expression was restricted because of Quaker traditions and regulations. During the annual meeting of the Friends in 1716, members were advised against "going to or being in any way concerned in plays, games, lotteries, music, and dancing."[4] Later in the century Philadelphia would become the cultural capital of America.

For the young James Ralph, however, only London could offer the literary challenges he desired. After leaving Philadelphia in 1724, he wrote *The Fashionable Lady; or, Harlequin's Opera,* and it was given its premiere on April 2, 1730, at Goodman's Fields. Although it was not staged on American soil, it is the earliest opera by an American to be both published and produced. Even more important, in its delineation of character, use of spectacle, and instrumental tone-painting it brought vital new dramaturgical dimensions to the history of English and American opera.

James Ralph's Fashionable Lady

James Ralph was born in 1695, either in Pennsylvania or what is now New Jersey.[5] While still in his teens he became a merchant's clerk in Philadelphia and a close friend of Benjamin Franklin, who found him "ingenious, genteel in his manners and extremely eloquent."[6] In December 1724 Ralph left his wife and baby daughter to follow Franklin to London, where he came in contact with nearly every one of that city's great artistic minds, including Alexander Pope, Samuel Johnson, and William Hogarth, whose book *Analysis of Beauty* (1733) Ralph edited. From 1733 to 1737 he served as assistant manager at the Little Theatre, Haymarket under Henry Fielding, author of the novel *Tom Jones* and the popular ballad opera *The Mock Doctor* (1732) staged years later in America.

Ralph wrote an impressive number of critiques, essays, and books, but his finest work is the two-volume *History of England* (1744–46), which is still a valuable reference for the study of Restoration and Revolutionary England. Ralph was also an accomplished poet. Several of his poems in blank verse, written a few years after he came to London, such as "The Tempest" (1728) and his elegiac "Night" (1727), have references to America. His dramatic works include a tragedy, *The Fall of the Earl of Essex* (1731), and two comedies, *The Lawyer's Feast* and *The Astrologer*, both staged in 1744. Of these, his ballad opera *The Fashionable Lady; or, Harlequin's Opera* was the most successful. It received sixteen performances within the five weeks that it was staged. When Ralph died on January 24, 1764, in Chiswick, he had managed to live the last years of his life quite comfortably through a sizable pension from the English crown.

The Fashionable Lady was written during one of the most exciting and progressive periods in English theater history. *The Beggar's Opera,* with text by John Gay and music arranged by Johann Pepusch, was taking all of London by storm. It was first produced at Lincoln's Inn Fields on January 29, 1728, and ran for sixty-two nights its first season, the longest run on the English stage for nearly a century. Its immense popularity and box-office appeal spawned similar works; more than one hundred ballad operas were written between 1728 and 1750.[7]

Why was the ballad opera so successful? It reached everyone. By using well-known airs, everyday characters, and spoken dialogue, it poked fun at the contemporaneous Italian *opera seria,* which employed long, elaborate arias and complex plots. Another aspect of the ballad opera, the element of parody, also contributed to its popularity. As in the seventeenth-century *comédie en vaudevilles,* the texts of many songs in *The Beggar's Opera* were set to familiar tunes. But the original source for a particular tune was important to the effect the song would communicate in the new dramatic context that the author supplied. Borrowing, in other words, became a unique form of dramatic symbolism and a highly effective art.[8] James Ralph was an especially skillful parodist and had a keen sense of the dramatic and lyrical content of a song. He also added a new element to ballad opera—the harlequinade, a special form of English pantomime that helped shape the dramatic spirit of American opera and music theater for decades to come.

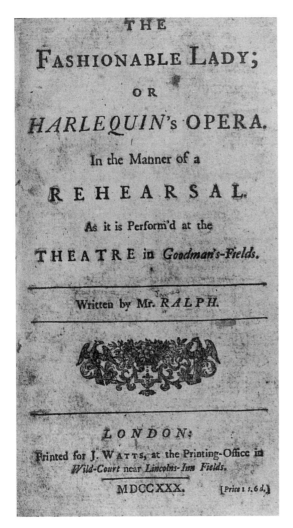

THE

FASHIONABLE LADY;

OR

HARLEQUIN'S OPERA.

In the Manner of a

REHEARSAL.

As it is Perform'd at the

THEATRE in *Goodman's-Fields.*

Written by Mr. *RALPH.*

LONDON:

Printed for J. WATTS, at the Printing-Office in
Wild-Court near *Lincolns-Inn Fields.*

MDCCXXX.   [Price 1 *s.* 6 *d.*]

Title page from *The Fashionable Lady; or, Harlequin's Opera* (1730) by James Ralph, the earliest extant opera by an American. *Library of Congress*

The Fashionable Lady is a musical and literary satire on the pleasures and pitfalls of the era. Its plot, although too lengthy, provides a witty and effective venue for Ralph's kaleidoscopic moods. His main target was the current ballad opera fad. But, like its modern counterpart, John Corigliano's *Ghosts of Versailles, The Fashionable Lady* is not so much a satire on opera as on the perception of opera. In that regard, Ralph moves into a different territory than Gay and his contemporaries with their political and social satire, bawdy rogues, and low-life overtones. Ralph was a masterful critic, and his characters, even though allegorical, live and breathe through some excellent dialogue and finely wrought poetry. There is plenty of humor but always with a touch of elegance.

Like most ballad operas, *The Fashionable Lady* is in three acts, each containing numerous short scenes. The story takes place during the rehearsal of a play being produced by Mr. Drama and Mr. Ballad, and all its characters bear names that personify the vicissitudes of the contemporary theatrical scene.[9] Mrs. Foible, representing popular tastes or "Fashion," is an arrant coquette who has a multitude of suitors. Among them are the lovesick Mr. Merit, the fashionable Mr. Smooth, and a coarse seaman, Captain Hackum. Mrs. Foible is also admired by Mr. Trifle ("the Virtuoso") and Mr. Whim ("the Humorist"). They all go to see the master conjurer himself, Harlequin, who startles them with a variety of spectacular tricks. After a long struggle between "passion and reason," however, Merit decides Mrs. Foible is not for him. He falls into the willing arms of her cousin Mrs. Sprightly, who is much more sensible, witty, and wise. One by one, Mrs. Foible's suitors desert her, and by the end of the play she is left with only Harlequin. Because Ralph in his writings attacked the current practice of bringing into opera the pantomime—which traditionally had only mime without speaking and singing—Harlequin, so to speak, is now caught in the spell of the current "Foibles" of fashion.

Because of the lines he gives them and the songs he chooses for them, Ralph's characters become distinct personalities through beautifully drawn caricature. Nuances abound in their picturesque language: "Confound your *Amphion's,* your dancing Rocks, and Italian Gimcracks!" rages Ballad. "Confound this Italian! It ties up a Man's Voice like the Appearance of a Ghost at Midnight." But English opera, he continues, "makes me as eloquent as Mr. Quibble the orator, and as valiant as Captain Macheath or a prime Minister." "There is more Wit in a fiery Dragon, than in all the plays in Europe," Ballad complains in another scene. "I love your loud Horse-Laugh most exceedingly. I always distinguish myself at the Play-house by my Laugh." Ralph's ballads, however, distinguish themselves less by raucous laughs than by gentle smiles. He never misses a chance to attack Gay and *The Beggar's Opera:* "I love a noise," affirms Ballad, "the Whores and Highwaymen in one Opera, the Beggars in another, and the Rustiks in a third, make a noble symphony . . . i'faith it sounds better than Church-Musick."[10]

There are sixty-eight short songs, or ballads, in *The Fashionable Lady,* and in the practice of the time each uses the tune of an older song with new lyrics provided by the author. Theater-goers not only knew the tunes but also the various previous parodies. Often the parodies were so numerous that the symbolism became layered upon layer. The true art involved varying the text to provide fresh ideas while still retaining an identity with the original song. Air No. 40, "Winchester Wedding" from *The Fashionable Lady,* for example, appeared with different texts in at least fourteen ballad operas between 1728 and 1733.

The parody in Ralph's poetry offers a higher order of sentiment than that found in most ballad operas. He prefers to place the humorous lines in spoken dialogue, allowing the songs to enlarge its deeper expression, much as the aria in romantic opera. Sometimes he deliberately reverses the original sentiment of the song, as in Air No. 6, which is set to the tune of "Alexis Shunned His Fellow Survivors," a pastoral elegy. Rather than the lamentation found in the song, Ralph provides celebration. The final lines of the original, for example, read: "He mingled his concern with theirs / He gave them back their friendly tears. / He sighed, but could not speak."[11] Ralph's poetry is a kind of mirror image: "But when I spoke her all divine, / Her soul became entranced with mine, / As mine with hers alone."[12]

Another parody is Air No. 59, to the tune of "Coal Black Joke." The song was originally associated with a type of English folk dance known as the morris dance or *moresca* (Moor's dance). It is traditionally performed by six men, sometimes with blackened faces, who had bells attached to their legs. The dance is suggested brilliantly at the end of the century in Mozart's *Magic Flute,* when the Moor, Monostatos, and his cohorts are charmed into dancing by Papageno's magic bells. Many earlier opera authors created lewd parodies of the tune. Ralph's desire to change the way the song was viewed reflects his own artistic goal: to progress from empty fashion to noble art. "No more the modish trifling Dame / Should lure my Vows, or taint my Fame," sings Merit. "Really," exclaims Mrs. Sprightly when the song is over. "This is a change indeed! I have hopes for you now. Before, I imagin'd one part of your Conduct was a Satire on the other."[13]

Because it was the practice to print the name of the author and not the arranger or "composer," one often must guess who assisted with the music. At the time *The Fashionable Lady* was being performed at Goodman's Fields, the music director there was George Monroe, a former pupil of Pepusch and Handel.[14] The author usually chose tunes in collaboration with a composer—or more accurately "arranger"—who realized them musically. Seated at the harpsichord, the arranger filled in the appropriate harmonies, accompanied by a violinist who would double the vocal line and a viol player or two who would render the bass. In rare instances, as in the case of Theophilus Cibber's *The Harlot's Progress* (1733), a more lavish instrumental ensemble was used.[15]

Ralph's cleverness in matching preexisting tunes with new texts shows his awareness of music's associative powers and its unique role in expressing character and mood. Air No. 23, for example, is in c minor with a key signature of two flats. The oscillation back and forth between pitches A and A-flat seems to reflect the psychological confusion that love causes a lover expressed in Ralph's poetry. His thoughts, so to speak, are "ever roving," and "Gay delusions cloud him over." Air No. 48, from "Over the Hills and Far Away," offers a musical getaway as the song begins in B-flat but ends in c minor. The poetry refers to the enchanting tricks of Harlequin but warns him in the final line: "Fly, wiley Traitor, far away."

The true theatricality of Ralph's creative imagination, however, shines most effectively in the Harlequin scenes. The harlequinade is a special form of English pantomime, which derived from the Italian commedia dell'arte as it was developed in France. Along with Harlequin, its stock characters included Columbine, Pantaloon, Scaramouch, Pierrot, and Punch, all of whom appear in *The Fashionable Lady*. Writing in 1728, John Weaver indicates that the early English pantomimes consisted of a story or fable "carried on by Dancing, Action, and Motion only . . . performed by Grotesque characters after the modern Italian."[16] The term *grotesque* was equated with "fantastic" and used to describe commedia dell'arte characters well into the nineteenth century. The earlier pantomimes were only mimed. Later, however, song, recitatives, and ensembles were added and then, toward the end of the century, dialogue. Weaver speaks of the "dances" as stylized, expressive "gesture." *"Admiration,"* he writes, "is discover'd by the raising up of the right Hand, the Palm turn'd upwards, the Fingers clos'd. . . . The left Hand struck suddenly with the Right; and sometimes against the Breast; denotes *Anger.*"[17]

An important period for the harlequinade was between 1714 and 1741, when John Rich was manager of Lincoln's Inn Fields. One of Rich's big hits, *The Necromancer; or, Harlequin Dr. Faustus,* staged in 1723, placed the harlequinade firmly in the sphere of mass popular culture for almost a century. Although eventually Harlequin was relegated to the role of circus clown, his modern spirit is not far from that of Charlie Chaplin in the silent film era. Indeed, the pantomime's use of spectacle and continuous music to underpin character and drama became the lifeblood of the theater, shaping ballet, melodrama, motion pictures, and opera well into modern times.

Body language was vital to pantomime, but what really attracted audiences in droves were the tricks and escapades of Harlequin. Here was the lure of fantasy—its penchant for the startling, the weird, the spectacular, and the daring. Harlequin leaped to the moon or descended into the underworld. His magic wand, or bat, could transform a palace into a hut, a man into a wheelbarrow, colonnades into beds of tulips, and mechanics' shops into ostriches. Witches, demons, and other bizarre creatures—even a seventeen-foot-long clockwork snake—inhabited the stage of Harlequin. Perhaps Richard Wagner knew the harlequinade. His *Ring* has its share of fantasy: a magic sword, an omnipotent spear, a giant turned into a dragon, and a dwarf transformed into a toad—not to mention the great ring of gold itself. Like Wagner's spectacle and the deus ex machina of Italian

Air, "Ghosts of Ev'ry Occupation," from Harlequin scene (act 2, scene 2) in *The Fashionable Lady*. *Library of Congress*

Baroque opera, the pantomime, too, must have required deft mechanical maneuvering.

James Ralph was a pioneer in bringing the harlequinade to ballad opera in a successful production.[18] His approach in *The Fashionable Lady* adds a new dimension of theatricality to ballad opera through Harlequin's phantasmal antics and mime, but even more important Harlequin provides lively action in a rather motionless work. Interposed within each act of the opera, his scenes contain the only stage directions printed in the libretto. The appearance of Harlequin, moreover, offers fresh opportunity for wit and satire—and most likely background or action music, thus sewing the dramaturgical seeds for melodrama, opera, and, eventually, the cinema.

Another aspect of the harlequinade that particularly attracted audiences was the scenery; the frequent scene changes that appeared to take place almost instantaneously by the raising and lowering of different backcloths were part of the fun. Toward the close of act 3, scene 14 of *The Fashionable Lady,* however, the staging appears overburdened with mythological and allegorical types—probably to poke fun at audiences' perennial fascination with spectacle and fantasy: "SCENE drawing, discovers Harlequin in his Chair, Punch, Scaramouch, Pierot [*sic*], Pantaloon, in the Manner and Posture of Statues, behind him: Two Giants, one on each side of the Stage; by one stands Cerberus, by the other Pegasus; beyond them Angels and Furies promiscuously ranged; the Devil and Death ending the Line: Above are Machines of Gods and Goddesses, Dragons and Witches astride them; the back Scene decorated with the Sun and Moon, one Range of Scenery a Colonnade, the other a Wood." "You little Dog!" Ballad says to Drama. "What a scene is here! Faith the Essence and Quintessence of every Entertainment extant."[19]

There would have been an overture to *The Fashionable Lady,* but like the instrumental score it has been lost. What role that instrumental music played, in addition to accompanying songs, remains a tantalizing question. Could the harpsichordist have provided transitional interludes between the dialogues and the songs? Quite possibly. That would not only have unified the drama but also enabled the singers to obtain their pitches. More important is the question of how closely allied the music was to the dramatic escapades of the harlequinades. Could instrumental music have been played during these scenes to underpin the actions? We know that around 1740 action designations such as "hurry" appear within "Comic Tunes" intended for miming. Later in the century, works such as Charles Dibdin's *The Touchstone; or, Harlequin Traveller* (1779) illustrate how expressive music had become in not only reflecting the action but also motivating it.[20]

Some of the stage directions in *The Fashionable Lady* offer clues about this characteristic alliance of music with gesture and action:"As they dance, Harlequin and his Companions join with them, in a humorous manner; and after playing them several Tricks, retire to their Places" (Air No. 41).[21] In another scene, lively antics take place during the jaunty, dancelike tune that Smoothly and Voice sing in Air No. 13:

> Smoothly:　While sweet, smooth, and clear'
> 　　　　　　Music charms your Ear,
> 　　　　　　Devils may be near'
> 　　　　　　　　Pois'ning the Sound
> 　　Voice:　Devils still are near'
> 　　　　　　Laughing in your Ear
> 　　　　　　When fools pay so dear,
> 　　　　　　　　Only for Sound.

"While he sings," continue the stage directions, "Harlequin and Pantaloon stand on his right Hand, mimicking his Action, Pierot [*sic*] and Scaramouch on his left, Voice behind; when he has done, they all Dance round him, till by degrees he is pushed into the Doctor's Chair; which rises towards the Roof of the House, while they continue dancing below."[22]

The opera closes with considerable action and "A GRAND DANCE," but Drama appears to have the last word in a brief closing epilogue:

> But now Muses fav'rite Sons arise,
> Politely learn'd and wise,
> Arise majestic to reform the Stage,
> And, with a nobler Scene, delight th' admiring age.[23]

If James Ralph did not "reform the stage," he did imbue it with "a nobler Scene." His elegant satire, understanding of music's role in underpinning character and mood, and use of the harlequinade to heighten fantasy, action, and drama brought ballad opera into a new, expressive terrain.

❧

Ralph's *The Fashionable Lady; or, Harlequin's Opera* never made its way to America, but its style and spirit were felt in the New World for almost a century. Only five years after *The Fashionable Lady* made its London premiere, America saw its earliest ballad opera, *Flora; or, Hob in the Well,* brought to Charleston, South Carolina, in 1735 from London. The performance was immediately followed by a "pantomime," *The Adventures of Harlequin and Scaramouch,* and for nearly a century other harlequinades like it drew audiences to the American stage. More important, these rather slight works pointed the way to later, more serious pantomimes and eventually to the nineteenth-century American melodrama, with its operatic arias, choruses, and especially its highly pictorial orchestral score.

2

The Earliest American Operas

For the future, the days of performance will be Tuesday and Friday. The Orchestra, on Opera Nights, will be assisted by some musical Persons, who, as they have no View but to contribute to the Entertainment of the Public, certainly claim a Protection from any Manner of Insult.

—*Pennsylvania Gazette,* Nov. 30, 1769

WHILE THE BALLAD OPERA and its many derivatives continued to "delight th' admiring age," important changes were taking place in the form itself. As it exhausted its supply of popular songs to parody, it gradually evolved into a pastiche that included more music by name composers and more attention to musical characterization and imagery. The new comic operas produced in London and Edinburgh during the second half of the century were often composed by one individual, but "composed" could still mean "compile." Thomas Arne's *Love in a Village* (1762), produced in Philadelphia in 1767, was a pastiche of forty-two pieces, only five of which were newly composed by Arne himself. But its musical settings were more elaborate than the earlier operas, with more complex duets, livelier finales, and richer orchestration.

If James Ralph had returned to Philadelphia in mid-century, he would have found a city quite different from the one he left in 1724. The colonial population, as a whole, had more than doubled, from 474,388 in 1720 to 1,207,000 estimated by 1750. In 1760 Philadelphia was the largest as well as the most rapidly growing city in America. Gilbert Stuart called it the "Athens of America."[1] Attracted by its industrial success and opportunities, settlers came from the southern Colonies, New England, the West Indies, and from England, Scotland, and Ireland. Many well-established merchant families lived in comfortable homes of fine red brick from the local clay bakes.

Philadelphia was also rapidly becoming the cultural capital of America, a position it held until about 1820 when it yielded its place to New York. Through the efforts of Francis Hopkinson and Gov. William Penn, a concert series was started in 1757 that included the works of the best English, Italian, and German composers of the time. In 1761 James Lyon published the first major book of music by an American, a collection of psalm tunes, anthems, and hymns entitled *Urania*. Six years later the American Company opened the Southwark Theatre and brought to the nation the finest comic operas of Thomas Arne, William Shield, Stephen Storace, Charles Dibdin, Thomas Attwood, and other popular English composers. By the time the Declaration of Independence was signed in 1776, Philadelphia was the "metropolis of the American continent." With thirty thousand inhabitants, it was second only to London as the center of the English-speaking world.[2] Philadelphia also saw the formation of the first nonsectarian college in America, the College of Philadelphia, chartered in 1755 and named the University of Pennsylvania in 1772. Associated with the young college were two historical musical events—the earliest operas to be composed in America. Harbingers of what was to come in the decades and centuries to follow, these works reflected the varied cultural moods of the nation—the one was lofty, spiritual, and heroic and the other, light, funny, and brashly American.

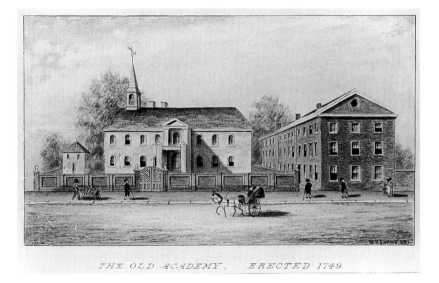

THE OLD ACADEMY,   ERECTED 1749

The Academy of the College of Philadelphia, where America's earliest attempt at serious opera, William Smith's *Alfred,* was produced in 1757. *Library Company of Philadelphia*

Modern universities are often centerpieces for innovation in the arts, but even in the eighteenth century theatrical expression was a vital part of the American academic life. Colleges such as William and Mary, Yale, Princeton, Dartmouth, and Harvard all performed dramas and oratorical pieces from time to time. But the story of Philadelphia's small college is particularly remarkable because its ambitious masque staged in 1757 was actually a serious opera. One of the key founders of the College of Philadelphia was James Ralph's friend Benjamin Franklin, who had returned to Philadelphia from London in 1727. An ardent music lover, Franklin contributed greatly to the cultural advancement of his adopted city. In addition to creating the American Philosophical Society, he became the first president of the trustees of the College of Philadelphia.

The fundamental ideals of the College of Philadelphia revolved around Franklin's conception of a purely English higher education that included a thorough understanding of the English language. Franklin's ideas were reinforced by the young provost he brought to the college, William Smith, who stated in the *Pennsylvania Gazette* on January 20, 1757, "Ever since the Foundation of the College and Academy in this City, the improvement of the Youth in Oratory and correct speaking has always been considered as an essential branch of their education." Like the practices of English universities and the Collegio Romano in Rome, student elocution at the college was enlarged through vital dramatic and musical expression.

Numbering only twenty students, the College of Philadelphia's first student body enrolled two Mohawk Indians, and its first graduating class in 1757 included a native Philadelphian, Francis Hopkinson (1737–91). Hopkinson was a remarkable public figure who had a wide variety of skills. Lawyer, inventor, and poet, he also became one of the signers of the Declaration of Independence and America's first secretary of the navy. From his earliest days at the college, he played the organ and harpsichord and composed songs in the current English comic opera and pleasure-garden style. One, "My Days Have Been so Wondrous Free" (ca. 1759), has been hailed as the earliest surviving American secular composition. It appears in a collection of nearly a hundred songs that Hopkinson copied out by hand. Housed in the Library of Congress, the collection provides valuable information on American taste in English song before the American Revolution. It comprises operatic excerpts, pastoral songs, duets, and hymns; among the composers represented are Handel, Arne, Purcell, Terradellas, Vinci, Palma, Giardini, Rameau, and Hopkinson himself, whose five songs are inscribed simply "F.H."[3]

Early Attempts at Heroic Opera

One of Hopkinson's earliest musical undertakings was participation in the College of Philadelphia's elegant dramatic production, the masque *Alfred* presented several times during January 1757.[4] Sometimes called "English opera," a masque was a form of court entertainment that employed solos, ensembles, recitatives, choruses, and sometimes dance. It was usually sung throughout, although at times spoken dialogue was included. Its plot was mainly allegorical and based on a classical theme or legend. In the history of American culture, the masque was to the development of serious opera what the ballad opera or pastiche was to comic opera. Both masque and ballad opera forms had dialogue, song, story, and staging, but each served a different aesthetic end.

When *Alfred* was performed at the College of Philadelphia in 1757, it was presented in costume and with "a set of new scenes that were painted for the representation."[5] Arthur Quinn describes the production as "the first native dramatic effort, containing original material and known to have been performed on the stage, that has come down to us."[6] To be sure, the story of the great ninth-century English monarch was highly dramatic, but even more important, it invited an abundance of wonderful music. A moving theatrical gesture overlooked by musicologists, *Alfred* is in essence America's first attempt at serious, heroic opera.

The libretto for *Alfred,* based on Thomas Arne's masque of the same name, was written by the college's twenty-eight-year-old provost William Smith, originally from Scotland.[7] Smith's rationale in producing *Alfred,* along with excerpts from his libretto, appeared in the *Pennsylvania Gazette* at the time of the performances: "We are a Mixture of People from almost all Corners of the World, speaking a Variety of Languages and Dialects," he wrote. The production, therefore, reflects the "Original Plan of the *English School,* that the *English* Tongue should be taught . . . in acting Scenes from our best Tragedies and Comedies." But Smith was also concerned with the moral message of the drama, and his comments offer a timeless image of the power of the arts in educating the young. "Nothing seemed fitter," he claimed, "than the story of The Redemption of England from the Cruelties of the Danish Invasion by Alfred the Great. . . . in *Alfred,* we have a finished Pattern of true heroism and diffusive Virtue; bold and steadfast to what is right in his own Case, yet patient, humane and tender to the Failings of his fellow mortals."[8]

Smith made several changes in the libretto to suit his resources, as did other authors and composers of the time who adapted their work to varying theaters and performers. For the all-male college, Smith omitted the women's speaking roles of the original. Two young women, however, were engaged from outside the college to sing the solo vocal portions: a "Miss Lawrence" and Hopkinson's eldest sister, Elizabeth. A fine musician like her brother, Elizabeth was married to Hopkinson's closest friend, Jacob Duché, who also played the role of Alfred. Smith also claimed that he added two hundred new lines to the original drama. Many gracefully reflected an emerging American spirit. As he stated in the *Gazette,* he "extended the Hermit's Prophecy of the future Greatness of England so far as to include these Colonies." In his epilogue he called upon Americans "to rise instantly with one heart and one hand, in the cause of liberty and their country."[9]

In his *Gazette* commentary, Smith states that *Alfred* had introduced several "new Pieces of Music."[10] "New" in those days usually meant "newly borrowed." Borrowing, however, not only signified parody in a literary sense but also in a musical and dramatic one. The substitution and addition of new songs, duets, and choruses can be operatic if they effectively underpin the emotions of the drama. In the Philadelphia production of *Alfred,* the interpolation of music by Arne, Handel, and especially from Italian opera seria allowed an otherwise turgid play to shine dramatically.

If James Ralph showed imagination in applying new texts to preexisting tunes, William Smith illustrates in *Alfred* how powerfully operatic a drama can become through the use of preexisting tunes with their original texts. In act 1, for example, he includes a pastoral song by Thomas Arne, "A Youth Adorned with Every Art," because of its "Tenderness of Expression, Dignity of Language, and force of real Woe." The song appears also in the 1753 London libretto and in Hopkinson's collection of songs (1759). Its doleful lament over a dead lover relates well to the anguish expressed in Alfred's soliloquy that follows:

How long! Just Heaven, how long
Shall War's fell Ravage desolate this Land?
All, all is lost—and Alfred lives to tell it!
His cities laid in dust! His Subjects slaughter'd
Or sunk to Captive Slaves![11]

The most striking use of music in *Alfred* occurs within the complex action of act 3, in which the opposing camp is attacked and the Danish monarch defeated. The action and feelings of the characters are so intensely drawn that Smith finds a contemporaneous Italian aria the most appro-

priate vehicle for expression. The aria, "Figlio ascolta!" (Hear Me, My Son!)
is from the last act of *Merope* (1743) by Domènech Terradellas, a Spanish
opera seria composer who became director of the King's Theatre in London in 1746.[12]

Terradellas's *Merope* dramatizes the chilling story of Merope, Queen of
Messenia, who is wrongfully accused of killing her two elder children.
Smith picks up on the opera's intense emotions in a scene that allows one
of the sopranos to sing the aria offstage. The Danish king has just learned
that his son, Ivar, has been killed. "My son—my son! Ah! Dead," he cries.
"My only child." Smith then gives him the following melodramatic lines:
"But ah! Who comes?—The miserable Mother—O bitterer far than
Death! She calls on Ivar who ne'er shall hear—Guards! Guards! She must
not see him; keep off the frantic Woman—Ah! 'Tis vain—She rushes forward, wing'd with wild Despair!" Smith's commentary explains: "Here the
Mother of Ivar, and Wife of the Danish King, supposed to be seen behind
the scenes, sings the famous Italian Disperata over the dead Body of her
son—'Figlio ascolta! Ah! Giace estinto!'"[13] Of all the scenes in *Alfred,* this
is the most interesting. Highly dramatic and expressive, it is a singular
example of an Italian aria used within prerevolutionary American theater.
It also offers a rare glimpse of musical characterization in an early staged
American production.

The exact role Francis Hopkinson played in this fine theatrical venture is hard to say. Historians have concluded that he played the harpsichord for the performance, but Smith only mentions "the kindness of the
Gentlemen who politely obliged us with the instrumental Parts of the
Music." Along with the harpsichord, there might have been one or two
violins, a cello, and perhaps a German, or transverse, flute. The conductor,
John Palma, was also the director of Philadelphia's first concert series, initiated on January 25 only days after the *Alfred* performances.[14] How important a role Palma played in choosing and arranging the music for *Alfred* is uncertain. Five of the eight arias known to have been used in the
performance—three by Arne, one by Handel, and one by Terradellas—
are found in Hopkinson's vocal collection of 1759. Whether the young
student musician had selected these for the college production of *Alfred*
or copied them later as mementos we do not know, but they were important enough for him to save.

Alfred must have had an impact on Hopkinson's life, as it did in the
life of the Philadelphia community as a whole. Smith refers to "the applause from crowded and discerning Audiences, during the several Nights
of its Representation." Cheyney claims audiences for the Philadelphia

College plays and oratory "were always available" and comprised a "learned, polite and very brilliant Assembly." Every part of the "great Hall" was usually crowded with spectators, he adds, "a vast concourse of people of all Ranks."[15] But perhaps the true success of *Alfred* belongs to the young performers themselves. "The songs were performed to great advantage by certain young ladies of this city," wrote one critic. "Having been taught music by an able master, Signor Juan Palma, they condescended to oblige their friends by adorning this performance with their musical voices."[16] As for the young men, Provost Smith provides the final encomium: They not only possessed a "true Relish for poetic Beauty," he remarks in the *Gazette* on January 20, 1757, but they "would be an honor to the Taste and Improvement of any Country."

America's First Comic Opera

American theatrical life was indeed making a gallant effort toward "Taste and Improvement," but its inroads were slow. Attempts to establish theater in Philadelphia had been made by the Kean and Murray Company in 1750, Lewis Hallam in 1752, and David Douglass, the talented actor-entrepreneur, in the 1760s. Although "oratorial" entertainments were allowed, rigorous blue laws promulgated that anyone who attended the theater would be fined 500 pounds. Plays and operas could be read publicly but not acted or staged, and songs had to be rendered by instruments alone.[17]

Opposition to the theater during this period was undoubtedly aggravated by poor audience behavior. During the raucous little ballad operas, theatergoers were not always well mannered. Oscar Sonneck noted, "Gentlemen, sportive or otherwise . . . were in the habit of crowding the stage during the performance and conversing with the actresses while they were waiting for their lines." If that trend was eventually rectified, other problems persisted, judging from an advertisement in a newspaper of 1762: "Pistole reward—to whoever can discover the persons who were so rude as to throw Eggs from the Gallery upon the Stage."[18]

With all these roulades of impropriety—and fines to boot—is it little wonder that America's first comic opera, *The Disappointment,* should have such a disappointing fate? Its real author remains unidentified, and the opera never reached the contemporaneous stage. It can, however, claim rights to being the first complete libretto published in America (New York, 1767). It is also the first opera to boast a truly American plot. As its title page reads, "The Disappointment: or the Force of Credulity. A New American Comic-

Opera of Two Acts, by Andrew Barton, Esq." Modern scholars have determined Andrew Barton was a pseudonym that whimsically reflected the opera's tall tale of piracy. The real Andrew Barton was an infamous Scottish pirate who died in 1511.[19]

There is also speculation that the opera was written by a "Son of Philadelphia College," as William Paterson claimed in 1766.[20] Who could this have been? Francis Hopkinson? Jacob Duché? These were "gentlemen amateurs," and the bawdy little opera was not their style. If it was another "son," he would have been well familiar with the ballad opera art because the work is a fine example of comedy, satire, parody, and nascent musical characterization—a kind of American *Beggar's Opera,* complete with its own brand of low-life characters. But the opera's gala premiere, scheduled to take place at the Southwark Theatre on April 16, 1767, was canceled. According to the *Pennsylvania Gazette* of that date, the opera contained "personal Reflections unfit for the stage." Its characters, such as Hum, Washball, Rattletrap, and Raccoon, supposedly poked fun at actual prominent Philadelphia personalities. In its place was substituted a serious play, Thomas Godfrey's *Prince of Parthia.* Godfrey had been a member of a little coterie at the college guided by William Smith that included Francis Hopkinson and Benjamin West. Thomas Godfrey, then, received the distinction of becoming the first American-born author to have his play staged in the New World. He did not live to see it, however. It was performed four years after his untimely death at age twenty-seven.

The lighthearted story of *The Disappointment* abounds in humorous escapades and clever satire, the latter more social than political. Four pranksters, Hum, Parchment, Quadrant, and Rattletrap, devise a tale about hidden treasure that belonged to Blackbeard and his crew. The pranksters, or "Humorists" as they are called, lure four "Dupes" into seeking the treasure, which they claim comprises "20,000 Spanish pistoles, a small box of diamonds . . . and 150 pounds weight of gold dust."[21] The gullible dupes agree to meet with the pranksters in complete secrecy near Stone Bridge, where the treasure is supposedly buried. In a long scene of astrological magic, Latin incantations, and ghostly apparitions, the treasure chest is exhumed. All hopes for becoming rich, however, are quickly dispelled as the dismayed and embarrassed dupes discover that the chest is filled only with rocks.

In his preface the author specifies that he wrote the opera for his own amusement and that of a few friends. He did not want to "put it in the power of gentlemen skilled in scholastic knowledge," but one of his aims was "to put a stop, if possible to the foolish and pernicious practice of

Engraving attached to 1796 edition of *The Disappointment; or, The Force of Credulity*, the first comic opera written in America. *Historical Society of Pennsylvania*

searching after supposed hidden treasure. . . . The moral: the folly of an over credulity, and the desire for money, and how apt men are (especially old men) to be unwarily drawn into schemes where there is but the least shadow of gain; . . . . mankind ought to be contented with their respective stations; to follow their vocations with honesty and industry—the only way to gain riches."[22]

Like James Ralph's *The Fashionable Lady,* Barton's characters bear metaphorical names, but instead of aesthetic ideals they reflect contemporary occupations. Quadrant is an instrument maker; Parchment, a teacher of penmanship; Washball, a barber; McSnip, a tailor; and Raccoon, a rustic militiaman (not an African American as has been erroneously interpreted).[23] Topinlift is a sailor, named after a piece of sailing tackle. Perhaps the most colorful name of all is that of the prostitute, Moll Placket. 'Placket' was common slang for vagina and provides a useful identity for this "woman of the town."[24] The use of different dialects for each of the dupes, moreover, cleverly delineates their personalities: Raccoon, Pennsylvania Dutch; Washball, English; Trushoop, Irish; and McSnip, Scottish.

In true ballad opera style, the songs, or airs, vary in age, form, and character. They appear in name only, without music. Dating from the sixteenth century to 1757, the year of *The Disappointment,* they range from traditional English, Irish, and Scottish tunes to the cultivated songs of William Boyce, Thomas Arne, and Samuel Howard. One American tune even surfaces— the perennial "Yankee Doodle," which might be called America's earliest surviving opera "aria." Believed to be associated with the early militia, the tune itself did not appear in print until about 1782.[25] When Raccoon, a military man, sings "Yankee Doodle" (Air No. 4) in *The Disappointment,* he provides the earliest reference to this age-old melody. To Moll Placket he confidently sings:

> O! How joyful shall I be,
> When I get de money.
> I will bring it all to dee;
> O! my diddling honey.
>
> Yankee doodle, keep it up,
> Yankee doodle, dandy;
> Mind the music and the step,
> And with the girls be handy.

Ranging not more than a tenth, the airs within *The Disappointment* are cast in binary or ternary design with occasional irregular phrases, such as those in James Ralph's *The Fashionable Lady.* They differ from Ralph's compilation, however, in their occasional kinship with the current, gently flowing English song style. Illustrating their durability in both the New World and Old, "Over the Hills and Far Away" (Air No. 8) and "Blackjoke" (Air No. 13) had been used thirty years earlier by James Ralph in London. *The Disappointment,* however, has few ensembles; only three duets, one chorus, and a country dance as a finale.

The Disappointment also displays many elements of skillful writing; above all, it shows creative delineation of characters through clever dialogue, plot progression, and appropriate associative tunes. As Oscar Sonneck noted, "The author possessed a surprisingly keen eye for what is effective on stage."[26] But the identity of the keen-eyed author remains a mystery. The opera's association with the College of Philadelphia, however, offers some tantalizing missing pieces in the puzzle. Based on a prank, the plot of *The Disappointment* has a boyish ring to it, rather like Cheyney's description of life at the college: "Much more mischief was chargeable to the boys . . . familiar childish tricks, such as the twitching off of Professor Beveridge's wig and the closing of the shutters from the outside so that in the dark the professor might be made the target for textbooks and blackboard erasers."[27]

If a "son" of the college were indeed the author, as Paterson stated, could he have been Thomas Hopkinson, the talented younger brother of Francis? Thomas, who graduated in 1766, a year before *The Disappointment* was to be staged, composed music for his commencement that was performed by his brother Francis on the organ. As Cheyney notes, "Boys in the Latin School sang odes on 'Liberty' and 'Patriotism' written by Thomas Hopkinson."[28] "Liberty" celebrated a popular recent visitor to the college, Col. Isaac Barre, one of the few English opponents to the Stamp Act. Barre's term, "sons of Liberty," became the name of numerous clubs formed throughout the Colonies. An unreasonable taxation of the Colonies, the Stamp Act, might have been parodied in the opera's preface with the reference to "this unconstitutional digging act." Digging for treasure, in other words, took many forms.

As noted in Smith's prologue to *Alfred,* the study of language, especially English, was one of the precepts of the college. Dialect to define comic characters was fairly common in comic opera, but the use of four dialects in *The Disappointment* might have been a fun-filled poke at lofty college ideals regarding the purity of the English language. The study of Latin, too, was important. A "Sylogistic Disputation, 'utrum praescientia deorum tollit Libertatem agendi'" was featured at Thomas Hopkinson's commencement ceremony. In the opera, one of the most important scenes (act 2, scene 2) is a long dialogue with Latin incantations as the infamous buried treasure is located and uncovered. "Cum meritantibus considerationibus, terrabandum ophagnum" intones the Harlequin-like conjurer, Rattletrap, as the ghost of Blackbeard rises up and spits fire. The diggers shriek and tremble. "Pray in English," advises Rattletrap. "Dese pirate spirits don't understand de Latin."

Another possible reference to academia takes place in this same scene with the use of the magnet as a superstitious, mystical tool—twenty-five years before Mozart tried the idea in *Così fan tutte*. Could this have alluded to the newly founded medical department at the college and the famous Austrian doctor, Friedrich Mesmer, inventor of animal magnetism or hypnotism? Mesmer's *De planetarum influxu* was published in 1766, moreover, and his views on astrology and the occult are reflected in several references to the twelve signs of the Zodiac. Mathematics, too, comes under the harmless attack in this same farcical scene: "Diapaculum interravo, testiculum stravaganza," intones Rattletrap, drawing a circle with his wand to outline the position of the treasure. "By my showl! My dear," exclaims Trushoop. "He spakes halgebra to it." Not only dialogue but also songs occasionally refer to the school. In "Granby" (Air No. 14), Rattletrap sings in pleasant internal rhyme: "'Tho the wisdom of schools damn our art and our tools / We can laugh at the fools of the college."

One person very familiar with both the English and American theatrical scenes was William Smith. If the young provost helped a "son of the college" write the opera, he had found a special venue to attack his enemy, Benjamin Franklin. The vitriolic struggle between the two men during the 1760s resulted in Smith's loss of his position as provost of the college not long after the opera libretto was published. Smith and Franklin also disagreed about the focus of language at the college. Smith wanted emphasis on Latin, and Franklin preferred an "English" college. Was Franklin, then, the "pirate spirit" who did not understand "de Latin"? Franklin was not very popular in Philadelphia at the time because of his accumulated wealth and his alleged support of the Stamp Act. It was rumored that he had been paid for recommending stamp officers and that the crown had promised him a high post.[29] Was the opera canceled because its "personal reflections unfit for the stage" referred to Franklin? Did the author have in mind Benjamin Franklin, then sixty-one, when he wrote in the preface: "The Moral: the Folly of . . . a desire for money, and how apt men (especially old men) are to be unwarily drawn into schemes where there is not the least shadow of gain"?[30] We may never know. Perhaps only the ghost of Blackbeard has the answer.

The libretto for America's first comic opera was published in New York and announced for sale in Philadelphia in the *Pennsylvania Chronicle* in April 1767. Apparently widely read and enjoyed in its literary format, the libretto was published in a new edition in 1796.[31] But it was not until 1937, under the auspices of the Federal Theater Project of the Works Progress Administration, that this charming, historic bit of Americana was finally given its world premiere.[32]

✍

There was little theatrical activity in the Colonies during the years leading up to the American Revolution. As British and American relations escalated toward open conflict, the theater became associated with loyalist diversions and English decadence, and audiences dwindled. The opera curtain remained virtually closed during the war years themselves, from 1775 to 1781, although plays were staged by British troops stationed in New York, Boston, and Philadelphia. After the war, however, the scene would change remarkably. Opera and music theater would take on exciting new directions as the strain of the Revolution subsided and laws against the theater were lifted. The pantomime and melodrama would bring a closer alliance between music and drama; plays would include more music, many approaching the realm of opera; comic opera would be sentimentalized; and a newborn American Romanticism would capture the creative spirit of a nation craving artistic identity.

The true voyage of discovery had already begun. *Alfred* and *The Disappointment* set the stage for the sublime and lighthearted elements that would shape the musical dramaturgy of American opera for decades to come. They also show how the study of opera must not be limited only to works called 'opera.' Designated a masque, *Alfred* is far more operatic in style, scope, and characterization than *The Disappointment,* a comic opera. Although its libretto is not as original as that of the latter, *Alfred* should nevertheless take its rightful place with *The Disappointment* as one of the two earliest operas written in America. *Alfred* not only predates *The Disappointment* but also has the added distinction of possessing an identified author and a documented contemporaneous American premiere. Both works, however, are important emblems of their era. They tell much about the people—their youth, daring, and exuberance, their fears, longings, and dreams—during a vital early period in the nation's history. No other art form was as convincing or persuasive.

3
National Themes and the American Image

Why should our thoughts to distant countries roam,
When each refinement may be found at home? . . .
Strange! We should thus our native worth disclaim,
And check the progress of our rising fame.
  —Prologue to *The Contrast* (1787) by Royall Tyler

WHEN THE PEACE TREATY with Britain was signed on September 3, 1783, the Revolutionary War officially ended and a new republic was born. The boundaries of the young republic comprised the Great Lakes to the north, Florida to the south, and the Mississippi River to the west, with an estimated population of more than two-and-three-quarters million. Philadelphia—birthplace of the Declaration of Independence and the national capital from 1790 to 1800—was still the largest city in the Republic, boasting fine streets lined with banks, warehouses, shops, and graceful trees. Outside the elegant two thousand–seat Chestnut Street Theatre, built in 1794, crowds of pleasure-seekers promenaded, the gentlemen with their long coats, striped stockings, and silver-buckled shoes and the ladies in rich brocades and taffetas. Philadelphia also had the finest church in the nation, Christ Church, and the largest public building, the State House. According to Thomas Jefferson, neither London nor Paris was as handsome a city as Philadelphia.[1]

By the 1790s, however, other American cities began to compete in the cultural and commercial arena—Baltimore, Charleston, Boston, and especially New York, which to one traveler seemed like Venice, "gradually rising from the sea."[2] With its array of balls, parades, concerts, operas, literary groups, puppet shows, comic lectures, and circuses, New York seemed the most cosmopolitan of the post-Revolutionary cities. As early as 1750, at least eighteen languages were spoken on its streets. Two years after the fine Park Street Theater opened in 1798, the city's population had swollen to seventy thousand, only ten thousand fewer than Philadelphia. By 1820 New York was first in the nation in population and commerce. "The

Chestnut Street Theatre, Philadelphia (right), where Susanna Rowson's opera *Slaves in Algiers* was given its premiere in 1794. *Library Company of Philadelphia*

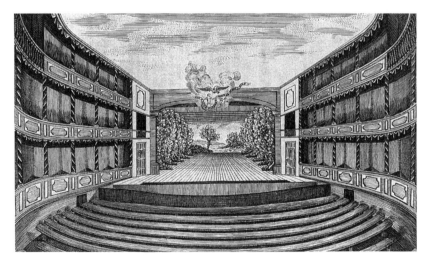

Interior of the Chestnut Street Theatre when it opened in 1794. The theater rivaled the major opera houses of Europe in size and elegance. *Library Company of Philadelphia*

Quaint old Dutch town into which Irving was born," remarked William Cullen Bryant, had by his time "become transformed into a comparatively gay metropolis."[3]

During these years especially there emerged the beginnings of a distinctly American social style, expressed in a wide variety of ways from the British and European. In effect, what had been a particular kind of British colonial way of life now became an American way, differing from the mother country not merely in dress, manners, mores, and speech but also in attitudes and point of view. Although there remained the ineffable staples of reference—Britain and the Continent—Americans after the Revolution were breaking away, leaving behind, and beginning anew. No art form seemed to reflect these new American tastes and values as acutely as opera. The prolific use of American patriotic and indigenous themes shaped the composition of new works—and often the arrangements of foreign ones—into a rich national tradition. American and "Americanized" opera manifested a romantic spirit of nationalism long before similar European trends were noted overseas.

After the war, the growth of imported opera production was phenomenal. More than a thousand different musical plays and operas were performed in America between 1785 and 1815; one hundred of these were produced between 1794 and 1800 in Boston alone.[4] Most were English or adaptations of English operas to suit American audiences. Americans, it seems, could not get enough of such works as *The Mountaineers, Rosina, Children in the Wood, The Duenna, Blue Beard,* and especially *The Poor Soldier,* which ran for half a century and played as far west as Detroit.

One of the most important factors contributing to this thespian effusion was that the ban on theatrical productions had been lifted. Although the antitheater law enacted by Congress in 1778 was repealed in 1789, it was observed in Boston until 1793. To skirmish around the restrictions, operas were produced throughout the Colonies under various guises such as 'lectures,' 'recitations,' or 'concerts.' Even the learned-sounding term *speculum vitae* was sometimes applied. Operas, moreover, were to uplift and offer provocative moral lessons said the critics. "Our stage," one reviewer maintained, "should represent to us the superior excellence of those manners which result from strict morality and the proper exercise of our political principles."[5] Perhaps these words explain why the Philadelphia composer Peter Markoe wrote his comic opera *The Reconcilliation* (1790) as an allegory on the virtues of charity, honesty, and repentance. Markoe's opera, moreover, was only a step away from early-nineteenth-century melodrama, with its accent on moral rectitude and the horrors of sin.

Composers, Compilers, and Librettists

With an increasing demand for music in all its varied forms and guises, especially opera, came the first major influx of musicians to American shores. Impresarios, composers, performers, and teachers settled in the major cities along the eastern seaboard and enriched the national cultural scene with their talent and professional experience. Arriving mainly from England but also from Holland, France, Germany, and Italy, they brought their European tastes and training. More important, they knew what would sell. They were craftsmen—musical sculptors who shaped their wares to satisfy the burgeoning demand for an all-pervasive product: theatrical entertainment. English plays were their primary raw material, and for nearly every new hit show in London they composed or compiled a special musical score that suited the needs of their adopted country.

It was in the theater, moreover, that most of these musicians found employment. But a theatrical musician had to wear many hats. Because most plays of this period contained music cues, a composer—who was usually also the conductor—had to write musical passages, very much as film composers do today. Composers were also responsible for providing patriotic music and popular tunes to fill in between the acts and also adapted or selected background music, incidental music, dance music, and songs if singers asked for them. Occasionally a composer would double as a scenic artist or dancer. Sol Smith tells of a certain musician-actor "who frequently played two or three parts in one play, and after being killed in the last scene [of *Pizarro*] was obliged to fall far enough off the stage to play slow music as the curtain descended." For all this he received the highest salary in the company.[6]

Just who were these adventurous creators—the American theater composers of the early republic? Many were young and at the start of their careers, others already had considerable experience in both concert and theater. Alexander Reinagle (1756–1809) was from a musical London family. At age fourteen he gave his first solo harpsichord concert in Edinburgh and soon thereafter became a fine teacher and respected member of the Royal Society of Musicians. He came to America in 1786, working mainly in Philadelphia where he was in great demand as a teacher and performer. With the English actor Thomas Wignell he formed Philadelphia's New Company in 1792 and modernized theater pit orchestras by replacing harpsichords with pianos. "He presided at his pianoforte," wrote the dancer Charles Durang, "looking the personification of the patriarch of music. . . . Such was Reinagle's imposing appearance that it awed the disorderly of

the galleries."[7] Reinagle was also the first in America to write piano so-
natas, and he shaped the scores of *La forêt noire* (1794), *Pizarro* (1800), and
at least fifteen other operas and theater works.[8]

Other important English immigrant musicians around the turn of the
century were James Hewitt (1770–1827), Benjamin Carr (1768–1831), John
Bray (1782–1822), and Rayner Taylor (1747–1825). Hewitt and Carr, at ages
twenty-two and twenty-five, respectively, arrived in America one year apart,
although Hewitt worked in New York and Boston and Carr chose Philadelphia. James Hewitt had played in Astley's Amphitheatre in London and
claimed he had studied under Haydn and Pleyel. Eventually he became
conductor at the Park Street Theater in New York and wrote and compiled music for fourteen operatic works. Of these, *Tammany; or, The Indian
Chief* (1794), with a libretto by Ann Julia Hatton, appears to be the earliest American opera with a libretto by a woman.[9] As for Benjamin Carr,
his early career included concertizing in London, where he had been a
pupil of Samuel Arnold. From a family of music publishers, Carr established in Philadelphia one of America's earliest music publishing houses,
Carr's Musical Repository. Among the 275 secular works that he composed
is his ambitious operatic realization of the William Tell story, *The Archers*
(1796), composed three years after he had arrived in Philadelphia at age
twenty-three.[10]

The new nation seemed to be a shaping force in the lives of these young
men, who managed from the start to immerse themselves in their jobs with
diligence and creativity. Like Benjamin Carr, John Bray also wrote one of
America's more important early operas only three years after arriving in
the new land. He was twenty-six when he composed his melodramatic
The Indian Princess; or, La Belle Sauvage, which was published in Philadephia
in 1808 by T. and G. Palmer, the first full piano-vocal score of an opera
published in America that has survived. Before joining the Chestnut Street
Theatre company in Philadelphia in 1805, Bray had performed with the
Royal York Theatre, London, as an actor and instrumentalist. Later he
composed and staged several operas in New York and Boston, receiving
considerable acclaim.[11]

Rayner Taylor, however, had already enjoyed an extensive and highly
successful career before coming to Philadelphia when he was in his forties. Trained at the Chapel Royal, he was only twelve when he sang at the
funeral of George Frideric Handel. He was active as a singer, composer,
and performer at Sadler's Wells, where in 1765 he was appointed music
director. In 1793, the year Taylor settled in Philadelphia, three of his comic operas were produced in Annapolis, Maryland. Taylor's most significant

work, however, was *The Aethiop; or, The Child of the Desert* (1813), an over-whelmingly successful, spectacular "Grand Romantic Drama" that provided Americans with an early prototype of modern musical dramaturgy.

The most important composer of these years, however—and the most prolific—was Victor Pelissier (ca. 1740-ca. 1820). Caught up in the great wave of dramatic expressivity at the turn of the century, Pelissier was a prime mover in the new melodramatic romanticism that shaped American opera for decades. With his influential *Ariadne Abandoned by Theseus in the Isle of Naxos* (1797), as Mates notes, "Pelissier had dropped the pebble which started an avalanche, and melodrama in nineteenth-century America would crush nearly every other stage form."[12] Very little is known about Pelissier's life and career before coming to America. A horn player in Santo Domingo, he most likely fled to America during the slave uprisings in 1792. He worked in both Philadelphia and New York as a composer and arranger, and contemporaneous critics maintained that his work displayed "variety of thought and readiness of invention, with the full knowledge of all the powers of an orchestra."[13] Throughout his long life, Pelissier wrote music for at least eighty-four theatrical works, ranging from spectacle and comic opera to pantomime and sentimental melodrama.[14] In the practice of the times, he either added new music—songs, marches, dances, and the like—to especially popular preexisting scores or wrote new accompaniments, harmonizations, and orchestrations. In addition to his theater works, Pelissier composed a symphony, a concerto, an overture for six wind instruments, and a variety of songs and solo instrumental pieces.

These then were the Bernard Herrmanns and Quincy Joneses of the early national period—but their medium was live theater rather than film or television. They were the "opera composers" of the day. They were also astute collaborators who worked prodigiously with their librettists—much like Mozart and Da Ponte, or Verdi and Piave. Like modern film composers, however, they did not always get top billing. The author, or librettist, was usually named in playbills and promptbooks before or immediately after the title. If mentioned at all, the composer was generally indicated at the end of the cast list and staging credits—in very small print. That changed as more composers wrote original music and music became more important within the drama. Rayner Taylor, for example, is listed prominently as "composer of original music and accompaniments" for *The Aethiop*.

The earliest American opera librettos were written by authors whose main professions were usually not in the literary field. Doctors, lawyers, painters, actors—nearly everyone, it appeared, wanted to get into the literary theatrical act. Unlike theater musicians who had to have professional

training in order to survive, anyone, it seems, could pick up a quill and
write a play or opera libretto. And unlike the musicians, who were immigrants, most important early American authors were native-born. A Har-
vard-educated lawyer from Boston, Royall Tyler (1757–1826) wrote the
first American comedy to be professionally produced: *The Contrast* (1787).
Written the same year, Tyler's comic opera *May Day in Town; or, New York
in an Uproar* (1787) brought local color to American opera by satirizing
New York's obsession with spring cleaning. Other librettists of the period
include William Dunlap (1766–1839), a portrait painter turned librettist;
Ann Julia Hatton (1764–1838), a novelist and poet; Elihu Hubbard Smith
(1771–98), a young doctor from Connecticut recognized for his popular
comic opera *Edwin and Angelina; or, The Banditti* (1796); and James Nelson
Barker (1784–1858), who wrote *The Indian Princess* at age twenty-four and
later enjoyed a distinguished public career as mayor of Philadelphia.

The Changing Relationships between Music and Drama

People and places are only part of the story. The real tale of American opera
lies in the works themselves—in the drama, the music, the interpreters,
and the impact they made. What were these operas like? Did the plots have
action and dramatic tension? Were the characters moving and real? Most
important, was there a close alliance, a dramatic compatibility, within the
relationship of text and music, action and imagery?

To study the operas of this period, one must look at a variety of sources
and put the pieces together like a puzzle. And there are many missing pieces.
For a few operas, such as Susanna Rowson and James Hewitt's *The Volunteers* (1795), the songs are extant but the libretto is lost. For the majority
of others, the librettos or promptbooks with references to the songs remain but the actual music is lost. Sometimes the music from an opera was
published later, attesting to its popularity; an example is James Hewitt's
songs and marches from *The Brazen Mask,* published in New York in 1811
following its premiere in 1806. Broadsides that printed only the words of
songs were often sold at theaters before performances. If an opera was
expected to be a big success, as in the case of *The Aethiop,* piano and vocal
scores were occasionally made available to theater audiences, but that was
rare. The earliest extant orchestral score of an American opera appears to
be William Dunlap and Victor Pelissier's *The Voice of Nature* (1803), which
was not reconstructed and edited from the manuscript parts until 1994.[15]

The period from the end of the Revolution to about 1810 is one of
the most fascinating eras in American operatic history. Important changes

were taking place in the role of music within the drama, and opera as it had emanated from the English ballad opera was being reshaped and redefined. It was a period of experimentation: trying, learning, adapting, and imitating. It was also an era of particular charm and delight. As the nation moved from the colonial period to the 1800s and beyond, music became more and more allied with the drama. Rather than dialogue interspersed with songs—as in the early ballad and pastiche operas—song, action, character, and mood became defined throughout by music that was more powerful catalyst than casual accompaniment. Both pantomime and melodrama used music lavishly throughout to heighten drama, but in pantomimes the story was largely mimed, whereas it was realized primarily by spoken dialogue in melodramas. Thus it is through the pantomimes and melodramas of the period that the nation moved in the direction of grand opera.

After the Revolution, the nation's artistic route turned from patriotic masque and comic opera to pantomime and melodrama, but the road was not always clearly delineated. Comic opera melded with serious drama, the harlequinade with the spectacle, pantomime with ballet, and musical plays with melodrama. The designation *opera* as a grand umbrella over all reigned supreme. Frequently the terms *opera* and *melodrama* were used interchangeably (as in the case of *Pizarro*) or in a combination (*The Indian Princess*). A similar practice is seen in certain works of Rossini, Donizetti, and Verdi (*Rigoletto, Un ballo in maschera,* and *Luisa Miller*) that are now called operas but were designated as melodramas at the time of their European premieres. Other nomenclature for American operas ranged from "grand operatic drama" (*Virgin of the Sun,* New York, 1800) to "grand, romantic, cabalistic, melodrama, interspersed with processions, pageants and pantomimes" (*The Wood Daemon,* 1808). Theater managers, publishers, and composers marketed their wares by any name that would sell.

What these varied and often confusing designations do not provide, however, are details of structure such as the balance and integration of song and dialogue. Whether called a play, opera, or melodrama—or a combination of all three—it is the role of music in defining character, emotions, and action that ultimately determines a work's operatic qualities. Very often it is not how much music is used but how it is used. With that ideology as a springboard, the operatic forms of the era can be investigated and defined.

The spirit of both nationalism and early romanticism shaped the operas of this period, but the way their influence was manifest changed with the times. At the close of the Revolution, when patriotic sentiment was strong, American themes were often dramatized in the allegorical masque. Francis Hopkinson's *America Independent* (1781), renamed *The Temple of Minerva* a few months after its premiere, is a short "oratorial entertainment" comprising two scenes, four characters, and thirteen musical numbers. Like *Alfred,* it is a pastiche of what is mainly the music of Arne and Handel. But unlike the earlier masque, which used spoken dialogue, *America Independent* appears to have been sung throughout in the manner of the all-sung masques known as "English operas."[16] *America Independent,* however, has virtually no plot, its staging is minimal, and its protagonists are allegorical rather than historic. The beauty in this little work lies principally in Hopkinson's skill in choosing elegant music that captures the poignant moods of America at the close of the Revolution—moods of struggle, hopes, dreams, and longing.

By the end of the century, the patriotic masque had become increasingly scenic and spectacular. *The Apotheosis of Franklin; or, His Reception in the Elysian Fields* (1796) and *Americania and Elutheria; or, A New Tale of the Genii* (1798) employed complex machinery that allowed clouds to float on the ground and characters to fly through the air à la Baroque opera and harlequinade. Both works eulogized Benjamin Franklin and were designed by a French- and English-trained artist named Monsieur Audin who was known for his opulent stagings. In the latter work, Franklin, discoverer of the lightning rod, is placed on a great rock in the Allegheny Mountains, and the god of lightning vanquishes the god of darkness with a shower of "electric fluid" from an "electrical rod" prop.[17] In the world of the theater, it was no mere coincidence that Franklin and Harlequin shared a common wizardry.[18] In the twentieth century, Albert Einstein would come to life in a similar phantasmagoric tableau through the wizardry of Robert Wilson and Philip Glass.

The Earliest Operas by Women

Although the new republic felt the impact of romanticism in the phantasmal and wondrous, its true myths and symbols were those of a self-proclaimed democracy whose mission was a seemingly endless quest for identity. "America flourished not in discovery," says Daniel Boorstin, "but in search. It lived with the constant belief that something else or something better might turn up. . . . When before had men put so much faith in the unexpected?"[19] That spirit of adventure or joy in the unknown formed a kind of survival mode for American artists. The creators and shapers of the nation's cultural life were a sturdy, self-reliant breed quite different from their European counterparts. As Francis Hopkinson put it, in Europe one could get any kind of work done by specialists, but average Americans were accustomed to doing everything themselves, from building a house to pulling a tooth.[20]

Women played a remarkable part in this diversification. Because there was a national shortage of women, especially in rural and frontier areas, women in early America had much more independence and freedom than they did in Europe. They were also more versatile, active, and, on the whole, more successful in activities outside the kitchen than were their English counterparts. Women were printers, publishers, apothecaries, and even practiced general medicine, but they were rarely composers or librettists. Because society considered female public performance immodest, women studied music as an accomplishment or social skill rather than for professional attainment. Two, however, Ann Julia Hatton and Susanna Haswell Rowson (1762–1824), made significant and creative contributions to early American theater and opera. Although both were originally from England, they lived most of their professional lives in the New World and are among America's earliest professional librettists.

The music theater works of Hatton and Rowson are fine early prototypes of modern American opera, that is, they are neither masque nor ballad opera but a new skillful literary form exhibiting yet another vital stepping stone within the development of American opera. Both works are distinguished by cohesive plots and strong characters. With its overture and music by James Hewitt, Hatton's *Tammany; or, The Indian Chief,* designated "a serious opera," was given its premiere at New York's John Street Theatre on March 3, 1794. Staged also in Philadelphia and Boston, *Tammany* is America's earliest serious opera on an American subject, and Ann Julia Hatton was a rare woman librettist to have her work produced on the American stage.

Ann Hatton came from a brilliant theatrical family. She was the daughter of Sarah and Roger Kemble and the younger sister of the great Sarah Siddons. Accounts of the time indicate that she may have been handicapped, for she felt it was because of her "squint and limp" that her family mocked her as "the Genius." She published her first set of poems at age fourteen. And while the London newspapers praised her "uncommon intellect" and "pround and strong mind," they also mentioned her "immoral avocation" of writing for the theater.[21] In 1792 she married a musical instrument maker, William Hatton, and went to New York with him the following year. That same year she collaborated with the talented singer and actress Mary Ann Pownell in the composition of the ballad opera *Needs Must; or,*

The Ballad Singers, which was performed in New York in December 1793. Hatton also wrote fourteen novels that reflected every popular subject of the day—nuns, social satire, moral progress, and a wide variety of female stereotypes, including bossy wife, doting mother, and crabby spinster.

Hatton's opera *Tammany* is an intriguing work not only because of its historic importance but also because of the political controversy that surrounded it. Not long after she came to America, Hatton allied herself with the powerful anti-Federalist Tammany Society that favored the French Revolution. She became known as "the poetess of the Tammany Society" and "bard of American Democracy," and her opera provoked much controversy, ranging from angry sarcasm to ebullient praise. More appeared in the newspapers and journals about *Tammany,* in fact, than any other theater work of the time. *New York Magazine* claimed in March 1795 that it was "one of the finest things of its kind ever seen," and the *Daily Advertiser* reported on March 6, 1794, that its language was "sublimely beautiful, nervous and pathetic."[22] *Tammany* also set the tone for operatic staging to come through its lavish, colorful sets by America's first full-fledged scenic artist, Charles Ciceri. Its libretto and music may always remain a mystery, however, for only the texts of the vocal numbers are extant.

A study of the song texts that were printed for distribution at the theater can tell much about the work, however.[23] What distinguishes *Tammany* from other operas of the time is its powerful heroic nature. Political messages in American musical theater were mainly either satirical, as in comic opera, or allegorical, as in masque. Hatton's opera tells the tragic story of Indian lovers, Tammany and Manana, who are burned in their cabin by the jealous Ferdinand, a member of Columbus's exploration team. Produced only a short time after the French Revolution with its ubiquitous cry of "Liberty, Equality, Fraternity," the opera became a strong symbol of republicanism. Factions were organized to hiss the play off the stage; others assembled to drive out meddling "aristocrats." Tammany, the downtrodden, and Columbus and his crew, the malicious Europeans, provided a powerful theme, and the love element and conflicting suitor added romantic melodrama.

Although the opera is a highly charged emotional piece, the idea of the dignity and virtue of Native Americans was not new. Among others, Philip Freneau, Robert Rogers, and Royall Tyler had used the theme earlier in their plays, and the Pocahontas story was repeated several times. Not until James Nelson Barker and John Bray's *Indian Princess* was there a vicious or vengeful Indian on the American stage.[24] More important than the political or social themes of Hatton's opera, however, are its literary and dramatic aspects. *Tammany's* large cast, grand choral finales, well-executed scenery, and lyrical song texts planted the seeds for an American grand opera tradition.

According to the song texts, the opera is constructed in three acts and contains twelve airs (or arias), two duets, and a choral scene closing each act. The choral finales appear to be more extensive than those of comic or pastiche operas. Additional cast was no doubt used for the chorus rather than using only the show's six or eight lead characters as in earlier opera choruses. A specified "chorus of women," "chorus of Indians," "chorus of Spaniards," and "chorus of Indian priests" appear. "Indian dances" were rendered by Charles Durang, the era's most famous dancer. John Hodgkinson, a noted actor and singer, played the role of Tammany; his wife, Frances Brett Hodgkinson, performed Manana. Two of the characters, Columbus and Perez, had speaking roles only, but with no extant libretto it is impossible to judge the proportion of speaking to singing throughout the opera.

A recurring motif that runs throughout the opera from its prologue to epilogue is the reference to "fire," both literal and metaphoric—a kind of mystical cyclic message like that in Wagner's *Ring*. Tammany perishes in a fire set by the violent and vicious explorers, a fire that serves as a torch to rally the world against tyranny and possession. Thus, as in Wagner, it is through fire that a new world will rise from the ashes of the old. But the idea that this "sacred flame" of liberty was implanted in the nation's soil long before the advent of white people is brought out in the opera's prologue—a poetic encouragement of public sentiment to support the "rising fire" of freedom in France: "Secure the Indian rov'd his native soil. . . . And seal'd the cause of Freedom with his blood":

> Can Freemen, friends to genius, e'er refuse
> To crown such efforts of a *stranger* muse?
> No.—they will cherish still the rising fire,
> And bid its blaze again more bright aspire.

There are also effective contrasting moments of characterization in the songs. A touch of humor is provided by Wegaw's air, a drinking song in lilting anapestic meter that has a special poetic charm:

> The moon she loves drinking 'tis plain
> She governs the tides of each flood
> And oft takes a sip from the main
> You may know by her changeable mood.

Manana's poetry is sensitive and lyrical, revealing her loving respect for Tammany and her joy in the beauties of nature. But the real fire is in the character of the bold Indian chief. When in act 3 he learns that Ferdinand has seized his beloved Manana, he sings five passionate stanzas: "Fury swells my aching soul," he begins, "boils and maddens in my veins." He hears "her shrill cries thro' the dark woods" and envisions her "struggles in lust's cruel arms":

> Come revenge! my spirit inspire,
> Breathe on my soul thy frantic fire,
> O'er each nerve thy impulse roll;
> Breathe thy spirit on my soul.
> . . . .
> Despair, the fiend of darkest night
> Fiercely urging on the fight,
> He thy sorrows shall avenge,
> And 'midst the carnage, howl revenge.

Although we may never know what the music of *Tammany* was like, we can confirm its foremost dramatic tool—the age-old power of grief and despair.

Like Ann Hatton, Susanna Rowson built her operas around national subjects, but her approach combines both political and feminist themes. Before coming to America in 1793, Rowson had already published two volumes of poems and five novels, among them her famous *Charlotte Temple* (1790).[25] In Philadelphia, she was employed as an actress and her husband as a prompter in Thomas Wignell's thriving theatrical company. It was at the spacious Chestnut Street Theatre, modeled after the Theatre Royal in Bath, that her first American musical play was staged. *Slaves in Algiers; or, A Struggle for Freedom* received its premiere on June 3, 1794, to celebrate the two-thousand-seat theater's gala opening season.

Rowson's life in America was a full one. As an actress, she reputedly played 129 different parts in 126 productions within three years, and she also continued to write a variety of novels, poems, song lyrics, and plays. Several of her plays contained music. *The Volunteers,* for example, which is based on the Whiskey Rebellion in western Pennsylvania, contains fifteen songs.[26] Her pantomime *Shipwreck'd Mariners Preserved* (1795), moreover, is one of the earliest American ballets. A dedicated reformer, Rowson openly proclaimed equal rights for women and was one of the first to advocate freedom for slaves. Many of her plays, such as *Columbia's Daughter; or, Americans in England* (1797) and *Female Patriot* (1795), combine both

feminist and patriotic themes. Later in her career, Rowson became a prominent educator. She ran a boarding school for females in Boston that employed such distinguished musicians as Peter van Hagen and Gottlieb
Graupner, a founder of the famed Boston Handel and Haydn Society.[27]

Slaves in Algiers was given its premiere in the same year that Mary Wollstonecraft's treatise *A Vindication of the Rights of Women,* was published in
Philadelphia. On its title page it was called "A Play Interspersed with songs,"
with the score composed by Alexander Reinagle. Rowson played the role
of Rebecca, a speaking part she created for herself. Part of the opera's story was inspired by Cervantes' *Don Quixote;* the rest, according to Rowson,
was "entirely the offspring of fancy."[28] The immediate setting was based on
a current political situation, the ignominious problems the nation faced because of Algerian pirates who had seized American ships during the 1790s.
Numerous Americans remained prisoners of the Barbary corsairs, and the
matter dragged on for years because John Paul Jones died before he could
carry out his assigned mission to ransom the captives.

In Rowson's opera the interrelationship between the Algerians and
their captives is played out mainly by the women, who, with their strong
feelings and attitudes, form the main dramatic thread of the opera. The
Algerian situation is seen through the eyes of women—a feminist approach
within American opera rarely seen before Gertrude Stein 150 years later.
In the story, the concubines Fetnah and Selima and the American captive
Rebecca are bonded by their common situation of slavery and longing
for freedom. In various portions of the opera they exchange thoughts about
the place of women in the world: "Woman was never formed to be the
abject slave of man," observes the spunky Fetnah. "Nature made us equal
with them, and gave us the power to render ourselves superior." Later, in
act 3 when Henry offers to protect Fetnah, she retorts, "What, shut me
up? Do you take me for a coward?" "We respect you as a woman and would
shield you from danger," explains Henry. "A woman!" cries Fetnah indig-
nantly. "Why, so I am, but in the cause of love or friendship, a woman can
face danger with as much spirit and as little fear, as the bravest among you."
Overhearing her, the Spanish slave Sebastian remarks, "It's a fine thing to
meet a woman that has a little fire in her composition."

Other women in the opera, Zoriana, daughter of the dey of Algiers,
and Olivia, another American captive, become good friends. There are
touches of romance when Olivia is reunited with her fiancé Henry. And
as the opera moves along amid moonlit Moorish gardens, disguises, escapes,
and emotional revelations of lost families, it closes with the joyous asser-
tion that "no man should be a slave." "Let us not throw on another's neck

the chains we scorn to wear," proclaims Rebecca. The story and action, however, are not as significant as the imagery and social messages of the provocative text.

Like most operas of the time, the musical score of *Slaves in Algiers* has been lost. All we know of it is what Rowson claims in her preface to the libretto: "I feel myself extremely happy in having an opportunity, thus publicly to acknowledge my obligation to Mr. Reinagle for the attention he manifested, and the taste and genius he displayed in the composition of the music."[29] The lyrics of the songs, however, indicate potential for musical characterization that is rare in early American opera. Only four of the twelve characters have singing roles: Zoriana, Fetnah, Ben Hassan (Fetnah's father), and Sebastian. But in giving these characters musical emphasis, Rowson provides each with a special life and individual personality. Ben Hassan, a Jewish corsair under the dey of Algiers, sings in the anapestic meter common in humorous songs of the period. Like many Jews in literature, he is portrayed as a Shylock-Fagin type of figure. Sebastian's song, also comic, reflects a "poor, little innocent boy" who never has much luck with women.

In the three songs of Zoriana and the two of Fetnah, the women's contrasting personalities are creatively delineated. Through her song in act 1, we come to know Fetnah—young, outspoken, and longing for freedom from the world of the concubine. She sings a straightforward ballad about women who "wither in slavery." But she is also sensitive and poetic, as her act 2 air in graceful trochaic meter attests. It is the dawn that can summon laughter and tears together, she sings. Zoriana's three songs present her as more delicate and fragile than Fetnah. She is a child of nature, and the lyrics of her songs contain frequent allusions to Greek mythology, beauty, and love. Of all the characters, she seems most representative of the emerging spirit of romanticism as the century draws to a close.

If the opera was not always well received, Rowson, at least, had the courage to respond to critics. In a lengthy coarse and brutal diatribe, William Cobbett lashed out against her literary abilities, feminist leanings, and even her patriotism. Women, he said, would soon be taking over the House of Representatives. In Cobbett's mind, Rowson was not only a hypocrite but also a "stupidly pretentious writer." *Slaves in Algiers,* he wrote, could serve as a most excellent potion to induce vomiting ("emetic"). Rowson responded with a bit of venom of her own: "The literary world is infested with a kind of loathsome reptile. . . . [who] spits out its malignant poison, in scurrility and detraction. One of these noisome reptiles has lately crawled over my volumes. . . . I say crawled over them, because I am certain it has never penetrated beyond the title-page of any."[30]

Tammany and *Slaves in Algiers* mark a fresh, innovative approach within the long, variegated skein of American operatic history. They were the first American operas to move away from the pastiche into the single-composer work—an important step toward modern opera. More important, Hatton and Rowson found truth and depth in their characters, and by placing them within the framework of American social and political ideology they endowed them with inner dramatic life.

The Role of Music in the Operatic Melodrama

However original their attitudes, composers and librettists still drew inspiration from the traditional theatrical forms of Europe. Often the results were every bit as imaginative as the operas staged in London, Edinburgh, Bath, or the surrounding provincial cities. America, after all, was the nation that could produce the buildings of Charles Bulfinch, the paintings of Charles Wilson Peale, the portraits of Gilbert Stuart, the furniture of Duncan Phyfe, and the sculpture of William Rush. Operas, too, were part of the American cultural image—operas and theater pieces created with flair and dramatic integrity. American producers hastened to capitalize on a rapidly expanding market.

One such producer was William Dunlap, the "Father of the American Theatre." Dunlap was the nation's first American-born professional entrepreneur. He was born in Perth Amboy, New Jersey, and before he turned thirty-eight he had written and staged almost fifty plays and operas, many with musical scores by Carr, Hewitt, and Pelissier. One of his major works was *The Archers; or, The Mountaineers of Switzerland* (1796) on the William Tell story.[31]

In 1796 Dunlap became a partner in New York's Park Theatre, but nine years later disastrous financial and managerial upsets forced him to close the theater and declare bankruptcy. He continued to write plays and librettos and in his later life turned to painting. It was through his adaptations of the works of the influential German dramatist August von Kotzebue, however, that Dunlap prepared the way for a rich romantic expression that the nation had never experienced in opera. For Kotzebue, it seemed, tears were the sure sign of inner virtue, and in the true romantic tradition, his characters, both male and female, shed them abundantly.[32]

Of Dunlap's twenty-five extant plays and operas, eleven are translations or adaptations of Kotzebue, all staged within only two years (1798–1800). The most popular of these were *Virgin of the Sun* and *Pizarro in Peru* (New York, 1800), heroic tales about Peruvian Incas during the Spanish conquest. Their exotic locales, historical pageantry, and rituals of sun worship, com-

Audiences reacting to a melodrama. From an engraving in *Le Melodrame,* a late-nineteenth-century monograph by Paul Ginisty. *Library of Congress*

bined with the dramatic themes of forbidden love and self-sacrifice, packed theaters. Although *Virgin of the Sun* is called a "play" in the original libretto and *Pizarro* a "tragedy," both illustrate the powerful three-way interaction of play, melodrama, and opera as the century turned.[33]

Of the two Inca stories, *Pizarro in Peru* is the more action-packed and popular, staged over and over for at least a quarter of a century. The three main characters that provide the ménage à trois in *Virgin of the Sun*—the Incas Cora, Alonzo, and Rolla—return in *Pizarro,* but added is the Spanish conquistador Francisco Pizarro and his lover Elvira, allowing more dramatic intensity and conflict. Pizarro provides the villainous intruder; Elvira, the virtuous woman; and Cora's child, domestic innocence—thus rounding out the characteristic ingredients of early-nineteenth-century melodrama. When Alonzo is taken prisoner by the Spaniards, so the story goes, the courageous Elvira attempts to rescue him only to discover that, disguised as a monk, Rolla has already helped him escape. Rolla, in turn, submits to the Spaniards' brutality and is eventually killed but not before bravely saving the child of his former lover, Cora, and her husband Alonzo.

Dunlap's version of *Pizarro in Peru,* based on Richard Brinsley Sheridan's London edition, provides a good example of the way popular theater works were altered and adapted as they crossed the ocean from the Old World to the New.[34] Kotzebue's drama *Die Spanier in Peru* (1789) is based on Marmontel's *Les Incas* (1777). When Sheridan adapted Kotzebue's play for Drury Lane, he made some of the dialogue more heroic to express current patriotic sentiment and softened the coarseness of Elvira, "little more than a soldier's trull in the original."[35] Seduced by Pizarro as a young novice in the convent, Elvira reminds him that he brutally killed her brother. She can still hear "the last shrieks" of her mother's breaking heart and "the blood-stilled groan" of her murdered brother. "That I could not *live* nobly," she cries, "has been Pizarro's act. That I will die nobly shall be my own!" As the play's most interesting character, Elvira resembles Leonora in Beethoven's *Fidelio* (1804), which also has themes of undeserved suffering and heroic resolve and even a debased Spaniard named Pizarro.

To Dunlap, the ennobling of Elvira's character served the piece well. But Dunlap also mitigated Pizarro's baseness and metamorphosed Valverde the priest into a private secretary because he felt wicked priests could be tolerated in the great theater of the world but not on the stage of a playhouse. He retained the long five-act structure of Sheridan, however, and, like his English counterpart, he understood well the ingredients for success: "pathos, spectacle, song and the peculiar attractiveness of the Germanic."[36] These ingredients are especially apparent in the staging. One of the most famous scenes of the century occurs in the last act, where Rolla makes his breathtaking escape from the Spaniards, Cora's child in his arms, by crossing the bridge over a cataract. With soldiers firing at him, he rips away the tree that supports the bridge and barely manages to escape. Significantly, this piece of exciting stage business in not in Kotzebue's original text and shows how Americans were lured then, as now, by a perennial grandiloquent chase.[37]

What is most interesting about *Pizarro* is the use of music that accompanied it, making it a heroic operatic work by any measure of the term. In both the Sheridan and Dunlap editions, the focus is on the large processional choruses that go hand in hand with the staging. There is only one solo song, "Yes, Be More Merciless Than Tempest Dire." Sung by Cora to the accompaniment of the harp during "a dreadful storm with Thunder and Lightning," the song has some dramatic "ad lib." designations reflecting her fear for the safety of her child. With the exception of this ballad and the glee, "Fly Away Time" (act 2, scene 2) sung by a small chorus of Peruvian women, music in the play primarily enhances the spectacle. The processional scenes take place in acts 2 and 3, with marches and choruses by Michael Kelly, Christoph Willibald Gluck, Antonio Sacchini, and Luigi Cherubini in the Sheridan edition.[38]

How much of the Sheridan-Kelly music is retained by Dunlap—and how much was newly composed, selected, or arranged by James Hewitt—one cannot be sure. But from all editions of the libretto, English and American, the dramatic processional scenes were elaborate and spectacular.

John Philip Kemble as Rolla in the London production of *Pizarro in Peru*. *Folger Shakespeare Library*

A fine singer and actress, Frances Brett Hodgkinson played Cora in the American production of *Pizarro in Peru* and Manana in Hatton's *Tammany. Harvard Theatre Collection, the Houghton Library*

Act 2, scene 2, for example, begins with a "Solemn March" in the Temple of the Sun, around which warriors, priests, and virgins assemble. Alternating with the choruses, the high priest sings a hymn to the sun as a flame descends and consumes his offering. The triumphal march in act 3, scene 1 is even more interesting because contrast is achieved not merely by solo and chorus but in the choruses themselves, which form an integral part of the drama. As the libretto describes:

> A wild Retreat among stupendous Rocks.—CORA and her Child, with other Wives and Children of the Peruvian Warriors, are scattered about the scene in groups. They sing alternately, Stanzas expressive of their situation, with a CHORUS, in which all join in. . . . The triumphant march of the army is heard at a distance.—The Women and Children join in a strain expressive of anxiety and exultation. The Warriors enter singing the Song of Victory, in which all join.—The King and ROLLA follow, and are met with rapturous and affectionate respect. CORA, during this scene, with her Child in her arms, runs through the ranks searching and inquiring for Alonzo.[39]

If there is any question about calling *Pizarro* an "opera" one need only consult the score for this scene. As the Peruvian warriors sing ebulliently "Victory now has made us free / We haste, we haste our friends to see!" the women sing:

> Hush! Hush! don't you hear?
> Some footsteps near
> A distant march assails the Ear;
> Hark! louder still from yonder Hill
> Encreasing sounds with terror fill.[40]

Each chorus retains its identity and mood in a dramatic scenario that could come right out of Meyerbeer or Verdi. Dunlap's twenty-five-piece orchestra of strings, brass, woodwinds, percussion, and harpsichord (or pianoforte) matched that of Sheridan's. And the lavish and colorful staging by Charles Ciceri would have worked hand in hand with the music to draw those tears so vital to early melodrama.[41]

Other operatic elements in the action are not indicated in the libretto. But there is reason to believe orchestral or piano music was used in the background to heighten some of the more dramatic scenes, as in the newer pantomime and melodrama styles. Dunlap's promptbook for *Virgin of the Sun* has several notations in his hand, such as "Solemn Music Ready" at the beginning of act 3, and where the libretto indicates "The Curtain Falls," his notes add "to Grand Music."[42] As early as 1796 there is indication that "on either side of the stage [was placed] a forte piano."[43] More commonly, however, a single piano was situated in the pit and may have improvised occasional music for mood or transition and provided contrast with the dialogue and larger orchestral scenes.

><

When Joseph Donohue called *Pizarro* a "grand operatic tragedy," he was not far off mark.[44] Its grand scenery, pageantry, choruses, and drama melded felicitously to draw the maximum empathy for the characters and their plight. *Pizarro in Peru* combined the heroic spectacle of the masque, the legendary heroism of *Tammany,* and the dramatic musical potential of the melodrama. From these fertile seeds would grow the American tradition of grand opera. But that is only part of the story. During these early national years, two women also made history. Ann Julia Hatton wrote the libretto for America's first serious opera on an American subject, and Susanna Rowson's feminist-tinged *Slaves in Algiers* was given its premiere in an elegant American opera house the size of Covent Garden during its important opening season in 1794. Both operas reflect American social and political thought through skillfully etched characters that have dramatic truth and inner life. Hatton and Rowson are the first of the American women whose work in the decades and centuries to come would comprise some of the nation's most innovative operatic gestures— Louisa Mars, Stella Stocker, Abbie Gerrish-Jones, Mary Carr Moore, Gertrude Stein, Meredith Monk, Libby Larsen, and many others. The history of America's opera is not only a study of its style but also a tale of its people—their dreams, creativity, and fortitude.

4

Mime, Melodrama, and Song

Gentlemen: The *Rubicon* is passed. *America* has produced an *opera*. A national feeling pervades us; we are becoming fond of ourselves. We begin to love *American* manufactures, *American* books, *American* plays. The audience . . . is excited to behold a *rara avis*—an *American* opera—performed by *American* actors—and the music composed in *America*. I was delighted.
   —*Baltimore American,* May 29, 1822 (on Arthur Clifton's *The Enterprise*)

WHEN *Arthur and Emmeline; or, The Prospect of Columbia's Future Glory* was advertised in the *New York Daily Advertiser* on May 19, 1800, it was not the arias, choruses, or singers that captured the headlines but the scenery. In only two acts the audience witnessed a Gothic temple; three Saxon gods on pedestals: Woden, Thor, and Friga; an enchanted wood "in which a tree being struck by Arthur spouts blood"; a golden bridge; and Merlin, "the British enchanter" who displays to King Arthur "the progress of the American nation, from its infancy to its present power and a prophetic view of Future Glory." Thus, with a shade of the patriotic masque, a hint of Harlequin's magic, and a foretaste of Wagnerian myth, music theater opened the nineteenth century with its own special variety of song and spectacle. But it remained for the melodrama to infuse these elements with new dramatic life and bring them into the sphere of grand opera.

The American melodrama drew dramatic strength from English and French pantomimes of the eighteenth century. From the English, it picked up elements of the harlequinade—popular in America from colonial days until about 1830—such as the delineation of character, a redefinition of comedy, focus on the phantasmal, and incorporation of "action music" newly composed for a particular work. From French pantomimes—fashioned in America during the 1790s—it inherited the gestures and grace of *ballet d'action,* expressive new acting techniques, provocative serious subjects, extravagant scenic effects, and a new dramatic use of the orchestra. From both English and French forms, however, melodrama derived its life's blood: the dramatic powers of music. As Anne Shapiro points out, cues for music in pantomime were often the same as for melodrama. Designations such as "hurry," "fright," and "battle" are used to underline the more intensely dramatic scenes. In both pantomime and melodrama, then, music is used "at the moments where verbal information becomes less important than action or feelings. These moments are the focal points of each of the forms . . . and they are prepared for emotionally, scenically, and musically."[1] Significantly, both pantomimes and melodramas were often called operas.

Elements of English pantomime, the harlequinade, made their way into opera as early as 1730, when the first ballad opera by an American, James Ralph's *The Fashionable Lady,* was staged in London. More commonly, English pantomime appeared as a separate theatrical form and had endless variations on a single storyline. Satire, highly colorful and phantasmagoric, was often at the heart of the harlequinade. Although the main character of Harlequin remained for the most part silent, he was accompanied by almost continuous orchestral music expressive of his every attitude and action. The role required extraordinary dexterity and dancing skills embellished by a set repertory of sighs, looks, and gestures. As Harlequin disappeared and reappeared through hinged traps in the stage floor, he worked his magic bat. With a slap he cued stagehands to alter an object, character, or setting, creating for the enraptured audience what might be called visual similes. Judges became applewomen, or a Yorkshireman who stole a horse became a clotheshorse. Such fleeting satiric images provided the veritable soul of wit—or so it seemed.

In February 1735 *The Adventures of Harlequin and Scaramouch* was staged in Charleston as an afterpiece to Thomas Otway's tragedy *The Orphan,* indicating a juxtaposition of tragedy and comedy in American performance practice similar to the English. In American practice, however, often only the comic portion was staged without the tragedy. Indeed, it was a magical world of surprises that drew audiences. Harlequin appeared in every possible adventure, as the titles of works staged in America between 1765 and 1815 suggest: *Harlequin Balloonist, Harlequin Barber, Harlequin Fisherman, Harlequin Freemason, Harlequin in the Sun, Harlequin Skeleton, Harlequin in Philadelphia, Harlequin in the Moon, Harlequin Traveler,* and *Harlequin's Invasion of the Realms of Shakespeare.* Most of the eighty-odd titles listed by Susan Porter are premieres created specifically for American audiences.[2] Several had American themes, such as *Columbus; or, The Discovery of America, with Harlequin's Revels,* which was staged in Baltimore in 1783. Clearly, a fascination with the unknown and outrageous captured American imagination time and time again, becoming a rich inspirational font for opera composers in the decades to come.

French pantomime differed considerably from English. Arriving in America from Paris via London during the late eighteenth century, "ballet-pantomime," as the French version was sometimes called, was a serious, noble, spectacular show, the action of which was carried mainly by elegant dance and pantomimic gesture. Speaking or singing was usually absent, and the instrumental music that flowed continuously throughout played an even more dramatic role than in English pantomime. The plots of French pantomimes were also serious or tragic, allowing little room for satire and the earlier buffoonery of the commedia dell'arte.

Although French pantomime may have played a more immediate role in the development of melodrama, the English form, or harlequinade, gave it its American flavor. The charm, humor, vocal interludes, and dramatic orchestral vitality of the harlequinade made their way into such serious early melodramatic works as John Bray and James N. Barker's *The Indian Princess; or, La Belle Sauvage* (1808) and Rayner Taylor's *The Aethiop; or, The Child of the Desert* (1813), offering a new operatic expression molded specifically to the American sensibility. Thus, with an abundance of grand gesture and sentiment, both English and French forms of pantomime brought to America the seeds of the early melodrama and an ever-increasing awareness of music's dramatic potential.

Like many pantomimes, early melodrama came to the new nation through French productions that were popular in England. Early melodramas (from the Greek *melos,* or melody with drama) had no particular plot and employed a technique that alternated short passages of music with poetry or dialogue. In these early works, mood, spirit, feelings, and "passions" become the springboard for dramatic musical representation. But when story and action come into the picture—and music that runs underneath the action—melodrama takes on a new expressive dimension that carries it well into the next century. The most successful example of this new style was Thomas Holcroft's *A Tale of Mystery,* first performed in London in 1802 and in New York and Philadelphia later that same year with new music by both James Hewitt and Victor Pelissier. Holcroft based his melodrama on *Coeline; ou, L'enfant mystère* (1800) by Guilbert de Pixèrécourt, father of popular French melodrama. Illustrating the close ties between melodrama and Romantic opera, Pixèrécourt's lavish scenic innovations and use of historic subjects later became hallmarks of French grand opera, while another popular French writer, Eugene Scribe, used towering melodramatic twists and turns in his librettos for the grand operas of Meyerbeer, Boieldieu, Auber, Cherubini, Donizetti, and Verdi.

Thus it was in England and France. But what happened when the first

American-born author, William Dunlap, produced a melodrama for his nation's theater-hungry audiences? Staged in New York on February 4, 1803, Dunlap's three-act *Voice of Nature* was adapted from the English version of a well-known biblical story as it appeared in L. C. Caignez's *Le Jugement de Salomon*. Like the English version by James Boaden, *The Voice of Nature* is set in Sicily rather than Jerusalem. It employs a large cast of ten principal roles and assorted laborers, peasants, courtiers, soldiers, and the like. A sure-fired audience-pleaser, its sentimental plot involves themes of motherhood, feminine virtue, and justice.[3] More significant than the plot, however, was the music—not merely instrumental music to underpin the story but vocal as well, as in America's first major dramatic melodrama, *Pizarro in Peru*.

The lyric power of song and chorus had now become a vital element of the American melodrama, allowing the form to approach the dimensions of grand opera—as grand in spirit and scope perhaps as Beethoven's *Fidelio*, Donizetti's *Lucia di Lammermoor*, or nearly half of Bellini's operas, which, in fact, bear the designation "melodrama."

Two works performed and published only a few years apart illustrate these expressive directions toward grand opera and also provide important insight into the close relationship between the early American melodrama and its sister art, the pantomime. Both John Fawcett and James Hewitt's *Brazen Mask* (1806) and Barker and Bray's *The Indian Princess* (1808) were given their premieres in Philadelphia, and both employ choruses, solos, and serious plots, although the latter adds touches of levity through the addition of comic characters. Unlike *The Indian Princess*, which is designated "an operatic melo-drame," *Brazen Mask* has no spoken dialogue and is meant to be danced or, more accurately, mimed. *The Indian Princess* also has a richer musical score, with more solos, ensembles, choruses, and, most important, precise indications of where melodramatic accompaniments take place within the drama. Both works are important early-nineteenth-century examples of American operatic forms and bring to light the variety of ways music was used as a dramatic vehicle.

Following the custom of the pantomime, *Brazen Mask* was published as a synopsis rather than a libretto. The twelve-page synopsis Russell and Cutler published for the Boston Theatre production of 1809 begins: "Sketch of the Fable, Arrangement of the Scenery, with the Songs and Choruses in the Grand Pantomimic Ballet called BRAZEN MASK: or, ALBERTO & ROSABELLA." Along with James Hewitt's piano-vocal score, published in 1811, the synopsis offers useful ideas about the way the work, and perhaps others like it, was performed.[4] It is in two acts, each with five or six scenes.

Act 1 opens with a chorus of peasants and interposed solo; act 2 begins with a "Mad Song" sung by the heroine, Rosabella. Act 2 closes with a chorus and alternating solo sections before the lengthy final mimed or danced scene. The story takes place near a village in Poland and concerns a family whose farm has been plundered and its inhabitants taken captive by a group of bandits led by Brazen Mask. In true rescue-opera style, there is horror, suspense, dank caverns, and combat. The most interesting character is that of Rosabella, the young wife who courageously manages to stab her guard, mortally wound Brazen Mask, and save her husband from imprisonment and death. According to the synopsis, placards ("scrolls") were regularly held up throughout the pantomime to inform the audience of situations that might not be understood by miming alone—a kind of early silent film or modern opera surtitle technique.

Playing through Hewitt's score, which has twenty-one short, dance-like instrumental passages interposed with vocal numbers, provides a good sense of the various changing moods in the story. Designations such as "plaintive," "andante," "agitato," or "combat" are reflected in the music that follows but do not tell exactly where in the story the music is used. The situation is similar to researching the French pantomime-ballets of Jean Georges Noverre, whose works were produced in London at the time. But from Noverre we do learn that the performer must make music "intelligible by the force and vivacity of his gestures, by the lively and animated expression of his feature." Only then will the two arts, music and mime, "mutually exchange their charms to captivate and please."[5]

Hewitt's score for *Brazen Mask* has a Mozart-like classicism, but its pervasive diatonicism offers little adventure in modulation or dramatic impetus. With its "Scottish snap," Rosabella's Mad Song is reminiscent of Thomas Arne's graceful Vauxhall style still popular in both England and America.[6] Despite the "dolce" marking on the words "'twas a dying husband's groan," the song's mood seems more delectable than delirious, far from the distraught Lucias, Aminas, and Elviras of later Italian opera.

After its premiere at the Chestnut Street Theatre in Philadelphia, *Brazen Mask* played in Baltimore, Charleston, New York, and Boston and enjoyed more than fifty performances. Barker and Bray's *Indian Princess* was less popular. After its Chestnut Street Theatre premiere on April 6, 1808, it appeared only a few times in major American cities. In 1820, however, it made its way to London, where in modified form it received the distinction of an English staging. *The Indian Princess* is not, as some have claimed, the first opera written by an American author on an Indian subject—Ann Julia Hatton's *Tammany; or, The Indian Chief* preceded it—but it appears to be the first complete surviving piano-vocal score of an opera published in America. That fact makes it especially valuable in enlarging the understanding of the subjects, techniques, and dramatic focus of early American opera.[7]

The Indian Princess combines the patriotic nobility of masque, the intensity of melodrama, and the gesture and wit of harlequinade. Barker's use of comic or light-hearted characters and Bray's lyrical set pieces bring their "operatic melodrama" into the sphere of comic opera, but with a new twist. *The Indian Princess* is a wonderfully varied, spirited work with fresh vigor and a Native American aspect that sets it apart from English counterparts. The nation must have a literature to prove its greatness, librettist Barker once wrote, a literature "to celebrate American achievements, and to record American events."[8]

The opera is in three acts, and music plays an important role throughout, especially in defining characters and their places in the story. The large choral scenes are sung mainly by settlers, who express joy and wonder at their new surroundings, and a chorus of Native Americans who entreat Aresqui, the god of war, at the closing of act 2. Choral scenes open the opera and form the finales of each act. For individual characters, Bray provides six tuneful arias, a jaunty trio, and a comic "dialogue quartet" in which characters sing alternately rather than simultaneously in a kind of pseudo-accompanied recitative. At the start of act 1, Larry confides that he prefers "skipping to the simple jig of an Irish bagpipe." His aria, which follows somewhat later, is in G minor and has a dronelike accompaniment reflecting the sound of a bagpipe and a decided Scotch-Irish flavor in rhythmic pattern. Walter's aria "Captain Smith Is a Man of Might" is a strong and martial "maestoso," and Pocahontas sings a particularly beautiful, plaintive lament.

In contrast to her Native American brothers, who are given overly repetitious phrases and strangely chromatic music, Pocahontas is "westernized" in an expressive da capo aria (*aba*). Changing moods are represented in the joyous allegrettos of the midsection ("when the lov'd one appears in her mind") and in the fioritura as the mockingbird "trolls the sweetly varying note." The outer, andante sections are more pensive and doleful, the first closing with a minor-mode inflection on the words "steeped in tear drops that fall from the eye of the night." Like the falling figures in Gluck's *Orfeo,* even the oboes seem to share the princess's grief.

The most intensely dramatic parts of *The Indian Princess,* however, are not cast in song, chorus, or dialogue but in melodrama. Music appears with the action as well as between blocks of dialogue. How that was maneuvered

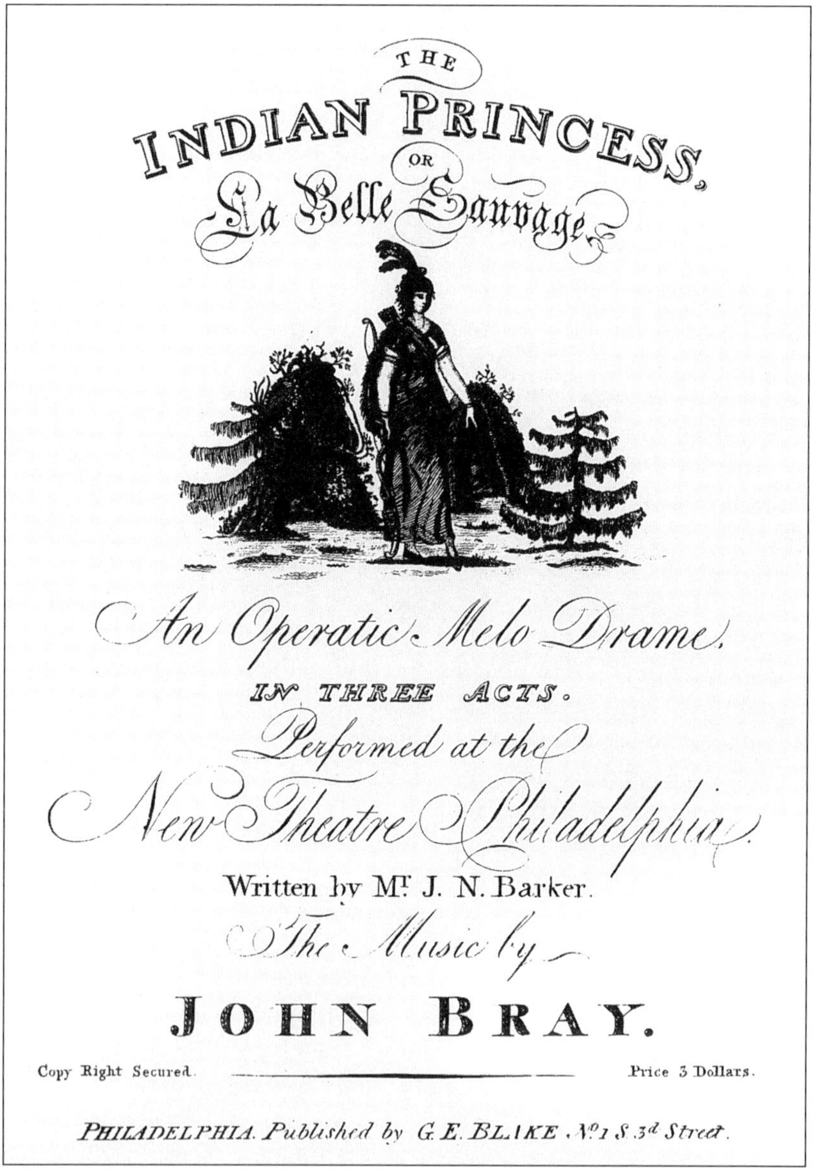

THE

INDIAN PRINCESS,

OR

La Belle Sauvage

An Operatic Melo Drame.

IN THREE ACTS.

Performed at the

New Theatre Philadelphia.

Written by Mr. J. N. Barker.

The Music by

JOHN BRAY.

Copy Right Secured.   Price 3 Dollars.

PHILADELPHIA. Published by G. E. BLAKE. No. 1 S. 3d Street.

Barker and Bray's *The Indian Princess; or, La Belle Sauvage* (1808), title page of original piano-vocal score. *Library of Congress*

can be learned from Bray's score, in which portions of the action are described above each short musical example. The pianist may have improvised transitions—a kind of "vamp till ready" technique—as in the measure marked "ad lib." in "Plaintive." Moreover, the short pieces in the libretto
may not have always followed each other immediately because of intervening action or dialogue.

There is also reason to believe that music played an even greater role in
The Indian Princess than the score indicates. Scattered throughout the libretto
are references to just "Music," with or without additional designations. Many
such references seem just as relevant to the drama as those printed in the
score, such as the "Music" accompanying the climactic tableau scene in act
3. Another musical reference that does not appear in the score (perhaps it
was improvised at the piano) has pantomimic overtones: "Music. Miami
stamps furiously; his actions betray the most savage rage of jealousy; he rushes
to seize the princess, but, recollecting that her attendants are nearby, he goes
out in an agony, by his gestures menacing revenge."[9]

The Indian Princess was not unique in its melodramatic use of music.
Although their scores have been lost, other plays and melodramas occasionally bear designations similar to those in Bray's opera. One of the earliest
and most interesting is John Turnbull's *Rudolph; or, The Robbers of Calabria*
(1804), "a Melodrama in three Acts, with marches, combats and choruses"
that was published by B. True in 1808 ("as performed at the Boston Theatre"). The importance of the character's subjective mental state is illustrated
in the large number of stage directions indicating not only how he should
react ("with astonishment," "with horror," and "with a scrutinizing eye")
but also how music should respond: "Music. Expressive of agitation and
mistrust" is indicated or "Music expressive of disappointment."[10]

From masque to mime and from melodrama to melody—America at
the turn of the nineteenth century was clearly a nation of theater and song.
The country was by no means culturally deprived, but efforts at culture
did have "gaps and mischances," as Constance Rourke notes.[11] Still, these
early works cannot be considered naïve or preliterate. They had their own
inner life and sprang from a clearly defined culture that had values and
spirit. John Bray, however, considered his *Indian Princess* a "plain-palated,
home-bred . . . urchin. . . . But do not, O goody critic," he warned in his
Preface, "apply the birch, because its unpracticed tongue cannot lisp the
language of Shakespeare, nor be very much enraged, if you find it has to
creep before it can possibly walk."[12] If American opera had learned to creep,
it would soon walk—and confidently, with a brisk Yankee stride.

Toward Grand Romantic Opera

The history of American opera is a history of its people and the manner in which they expressed their attitudes in song and drama. As the nineteenth century moved forward, music became more strongly linked with theater. Composing for opera—or "plays," as they were often called—no longer meant just arranging what already existed, but writing new music that captured the action and dramatic focus of the libretto in a unified score. Illustrating this new style along with *The Indian Princess* were such works as Rayner Taylor's *The Aethiop,* John Howard Payne's *Clari; or, The Maid of Milan,* and Micah Hawkins's *The Saw-Mill.*

Other elements of style provided new unity within the operas: the influence of the melodrama, tales of Gothic mysticism and horror, integration of comic and serious themes, the development of the American character, and a new attitude toward just what music should be in opera. Spoken prologues and epilogues, with their moralizing rhetoric, were rapidly going out of style. Instead, large ensemble finales with more elaborate staging and spectacle rounded out the drama with color and flair. Arias for more highly skilled singers and richer orchestration added to the dramatic effect. Yet always at the heart of these works were the people—Americans reflecting a new national pride and never-ending wonder in the surprises they experienced at every turn of the way.

One of the great ironies in the English-American theater connection was the production of William Dimond's *The Aethiop; or, The Child of the Desert,* with music by Henry Bishop. Advertised as a "New Grand Romantick Drama," it was a complete failure when it was staged at Covent Garden on October 13, 1812, but a brilliant success after it came to America. *The Aethiop* was produced first in New York in 1813, but its true impact came with its Philadelphia premiere on New Year's Day 1814, triggering a popularity that lasted until the Civil War. Even more surprising is the fact that *The Aethiop* crossed the seas at the height of the War of 1812. It was presented in Philadelphia's elegant Chestnut Street Theatre in "a style of splendour never exceeded on the American stage . . . with entire new scenery, dresses and decorations."[13] But its extraordinary success was more likely due to the fine musical score supplied by Rayner Taylor, advertised as the "composer of original music and accompaniments."

Undoubtedly Taylor's most important tool in molding his score for *The Aethiop* was the piece's complex dramatic structure. Its double plot—one serious and the other comic—derives from the contemporaneous English pantomime or harlequinade, but separate groups of comic and serious characters are also seen in the earlier seventeenth- and eighteenth-century commedia dell'arte and in some of Shakespeare's plays, such as *Love's Labours Lost* and *The Tempest*. What is unusual about *The Aethiop* is its use of a Harlequin-type character for a serious plot rather than a comic one. In *The Aethiop,* it is the noble Haroun Al-Raschid, the former caliph of Baghdad and disguised as the Black Necromancer (the Aethiop), who regains the throne through his ebony magic wand. Woven into a tale of intrigue and mystery is a light domestic comedy about a young Greek couple, Zoe and Alexis, who sell contraband liquor in Baghdad. Zoe resembles the perky comic servants in eighteenth-century operas, such as in Mozart's *Marriage of Figaro.* She saves her husband through her wit while the caliph saves the throne with his magic—a kind of English-American parody of aristocrat versus commoner seen in operas from *La serva padrona* to *Der Rosenkavalier.*

Comic and serious characters are delineated further through speech and song. Like Captain Smith in *The Indian Princess,* the caliph speaks in blank verse. Choral scenes are given to the serious characters, and the three songs, single duet, and trio are sung by the comic characters, who have the only major singing roles. Assigning solo songs to comic roles was undoubtedly a holdover from ballad opera practices. Large choral and instrumental scenes outnumber the solos three to one. There is also a "Corps de Ballet" integrated into the action, several marches and instrumental interludes, and a wide variety of intricate staging, usually with the choruses and finales working well into the action. A "Subterranean Chorus," for example, intones eerily, like the Furies in Gluck's *Orfeo,* as the tomb of the former caliph opens ominously amid "thunder, lightning and a hurricane."[14] Called a "Musical Colloquy," one of the most suspenseful operatic scenes takes place among Caliph Benmoussaff, Zoe, and Alxis in act 1. The sung dialogue resembles a form of accompanied recitative, as Alexis is dragged off to jail. When Zoe frantically enters, pleading for her husband's freedom, the music changes to minor mode, and the scene concludes with a short chorus sung by the Turkish guards.[15]

The Aethiop comes closer to grand opera than any of the earlier American works. It offers complete musical scenes, more clearly defined characterization, touches of accompanied recitative, and an orchestral fabric that supports the drama as never before. As one anonymous American wrote in an essay entitled "Thoughts on the Power of Music" in 1800: "The mere combination of agreeable tones, is capable of exciting an agreeable action in the organ of hearing; but the greatest pleasures we experience from music, are probably derived from the associations of ideas."[16] *The*

Aethiop proved that not only could Americans creatively associate music with ideas but also that they could write a convincing opera that would have staying power for decades to come.

Yankee Roles and Characterization

During the first quarter of the nineteenth century, the American operatic character took on new meaning for the young nation. As music theater and opera moved away from the Romantic themes of horror, bandits, specters, and far-off lands, it began to embrace sentiments closer to home—the humble cottage, industrious saw mill, rural singing schools, and the vastness and variety of the American landscape. Heroes and heroines were now the nation's cowboys and farmers, whether white or African American.

The most popular character of all, however, was the "Stage Yankee." He appears first in Royall Tyler's *The Contrast* (1787), singing lyrics now known as "Yankee Doodle." His most enduring image is found in Samuel Woodworth's *The Forest Rose; or, American Farmers* (1825). "A Pastoral Opera," as its title page indicates, the work is set in rural New Jersey. The opera is a light domestic comedy that pits the awkward shrewdness of an American farmer with the polished stupidity of an Englishman. It owes its highly successful run of more than forty years chiefly to an earthy Yankee character, Jonathan Ploughboy, who gives the play humor, stability, and conviction. The Stage Yankee became a stock character for comedians for decades. Another new twist in casting is the role of a young African American, Rose. Although her part is small, she achieves prominence in the opera's title.

The score for *The Forest Rose* was "newly composed" by John Davies, a prominent New York organist, pianist, and teacher.[17] Davies's songs, trio, duet, and two large choral finales are well integrated into the action; more important, eight of the ten major characters have singing roles—placing importance on the singing star. A new influence of the American earth, moreover, is captured in the instrumental sounds and colors of the score. Jonathan plays a jew's harp and Caesar a country fiddle. Even the overture "expresses the various sounds which are heard at early dawn in the country," as the libretto indicates, "the singing of birds, the shepherd's pipe, the hunter's horn." Described in the opening stage directions, the overture takes on new significance, both in its programmatic overlay and its links with the story.[18]

Samuel Woodworth is usually credited with founding a new American school of playwriting with *The Forest Rose*. But theater historians have

Designd & drawn on Stone by I. Baker

Scene from Samuel Woodworth's pastoral opera *The Forest Rose; or, American Farmers* (1825). *Museum of the City of New York*

often overlooked a significant work that predated it: *The Saw-Mill; or, A Yankee Trick.* Called "a comic opera" in the libretto, *The Saw-Mill* was both "written and composed" by Micah Hawkins (1777–1825), with the orchestral arrangement by James Hewitt.[19] Born in a small village near Stony Brook, New York, Hawkins was a versatile and original musical figure, largely self-taught. He was primarily a carriage-builder but also ran a grocery store where supposedly he kept a piano under the counter to entertain customers. In Hawkins's collections of songs are several in black dialect—among the earliest known to have been sung in blackface on the American stage.[20] Like his nephew, the American painter William Sidney Mount, Hawkins's main interests lay in creating distinctly American cultural forms, and his unique insight provided indigenous American personalities with new, republican dignity.

The Saw-Mill was first staged at New York's Chatham Garden Theatre on November 29, 1824, and was performed only a few times thereafter. Its scenery—designed by Alexander Reinagle's talented son Hugh—featured horse-drawn canal boats that crossed the stage, a farmhouse and a cascading waterfall, and a saw mill with all its machinery in motion.[21] The story takes place in northwestern New York state during the building of the Great Western Canal and abounds in colorful local characters. Dutch settlers, canal lockmen, saw mill workers, and a bevy of rustics all tie the plot into a cohesive whole.

The story concerns a wealthy patron, Baron Schafferdwal, who offers to give one hundred acres of land to anyone who will put up a saw mill on Oneida Creek. Two young men, Bloom and Herman, disguise themselves as "Yankees" and devise a scheme to claim both the land and the women of their choices. Through a variety of escapades, Bloom wins the baron's daughter, Elena; Herman wins Louisa; and both win the property. Two characters, Baron Schafferdwal and Norchee, speak in Dutch dialect, but what is most distinctive about the opera are its musical numbers. Although only one song from *The-Saw Mill* remains, "The Boys and Girls Must Love Each Other," the libretto indicates twenty-eight musical numbers ranging from duets and dances to songs and choruses. There are also occasional indications for melodramatic background music, unusual in a comedy. Many of the vocal ensembles are imitative—glees, catches, rounds, and fuging tunes—in other words, exercises from the American singing school tradition of Lowell Mason and Andrew Law. One scene even parodies the music lesson. "What joy breaks forth when friends do meet" sings Jacob in act 1:

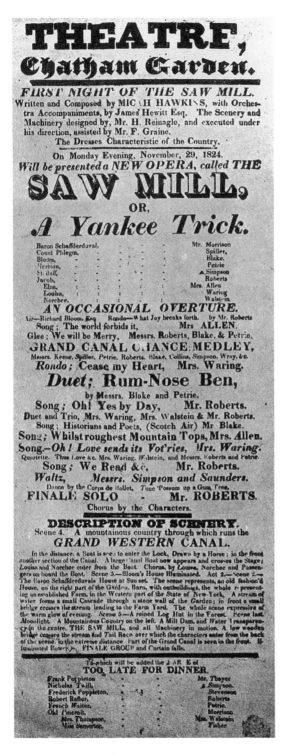

Playbill for Micah Hawkins's *The Saw-Mill; or, A Yankee Trick* (1824). *Library of Congress*

Micah Hawkins by Louis
Child. *The Museums at
Stony Brook*

> For many years, I liken their delight
> To girls and boys a singing, fa mi la sol. . . . (Sings the common chords
>   etc. with their relative minors, or otherwise, of many keys.)
> How innocent and pretty they do look
> All seated round the school-room. . . . Now the bass is here, the tenor
>   there—the counter here—the treble yonder. . . . Then, the master
>   sounds. . . . (Imitates all the different parts in the manner of a sing-
>   ing master's commencing tunes).[22]

With Hawkins, not only the characters and settings of American opera use
indigenous sources but also the music.

Early Tunes and Arias from Opera

With changes in types of characters came new developments in the music they sang. Solos, small ensembles, and choruses became more expressive and more effectively integrated within the text and action. As in the

past, lighthearted or comic songs tended to be simpler and more folklike than songs of love, anguish, and warm sentiment. "The Camel's Bell" from *The Aethiop*, for example, is constructed in three equal sections of ten bars each (*abc*) and unified by similar motifs on the words "sweet ding, ding, dong." Serious songs were given more freedom, not only in structure but also in use of embellishment. Cast in da capo form (*aba*), "If 'Tis Joy to Wound a Lover" from Peter Markoe's *The Reconcilliation* (1790) contains florid passages in the Italian gallant style.[23]

Markoe's use of the da capo aria form was rare in America at the time, although John Bray also used it in *The Indian Princess.* More common was the binary design (*ab* or *aa'*). Serious binary arias often contained segments of embellishment for dramatic enhancement. In Angelina's air "Few Are the Joys and Great the Pain" from Pelissier's *Edwin and Angelina* (1796), the B section is expanded, and the vocal line, with a flute obbligato, is embellished to reflect the "bird when summer charms no more." Touches of chromaticism on the phrases relating to "jealousy and woe" and broken vows add further color to the line.[24] The duet "Stay Lov'd Arbina" from Arthur Clifton's *The Enterprise* (1822), however, is cast in *aba'c* design, which allows phrase expansion and melodic variation in its B and C sections. The overall mood of the duet reflects the lovers' sentimental concern: "Stay Lov'd Arbina / And strew the way with flowers . . . should you in anger haste away, peace or joy no more are ours."[25]

Whether written into the score or improvised by the singer, it was taken for granted that some degree of "gracing" would be added to songs of all types. But theater-goers reacted variously. According to a review of 1810, the audience was riotous and noisy, "throwing a fork at Mrs. Oldmixon, when singing the bravura song. . . . Our taste is not yet sufficiently refined," said the critic, "to enjoy this style of singing; and a New York audience, in their soberest moments, will only listen to it from respect for the performer."[26] Another singer, Elizabeth Billington, received a somewhat kinder critique: "Though the pit yawned, and the galleries gaped in amazement, the musical world were enraptured; the effect produced in the orchestra, by her performance, is said to have been magnetic;—though, during one of her beautiful cadences, every musician (and especially the leader) was so wrapt, that he neglected to give his chord at the close of it, and proceed with the air, until the cessation of sound woke him to his senses."[27]

Opera airs that became imbedded in the minds and hearts of the American people, however, were neither spectacular nor florid but simple and tuneful. Both the tune and its associative powers, its unique role within the drama, helped songs endure. That is evident in two from operas of the period that became all-time hits: James Sanderson's "Hail to the Chief" and Henry Bishop's "Home, Sweet Home." One is America's primary ceremonial march, and the other is one of its most enduring sentimental ballads. The composers, both British, are largely forgotten, yet each song found a special place in American life and illustrates how opera and music theater reach out to everyone.

"Hail to the Chief" is still played every time an American president appears at a formal state ceremony. It is one of America's oldest patriotic traditions, harking back to the earliest days of White House history. Based on an old Scottish air, the song was written by James Sanderson, a prolific theater composer and director of the Surrey Theatre. The earliest reference to an American appearance is from a Baltimore playbill: "On Friday evening, April 3, 1812, will be performed for the first time here a celebrated dramatic romance in three acts called *The Lady of the Lake* written by John Edmund Eyre from the much admired poem of that name by Walter Scott, Esq . . . Music by the celebrated Sanderson and Dr. [John] Clarke of Cambridge and M. Pelessier, the accompaniments by the latter."[28]

But what elements in the drama gave rise to "Hail to the Chief's" time-honored association with the American presidency? Most likely it was the ceremonial flavor and colorful pageantry of the spectacle heralding the arrival of the heroic protagonist at the opening of the melodrama. Called "THE LAKE," the scene is described in the 1811 Longworth libretto printed in New York:

> Four manned and masted barges, in perspective, are sailing towards the island—above their spears, pikes, and axes, waves the bannered pine of Sir Roderick—on the opening of the scene, the pipers on the bows of the vessels play the bag-pipes; but when those cease, the following chorus is sung by the boatmen, and joined by numerous clansmen on the surrounding hills, in groups of figures on the sides and summits of the mountains:
>> Hail to the Chief who in triumph advances!
>> Honored and blessed be the evergreen Pine!
>> Long may the tree in his banner that glances
>> Flourish, the shelter and grace of our line![29]

Although the score of *Clari; or, The Maid of Milan* was written by an English composer, Henry Rowley Bishop (1786–1855), the opera's librettist, John Howard Payne (1791–1852), is considered one of the earliest popular American playwrights. He was born in New York City but wandered, living in London and various other European cities as well as Tunis, where he served as U.S. consul. His lyrics for "Home, Sweet Home" seem

The chorus "Hail to the Chief" (New York, 1817–18) by James Sanderson. *Library of Congress*

to reflect not only his own loneliness but also the longings of millions of Americans who had felt the pain of separation resulting from emigration, war, or death. The song was first sung during *Clari*'s premiere at Covent Garden on May 8, 1823. Only six months later, on November 12, the opera was staged at New York's Park Theatre. The simple, folklike structure of the tune, sung with "inexpressibly tender" emotions by "Miss Johnson," added to the success of the song.[30] But it was its creative position in the drama that made the song especially memorable. It recurred, in whole or part, throughout the story in a kind of recall technique similar to that found in the operas of Méhul and Cherubini—a unifying musical message, tying together themes of longing that American audiences had not yet experienced.

In its storyline, *Clari* resembles Augustus von Kotzebue's *The Stranger,* which William Dunlap had produced in 1798: a woman deserts her husband and children for another man, repents, and comes back to the bosom of her home. The theme of domestic life with a touch of pathos returns time and again in the stage works of the era. If characters—usually women—knitted socks, set the table, swept the floor, or trimmed the hedge they were also in the midst of some heartrending experience.[31] Clari, the pretty young daughter of an Italian farmer, is seduced by a lecherous nobleman, Duke Vivaldi. She leaves her home to live with him in his sumptuous castle but soon learns that his promise of marriage is nothing more than a hoax. Despondent and near suicide, she eventually escapes and returns to her family. The situation is happily reconciled when the duke admits his deception and asks Clari's father for her hand in marriage. For all its musty language and virtuous themes of repentance, the story has modern overtones. Real-life dramas, made visible in movies and on television, all too often find vulnerable young girls lured from their homes into tragic, abusive relationships.

As in the score of *The Indian Princess* staged fifteen years earlier, the piano-vocal edition of *Clari* contains several short instrumental passages with accompanying descriptions of the action.[32] The libretto and promptbooks, moreover, indicate that music was used almost continuously throughout the opera to underpin dramatic scenes and heighten the emotions of the characters. The score also contained twenty numbers, including solos, duets, and choruses. Yet only "Home, Sweet Home" recurs. The melody first appears in the overture and is then introduced as a song by Clari near the beginning of act 1. When the same song is sung later by Leoda, a character in the play that Clari attends at the castle, Clari is driven to near madness with guilt and grief. The most interesting treatment of "Home, Sweet Home" is its thematic recurrence in the flute's ghostly utterances as Clari sings "In the Promise of Pleasure" or in the strings' gentle reminiscence of Clari while her distraught father crosses the bridge to his farmhouse.

When Clari arrives at the farmhouse gate, a hidden four-part chorus sings "Home, Sweet Home" during a long soliloquy in which she tearfully implores her family to accept her mistakes. The chorus thus becomes less essential to the action than to the mood. As Laurence Berman notes, "The basic obligation of melodrama, as with any authentic art, is to be faithful not to 'everyday life,' but to 'inner life,' which is a reality not actually seen, but envisioned."[33] Much of *Clari*'s inner life is experienced through the recurrence of one song, a simple ballad that becomes a true operatic reminiscence aria, unifying the drama and clarifying its messages. Both "Hail to the Chief" and "Home, Sweet Home" would undoubtedly have escaped the public's notice had they not been so integrally bound into popular dramas.

With *Clari, The Forest Rose, The Saw-Mill,* and *The Aethiop,* Americans brought originality and creativity to melodramatic form by accenting its liveliest resources: laughter and music. The American stage was changing rapidly, however. Although its charm, colorful instrumentation, and magical stage effects were part of opera for decades, the harlequinade went out of fashion as its London model—replete with "dandyism" and a new character, "Dandy Lover"—became too flamboyant for Victorian American tastes, leading to speculation that the original Harlequin character may have been transvestite or gay.[34] Melodrama, however, branched into two roads: one led to the silent and early sound film of the twentieth century and the other to grand opera and the verismo style.

Ironically, the form that gave rise to both roads, the melodrama or stage play, began to contain less music as the century turned. Only during the twentieth century was music separated from dramatic performance. "We in this century [the twentieth] with our musicless theatre are the radicals, not our nineteenth-century predecessors," observes David Mayer.[35] Fortunately, the seeds were well sown early. By the early nineteenth century, the spoken monologue of the melodrama was on its way to becoming an operatic aria. What music Reinagle, Hewitt, or Pelissier played when the word *music* appeared in a libretto may never be known, but clues may lie in the dynamic musical messages that gained vitality and momentum as the century moved forward.

5
Grand Opera—the American Way

She sang, of course, "M'ama!" and not "he loves me," since an unalterable and unquestioned law of the musical world required that the German text of French operas sung by Swedish artists should be translated into Italian for the clearer understanding of English-speaking audiences.
—Edith Wharton, *The Age of Innocence*

TWO MONTHS AFTER Woodworth's homespun Jonathan Ploughboy captured the stage in *The Forest Rose,* another character not too unlike him in social status and spunk appeared—Figaro. Their worlds were far apart— both geographically and aesthetically—but Figaro, Rosina, and Basilio and their antics created a sensation in America. One of the "highest and most costly entertainments" of the Old World would at last be heard in New York, proclaimed the *American* on November 7, 1825.[1] "Until it is seen," added the *New York Evening Post* on November 30, "it will never be believed that a play can be conducted in recitative or singing and yet appear as natural as the ordinary drama."

The work to which the *Post* referred was the first fully staged performance in America of an Italian opera in the original language: Gioacchino Rossini's lighthearted masterpiece *Il barbiere di Siviglia.* It was staged at the Park Theatre on November 29, 1825, under the direction of Manuel Garcia, the noted Spanish tenor who had sung Count Almaviva in *Il barbiere*'s premiere in Rome in 1816. Numbering twenty-five members, the orchestra for New York's staging was one of the largest and most complete of its time.[2] From London, Garcia had brought his wife, the soprano Joaquina Sitches; his son, Manuel Patricio; and several other fine singers. But the prize of his troupe was his seventeen-year-old daughter Maria, who sang the role of Rosina. Later known as Madame Malibran, she brought to America a dazzling range and coloratura style that would establish her as one of the century's most celebrated singers.

The furor over *Il barbiere* was unprecedented, but New York was ready for Italian opera. With a population of 166,000, it was one of the fastest-growing cities in the world. The opening of the Erie Canal in 1825 enlarged the commercial welfare of the city, and new visions of American culture began to take hold in the arts. In 1831 the New York Sacred Musical Society performed the city's premiere of Handel's *Messiah,* and eleven years later the Philharmonic Society of New York was formed, the same year as Vienna's great Philharmonic. Most important, New Yorkers were developing a strong sense of civic pride. As James Hardie observed in 1827, "The City of New York, from its rapid growth, commercial character, and unrivalled prosperity, has justly been called the London of America. But it is now high time to change the appellation. The extensive patronage afforded to the liberal arts, and works of taste: the unexampled increase in public amusements, with the consequent progress of morals and refinement: have, at length, rendered New-York the *Paris of the New World.*"[3]

Il barbiere ran successfully for twenty-one performances, but in his single New York season Garcia also produced Rossini's *Tancredi, Otello, La Cenerentola,* and—at the suggestion of Mozart's librettist Lorenzo da Ponte, who lived in the city at the time—*Don Giovanni.* Staged on May 23, 1826, *Don Giovanni* was the first complete performance, in the original version, of any of Mozart's major operas in America. When the season ended, Garcia had given New York seventy-nine performances of nine different Italian operas, including two of his own, *L'amante astuto* (1825) and *La figlia dell'aria* (1826).[4] After Garcia left New York for Mexico City, da Ponte continued the cause for Italian opera. He raised funds for the construction of the elegant Italian Opera House, which opened its doors on November 18, 1833, with the New York premiere of Rossini's *La gazza ladra.* By the close of the first season, some eighty performances of Italian opera had been given there.[5]

As the century progressed, the new, florid Italian operas, with their bel canto arias, recitatives, and ensembles rendered by agile professional singers, became enormously popular. Many, such as Vincenzo Bellini's *La sonnambula* (Milan 1831 and New York 1835) and *Norma* (Milan 1831, New Orleans 1836, and New York 1841), were produced in America only a few years after their world premieres.[6] Singers became veritable superstars whose images decorated the covers of countless pieces of sheet music arrangements of arias and other gems from favorite operas. Fine opera houses were constructed, notably in New York City. Palmo's opened in 1844, and the Astor Place Opera House three years later with Giuseppe Verdi's *Ernani* (1844). In 1854 the 4,600-seat Academy of Music was built "for the purpose of cultivating a taste for music."[7] Its stage was the largest in the world, and it remained New York's main venue for opera for the next thirty

years. The mystique of foreign-language opera and fashionable new theaters with private boxes, moreover, encouraged a new, upper-class audience. It also created a social custom—and power base—that would shape
the nation's important operatic institutions, such as the Metropolitan Opera,
in the decades to come.

Still, there were those who resented the invasion of this foreign art—
sometimes even patrons themselves. Philip Hone, a former mayor of New
York and an important fund-raiser for the Italian Opera House, wrote in
1835, "We want to understand the language; we cannot endure to sit by
and see the performers splitting their sides with laughter, and we not take
the joke; dissolved in 'briny tears,' and we not permitted to sympathize with
them; or running each other through the body, and we devoid of the means
of condemming or justifying the act."[8] Yet some nineteenth-century
American composers had an answer to Hone and those like him: write
new "Italian operas" in English—grand opera, in other words, American-
style. The term *grand opera* in the 1830s and 1840s referred to long, elabo-
rately staged operas that had large casts and serious dramatic content, as
in the operas of Meyerbeer, Spontini, Auber, and many of Bellini and
Donizetti. That definition might apply also to melodrama, with the vital
exception that there was no spoken dialogue in grand opera. As Vincenzo
Bellini once remarked, "Opera, through singing, must make one weep,
shudder, and die."[9]

William Henry Fry

Plots in grand opera were heroic, with shifting moods often laced with
violence, intrigue, and tragedy. The major characters might be from a lower
class but able to rise heroically through wit and perseverance, like the re-
sourceful servants in comic opera. As for musical style, some arias might
abound in florid vocal fioritura, whereas others could be simple, folklike
ballads. Ballet, large choruses, pageantry, and varied orchestral colors also
figured prominently in this exciting new entertainment force.

The first American composer to attempt this style of opera with a
modicum of success was William Henry Fry (1813–64). Fry's *Leonora* was
given its premiere at the Chestnut Street Theatre in Philadelphia on June
4, 1845. Conducted by Adolph Schmidt, the production had an orchestra
of sixty and a chorus of eighty and received at least fifteen more stagings
during its first two years.[10] On March 29, 1858, at New York's Academy of
Music, *Leonora* was produced again in a revised version in Italian. Fashioning his work mainly after Bellini and Donizetti, Fry had taken a suc-

cessful—but for Americans still relatively exotic—art form and offered it to the nation's ever-expanding audiences. As he explains in the score's "Prefatory Remarks":

> This lyrical drama was produced on the stage with a view of presenting to the American public, *a grand opera,* originally adapted to English words. . . . Its peculiarity lies in the absence of all spoken monologue or dialogue; every word being sung throughout and accompanied by the orchestra. This is essentially the high, complete, and classic form to give to the opera; it imparts proper uniformity of style to the entire declamation; does not confound the strictly musical with the acting drama; and with an artistic performance confirms the interest of the representation. . . . I have, indeed, too much admiration for the English language, to admit of the supposition that it is excluded, by its nature, from the highest form of opera; and I believe that the original grand opera . . . would, if produced by English composers, take permanently as a class the preference over mixed speaking opera. . . . It is a clear proposition, that no Art can flourish in a country until it assumes a genial character. It may be exotic, experimentally, for a time, but unless it becomes indigenous, taking root and growth in the hearts and understandings of the people generally, its existence will be forced and sickly, and its decay quick and certain.[11]

Fry's concern for the staying power of a new art form was prophetic. America's earliest and most vehement champion of American musical culture was born and raised in Philadelphia. He received his master's degree from the University of Pennsylvania in 1833 and was eventually admitted to the bar, but music and journalism were his real passions. Fry studied piano and composition with Leopold Meignen, formerly of Paris, and worked on the editorial staff of his father's newspaper, the *Philadelphia National Gazette,* covering music, theater, and art. Fine touring companies were bringing French and Italian opera to the city, and Fry was able to hear the newest works of Auber, Rossini, Bellini, Mercadante, Hérold, Méhul, Grétry, and others. Caught in the spell of grand opera, he brought to Philadelphia in 1841 the city's first production of Bellini's *Norma.*[12]

During the years he spent in Europe as correspondent for the *New York Tribune,* Fry heard and reviewed literally hundreds of Romantic operas. Returning to New York in 1852, he continued to write for the *Tribune,* and these "fusions of wisdom and unwisdom" provide a kaleidoscope of American operatic activities during the antebellum era.[13] Fry also presented a well-attended series of eleven lectures for the general public on all aspects of music. The series was ambitiously illustrated by a large chorus, fine

Philadelphia-born composer, William Henry Fry, whose grand operas attracted more attention than any other American operas of the time. *Library of Congress*

soloists, and the New York Philharmonic, making Fry a kind of nineteenth-century Leonard Bernstein. "For two hours and a half," wrote the *Boston Courier,* "did he talk brilliantly, quaintly, convulsingly, learnedly, button-holedly, prophetically, half-inspiredly, whimsically, conceitedly, bravely, truly, about everything—and *music.* "[14]

Thus was the image of this variegated American personality. But Fry was also a composer of symphonies, overtures, chamber music, and choral works, among them the *Stabat Mater* (1855) and Mass in E-Flat, which was left incomplete at his death on December 21, 1864. Most significant among his works, however, are the grand operas. Although his *Bridal of Dunure* and *I Cristiani e Pagani* have been lost, scores remain for three completed works: *Aurelia the Vestal* (1841), *Leonora* (1845), and *Notre-Dame of Paris* (1862). *Aurelia,* the familiar story of the love of a vestal virgin for a Roman Christian nobleman, was never performed. But both *Leonora* and *Notre-Dame* were not only staged several times but also attracted more press attention—pro and con—than any American opera thus far.

In three acts, *Leonora* is based on a popular play, *The Lady of Lyons* (1838), by the English novelist Edward Bulwer Lytton. Its libretto was written by Fry's brother, Joseph Reese Fry, who had recently fashioned an English libretto for the Philadelphia staging of Donizetti's *Anna Bolena.* One of the main changes in *Leonora*'s libretto concerns the setting. No longer set in revolutionary France, the action is moved to sixteenth-century Spain during the early conquests in America and, as Fry explains, "to a more distant and hence romantic era."[15] The story is the old three-way conflict—popular from harlequinade to melodrama—of young woman, rival suitors (often one rich, the other poor), and controlling father. In *Leonora* there is intrigue but not the blood and thunder of many melodramas. Rather, the story hinges upon the triumph of sincere love over deception and greed—with a touch of American-style derring-do in the character of Julio, a humble young peasant.

For Americans, the basic story was not at all new, nor were the lyrical sounds of Bellini and Donizetti that shaped Fry's musical style. What was new was the challenge to the American composer of relating music and drama within a fresh theatrical framework. The relationship between voice register and characterization, common especially in grand opera, is important to Fry. Lithe and young, Leonora is cast as a colorature soprano; the villain, Montalvo, is a bass; and the lover-hero Julio is a tenor. A mezzo-soprano or contralto role, often reserved for darkly mysterious parts, is absent. To realize fully these contrasting vocal timbres, Fry employed the finest singers in America. The excellent young English tenor John Frazer played Julio, and Leonora and Montalvo were played by Anne and Edward Seguin, a famous English married team who toured the East Coast with their Seguin English Opera Company. Professionally trained at the Royal Academy of Music in London, both Seguins had sung the major repetoire and had strong star appeal.

In placing his singers within the opera, Fry found a model in the scena-ed-aria structure common in nineteenth-century Italian opera. A typical scena might have several parts, such as recitative, aria, or cavatina (a short aria); a chorus sometimes interrupted by a solo; and a final bravura solo, sometimes called a cabaletta. Thus the rapidly changing moods of the drama were unified and enhanced by a variety of connecting vocal styles. Solos were often embellished by highly florid singing. Published separately, the cavatina "My Every Thought" from scene and cavatina (no. 5) contains vocal fioritura that illustrates how ornamentation is often as much text painting as showmanship. "My heart as free as soaring bird," sings Leonora, and on the words "exulteth proudly in liberty" she soars jubilantly.

The orchestra, too, often has dramatic—and melodramatic—function in the opera. As Leonora meets Julio in the wedding scene in act 2, for example, we hear the "Dies Irae" melody in the organ, then a rising bass line and tremolo strings as ominous harbingers of what lies ahead for the young couple. That technique of melodrama, using the orchestra to forcast what is to come, moved directly into Wagner and on into modern film scores.

The key elements of any drama are, of course, the finales, which in *Leonora* show considerable interplay among characters and musical styles. The act 2 finale, for example, alternates chorus, solos, quintet, and quintet with chorus, all joined by often long passages of recitative. In his "Prefatory Remarks," Fry justifies the use of recitative in English and adds, "All language which has sufficient dignity to merit a place in such an opera, may be sung in *recitative accompanied by the orchestra.*"[16] Thus the recitative does more than link arias and ensembles. It furthers the action through vocal lines as well as orchestral support. In the dramatic "Recitative and Duet" (no. 15) before the finale of act 2, shifting orchestral colors, tempos, and dynamics underscore the scene in which Leonora learns of Julio's deception. The recitative is especially stormy and agitated, and the score's descriptive markings resemble those of melodrama: "Julio agitated, Leonora surprised," "Julio with restrained calmness," "Julio with a groan," and "sinks into a chair." Use of the tri-tone to imply impending evil, string tremolos, rising chromatic scales, and other melodramatic orchestral effects add to the dramatic impact of the scene.

But how dramatic and effective was *Leonora* to audiences of the time?

Reviews were mixed. Philadelphia in general supported its native son. The *Public Ledger*'s critic wrote on June 12, 1845 that "Leonora improves with each subsequent repetition, and is now universally pronounced the most brilliant spectacle of the opera kind ever afforded in this city. The audience, which have nightly increased in numbers, as well as in fashion and gayety will, we have no doubt, on this occasion, fill the house to overflowing." And overflow it did. Among the notables were the vice president of the United States, George M. Dallas, and his family. But New York—its nose out of joint in not hosting the premiere of America's first grand opera—felt otherwise. The *New York Herald*'s reviewer observed on June 8 that the opera was "a warm hash of Bellini, with a cold shoulder of 'Rossini' and a handful of 'Auber' salt."[17] As Giovanni Pacini once remarked about composers' ubiquitous practice of imitating the florid style of Rossini, "There was no other way to make a living."[18] Sixteen years later, however, *Leonora* did make the stage of New York—and in Italian. "What an infinite relief it is to be bathed in melody," wrote a New York critic, "after being dry-rubbed with mere sound, as in the case of some of our modern composers."[19] Who those dry modern composers were the critic does not say.

Fry's last opera, *Notre-Dame of Paris,* tells quite a different story.[20] In many respects it is a better work than *Leonora,* more compact dramatically and with fewer Bellini-like conventions, more vivid text-painting, and greater harmonic richness. Composed nineteen years after *Leonora,* it also shows more maturity and originality in handling the enormous creative forces required of the grand opera style.

Based on Victor Hugo's work of 1831, *Notre-Dame de Paris* (*The Hunchback of Notre Dame*), Fry's opera is rich in romantic imagery and contrasting moods—a story that provided the composer felicitous memories of his beloved Paris. It is set in the late fifteenth century, and although it abounds in the usual melodramatic tools of dungeons, daggers, and death, its colorfully contrasting main characters provide a new twist: Quasimodo, the pathetic, deformed bell-ringer of Notre Dame, and Esmeralda, the voluptuous gypsy dancing girl whom he loves.

Joseph Reese Fry was again the librettist for one of his brother's works, and *Notre-Dame of Paris* was presented for the first time at the Academy of Music in Philadelphia on May 4, 1864. It was staged during the Grand Music Festival opening the Sanitary Fair to benefit the servicemen of the U.S. Army and Navy while farther south the armies of Lee and Grant wrought mutual destruction in the Battle of the Wilderness. Directed by Theodore Thomas, future conductor of the New York Philharmonic, the production featured outstanding talent. Edward Seguin (bass), son of *Le-onora*'s Montalvo, sang Quasimodo; Mme. Compte Borchard (soprano) portrayed Esmeralda; and William Castle, who was to become one of America's most popular singers, sang the role of Captain de Chateaupers of the Royal Guard. Jenny Kempton (contralto) played Gedule, the mysterious stranger who eventually finds her lost child, Esmeralda, only to witness the young girl's death sentence.

Notre-Dame has all the features of French grand opera: festive celebration scenes; on-stage military bands; the use of an organ (as in *Leonora*); colorful solo instrumental passages, such as the saxophone used in act 1; and an extensive ballet in act 4. Newspapers advertised a chorus of one hundred and orchestral forces of ninety-five. A large cast included the king and royal family, Flemish ambassadors, judicial officers, showmen, and grotesque characters for the king of fools scene; costumes must have been lavish. A team of designers realized the scenery, and "the Cathedral was accurately painted in proportion and details from an imperial photograph by Mr. Hawthorne," reported the *Philadelphia Ledger* on May 3 and 2, 1864.

Perhaps most significant in Fry's work is his technique of musical characterization. Characters come to be known not only through their lyrics but also by their music. Like Georges Bizet's *Carmen* almost a decade later, Esmeralda is introduced in act 1 with a folklike tune that is sung with lyrical abandon:

> Born where the summer's
> Perennial power
> Laughs in the homage
> Of bird and flower;
> Where'er I wander
> Joy aye attends me,
> Music my herald,
> Love is my train.[21]

Later in the same act, the audience meets Quasimodo, king of fools, who "is borne aloft, attired as the King, with burlesque paraphernalia of a royal court—banners, music, heralds, guards, pages, and so forth." His aria, almost a caricature, introduces him through a grotesque, limping melodic line that has widely spaced, awkward intervals. Contrasting with both Esmeralda and Quasimodo, Chateaupers, the tenor and lover, is given lyrical, sustained melodic lines in his act 3 aria "Vision of Love," with its romantic accompaniment of strings and harp. In act 1, Chateaupers sings:

What nameless spell is on me
With this strange maiden, darkly blending;
What potent charm hath won me
To ardent longing for her heart.

With its emotional climax, as Upton claims, even Caruso would have done the aria "sumptuously and would have gloried in it."[22]

Rare for American operas of this time, *Notre-Dame of Paris* received an abundance of excellent reviews. On May 7, Philadelphia's *Evening Bulletin* placed *Notre-Dame* "among the front rank of modern operas—better than some of Verdi's, Donizetti's and Bellini's, and far before those of Pacini, Petrella and others that have won popularity." "The audience was astounded and delighted in hearing such a gigantic body of sounds, and witnessing stage displays stately and grotesquely eccentric, by turns, such as are unparalleled," reported the *Philadelphia Ledger* on May 6. "Not even in England are so many persons on the stage in grand opera, and it is the general sentiment of travelled connoisseurs that in freshness and resonance, the chorus exceeds even that of the Paris Academy, while its accuracy is perfect." "There are processions of ecclesiastics, soldiers, peasants, maskers and others; a military band, and an organ pealing through the open portals of the church," added the *New York Times*. "Mr. Fry has been most successful in writing for the low-pitched voices. The barytone, bass and contralto parts are the best. The gayety and brilliancy of the soprano is sometimes a little overstrained and the tenor is likely to fall in love with himself. In the important matter of instrumentation, Mr. Fry is particularly happy. Some of the scenes are tone-colored with absolute felicity."[23] But on May 6 the *Philadelphia Ledger* seemed to grasp the true significance of the event: "Mr. Fry has given his time and his labor gratuitously for the benefit of the soldiers, and he has presented an opera which, as a work of art, is really an honor to his country, and especially to the city of his nativity."

Impresarios, Politicians, and Parodists

Few American composers of the era came even close to Fry's achievements in the grand opera form. Others tried their hand at it but with varying levels of success. They had competition. New operas from Europe were steadily pouring into the country, and older ones were revived again and again. By 1855, the year Verdi's *Il trovatore* (1853) was given its premiere (in Italian) in New York, *The Bohemian Girl* (1843) by the Irish composer William Balfe was well on its way to becoming America's most popular opera of the century. Too, there were all the "Dramatic, Operatic, Hippo-dromatic, Panoramatic, Minstrelatic, and Concertatic amusements," as the *Evening Mirror* reported on November 4, 1848, that managed to fill the city's some fifteen theaters. How could an American composer compete? Yet they did—and why and how they composed is often as interesting as the works themselves. Whether impresario, politician, or parodist, all were caught up in the mesmerizing spell of Italian grand opera, with its melo-dramatic inflections and florid vocal lines that singers loved to display.

Not long after they had emigrated to America, three important con-ductor-impresarios—Luigi Arditi, Maurice Strakosch, and Max Maret-zek—composed operas in the Italian style, lyrically featuring the flexible voices of their fine singers.[24] Arditi (1822–1903), who had conducted the fine Havana Italian Opera Company and at Covent Garden, could boast under his baton Marietta Alboni, Adelina Patti, and many other vocal su-perstars who entertained American audiences at the time. Arditi's *La Spia,* from James Fenimore Cooper's popular novel *The Spy* (1821), was admi-rably received at its premiere at New York's Academy of Music on March 24, 1856, as was an opera by the Czech impresario Maurice Strakosch, whose *Giovanna prima di Napoli* (1850) was considered especially "sing-able."[25] Maretzek did not fare as well with the critics, however. A noted musician who had conducted the American premieres of Verdi's *La travi-ata* in 1856 and *Don Carlos* in 1877, Maretzek found only modest recep-tion of his opera after Washington Irving: *Sleepy Hollow; or, The Headless Horseman* (1879). Americans had tired of the Italian bel canto style. "Maretzek leads us back at least twenty-five years," wrote J. S. Dwight on October 4, 1879. "New York with its cosmopolitan character, with its mixed population, can digest stronger food. But we must not forget that Maretzek has written for the whole country. . . . It is no use to present an opera on an American subject to a farmer out West, and give him high-toned mu-sic, which this poor man will not understand at all."[26]

At least one famous man from "out West," however, proved that grand opera could reach many levels of the American spirit. Abraham Lincoln's tastes form a barometer of the operatic life of the nation's capital during the Civil War. Shortly before his inauguration, Lincoln attended in New York the American premiere of Verdi's *A Masked Ball,* originally the story of a monarch's brutal murder—and a chilling prophecy of his own assas-sination. A passionate opera-lover, Lincoln was also the first to invite an opera singer to entertain him in the White House and the only president in history to have had an inaugural opera staged for him. Friedrich von Flotow's *Martha* was presented for his second inauguration in 1865. Between 1861 and his assassination in 1865, Lincoln saw at least thirty productions in Washington. Among them were Bellini's *Norma,* Rossini's *Barber of Seville,* Donizetti's *Daughter of the Regiment,* Mozart's *Magic Flute,* Beethoven's *Fidelio,* Weber's *Der Freischütz,* and Gounod's *Faust.* When criticized for attending the opera so frequently during the turbulent years of the Civil War, he said simply, "I must have a change, or I will die." It was a poignant tribute to music's enduring therapeutic powers.[27]

Lincoln appointed a prominent American composer, James Remington Fairlamb (1838–1908), to be U.S. consul in Zurich from 1861 to 1865. When Fairlamb's *Valerie; or, Treasured Tokens* (1869) was performed in Washington, it became the first American opera to be staged there. Born in Philadelphia, Fairlamb studied music in Paris and Florence and became a prolific composer; more than 150 of his songs and organ pieces are published. His *Te Deum* for double chorus and orchestra, moreover, won him decoration by the king of Württemberg. Upon returning to the United States, he worked primarily in Washington, D.C., and New York City and was one of the founders of the American Guild of Organists.[28] The date of *Valerie*'s performance in Washington is unknown, but the opera was staged in Philadelphia on December 13, 1869, and advertised in the *Evening Bulletin* on that same date as having "a large chorus and a first rate orchestra under the direction of Mr. Fairlamb . . . a musician of a great deal of natural ability."

Combining traits of Italian grand opera with those of light comic opera, *Valerie* contains thirty-three musical numbers and four acts and uses both spoken dialogue and recitative.[29] The story, set in Lyons, France, during the early nineteenth century, is light and superficial, but judging from the libretto's detailed descriptions of the costumes and staging the production was an ambitious undertaking.

The Italian influence was manifest in several other operas by American-born composers of the period, but it also lent itself to an abundance of ridicule and satire. One of the most popular was John Brougham's *Po-Ca-Hon-Tas; or, The Gentle Savage* (1855), called "An Original Aboriginal Erratic Operatic Semi-Civilized and Demi-Savage Extravaganza. . . . The Music Dislocated and Re-set by James G. Maeder."[30] Brougham's famous burlesque pokes fun at the current fetish of theatrical works on Indian subjects, and its stage directions are often whimsical spoofs on Italian opera. "I see [Music in orchestra] and hear a famous opera-tunity," says Captain Smith. What follows is a "GRAND SCENA COMPLICATO, In the Anglo-Italiano Style" that would make even Peter Schickle envious. Similar markings dot the libretto: "Recitativo—Italiani doloroso," "GRAND SCENA PERTURBATO,

Aria—Hibernoso affettuosamente," and reference to "an exhibition of tra-cheotomous gymnastics." After the "Air—Pop goes the Weazle," Poca-hontas enters, and "her overburthened soul bursts forth in melody."

Other burlesques are parodies of Italian operas themselves, such as *Mrs. Normer* (*Norma*), *Sam Pari* (*Zampa*), *The Roof Scrambler* (*La sonnambula*), or *Buy It Dear, 'Tis Made of Cashmere* (*The Bayadere; or, The Maid of Cashmere*). The cleverest parody of all is not a stage work but a literary publication, *Physiology of the Opera* (1852) by one "Scrici," whose persona remains ob-scure. The book of nine chapters is a sort of American *Il teatro alla moda* (Benedetto Marcello, 1720) and covers voice ranges, audiences, conduc-tors, orchestra, acting, plots, and even the prompter. "The primo basso is to the primo tenore what the draught horse is to the racer," writes Scrici. "His features are gross and sensual, exhibiting about the amount of intel-ligence which may be looked for in one of those bedecked and garlanded animals, whose appearance among us announces the future sale of show beef."[31] The prompter (*suggeritore*), adds Scrici, must be a thin man: "It does not require a Paxton to know that a hole in the stage two feet square, will not hold Barnum's obesities. He must also be short and supple-necked, to allow the green fungus which excresces from the stage to cover him; and he must be the fortunate owner of a right arm as untiring as a locomo-tive crank or the sails of a windmill."[32]

As for the characters in the opera, the chieftain, always a tenor, "has from time to time indulged in gestures about as strong as we can well conceive of, but now and then when an extraordinarily deep sentiment, and a very high note, choose the same moment for their expression, he is obliged to poise himself on one foot, extend the other behind him, ele-vating the heel and depressing the toe, fold his hands over his breast, throw back the head and shake the body like a Newfoundland dog just issuing from the water—the refractory note and the hidden emotion are always brought to light by these gesticulatory expedients." The distressed female sings a cavatina with "some very high singing." She, too, makes a "great many of the Newfoundland dog shakes, the lady part of the audience sit-ting up wrapt in admiration, with the eyes fastened on the stage as intent-ly as if they were witnessing a marriage ceremony, gently murmuring their approbation in detached sentences, such as 'sweet, lovely, charming, ex-quisite;' while the fast men by the door, utter the words 'knocker, fast nag,' and declare that her time is 'two thirty.'"[33]

For all the zany pokes at it as a fad, Italian opera provided American composers with a lyrical and dramatic springboard. It became a model to emulate and shape into their own expressive creations for years to come—

no better model for opera could be found. It was what drew the best singers. It was what was known. It was what worked.

Grand Opera and American Literature

While Fry and other American composers based their operas on European literature and themes, others were turning to sources closer to home.
"Why," demanded one critic of the era, "cannot our literati comprehend
the matchless sublimity of our position among the nations of the world?"
Why should the nation "bend the knee to false tastes and foreign idola-
try," he asked, when it had its own magnificent scenery, heroes, and experiences?[34] Others asked why it was necessary for the sculptor Horatio
Greenough to clothe his statue of George Washington in a toga. Why
should the nation's capitol be infused with figures from mythology—where
were America's birds, trees, and flowers?

Although the period from about 1830 to the Civil War abounded in
cries for a distinctively American culture, it also found answers in broad,
highly individual expressions of American literature. "We will walk on our
own feet," asserted Ralph Waldo Emerson. "We will work with our own
hands; we will speak our own minds."[35] By the start of the Civil War, Henry
David Thoreau had completed *Walden,* Walt Whitman his *Leaves of Grass,*
Harriet Beecher Stowe *Uncle Tom's Cabin,* Herman Melville *Moby-Dick,*
Nathaniel Hawthorne *The Scarlet Letter,* and Washington Irving *Rip van
Winkle* and *The Legend of Sleepy Hollow,* both of which were published in
England and America. Although their locales are American, the latter two
works were based on familiar European sources. Irving had spent much
of his active life abroad, and European critics came to admire him as an
eminent American author.[36]

Like Edgar Allan Poe, Washington Irving delighted in the mystical and
obscure. But he was also one of the first American authors to discover the
romantic potentialities of the expanding American frontier. His work inspired at least four American operas of this period: Max Maretzek's *The
Legend of Sleepy Hollow;* Charles Edward Horne's *Ahmed al Kamel* (1840),
which was from Irving's *Tales of the Alhambra;* James Gaspard Maeder's *The
Peri; or, The Enchanted Fountain* (1852) from *A History of Columbus;* and
George Bristow's *Rip van Winkle* (1855), after Irving's short story of the
same name. None quite matched Bristow's in importance, however. The
score and libretto of *Rip van Winkle* tell much about how literature became opera through the collaborative craft of early American composers
and librettists.

When George Frederick Bristow (1825–98) composed *Rip van Winkle,* he and his librettist, Jonathan Howard Wainwright, had to alter Irving's story to accommodate the exigencies of the musical stage. In the opera, Irving's story develops in acts 1 and 3. Events involving Rip, his shrewish wife, and the burgomaster's plot to marry his son to Rip's eventually wealthy daughter, Alice, occur in act 1. The act closes as Rip, wandering into a dark ravine, succumbs to the ghostly spell of the lost explorer Hendrick Hudson and his strange cohorts. In act 3, Rip awakens from a twenty-year sleep, his wife and old friends gone. By a stroke of luck, he returns home just in time to annul Alice's marriage contract, and she is free to marry her true love.

New to the tale are the events in act 2. Wainwright cleverly added a love story between Alice and Edward, a young captain in the Continental army. That provided an opportunity for some lyrical duets between the young lovers. By placing act 2 during the Revolutionary War, he not only ties together the two outer acts by repeating some of their characters but also gives the opera an American patriotic flavor, allowing for spirited musical numbers such as martial rhythms, a soldiers' chorus, and a vivandière song.

Like William Henry Fry, Bristow was an avid champion of American music. Born in Brooklyn, he played in the violin section of the New York Philharmonic for thirty-six years. He was not only active as a choral director, organist, and composer of symphonic works but also contributed significantly to New York's music education in his work as a public school teacher and pedagogical author. Decrying the lack of American works in the Philharmonic's repertoire, Bristow once complained that "the Philharmonic Society has been as anti-American as if it had been located in London during the Revolutionary War, and composed of native-born British tories."[37]

Rip van Winkle, Bristow's only completed opera, was first produced at Niblo's Garden in New York City on September 27, 1855, by the Pyne and Harrison troupe. The composer had barely turned thirty. It was an immediate success. "Sebastopol has fallen, and a New American Opera has succeeded in New York!" hailed the *Musical Review* with wry reference to the concurrent Crimean War.[38] The elaborate sets were "all painted from nature," and the tableaux were based on illustrations by F. O. C. Darnley. Lighting had become a major feature in opera production, as stage directions for the extensive act 1 finale attest: "Back drop painted on scrim, to light up at cue [during the chorus], showing 'storm king' in chariot drawn by horses in mid-air. . . . Full stage. one-half dark, calcium light etc.; blue mediums. Hendrick Hudson and companions, spirits, etc. are discovered in various picturesque attitudes. Blue lights thrown on scene—the whole to produce a weird and supernatural effect."[39]

Rip van Winkle is designated a "grand romantic opera" in the piano-vocal edition published in 1882.[40] There are ubiquitous "Italianisms": bel canto arias with vocal cadenzas; passages of recitative; and scenae, such as number 13, "I Cannot Wait," with Alice, Herman, and Edward. The reminiscence-aria technique, becoming more common in Italian opera, is apparent when the tune from Alice's important aria in act 2, "Yes, I'll Follow to the Battle," returns to reinforce her happiness in her final number. What gives the opera its special American flavor, however, is its main character, a folklike American hero—a Catskills farmer, a little tipsy and a little henpecked—who in the end saves the day. Washington Irving provided Bristow with what Daniel Boorstin calls the "comic superman." "What made the American popular hero heroic also made him comic," he writes. "The pervasive ambiguity of American life, the vagueness which laid the continent open to adventure, which made the land a rich storehouse of the unexpected . . . suffused both the comic and the heroic. Both depended on incongruity: the incongruity of the laughable and the incongruity of the admirable."[41]

That incongruity furnishes the interest and color in Bristow's variegated score. There are touches of melodrama (with music both accompanying and alternating with the dialogue); a drinking song; a morris dance; lyrical parlor ballads; tuneful Protestant hymns; bouncy comic-opera rhythms; and a shivering finale complete with thunder, dancing spirits, and the orchestral rumblings of ninepins. Bristow provides a fascinating panorama of mid-century American culture.

Not all critics of the day understood the new kind of American opera, however. Waldemer Rieck noted that "the work has the length of a grand tragic opera, while it is in itself only a melodrama."[42] John Sullivan Dwight questioned the use of spoken dialogue—"a shabby practice," he said. "I rejoice even at the production of works like this," he added, "because the public will learn in time that all inspiration was not given to the Italian and Teutonic races. If we are ever to have any national operas, they must be based upon our own language; the union of intelligible, vigorous and attractive plays with kindred music."[43]

None of the nineteenth-century literary works that inspired operas was as far-reaching as Harriet Beecher Stowe's *Uncle Tom's Cabin*. When that brilliant work was published in 1852, it aroused so much anger and emotional fervor that it played a major role in fanning the flames of abolition.

During its first year, it sold more than three hundred thousand copies and was translated into twenty-one languages, including Welsh, Wallachian, and Armenian.[44] Rarely had an American play dealt with current social problems. Thus, when Stowe's novel became a stage play the same year, it inaugurated a theater phenomenon unparalleled in American history. "Tom shows," extravaganzas, plays, and variety acts based on the story continued to draw audiences in droves well into the twentieth century. Songs relating to the novel and its dramatic offshoots became mainstays of nearly every mode of musical expression, from parlor piano to circus organ and from dance orchestra to military band.

Two of the most interesting stage realizations of the novel were first produced thirty years apart: George Aiken and George C. Howard staged their melodrama *Uncle Tom's Cabin* in Troy, New York, on September 27, 1852, and Caryl Florio's opera of the same name had its premiere in Philadelphia on May 27, 1882. The two works not only illustrate the interrelationship between the melodrama and opera as nineteenth-century theatrical forms but also show different approaches to the same highly popular subject. Of the two composers, Howard had a far better grasp of the audience; his melodrama and its derivatives remained popular for almost eight decades. Roughly, the melodrama (or "play" as it was often called) follows the events of the novel, but it is more a series of scenes than a consistent drama with motivation. Even lacking taught dramatic ebb and flow, it remained a powerful social force. "I wish every abolitionist in the land could see this play as I saw it," wrote one New York correspondent, "and exult as I did that, when haughty pharisees will not testify against slavery, the very stones are crying out!"[45]

Music played a vital role in the emotional impact of Howard's *Uncle Tom*. As in other melodramas of the time, it was used to enhance or heighten the spoken dialogue and dramatic action and to express the characters' feelings through song. Although the work's four poignant songs became so popular that they were published separately, it was the "expressive" instrumental music running throughout the text that intensified the play's social and religious messages. Scripts and promptbooks usually did not indicate the exact music to be used, only cues for the moods to be conjured up. Those moods graphically defined each character, whether the dancing antics of Topsy or the vicious inhumanity of Simon Legree.[46]

Probably the most famous scene in all of nineteenth-century drama comes at the end of act 1, when Eliza escapes over a snowy landscape with her little boy in her arms. All staging restraints were let loose: Dramatic lighting effects, howling winds, and an array of mechanics thrilled audiences. As stage directions indicated, "The entire depth of the stage, representing the Ohio River, is filled with floating ice . . . Eliza appears, with Harry [her child] on a cake of ice, and floats slowly across." Everything contributed to the excitement: the directions for "Music, chord" as Eliza screams; "Music" as the vicious slavers Haley, Loker, and Marks leap through the window ("She's making for the river . . . Let's go after her!"); and "Music continued" ("Courage, my child! We will be free—or perish!").[47] Stowe managed to squeeze every bit of melodramatic sympathy and pathos she could from readers, but Aiken and Howard drew even more from theater audiences through the expressive techniques of music.

When Caryl Florio's opera version of *Uncle Tom's Cabin* was given its premiere in Philadelphia at the Chestnut Street Theatre in 1882, a modernized version of the Aiken-Howard melodrama was enjoying a run in the same city at the Academy of Music. In the Aiken-Howard show, not only a live donkey appeared onstage but eight live bloodhounds were also set loose to chase Eliza and little Harry in act 1's closing scene.[48] Florio's opera contains neither that scene nor the usual spectacles and tableaux that

Nineteenth-century poster, from a musical theater version of Stowe's *Uncle Tom's Cabin*, shows Eliza's sensational escape across the ice. *Library of Congress*

enthralled audiences. Presented "for the first time as an opera!" as the Chestnut Street Theatre touted, it did, however, contain "entire New Scenery, Costumes and a Grand Chorus and orchestra of 100."[49] Wayne Ellis, Florio's librettist, drew his drama from Stowe's novel but with one major departure: the introduction of Rosa, a young octoroon who has a white father and an African mother. Sold with Uncle Tom to the trader Haley, Rosa adds further poignancy to the story. She is "frightened and shrinking like a wild animal at the brutalities," as the theater playbill describes her. As the leading soprano, Rosa also provides sonorous brilliance within the opera's numerous ensembles.

Little appears in modern sources about the composer, who apparently was highly esteemed. Caryl Florio (1843–1920) was born William James Robjohn in Devonshire, England, and came to America when he was in his teens. He worked first in New York and then eventually settled in Ashville, North Carolina, where he taught music and directed choirs for almost twenty years. In addition to *Uncle Tom's Cabin,* he wrote six other operas although details about their music and production are for the most part incomplete.[50] He also composed close to two hundred choral pieces, both sacred and secular, as well as several instrumental works. The Steinway Hall concert he presented in 1888 with a full orchestra conducted by Theodore Thomas consisted of his own compositions and featured two symphonies and a piano concerto. "This is the first time in memory of the present generation that a resident musician has attempted so ambitious an achievement," extolled the *Commercial Advertiser* on March 18, 1888. "A concert of such magnitude is certainly important in the march of musical events in this country."

Like the Aiken-Howard melodrama, Florio's opera contains dialogue and some dramatic moments of melodrama technique. The main difference between the melodrama and the opera, however, lies in the amount of music sung. Florio's five-act opera contains thirty-four vocal numbers and emphasizes choral scenes that would be difficult to extract and hence popularize as sheet music. Of the many musical numbers in the opera, only five are separate arias or ballads; the rest are concerted scenes woven throughout with arias, duets, and choruses.[51] In act 1, Rosa sings a da capo aria (no. 4) that begins "O how happily the days pass on." The mid-section (B section) reflects the text "still have I felt a touch of sadness" in key change and a more "cantabile" mood. Chromatic alterations, shifts in tonal focus, and fioritura in the passage marked "cadenza" underpin her "yet, why shall I sigh when all is bright?" as the aria moves back to the reprise of A. Rosa is also given an alternative aria: "Old Folks at Home." Uncle

Tom's song in act 2 (no. 14), which begins "Look! de golden stairway lead-ing / Way up in de clouds" is rhythmically interesting in its repeated shifting interplay between duple and triple meter.

The chorus plays a prominent role in *Uncle Tom's* action and moods. "Gib' me de water from the Jordan ribber to wash away the sins of my youth" sings Tom to the children while seated on a bench near the door (no. 6). "For we're all little children, and we don't know the road" responds the adult chorus behind the scenes. A lovely unaccompanied seven-part madrigal (act 2, no. 13) indicates Florio's interests in early music (he founded New York City's Palestrina Choir). In the Mississippi steamboat scene (act 2, no. 11), a double chorus pits two contrasting moods and musical styles. A chorus of passengers sings the words "gaily along the stream we glide" in five-part harmony. In counterpoint, the chorus of slaves weaves a sin-gle, doleful, monophonic line to words taken directly from Stowe's novel: "Oh, where is weeping Mary, 'rived in de goodly land / She's dead and gone to heaven, 'rived in de goodly land."

The novel contains many references to music, ranging from Latin chant to Methodist hymns and slave songs. References to religious music rein-force Stowe's deeply felt messages of Christian responsibility, her indig-nation over the immorality of slavery, and her belief in the brotherhood of humanity. The opera captures the spirit of hymnody from time to time through both music and text. Like Stowe, whose novel is occasionally re-freshed with comic relief, Florio also adds humor, such as with the Laugh-ing Quartet (no. 19) and a spirited song and dance for Topsy at the close of act 2.

For especially dramatic scenes and passages of conversation Florio chooses either accompanied recitative or spoken dialogue with orchestral underpinning in the style of the melodrama. When melodrama techniques appear in operas of the period, the music is usually written into the score and not left up to an accompanist to choose or improvise, as was the case in plays or melodramas. In number 8, marked "Scene and Duett" with Tom and Eliza, stage actions are written over the orchestral score, which shifts melodramatically to reflect Eliza's grief as she learns that her son has been sold. Techniques of melodrama are also important in scenes with Simon Legree. It would seem that the vicious, evil nature of the slave trader is better represented with dialogue spoken over the orchestra than with song, as in the scene with his whip (no. 29) in act 5.

For all its merits, Florio's *Uncle Tom's Cabin* had only a single perfor-mance. Future interest would no doubt have been dampened by the work's unfortunate, poorly organized presentation by an amateurish cast that could neither act nor sing. Perhaps, too, the cause lay in competition from the world of circus extravaganzas—wild animals, drill teams, and pugilists that supplemented the usual run of Tom dramas—those trappings of bravado and bluff that dominated American culture. Florio's *Uncle Tom's Cabin,* however, was an important emblem of an era, a work infused with passionate social issues that occupied the hearts and spirits of Americans for decades. It was the earliest American opera to realize the dramatic and musically expressive potential of human oppression and the plight of the nation's blacks. Its ambitious choral-solo interaction and narrative tension make it a modest forerunner of far more important American works to come, such as *Showboat* and *Porgy and Bess* in the twentieth century.

The craze for Italian grand opera had an important place in the development of American opera and its composers—not so much because it was Italian or even grand but because it was melodramatic in the noblest sense of the term. The use of music to heighten drama, dialogue, recitative, and mood became a true art to be reckoned with and a vital part of American composers' operatic language and sensibility. To the critics of the time, however, the term *melodrama* denoted a popular theatrical spectacle that drew audiences and hence made money. About the time Florio's opera appeared, the *Philadelphia Evening Bulletin* boasted on May 20, 1882, that the theater season had been a smashing success: "Melo-drama and comic opera have been the favorites, and the managers . . . are chuckling over the piles of checkers which they have stored away in their fireproofs." Melodrama and grand opera—the vernacular and the cultivated—had begun to go their separate ways. Yet through the lighthearted gestures of operetta and comic opera they would remain friends.

6

In the Spirit of Comedy

I have seen wimmen in opera, and also hav seen them in fits, and I prefer the fits, for then i know what tew do for them.
—Josh Billings

COMEDY WAS ONCE described by the literary scholar Louise Cowan as "that vital rhythm of life," which on its most basic level speaks of endurance and survival and on its highest level of love and salvation. "We may have our lyric moments of vision," says Cowan, "our tragic moments of defeat, our heroic moments of creation, but we live by the comic rhythm of action—that persistent and irrational urge to go on in the face of difficulty, to look at our situation in a new light, and so to find a solution to it; to use imagination, wit and ingenuity—and hence finally to make the narrow escape into grace."[1]

In opera, it is the music that allows experiencing that "narrow escape into grace." Ultimately, whether in the tragedies of Verdi and Wagner or the roulades of Rossini and Offenbach, it is the music that offers that touch of faith and hint of hope, that "irrational" sense of wit and ingenuity. As the term *comedy* implies, comic opera, far more than mere buffoonery, relies on a multiple array of forces to reach its audience. It lives by that persistent "rhythm of action" through its melodies, which are tuneful, flowing, jaunty, and enticing; its orchestration; and its harmonic palate. But like its more serious counterpart, comic opera was also shaped by the role music played in the drama—that is, where and how it occurred. Through its light, humorous plots with spoken dialogue rather than recitative, moreover, comic opera was often more intelligible to audience and composer alike. During the nineteenth century's final decades in particular, American composers, both men and women, were attracted to the witty and lighthearted.

Comic opera from the antebellum era to about 1900 could be designated in any number of ways: musical extravaganza, farce, operetta, opéra bouffe, or, as in Nate Salisbury's *The Brook* (1877), a "rural operatic jubilee." One of the most successful early efforts within American light opera tradition was Julius Eichberg's *The Doctor of Alcantara* (1862), which was called an opera, comic opera, opéra bouffe, operetta, light opera, and light operatic entertainment. Other works that came under the all-encompassing umbrella of "comic opera" were plays with music, for example, the sketches, burlesques, and parlor operettas of Alfred B. Sedgwick and the shows of Ned Harrigan and John Braham. The spectacle, too, was a genre of music theater that had all the trappings of opera—elaborate scenery, costumes, dance, lighting, sound effects, and musical numbers—but had little or no plot. Derived from the earlier English and French pantomime, the spectacle wallowed in supernatural stage effects and mind-boggling transformation scenes that would have humbled old Mr. Harlequin.

Unlike many spectacles of the time, Charles M. Barras's popular *The Black Crook* (1866) did manage a semblance of a plot. Loosely based on the Faust legend, the show (all five and a half hours of it) contained dazzling scenery, a grand ballet of gems, a hurricane through the mountains, angels transported in gilded chariots, a breathtaking transformation scene, a ritual by demons, and, most wicked of all, an abundant display of female legs. Running for a year in New York and twenty-five more years on the road, *The Black Crook* became one of the great hits of all time.[2] By coincidence, one of the most successful French operas ever written—Gounod's great *Faust*—had been given its American premiere in New York only three years earlier. It opened the Metropolitan Opera in 1883, America's longest-running grand opera company.

If there were those who preferred another kind of music theater, one not as esoteric as grand opera yet not as shallow as spectacle and burlesque, there were always operettas. A craze for operetta, or opéra bouffe, took hold in America when Offenbach's *La Grande Duchesse de Gérolstein* received its premiere in New York City on September 24, 1867, not long after the Civil War.[3] The French composer's airy, sparkling operettas, particularly *La Belle Hélène* and *La périchole,* continued to attract the public for nearly a decade. One of Offenbach's tunes, the "Duet of the Queen's Guards" from *Geneviève de Brabant* (1861), even became the origin of the Marines' Hymn.

The Offenbach mania, however, was short-lived. It soon yielded to other fads that swept the nation. After William S. Gilbert and Arthur Sullivan's *H.M.S. Pinafore* was given its American premiere in 1878, "G and S" seemed to be everywhere. During the late 1880s Boston boasted 163 performances of the *Mikado,* and New York saw *Pinafore* produced by churches, black companies, twelve-year-olds, and Yiddish theaters. By 1900 Viennese and Central European operettas had swirled their way onto the stages of America. From New York to San Francisco, Merry Widow shoes,

Merry Widow hats, and Merry Widow waltz classes became as "in" as Franz Lehar's colorful music.

It was in the light, lyrical framework of operetta that several American composers prodigiously worked, some now forgotten and others immortalized. It was a theatrical form that was not only appealing and romantically graceful but also served another important function in American life: education and community enrichment. Operettas were especially attractive to young performers, amateurs, and church and community groups, always eager for material to perform. Music education, too, was becoming increasingly important, and more schools of music, colleges, and universities were founded as the century closed. In its own way, the trend seemed to be a felicitous harbinger of the chamber opera and opera workshop programs that spread across the country after World War II.

The American Operetta

Many operetta composers were prominent educators, and their works represent a growing, conscientious urge to reach out into the far corners of America's didactic and aesthetic terrain. A New Hampshire music teacher, George W. Stratton (1830–1901), was one of the earliest and most successful composers of operettas for children. Stratton's *Laila* (1867), *Genevieve* (1870), and *The Fairy Grotto* (1872) were widely performed showpieces with phantasmal plots enhanced by choruses, solos, duets, and even recitative. Other educators focused more on community outreach and adult amateurs than on children. A professor at the University of Missouri and critic for St. Louis's *Reedy's Mirror*, William Henry Pommer (1851–1937) composed at least eight operettas for his university and community, among them *The Daughter of Socrates, The Fountain of Youth,* and *The Queen of the Buccaneers.* On the East Coast, Thomas Whitney Surette (1861–1941) staged his highly successful operetta *Priscilla; or, The Pilgrim's Proxy* in Concord, Massachusetts, on March 6, 1889. Based on Longfellow's *Courtship of Miles Standish,* the operetta enjoyed more than a hundred performances in New Hampshire, Connecticut, and New York.[4]

On the other end of the operetta spectrum were the late-nineteenth-century works on a far more elaborate scale than those of Pommer and Surette. These operettas approached the style and scope of grand opera. They contained demanding vocal pieces and full orchestral forces as well as recitative, melodrama, and scena-like finales. They also fell under the influence of the spectacle, with its transformation scenes, tableaux, and other visual attractions. Between 1879 and 1912, Gustav Kerker (1857–1923) poured out twenty-three operettas that were all staged in New York. He is perhaps best remembered by *The Belle of New York* (1897), which also became popular in London and was supposedly performed seven hundred times. Many of Alfred Robyn's twenty-some operettas approach the domain of grand opera, such as *Merlin* and *Will o' the Wisp,* both produced after 1900. And although he composed few stage works, William Spenser could take pride in *The Little Tycoon* (1886), which received more than five hundred performances in its first run. His *The Princess Bonnie* (1894), also successful, was produced in Philadelphia, reputedly 1,039 times.[5] Now forgotten, these works illustrate the great popularity of operetta as the century turned, a form that had many shapes and guises and served the community well.

For audiences of the time, the spirit of comedy implied romance—the romance of lighthearted lovers and far-off lands. The word *romantic* not only advertised the product but also defined what the audience came to expect. Richard Stahl's *Said Pasha* (1888), "An Original Romantic Opera in Three Acts," takes place in the exotic locale of Constantinople and concerns the three-way conflict among a Turkish diplomat, his daughter, and her lover. Stahl's operetta, however, did not have the appeal of Noah Brandt's "Romantic Historical Opera" *Captain Cook* (1892), set in Hawaii and inspired by Cook's landing on that island in 1778. Brandt provides not only the usual spoken dialogue and arias but also large-scale processional scenes, several tableaux, a fiery tarantella, and lavish melodramatic pantomimes or ballets.[6] Performed at San Francisco's Bush Street Theater in 1895, the work was so popular that even the deposed Queen Lili'uokalani occupied a box at the premiere. Especially significant, however, is the location of the premieres of both the Stahl and Brandt operettas, illustrating that operas composed by Americans now reached as far west as San Francisco.[7]

Reginald De Koven and John Philip Sousa

As the century closed, audiences came to expect more for their money in all areas of theater—acting, singing, scenery, and story. Realism was now an essential element in the visual aspects of the theater, yet realism should always serve the spirit of romanticism that formed the heart and breath of American lyric theater. Exaggeration in both comedy and tragedy was becoming passé, replaced by a quieter, more restrained style of acting. Why, asked the *Galaxy,* should "everybody in intenser moments do everything as no rational human creature ever did, could do or will do?" Why should kings and queens "get about the stage with a hobbling strut, which could only naturally result from a complicated attack of lumbago? There is no reason," continued the *Galaxy,* for actors "to spout their lines with the sing-song intonation of a chanting friar" or that "Lady Macbeth should snatch the daggars with the frenzied gestures of an equestrian in her bareback posing."[8]

Singers, too, were viewed in a more discriminating light. "Hilda Clark," wrote the critic after the premiere of De Koven's *The Highwayman,* "should cut out her coloratura aria at once . . . New York does not tolerate singers who cannot do that sort of thing better than she does."[9] Many fine American singers were members of American operetta casts, however. Jessie Bartlett Davis by means of her beautiful voice kept herself in the lead among light opera contraltos.[10] Other popular American singers and comedians included De Wolf Hopper, Eugene Cowles, and Alice Nielsen, a soprano who later joined the distinguished roster of the Metropolitan Opera. The famous American baritone John Charles Thomas was only twenty-six when he sang the role of the Irish soldier of fortune Dick Fitzgerald in a revival of *The Highwayman.* The part, originally written for a tenor, was transposed to baritone to accommodate his rich, lyrical voice. Singing opera and operetta in English appealed to Americans, for often foreign artists either did not know the English language or felt that American operatic works were not prestigious enough for them to bother learning—a trend that still continues.

As earlier in the century, costumes were often the property of the singer because producers were sometimes reluctant to spend money on costumes for an untried new opera or operetta. In the premiere of De Koven's *Robin Hood* (1890), recalls the librettist Harry B. Smith, "the tenor sang in his *Il trovatore* costume, and the dresses of all the principals had seen service in 'Martha,' 'The Bohemian Girl' and other operas."[11] Scenery, however, was another matter. Producers often did not hesitate to spend hundreds of dollars to startle the public. From the century's earliest decades, American opera was rarely without spectacular scenes of battles, demolitions, and processionals. Thunder and lightning, roaring cataracts, and rain and snow were standard props for melodramatic action, and new and ingenious spectacular effects were continually being invented. There were dioramas, panoramas, and cosmoramas; given the nation's quest for visual thrills, it is not surprising the next step was motion pictures. Techniques at the close of the century allowed sunset, twilight, and moonlight to enhance romantic scenes with realism and wonder. As Richard Moody notes, "In the last half of the century, realism and romanticism were simultaneously in evidence, and . . . we find in the theatre and drama of this period a searching for realistic detail to be exhibited within a general romantic design."[12]

John Charles Thomas. *Library of Congress, Prints and Photos Division*

The romantic plots and characters of late-nineteenth-century operetta were more vehicles of escapism than realism, however. Two of the most popular and prolific American operetta composers, John Philip Sousa (1854–1932) and Reginald De Koven (1859–1920), set most of their stories in foreign locales. No longer was the heroic backwoodsman Davy Crockett the center of attention, or even the homespun Yankee, Jonathan Ploughboy. More sophisticated heroes, made enticing and romantic by their associations with far-off lands, replaced them. In Sousa's operettas were leading characters such as Don Medigua, viceroy of Peru (*El Capitan,* 1895); Prince Boris of Bokhara, Russia (*The Charlatan,* 1898); Marquis de La Varée of the French musketeers (*Désirée,* 1883); Princess Minutezza of Capri (*The Bride Elect,* 1897); and the Emperor of Braggadocia (*The Free Lance,* 1905).[13] In one of Sousa's rare American settings, *Chris and the Wonderful Lamp* (1899) takes place in New England but features Aladdin, the genie of storybook fame. *The American Maid* (1909, formerly *The Glass Blowers*) was memorable less for its characters or music than for its novel staging. Actual motion pictures were used along with traditional scenery, perhaps for the first time in American musical theater.

Many of both Sousa's and De Koven's stories center around love triangles colored by intrigue, disguise, and villainous pursuits, with the "right" couple happily paired at the end. Male characters provided courageous deeds and women the necessary love angle; as the *New York Times* expressed on December 14, 1897, "without them there would be no prima donna." Comedy was usually played out in secondary characters such as Little John in *Robin Hood* or Detective Foxy Quiller in *The Highwayman.* Accompanied by a chorus of constables, Quiller sings his jaunty "On the Track" in act 3 with a bit of Gilbert and Sullivan spoof:

> If a wretch in anguish utter
> Steals a slice of bread—no butter—
> 'Cause he's starving and of pie he hasn't got any,
> He has time for deep repentance,
> For the justice in his sentence
> Gives him twenty years in that far Bay called Botany.
> But it's very much more healthy
> For the tolerably wealthy
> To appropriate, embezzle and conceal
> For Dame Justice sits and grieves,
> Never calling people thieves
> If they do not really need the things they steal.[14]

Reginald De Koven wrote twenty-eight operettas and John Philip Sousa fifteen, but only a single work from each composer was a complete success: De Koven's *Robin Hood* and Sousa's *El Capitan*. Both lie firmly under the shadow of Gilbert and Sullivan, but each also shows the composer at his dramatic best. After its premiere at the Chicago Opera House on June 9, 1890, *Robin Hood* ran for more than three thousand successive performances, including a successful run in London and twenty years of stagings in Boston.[15] De Koven's best-known song from *Robin Hood,* "Oh, Promise Me," was not part of the original production but was added later for the character Allan à Dale, a trouser role sung by Jessie Bartlett Davis. Especially notable within *Robin Hood* and in many of De Koven's other operettas are the elaborate ensemble finales that close, and sometimes begin, each act in the tradition of Italian grand opera. The extended finale to act 1 of *The Highwayman,* for example, includes nine characters who interact with the chorus through changing tempos, keys, and lyrics in a continuous musical tapestry.[16] That and other De Koven finales underpin action, text, and mood through music in a way that opened the very nature of opera to thousands.

John Philip Sousa's operettas lack the soaring, lyrical lines that are gratifying for singers, but they have many passages of clever tunes, sparkling orchestration, and—as would be expected of America's favorite icon of the concert band tradition—spirited marches. Born in Washington, D.C., Sousa was the first American to break into the long line of foreign-born Marine Band leaders, whose nationalities had encompassed Italy, Germany, France, Spain, and England. As director of the Marine Band from 1880 to 1892, Sousa managed to widen the repertoire, instrumentation and polish of "The President's Own" as never before. In his performance catalog are lists of works from operas by Rossini, Gounod, Offenbach, Bellini, Wagner, and eighteen of Verdi's operas. Some of his own music also appears, notably the music from *Désirée,* first staged in Washington, D.C., in 1884.[17] When Grover Cleveland married the twenty-one-year-old Frances Folsom in the White House in 1886, he asked Sousa to play "And He's Going to Marry Yum Yum" from the *Mikado* as well as "Student of Love," the quartet from the last act of *Désirée,* at their wedding reception. The latter number presented a problem: Could Sousa merely call the piece "Quartette" and eliminate the reference to "student of love"? Sousa complied.

El Capitan was written after Sousa had left the White House as Marine Band director and formed his own highly successful civilian band that toured the world. With a libretto by Charles Klein and lyrics by Thomas

The illustrious "March King" John Philip Sousa composed several operettas, among them *Desirée, El Capitan,* and *The Bride Elect*. *"The President's Own"* United States Marine Band, Washington, D.C.

Frost, the operetta was given its premiere in New York in 1895. It ran for four years in Boston, played 140 times in London, and has been presented several times by various American opera companies since the 1990s. Some of the songs in *El Capitan* are adaptations from earlier works, such as the lovely "Sweetheart, I'm Waiting," which was taken from *The Smugglers* (1882). But all pale in comparison to the rousing "El Capitan March," which has become a staple of almost every concert band across the nation and abroad.

John Philip Sousa and Reginald De Koven carved a special niche in the history of American opera. Perhaps a critic of De Koven's *The Highwayman* with its libretto by Harry Smith summed up the operetta phenomenon as well as anyone. In the December 12, 1897, *New York Times Illustrated Magazine,* he said, "Comedy is quite capable of most artistic development. If you do not believe that, go and study the libretto and scores of 'La Belle Helene,' 'Fatinitza,' 'Die Fledermaus,' and 'Iolanthe.' Smith and De Koven are not Gilbert and Sullivan. But they have given us some pretty good work."

Opera and Victorian Women Composers

While the illustrious American soprano Clara Louise Kellogg was running her own opera company and winning international accolades for her singing, another American woman was accomplishing near-miracles: Susan Brownwell Anthony. A former teacher in the New York school system, Anthony was an officer of the National Woman Suffrage Association from 1869 to 1892. Her motto was "the true republic—men, their rights and nothing more; women, their rights and nothing less." For casting a vote in the presidential election of 1872, she was arrested and fined. Yet until her death in 1906 Susan B. Anthony continued to be a major force in the struggle for suffrage and coeducation.

The period from 1870 to about 1920 was a time of great change for American women. Victorian women were conditioned to be docile, submissive, and the rightful property of fathers and husbands. Their lot in life was to accept illness and pallor, but their highest duty was to suffer. Writers of the time also noted that females died more "beautifully" than men. As Henry James observed in *The Wings of the Dove,* "The generous woman, dead, is noble, whereas the shrewd female survivor will always be unhappy."[18] In romantic opera, heroines usually die—the Toscas, Sentas, Brünnhildes, Violettas, and Mimis. "If tragic opera is the form where the men usually win and the women die," writes Joseph McLellan whimsically, "comic opera is a form where the women usually win and the men get married."[19] Innocence was also a cherished female virtue, and the constant threat to this loss of innocence was the emotional core of American melodrama.

And so it was in the world of Victorian women. But times were changing. The phenomenal upsurge in urbanization and industrialization from approximately 1870 to 1920 expanded the sphere of activity for middle-class women and eclipsed the narrow dimensions of her "proper place" that had dominated during the Victorian era.[20] By the 1880s the Gibson Girl—with her "free stride, her direct glance, the arrogant swing of her wide shoulders and the haughty tilt of her head"—epitomized the New American Woman. "Hers was the first generation of American women who had experienced coeducation . . . who had dared to think of 'going to work' . . . or . . . remaining 'bachelor girls' . . . who had used slang, played basketball, ridden a bicycle-built-for-two."[21]

City life, with its numerous technological innovations, changed women's lives dramatically. As the century turned, a nation that had been predominantly rural had become almost 50 percent urban. The telephone was still a novelty, but electric trolleys had replaced most horse-drawn transportation and the proliferation of electric streetlights gave women greater freedom to go out at night. "Ready-mades," such as food and clothing, made life easier, and beginning in the 1880s more and more middle-class city homes had indoor plumbing, which eliminated the traditionally female task of hauling water. The expanding resources of the city, moreover, offered a growing array of job opportunities for women in restaurants, bakeries, and department stores and also in the professions. Frances Willard and Mary Livermore's *American Women* (1897) includes 1,500 biographies and an index that classifies the women according to profession. Among them are actors, authors, archaeologists, businesswomen, composers, educators, inventors, journalists, lawyers, ministers, musicians, physicians (one hundred are listed), temperance workers, and a single "train dispatcher."[22]

In the field of music theater, female performers were needed to balance the drama and bring diversity and color to musical scores. Professional women singers were thus accepted much earlier than women instrumentalists. "Women cannot possibly play brass instruments and look pretty" observed the *Musical Standard* in 1904. Although female chamber groups and orchestras were formed in the late 1890s, women were not hired to play with major male orchestras until the close of World War II. Teaching music was an attractive profession for women, but composing was another story. Although many nineteenth-century women composed songs and short piano pieces, it was not until the end of the century that several tried their hands at larger symphonic forms. During the 1890s, Amy Marcy Beach, Margaret Ruthven Lang, and Clara Kathleen Rogers were the first to hear their work performed by major American symphony orchestras.

The job market for women composers, however, was much more limited than for men. As Judith Tick observes, "The issues involving the debate about women composers were weighty intellectual concepts about creativity and biological determinism rather than social propriety and money."[23] Writing in 1880, George P. Upton, a prominent critic with the *Chicago Tribune,* concluded that women could feel music but not create it. His reasons: "She feels its influences, its control, and its power, but she does not see these results as man looks at them. He sees them in their full play . . . ; to treat emotions as if they were mathematics, to bind and measure and limit them within the rigid laws of harmony and counterpoint, and to express them with arbitrary signs, is a cold-blooded operation, possible only to the sterner and more obdurate nature of man."[24] More than thirty years later, Otto Ebel had a different view, which he aired in 1913: "The scarcity of women's work in music is . . . not owing to their inability to grasp and apply the science, but it may rather be attributed to prejudice and the rules of fashion and custom, which so long debarred her from entering this field of useful and profitable work and study."[25]

It is surprising, though, how many women actually did enter this "profitable work and study." Because grand opera required expensive performing and staging resources, few American companies were willing to produce anything but tried-and-true European works. Yet operetta, or comic opera, had more potential for production, and by the 1880s several women composers had ventured into that field. Because most of their scores and librettos are lost, these achievements must remain less a tribute to the creative process than to the women's imagination, productivity, and determination.

At least forty operas came from the pens of women composers of the period. The earliest appears to be *Mr. Samson of Omaha* (1880), a comic opera by Eliza Mazzucato Young (b. 1858) with libretto by Frederick Nye. Young's father, Alberto Mazzucato, was the director of Milan's famous Teatro alla Scala. *The Joust; or, The Tournament,* written by a composer who called herself "G. Estabrook," is the first complete opera by an American woman to be published (Chicago Music Company, 1885). Among its thirty musical numbers is "Return My Love" for soprano and violin obbligato. With its delicate interplay of string and vocal lines, it reflects the best in American art song tradition. Three women shared honors for being the first to have their operettas produced, each staged in 1889: *Dovetta* by Emma Marcy Raymond (1856–1913) in New York; *Fleurette* by Emma Roberts Steiner (1852–1929) in San Francisco; and *Leoni, the Gypsy Queen* by Louisa Delos Mars in Providence, Rhode Island. Although John Thomas Douglass's *Virginia's Ball* (1868) appears to be the earliest opera by a black composer, Mars's premiere is especially notable because she was the first black woman whose work was staged and produced.

Many women opera composers of the period were well educated and had studied with excellent teachers. Emma Marcy Raymond studied piano with Louis Moreau Gottschalk, voice with Giorgio Ronconi, and "harmony and counterpoint with the best German masters."[26] Margaret Williams, composer of the five-act operetta *Columbus,* studied at the Peabody Conservatory of Music in Baltimore. Addie Anderson Wilson, who won many prizes for her songs, was a carillonist and organist in her home state of Alabama as well as the composer of several operettas. She studied under Mary Carr Moore. Bessie Marshall Whitely, a Kansas City music teacher, studied at the Oakland Conservatory of Music. Her operetta *Hiawatha's Childhood* won a prize from the National Federation of Music Clubs in 1913, and two of her theater works—*Pandora,* based on Longfellow's "Masque of Pandora," and *Sarita* on a Mexican subject—were described as "grand operas."[27]

Many women also wrote their own librettos, such as Marie Mansfield Townsend (or Marie Townsend Allen), whose *Hawaii* is a comic opera of thirty-eight musical numbers, comprising choruses, quartets, duets, solos, "recitations," and concerted finales.[28] Constance Faunt le Roy Runcie (1836–1911) also wrote both libretto and music for her three-act *Prince of the Asturias* (1894). Runcie grew up in New Harmony, Indiana, a colony of intense religious and cooperative spirit founded by her grandfather Robert Owen. She studied literature and music in Germany and is one of the earliest American women composers to achieve recognition for her many songs, instrumental works, and cantatas. Her only opera, however, *The Prince of the Asturias,* remains in manuscript and was probably not performed. Called by some of her biographers a "romantic opera," its only surviving score appears to be a piano-vocal draft, containing a small amount of spoken dialogue, a few stage directions, a solo ("O Prince Remember"), a "Chorus of Country Folk and Gypsies," and a habanera from the last act.[29]

Louisa Melvin Delos Mars (dates unknown) is especially interesting because she is one of the earliest black musicians to achieve recognition as a composer. Details of her life are scant. She was born Louisa Melvin, and during the 1880s she and her sister, Carrie Melvin Lucas, formed a duo, with Carrie playing violin and cornet and Louisa singing. Louisa also directed, produced, and performed in her own operettas, which were staged in the Boston and Providence areas. She composed five full-length operettas. Three of these, *Fun at a Boarding School, Love in Disguise; or, Things Are Not What They Seem,* and *Leoni, the Gypsy Queen,* are mentioned in *The Woman's Era* of Boston in January 1896 along with encomium about her work: "Too much cannot be said in praise of Mrs. De Los Mars, who possesses rare talent, both as a musician and an authoress. She has written five Dramas, which have been presented to the public with grand success, both in Providence, R.I., Boston and elsewhere."[30] Although her works are no longer extant, Mars must be recognized with other nineteenth-century black women, such as Sissieretta Jones, Marie Selika, Lulu Richards, and Amelia Tilghman, as a pioneer in the history of American music and the culture of the operetta.

As the twentieth century opened, changes occurred within romantic operetta storylines and styles. Native American and Japanese settings, along with mythology and fantasy, drew operettas away from their European melodramatic roots. That is especially apparent in the works of Abbie Gerrish-Jones, Emma Roberts Steiner, and Stella Stocker.

One of the most prolific female opera composers of the time, Abbie

Gerrish-Jones (1863–1929) wrote nine music theater works that ranged from children's operettas to a large-scale grand opera. Born in Vallejo, California, she spent most of her professional life on the West Coast. She came from a remarkably musical family, played the piano by ear at age five, and went on to study with Charles Winter, a pupil of Mendelssohn. Her strong literary aptitudes and excellent education provided the background for her work as a music critic for *Pacific Town Talk* and later the *Pacific Coast Musical Review.* She was also the Pacific Coast representative for the *Musical Courier,* published in New York. She wrote more than a hundred songs, and one of her piano pieces won a prize in the prestigious Josef Hofmann Competition for the best American piano work. But her forte was opera, and her lyrics were considered among the best in their field.[31]

Especially characteristic of Gerrish-Jones are eerie, Poe-like stories that place her works within a new realm of comic or light opera. *Priscilla* (1887) tells of a young woman's agonized vigil for her dead lover, who had perished through the wiles of a sea witch. *Sakura* and *The Snow Queen,* both written in collaboration with Gerda Wismer Hofmann, are similarly strange and other-worldly in their moody plots. The former is the diabolical tale of various personalities whose lives revolve around their reflections in a strange mirror. The latter, a "Fairy Music Drama" in five acts, is based on Hans Christian Anderson's story of the power of love and song over evil. Like *Priscilla,* it involves an Orpheus-like search for a lost lover—in this case one who has been encased in ice at the North Pole by the virulent Snow Queen and is set free only by the determined heroine's beautiful singing. *The Snow Queen's* lavish production required a cast of fourteen, a large chorus, and a corps de ballet. Its premiere in San Francisco in the new Children's Theater on February 9, 1917, was supported by an array of dignitaries that included California's governor, the mayor of San Francisco, and the presidents of Stanford University and the University of California.[32] The production ran for twelve weeks and then toured across the country, playing in major cities with great success.

With the operas of Emma Roberts Steiner (1850–1928), comedy often takes the form of satire. Emma Steiner was America's first professional woman conductor. Her successful career was particularly remarkable, and, felicitously, it provided her with both dramatic and orchestral skills in her work as a composer. Edward Everett Rice engaged Steiner to conduct Gilbert and Sullivan's *Iolanthe* with his company, and from there she went on to posts in Boston and Toronto. Reputedly, she conducted more than six thousand performances of fifty different operas throughout her long life. The manager of the Metropolitan Opera, Heinrich Conried, was so

impressed with her talents that he would have let her conduct a performance "had he dared to put a woman armed with a baton in front of a
totally male orchestra."[33] Steiner did, however, make her way to the Met,
but not until she was in her seventies. On February 28, 1925, she conducted
a concert there to celebrate the fiftieth anniversary of her conducting debut.
She was recognized as "a composer of great merit, a conductor of much
ability and a musician whose abilities are marked in every branch of the
art."[34]

Among Emma Steiner's numerous vocal and instrumental compositions are seven operettas. Her earliest, *Fleurette,* was performed in San Francisco in 1889 and in New York two years later and contained music far
superior to that usually heard on the comic opera stage wrote one reviewer.
Among her works, one in particular stands out for its wit, feminism, and
clever subject. Bearing the somewhat new designation "Musical Comedy," Steiner's *Burra Pundit* (1908) is in three acts with a libretto by Margaret I. MacDonald. It remains in manuscript, although the title page indicates that "some of the leading musical numbers are now being prepared
by the publishers and can be had at the music stores."[35] The manuscript
contains twenty-eight musical numbers (tunes and texts only), casting
information, costume descriptions, and the full libretto. Occasional notations indicate that the music was "composed and orchestrated by Emma
Steiner," and for the performance "Mr. Frank Windsor's Full Orchestra "was
to be "enlarged and completed by solo players from Toronto and Buffalo."
Whether the opera was ever performed remains unknown.

Steiner's opera centers around the Burra Pundit ("Great Wise One"
in Hindi) who has invented a "chemical" to make people perfect. He is a
"professor" who manufactures brains and brawn, like the wizard in L. Frank
Baum's *Wizard of Oz,* which itself appeared as a musical show in 1903. The
phantasmal atmosphere of Steiner's show is reflected in its stage directions.
Act 2, for example, was to be "arranged as a drug store, with shelves full of
jars, labels large enough to be read by audience: Farmers' Brains, Critics'
Brains, Actors' Brains, Lovers' Brains. . . . Tubs standing about labeled Sa-
gacity, Instinct, Horse Sense, Common Sense, etc. . . . Surgical chair with
laughing gas apparatus. . . . Wigs of patients to be operated on have square,
trap-door-like arrangement, which after the operation with chisels etc.,
opens up allowing old brain to be removed and new one inserted. Over
all are signs: Brains, while you wait. Prices paid for good, old brains. Dudes'
brains at a discount. Liars made Truthful etc."

Song lyrics and dialogue in *Burra Pundit* often have a fanciful bent as
well. The opening chorus sings:

Political, Musical, Critical, Farcical
Brains no one can score
Tammany bosses, Republican losses
Sunday school teachers, rhapsodic preachers
deep river divers, and cable road drivers.

"I should call you underdone," says the Professor later on. "Go get Diana and bring her here. I sent her five tons of Beethoven-Wagneronic Hydrate and that easily made her the greatest living Prima Donna." In a take-off on black-faced minstrelsy, a "darky" sings "jus make me white all ober / And don't stop at de neck." Another character philosophizes, "We have eclipsed the wizards of the past, but happiness still baffles our search."

Perhaps the most interesting portions of the opera are those that reveal Steiner's feminism. A Chorus of Spirits in the last act includes "shades of women who gave their bodies to bad men." Later Alco, now an "intelligent man," reveals, "The woman I should like to marry has a brain—an intellect. She is not a mere doll; four walls cannot hold her mind. The ideal marriage is based on companionship. Passion serves its turn—intermittant, unstable. But companionship, soul affinity, mind marriage—this is God's own."

Quite a different subject inspired Stella Prince Stocker (1858–1925). In her *Ganymede* (1893), which she calls a "light opera," Stocker draws upon a mythological subject: the legend of Ganymede, the beautiful youth snatched up by Zeus in the form of an eagle to be the cup-bearer of the gods. Greek mythology was not a favorite theme for light operas of the period, although Edward Everett Rice used it in *Adonis* (1884) and Julian Edwards in *Jupiter* (1892). Set in Christian times, the plot of Ganymede is difficult to reconstruct from the surviving collection of thirteen musical pieces published in New York in 1902. But the collection does reveal several choruses for women's voices (a chorus of nymphs and another of nuns), a "Nectar Song" for soprano and alto, and the comic "Macaroni Song" for baritone solo ("Do not hesitate or wonder what his Majesty will please / Give the great Italian sovereign Macaroni served with cheese"). The dichotomous mixture of pagan and Christian is plaintively sketched in the lyrical "Song of the Novice," published separately in 1897.[36] In minor mode, chromatic alterations and delicate embellishments color the text on such lines as "'tis strange, but since I saw that youth who gazed so long on me / Which ever way I chance to turn, his features I can see!" The Cecilian Society of Duluth performed the song on June 21, 1893, along with three other pieces from the opera.[37]

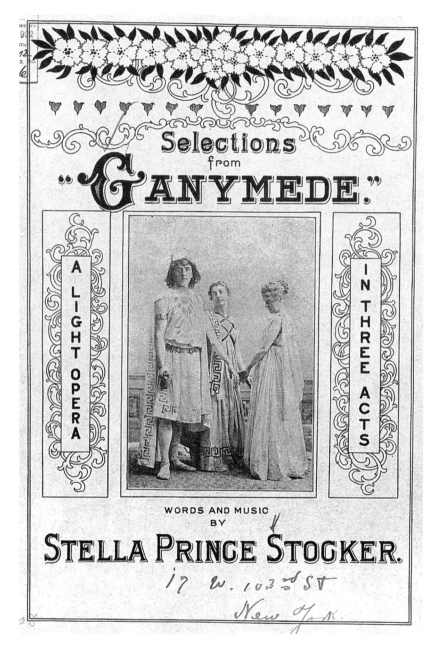

From Stella Prince Stocker's light opera *Ganymede* (1893), title page of piano–vocal score. *Library of Congress*

In addition to *Ganymede,* Stocker's operettas include *Beulah, Queen of Hearts,* and *Raoul,* but her true interest concerned Native American music. In order to bring ethnographic authenticity to her work, she lived among Native Americans and eventually became a member of one of the Ojibway tribes. She took the name O-mes-qua-wi-gi-shi-go-que ("Red Sky Lady"). Two of Stocker's dramatic musical works include transcribed Native American chants: a three-act "Indian pantomime" entitled *The Marvels of Manabush* and *Sieur du Lhut* (1916), a "Historical Play in Four Acts with Indian Pageant Features and Indian Melodies."[38]

Sieur du Lhut tells of the French explorer Daniel de Gresollon du Lhut. The action takes place in the western corner of Lake Superior, where the Sioux and Chippewas fought their last great battle over the village of Kathio. It is an expansive colorful pageant reinforced by elaborate scenery and a large cast of twenty-nine individual roles. In the appendix of her libretto, Stocker reproduced ten Native American chants and indicated their position in the play alphabetically: (A) Indian march, (B) moccasin game song, (C) melody for peace pipe, (D) Nett Lake dance, (E) theme for wooing flute, (F) "He has gone to Sault St. Marie," (G) loon cry, (H) death chant, (I) love charm song, and (J) music for skull dance. "These melodies," she adds, "are sung in unison and repeated several times, a single note reiterated as a bass foundation on piano or kettle drum. The piano or other instruments used for the support of the voices in the unison singing, also for the French incidental music of Act III, must be placed behind the scenes."

Stella Stocker wrote at a time when American composers—Arthur Nevin, Charles Wakefield Cadman, and others—were beginning to realize the value of their indigenous culture as a source for representative American music. Commenting on the premiere of *Sieur du Lhut,* which drew large crowds, on July 14, 1917 *Musical America* added, "Throughout the whole play ran a thread of Indian melodies, weird strains sung in unison or in octave with a tom tom for accompaniment. The singing of Indian melodies, which Mrs. Stocker has been collecting and transcribing for years, was a feature of the production which is one of the most important additions to the praiseworthy work of preserving the traditions and customs of a people that have played such an important part in the historical life of the Northwest."

✍

Lighter in mood and more intelligible to audiences than grand opera, comic operas provided an important function: They reached out to all, young and old alike. As a result, by the late nineteenth century numerous teachers and music educators throughout the United States were composing comic operas and operettas. Their work was staged in schools, churches, and city auditoriums. While American grand opera drew mainly from Italian and German models, American operettas were inspired more often by English and French styles, as in the operettas of John Philip Sousa and Reginald De Koven. One rarely studied aspect of the comic opera form was its use by American women composers. The first black woman to write and stage her own operas, for example, favored the romantic levity and grace of the comic opera. Many of the era's most innovative and creative trends—feminism, wit, mysticism, and Native American ritual—molded comic operas by the educated, productive women of Victorian America.

Although romantic operetta withered somewhat as the nineteenth century closed, its sister art, musical comedy, became increasingly revitalized through the fresh vigor of ragtime. The dramatic changes taking place on Broadway can be seen in the thirty-year period between 1894 and 1924, when Victor Herbert composed his operettas. Although Herbert never lost his fondness for large-scale operettas with grand finales and happy endings, his scores reflected changing popular styles. Ragtime is especially pronounced in a show such as *Her Regiment* (1918), and Herbert, in his connections with Jerome Kern, Irving Berlin, and George Gershwin, could apply the most recent popular song styles of the day to his later work.

Yet the early twentieth century was also a time of great visibility and potential for American grand opera composers. The Metropolitan Opera had opened in 1883 and offered not only a new showcase for serious opera but also an exciting venue for the nation's finest composers. The Wagner craze that escalated during the later nineteenth century lured many American composers into the German master's lush hypnotic den and would provide inspiration and emulation for decades to come. It also separated popular music from classical in a way not seen before. As the world of American composers was enriched and recharged, the term *opera* took on new luster. Harlequin's magic sword had a decidedly Germanic sheen.

PART 2

The Signposts, 1880 to 1960

I believe that a great many operas are tragic, sordid, or even superficial in their story and environment, but it is the music and the music alone that decides whether or not they are immortal works.
—George Antheil to Mary Curtis Bok, 1921

The role of music in opera, no mater how extended, is governed finally by the needs of the drama. So it is with the best film music. It identifies itself with the action, and becomes a living part of the whole.
—Bernard Herrmann, "Music in Motion Pictures," 1945

If I were writing a libretto, I should be careful to make the measure dance or languish or stalk loftily or creep mysteriously according to the feeling, as suggestively as possible for the musician.
—George Bernard Shaw, *Collected Letters*

7

Wagnerism and the American Muse

They come, with their thunder-chorus,
   Vast shapes, of a stronger race;
An alien throng from some star of song
   In the undiscovered space.

I thrill to their eager calling,
   I shrink from their fierce control.
They have pressed and pried the great doors wide
   That were closed to guard my soul.
   —"At the Concert: A Wagner Number" (1894), Marion Couthouy Smith

OF ALL THE FORCES that shaped the creative process of American opera composers as the century turned, none was quite as powerful as the art of Richard Wagner. From the *Flying Dutchman*–like ghostly crew in Reginald De Koven's *Rip van Winkle* to the quasi-Rhinemaidens in Silas Pratt's *Triumph of Columbus* and from the leitmotifs of Victor Herbert's *Natoma* to the chromaticism of John Knowles Paine's *Azara*—Wagnerian influences were rampant. "Everything reminds one of Wagner nowadays," wrote Rupert Hughes in 1914, "even his predecessors."[1] The sounds of the modern French and Russian schools began to appear in American instrumental music of the time, but in both opera and early motion picture scores it was generally Wagner who provided dramatic and musical dynamism well into the 1930s and beyond.

Why this love affair with Richard Wagner? He promulgated a new kind of visionary morality in what was to Americans a familiar format—the melodrama. His operas were, in essence, the final cry of waning nineteenth-century melodrama—provocative, spiritual, and uplifting.[2] Other aspects of Wagner also appealed to Americans. Women especially were drawn to him, both through the passion of his music and the courage of his heroines. And then there was that "Yankee push" that Joseph Musselman noted. Wagner seemed to inspire ambitious Americans who felt they were following a genuine cultural hero. The younger generation especially, wrote a critic in 1882, "thinks and feels and sees with Wagner by instinct and not by effort."[3] For Americans, Richard Wagner's "Music of the Future" was also the music of the present.

Much of Wagner's success in America was also due to the fact that he had a ready-made, built-in audience. During the latter part of the nineteenth century, immigrants from Germany began to outnumber those from other countries, and German influence on American cultural life escalated. By 1890, the height of the Wagner craze, close to 27 percent of the population of New York City was German-born. These were New Yorkers who discussed Schopenhauer, enjoyed songfests, and attended their own theaters, schools, and churches. One of the earliest enterprising Germans to bring the music of Wagner to America was Carl Bergmann, conductor of the fine Germania Orchestra, who on April 4, 1859, conducted the entire *Tannhäuser* at New York City's German-language Stadt Theater—the first staging of a complete Wagner opera in America.

America's first staging of *Lohengrin* brought yet another dimension to the nation's cultural life. The opera was conducted by twenty-eight-year-old Adolf Neuendorff on April 3, 1871, also at the Stadt Theater—a dusty old place, some thought, with "dingy benches." But "at a quarter past eight the lights were turned up, motherly dames put their half-sucked oranges away, a glow of pleasure suffused the faces of the red-handed damsels, and a great crowd of men, smelling of tobacco, came in from the lobby." As for the music, "The wonderful orchestral accompaniment grows more and more eloquent; the declamation becomes impassioned. . . . We do not envy the man who can hear and see this closing scene unmoved," said Frederic Ritter.[4] The opera was so popular that a few years later the Marine Band performed selections from it on the White House lawn for President and Mrs. Grover Cleveland. "The President stood up and held on to the window as though he were afraid it would get away from him," recounted John Philip Sousa. "His pretty young wife sat down facing him, enthralled."[5]

On October 22, 1883, the Metropolitan Opera opened its doors for the first time, and from its next season until 1891 all the operas were sung in German, even *Aida* and *Faust*. Wagner accounted for nearly half the repertoire. *Tristan und Isolde* was given its American premiere on December 1, 1886, and the complete *Der Ring des Nibelungen* (1876) during the 1888–89 season, both conducted by Anton Seidl. Because of his attention to authenticity and brilliance of interpretation, Seidl was called a "demigod." He gave America "a new Wagner, the real Wagner," raved critics.[6] In *Tristan* itself they found a new "poetic work of art" in the leitmotifs, orchestration, story, medieval legends, and symbolism.

Caricature by Joseph Keppler from *Puck* shows Anton Seidl, America's noted Wagnerian conductor, at odds with the conductor Claudio Muzio, known for his interpretations of Italian opera. *Opera News*

Before its complete staging, the *Ring* had captivated audiences in pieces. Favorite scenes from *Die Walküre* reached both home and bandstand in transcriptions ranging from concert band to harmonica, melodeon, and banjo. Theodore Thomas's "Ride of the Valkries" "electrified the house," wrote Rose Fay Thomas. "People jumped on their chairs, shouting and waving hats and handkerchiefs until he [Thomas] was obliged to give it a second time."[7] After its successful premier at the Metropolitan Opera, the complete *Ring* tetrology toured Philadelphia, Boston, Milwaukee, Chicago, and St. Louis to packed, enthusiastic houses. The further west it traveled, the more its advance publicity seemed to expand, Barnum-style, like a genie out of a bottle. In St. Louis, for example, the *Ring* was advertised as "the greatest Operatic Attraction in the World."[8]

But as for Wagner mania and media attraction, nothing matched the American premiere of *Parsifal*. Staged at the Metropolitan Opera House on Christmas Eve of 1903, Wagner's mystical last opera was presented for the first time outside Bayreuth, where it had been given its premiere on July 26, 1882. Requests for opening night tickets numbered more than seven thousand, and five hundred people had to stand for the entire five-hour performance. The manager of the Metropolitan Opera, Heinrich Conried, had procured the top *Parsifal* singers and production personnel from Bayreuth, resulting in what Richard Aldrich of the *New York Times* of July 18, 1882, called "the most perfect production ever made on the American lyric stage." At age thirty-one, Alfred Hertz conducted "as though Wagner were looking over his shoulder." But for all of *Parsifal's* glittering success, Conried had to ride out a lawsuit by Cosima Wagner, who tried to stop the performance claiming her husband intended the opera only for Bayreuth. Calling Conried an "audacious Barnum from Vienna," she could do little to prevent what she considered a sacrilege on her husband's work.[9] She worried about America commercializing a quasi-sacred drama, and perhaps she had a point. In New York, for example, a veritable "Parsifalitis" epidemic broke out, replete with Parsifal hats, Parsifal cigars, and Parsifal cocktails.

How did such Wagner furor affect American opera composers? They were, first, caught up in what was new and attracted the public, and they also sought what suited their own creative energies. Wagner epitomized new music and the theater of the future, with lush orchestration, blatant emotional impact, sensuous imagery, powerful characters, and timeless tales. It was the ultimate melodrama. Americans' ongoing joy in theatrical melodrama that had dramatic musical underpinnings was undoubtedly a prime factor in Wagner's drawing power. There were significant parallels in the role that music played in his operas and in concurrent American melodramas. Indeed, Wagner's unique genius in understanding music's symbolic and associative powers was at the core of his popularity in America.

By the late nineteenth century, the term *melodrama* had become equated with the trappings of asides, sensational incidents, and the clichéd plot of "spoiled" female honor. Dramatists often preferred the phrase *play with incidental music* to *melodrama*. But if the term itself was becoming outmoded, the form was not. Melodrama continued to pack theaters up to the end of the century and "became the projected fantasy life of an America caught up in a period of unprecedented flux."[10] *Monte Cristo, The Blackbird, How Fair, How Fresh Were the Roses,* and the turgid melodramas of Augustin Daly, such as *Under the Gaslight,* were theatrical fare during the later nineteenth and early twentieth centuries. In *Theory of Drama,* Allardyce Nicoll draws the distinction between melodrama, with its "undue insistence upon incident," and high tragedy, which has an "inner quality" that "moves progressively toward an ideal."[11] It is, then, some inner quality—the spiritual as opposed to the merely physical—that makes tragedy out of melodrama and comedy out of farce. The enormous popularity of melodrama went hand in hand with the Wagner fad—the former with its "undue insistence upon incident" and the latter with its spiritual and "inner quality." The task for American opera composers was to draw from both worlds without sacrificing dramatic veracity and artistic worth.

Another aspect of the melodramatic and the Wagnerian worlds attracted American composers—the use of leitmotifs, short musical figures associated with specific characters, moods, ideas, or objects within a drama. But mere association is meaningless unless a leitmotif tells something about a character's feelings or rationalizes action—in other words, it must be symbolic of a deeper dimension of human experience. Besides enlarging the dramatic expression, the leitmotif technique also unified the score, which in Wagner's later music dramas flowed continuously without breaks. The term *leitmotif* appears in a description of a melodrama in 1881: "The music that illustrates the progress of a drama, though perhaps little recognised, is often of much merit and interest. Full of grace and colour, it lingers on the ear and reflects the dramatic passion of the situation. It is surprising to find some obscure leader devising a truly dramatic 'leit motive,' which is thereafter associated with the play. . . . In a good dramatic melodrama the entrance of a hero is attended by some particular melody, and always with good effect."[12]

As David Mayer points out, "Nowhere is the use of musical accompaniment more pervasive and continuous, from ten years before the start of the nineteenth century until well after the First World War, than in the melodrama."[13] He describes pantomimes in London in 1888 having "about sixty 'melos' numbers . . . 'agits,' 'pathetics,' 'struggles,' 'hornpipes,' 'andantes.'" What is notable is that Mayer asserts that with the new dramas of Henrik Ibsen, Arthur Pinero, Oscar Wilde, and others, "Serious drama . . . was suddenly music-free." They instituted a comparatively new practice: stage plays that had only dialogue and no music. As the melodrama died out, the associative role of music went directly into motion picture scores—and, as always, into opera.

Wagner's Spell on American Opera Composers

American opera composers in the years surrounding the turn of the twentieth century responded to the spell of Richard Wagner in a wide variety of ways and with varying levels of success. Some relied on the leitmotif technique to provide unity and dramatic coherence to their scores, for example, Frederick Grant Gleason, John Knowles Paine, Walter Damrosch, and Victor Herbert. Others, such as Edgar Stillman Kelley, turned to the melodramatic pantomime as a vehicle for their associative musical ideas. Still others managed to escape the Germanic influence and embrace mainly the French, as did George W. Chadwick, or turn to original styles of their own, as did Silas G. Pratt. "My work has borrowed neither its plot nor situation from the European Opera," Pratt claimed in his preface to *Zenobia* (1882). "The music owes no allegiance to any special school. I trust this fact will make it none the less acceptable to American audiences."[14]

Wagner's courageous heroines—Senta, Elsa, Elizabeth, and Brünnhilde—encouraged fresh focus on female protagonists in American operas of the period. Innocent passivity was no longer the issue; what mattered were pride, bravery, accomplishment, and intelligence. Many operas are named after their heroines: *Lucille, Zenobia, Azara, Natoma, Judith, Mona,* or *Narcissa.* Lucille, daughter of France's noted Comte D'Auvergne, uses ingenuity to free her imprisoned lover. The medieval noblewoman Azara manages to escape her pursuer and cleverly disguise herself to win back her lover. And Narcissa was the first female protagonist to play a role in winning the American West. But like *Parsifal's* Kundry, George Chadwick's Judith is both fin-de-siècle seductress and sublime heroine. The *Jugendstil* woman also is reflected in Native American heroines as the century turned. Natoma, for example, kills the abductor of her mistress—a departure from Wagnerian heroines who save men through virtue rather than violence.

Both virtuous and noble, however, Pratt's Zenobia, whom the composer describes as "learned and beautiful," is one of the period's most interesting characters. In her entrance recitative in act 1, the proud rebel queen of the third-century Roman province of Palmyra sings, "The sun has gone down in their hearts, Alas! My own is like a starless night! I must feed them with hope, Tho' I myself do starve. [With a great effort assumes a queenly bearing.] Arise! my people, cease lamanting, Palmyra yet must be defended! Each one must now a hero be! As tho' his soul from Mars descended." American opera heroines as strong leaders create speculation that not only Wagnerian heroines played a role in the ideology of composers but also the tenor of the times—the new and growing assertiveness of American women and their quest for equal rights and suffrage.

Wagner "Out West"

Although not a cultural rival of the East Coast, the City of Big Shoulders was beginning to occupy a prominent position in the world of opera. Chicago saw Bellini's *La Sonnambula* staged by a touring company in 1850, and fifteen years later the city could boast an opera house larger than La

Scala. With the opening of the four-thousand-seat Auditorium Theater in 1889, Chicago housed the nation's first cultural center. The same season, the opulent Auditorium witnessed Wagner's complete *Ring* during its Metropolitan Opera tour and Verdi's *Otello* (1887) before it appeared in Paris. Many great singers, moreover, made debuts in the Auditorium, notably the Polish tenor Jean De Reszke and the American soprano Emma Eames. Thus, by the opening of the new century, Chicagoans could hear opera of a quality comparable to any in the country.

Two composers were prominent in Chicago's operatic history: Silas Pratt (1846–1916), a distinguished local organist who later founded Pittsburgh's Pratt Institute of Music and Art, and Frederick Grant Gleason (1848–1903), a respected Chicago music critic and composer. Both fell under the influence of Wagner, but of the two Pratt was the more adventuresome and possessed a surer sense of theater. His *Zenobia* was the first "grand romantic opera" composed by a Chicago resident, and it forecast the city's growing position as a center for American opera.

Zenobia was presented unstaged on June 15 and 16, 1882, at the Central Music Hall and fully staged at McVicker's Theater on March 26, 1883. It is a majestic, ambitious grand opera (a "lyric opera" as Pratt called it) with a large chorus, ensembles, through-composed and strophic arias, dramatic accompanied recitative, spectacular tableaux closing most of the acts, and no spoken dialogue. It is cast in the older "number-opera" framework, with individual sections rather than continuous musical flow. Although often lacking in soaring melody, the score is colored by rich, post-romantic harmonies and often-surprising tonal juxtapositions.

There were many numbers "of positive merit, well scored and effective," the *Chicago Tribune* reported on March 27, 1883, but what seemed most disturbing was Pratt's highly colorful harmonic language:

> Mr. Pratt's harmonies are beyond our comprehension or apprehension. Compared with Pratt, Wagner is in some respects but another Rossini. Instances of Mr. Pratt's absurd modulations are to be found on almost every one of the 203 pages of the score. . . . The most remarkable example perhaps is on page 159. In Longinus' air, "Calm and Serene," there are modulations of frightful proportions written to a text calling for the simplest harmonies. There is not a singer in this city who could sing the first four measures of this air at sight.

If Pratt's "absurd modulations" were not understood at the time, they reflected a composer straining to create a new, American, post-romantic style that was his own style and owed no allegiance to any special school.

A contralto with a lovely,
wide-ranging voice,
Annie Louise Cary was
America's first native-
born Wagnerian singer.
Pratt wrote the title role
of *Zenobia* for her, but
she retired from singing
shortly before the opera's
premiere. *Library of Congress*

His use of dissonance to obscure tonal centers, often in the most expressive arias ("Most Gentle One" in act 4), places him ahead of his American
contemporaries in the use of innovative sonorities. Yet in spite of the critic's comments, Pratt was still well rooted in the Wagnerian tradition.

While *Zenobia* was playing in Chicago, Frederick Grant Gleason was
working as music critic for the *Tribune*. More than likely, Gleason wrote
the *Zenobia* reviews. As one of the nation's most distinguished music critics, he drew from vast experience and extensive studies in Leipzig, Berlin,

and London. He composed songs, choral works, a piano concerto, two symphonic poems, and various instrumental pieces. He was both composer and librettist for his operas *Otho Visconti* (1877) and *Montezuma* (1885), the latter so rich with leitmotifs that Gleason had to provide an elaborate key to their symbols. Both operas, however, remain in manuscript. Only the former has been performed—and not until June 6, 1907, seven years after Gleason's death.[15]

Otho Visconti, like *Zenobia,* is grand opera in the tradition of Wagner and Meyerbeer but also at times reminiscent of Verdi, especially in its arias. The orchestration is skillfully executed and has considerable contrapuntal interplay. Theodore Thomas thought so highly of the Vorspiel that he conducted it during Chicago's World's Columbian Exposition of 1893. The story is set in Florence during a period of war between the Florentine Guelphs and the Ghibelines and is a tale of love, betrayal, and murder between Otho and Bianca, the leaders of rival factions.

The opera has action, dance, bridal processions, crowd scenes, and a variety of vocal forms characteristic of grand opera, but many details in the libretto seem to need follow-up or rationalization. Why, for example, should Bianca give Otho her scarf as "a token of friendship"? Although the scarf seems to have some significance in this scene, it never again appears. Bianca's personality, moreover, is not developed enough to justify her violent actions at the close of the opera, and Otho, the lead character, is more a man of action than perception. He is killed in the end. Yet unlike the king in Verdi's *Masked Ball,* who is also murdered but has gained the audience's empathy musically, Otho has no emotion-packed arias that display his feelings and thus heighten the audience's. At question is whether *Otho Visconti* is perhaps more melodrama than tragedy—more outward action than inward spirituality.

Paine, Damrosch, and Late-Nineteenth-Century Wagnerists

Many American composers worked prodigiously between 1898 and 1912, but only a handful stand out for their originality and importance within the operatic form: Edgar Stillman Kelley (1857–1944), John Knowles Paine (1839–1906), Walter Damrosch (1862–1950), George Whitefield Chadwick (1854–1931), and Horatio Parker (1863–1919). All five were prominent leaders in American musical life and enriched the nation's culture through teaching, composing, conducting, and writing. Paine, Damrosch, Chadwick, and Parker worked mainly in New England, while Kelley divided his time among California, Ohio, New York, and Berlin, Germany. The door to the

twentieth century had begun to open, and a place of permanence was established for American composers. Several of their works still appear in
concert repertoire, although modestly when compared with those of European composers. More relevant about the composers, however, is the
characteristic American spirit of adventure in their operas. Although Wagner may have guided them, they forged individual paths: Kelley in his cinematic visions; Paine as a builder of large-scale dramatic structure; and
Damrosch, Chadwick, and Parker in their vision of the female protagonist,
with all her fascinating ambiguities, whether sinner/victim, murderer/hero,
or winner/loser. Wagner's heroines may be more noble, but the women in
turn-of-the-century American opera are every bit as engrossing.

Among the five composers, Edgar Stillman Kelley can be singled out
as a true pioneer in what would become paramount in the sensibility of
American creative minds—the association of film techniques and aesthetics
with live opera. What is especially interesting about Kelley's music is its
ties with motion pictures. His music for *Ben-Hur* (1899) foreshadows the
great epic film scores of decades to come, even William Wyler's *Ben-Hur*
in the 1950s. Called a "melodrama-pantomime," Kelley's *Ben-Hur* contains
more instrumental music, pageantry, and dance than vocal music, distin-
guishing it from grand opera. Yet it also has some impressive large choral
scenes and occasional solo numbers. Kelley had once planned to write a
grand opera on the subject of Ben-Hur, but the idea never materialized.
A great admirer of Wagner, he also associates musical motifs with various
characters and incidents throughout the work. An Oriental-sounding motif
first heard in the Prelude, for example, later reappears in "The Spinning
of Arachne" scene as Iras ominously ensnares Ben-Hur.[16] Kelley also composed music for several melodramas such as *Macbeth* (1885) and *Puritania*
(1892), but *Ben-Hur* was his most popular. Based on Lew Wallace's biblical
novel, it reputedly ran more than five thousand times in various parts of
the country. Clearly, Kelley knew what the public wanted.

John Knowles Paine was not as fortunate. His last major work, and only
grand opera, *Azara* (1898) was never staged. It received only three performances, all in Boston. Two, in 1903 and 1905, were with piano accompaniment; the other was with orchestra at Symphony Hall on April 9, 1907.
The Metropolitan Opera almost staged *Azara* that same year, but good
singers who knew the English language could not be found for either the
demanding solo roles or the chorus. It took Paine fifteen years to complete the opera. By that time, he was an experienced composer of almost
seventy opus numbers that included eloquent symphonies, choral works,
and dramatic music for melodramas, notably Aristophanes' *The Birds*. A

An advertisement for an early production of *Ben Hur,* the subject also used by Edgar Stillman Kelley in his melodrama-pantomime *Ben Hur* (1899). *Library of Congress*

member of the Harvard University faculty, Paine's students—John Alden Carpenter, Arthur Foote, Thomas W. Surette, Edward Burlingame Hill, Frederick S. Converse, and many others—formed a coterie that shaped American music well into the twentieth century. As his friend John Fiske observed, "It is due to Paine that music has been put on the same level with philosophy, science and classical philology. . . . It was not easy to accomplish."[17]

Paine wrote his own libretto for *Azara,* effectively alternating prose with rhymed verse. The published piano-vocal score includes both English and German text. Based upon an early thirteenth-century French *chante-fable* entitled *Aucassin and Nicolette,* the story is at times tumultuous and stormy, pitting "rays of fight and conquest and the animosities of races and peoples."[18] It also confronts daughter with guardian, son with father, and pursuer with fugitive. Set in medieval Provence, the opera follows the original fable about a lovely Moorish girl, Azara, who is separated from her lover Gontran, son of King Rainulf. Pursued by the Saracen chieftain Malek, Azara is captured, manages to escape, and, disguising herself as a minstrel, eventually reunites with Gontran in the opera's brilliant and highly dramatic conclusion.

Paine uses the leitmotif technique skillfully to accentuate dramatic moments and provide unification in a score that is through-composed (that is, it flows continuously, one number into the next).[19] The most interesting motifs are those associated with Azara and Malek, which through musical imagery separate heroine from villain. Azara is announced through a delicately scored motif as Gotran announces his plans to marry to his father. The motif is then transformed to reflect Azara's various moods throughout the opera, such as its climatic ascent in the daybreak scene in act 2 and pensive iteration as Azara grieves over the loss of Gotran. As in Wagner, the leitmotifs are almost exclusively instrumental. Although Azara is disguised in the final scene, Paine allows her to sing her motif in a lyrical troubadour ballad, thus heightening her true identity and providing her with feminine imagery, as Verdi did in allowing Aida to sing her motif long after it is first heard in the orchestra. Malek, too, is effectively characterized throughout the score. The Saracen chief is given a touch of exoticism through a motif sometimes infused with modal inflections, and at times it appears more rhythmic and sharply defined than Azara's.

Underpinning the well-constructed libretto is Paine's especially rich and sonorous orchestration. An even larger orchestra is required for *Azara* than for the composer's earlier *Mass in D* and *St. Peter*. The opera has parts for tripled woodwinds, increased brass and percussion, and more extensive *divisi* passages in the strings. In his earlier years, Paine drew mainly from the German romanticists such as Mendelssohn and had little use for Wagner. Later he admitted, "You will find that I have entered upon a new path in all respects—in form, thematic treatment, instrumentation, etc. All dramatic composers must learn from Wagner, yet I have not consciously imitated him . . . I have followed throughout the connected orchestral rhythmic flow, and truth of dramatic expression characteristic of Wagner."[20] Paine's importance in the field of American opera lies not in his emulation of Wagner but in his ability to assemble highly individual dramatic impulses within a work of large-scale, skillfully organized proportions.

Eroticism and the Female Protagonist

With Walter Damrosch's *Scarlet Letter* and George Chadwick's *Judith,* noticeable changes in American opera began to appear—notably, the acceptance of plots revolving around the strong sexual motivations of heroines. Changes were in the air as the century turned through the lure of the powerful although short-lived art nouveau or *Jugendstil* movement. Many later-nineteenth-century European painters, architects, and graphic designers shared the common aesthetic bonds of art nouveau and its exotic sub-jects: long, flowing lines (as Mélisande's hair); organic, Darwinian floral motifs; and often blatant eroticism.[21] In America, the spirit of art nouveau was manifest in James McNeill Whistler's Peacock Room and the deco-rative glassware of Louis Comfort Tiffany. Music and dance responded through the "exotic" sonorities of Charles Griffes's *White Peacock* and the symbolic sensuality of dancer Loïe Fuller.

In art nouveau, women are often viewed through misogynist eyes and portrayed as sinful or evil, as in the work of Jan Toorop, Frantisehak Kup-ka, or Gustav Klimt. Women's sexuality was feared as a tool of the devil, a concept stemming from early Christian times when the leaders of West-ern civilization were celibate clergy. Decadent women of antiquity—for example, Delilah, Elektra, and Salome—fascinated such composers as Richard Strauss and Camille Saint-Saëns. Even Wagner, whose earlier heroines were noble, broke new ground with the sublimely erotic Kun-dry in his last opera, *Parsifal*. Damrosch and Chadwick approached the sexuality of women from different perspectives—Damrosch from the time-honored viewpoint of Wagnerian romanticism and Chadwick in the light of the new, fin-de-siècle eroticism. The former closed an era while the latter opened one.

The Scarlet Letter is a "Wagnerian" opera based on an American novel. Damrosch was only thirty-four when portions of his work were performed in concert in Carnegie Hall on January 4 and 5, 1895. Produced by the Damrosch Opera Company, staged productions of the full opera followed in Boston on February 10, 1896; at Philadelphia's Academy of Music on February 22; and at the Academy of Music in New York on March 6. Born in Breslau, Germany, Damrosch had come to America at age nine. He was only twenty-three when he succeeded his father, Leopold Damrosch, as conductor of both the Oratorio Society and the Symphony Society of New York (later the New York Philharmonic), remaining the conductor of the latter for forty years. Between 1894 and 1900 he introduced Wag-nerian opera to cities as far west as Denver through the two-hundred-member Damrosch Opera Company. A distinguished music educator and champion of American music, Damrosch also commissioned George Gershwin's Piano Concerto in F, crusaded tirelessly for the production of opera in English, and was one of the earliest composers to recognize the potential of radio.

Damrosch was also the first American composer to have two of his operas produced at the Metropolitan Opera: *Cyrano de Bergerac* (1913) and *The Man without a Country* (1937).[22] But none of his later operas had quite

Walter Damrosch, com-
poser of *The Scarlet Letter,*
an opera Anton Seidl
facetiously called a "New
England Nibelung Trilo-
gy." *Library of Congress*

the dramatic integrity and musical impact of his earliest, *The Scarlet Letter.*
Instead of heroic legends of distant lands, Damrosch turned to Nathaniel
Hawthorne's brooding psychological romance set in colonial Boston.
George Parsons Lathrop, Hawthorne's son-in-law, wrote the libretto, and
the result is a taut and masterful image of the novel. Lathrop's poetry for
the libretto is often free, unrhymed, and "molded by the sentiment, passion or situation of the moment," as he states in the introduction. "Besides the metre and rhythm of each line," he adds, "there is often a complicated word melody, or a scheme of emphases and pauses, running
through several lines. . . . Such 'over-rhythms' correspond frequently to
continuing strains of music in the text."[23]

Lathrop constructs his story around the primary themes of the novel:
sin and its effects on individuals and society. Specifically, Hawthorne traces
the effect of sin on the lives of three characters: Hester Prynne, who has
been convicted of adultery; Arthur Dimmesdale, the minister whose dis-
tressing secret eventually kills him; and Chillingworth, Hester's malicious

husband. With its somber allegorical overtones, the story parallels the guilty lovers in *Tristan und Isolde,* first produced nine years after Hawthorne's novel. It also anticipated Sigmund Freud's theories of the effects of guilt on the human spirit. Like Wagner's operas, the novel abounds in symbols: the scarlet *A* that Hester must wear to mark her sin, the scaffold of public notice, the sunlight in the forest, and the main characters themselves. Wagnerian "redemption" is realized as Hester takes poison and dies with her lover. "The flow of sacrifice / Blooms in no earthly garden / Thou, Hester, over us triumph has won" sings the chorus of townspeople, their attitudes changed from scorn to reverence.[24]

Obvious weaknesses in the cast are the omission of Hester's child and the dominance of male roles, especially in the lower registers. Of the seven main characters, Hester (soprano) is the only woman's part and Dimmesdale the only tenor. The score calls for a large orchestra and double choruses of four parts each.[25] Wagnerian aspects come to play in the harmonic language, orchestral fabric, and continuous structure of the work. Even more extensively than in Paine's *Azara,* characters, objects, and passions are heightened by leitmotifs molded and transformed throughout the opera. The symbolic nature of the "scarlet letter" motif is illustrated in act 1 when the chorus calls Hester a "child of error." As in *Azara,* characters are delineated through motifs. Hester's, marked initially "andantino grave," is usually in E minor; Arthur's motif is often oddly detached and dissonant; and Chillingworth's, first sounded by the oboes, is melodramatically sinister.

Touches of dissonance and polytonal inflections underpin text or mood during tense dramatic moments such as the chorale ("praise God from whom all blessings flow") pitted against agonized soloists in the closing scene of act 1. Certain arias have special charm. Hester's "Ripple of the Brook" at the opening of act 2, for example, follows the symbolism of the brook in the novel. And the "Shipmaster's Song" in act 3 is colorful and dramatic. In general, throughout the fiery roulades of Hawthorne's drama, score and libretto are felicitous partners.

For the concert performance at Carnegie Hall, the role of Hester was sung by the noted American soprano Lillian Nordica; in staged productions that followed, the twenty-three-year-old Wagnerian star Johanna Gadski sang Hester. In Philadelphia where he was born, David Bispham brilliantly portrayed the demanding role of Chillingworth. Bispham, like Lawrence Tibbett, would become one of the twentieth-century's top stars of American opera. Although Damrosch was praised for "blending the elements of his composition with a freedom and daring quite astonishing

in their exhibition of mastery," he was criticized for adhering too closely
to Wagnerian ideals.[26] Anton Seidl called *The Scarlet Letter* "a New England
Nibelung trilogy."[27] Alfred Remy found the orchestra "a tempestuous
ocean in which a few musical phrases—chiefly Wagner's—float like de-
bris after a shipwreck."[28]

If Wagner was no longer a novelty, Americans needed to turn elsewhere
for fresh inspiration if their work was to survive. George Whitefield Chadwick did just that when he turned to French styles for *Judith* (1901). Still,
the opera never traveled beyond the concert stage. An America that embraced the noble Wagnerian heroine would not accept a murderous female who chose the dripping, severed head of her male antagonist. If
Strauss's *Salome* would be pulled from the Metropolitan Opera after a single
performance in 1907, *Judith* hardly stood a chance. Chadwick clearly hoped
to see *Judith* in operatic form but did make some initial compromises
because of the difficulties he anticipated in seeing the work staged. He
conceived *Judith* as a hybrid form modeled after the French *drame lyrique,*
such as Saint-Saëns's oratorio *Samson and Delilah,* which he had recently
conducted.[29]

The extraordinary sensual scenes of seduction and murder in *Judith*—
heightened by a score of exotic and erotic musical imagery—cry out for
staging, however. One great climactic effect, Judith's victorious slaying of
Holofernes, is illustrated in graphic detail by the strategic placement of
percussive effects, cross rhythms, and explicit orchestral contrapuntal
figures.[30] Nothing like it had ever been conceived for the American stage.

Judith's libretto by William Chauncy Langdon follows the apocryphal
tale of the beautiful Israelite, who goes to the Assyrian camp to seduce its
general Holofernes, proudly defying the admonition of her people that
"lust digs every grave." She avoids submitting to Holofernes' passions by
intoxicating him and then beheading him with his own sword. She presents the head to Israel's chief, Ozias. "Ah, noblest of Judah's women," sings
the chorus, offering a parallel between Judith and Hester Prynne. Both
women, earlier shunned, are now extolled. But there is a difference: Hester is redeemed through her sacrifice and Judith through her courage. What
Jane Marcus says of Salome is true of Judith: "Only a little leap of the
imagination transformed this furious girl into a suffragette with a rock in
her hand."[31]

Horatio Parker's character Mona is also strong in her achievements, but,
unlike Azara and Judith, the young first-century princess of Britain is
imprisoned by conflicting emotions that eventually destroy her. Her lover Gwynn is killed in a revolt that Mona leads against the Romans. "I could

not be a woman," she sings passionately as Roman soldiers bind her hands at the end of the opera, "loved and loving, nor endure Motherhood and the wise ordinary joys of day by day. . . . I have had dreams," she cries out in arching, eloquent melodic lines. "Only great dreams!" The tragedy is neither in Mona's actions nor in her fate but in her attitudes.

By the time *Mona* was given its premiere at the Metropolitan Opera in 1912, audiences had wearied of German ideology. Parker's heroic libretto was "somewhat gray," some said, although he handled musical imagery with finesse and flair. Parker admired Richard Strauss even more than Wagner. "In *Salome,*" he once said, "we have an orchestra with its lid entirely removed."[32] The orchestra in *Mona,* too, plays with all lids up, allowing a vivid instrumental sheen to highlight the dramatic flow of events and characters. The texture is dense with leitmotifs that often appear as successions of chromatically altered chords rather than only melodic fragments. The character of Mona is portrayed by several themes or groups of themes, creatively varied and expressive of her every mood and action. A harmonic transformation of the sword motif reflects the abusive personality of Arth,

Horatio Parker's *Mona* included among its cast the noted American contralto Louise Homer (second from left) as Mona and Albert Reiss (far right) as Nial. *Metropolitan Opera Archives*

and Nial dances with his shadow to light, fleeting melodic phrases and amorphous instrumental colors. "I have employed leitmotifs in *Mona,* of course," said Parker. "For I can't conceive of anyone's writing an opera nowadays without them."[33]

✂

Wagnerian ideals of music drama continued to influence American and European composers despite periodic charges of anti-Wagnerism. "Only a phase," said Krehbiel. "It stands for nothing." Yet William Henderson emphasized that the "New School of Italian Opera" represented the new taste, a combination of the "powerful expressiveness of the Teutonic dec-lamation with all of the vocal elegance and essentially singable qualities of the Neapolitan manner."[34] The remarkable success of *Cavalleria* and *Pagliacci* were attributable, he said, to widespread public demand for dra-matic brevity and tragic intensity. Another critic, George William Curtis, gently mocked the more cerebral Wagnerites: "Do you think that you hear music sufficiently with your mind?" he chided. "Instead of being absorbed in the *Leitmotiven,* are you not really hankering for the flesh-pots of mel-ody—of gross *tune?*"[35]

"Gross tune," however, is not what opera is about—at least not for Wagnerites in America. In their enduring romance with the Wizard of Bayreuth, American opera composers managed to keep the dramatic flavor of the melodrama alive for decades but always seasoned with their own individual attitudes. In their emphasis on the role of the orchestra to en-hance drama; to explore the inner feelings of the characters—especially the heroines; and to draw the audience into scenes of action, serenity, or suspense, Paine, Chadwick, Damrosch, and the other American Wagner-ites anticipated the aesthetic approach of the American operatic style that would shape the nation's finest works in the decades to come.

8

Native Americans through Symbolism and Song

Hehaka spirit is a flute spirit. The girl hears it and comes running. She can't resist. The elk flute is for making love. You play the flute, the next morning the deer are around and a good spirit comes.
   —Henry Crow Dog, from *Crying for a Dream,* 1969

BY 1900 THE MUSICAL dramaturgy of Richard Wagner had become such an integral part of American opera composers' vocabularies that it was no longer a trend but a tradition. Composers began to look beyond Germanic culture for a more "American" image. They readily found it in Native American aesthetics and art. But in discovering their indigenous cultural treasures, Americans also found a new, modern mode of dramatic expression. Native American music became exotic and Wagner commonplace—and that unique interplay allowed fresh new dimensions in American opera.

When John Comfort Fillmore returned from many months among the Omahas, studying their music, he found a "cosmic connection" between Indian and Wagnerian styles: "In the absolute supremacy of the imaginative and emotional elements which dominated every moment of the Indian's criticism of my work, I was continually reminded of [German Romanticism]. Here, as with . . . Wagner, the all-important matter was the feeling to be expressed."[1] Charles Hamm's description of the functional nature of Native American music conveys something of the inner, numinous life of opera: "For the Native American, music was not rational, but a matter of faith; not personalized, but a gift from the gods; not specialized, but one component in ceremonies involving large groups of people . . . song was not simply self-expression. It was magic which called upon the powers of Nature and constrained them to man's will."[2]

The multidimensional nature of opera has always encouraged the rich interplay of periods, characters, and musical styles. Giacomo Puccini's *Girl of the Golden West* (1910), from David Belasco's famous melodrama about the California gold rush, is an early-American setting with a modern Italian score. Ferruccio Busoni's *Turandot* (1911) is based on an ancient Chinese legend captured within an eighteenth-century Italian *fiaba* set as a German singspiel with a contemporaneous score. Americans, too, were becoming more experimental in melding styles and forms as the twentieth century began. Native American culture provided many options. It reinforced their ever-expanding national consciousness, gave them what they believed to be a strong American identity, and provided librettos with mysticism and melodrama—sure-fire audience-pleasers. The modes, chants, and instruments of Native Americans, moreover, offered new musical sonorities to enrich their scores.

With the advent of sound recordings around 1890, composers could retain and better understand a musical culture that had been transmitted mainly orally for generations. The study of Native American music (and its transcription into Western notation) began in 1893 with Alice Cunningham Fletcher's *A Study of Omaha Indian Music.* In 1907 Natalie Curtis (Burlin) published the most comprehensive collection of Native American music to that date. Her efforts were an attempt to preserve a culture that would soon be lost forever through devastating destruction brought about by whites. As one grim Navaho put it, "They came with the Bible in one hand and the gun in the other. First they stole gold. Then they stole the land. Then they stole souls."[3] Curtis appealed directly to President Theodore Roosevelt, and her influence resulted in the shaping of an enlightened policy in the administration of Native American affairs and the adoption of many of the reforms she advocated. "At last," she said, "the Indian child in the government school and the adult on the reservation were allowed a freedom of racial consciousness and a spiritual liberty theretofore almost tyrannically denied."[4]

About the time of Curtis's work, American composers, notably Charles Wakefield Cadman, Harvey Worthington Loomis, and Charles Sanford Skilton, began to incorporate Native American chants and ceremonial rhythms in their piano pieces, songs, and orchestral works, usually within a Westernized harmonic framework. In 1910 Cadman organized a series of popular lecture recitals, "American Indian Music Talks." Presenting more than four hundred programs within a fifteen-year period, he illustrated his talks with the singing of Tsianina Redfeather, a descendant of Tecumseh. Arthur Farwell was also deeply attracted to Native American lore, which he believed was close to the true "art-spirit" of Western civilization. Founded in 1901 to encourage work by young American composers, Farwell's Wa-Wan Press was named after a ceremony of the Omahas to celebrate "peace, fellowship and song." His own concert music often used material from not only Native Americans but also other folk-ethnic traditions—traditions drawn creatively from the sea, soil, and heart of America.

How then was Native American music—through technique, form, style, and philosophy—absorbed by early-twentieth-century American opera composers? Was it a relatively superficial, external influence, or did it provide composers with new musical and dramatic directions? Did it involve plot and characters, scales and modes, or mainly spirituality and symbolism? Finally, did it help solve the age-old problem that faces every opera composer—problems regarding the relationship of action and music and the confluence of imagery, characterization, and dramatic truth, in short, the creation of a viable operatic dramaturgy?

During the early decades of the twentieth century, colorful Native American legends and music provided starting points for what amounted to an array of Americanized, or Westernized, "Indianist" operas. But such themes were hardly new. *Tammany,* composed in 1794, was America's first serious opera, and others inspired by Native Americans followed. Even before American composers, Europeans were drawn to the subject.[5] These operas, however, made no pretext of ethnographic authenticity. Not until the early twentieth century did composers such as Puccini, who used "Oriental" melodies in *Madama Butterfly* and *Turandot,* strive for more authentic ethnographic coloring. In the United States between 1910 and 1930, Native Americans inspired more than twenty operas. Composers, in a sense, became ethnomusicologists and explorers. Like Arthur Nevin, they tried "not so much to reproduce the actual music and words of the Indians," as Hipsher observed in 1934, "as to create, through the use of figures of speech and of musical idioms, an art work which would interpret the Indian in his life and manner of thought, and at the same time to mold the work to the requirements of the operatic stage."[6]

To gain insight into Native American culture, several composers, such as Stella Stocker and Henry Schoenefeld, lived among the tribes for extended periods. Cecil Fanning, the librettist for Francesco de Leone's *Alglala* (1924), spent several months on a Crow reservation, and Arthur Nevin, composer of *Poia* (1910), worked for four summers among the Blackfeet. Charles Wakefield Cadman made cylinder phonograph recordings during a visit to the Omaha reservation in Nebraska. Alberto Bimboni researched his Chippewa melodies for *Winona* (1926) from Native Americans in Minnesota and the comprehensive collection of the Smithsonian Institution. William Hanson drew from the vast knowledge of several contemporaneous Sioux women for his spectacular *Sun Dance,* staged in Vernal, Utah, in 1913. The various opera librettos themselves are a compendium of tribal diversity. From the Chilkoots of Alaska to the Seminoles of Florida, from the Pueblos of the Southwest to the Blackfeet of the northern Plains, and from the Hurons and Delawares to the Utes and Chippewas—each opera plot reflects a different Native American culture and regional expression.

Most of the librettos are inextricably bound into the well-worn American melodramatic love triangle but with new twists and turns. The young woman is now an Indian maiden, the lover is often white, and the jealous rival or angry father is sometimes the tribe's chief, creating the intense conflict and highly charged emotions Americans came to expect. Significantly, with the exception of *Poia,* the operas focus on female leads, as their titles indicate: *Natoma, Narcissa, Daoma, Osseo, Shanewis, Atala, Alglala, Winona, The Sun Bride, The Chilkoot Maiden,* and *The White Buffalo Maiden.* Once again, it is a woman—jumping off a cliff or dying for her man (or lack of him) in true Wagnerian style—who is the source of the drama. Winona leaps into Lake Pepin rather than marry the Dacotah chief Matosapa; Natoya saves Poia but is killed in the process; Atala takes poison and dies in her lover's arms; and Alglala is killed along with her white lover by her angry father, a Chippewa. Even if she herself bravely kills her opposition, she dies. An Indian heroine is the ultimate loser. Either, like Natoma, she is relegated to life in a convent, or, like Shanewis, she loses the one she loves. If the female protagonist carries the action, she also bears the agony.

Arthur Nevin's Poia

Native American–inspired operas went through several changes in style and focus as they moved through the first decades of the twentieth century. Many earlier ones such as Nevin's *Poia* were based on legend and concerned Native American characters. Later operas, *Natoma, Shanewis,* and others, began to take on a more realistic or historic aspect using white characters as well. Others, especially those after World War I, returned once again to legendary and ceremonial subjects.

Many earlier operas fell under the influence of Wagner. Of these, one in particular stands out, the lyrical *Poia* by Pennsylvania composer Arthur Finlay Nevin (1871–1943). Although he uses carefully researched Native American music and lore, Nevin also shows strong Wagnerian influences in *Poia's* mystical plot, leitmotif technique, and through-composed structure, with flowing interplay among narrative, dramatic, and lyrical moments. More significant is that the work draws beholders into its drama through a marvelously rich and exuberant score. Because it surpasses many American operas of the time in dramaturgical substance and employs an especially interesting blend of legend with character, it merits consideration at some length.

Poia's performance history is particularly fascinating because its staged premiere took place overseas. It was first produced in concert form in Pittsburgh on January 15, 1906, with predictions that it would "take its place among the greatest of the world's classics."[7] The next year, the composer presented it as a lecture-concert for President and Mrs. Theodore Roosevelt at the White House. Ironically, its staged premiere occurred not in America but in Berlin and was conducted by the brilliant German maestro Karl Muck. Muck had also conducted another of Nevin's compositions in Berlin, the Lorna Doone Suite. Neither conductor nor composer, however, was prepared for the hostile reception *Poia* received after its premiere on April 23, 1910. As Nevin recalled, "That first night was an event I shall not forget. The applause for a time seemed strong, and with Randolph Hartley, the librettist, I was called before the curtain. Right away there were hisses. I have heard hissing in other theaters, but never anything like that. It sounded like steam whistles. People in the upper part of the house used large keys they carry in Berlin to blow across the cup-shaped ends. It produced a terrible noise, and I was thunderstruck."[8]

Nevin believed the insidious reaction may have been due to either the false report that the crown prince of Germany was providing the opera with undesirable political backing or to European jealousy of rival American singers. The fine American baritone Putnam Griswold was the Sun God. After a young German whose opera had been refused by the Royal Opera House committed suicide, Berlin newspapers protested: "The stage of the Royal Opera House should not be made a checkerboard for political games, while our own artists are driven to suicide."[9]

After a sold-out opening night attended by both American and German dignitaries, however, *Poia* did manage to run for three more evenings, "more than any recent opera has had in Berlin," Nevin claimed. He also indicated that *Poia* had received less lambaste than other recent new operas. Perhaps he meant the Berlin premiere of Strauss's *Elektra,* that icon of matricide that had created a furor the year before.

In addition to Griswold, *Poia*'s stellar cast included the English soprano Florence Easton as Natoya and the powerful young Wagnerian tenor Walter Kirchhoff as Poia. Years later, Kirchhoff would gain further recognition as Max in the American premiere of Ernst Křenek's *Jonny spielt auf.* *Poia* also bore the distinction of being not only Berlin's first American opera but also one of the first full scores of an American opera to be published overseas, preceded only by Frederick S. Converse's *The Pipe of Desire* (1908). *Poia* was printed in Berlin by Adolph Fürstner in 1910.[10] The opera's staged performance history, however, is uncertain. According to some sources, rights to it had been disposed of, and its future, accordingly, was out of the composer's control.[11]

The opera's story is drawn from the Blackfeet legend of Poia, grandson of the sun god and savior of his people, as interpreted by the explorer Walter McClintock. The original legend has many versions, and the opera offers yet another, mainly in the addition of a rival lover, Sumatsi, and Natoya's self-sacrifice in the closing scene.[12] The traditional legend also appears to meld Native American, Christian, and Greek beliefs, yielding a scenario rich in imagery and dramatic potential. As the various legends intertwine within the opera's expressive narrative, symbolism, pageantry, and passion play themselves out in grand design.

The action takes place in the far Northwest before the advent of whites. Poia, a prophet of the Rocky Mountain Blackfeet tribe, is cursed with a facial scar that impairs his courtship of Natoya ("The Blessed One"). "Ha, ha! Natoya as lover?" the chorus taunts. "Whence came the wound?" asks Natoya. "I know not," admits Poia. "He who bears a scar unblessed by valiant deed in chase or fray," sings Natoya scornfully, "is by dishonor's cloud oppress'd." In agony and despair, Poia decides to undertake a dangerous journey to the realm of Natosi the Sun God to seek removal of the scar. Doing so is his only hope of winning Natoya, because the boastful young Sumatsi loves her too.

As act 2 begins, Poia makes his way along the arduous path to the sun god's mysterious domain in the forest. Exhausted, he imagines he hears Natoya's voice in the distance. As the sun rises gloriously, the chorus sings a ceremonial song, and the audience witnesses a "transformation—a cavern like hall, the walls and roof are of clouds upon which varied lights play. Natosi, the Sun God, is seated on Throne. On both sides are the four seasons, Mota, Nepu, Moku, Stuyi and four Heralds." Adament, Natosi refuses to hear Poia's plea ("Thou shalt bear the scar, 'till men's tears have washed away the stain"). Poia pleads again:

> At birth thou dids't destroy me with this scar
>> That makes me fear the guilt of all mankind.
> I sought a God of justice, journey'd far
>> And now a God of all injustice find."

Suddenly, Kokum the Moon cries out that a monstrous bird is attacking her son Episua (Morning Star). Poia courageously slays the bird with his arrow, and in gratitude Natosi grants Poia's request. "Come, thou shalt change thy wound for beauty," he sings. "Teach your people to love as you have loved." Episua then evokes the god of slumber to "spread the veil of sleep before his eyes" and summons the gods of thunder and lightning to give him power. During a colorful four-part dance scenario, Ballet of the Four Seasons, Poia's accursed scar disappears. Episua then hands Poia a magic flute ("it's song hath charm and witchery, that bids a maiden's soul rejoice"). Slowly and majestically, the sun god and his court begin to sink from view. Episua takes Poia's hand and carefully guides him through the clouds and back to earth by the trail of the Milky Way while the chorus sings praise to Natosi, "Lord of Light."

Act 3 opens as the tribe laments "weary and old is our mother, the world, and weak are the children she bears in her age." "The tribe is a forest of dying trees," sings an old man. "The curse that Poia bore alone has fallen now upon the race." But when Poia arrives, his dreaded curse removed, he is now a hero. He plays upon his magic reed pipe, and when Natoya hears its plaintive call she rushes to his arms. Sumatsi, enraged with jealousy, raises his hand to kill Poia, but Natoya flings herself in his way and the blade strikes her instead. As Poia leans over the dying Natoya ("in this sweet refuge of thy breast, my life shall end in ecstasy," she sings, Isolde-like), Sumatsi starts to plunge the dagger into Poia's back. Suddenly, Natosi the Sun God intervenes, and a brilliant shaft of sunlight falls on Sumatsi, striking him dead. Gently carrying the body of his beloved Natoya, Poia makes his way to the glorious land of the sun god, never to return.

In Native American belief, John Collier observes, symbol systems were "the conservers and propellers of the deep life of man, the definers and molders of personality, and the pilots of societies in their movement toward half-conscious goals." "The Earth is a living thing," says a contemporary Native American, Lame Deer. "The Mountains speak. The trees sing. Lakes can think. Pebbles have a soul. Rocks have power."[13] Plains Indians believed that all power came from Wakan-Tanka (the Great Mystery), and their gods were nearly always Sun, Earth, Moon, Morning Star, Wind, Fire, and Thunder. The greatest ceremony of the year, the Sun Dance, was held in midsummer and featured symbols of fertility such as a large pole, the tree of life, around which dancers circled. Lasting almost a week, the Sun Dance also comprised processions and the voluntary self-mutilations of warriors carrying out their vows. In the legend, Natosi teaches Poia the Sun Dance, which he in turn brings to his people on earth. Perhaps Nevin entitled his work "the Ballet of the Four Seasons" because the American authorities had criticized the Sun Dance and nearly abolished it as being too "barbaric."

Like Wagner's pervasive use of symbol and myth, Nevin's occurs on many levels: in the legend, characters, staging, and music itself. Symbols, such as the sun, the flute, and the wound, are shared by many civilizations but are central to the dramatic imagery of *Poia*. The interplay of gods and mortals is seen not only in Wagner's *Ring* but also in Skilton's *The Sun Bride*. "My mate is Light, but I know only darkness," sings the lonely young Pueblo woman. And there is more than a touch of Schopenhauer in the metaphysical realization that two people are aspects of one life—so vital to both Wagner and Native American–inspired opera.

Natoya's sudden change from hatred to love for Poia is justified when one understands the nature of the flute in Native American tradition. The flute, or reed pipe, was not only the primary melodic instrument but also held strong magical or spiritual properties linked closely to the semiotics of sexual desire. In non-Native American cultures, too, the flute becomes a kind of phallic symbol—from Dionysus to Papageno—and fills the air with sensuous and enticing tones, like mating calls. In De Leone's *Alglala,* the young Native American imitates a flute obbligato in florid cadenzas that become her "Bird Song." Skilton's *Kalopin* features an aria and love scene emanating from the strange flute serenade of a Chickasaw chief. The symbol of the scar, or facial "pox," in *Poia* also has spiritual and sexual overtones, although they are more obscure. Reference to diseases of sexual excess, especially syphilis, appear in works somewhat earlier, such as Ibsen's *Ghosts* and Wagner's *Parsifal* (Amfortas'"wound").[14] Poia, like Christ, frees humanity from its sins. The emblem of that redemption is, in Poia's case, a scar ("he who bears an unblessed scar . . . is by dishonor's cloud oppress'd") and its eventual removal through self-sacrifice and sublime love.

The musical messages of *Poia* are evident in colors as vivid as the legend. The opera's scoring is rich, sonorous, and lyrical. Splashes of harp glissandi heighten images of sunlight, and other orchestral colors underpin Natoya's voice and the imposing moods of the Sun God. As the four dances, Spring, Summer, Autumn and Winter, progress, the overall tempo gradually increases. Summer, marked "allegretto grazioso," is embellished by glockenspiel, tambourine, and triangle, simulating Native American idiophones. Winter is reflected in a repeated ostinato timpani beat marked "presto, Indian melody." Native American tunes—more precisely, quasi-tunes—are woven throughout the score, some insistent and narrow in range, others lyrical and modal. Yet overly melodramatic, pictorial use of Native American material occasionally mars dramatic moments. The brief war dance motifs following Poia's determination to seek the Sun God ("then I shall game with death") seem contrived, almost cinematic "Mickey-Mousing."[15] Still, it is not hard to see why conductor Karl Muck, the great Wagner and Mahler interpreter, was attracted to *Poia* and its postromantic Wagnerian idioms.

Victor Herbert and the First Waves of Realism

Because mysticism, symbol, and legend no longer seemed to serve the creative needs of Indianist composers, many turned to the everyday life of Native Americans in portrayals they felt were more realistic. It is significant, moreover, that the earliest verismo operas in America were inspired by the culture of Native Americans. Modern or historic locales and characters in intense emotional conflict were the substance of these new librettos, and American composers Victor Herbert (1859–1924) and Charles Wakefield Cadman (1881–1946) were especially attracted to what they felt was a truly indigenous subject with fresh operatic potential and colorful sonorities.

From *Prince Ananias* (1895) to *The Dream Girl,* staged the year he died, Victor Herbert wrote more than fifty works for the musical stage, including one of the earliest orchestral scores for film, *The Fall of a Nation* (1916). His *Natoma,* completed in 1910, is a serious, lyric opera in three acts, one of only two operas he wrote. Herbert's other opera, the lighter, one-act *Madeleine,* was staged at the Metropolitan Opera in 1913. *Natoma* was given its premiere in Philadelphia on February 23, 1911, by the Philadelphia and Chicago Opera Company under the management of Andreas Dippel. It then toured New York, Chicago, and other cities, totaling more than forty performances. The brilliant original cast included the young Metropolitan Opera tenor John McCormack as Paul and the celebrated Mary Garden—who had sung Mélisande in America's first *Pelléas et Mélisande* the year before—as Natoma.

Natoma was composed at the peak of Victor Herbert's popularity as the nation's noblest man of the theater, and its production was awaited eagerly by both public and press. Here, at last, was an American opera composer and a successful and beloved American musical figure. Surely, people thought, he could put America on the European-dominated operatic map. But *Natoma* did not live up to its expectations. Although some critics praised Herbert's musicianship, dexterity, and brilliant scoring for the orchestra, others were far less complimentary.[16] Mary Garden felt the work was not successful because of the cast, many of whom were foreign-born and had to wrestle with an English text. To the press, the problem lay in the libretto. Written by Joseph D. Redding, a San Francisco lawyer, it was dubbed "futile, fatuous, halting, impotent, inane and puerile . . . its verbiage, cheap colloquialism or jingling balderdash."[17] Such a harsh diatribe was unfounded and no doubt illustrated American critics' unwillingness to accept the new verismo libretto as viable opera. Perhaps what they missed was operatic thunder, as in the work of Verdi, Wagner, and Puccini. What they got was closer to Viennese operetta with recitative.

   Natoma tells of a young Native American during the early mission days of California and her violent act of murder to protect her young white friend and mistress. The libretto offers a great deal of potential for dramatic scenarios, choral interaction, colorful Spanish and Native American visual effects, and lyrical musical moments. Herbert provided all of these—and more. He knew very well how to write for the voice, and by struc-

Victor Herbert, composer of nearly fifty operettas, wrote only one serious grand opera, *Natoma* (1910). *Library of Congress*

turing his opera in number format rather than continuous Wagnerian flow he could feature individual arias and enhance musical characterization.

Two arias are perhaps the earliest American ones to have been recorded: Barbara's "I List the Trill" and Paul's "No Country Can My Own Outvie," both from act 2.[18] Each reflects its character's moods and personality, Barbara through her light operetta style and Paul in his confident, military, rhythmic bounce. Natoma, the most interesting character both musically and dramatically, is often portrayed through orchestral motifs and melodies sometimes built around the "exotic" pentatonic scale.[19]

One of the finest dramatic scenes in the opera takes place in the last act when Natoma huddles on the steps of the church, her head between her knees. Anguished and dazed, she sings a plaintive lullaby: "Beware of the hawk, my baby, Beware of the hawk, my child! It flies in wide, wide circles, And turns upon the wing." Gradually coming to her senses, she sings of the injustice to her people in the coming of whites. Her lyrical recitative becomes more impassioned as she calls upon the Great Spirit to give her strength and power to join her people. Herbert once commented, "In *Natoma* I have tried to make every character sing differently. My early training has led me to consider Mozart's masterpiece as the most glorious example of characterization."[20] He came very close to his aims.

Characterization was also a formidable concern for Charles Wakefield Cadman in *Shanewis, the Robin Woman,* partially based on the life of a woman who still lived. Given its premiere at the Metropolitan Opera on March 23, 1918, *Shanewis* became the Metropolitan's first production that had a contemporary American setting and the earliest opera staged there featuring a libretto by an American woman. Nelle Richmond Eberhart (1871–1944), Cadman's lifelong friend and collaborator, wrote the lyrics for more than a hundred of his best songs, one of which, "From the Land of the Sky Blue Water," was popularized by the American soprano Lillian Nordica. Her finest literary achievements are her librettos for all five of Cadman's operas: *Daoma* (1912), *The Garden of Mystery* (1915), *Shanewis* (1918), *A Witch of Salem* (1926), and *The Willow Tree,* the first American opera composed specifically for radio. It aired on NBC on October 3, 1932.

One problem for composers and librettists who used Native American subjects concerned how to portray their characters through the text. Some, as the librettist of *Natoma,* resorted at times to a kind of *Hiawatha*-style sing-song. Others, such as Eberhart in *Daoma,* preferred a dichotomous mixture of archaic thees and thous combined with modern English, which did nothing for character portrayal. *Shanewis* is felicitously endowed with poetic imagery that often delineates the characters' attitudes and

Charles Wakefield Cad-
man. *Library of Congress*

thoughts. As Lionel sings in his love scene with Shanewis in act 1, "Do you know the diff'rence between moonlight and starlight? Between reflected glow and burning flame? Ah, moonlight is ghostlight. It is like a candle shining on a white, dead face. While starlight is a beacon which guides to the heart of fire!" Characters and moods throughout the opera, moreover, are painted through music—perhaps most effectively in the use of Native American themes, which Cadman researched in the work of Alice Fletcher, Frances Densmore, and others. Whether full, partial, or fragmentary, such themes add rhythmic interest and color to key episodes and characters.

The essence of Shanewis—her sensitivity, courage, and intellect—remained problematic dramaturgical challenges. Although the more interesting aspects of her life never made their way onstage, *Shanewis* is loosely based on incidents that happened to Tsianina Redfeather (Blackstone), the young Cherokee-Creek singer described as a "wonderful mezzo-soprano with fervor and realistic charm." For many years she appeared as part of Cadman's popular lectures and concerts devoted to Native American music.

Far ahead of her time in seeking a better way of life for Native Americans, Redfeather also founded several philanthropic organizations, among them the Foundation for the Education of American Indians. She was 102 when she died.[21]

Tsianina Redfeather's forward-looking attitudes toward helping Native Americans extended elegantly to her art. Both Eberhart and Cadman had particular problems with the opera's conclusion. How, they mused, does one end the opera as a melodrama yet preserve the heroine's integrity? Eberhart suggested manufacturing an ending based on "resignation" or "sacrifice," but Cadman rejected that as "an old chestnut . . . worn threadbare." He encouraged Eberhart to think in terms of what seemed more realistic and in the tenor of the times. "I had hoped that you would carry out the tragic ending," he wrote, "with the Indian girl either killing herself or being killed or else stabbing the false lover in a passion or frenzy at the revelation of his perfidy. That would give an opportunity for BIG MUSIC and dramatic music."[22]

Tsianina Redfeather and Eberhart, however, did not agree. Cadman wrote, "Tsianina said you felt the tragic ending or the killing or being killed business was not 'Indian' or 'civilized Indian' for this age and day. . . . I have never at any time associated this plot of hers with *her life story* save ONLY the opening which is that drawing room scene and the fact of her having a 'benefactress.' Outside these two TRUE events I had pictured the whole plot in the nature of a tragedy or melodrama such as one thinks of and associates with the grand opera stage."[23] Thus, as the final version attests, Shanewis became the rare Indian heroine who does not kill or is not killed herself. The violence instead is at the hand of her jealous suitor Philip Harjo, who murders her non-Native American lover with a poisoned arrow.[24]

The Popularity and Spread of Indianist Operas

As the popularity of the Native American–inspired opera escalated, it spread throughout the United States. The colorful topic opened new channels, drawing new audiences for opera that perhaps would never have heard one otherwise. The radio helped, and as early as 1928 *Shanewis* was broadcast on NBC. Two years later, Charles Sanford Skilton's *The Sun Bride* became the first opera to receive a premiere on American radio.[25]

Native Americans became an interesting theme, especially for composers who had lived and worked among them, and operas about them often attracted large and enthusiastic audiences. In the decade following World War I, the West Coast, especially California, became a focal point for the composition and production of operas on Native American themes. In the summer of 1927, California composer Samuel Earle Blakeslee saw his only opera, *The Legend of Wiwaste* (1924), staged at the Hollywood Bowl. Based on Dakota Sioux legends, the opera featured ceremonial customs, such as the Feast of the Virgins, the Feast of Hekoya, the Calumet Ceremony, and characteristic Native American dances within a Wagner-Puccini musical framework. In 1928, *Shanewis* with Tsianina Redfeather and Chief Os-ke-non-ton, a Mowawk baritone, appeared at the Hollywood Bowl, drawing an audience of twenty-two thousand.

Thousands also witnessed Mary Carr Moore's *Narcissa, The Flaming Arrow,* and *Los Rubios,* all inspired by Native Americans. Not only were these operas performed frequently but they also won several important prizes for Moore. Born in Memphis, Mary Carr Moore (1873–1957) spent most of her life in Seattle, San Francisco, and Los Angeles. A person of enormous energy, for more than half a century she taught voice, counterpoint, theory, composition, and music history "virtually nonstop through marriages, childbearing, divorces and even grandchild-rearing."[26] She wrote at least 225 songs and sixty short piano pieces but was at her best in larger symphonic and dramatic forms, among them a fine piano concerto and eleven works for the stage.

Moore's gifts in dramatic composition, however, are most apparent in the opera *Narcissa,* which features one of American opera's most human characters, Narcissa Whitman. Rather than the usual love triangle, Moore infuses the work with a profound sense of tragedy through the desolation and terror that were part of Whitman's missionary life in the Great Northwest.

Narcissa was the first grand opera to be composed, orchestrated, and conducted by a woman. It is artistically significant because of Moore's skillful and innate sense of music theater and character portrayal within an ambitious four-act work. The libretto, in rhythmic prose, written by Moore's mother Sarah Pratt Carr, is based upon the true story of Marcus Whitman, a Presbyterian minister who with his bride Narcissa took the Oregon Trail in the 1840s to bring the Gospel to the Great Northwest. As Congress prepared to sell the vast Oregon Territory to Great Britain, Whitman made a perilous journey to the nation's capital to save the territory for the United States. He returned to Oregon, where, during a violent uprising, Native Americans battered down the mission's door and massacred both Whitmans. In the opera's final moments, Chief Yellow Serpent, who was friendly with the missionaries, swears an oath of vengeance: "So shall each Cayuse who slew a white himself be slain!"

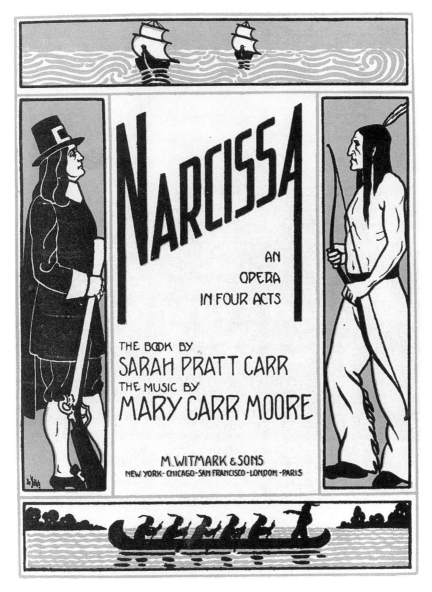

Narcissa (1912) by Mary Carr Moore is based on a true story. *Library of Congress*

What is important about the opera is not its action but its characters and the music Moore ascribes to them. Native Americans called Narcissa Whitman their "Golden Singing Bird" because she often sang poignant hymns, strange and new to them. "By the rivers of Babylon / There we sat down, yea, wept. . . . How shall we sing the lord's song in a strange land?" the opening chorus sings as a grim prophecy of her coming desolation.[27] Later her torment is revealed through her lines, their position in the drama, and her music. Weary and heartsick over the loss of her baby, she opens act 3 with a somber recitative: "Ah! Another weary day, that but repeats the weary yesterdays / God knows how hard it is to win these children of the plains." Startled, she looks around. Native American faces press against the window. "Eyes!" she cries out. "Eyes! Everywhere they are! No hour of day or night may we escape them, save in darkness, sleep."

Her lovely singing serves both dramatic and symbolic ends. Song and the sound of birds and the flute are sensuous, enticing, and powerful— ways to convert and bring love. But the allusion to Narcissa's song provides other dimensions of her character—strength and power. Although both Whitmans are noble advocates of their mission, it is Narcissa's personal sacrifice that provides the focus of the story. Through Moore's eloquent perceptions, the heroine assumes humanity and warmth rare among operas of the period.

Moore herself conducted *Narcissa*'s premiere, staged at Moore Theater in Seattle on April 22, 1912. The cast included Charles Hargreaves from the Metropolitan Opera (Marcus Whitman), Luella Chilson-Ohrman from Chicago (Narcissa), and Anna Ruzena Sprotte, formerly of the Berlin Opera (Waskema). The opera enjoyed nine successful performances in San Francisco during California's Diamond Jubilee in September 1925 and a revival in Los Angeles in 1945. Perhaps the long-awaited American opera finally had arrived. "Certainly it is American grand opera," said Cyril Player, "and the only one worthy of the name."[28]

None of the American operas of the time, however, created quite the furor of Alberto Bimboni's *Winona,* which had its debut in Portland in 1926. Its enthusiastic reception in Oregon and Minnesota illustrates the attraction of American opera as it related to regional pride. In Minneapolis, where the opera was staged in below-zero weather two years after its premiere, throngs of music-lovers poured into the city from all over the Midwest. "Audience of Nine Thousand Hail 'Winona'" heralded a newspaper headline, and displayed across its front page was one of the opera's grandest scenes.[29]

Indeed, Bimboni (1882–1960), who had come to the United States in 1911 to conduct the first American tour of Puccini's *Girl of the Golden West,* created an opera that reflected his Italian heritage and gift for dramatic contour. Its score is rich and flowing. He gives Winona—an impressionable young Native American who relives an ancient tribal legend to avoid marrying the Dacotah chief Matosapa (her father's choice for her husband)—expansively lyrical and expressive music.[30] Before the close of act 1, for example, Winona's loyal friend Weeko sings the legend of the moccasin flower as Winona and her friends gather around her, reminiscent of Senta's ballad in Wagner's *Flying Dutchman.* In an expressive declamatory arioso, Weeko tells of Minneopa, the brave young huntress who one day wore her magic moccasins into the forest. As a devastating fire broke out, the legend continues, she leaped from a rocky ledge to her death. On that spot a moccasin flower grew up. Sensing the loss of her lover, Winona interjects lyrically, "Love is a burning forest, if lost is the hope of fulfillment." In the suspenseful closing scene of act 3, Matosapa follows Winona to the top of the ledge, pleading for her attentions. Despairing, she cries out, "And you would have my heart, when you have robbed its love? I'll test you. Follow me to death. Like Minneopa, I shall cheat the flames." Soaring to a high B on the word *cheat,* she leaps into the lake, horrifying all.

Like most Indianists, Bimboni weaves into his score several traditional chants, such as hunting songs, war songs, moccasin songs, a Chippewa lullaby, Indian flute calls, and Sioux serenades. The score is pliant and melodious, with accents on lyrical vocal parts rather than a multi-hued orchestration. Bimboni uses frequent and fluid metrical impulses to reflect changing declamations in the libretto. He also uses shifting meters and interesting rhythms not only to express the text but also for sheer delight in grace of motion. Matosapa's haunting serenade, for example, is cast in a flowing, five-eight meter. These and other types of flexible, compelling rhythms provide great theatricality and warmth.

The lives and legends of Native Americans gave American opera of the early twentieth century its most popular subject and drew audiences as never before. After *Winona,* the Indianist movement in opera waned and was not revitalized until the final years of the century. As the decades moved forward, American opera turned to other sources of inspiration, especially the riveting culture of jazz. Not until seventy years after *Winona* did David Carlson and Stephen Paulus, among others, return to Native American subjects, but with new approaches to both the musical and spiritual messages of their works. In *Dreamkeepers* (1996), commissioned and presented by Utah Opera for the centenary of Utah's statehood, Carlson places a modern Native American protagonist into an urban environment, where she attends law school. Tackling the difficulties of assimilating the microtones and vocal inflections of Native American music within a lush, postromantic score, Carlson uses distinctive Ute rhythms, dance steps, and instruments, including a river-cone flute.[31]

Stephen Paulus (b. 1949), however, avoids ethnographic authenticity in his score for *The Woman at Otowi Crossing* (1995), which is based on history. He finds a natural bonding with Native American culture without consciously using indigenous themes and instruments. When Paulus showed his score to a Native American friend before its premiere, the friend was pleased to note the special use of timpani and bass drum to mark the heroine's passage to the next world. "See," the friend remarked, "it's universal." "For me," says Paulus, "it was one of those spine-tingling moments, because I had intuitively come up with a musical realization of the life and death of this character, just as the Indian would approach it."[32]

Stephen Paulus. *Photo by Jennifer Borg*

World premiere of Stephen Paulus's *The Woman at Otowi Crossing* at the Opera Theatre of St. Louis, with Andrew Wentzel (kneeling), Sheri Greenawald, and Kimm Julian.
Photo by Ken Howard

Perhaps it is the bonding of cultures through mysticism, legend, and imagery that gives inner life to operas inspired by Native American culture. If they are too closely tied to stereotypes and clichés they will not serve future audiences. Legend, as Wagner knew very well, gives timelessness and permanence to art, a universal springboard for characterization and music that composers from Nevin and Moore to Carlson and Paulus understood. Native Americans would say that "the White Man is all square. Square is his house and its rooms. Square is his dollar bill. Square is his mind. It has sharp corners. The Indian's symbol is the circle. The universe and the Earth are round. Round is the camp circle. Round is the tipi with the humans forming a circle within it. Round is the human hoop of the sun dancers."[33] "Round," too, are Wagner's *Ring*, Hansen's Sun Dance, and the Ute's magical flute—all sharing the same legendary world of symbol and song. It was that legendary sphere of Native Americans that gave American opera during the first decades of the twentieth century an individuality that no other country could claim.

Americans in the early days of the twentieth century became cultural explorers in their use of Native American materials in opera. Hardy individualists, each composer and librettist approached the subject from a somewhat different vantage point, producing work that differed in use of symbol and in how Native Americans should be portrayed within opera. If their viewpoints now seem distorted and narrow, they are perhaps no more so than those that defined African Americans in such nineteenth-century classics as Mark Twain's *Tom Sawyer* or Stephen Foster's minstrel songs.

If early-twentieth-century composers failed to interpret the real-life tragedy and oppression of Native Americans, their signposts were the messages of art and the quest for new and expressive sounds and colors within opera. Whether through mysticism and legend or history and realism, the creative blend of music and drama remained their essential goal. Composers also reflected the tenor of the times and wished to preserve the customs and traditions of those who had played an important part in the nation's historical life. They were beginning to "taste of the regenerative sunlight flooding the wide stretches of our land," observed Arthur Farwell, and realized that "justice must be done at last to the myriad sights and sounds of our own country."[34]

The intensive research into the culture of Native Americans during the early twentieth century by Curtis, Fillmore, and others enlarged the harmonic, rhythmic, instrumental, and dramatic pallet of American composers and provided their operas with the strong new identity they sought. The Indianist movement waned as the importance of jazz as an inspirational force within classical music escalated. But it remained significant for American cultural history. The operas inspired by Native Americans attracted thousands across the country—in remote regions as well as accessible ones—to an art form many had yet to experience. In using indigenous sources, a new frontier for opera had been opened. The groundwork had been laid.

9

American Opera at the Met: The Gatti-Casazza Story

A national music is to a nation what a song is to the singer who conceives it, a trustworthy expression of the quality and strength of his spirit.
　—Arthur Farwell

THE UNITED STATES in the early twentieth century was no longer a rural nation, but in the eyes of President Theodore Roosevelt "an industrial giant run amok." By 1920 more than half the population resided in cities—thriving, bustling urban centers that shaped the values, attitudes, and behavior of the nation. Sixty-eight cities had more than a hundred thousand residents, and with its population of 5.6 million New York took the lead. Not only was there a change in the size of American cities but also a dramatic alteration in the ethnic mix of their people. City theatrical life took on new dimensions as many small regional opera companies reflected the cultures of urban immigrant communities. Especially active were Chicago's Swedish Theatre and Lithuanian Opera Company; New York's Yiddish Theater, established in 1882, also continued to thrive. Along with these fruitful ethnic impulses, an explosion of knowledge, vast increases in prosperity, and sense of discontinuity that the modern age stimulated also helped mold the new shape and spirit of American cities.

As the cities contained the poor and depressed they also housed powerful, reckless, and openly flaunted wealth. America was feeling its imperial oats. Philanthropy wore a new top hat. Between 1890 and 1917 Andrew Carnegie donated $41 million to construct 1,600 libraries in cities and towns across the nation. During the first two-thirds of the nineteenth century, audiences of all classes patronized plays, operas, musical shows, and other forms of culture. Toward the end of the century, however, culture became, as Ralph Bogardus observes, "sacralized and segregated" in terms of taste groups, and the gap widened between the fine and the popular arts.[1] Operas were performed in "opera houses" and popular shows in "theaters."

Philanthropy replaced politics, and art and intellect were "seized upon to correct wayward sensibilities." Those who had grand visions were separated from—as a new term of the 1920s put it—"the man on the street." Marketing professionals often seemed to be viewing "the masses" from the thirtieth story of a midtown Manhattan skyscraper, says T. J. Jackson Lears. How great were the electric signs that transformed Broadway! "Delicate jewels of ruby, gold, and turquoise, wrought in tiny lamps, are suspended over dingy buildings in the sight of the hurrying ants called men."[2]

As the nation's financial center, New York in 1920 was considered the "Capital of Capitalism." It was also at the vortex of a vital arts conglomerate. Theater, Broadway, painting, architecture, industrial design, museums, libraries, opera, concerts, and dance all enlivened life in this amazing city. New York in the early twentieth century was as active culturally as any large city in Europe—or so it was said. From the opulent glamour of the Ziegfeld Theater to the aquatic shows in Madison Square Garden, New York seemed to have it all. Carnegie Hall, which opened in 1891 with Tchaikovsky as honored guest, hosted practically every major European and American concert artist. And with the opening of the elegant 3,625-seat Metropolitan Opera House on October 22, 1883, a new era of American operatic history had begun. Through the backing of the Morgans, Vanderbilts, and other wealthy patrons, the Metropolitan Opera reflected the nation's changing face of finance and industry. This, in turn, enlarged the power base for the arts, encouraging a cultural hierarchy around opera that has, for better or worse, defined its image and created notions of class distinctions that are peculiar to Americans even now.

New York was also caught up in the great focus on American music, which along with its performers was making vital new inroads, not only at home but also overseas. As the United States became an internationally recognized economic and political force, its culture, too, attracted attention. American singers and instrumentalists appeared with increasing frequency in European halls. Mary Garden's Mélisande in 1902 is legend, and in 1908 Henry Hadley became the first American to hold a conducting position in Germany.

On May 21, 1910, the Metropolitan Opera took Paris by storm by presenting that city's first staging of Puccini's *Manon Lescaut* conducted by Arturo Toscanini. The stellar cast included Enrico Caruso, Geraldine Ferrar, and Emmy Destinn, and the lavish scenery had been transported from New York. But the two most sensational events of 1910 in the world of American composition, noted *Musical America,* were the performances of Frederick Converse's *The Pipe of Desire* at the Metropolitan Opera House in New York and Arthur Nevin's *Poia* at the Royal Opera in Berlin. "American grand opera may now be regarded as fairly launched," *Musical America* reported, "and with the increasing interest in opera in America, American composers will undoubtedly make operatic history from now on at a rapid rate."[3]

Poia was not the only early-twentieth-century American opera to be staged in Europe. *Zenobia* (also Silas Pratt's subject) by the New Jersey–born Louis Adolphe Coerne was produced to great acclaim in Bremen in 1902. Others followed: Henry Hadley's *Safié* (Mainz, 1909), John Beach's *Pippa's Holiday* (Paris, 1915), and Paul Allen's *Last of the Mohicans* (Florence, 1916). Allen's *Cleopatra* (1921) is also historically significant, for it was the first American opera commissioned by an Italian publisher. Not until 1935 did Vienna welcome its first American opera, however: *Caponsacchi* by Richard Hageman, a former Metropolitan Opera and Chicago Opera conductor, was produced at the Volksoper on March 19 and drew rave reviews. The opera had been given its premiere three years earlier at the Stadttheater of Freiburg-im-Breisgau in Germany. With a libretto by Arthur Goodrich after Robert Browning's *The Ring and the Book,* it was a work of fine dramatic proportions and received no less than forty curtain calls. The fact that American opera had begun to attract European opera producers was a sure barometer of its growing visibility and success.

If all seemed to be going quite well for American composers, the outbreak of World War I in 1914 helped their course and cause still further. The powerful hold of German repertoire weakened temporarily during the war, and by the Armistice in 1918 important musical figures were making their manifestos clear. "I believe this is the opportune moment for American music," asserted Reginald De Koven. "A nation that can send eighteen hundred thousand men to battle for an ideal must surely rise above the sordid things, and produce something great in art. I have always believed that a country's art depends upon the national feeling of unity."[4] "The war has brought us nearer to the ideals of a National Music," added Geraldine Farrar. As for opera, "American composers will have a wonderful opportunity after the war if they first will learn to take an absolutely practical view of the limits and purposes of the theater," said Metropolitan Opera manager Giulio Gatti-Casazza. "If the public is induced to attend the theater to go to sleep, after a while it will discover that it is much more comfortable and less expensive to stay at home and go to bed."[5] What form this "practical view" should take to keep audiences awake Gatti-Casazza did not say.

It was Giulio Gatti-Casazza, however, who put American opera on the national cultural map. The spotlight on New York as a center for American opera for more than three decades was due to this savvy manager, who, ironically, spoke no English himself. He was "a gracious, but solemn presence . . . a large man with a square-cut beard and sad eyes, thumbs in vest, walking ponderously, nodding occasionally but rarely speaking."[6]

Coming from La Scala in 1908, where he had served as director for ten years, Gatti at first shared managerial control of the Metropolitan Opera with Andreas Dippel. When the prosperous banker Otto Kahn became president, Gatti took over as sole director from 1910 to 1935—the longest tenure in the history of the Metropolitan. These were "golden years" indeed. Conductors during the early seasons included Gustav Mahler, Alfred Herz, and Arturo Toscanini, whom Gatti brought with him from Italy. The orchestra consisted of 135 musicians, and choral forces numbered more than two hundred voices. The world's finest singers graced the stage in a repertoire of forty to fifty different operas each season. By the time Gatti retired to Italy, he had witnessed an exciting momentum at the Met and weathered the rigors of war and the production cuts of the Great Depression.

Giulio Gatti-Casazza, manager of the Metropolitan Opera, produced many fine American operas during the company's early-twentieth-century seasons. *Metropolitan Opera Archives*

Felicitously, Gatti-Casazza brought from La Scala the practice of augmenting traditional repertoire with new works. He insisted that an opera company must create as well as repeat. Eight months before he gave the world premiere of Puccini's *Girl of the Golden West* on December 10, 1910, he had produced the first English-language opera to be staged at the Metropolitan—Frederick Converse's *Pipe of Desire*. As he wrote in his memoirs:

> My hope, when I came to America was to be able to discover some good American operas, which I could produce and maintain in the repertoire. . . . It seemed to me that one of the inescapable obligations of the great American lyric theatre was to foster and promote the development of American opera. No national school of opera has ever developed without the incentive of performances. In America the conditions are harder for the native composer than in any other country, chiefly because there are so few stages upon which his works can be presented.[7]

Gatti-Casazza also had great faith in American singers. "Americans have beautiful natural voices," he once remarked. "They are extremely intelligent; they have unusual educational advantages." But, he added, "They demand action, and are often so impatient that they ruin their opportunities by failing to work hard enough." At a time when fine American opera singers were still a rarity, Gatti brought to the Metropolitan such great artists as Rosa Ponselle, Lawrence Tibbett, Grace Moore, Gladys Swarthout, and John Charles Thomas. One brilliant young diva from Missouri, Marion Talley, made her debut as Gilda at the age of eighteen. The coloratura was always the preferred voice, Gatti claimed. It usually left him cold, he said, but "the public goes mad when it hears the high notes."[8]

The Earliest Gatti Seasons

The fourteen American operas staged under Gatti-Casazza reflect the vast and varied horizons of the nation's creative spirit over three decades. It was a spirit in flux, caught up in changing styles, subjects, characters, dramaturgy, and stage designs closely tied to the vicissitudes of American life and times. From Wagner to verismo and from romantic to ultramodern, the Gatti years are a capsule history of American opera during the early twentieth century. With the exception of Converse's *Pipe of Desire,* first produced in Boston in 1906, all the operas were world premieres. More than half were in one or two acts and appeared with other works in double or triple bills. Charles Wakefield Cadman's *Shanewis,* for example, was

Victor Herbert and cast for the Metropolitan Opera production of Herbert's one-act light opera, *Madeleine* (1914). Seated is Maestro Polacco, with Victor Herbert on the left and soprano Frances Alda on the right. *Metropolitan Opera Archives*

first staged with Henry Gilbert's wildly brilliant ballet *Dance in Place Congo,* but for its second season it was placed with Joseph Breil's *The Legend* and *The Temple Dancer* by John Hugo. During its nine appearances at the Met, Henry Hadley's *Cleopatra's Night* occasionally appeared with Rimsky-Korsakov's *Le coq d'or* in the Fokine version, in which singers performed in the orchestra pit while dancers portrayed characters onstage. John Laurence Seymore's *In the Pasha's Garden* was paired with *La bohème,* and Victor Herbert's *Madeleine* was a curtain-raiser for *Pagliacci,* with Caruso in the leading role.

All the Gatti operas won the Bispham Memorial Medal for American Opera except De Koven's *The Canterbury Pilgrims* and Horatio Parker's *Mona,* the latter already the recipient of a prestigious prize from the Metropolitan Opera. The following list provides the Gatti American repertoire, the number of their acts, and the dates of their premieres at the Metropolitan:

Frederick Converse	*The Pipe of Desire* (1)	March 18, 1910
Horatio Parker	*Mona* (3)	March 14, 1912
Walter Damrosch	*Cyrano de Bergerac* (4)	February 27, 1913
Victor Herbert	*Madeleine* (1)	January 24, 1914
Reginald De Koven	*The Canterbury Pilgrims* (4)	March 8, 1917
Charles Wakefield Cadman	*Shanewis* (1 or 2)	March 23, 1918
Joseph Breil	*The Legend* (1)	March 12, 1919
John Adam Hugo	*The Temple Dancer* (1)	March 12, 1919
Henry Hadley	*Cleopatra's Night* (2)	January 31, 1920
Deems Taylor	*The King's Henchman* (3)	February 17, 1927
	Peter Ibbetson (3)	February 7, 1931
Louis Gruenberg	*Emperor Jones* (1)	January 7, 1933
Howard Hanson	*Merry Mount* (4)	February 10, 1934
John Laurence Seymour	*In the Pasha's Garden* (1)	January 24, 1935

Gatti spared little in providing his American operas with the finest casts, conductors, and staging. All were brilliantly produced and drew sizable, often capacity, audiences. They also received extensive advance press notices, articles, and reviews—more than any other American works of the time. The variety and scope of the operas Gatti selected are apparent from the subjects and styles of the productions during the early seasons.

Frederick Converse's *The Pipe of Desire,* the Metropolitan's first American opera, is a mystical one-act work about the fatal powers of an elfin king's magical flute and the greed of the mortal who covets it. Its superb cast starred the Pittsburgh-born soprano Louise Homer, who sang the lead in Horatio Parker's *Mona* produced two seasons later.[9] *Mona,* by contrast, is a far more ambitions work than *Pipe of Desire* and also more interesting musically and dramatically. It was criticized for having too much recitative and too little melody, but lyrical moments are frequent and occur at key dramatic points. The striking Druid chorus closing act 2, Mona's monologues in acts 1 and 3, Gwynn's solos, and Nial's arioso-like passages are only a few of the effective melodic segments in the score.[10]

Unlike his earlier *Scarlet Letter,* Walter Damrosch's *Cyrano de Bergerac,* after Rostand, comprises set pieces—arias, duets, ensembles, and choruses—and falls more clearly under the romantic Italian and French tradition than the German. But of all the Metropolitan's American works during the first few seasons, Charles Wakefield Cadman's lyrical *Shanewis* was by far the most successful. Its contemporary setting, Native American themes, and modern English libretto fascinated audiences. Paul Althouse, the first American tenor without European experience to sing at the Metropolitan, played Lionel, and Sophie Braslau enhanced her career with the role of Shanewis and her interpretation of the popular "Spring Song of the Robin Woman" from act 1. Critics noted a Puccini-like sweetness in the love music; more important, the singers did not have foreign accents and could be understood.

The Gatti period was as important an era for American stage designers as for composers. Always interested in new staging techniques, Gatti employed the twenty-five-year-old Norman Bel Geddes to design act 2 of *Shanewis* and later Hadley's *Cleopatra's Night*. Bel Geddes soon attracted the attention of Broadway and eventually designed more than two hundred theatrical productions, specializing in dramatic lighting effects with lamps and lenses of his own invention. His earliest work, however, was in American opera, and he brought exciting new dimensions to its visual aspects. Rather than a pictorial representation, the set for *Shanewis* was more abstract and stylized—a psychological interpretation of the attitudes and environment of Native Americans that helped the overall impression of the work.

What likely drew audiences even more than *Shanewis* alone was a triple bill.[11] Gatti added *Dance in Place Congo* to the program, which had music drawn from Creole songs and slave dances of New Orleans. Originally

The Metropolitan Opera's premiere of Charles Wakefield Cadman's *Shanewis* (1918) with Sophie Braslau (Shanewis) and Paul Althouse (Lionel), both far right. *Metropolitan Opera Archives*

written as a symphonic poem, the ballet featured the superb dancing of Rosina Galli, who later became Gatti's second wife. Rounding out the bill was Franco Leoni's one-act opera *L'Oracolo* (1905), which told a sinister tale about Chinese Americans in San Francisco. Some said that Gatti had presented four races on one program, but the unique thrust of the venture brought far more. It added a fresh new American vitality to the nation's performing arts.

Staging Innovations and Influences from Film

After World War I, Gatti produced several short operas that were more experimental than the longer, more conventional works of the period. They were less lavish and more in tune with the economy of forces required during the years of war and depression. They also had small casts and contained no ballets or choruses, although *Cleopatra's Night* included the Arabian-style dancing of Galli. John Adams Hugo's one-act *Temple Dancer*—the story of a Hindu woman driven by passionate love to steal a temple's jewels—was performed only three times at the Metropolitan. It did, however, move on to Chicago and in 1925 became the first American opera to be staged in Honolulu—with sensational success.

Many short American operas of the period reflected the new technology of the burgeoning motion picture industry. Postwar American composers Frederick Converse, Eugene Adrian Farner, Joseph Breil, Louis Gruenberg, and others found a place for their creative energies in motion picture scores. Writing in 1923, Eugene Adrian Farner, composer of the one-act opera *The White Buffalo Maiden,* commented on opera's affinities with the methodology and aesthetics of early film. As ways of making opera an "appealing medium" he listed:

a. Brevity (one hour); avoiding narrative in recitative, using instead pantomime with musical accompaniment; condensation of material to a series of "big screens" with opportunities for each singer, the chorus, and orchestra; by
b. Being *to the point*—striving for the self-unconscious naturalness of Gilbert and Sullivan, the direct and simple description of Gluck; the vocal opportunity in Mozart, the action of the "movies"; by
c. Use of small cast, small chorus and small orchestra, facilitating productions on tour; and by
d. A full measure of popular dramatic interest.[12]

Joseph Breil, composer of *The Legend* (1919), argued that "an opera libretto should be chockfull of action. Action, action, all the time. The story should be simple and straightforward, like a film play, only more so, since the scenario writer can explain himself, whenever he gets involved, by throwing a line or two of print on the screen. . . . Certainly his opera will be melodramatic; indeed it is a sort of art which has a peculiar attraction for the Yankee temperament, in which a vein of melancholy and sentiment closely underlies the quaint surface humor."[13]

Traditional melodrama was alive and well for Breil, who composed scores for D. W. Griffith's ground-breaking *Birth of a Nation* (1915) and *Intolerence* (1916) as well as fifteen other early film scores. Shortly before he died, he worked on the score for *The Phantom of the Opera* (1925). *The Legend,* a fascinating mix of motion picture and opera ideology, was not fully understood in its day. One critic complained that it contained "too much of the rapid outlines of the moving picture."[14] What brought distinction to *The Legend,* however, was the magnificent full and lustrous voice of Rosa Ponselle, who portrayed Carmelita, the distraught daughter of a nobleman-turned-bandit.

The brilliant American soprano Rosa Ponselle appeared in Joseph Breil's *The Legend* at the Metropolitan Opera during the same season she made her Met debut at age twenty-one as Leonora in Verdi's *La forza del destino. Metropolitan Opera Archives*

By the time Gatti had staged his last American opera, John Seymour's *In the Pasha's Garden* (1935), the aesthetic ties between opera and film noted in Breil's *The Legend* had become technological as well. Carleton Smith called *Pasha's Garden* "the most economical opera ever produced in the Metropolitan." It ran only forty-five minutes, but what attracted attention was its staging by Frederick Kiesler. On a seventy-by-forty-foot screen, a scenic pattern was projected from what amounted to glorified lantern slides. "Instead of the conventional minarets, marble pillars, statues, and other bric-a-brac," Kiesler explained, "the background was a simple white canvas curtain." Three overhanging leaves flashed across the screen, "threatening, sinister, watchful, even as the spying eunuch is watching." In the libretto, which is about a pasha's revenge on his unfaithful wife, "the whole movement of the plot is carried out in the movement of the background. . . . But unlike the old peep-show settings of the proscenium theater, the motion of the setting is cued to the music, singing and acting on the stage."[15] From that description it appears that Kiesler set the stage for the innovative projections and film technology of Dominick Argento, Philip Glass, Libby Larsen, and other American opera composers of the later part of the century.

Deems Taylor's Metropolitan Opera Premieres

The most successful enterprises of the Gatti years took place during his final decade with the company. The operas of Deems Taylor, Louis Gruenberg, and Howard Hanson were smash hits that brought unprecedented visibility and distinction to American opera. Not all credit can be attributed to the works themselves, however. Lawrence Tibbett, the star singer for Gatti's last five American operas, enhanced the roles with considerable glamour and theatrical power. Born in Bakersfield, California, Tibbett made his Metropolitan debut as Lewicki in *Boris Godunov* in 1923. Before he left the Met in 1950 he had given 384 performances in that opera house alone. Tibbett possessed a smooth, flexible baritone voice and had virtually flawless diction. He enjoyed singing in English at a time Americans were debating the viable vocality of their native tongue. "Many American singers," he said, "are cursed with this feeling of shame when they sing in English. I can roar out 'I *love* you!' with all the passion of a Don Juan whose lady love is confined on a desert at the top of a high tower. But many American singers cannot become emotional in English. They will put their very souls into *Io t'amo, Ich liebe dich,* and *Je t'aime,* but on 'I love you' they stammer like a schoolboy with his first sweetheart."[16]

Lawrence Tibbett as Eadgar in the world premiere of Taylor's *The King's Henchman* (1927). *Metropolitan Opera Archives*

Deems Taylor (1885–1966) also added luster to the American operatic scene by being a kind of an early-twentieth-century Leonard Bernstein. A native New Yorker, Taylor was the brilliant editor-in-chief of *Musical America,* but what brought him into the public eye about the time his operas were produced at the Metropolitan were witty and informative opera commentaries on NBC. In 1933 he began the first of several radio series, among them the popular Chase and Sanborn Opera program in which two casts were employed, one to sing and the other act. Taylor, like Leopold Stokowski, was always something of a showman, a fact well illustrated in his narration for Walt Disney's *Fantasia.* Taylor also was a director of the American Society of Composers, Authors and Publishers (ASCAP). The year after he died, the society established in his honor the ASCAP–Deems Taylor Award for outstanding literature in the field of music. Taylor composed choral works, operas, and a film score, and likely no other American symphonic work of the time received as many performances across the nation as his *Through the Looking Glass* suite (1922) after Lewis Carroll.

Taylor's *The King's Henchman* (1927) and *Peter Ibbetson* (1931) were the first American operas commissioned by the Metropolitan and the longest-running. *The King's Henchman* enjoyed three consecutive seasons and seventeen performances (half were sold-out houses), and *Peter Ibbetson* ran for four consecutive seasons and twenty-two performances.[17] Both operas toured extensively after their premieres. *The King's Henchman* gave ninety performances in forty-six cities during the 1927–28 season. It was also the first opera to be broadcast by CBS in 1927. It not only brought in an unheard of $15,000 for opening night alone but also set another record for American opera by selling out weeks in advance of its premiere. In 1932 *Peter Ibbetson* became one of the earliest operas to be broadcast from the stage of the Metropolitan, and six years later it was the first American opera to be broadcast overseas via Italian radio. The two productions made Deems Taylor the most successful American opera composer of his time.

Both *The King's Henchman* and *Peter Ibbetson* are three-act neoromantic operas with full, lush melodic and harmonic sonorities and skillfully written orchestrations. *Ibbetson,* however, has a more telling libretto and is a more successful work in theatricality and musical dramaturgy. Its characters also have more depth and inner life than those in *Henchman.* If both operas are eclectic, dipping into the perennial Wagner-Debussy-Massenet-Puccini stew, they only reflect Taylor's views about there being no "American" music and music transcending national boundaries. "We love Italian opera, not because it is so Italian," he said, "but because it is so singable." He also believed that "simple, plausible, melodrama" is indispensable for opera and that opera could "use stories of any period if they fit its needs and limitations."[18]

The libretto for *The King's Henchman* was fashioned by the poet Edna St. Vincent Millay, who had won a Pulitzer Prize in 1922. It was published in book format, and within twenty days four editions had been exhausted. The story is based on a tenth-century Saxon tale similar to that of *Tristan and Isolde* although with important differences. In *Henchman,* the lovers marry, and the "Isolde" (Aelfrida) is prouder and more lively than noble and self-sacrificing. As Millay's story goes, the lonely King Eadgar asks his trusted friend Lord Aethelwold to seek the hand of the beautiful Aelfrida on his behalf. When they meet, however, Aelfrida and Aethelwold fall immediately in love. Departing from opera's usual lovers (and from the Tristan legend) Aelfrida is restless and unhappy with marriage. "My life has been but a heaping of sticks under an empty pot," she moans.[19] Eadgar learns that his trusted henchman has deceived him, and Aethelwold, consumed with guilt, draws his sword and kills himself. The opera closes with a long lament by King Eadgar, more anticlimactic than peroration. The audience, moreover, is left wondering what will follow in the relationship between Aelfrida and King Eadgar. As one reviewer noted, Millay's story is about "honor rather than sexual love. . . . It is more convincing to talk about honor, than to sing about it."[20]

Deems Taylor (center), composer of *The King's Henchman,* with librettist Edna St. Vincent Millay and Edward Johnson, who sang the role of Aethelwold. *Metropolitan Opera Archives*

The performance received nearly fifty curtain calls. The excellent cast was led by Lawrence Tibbett (Eadgar), Edward Johnson (Aethelwold), and Florence Easton (Aelfrida) and conducted by Tullio Serafin, who would also direct *Peter Ibbetson, The Emperor Jones,* and *Merry Mount* and then leave for Rome's Teatro Reale—and more than fifty years of conducting. Josef Urban, well known for his three-dimensional sets that integrated architecture and painting, designed both Taylor operas. He had previously designed Wagner's *Ring* for Budapest, and, the same year as *The King's Henchman,* produced the design for Jerome Kern's enduring masterpiece *Show Boat.*

Taylor's score is expertly crafted, and its grace, rich textures, and romantic warmth no doubt contributed to its extraordinary success. Wagnerian leitmotifs flowed throughout, and were presented in various articles of the era almost like a dictionary, similar to Erno Rapee's *Motion Picture Moods* for movie pianists (1928). What is difficult to discern in either articles or opera, however, is the layering of motifs, the contrapuntal semiotics, that are so exciting in Wagner. Where in *The King's Henchman,* for example, are passages such as those at the end of *Die Walküre,* where Brünnhilde's sleep motif falls gracefully from the upper strings while the Siegfried motif wells up gloriously in the lower brass? It is through the motifs and their intrinsic structure and symbolism rather than the text that the audience learns that Siegfried will awaken Brünnhilde—but in the next opera.

There was also much discussion in the press about whether the text could be grasped if the opera were now in English. One writer brushed off the question by admitting that "certain passages in *Aida, Otello,* all the Wagner works and even *Pelléas et Mélisande"* could not be understood.[21] In general, audiences preferred poetic English to colloquial text (*Shanewis* "sounded like burlesque"). According to one source, "Miss Millay succeeded in fashioning what is surely the most remarkable opera book in existence, and the most poetic since *Pelléas et Mélisande.* It is remarkable as a linguistic tour de force. . . . It is more intelligible to a modern reader than Chaucer's *Canterbury Tales.* It abounds in lines of verbal music. And it is easier to sing than Wagner's German poetry."[22]

What critics failed to grasp about *The King's Henchman* is the touch— just a touch—of whimsy, almost satire, in its score, story, and even the characters themselves. Is Aelfrida an "anti-Isolde"? Is Aethelwold a "quasi-Tristan"? And the music? The lively interplay of orchestra and voices in act 1 resembles Eva's visit to the shoemaker Hans Sachs in *Die Meistersinger.* But the act closes with a rousing chorus far more at home in musical comedy than grand opera.[23] To accompany the text "O Caesar great wert thou," Taylor chose a Cornish folk song, "My Johnny Is a Shoemaker."

Was there still some ballad opera tomfoolery in modern American sensibility?

Peter Ibbetson differs substantially from *The King's Henchman* by virtue of its mystical, darkly romantic libretto. It is based on George du Maurier's novel of 1891 and the play adapted from it in 1917 by the actress Constance Collier for herself and the Barrymore brothers. The novel reveals "an author romantic with Goethe, realistic with Thackeray, symbolistic with Maeterlinck and sentimental with all three"—or, like Taylor's score, eclectic.[24] Using the play as the framework, Taylor wrote the actual text of the libretto himself. In a free verse more rhythmic than ordinary prose, the opera draws many lines from the original novel. The result is a taut, effective story about the bonds between childhood sweethearts and the mystical melding of dream and reality.

The locale of the opera is primarily mid-nineteenth-century London, with occasional scenes and flashbacks near Paris in Passy. Peter Ibbetson is a young English architect raised by his egocentric and intimidating uncle, whom Peter accidentally kills during a violent quarrel. Sentenced to prison for thirty years, Peter is sustained by repeated visions of the elegant Duchess of Towers—Mary, or "Mimsey" as Peter called her—whom he has loved since childhood but who had married another. In the moving final scene of the opera, Peter, old and frail, lies dying in his cell. As in a dream, Mary appears to him, smiling and holding out her hands, and from Peter's dead body rises the young Peter Ibbetson, who goes to her and happily takes her in his arms.[25]

With its eight scenes (four in the last act alone), the opera required deft scene changing. What is unique about the work are its three references to Peter's childhood in France, creating warm French inflections in both text and music. Adding to the charm of the dream scenarios, for example, are lyrical French melodies—including the ineffable "Jardin d'amour"—woven gracefully and subtley throughout.

Most of the musical interest in Taylor's score, however, lies in the orchestra rather than the vocal lines. The ninety-piece orchestra is a protagonist in its own right—commenting on every nuance of mood, dialogue, and action onstage. It sighs, chuckles, moans, snarls, and gasps right along with the characters in a masterful array of colors, always transparent and never competing with the singers.

Peter Ibbetson required a large cast of 320 participants that included a stage crew of forty-five, a directing staff of ten, and an off-stage chorus of 105. In the waltz sequence in act 1, a thirty-piece stage band is indicated. There are twenty solo parts, but only four are principal roles. These were

Spanish soprano Lucretia Bori as Mary in Deems Taylor's *Peter Ibbetson*. *Metropolitan Opera Archives*

sung by Edward Johnson (Peter Ibbetson), Lawrence Tibbett (Peter's uncle, Colonel Ibbetson), Lucretia Bori (Mary), and Marian Telva (the young English widow Mrs. Deane). Critics agreed that Peter Ibbetson was one of the finest operas the Metropolitan had ever produced. Indeed, its combination of moody mysticism and modern melodrama make it one of the most interesting American operas of the time.[26]

Merry Mount *and* Emperor Jones

After the extraordinary success of the Deems Taylor operas, Gatti-Casazza turned to two other highly esteemed American composers, Howard Hanson and Louis Gruenberg, whose operas were to serve as the grand finale of his long career with the Metropolitan. Hanson's *Merry Mount* and Gruenberg's *The Emperor Jones* were not as long-running as the Taylor operas, but they were initially very well received with a multiplicity of curtain calls and bravos. Opening nights for both were standing-room-only. *Merry Mount,* noted Olin Downes, had the most enthusiastic reception given any native music drama. Its audience was of a new, "uncommon character . . . more thoughtful than customary."[27] Like the Taylor operas, *Merry Mount* and *Emperor Jones* were broadcast nationwide and reached audiences estimated at two million. Both operas were staged elsewhere after their premieres. After two seasons and fifteen performances at the Metropolitan, for example, *Emperor Jones* played in Chicago, Los Angeles, and in major houses overseas, notably at Milan's La Scala after the war.

Although their scores were very different—Hanson's lyrical and post-romantic and Gruenberg's declamatory and atonal—their librettos similarly explored the inner workings of the mind and heart. Each featured a lone male protagonist, tortured, passionate, and dramatically convincing, who carries his audience into gripping theatrical scenarios. There is a darkness about these characters, each obsessed with impotence either to love or to control and both disintegrating emotionally and spiritually as the operas progressed. And with this darkness came new and expressive ways to treat characters musically. In its own way, each opera opened the door for the exploration of new avenues in lyric theater in the decades to come.

Merry Mount and *Emperor Jones* were composed and initially performed about the same time, although their Metropolitan Opera stagings came a year apart. When *Merry Mount* was given its Metropolitan Opera premiere on February 10, 1934, Howard Hanson (1896–1981) was director of one of the nation's finest schools, the Eastman School of Music, a post he held for

forty years. In 1964 he founded the Institute of American Music at Eastman and was recognized for his long dedication to the cause of American
music. *Merry Mount* had been commissioned by the Metropolitan Opera
although the Chicago Symphony had performed a concert version the year
before at Ann Arbor's May Festival. It is Gatti's only four-act American opera,
a revision of the original libretto in three acts and six scenes.[28]

The librettist Richard Stokes, the former music critic of the *New York
Evening World,* based his text on Nathaniel Hawthorne's grim tale of witchcraft and sexual obsession, "The Maypole of Merry Mount." Like the original story, the libretto derives from a historical episode involving Puritan
belief that a Saturnalian maypole, invented by the devil, had been built in
1625 near what is now Quincy, Massachusetts. The opera's main character, Wrestling Bradford (Lawrence Tibbett), is a fanatical Puritan clergy-
man haunted by demonic dreams that ultimately cause him to immolate
himself and his lover in a church consumed by flames. As the composer
described:

> *Merry Mount* is a somewhat Freudian story of the gradual change of char-
> acter of the pastor of the Puritan flock [Bradford] from a stern ascetic to
> a half-mad fanatic who, in the end, due to the violence of his own emo-
> tions, changes from a minister of God to a self-constituted bondsman of
> Satan. The harmonic technic which is used in this process of character
> change, attempts to work out in tone the basic underlying motives and
> emotions within the mind of the character itself. The musical background
> for the minister, therefore, changes gradually according to the change
> within the man's own nature.[29]

Merry Mount is essentially a lyric opera containing arias and choruses
cast in definite musical forms. Hanson felt it paralleled Mussorgsky's *Boris
Godounov,* which also has a lone protagonist and extensively uses a chorus. Indeed, the choruses throughout *Merry Mount* are especially powerful
and have considerable dramatic breadth and depth. The overall score, colored with rich harmonies and modal inflections, demands a large orchestra that features a wind machine and Oriental percussion effects. The ballet sequences, choreographed by Gatti's second wife Rosina Galli, were
apparently lavish. Bradford's vision, or the "Hellish Rendezvous" (act 3,
scene 2), is a sumptuous spectacle that climaxes in a ballet lit with bright
red "fire." The scene was made perilously alluring by a satanic and beautiful corps de ballet whose charms were "so liberally disclosed," said
Lawrence Gilman, "that one could almost hear the commiserating gasps
of an audience shivering in its protective mink."[30]

Louis Gruenberg (1884–1964) moved in quite a different direction from the other American composers of the Gatti regime. More innovator than iconoclast, he was nevertheless well in tune with the contemporary styles of Charles Ives, Edgard Varèse, Henry Cowell, and Igor Stravinsky. He was also one of the first to use jazz in concert music and the first to charm the audiences of Europe with it. As a man of the theater, Gruenberg applied his innovations creatively to dramatic ends. Included among his plethora of theater works—pantomimes, ballets, operas, operettas, and film scores— is a children's opera, *Jack and the Beanstalk* (1931), which was given its premiere at the Juilliard School. In 1937 he composed the radio opera *Green Mansions,* which used a musical saw in its score. Gruenberg had been born in Russia and was taken to America when he was two. He was a part of the great Russian-Jewish community of immigrants that increased dramatically as the century began.

In 1923 Gruenberg conducted the American premiere of Arnold Schoenberg's *Pierrot Lunaire,* which no doubt provided a springboard for the unusual *sprechgesang* style of *The Emperor Jones.* His characters in the opera employ not only dialogue and recitative but also a new declamatory style somewhere between dialogue and recitative. If Hanson's opera had Freudian overtones, Gruenberg's dramatic themes were Jungian and drawn from the theories of Eugene O'Neill, whose play inspired the opera. "As far as I can remember," O'Neill observed, "of all the books written by Freud, Jung, etc . . . Jung is the only one of the lot who interests me. Some of his suggestions I find extraordinarily illuminating in the light of my own experience with hidden human motives."[31]

The opera is in two acts but was performed at the Metropolitan in a single act lasting about an hour and a half. The libretto, shaped by Kathleen de Jaffa, takes its lines almost directly from the play. It is the story of Brutus Jones, an African American ex-convict and Pullman porter who escapes to an island in the West Indies and by devious means declares himself emperor there. He exploits the natives until they rebel and force him to take refuge in the jungle. Tormented by the ominous beating of voodoo drums, he flees in terror, perpetually haunted by the grotesque apparitions of his murdered victims. In desperation, he ends his miserable existence with the silver bullet that, ironically, was to help him live a "charmed" life. In the original play, the natives murder Jones, but the opera's ending is more effective because it allows him to find the ultimate control he seeks by taking his own life.

The actual events of the story are far less significant than what happens to the protagonist's inner spirit as his egotistical outer self gives way to the dark, inner terror of his unconscious. The symbolism in the opera occurs on many levels, visually, aurally, and psychologically. Jones's flight into the unknown, fearsome jungle symbolizes the gradual breakdown of his spirituality and psyche. Even his appearance and dress tell a story. One by one, his gaudy, gold-braided military trappings are shed, and he emerges a pitiful, half-naked barbarian in only a loincloth.

The sets, too, move from Jones's plush throne flanked on either side by gigantic cannons and balls—huge phallic symbols—to ghostly jungle vegetation embellished with eerie hands and weaving fingers. Thirty-two-year-old Jo Mielziner, also the designer of *Merry Mount,* would eventually create more than three hundred sets for plays and Broadway shows, among them *Death of a Salesman* and *Guys and Dolls.* For *Emperor Jones,* he felt it was essential to bring the audience "completely into the mood of fantastic imagination":

> In the second half of the opera, I propose to make the sense of scene change in the jungle by three methods: 1) By constant and varying light, both in the jungle and on Jones, 2) By back drops which may be slowly raised during the action . . . 3) By the non-singing chorus costumed in abstract vegetable and animal forms in a fantastic manner, such as the "Formless Fears" [Jones's apparitions]. In rhythm with the drum beats, they always can be moved in groups in an eerie light or lost completely in the background.[32]

What truly heightens the expressionistic imagery in the opera is Gruenberg's remarkable score. The fast-moving drama is underpinned by dissonance, tonal ambiguity, syncopation, and the intense rhythmic color of a tom-tom.[33] The chorus "yells and chants in conflicting rhythms and keys," noted Olin Downes, a magnificent effect that "always hurled forth the action."[34] In the O'Neill play, Jones's flight from emperor back to the atavistic dust that made him is circular. Gruenberg picks up the metaphor by placing the drums in a semicircle from the center of the stage to each side of the opera house. As in the play, the drums simulate Jones's heartbeat, pulsating ever-faster and louder. The addition of the chorus, with its dissonant threats and torments, powerfully reinforces his terror. The chorus thus becomes a vehicle that carries the opera far beyond the play in dramatic intensity.

In the score's syncopated nervous energy, Gruenberg felt he had given the opera a true "American sound." There were other American qualities, he noted: "speed, restlessness, mystery, ballyhoo, display and uplifting quality." But American composers should not merely "exploit a characteristic

Jo Mielziner's fantastic sets for *Emperor Jones* by Louis Gruenberg included a large metaphoric throne for the emperor, played by Lawrence Tibbett (shown). *Metropolitan Opera Archives*

melody." They should also invent a new technique that would "combine a knowledge of tradition and the modern experiment."[35] Gruenberg heightens the one melodic segment by saving it for the end of the opera. As Jones falls to his knees, terrified and obsessed with the "Formless Fears" of his corrupt past, he raises his hands and sings in a voice of agonized prayer a simple song that Gruenberg found in James Weldon Johnson's first book of spirituals: "It's a-me, Oh, Lawd, standin' in the need of prayer." The melody, the only aria in the score, provides a brief moment of lyrical effusion that yields a glimpse into a decaying soul's last breath. It is a glimpse of Jones the human being. After he falls lifeless, the savage mob prods his body with bayonets, lifts it to their shoulders, and disappears into the forest. The curtain falls on a silent, empty stage.

An explosion of applause followed the accumulated excitement, but some wondered what indeed they had seen. Was it a melodrama? Was it a motion picture? Or was it a music drama? Hipsher provided one answer when he called it "a highly developed monologue, accompanied by music." "I found the opera gruesome when not ludicrous," wrote one opera-goer to the *Herald-Tribune*. "How can such a piece of insanity be given on the stage of the Metropolitan?" said another. "Let us put Gatti-Casazza, Gruenberg and your music critic in a sanatorium. And I paid $5 for it. Heavens!"[36]

Yet critics had no doubt that the opera and its realization were triumphs and discussed it in lengthy reviews. Lawrence Tibbett's impersonation "was commanding," wrote W. J. Henderson. "It mastered and moved, excited and thrilled the great audience. It was brutality incarnate and plasticity perfected." Olin Downes found Tibbett's difficult task of "mastering the transitions from speech to song discharged with remarkable intelligence," and Leonard Liebling thought it was Tibbett's best performance; there was "nothing more affecting in his entire career."[37]

And the opera? Henderson compared Gruenberg's approach to Alban Berg's in *Wozzeck*, "but it is in no sense imitative. The form and the idiom of the music are Mr. Gruenberg's own." "This score is easily the most distinctive, convincing, artistically powerful that has been written by any American composer," Liebling added. "It's worth a dozen of the new, modern foreign importations which we have heard at the Metropolitan during the past decade." Downes believed that *The Emperor Jones* was "the first American opera by a composer whose dramatic instinct and intuition for the theatre seems unfailing, and whose musical technique is characterized by a very complete modern knowledge, and a reckless mastery of his means."[38] Clearly American opera had finally arrived in the twentieth century.

✑

By the time Gatti-Casazza left for Italy in 1935 he had commissioned and produced more American operas than any other Metropolitan Opera director—then or since. Not only did he bring innovative stage designs to his American works but he also gave a boost and visibility to American composers. By producing their operas on the stage of America's great Metropolitan Opera, Gatti afforded them a prominence they could gain by no other means. *Merry Mount*'s librettist Richard Stokes summarized their feelings in a letter to Gatti shortly before the director sailed for Italy: "While others have prated and railed on behalf of native music, you have contented yourself with nothing less than the heroic deed, boldly reiterated, of flinging into support of that cause the Metropolitan's giant resources. When American opera achieves equality of value with that of other peoples, you will be remembered with gratitude as one of its truest begetters."[39]

10

From the Black Perspective

So be of good cheer, composers of my race of people, for you stand on the threshold of a new world of art. . . . The Negro composer has within his possession, today, the inherent bequest of a rich and practically inexhaustible mine of musical soil upon which to build.

— Harry Lawrence Freeman, *The American Musician,* October 1920

LOUIS GRUENBERG's *Emperor Jones* brought an African American storyline and chorus to the Metropolitan Opera for the first time, but it was not New York's earliest opera on a black subject. On September 10, 1928, *Voodoo* by Harry Lawrence Freeman was staged at the Palm Garden Theater at Fifty-second Street. With far less visual panache and production aplomb than *Emperor Jones,* Freeman's grand opera was the first composed by a black to join the Broadway circuit. In the earlier years of the century, black audiences were exiled from downtown New York theaters, and African American composers and performers, playing to white audiences, were restricted in their creative endeavors. Love scenes were one of the well-known taboos; romance, it seemed, was for comedic stereotypes such as those of the minstrel traditions. But as all-black theaters opened in New York City, a new era in American drama began. In 1917 the Coloured Players at the Garden Theatre in Madison Square Garden gave three plays, and, as the lyricist James Weldon Johnson noted, "The stereotyped traditions regarding the Negro's histrionic limitations were smashed."[1] It was the first time anywhere in the United States that African American actors in the dramatic theater had commanded the serious attention of both critics and the public.

During the early years of the century, black writers, poets, and musicians, eager to gain access to New York's publishers, came to Harlem from all over the country, forming what came to be known as the Harlem Renaissance. With its roots dating back to 1910, the creative outburst spawned a vital Broadway connection that withered only in the throes of racial tensions and the Great Depression. "In the history of New York," wrote Johnson in 1930, "the name Harlem has changed from Dutch to

Irish to Jewish to Negro; but it is through this last change that it has gained its most widespread fame." Harlem was not merely a quarter or a slum, but an African American city located in the heart of white Manhattan. "It strikes the uninformed observer as a phenomenon," said Johnson, "a miracle right out of the skies."[2]

Awareness of music's dramatic potential could be seen in every aspect of African American cultural life: storytelling, spirituals, slave songs, ancient dance rituals, expressive blues, and musical plays. Christian traditions and European classical genres added other dimensions to an already highly creative sensibility. But the world of classical music was not always an easy one to enter. The post–Civil War opera singers Marie Selika and Sissieretta Jones sang in Europe for crowned heads of state and for American presidents, yet they never appeared in staged opera. "My color is against me," said Jones, who admitted her constant longing to sing on the operatic stage.[3] Black singers usually gave concerts, sometimes in costume, in their churches and at theaters and local halls. The impresario James Henry Mapleson provides an intriguing account of Marie Selika's singing "in the extreme quarters" of Philadelphia: "On entering, I was quite surprised to find an audience of some 1,500 or 2,000, who were all black, I being the only white man present. I must say I was amply repaid for the trouble I had taken, as the music was all of the first order. . . . She [Selika] sang the Shadow Song from *Dinorah* delightfully, and in reply to a general encore, gave the valse from the *Romeo and Juliet* of Gounod. In fact, no better singing have I heard."[4]

If Mapleson's account raises doubts about opera being an elitist art for white society, so did Harry Lawrence Freeman:

> When we say Grand Opera, it doesn't mean musical operetta, but Grand Opera in every sense of the word. Speaking of Negro originality, here is the greatest field in which to prove it. It goes without saying that such a venture would mark for the Negro the most wonderful of any undertaking, inasmuch as he has already crossed into the fields of most all the modern arts, and Grand Opera which is not of today, has remained unchallenged in his fight to prove equality in this field. There are those of narrow minds who would say that Grand Opera does not belong to the Negro, and for that reason this field has been passed over. But they are wrong entirely. Grand Opera belongs to all; that is, the themes first for the story are among the race, or can be taken from our foreparents. . . . Each day brings us new adventures successfully floated; and surely we have learned the meaning of "patronize your own," and would push over such a proposition as an all-Negro Grand Opera Company and carry it through to success.[5]

Freeman did organize his own opera company—several in fact. Although they were short-lived, they provided a practical and necessary venue for his own work. All-black opera companies, though, were not new to America. The earliest, Washington, D.C.'s fine Colored Opera Company, was founded in 1872, eleven years before the Metropolitan Opera. Another was the Theodore Drury Opera Company, which presented *Carmen, Aida, Faust,* and the like at the Lexington Opera House in New York from 1910 to about 1915. Some nineteenth-century African American opera composers, such as John Thomas Douglass and Louisa Mars, wrote operettas; a few others tried their hand at grand opera. One of the earliest was Edmund Dede, born in New Orleans in 1829. From its only surviving aria, Dede's grand opera *Sultan d'Ispaha* appears to be cast in the style of Verdi and the Italian school. Another gifted African American was Lucien Lambert, the eldest of six children, all of whom were talented musicians. Lambert wrote at least four operas, among them *La Spathi* (1897), a "poem lyrique" in four acts.[6]

Harry Lawrence Freeman

In operatic output, no African American composer matched the ambitions of Harry Lawrence Freeman (1869–1954). Between 1893 and 1947, Freeman composed more than twenty works for the stage, mainly grand operas in the neoromantic tradition. He was known as the "colored Wagner," not so much for his musical style as for his ambitious undertakings. He fashioned two enormous *"Ring"* tetralogies, one at the start of his career and the other at the end. From 1895 to about the turn of the century, he worked on a cycle of four operas that would introduce black characters progressively; the final opera would have an all-black cast. *Valdo* was produced in 1906, but the remainder of the cycle was left unfinished. With a piano-vocal score numbering 2,150 pages, Freeman's second cycle, *Zululand* (1941–44), was completed but never staged. Derived from Henry Rider Haggard's *Nada, the Lily,* it included *Chaka, The Ghost-Wolves, The Stone-Witch,* and *Umslopogaas and Nada.*

Harry Lawrence Freeman was born in Cleveland, Ohio, a prosperous city that contained the Standard Oil Company, Otis Steel, and as early as the 1870s could boast electric streetlights. His father was a master carpenter, and by the standards of the day the family was considered well-to-do.[7] Naturally gifted musically, Freeman landed a job as church organist by age ten. He taught music and then toured as music director with various popular theatrical groups. In the early part of the century he took his wife and small son to New York, where he remained in "delightful Harlem" for the rest of his long life. There he established the Freeman School of Music and the Freeman School of Grand Opera and organized the Negro Grand Opera Company that opened in 1928 with *Voodoo.*

For Freeman, the lifestyle in Harlem initially had a sophistication and dignity that corresponded to his love of great opera. But by the time he died at age eighty-four, he had witnessed his delightful Harlem change from a miraculous enclave of second-generation respectability to a jaded community of dubious ambiance. In the early days, average Harlemites took pride in themselves and their homes, wrote Arthur P. Davis. A male resident of Harlem "would not appear on the avenue improperly dressed or wearing a 'headrag.' He seldom went downtown to *work,* but to *business,* carrying not a lunch pail but his overalls and lunch in a *brief case.* Perhaps, he tended to overdo this respectability, but he was of a generation and class which felt that the whole race was judged by individual conduct, and he was determined to hold up his end."[8] Young people "hung out" on the Harlem street corners in those days not to sell drugs but to ogle jazz greats. From the corner of 135th Street and Seventh Avenue ("the Campus"), one could see Fats Waller stroll by, or perhaps Roland Hayes, Paul Robeson, or Florence Mills. At the Lafayette Theater on 132d Street, Ethel Waters, Fletcher Henderson, or Eubie Blake played regularly, and Duke Ellington was a staple at the Cotton Club.[9] In the domain of classical music, the Harlem Symphony Orchestra presented concerts of Beethoven, Weber, and Mendelssohn as early as 1925. This then was the atmosphere that shaped the life and thought of Harry Freeman.

Freeman composed songs, ballet music, two works for chorus and orchestra, and two symphonic poems, making him one of the first African Americans to write in a serious concert idiom. He also wrote a play, a "race drama" as he called it, about a light-skinned young man who is taken in by a black family to escape a lynch mob and eventually becomes a respected judge. Freeman's main interests, however, lay in opera. He composed at least twenty-three, although only eight appear to have been performed in entirety. Because Freeman sometimes changed the titles of his operas and many of his scores have been lost, information about his work is often incomplete.[10] Harry Lawrence Freeman, however, shares honors with Deems Taylor and Charles Wakefield Cadman as being one of the first American composers to have an opera broadcast. *Voodoo* was aired on May 20, 1928, on New York City's WGBS.

Freeman not only conducted and produced his own operas, but he also wrote his own librettos, and his son Valdo and wife Carlotta were usually part of the casts. His stories are by and large ultra-dramatic tales of love, jealousy, and murderous revenge in the romantic grand opera tradition. Exotic locales—Mexico, Egypt, Africa, and the Orient—share the spotlight with American themes, but many of Freeman's librettos turn in upon themselves and lack forward direction and dramatic thrust. His overall musical style is romantic, with melodramatic leitmotivic segments and little distinction between aria and recitative. In most of his extant scores the choral writing is excellent, often polyphonic and fairly complex.

With *Voodoo,* Freeman brings to life a new operatic form—grand opera embellished with jazz, blues, spirituals, and voodoo chants. The "ballets" in the opera are cakewalks, tangos, and clog dances. Leaving behind his cherished Wagnerian traditions, Freeman employs number arias, ballads, and ensembles in a somewhat simpler harmonic framework than earlier. The story is based on the ancient African *voudoum* (*vaudoux*) cult, whose ceremonies were practiced traditionally in Louisiana on St. John's Eve. The opera takes place on a plantation near New Orleans not long after the Civil War and develops along the lines of the ubiquitous love triangle but one stained with jealousy, occult powers, and murder. Although the opera's literary mode is clumsy, its plot provides a useful vehicle for Freeman's varied mixture of styles.[11]

Given its premiere at Palm Garden in New York City on September 10 and 11, 1928, with an all-black cast, *Voodoo* attracted more press coverage than any of Freeman's operas. Even Baltimore, Cincinnati, and Syracuse newspapers picked up the story. Some were puzzled, others charmed. The novelty of the score attracted attention. "The production is an experiment," wrote the *New York American,* "an endeavor to prove that the American Negro is creating an art that is peculiarly his own." Robert Garland described the "crashing cymbals and sounding brass, shrilling reeds and strings that scrape excitedly, discords all but unbelievable. You may not admire 'Voodoo,'" he said, "but it'll seldom bore you." The *New York Sun* found this "unbeautiful discord . . . somehow right and natural; against it the molasses of the old 'negro songs' seemed oddly synthetic, Nordic romances." There is "perfect blue harmony" and a "sharply hot banjo that can swing a theme crazily about."[12]

Although written in 1913, *Voodoo* had to wait fifteen years for a performance. America—as Scott Joplin also learned—was not quite ready to accept a serious opera that contained what was still considered a "low-class" art form: jazz.

Scott Joplin's Treemonisha

Harlem was not as kind to Scott Joplin as it was to Lawrence Freeman. During the period when Joplin was desperately trying to find backing for *Treemonisha,* Freeman and his son Valdo found him "lying in the doorway, a white shirt, no coat or anything." It was winter, and snow was on the ground, recalled Valdo. "My father took his coat off and put it around him. . . . He'd been knocked on the head and robbed. . . . We took him home. . . . My father knew him very well."[13] A few years later, Joplin died, broken and devastated over the failure of his beloved *Treemonisha.* The opera slumbered in oblivion for more than half a century before making a triumphant Broadway debut. It was also recorded commercially in entirety—the earliest African American opera to achieve that distinction and the earliest to receive widespread modern recognition and performance. In

Scott Joplin. *Astor, Lenox and Tilden Foundations, New York Public Library*

1976 Joplin was awarded a posthumous Pulitzer Prize. "Somewhere," stated a *New York Times* headline, "Scott Joplin's Just Gotta Be Smilin'!"

Scott Joplin (ca. 1868–1917) grew up in Texarkana on the Texas-Arkansas border. He was the son of a former slave whose home reverberated with singing, fiddling, and banjo strumming. Young Scott was blessed with an amazing ability to improvise at the piano, talents enlarged by all he heard around him that characterized black musical expression in the antebellum era—the "patting Juba," spirituals, shouts and hollers, ring plays, plantation songs, syncopated rhythms, blue notes, and strings of choruses. Because of his remarkable talent, Scott was given free lessons in harmony, theory, and keyboard technique by a German professor of music believed to have been Julius Weiss. No doubt the lessons opened the world of opera to the boy. They also demonstrated the joys of education, learning, and exploring—joys that would later form the vital message of *Treemonisha*.

Few opportunities existed for black pianists. There was, of course, the church, but brothels offered steadier and more lucrative work. And so, while only in his teens, Joplin left home to become an itinerant pianist. He played pre-ragtime ("jig-piano") in various red-light districts throughout the mid-South. He also took classes in composition and counterpoint at one of the nation's first all-black academic institutions, the George R. Smith College for Negroes in Sedalia, Missouri. With the ebullient, ever-popular "Maple Leaf Rag," published by John Stark in 1899, Scott Joplin soon became known as the "King of Ragtime." Throughout his life, he composed at least forty similar rags, all creative miniatures that he considered "classical" music. He wanted to elevate ragtime and compose music that would reach beyond the cheap bordello forms. And he succeeded. Joplin's piano rags are more tuneful, contrapuntal, infectious, and harmonically colorful than any others of his era. It was that persistent striving, that quest for artistic merit, that gave *Treemonisha* life of its own.

Joplin moved to New York in 1907, believing that it was the best possible place to find a producer for his new opera. He had written two previous theatrical works, the six-minute *Ragtime Dance* (1899) and the opera *Guest of Honor* (1903). Although the former was performed and published, the latter's history remains inconclusive.[14] *Treemonisha* was an obsession, however. Joplin seemed to cherish it beyond all his other works. It was dignified, and beautiful; it embodied a classical elegance, myth, message, and buoyancy; and it both reflected and reinforced his inner life and spirit. He could identify with its characters. To him, they were real, and his music richly promulgated that reality.

Reality became bitter for Joplin. As Vera Lawrence notes, "It was the rejection after rejection that came to erode the very foundations of his existence. He gave up his public playing, dismissed or lost his students, and eventually even sacrificed his composing to his monomania. He plunged feverishly into the task of orchestrating his opera, day and night, with his friend Sam Patterson standing by to copy out the parts, page by page as each page of the full score was completed. Perhaps Joplin was aware of his advancing deterioration and was consciously racing against time."[15]

In 1911 Joplin undertook the financial burden of publishing *Treemonisha* himself in piano-vocal format, and in a last, desperate effort to see it staged he invited a small audience to hear the opera at a rehearsal hall in Harlem. *Treemonisha* was given its premiere in 1915, unstaged and with only piano accompaniment. It was a miserable failure. Two years later, on April 1, 1917, Joplin died in a state of mental deterioration from conditions related to syphilis.

Had Scott Joplin lived into the 1920s and 1930s, as did Lawrence Freeman, he might have found a producer. Freeman, too, had difficulties seeing his operas staged, especially those that mixed black and European styles. *Voodoo* and *The Plantation* were both composed about the time of *Treemonisha*. The public, it seemed, was not yet ready for "crude" black musical forms to invade the sacrosanct domicile of European-style grand opera. What sets *Treemonisha* apart from Freeman's works, however—and, for that matter, all else before or after him—is its excellent craftsmanship in the balance and integration of musical styles. Overture, ragtime, sentimental parlor tunes, Italian lyricism, melodramatic chromaticism, recitative, barbershop quartet, thematic associations, dance, chorus, and musical characterization all miraculously combine to form a unified dramatic whole. The story itself is timeless. All can relate to its message, making it one of America's earliest family operas. *Treemonisha* is an excellent vehicle for introducing children to both opera and their national heritage.

Treemonisha is not an opera in the conventional sense, but it is much more interesting. It is what Joplin conceived an opera as being.[16] There are no transitions between the twenty-seven numbers, and there is no spoken dialogue in the three acts. Showing a kinship with early silent screen practices, many numbers bear such titles as "Surprised," "Confusion," "Treemonisha in Peril," "The Rescue," and "Conjurors Forgiven." The story is mythical rather than melodramatic. There is no murder or death, no love conflict or conquest, yet its protagonist emerges a true conqueror. A heroine of the spirit, she leads her people from superstition and darkness to salvation and enlightenment. With its magical mélange of song and dance and its translucent message of hope, *Treemonisha* becomes a kind of American *Magic Flute*—with a touch of the old English harlequinade.

As Joplin outlines in the preface to the libretto, the story takes place on a plantation somewhere in Arkansas, northeast of the town of Texarkana in the 1880s. Ned and Monisha long for a child whom they can educate to teach people "to aspire to something higher than superstition and conjuring."[17] Their prayers are answered when they find a baby girl under a sacred tree (the mythical tree of life?). Named Tree-monisha, the baby grows into a lovely young woman. In the first two acts, Treemonisha is kidnapped by evil conjurors and saved by her friend Remus, disguised as a scarecrow, just as she is about to be thrown into a nest of killer wasps. In act 3 the conjurers are brought to justice, but when the townspeople start to beat them mercilessly, Treemonisha advises:

> You will do evil for evil
> If you strike them you know.
> Just give them a severe lecture,
> And let them freely go

Remus adds:

> Never treat your neighbors wrong,
> By causing them to grieve.
> Help the weak if you are strong,
> And never again deceive.[18]

The people then joyously make Treemonisha their leader. "If I lead the good women," she asks, "tell me, who will lead the men?" "You, you, you," sing the men. "Women may follow me many days long," answers Treemonisha. "But the men may think that I am wrong." "No, no, no," the men reply. "We all agree to trust you," adds the chorus. The opera closes with "A Real Slow Drag" ("Dance slowly, prance slowly / While you hear that pretty rag"), one of the few true ragtime pieces in the score and a powerfully effective closing that brought charmed audiences of the 1970s' revival to their feet.

Joplin gives his characters special musical life and depth, perhaps because they represent those closest to him in real life. Like Ned, his own father had been a slave, and like Monisha, his mother took in washing and ironing so her child could have an education. And perhaps Treemonisha represents Joplin's only child, a daughter from his first marriage, who had died in infancy in 1905. Joplin may have made the little girl live again in the noblest character he could invent, a leader of wisdom, grace, and power—as he hoped he, too, would be through his music.

The magical musical moments in the score are numerous. The overture, a mini-reincarnation of the opera itself, presents three major themes. The Treemonisha theme or motif represents the happiness of people free from superstition. A ragtime tune, it recurs at key moments, as in the opening of number 15, "The Rescue," and in number 21, "Treemonisha's Return." Other melodic ideas in the overture are the ominous contrasting theme of number 14, "The Wasp-Nest," and the noble celebration of ragtime in the grand finale, number 27, "A Real Slow Drag." A fourth, more fragmentary, musical idea weaves in and out of the overture and in the opera heightens the story's more somber and dramatic moods. Directly from melodrama and silent film, moreover, are frequent patterns of diminished seventh-chords descending chromatically whenever the scene becomes eerie or frightening.

Whether individually or as a chorus, Joplin's characters are skillfully illuminated through his music. The five major characters appear in the opening scene's number 2, "Bag of Tricks." The bass Ned and soprano Monisha have brief, arioso-like dialogues. Zodzetrick, a high baritone, is slyly declamatory ("I am de Goofer dus' man . . . strange things appear when I says 'Hee-hoo!'")—a legendary con man not too far removed from Sportin' Life in George Gershwin's *Porgy and Bess.* For Treemonisha and Remus, soprano and tenor, Joplin writes warm, lyrical lines with loving care. Treemonisha's opening cavatina (short aria), for example, soars as she reprimands the conjurer for "doing great injury" to her people.

This well-defined musical characterization is retained throughout the opera in solos, duets, and choral numbers. Often action dictates form. Traditional declamatory recitative is the vehicle for Monisha's tale of how her daughter was raised and educated: number 8, "Treemonisha's Bringing Up." For dramatic moments, vocal outbursts are employed. "No, not a leaf from dat tree take!" Monisha cries out angrily to her daughter in number 5, "The Wreath." Melodic beauty often adds dignity and grandeur to both characters and text. Ned's aria in act 3, number 24, "When Villains Ramble Far and Near," is one of the finest bass arias of the period. To accent the opera's message "Wrong Is Never Right (number 22), Remus sings a melodically effusive, almost Italian, aria whose lines are lyrically reinforced by the chorus.

The chorus in *Treemonisha* is present in some format in nearly every number. Joplin uses it for dramatic action and musical show, but especially as a showpiece for spirited black traditions and current popular styles. Number 3, "The Corn-Huskers," uses a stop-time accompaniment, one of Joplin's favorite devices from vaudeville dance. Number 4, "We're Goin' Around," has a call-and-response pattern and typically black melodic inflections. The most powerful choral number comes at the close of act 2: "Aunt Dinah Has Blowed de Horn" (number 18). Its syncopated tune is similar to the Treemonisha theme, and, as the workers finish their day, it has a powerfully joyous tone. Harold Schonberg called it "one of the great curtains of American musical theater. . . It hits the listener like an explosion," he wrote, "exultant, swinging, wonderfully spiced harmonically. This is the real thing."[19]

Treemonisha was given its staged premiere at the Memorial Arts Center in Atlanta on January 28 and 29, 1972, with Robert Shaw conducting the Atlanta Symphony Orchestra. The cast included Alpha Floyd, Louise Parker, Simon Estes, and Seth McCoy. Because Joplin's original orchestration had been lost, the score had to be thoughtfully reconstructed. The following August, the opera was presented at Wolf Trap Park near Washington, D.C., and orchestrated by William Bolcom. The most successful production, however, was that of the Houston Grand Opera Association on May 23 through June 4, 1975, with a new orchestral score by Gunther Schuller, and Carmen Balthrop singing the title role. Frank Corsaro directed the production, Franco Colavecchia designed the sets and costumes after the fanciful paintings of Romare Bearden, and Louis Johnson devised the choreography. In the joyous "Aunt Dinah Has Blowed de Horn," Johnson had dancers leaping, whirling, and throwing cotton bags in the air until, in a chorus line at the end, they fell backward like a pile of dominoes. The Houston production was taken to Kennedy Center and then on to Broadway, where it ran triumphantly for two months and was recorded by Deutsche Grammophon.

Scott Joplin's "Sleeping Beauty" might still be slumbering had it not been for the efforts of Vera Brodsky Lawrence, whose monumental two-volume *Collected Works of Scott Joplin,* published by the New York Public Library in 1971, sparked the craze for Joplin's music. It even inspired a soundtrack for the popular film *The Sting,* starring Robert Redford and Paul Newman. If *Treemonisha* was not sophisticated enough for Harlem in 1915, it has felicitously found a place in the ever-widening terrain of respected and enjoyed American operas. It occupies a special place in American history as well. The opera's young heroine is a startlingly early voice for modern civil rights' causes, notably the importance of education and knowledge to African American advancement.

Act 2 finale from Scott Joplin's *Treemonisha* with Carmen Balthrop (Treemonisha), Ken Hicks (Andy), and Walter Turnbull (Remus) in the Houston Grand Opera production (1982). *Houston Grand Opera Archives,* © *DUPL 1982 Jim Caldwell*

Cults, Cultures, and Haitian Themes

The ever-fascinating interpenetration of cultures during the interwar years is nowhere more evident than in American opera and theater. Darwin T. Turner has observed that black dramatists of the 1920s and 1930s often found it necessary to work with characters and themes popularized by white dramatists.[20] Often these dramatists turned to themes of voodooism, as Eugene O'Neill did in *Emperor Jones,* Mary Wiborg in *Taboo* (1922), and Em Jo Bashe in *Earth* (1927). W. Frank Harling's *Deep River* (1926), called a blend of melodrama and grand opera, contains a frenetic voodoo scene that takes place in New Orleans on Place Congo during the 1830s. Perhaps the most popular realization of the mystical subject was John Houseman's electrifying production of *Macbeth,* known as "The Voodoo *Macbeth*" (1936), which was directed by Orson Welles with music by Virgil Thomson.[21]

Why the obsession with the arcane ritual of voodoo? The cult had become a kind of African American mythology that played a role in twenti-

eth-century black theater history, as Greek mythology did in seventeenth-
and eighteenth-century Western opera and drama. Voodooism, as woven
into the action, placed characters within intense dramatic postures of love,
conflict, and heroism, always with a certain mythic presence. Of African
origins, voodooism is believed to involve serpent worship, magic spells, and
necromancy and was especially prevalent in the West Indies, notably Haiti.
While the power of superstition became exotic, sometimes stereotypical,
fuel for white dramatists, for black composers it was also a symbolic voice
from the past—a symbol of ignorance and bondage from which blacks such
as Treemonisha longed to break free. Through the medium of opera, they
expressed anguish, joy, and faith, each in their own individual way.

After the success of Gruenberg's *Emperor Jones* in 1931, two operas by
black composers were staged in 1933, both with voodooism within their
plots: Shirley Graham's *Tom-Tom*, with a cast of five hundred, and Hall
Johnson's *Run, Little Chillun.* Johnson (1888–1970), who had studied at the
Juilliard School and the University of Southern California, was a distinguished choral conductor and composer of spirituals. He wrote only one
opera (sometimes called a "folk opera"), which contained singing, chanting, intoning, dancing, spectacle with spoken dialogue, and a cast of twenty-
nine solo roles. The work was provocative in a fresh, mythic sense and
differed from current popular black revues such as *Shuffle Along* (1921) or
Blackbirds (1928). *Run, Little Chillun* dealt with the conflict and interplay
of intense religious experiences. In general, Johnson tried to differentiate
a newer cult, the New Day Pilgrims, from old-fashioned voodooists. Spirituals in the score include "Amazing Grace," "Done Written Down-a My
Name," and "Run, Little Chillun" ("cause de devil done loose in de lan'!"),
which gave the work its title. But of special interest is the kind of "New
Day" voodooism that becomes central to the story. As the composer describes it in the opening of act 1, scene 2:

> The general impression should be something approaching voodoo—not
> too directly African, but with a strong African flavor. Since the cult is not
> designated by any familiar name, any features may be introduced which
> serve to make the whole scene more striking without any chance of con-
> troversy or any possibility of offense to any existing religious group. There
> should be no suggestion of actual idol-worship or animal sacrifices, but
> rather references (in the chants) to Sun, Moon, Water, etc., joys of life with
> nature—joys of love. The whole betokens and partly expresses a religious
> attitude of joy and freedom toward life, in sharp contrast to the well-known
> spiritual joy in suffering which characterizes the more orthodox religious
> services of Negroes.[22]

A scene from act 2 sets a revivalist mood not often seen on an opera stage: "This is impossible to describe in words as it soon becomes more music than anything else. It drones, wails and then mounts. There are groans, sobs, screams—all over an undercurrent of harmony with Elder Jones' [the Baptist pastor] voice soaring above the whole in an impassioned plea to God to 'Turn this boy around then and there, before it is everlastingly too late.' The storm is at the height of its fury."[23] The *New York Times* noted on March 2, 1933, that the revival scenes and the "orgiastic dancing" in the Pilgrims' forest scene "could not be excelled."

Stories involving voodooism attracted not only Freeman and Joplin but Clarence Cameron White and William Grant Still as well. Although the former two composers based their operas on fictitious tales set in the antebellum South, White and Still preferred the more exotic atmosphere of Haiti for *Ouanga* and *Troubled Island*. Coincident with the American occupation of Haiti from 1915 to 1934, both are about Jean-Jacques Dessalines, the black emperor of Haiti who proclaimed that country's independence from the French in 1804. Like Indianist composers who visited indigenous locales, White traveled to Haiti to gain familiarity with local history, culture, and musical styles. Exoticism as an enlarging artistic dimension was in the air at the time, and African American composers were finding their own métiers within the expressive challenges of opera.

Recognized as an important music educator, Clarence Cameron White (1880–1960) was the first African American opera composer to study extensively in Europe. Born in Clarksville, Tennessee, White was the son of highly educated parents who had graduated from Oberlin College. His father became a physician, and after receiving her bachelor of arts degree in 1876 his mother taught in Indianapolis. While still in his teens, White studied music at Howard University in Washington, D.C., and at the Oberlin Conservatory of Music. Later he taught violin at the Washington Conservatory of Music, which had been founded in 1903 and was a unique, privately owned institution operated solely by black musicians.[24]

Noted artists such as Jascha Heifetz and Fritz Kreisler featured many of Clarence White's compositions for violin. His *Elegy,* performed by the National Symphony Orchestra in 1954, won the Benjamin Award, and his only published opera, *Ouanga,* the prestigious David Bispham Medal in 1932. Performed successfully in several major American cities, *Ouanga* made history when it was produced, semi-staged, in New York City on May 27, 1956, by the National Negro Opera Company—the first production by an all-black organization to appear at the Metropolitan Opera House.[25]

Ouanga reflects not only the struggle of black composers and librettists to find a place in the world of grand opera but also illustrates how talented black singers were securing eminent positions on the American operatic stage. The National Negro Opera Company, founded in 1941 by Mary Cardwell Dawson, had performed in Pittsburgh, at the Chicago Civic Opera House, in Madison Square Garden, and at Griffith Stadium in Washington, D.C., with a repertoire that included *Aida, Faust,* and *La traviata.* Among its stars was baritone Robert McFerrin, the second black after Marian Anderson to sing with the Metropolitan Opera. In *Ouanga,* the role of Dessalines was sung by bass-baritone McHenry Boatright, and the dramatic soprano Defilée by Juanita King. At the Metropolitan Opera House, Adelaide Boatner played the terrifying voodoo priestess Mougali, but Carol Brice sang that challenging contralto part at Carnegie Hall.[26] Brice's impressive repertoire included *Regina, Showboat, Porgy and Bess,* and *Carousel,* and she was the first African American to win the distinguished Naumberg Award.

Ouanga—which in Haitian Creole means "charm" or "spell"—is cast in the postromantic operatic tradition favored by many American composers of the early twentieth century. But it moves beyond Freeman and others in its use of a wider, expanded harmonic vocabulary. Polychordal effects, Debussyan parallelism, pentatonic and whole tone scales, and clashing dissonance add excitement and tribal frenzy to a plot that, like Gruenberg's *Emperor Jones* a year later, audiences found exotic and novel. White had an advantage over Freeman and Joplin from the start because his libretto had been crafted by an experienced literary talent, the prize-winning black author John F. Matheus.[27] When White won the Harmon Award that enabled him to go to Haiti, Matheus went with him. Together they delved into the colorful history of the Haitian liberation. "We found the true story of this forceful character [Dessalines], marvelous material for an opera libretto," White said.[28] Libretto in hand, he completed his musical score in 1931 during an interlude in Paris.

Among the most distinctive traits in the opera are the composer's gift of melody and skillful writing for the singer, somewhat in the vein of Jules Massenet. Several arias could be sung effectively as separate vocal pieces. The story is about conflict—conflict between passionate love and heroic mission, masculine power and feminine sacrifice, and time-worn traditions and a brave new order. A particularly moving scene unfolds at the end of act 1 when Dessalines tells Defilée of a vision that warned him "to shun vain glory and tyrannical ambition, to hold steadfast to the ancient heritage of the Ouanga, to beware of the new order of things and of the bloody strife which will surely follow."[29] "Dessalines, Dessalines," Defilée cries out in a melodic motif that reappears throughout the opera. "All day I have caressed you in my thoughts, and now when night and darkness come, my heart is torn by terrors wild and distraught." Ending the act with perhaps the longest aria in the opera, "O Love of My Life," Dessalines sings, "For as a snake works its way beneath the ground, the Ouanga [the spell of the Python of Dambala] would try to coil itself about us and crush our hearts."[30] The aria offers the baritone an effective showpiece of emotional breadth and lyricism.

In his libretto, Matheus manages to paint the character of Defilée (the "Defiled One") in vivid native colors and imagery. She is no weakling, nor is she mad as some legends attest ("she was a butt for children's laughter and the snarls of dogs").[31] In lovely poetic simile, she warns her king:

> You can no more pay for some favors than you can atone for the dead or stop the "Ouanga." Listen to the drum beats. Can you destroy the wind, or stop the rain and the sea, Dessalines? The palm trees dance in the breezes, like tall mulatto women before the sacred altar. The mahogany trees rustle like the skirts of the mamaloi [voodoo priestess]. The rains beat upon the banana leaves like the hands of the beater on the small drums. The ocean pounds upon the shores of the Cape with the rhythm of the big drums. We are children of the forests. You cannot kill the jungle in us. Ah! Dessalines—you can not smother the "Ouanga" rhythm lurking in your own bosom.[32]

William Grant Still

In William Grant Still's *Troubled Island,* composed between 1937 and 1949, Defilée, the rejected but ever-loving wife of Emperor Dessalines, becomes the character Azelia. The mulatto Empress Claire, who secretly loves the traitor Vuval, is a vital conspirator in Dessalines's assassination. The ill-fated emperor is not as closely tied to mystical voodoo traditions in *Troubled Island* as he is in *Ouanga,* although the high priest and priestess of voodoo are still prominent in the cast. Still's librettist Langston Hughes saw the downfall of Dessalines in a somewhat different light: "The issue of the play is not solely the struggle against the whites but also the manner in which Dessalines becomes corrupted by his sense of power and desire for luxury. Important to his failure was the interracial rivalry between the blacks and the mulattoes of Haiti. By describing Haitians' excessive concern about distinctions based on color, class, and culture, Hughes warned African Americans against the destructive divisions which such prejudices can create."[33]

By means of the various "emperors" we are carried along in the cultural idioms of the century—from the O'Neill-Gruenberg Jungian and expressionistic approaches, through Freeman's and White's melodramatic view, to the modern social consciousness of Hughes and Still. The true tragedy of the Dessalines story, however, is that he exterminated thousands of whites after declaring himself emperor—events that do not become part of the opera's librettos.

Langston Hughes's libretto for *Troubled Island* closely follows his play *Emperor of Haiti* (1938), a revision of his *Drums of Haiti* first produced in 1935. Educated at Columbia University, Hughes was a talented and versatile author of plays, radio scripts, and opera librettos. His *Mulatto* (1935) was the first drama by an African American to have a long run on Broadway, and his lyrics for Kurt Weill's *Street Scene* (1947) added a special dimenson to the opera. Hughes had worked on the subject of Dessalines and the Haitian rebellion against the forces of Napoleon Bonaparte for nearly a quarter of a century. He offered the idea to Clarence Cameron White for a possible musical setting, but White preferred John Matheus's version, which had a stronger focus on voodooism. Hughes then approached William Grant Still with the subject, and their collaboration moved along well until Hughes became unable to complete the libretto. Still's wife, the writer and lyricist Verna Arvey, supplied the missing text and thus became his librettist for his remaining six operas.[34]

William Grant Still (1895–1978) has been called the dean of American black composers. His long and distinguished career included a wide spectrum of achievements. He was the first black to conduct a major symphony orchestra and one of the first to write for films and television. His *Troubled Island* (1937) was the first opera by a black composer to receive a world premiere by a major company. In 1949 it was staged by the New York City Opera, the third of eventually forty operas by American composers that the adventuresome young company would produce before 1972. Still studied at Oberlin and then with George Chadwick and Edgard Varèse. His early musical experiences were mainly in the commercial field as an arranger for Paul Whiteman, Sophie Tucker, and Artie Shaw and for both Columbia and Warner Brothers motion picture studios. Still composed five symphonies, nine operas, and numerous other works in almost every medium, drawing praise from musical luminaries such as Leopold Stokowski and Howard Hanson. "William Grant Still brought to music a new voice," said Hanson, "a voice filled with lovely melodies, gorgeous harmonies, insidious rhythms, and dazzling colors. But it was music deeply rooted in the traditions of the past. . . . His music speaks to the common

Scene from William Grant Still's *Troubled Island* (1949). *Astor, Lenox and Tilden Foundations, New York Public Library*

William Grant Still. *Van
Vechten Collection, Library
of Congress*

man. . . . [Those who listen] need no analytical tables, seismographic charts
nor digital computers. It is necessary only to bring a sensitive ear, a mind,
and a heart."[35]

All eight of Still's operas are basically tonal, dissonant when the drama
dictates, grand and eloquent in scope, and, most important, flowing in
supple melodic contour. More fortunate than most black composers—
indeed, most American composers in general—Still saw many of his instrumental works performed. Yet new American operas, which have complex and expensive production requirements, are a different matter, and
Still was not as fortunate with them as with instrumental works. Only three
of his operas were staged during his lifetime, and then many years after he
wrote them. *Troubled Island* waited twelve years, *Highway No. 1, U.S.A.* (1943)
twenty years, and *A Bayou Legend* (1941) thirty-three. Perhaps spurred by

the *Treemonisha* craze, *A Bayou Legend* was produced at Jackson State University in 1974 and six years later gained national visibility on PBS television. *Minette Fontaine* (1958) was first staged in 1984, and *Costaso* (1949) in 1992.[36] America, it would seem, was at last beginning to recognize one of its finest operatic craftsmen.

What was perhaps most remarkable about William Grant Still was his understanding of the sensuous nature of opera. His experience in the film industry and his use of the term *melodrama* for operas were only superficial. He knew well both the noumenal and phenomenal aspects of opera, the inner and outer, the symbol and action. He valued not only what the characters and audience saw and heard but also what they did not. Others, too, delved into love triangles, power plays, and legends and trickery. Still's stories seem to work, perhaps because there is always a mystical, even chilling, irony about them. If voodoo or superstition wins in the end, the tragedy comes about through ironical circumstances that allow subtle interplay and development of character.

The music Still weaves into these tales manages to enliven and lighten them with grand, sweeping gestures. Whether as recurring motives in an orchestra, lyrical effusion in a voice, or ethnic colors in chorus and ballet, music in Still's operas is the ultimate protagonist. It is a dramatic partner that interacts and intensifies with the diverse emotions of the characters. Recitatives are closely allied with the arias, often creating a dramatic framework for singers' more sustained reflections. Still also uses recitative for emphasis at key dramatic moments, as in act 2 of *Costaso* when Manuel and Costaso realize they are victims of a sinister plot. Earlier in the same opera, fluid vocal lines become increasingly angular and distorted and climax with Armona's agonized confession: "A map I cannot give you. The desert is uncharted!"[37]

Arias in Still's work are often symbolic, poetic character studies. Many are in a da capo form modified to suit the shifting moods of the text. Set in Spanish-Colonial America, *Costaso* tells of the treachery of Felipe Armona, who is in love with the wife of his assistant, Ramon Costaso. In order to win her, Armona sends Costaso into the desert to search for a nonexistent city of gold. The desert, in turn, becomes an ironic symbol permeating the entire opera. Ultimately, it is not Costaso whom the arid desert claims but the deceitful Armona himself. In his "Songs of the Desert" (act 2, scene 1), we discover the character and mental processes of Armona. The desert, too, is outwardly romantic yet false and capricious, and the asymmetrical da capo form allows these aspects full play. The outer two sections (A and A') explore the attractions of the desert, and the inner sec-

tion (B) the horror and desolation through shifting tempos and harmonies and a wider vocal range. As Armano's final lines grimly attest, "The
desert will serve us well."

In all of his operas, Still considered melody the most important element of musical fabric. "After melody comes harmony," he continued,
"then form, rhythm and dynamics."[38] Critics seemed to agree. Respond-
ing to the enormous vocal demands of *A Bayou Legend,* John De Mers
wrote, *"Bayou Legend* is a lyrical wonderland, deeply rooted in the American idiom while sharing with Italian and French masterworks the love
of sumptuous melody."[39] *Highway No. 1,* a verismo opera about family
conflicts and violent abuse, requires a cast of only four principals and a
small orchestra and chorus. It is easier to sing than Still's larger three-act
operas and contains interesting melodic cross-relationships that illuminate
the somber moods of the characters.

Although *Troubled Island* and *A Bayou Legend* work appropriately with
a black cast, Still's other operas need not be restricted by race or ethnic
identity. He intended his work to transcend race or color and felt that his
artistic roots were as European as they were African. Stylistically, he managed to assimilate the best from both black and white cultures, drawing
creatively from folk, blues, polytonality, and even occasional motion-pic-
ture Mickey-Mousing for special effects (honking horns, for example).
Following Still and alongside him as well were other fine black composers: Mark Fax, Ulysses Kay, Shirley Graham, Arthur Cunningham, Clarence Jackson, Lena McLin, Emory Taylor, and many more. Somewhere
along the road, they stopped to dream opera as opera. Arthur Cunningham made the point eloquently:

> Let others dream
> What they dream
> I dream music
> I am a source person
> My body
> Its height width length and color
> Is my house
> The earth
> My estate
> The universe
> My place
>
> Call me what you will
> Call my music
> Music.[40]

African American opera composers during the first half of the twentieth century viewed the operatic form as a means of expressing the inner spirituality that allowed characters to move, feel, and grow. Theirs was a highly romantic art, an intensely personal one formulated often through various interpretations of the myths of Haiti and the protagonists of its history that became the hallmarks of their best-known work. Like the case of many American women opera composers, African Americans found it extremely difficult to see their works staged. Harry Lawrence Freeman had to form his own opera company to realize most of his productions; decades later, William Grant Still waited many years for the premieres of his works. It was the African American composer, however, who brought jazz styles to opera for the first time, creating a new dramatic expression that would become the signature of George Gershwin, Marc Blitzstein and other modern American opera composers. Perhaps, as Freeman observed, African American composers first turned to grand opera because it "remained unchallenged in [their] fight to prove equality in this field." Whatever their rationale or style, black opera composers have illustrated lyrically that American opera is not the elitist property of a few but an expression of beauty for all.

11

Innovators and Iconoclasts; or, Is It Opera?

Pigeons on the grass alas.
Short longer grass short longer longer
    shorter yellow grass. Pigeons large pigeons
    on the shorter longer yellow grass
    alas pigeons on the grass.
    —Gertrude Stein, *Four Saints in Three Acts*, 1934

"I LIKE *Porgy and Bess*'s lack of respectability," Virgil Thomson wrote after the New York premiere of George Gershwin's opera in 1935, "the way it can be popular and vulgar and go its way as a real professional piece does without bothering much about the taste-boys." Although Thomson found no pleasure in the opera's "fake folk-lore, fidgety accompaniments," or "plum-pudding orchestrations," he did like "being able to listen to a work for three hours and be fascinated at every moment."[1] Merging popular and classical elements in opera—what Thomson called "the vulgar" and "the real professional"—was hardly new, nor was the use of African American dramatic and musical idioms. What was new was Gershwin's ingenious handling of these elements. His grace and joy brought fresh vitality to opera, making *Porgy and Bess* the most popular and longest-running American opera in history.

One of Gershwin's primary sources of inspiration came via Harlem, for it was during the Harlem Renaissance that intense social interaction between black and white musicians produced far-reaching artistic results. Paul Whiteman and Aaron Copland attended Harlem clubs and parties, and Gershwin "was often to be seen sitting on the floor, agape at the dazzling virtuosity and limitless improvisation that clamored around him."[2] As Samuel Floyd relates, "Just as modernists in painting—Picasso, Matisse, Brancusi, and others—had used black art as a basis for composition, the process was duplicated in music to some extent by Copland, Stravinsky, Virgil Thomson, and others. . . . the borrowings and verisimilitude were great, and had it not been for those well-known intangibles of Afro-American musical performance practices [jazz], who knows what might have happened."[3] For Gershwin, jazz was a powerful form of what he called "American folk-music," and it infused his Tin Pan Alley songs, numerous Broadway shows, and concert works, from the enduring *Rhapsody in Blue* and *Concerto in F* to the inimitable *Porgy and Bess.*[4]

Rich inspirational sources emanating from African American culture were available long before *Porgy and Bess,* and white playwrights and producers were quick to draw from them. Eugene O'Neill's *Emperor Jones* cast a black actor in a leading serious role for the first time, and Dorothy and DuBose Heyward's *Porgy* featured Paul Robeson in 1928. David Belasco's production of the sensational melodrama *Lulu Belle* had a cast of sixty, three-quarters of whom were black. Other plays with African American themes were O'Neill's *All God's Chillun Got Wings,* John Wexley's *They Shall Not Die,* and Paul Green's *In Abraham's Bosom,* which won the Pulitzer Prize in 1927.

Music theater, too, was influenced by African American culture. Marc Connelly's immensely popular *Green Pastures* (1930) featured a large, all-black cast and spirituals by the excellent Hall Johnson Choir. The play was "so simple and yet so profound," said James Weldon Johnson, "so close to the earth and yet so spiritual," that for an actor it was "a higher test than many of the immortalized classics."[5] And with its powerful story of miscegenation, expressive melodic imagery, and creative musical dramaturgy, Jerome Kern's *Show Boat* (1927) changed the face of musical comedy. Hall Johnson's *Run, Little Chillun* and Harry Lawrence Freeman's *Voodoo*—with its spirituals, blues, jazz rhythms, recitative, and arias—were also produced before *Porgy and Bess.* Thus, not only jazz but also another, lesser-known art of black musicians played a role on New York's kaleidoscopic stage—opera.

George Gershwin's Porgy and Bess

Gershwin had many models from which to draw. Perhaps the most poignant was the character of Porgy himself. An earlier verismo opera, Ernest Carter's *The White Bird* (1917), featured a dwarflike protagonist, but *Porgy* marked the first time that a hero in American opera was crippled and of humble birth. Porgy was drawn from a real-life figure, Samuel Smalls ("Goat Sammy"), who had lost the use of his legs and went about the streets of Charleston, South Carolina, in a goat-drawn cart fashioned from a wooden soapbox. Gershwin became familiar with Porgy and the other characters of Catfish Row when he read Dubose Heyward's novel *Porgy* in 1926. Heyward had lived in Charleston most of his life and from the city's working people and their families he fashioned the plot for his novel. With his wife Dorothy, he also wrote a play on the subject, and the project was staged with spirituals and other songs. When George Gershwin (1898–1937) approached Heyward with his idea for an opera, Heyward responded enthusiastically, agreeing to be the librettist.[6] Thus began a long, joyous collaboration between the outgoing Jewish New Yorker and the reserved southern intellectual—a collaboration reminiscent of another great team of contrasting personalities, Richard Strauss and Hugo von Hoffmansthal.

The story of *Porgy and Bess* is a familiar one. More important for the purposes of this discussion is an investigation of the characters and the way Gershwin brings them to life through music. The action takes place in the 1920s in a black community on the Charleston waterfront. During a rough game of craps, the contentious blowhard Crown uses a cotton hook to kill another player. Frightened and vulnerable, his lover, Bess, takes refuge with Porgy, and soon they fall in love. "Bess, you is my woman now," sings Porgy in one of Gershwin's most beautiful duets. "An' you mus' laugh an' sing an' dance for two instead of one." When Bess sees Crown again at a community picnic, however, she succumbs to his belligerent demands and stays with him. Distraught and ill, she eventually returns to the lonely Porgy. To protect Bess from Crown, Porgy, in an outburst of rage, stabs and kills the abusive stevedore. "Bess, Bess," he cries, "you got a man now. You got Porgy!" Returning to Catfish Row after his release from jail, Porgy learns that Bess has gone off to New York with the local drug dealer, Sportin' Life. He is convinced that he can find her and sets out in his rickety goat cart for the big city "way up north pas' de custom house." "Which way Noo York?" he asks. "A thousand mile from here."

Like many operas, *Porgy and Bess* is based on a dramatized version of the story rather than the novel. Samuel Smalls was only a springboard for Heyward, who wrote in the introduction to his play: "To Smalls I make acknowledgment of my obligation. From contemplation of his real, and deeply moving tragedy [Smalls had been arrested for the attempted shooting of a woman] sprang Porgy, a creature of my imagination . . . upon whom . . . I could impose my own white man's conception of a summer of aspiration, devotion and heartbreak across the colour wall."[7]

Dramatizing a novel usually requires extreme condensation and the portrayal of character through dialogue rather than description. For the play, the Heywards made many changes that sharpened the impact of the story and were attractive to Gershwin. At the end of the novel, Porgy

Scene from Houston Grand Opera's production of *Porgy and Bess* (1995): Left to right: Stacey Robinson (Crown), Marquita Lister (Bess), and Alvy Powell (Porgy), with ensemble. *Houston Grand Opera Archives*

George Gershwin. *Van Vechten Collection, Library of Congress*

returns to Catfish Row and, learning Bess is gone, gives up. In both the play and the opera, however, the ending is more upbeat: Porgy sets out to find Bess. This allowed Gershwin to bring down the final curtain with one of his brightest spirituals. The play also compresses several of the novel's minor roles so those of Bess, Sportin' Life, and Crown can achieve more prominence. In the hands of Gershwin, Sportin' Life is less a sinister drug dealer and more a "humorous dancing villain"—as the composer related, "likable and believable and at the same time evil."[8] Sportin' Life brings an ingenious touch of comic relief to the opera, notably in his mildly sacrilegious "It Ain't Necessarily So." But what Gershwin brought to the story was more than just music. He gave it an immortality that neither novel nor play had achieved.

Like other plays of the time with black themes, the Heywards' *Porgy* was embellished with spirituals. "Throughout the entire play of the Heywards [*sic*]," wrote Charles Isaacson in the *New York Morning Telegraph* on May 30, 1928, "music is literally woven into the entire texture of the atmosphere and action. From the first curtain to the end, the negroes are singing in joy and sorrow. To eliminate the singing were to rob the production of its power." These were provocative words that would seem to have given Gershwin a running start. Indeed, portions of the lyrics and style, although not the tunes, of three songs from the play made their way into the opera. "Lullaby," with its text "hush, little baby don' yo' cry (mudder an' fadder born to die)" became the springboard for "Summertime"; "Promise Lan'" inspired the revivalist mood that closes act 1; and "Ah'm on Mah Way (to a heabenly lan')" animates the opera's poignant grand finale.[9]

Gershwin's opera is fashioned not just from spirituals but spirituals that he himself composed specifically for the opera. He had known about spirituals from spending time on Folly Beach near Charleston and listening to the music of the African Americans who inhabited James Island not far from where he stayed. Like the play, music is woven into the texture of the opera, but the opera is remarkable for the fluid way music moves throughout its dramatic fabric through aria, recitative, and an expressive vocal style that seems to lie somewhere between. Gershwin's work also features operatic voices and a symphonic orchestral score that becomes as much a part of the story as the characters themselves. Gershwin called *Porgy and Bess* a "folk opera." He had created, he told the *New York Times* on October 20, 1935, "a new form, which combines opera with theater."[10] Although the form was not as new as Gershwin claimed, America's icon of popular song—with such dazzling hits as "Swanee," "Somebody Loves Me," "S'Wonderful," "Someone to Watch Over Me," and "I Got Rhythm"— could define innovation on his own terms.

In *Porgy and Bess,* it is mainly through song that Gershwin opens the life and breath of his characters. We learn of Porgy's loneliness ("when Gawd make cripple, He mean him to be lonely") in his brief dramatic recitative in act 1, scene 1, an intense outburst set within the patter of the opera's opening crap game scene and underscoring not only Porgy's feelings but also the pathos of his life. We learn of Porgy's happiness in "I Got Plenty o' Nuttin'," his jaunty banjo song in act 2, scene 1. "It's OK if they steal the rug from the floor," he sings, "'cause the things dat I prize / Like the stars in the skies / All are free." And his melody line rises in sympathetic joy. Finally, we learn of his courage as he leaves to find Bess. "I'm on My Way" in act 3, scene 3, is about a "land" that for Porgy becomes a source of spiritual redemption.[11]

Bess, too, has important musical moments that define her character and attitudes. Often they appear in the recitatives, which have been called "potential song." One of Gershwin's most inspired dramatic passages occurs at the end of act 2, scene 2 as Bess tries to convince Crown to let her return to Porgy. She knows Porgy needs her and understands her own need for the kindness and tenderness he has shown her. "I livin' wid Porgy now, an' I livin' decent," she sings. Her torment is expressed in a brief dramatic passage of recitative as Crown grabs her forcefully, and her emotions rise to the point of despair. Then, in an anguished aria she pleads, "Oh. . . . What you want wid Bess? These five years I been yo' woman / You could kick me in the street / Then you wanted me back. . . . Oh, Crown, won't you let me go to my man."

Fortunately, Gershwin did not give in to Heyward's original preference for spoken dialogue underscored with orchestral music throughout the opera in place of recitative, as in nineteenth-century melodrama or perhaps Hayward's play. Through Gershwin's recitatives even more than his arias, singers are able to demonstrate their true expressive powers.

Like other famous lovers—Romeo and Juliet, Dido and Aeneas, and Mimi and Rodolfo—Porgy and Bess are victims of uncontrollable forces that tear at their love. Porgy is marked by disability, frustration, and jealousy and Bess by her attraction to drugs and inability to leave an abusive relationship. Yet both are elevated to heroic heights in their beautiful duets from act 2, "Bess, You Is My Woman Now" (scene 1) and "I Loves You Porgy" (scene 2). The first reflects their similar feelings of love and devotion. Puccini-style, Gershwin gives each the same or similar soaring lyrical melody. In the second duet, Bess has returned to Porgy after being with Crown. "I loves you, Porgy," she sings. "Don' let him take me, Don' let him handle me. . . . I got my man." Her vocal line is sustained and emotionally effusive, whereas Porgy's is shorter and more agitated and emphatic as he sings in counterpoint: "What you think I is, anyway / To let dat dirty houn'dog steal my woman? You got a home now, Honey, an' you got love."

Other characters—Sportin' Life, Clara, Jake, and Serena—are likewise delineated, although not as poignantly. Because the villainous Crown is given dark, ominous vocal lines and orchestral support, his folksy "Redheaded Woman" seems to mark a sudden (and misplaced) change of mood and character. Gershwin, however, draws once more on African American church practices and within Crown's jazzy tune interjects a soulful protestation from the crowd: "Lawd, don't you listen to dat Crown, Lawd!" It is a wonderful touch of dramatic contrast and musical interplay. Two minor characters, the detective in act 1, scene 2 and Archdale in act 2, scene 1, are defined by brief passages of spoken dialogue. The fleeting interpolation of a new texture and sonority within the opera effectively pits the two cold, white characters against warmer ones, African Americans, who express themselves only through song.

Choruses, whether men's, women's, or mixed, are rarely absent but play a more important role than merely adding local color or commenting on dialogue, as in many earlier operas. They enlarge the attitudes and feelings of the soloists, bringing them into sharper focus. They mourn with Serena upon the death of her man ("he's gone, gone, gone, gone, gone"); they reinforce Porgy's optimism ("got his gal, got his Lawd"); and they placate dead Clara's spirit ("Clara, Clara, don't you be downhearted"). Their frequent interjections within recitatives provide contrast as well as musical and dramatic identity. Often the choruses reflect the antiphonal and polyphonic techniques that Gershwin heard in the black churches of Charleston. Sportin' Life's "It Ain't Necessarily So" bounces along with the chorus in a call-and-response pattern. The storm scene in act 2, scene 4 opens with six different prayers being sung simultaneously by different individuals, an effect that expresses grim, barren fear unlike any other moment in the opera.

Bringing back the opera's "hit tunes" occasionally throughout the opera—à la Verdi and Puccini—not only provides the work with musical and dramatic unity but also gives the audience something to hum long after the curtain descends. If the songs are general enough in mood and not bound too closely into the libretto, they sell well as sheet music on the commercial circuit. Broadway composers understood that well. So did Gershwin. He, however, had yet another motivation. He also uses thematic recurrence for dramatic ends. The graceful "Summertime" has been called the opera's "portal," as Clara sings to her baby with flowing warmth and charm. When Bess sings the song at the opening of act 3, however, it becomes a somber reminder of Clara's death in the violent storm.

Other thematic recurrences illustrate how Gershwin allows the orchestra to share the thoughts and feelings of his characters. Two more important tunes return to accentuate Porgy's torment during his final aria or long passage of dramatic recitative. As he unwraps the red dress he bought for Bess with money won in a crap game in jail, he sings a declamatory melodic line, and underneath is the confident "I Got Plenty o' Nuttin'" from the orchestra. As his doubts and fears about the whereabouts of Bess mount, his vocal line becomes increasingly anguished. When the theme of the first love duet "Bess, You Is My Woman Now" appears in the orchestra, it is apparent that she is indeed with him, but only in his broken dreams.

The orchestra is one of the most important and colorful features of the score. Like the actors themselves, it plays a role. Instruments such as the banjo, xylophone, and tom-tom stand out in important scenes. Creating a Stravinskian effect, the occasional addition of the piano gives crowd scenes a *Petrushka*-like flavor, and moments of fear and confrontation recall the pounding frenzy of *Le sacre du printemps*.[12] Just when the orchestration glows and swirls in neoromantic bliss, moreover, Gershwin recalls the "Porgy motif," with its flatted third scale step ("blue note").[13] The orchestra also provides eclectically expressive pantomime music as Porgy stabs and kills Crown. And it sets up important passages of dialogue and recitative, very much like a film score that reaches a chilling crescendo before a murderer opens the door.

Porgy and Bess played first in Boston in a kind of trial run that began on September 30, 1935. Ten days later, on October 10, it received its premiere at New York's Alvin Theatre in a version cut to about three-quarters of its original length. Gershwin was thirty-seven. It was his final big work, and he died two years later, never realizing how successful it would become. After his death, Ira Gershwin, who wrote some of the lyrics, specified that future American productions always retain a black cast, as the original staging. For the premiere, the young baritone Todd Duncan played Porgy, and a gifted twenty-year-old Juilliard student, Anne Wiggins Brown, sang the role of Bess. Sportin' Life was played by John W. Bubbles (né John William Sublett), who created complications through being unable to read music. His pop-style vocal numbers, however, gave him a special characterization by adding contrasting sonority within the score of lush operatic voices.

Boston liked the production, but New York had problems with it. Critics could not seem to decide whether *Porgy and Bess* was an opera or a Broadway musical. Americans seemed to be floundering around for a definition of opera rather than accepting the work on its own terms. Broad-

way critics thought the recitatives were monotonous and that the work
had too much of a "conservatory twang." Opera critics such as Virgil Thomson claimed it was an example of a "libretto that should never have been
accepted on a subject that should never have been chosen by a man who
should never have attempted it."[14] African Americans argued that the opera degraded their race, and even Duke Ellington complained that "the
music does not hitch with the mood and spirit of the story."[15] Even the
dialect came under attack. Drawn from the Gullah tongue of James Island,
it was criticized for not being true to the original. Gershwin responded
by saying that he and his brother Ira were striving for flavor rather than
authenticity, just as they were in the music itself.

After a short Broadway run, *Porgy and Bess* closed. It would take several years for its treasures to take hold. In 1938 it toured the West Coast
with good reception, and in 1942 it was staged successfully with spoken
dialogue instead of recitative. To glittering reviews, it toured Europe during the 1950s, becoming America's most successful musical export. The
New York City Opera staged it for the first time in 1962, and the Metropolitan Opera in 1985. Altogether, performances of *Porgy and Bess,* both
with and without recitative, have numbered in the thousands.

Now we can stand back and see the work for what it is: a story for all
time that crosses racial lines and deals with all-too-true human emotions.
It has all the mechanics of opera—plot, staging, aria, and recitative. More
important, it has the creativity—characterization, suspense, sentiment,
melodrama, and a score filled with glorious melody. It is indeed opera and
much more. *Porgy and Bess* is Gershwin's enduring gift to his nation and a
rare legacy that has placed American opera firmly on the world's cultural
map.

The Operas of Virgil Thomson and Gertrude Stein

George Gershwin and Virgil Thomson approached the creation of opera
from opposite ends of the spectrum: Gershwin from the dramatic and
associative, Thomson from the sonorous and abstract; Gershwin from the
story, Thomson from the symbol; and Gershwin as the savvy Brooklynite,
Thomson as the homespun Missourian. Both composers, however, produced operas that are stunning milestones in American operatic history.

Gershwin and Thomson began their careers during one of the most
exciting periods in American cultural history—the Roaring Twenties, the
Jazz Age, or the New Era as it was variously called. American artists, writers, and musicians flocked to Paris to the salon of Gertrude Stein and the

studios of Nadia Boulanger and Jean Cocteau. Young composers such as George Antheil chatted in Parisian cafes with James Joyce, Ezra Pound, Pable Picasso, and other luminaries. Earlier, during the fin de siècle, the prophetic voices of Erik Satie and the symbolist poets had been generational forces of a new "libertarian" attitude toward the arts. As Roger Shattuck pointed out in his charming discourse *The Banquet Years:* "The cafe came into its own, political unrest encouraged innovation in the arts, and society squandered its last vestiges of aristocracy. The twentieth century could not wait fifteen years for a round number; it was born, yelling, in 1885."[16]

Paradoxically perhaps, it was the French, who first recognized one of the newest creative forces—American jazz. Jean Cocteau called it "une sorte de catastrophe apprivoissée" (a sort of catastrophe tamed). The sounds of jazz, blues, and ragtime permeated the work of Debussy and Stravinsky as well as that of Ravel and Milhaud. Jazz crossed and recrossed the Atlantic, gaining respectability among serious modern composers, audiences, and critics.[17]

During the interwar years, experimentation and social commentary brought new avenues of creative thought to music. The work of many American experimentalists was performed for the first time in Paris. Antheil's iconoclastic *Ballet mécanique* (1926), for example, used amplified pianola, two pianos, anvils, xylophones, drums, doorbells, and two wooden airplane propellers. "One fat bald old gentleman . . . to the glee of the audience, lashed out his umbrella, opened it and pretended to be struggling against the imaginary gale of wind," wrote Bravig Imbs about the performance. "At the end of this most sweaty concert," added Virgil Thomson, "champagne was served in great quantity, and people were very thirsty, not to say shaken and distraught."[18] For all its experimentalism, futurism, Dadaism, surrealism, cubism, and every other "ism," Paris teamed with fervid excitement. "If you are lucky enough to have lived in Paris as a young man," wrote Ernest Hemingway, "then wherever you go for the rest of your life, it stays with you, for Paris is a movable feast."[19]

It was in Paris in 1925 that Virgil Thomson (1896–1989) met Gertrude Stein (1874–1946), the radical poet from California who would become the librettist for two of his three operas. He thought that she consumed people "like tea and cookies," but he also admitted that they had much in common. Stein's often-elliptical phrasing and approach of a subject from all possible angles fascinated him. She strove to free literature from the turgidity of romanticism, not unlike others around her—the avant-garde composer Erik Satie for one. Satie's clarity, restraint, and no-frills style was often manifest in short pieces bearing such whimsical titles as "Three Pieces in the Shape of a Pear" or "Four Flabby Preludes for a Dog" (models for Thomson's *Four Saints in Three Acts* perhaps?). His interest in language is seen in certain songs in which he pokes fun at the vocalized mute *e* in sung French.

Thomson admired the new ideology of both Stein and Satie but had fresh ideas of his own. Born in Kansas City, he grew up in a simple, homespun atmosphere of hymns and folk traditions that give his operas individuality. With Stein, he worked on *Four Saints in Three Acts* during 1927 and 1928. She wrote poetry, he noted, as a composer wrote music and let the words "develop themselves through the free expansion of sound and sense. . . . I took my musical freedom," he said, "following her poetic freedom, and what came out was a virtually total recall of my Southern Baptist childhood in Missouri."[20]

Virgil Thomson. *Van Vechten Collection, Library of Congress*

Gertrude Stein. *Van Vechten Collection, Library of Congress*

With its "sassy but classy" prose style, *Four Saints* was given its premiere in Hartford, Connecticut, on February 8, 1934, by an organization called the Friends and Enemies of Modern Music. It was a great success. That same year it was staged on Broadway and in Chicago, receiving sixty performances, and has had many revivals, including a magical staging by Robert Wilson at Lincoln Center in 1996. In 1947 Stein and Thomson produced another opera, *The Mother of Us All,* which was inspired by Susan B. Anthony. Stein died the year before the opera was performed, but Virgil Thomson lived to be ninety-three. Together they had produced one of the most innovative and creative operas of the century.

Four Saints in Three Acts contains many more saints than four and one act more than three. But its almost–title suits an almost–opera that has an almost–libretto very well. There is no real plot, only a series of tableaux that depict imaginary events in the lives of the saints. Stein and Thomson set the opera in sixteenth-century Spain and chose an all-black cast because they found African Americans to have clear diction, fine carriage, and a natural approach to religious themes. The main characters are Saint Teresa (represented by two singers, a soprano and an alto, dressed alike), Saint Ignatius (baritone), and their respective confidants Saint Settlement (soprano) and Saint Chavez (tenor). The characters Commère (mezzo-soprano) and Compère (bass) comment on the progress of the opera as it moves along. Other novelties were the cellophane sets by Florine Stett-heimer and Frederick Ashton and John Houseman's choreographed stage movements.

Maurice Grosser devised and developed the opera's unusual scenario, which was far more colorful spectacle than dramaturgical melodrama. In his full-score manuscript, Grosser noted that Tableau 1 takes place at Avila in early spring: "There is a wall and a tree. St. Teresa II [is] seated under the tree painting flowers on very large eggs." In Tableau 2, "St. Teresa I [is] being photographed by St. Settlement who holds a large pigeon in her

Original Hartford production of Virgil Thomson's *Four Saints in Three Acts*. The cello-phane sets were by Florine Stettheimer. *Astor, Lenox and Tilden Foundations, New York Public Library*

hands." For Tableau 5, "St. Teresa II and St. Ignatius motionless looking at blackboard. She seated. He standing with arm around her shoulder."[21]

Throughout the opera, two choruses, one large and the other small, sing alternately such profound lines as "Saint Teresa half in and half out of doors," and in act 3 sailors and young girls with castanets dance a very unsaintly tango. There are many inside jokes. Commère sings along in a Gregorian chantlike monotone in which only one word is raised by a step: "not." Saint Ignatius's vision of the Holy Spirit, joyfully irreverent in its reference to pigeons rather than doves ("pigeons on the grass alas"), is a jaunty, old-time hymn tune spiced with syncopation drawn from the word *pigeon.* The humor throughout the work is whimsical not crass and charming not sacrilegious. Thomson's satire of grand opera draws one in irresistibly through grace of motion, beauty of voice, and elegance of musical material. If the text makes no sense as an opera libretto, the music follows suit. It is a collage, a kaleidoscope of musical styles and sounds that, like the words, forms a unique drama found in no other opera then or since.

Thomson had a true genius for understanding the important element of prosody, or the rhythm of language, in opera, a talent American opera composers often lacked. He chose melodic lines, harmonic progressions, and rhythmic momentum that tied in closely with Stein's syllables, words, phrases, and stanzas. "With the text on my piano's music rack," he said, "I would sing and play, improvising melody to fit the words and harmony for underpinning them with shape."[22] Thus Stein's "fanciful cubistic text," in Victor Yellin's term, received in the hands of Thomson music that supplied continuity that was missing in the text. As in opera not sung in English, it provided "a feeling of structure and logic even though we do not understand the words."[23]

But how would structure and logic be achieved in this zany, elusive, almost-but-not-quite opera? There are no leitmotifs, thematic recurrence is minimal, and attempts at musical characterization are equally scant although Commère and Compère mainly chant or speak. Yet both wordsounds and music-sounds play important roles in overall continuity. Whether as sound or symbol, reference to numbers provides a subliminal sense of unity: "Four saints are never three . . . four saints are leave it to me three saints when this you see"; or "ten saints can"; or "one two three four five six seven all good children go to heaven." Compère boldly announces the number of each scene. There are also tongue twisters. "Between thirty five and forty five between forty five and three five as then when when they were forty five and thirty five when they they were forty five and" sings the chorus in act 3—lines that would challenge the memory of any seasoned singer.

Singers render the text in various musical styles that dip in and out of the musical landscape like so many lightning bugs flickering on a warm summer night. It is a rapidly changing landscape to be sure. There are fleeting moments of medieval chant, old-time hymn tunes, madrigal-like choruses, and even Handel-oratorio effects. But it is the small orchestra of about twenty-five players that offers the richest continuum throughout the opera. It is spiced with alto and tenor saxophones, cymbals, snare drums, and accordion, and the sound of a harmonium frequently adds a generous early American touch.

Much of the beauty of the score lies in the sudden contrasts of voice timbres and ranges and in the myriad of sounds that some modern critics say forecast minimalism. Bravig Imbs's was no doubt the most perceptive view of the work. After hearing Thomson himself sing and play it, he reported, "We were delighted with it, enjoying its quiet humor, its drollness, its simple melodies, its lyricism, which sounded so strange and so refreshing in 1928 after all of modern music's headlong excursions into discord."[24] Thirty years later, John Cage added a word of advice about the opera. "To enjoy it," he said, "one must leap into that irrational world from which it sprang, the world in which the matter-of-fact and the irrational are one, where mirth and metaphysics marry to beget comedy. And like any other work of high comedy, it leaves few traces. It does not clutter up the memory, but it elevates the spirit."[25]

The Mother of Us All presents quite a different landscape from the earlier Stein-Thomson opera yet still bears the unmistakable signature of their style. It includes "saints"—now Americanized—and a variegated, Thomsonian score, but its libretto is less abstract. The characters, drawn mainly from nineteenth-century American history rather than sixteenth-century Spain, are closer to home. The visual elements of the opera (again by Grosser) also reflect Thomson's aims to evoke an old-fashioned parlor album. Costumes recall the hand-tinted photographs of the period, and stage movements are choreographed to suggest photographic poses that evoke a sense of nostalgia.

The music also seems familiar. "Everybody thinks he remembers the tunes, but no one knows what they are," John Cage once noted.[26] With the exception of "London Bridge," the tunes are all original and suggest those Thomson knew from his Southern Baptist–Kansas City heritage. He called the score "a memory-book of Victorian play-games and passions . . . with its gospel hymns and cocky marches, its sentimental ballads, waltzes, darned-fool ditties and intoned sermons . . . a souvenir of all those sounds and kinds of tunes that were once the music of rural America."[27] In melding Americana and touches of bitonality, Thomson would seem the dramaturgical reincarnation of Charles Ives—who never wrote an opera. On the other side of the spectrum, *The Mother of Us All* is a harbinger of W. H. Auden and Igor Stravinsky's *The Rake's Progress.*

The Mother of Us All deals with the life and career of Susan B. Anthony. It is a panorama—Thomson called it a "pageant"—of a particularly critical era in American life and also reflects Gertrude Stein's feminism. Her personal relationship with Alice B. Toklas paralleled that of Susan B. Anthony and Anna Howard Shaw, another crusader who appears in the opera as Anthony's constant companion. The large gallery of characters anachronistically juxtaposes historical figures from different eras with incongruous imaginary personalities. Most had nothing to do with the real Susan B. Anthony. They seem to address the audience more than each other, expressing what they find urgent, so interrelationships rarely develop. Their promulgations, however arcane, give the opera a message and a mission that *Four Saints* lacks. The character of "Susan B." herself—a heroine of American social concerns—also creates a dramatic pulse beyond that of *Four Saints.* Natural empathy for her is shaped by many of her lines ("I enter a tabernacle, I was born a believer in peace. I say fight for the right, be a martyr and live, be a coward and die") and by the lovely, flowing lyricism Thomson ascribes to them.

The other characters are cleverly enigmatic. They keep their distance, yet at times Thomson places them in the spotlight by virtue of his wonderful music. The dignified and somewhat pompous Daniel Webster (bass) is often given martial-sounding music; Lillian Russell (soprano), costumed in picture hats, long gloves, and feather boas, is given a waltz; Thaddeus Stevens (tenor), the political opponent of Andrew Jackson and a "tactless, blustering man," has rhythmically disjointed phrases; and Susan B. Anthony (dramatic soprano) has elegant, melodious vocal lines. The narrators, Virgil T. (baritone) and Gertrude S. (soprano), have declamatory parts similar to Commère and Compère in *Four Saints.* Among the other characters are John Adams (romantic tenor), who courts Constance Fletcher (high mezzo-soprano), a minor novelist of Stein's day. Adams cannot kneel to her, however, "because his knees are not kneeling knees." Angel More (light lyric soprano) is part ghost, part ingenue and flits about in a pale pink and blue dress, tiny wings springing from her shoulders. Ulysses S. Grant (bass); Anthony Comstock (bass), a sturdy Victorian capitalist; and ten or more solo roles complete the cast.[28]

The orchestral sonority of *The Mother of Us All,* minus the persistent harmonium sound of *Four Saints,* is more romantic and universal than *Saints* and matches the longer, more sustained vocal passages in the score. There is the usual Stein-Thomson wit, to be sure. After Daniel Webster sings "when my eyes shall be turned to behold for the last time the sun in heav'n," Susan B. and others retort, "I hate mice." The curtain abruptly descends. Some moments seem quite modern. "[Men] have kind hearts but they are afraid," begins Susan B. in a long soliloquy that opens act 2, scene 2:

> They fear women, they fear each other, they fear their neighbor, they fear other countries and then they hearten themselves in their fear by crowding together and following each other, and when they crowd together and follow each other they are brutes, like animals who stampede, and so they have written in the name male into the United States constitution, because they are afraid of black men because they are afraid of women, because they are afraid. . . . Women often have not any sense of danger, after all a hen screams frightfully when she sees an eagle but she is only afraid for her children, men are afraid for themselves, that is the real difference between men and women.

"Life is strife," Susan sings in a fortissimo reminiscence of "Rock of Ages" at the end of the opera. "I was a martyr all my life not to what I won but to what was done. Do you know because I tell you so, or do you know"—as she soars delicately to a high G—"do you know? My long life, my long life," she sings in a near-whisper. There are few lovelier or more provocative moments in all opera than these simple, poignant closing passages.

Commissioned by the Alice M. Ditson Fund, *The Mother of Us All* was given its premiere at Columbia University on May 7, 1947, with Dorothy Dow as Susan B. Anthony. It was twenty-five years before Thomson would write another opera. *Lord Byron,* his last, was staged at the Juilliard School of Music in 1972, but lacked the magic of his earlier successes. "I came to realize that writing a libretto is in the end like working inside someone else," admitted the librettist Jack Larson. "The words have to make the bird sing, or they're of no use."[29] *Lord Byron* does not have Stein's sophistication and charm. More significantly, Larson's libretto gives little opportunity for dramatic dimension or lyricism. The audience is kept at arm's length from the characters and rarely senses the romantic, mythical aspects of the aristocratic poet-hero Byron. There is no lack of distance, however, between the audience and Thomson's living, breathing, ever-joyful saints.

The Impact of Jazz

The study of jazz within so-called classical or art music has been, for the most part, limited to instrumental forms whose scores are perhaps more accessible than those of American opera. But jazz idioms gave many early-twentieth-century American operas vital new dramatic dimensions that moved them beyond outmoded melodrama and into the realms of realism, expressionism, and social commentary. Jazz carried American opera far adrift from Wagnerian riptides. Still under the powerful musical dramaturgy of late romanticism, Gershwin's *Porgy and Bess* was the most important and successful jazz-inspired opera. But there were others that have been pushed to the background of music history and performance because of their radical departure from the norms of opera. They deserve a better place.

If aspects of ragtime and blues merged with popular music in the early decades of the twentieth century, elements of all three found their way into European and American concert works. The sounds of jazz were many: the lonely blue note (the lowered third and seventh degrees in major keys) and vibrant instrumental colors—trombone glissandi, clarinet solos with high tessitura, muted brass timbres, the wailing voice of the saxophone, and the relentless rhythms of the trap drum. Syncopation and call-and-response techniques added new rhythms and textures to symphonic scores. The harmonic vocabulary of jazz enriched composers' language, leading them to the bitonal and polytonal inflections of the modern age. For many instrumental composers, jazz was the key to experimentation and innovation within a new mode of sonorous clarity. Stravinsky's *L'Histoire du soldat* (1918), Darius Milhaud's *Le Boeuf sur le toit* (1919), John Alden Carpenter's *Krazy Kat* (1921), and Louis Gruenberg's *Daniel Jazz* (1924) were only a few of the many jazz-inspired works before 1925.

There was also the *drama* of jazz, its intensity, excitement, bravura, and joy. Did opera find in jazz a new means of dramatic expression? A new method of characterization? A new libretto? New scenarios? A new way to relate opera to American life? To many, jazz meant the modern age. The critic Sigmund Spaeth wrote in 1928 that jazz was thoroughly characteristic of American civilization: "Jazz is not a form of music. It is a treatment applied to music, and . . . to modern life in general." Spaeth compared jazz with a "jazzed" life, stating that both distort the conventional and revolt against tradition.[30]

Perhaps that is why Frederick Shepherd Converse's "The Immigrants" (1914) was called a "jazz opera" at the time, although its score has little to

justify that designation. It was, however, "a distortion of the conventional" because of its focus on progressive contemporary social issues and realistic situations. It tells of the disillusionment and tragic fate of a small
group of Italian immigrants who in the early part of the twentieth century arrive in America only to find slums, deception, and, ultimately, murder ("O Liberty, when will you cease to destroy the souls that seek you?").[31]
The use of real-life characters and violent passions makes "The Immigrants"
one of America's earliest verismo operas.

"The Immigrants" was commissioned by the Boston Opera, reputedly the first opera to be specifically commissioned by a major American
company. It was never produced, however. It may have followed the fate
of *The Padrone* (1912), George W. Chadwick's opera also about Italian immigrants, which was rejected by the Metropolitan Opera for its "unsuit-
able subject matter." A few years later the Metropolitan turned down another verismo work, Frank Patterson's *A Little Girl at Play: A Tragedy of the
Slums* (1918), because its libretto was "too gruesome." Such subjects were
too real, too close to the problems of American society, to be a part of major
grand opera seasons—or so it seemed. But they played a part in the "jazzed
life" that formed the spirit of many operas of their time.

What brought verismo opera more positively into American culture,
however, was the use of jazz within musical scores themselves and not
merely for atmosphere, as the onstage jazz band in Charles Wakefield
Cadman's *Shanewis* of 1918, but for dramaturgical power and expansion.
Between 1911 and 1913, Scott Joplin and Harry Lawrence Freeman used
forms of early jazz in their operas, but not until the 1920s did it become a
trenchant vehicle for realism. Frank Harling, a prolific symphonic composer and former music director at West Point, based both *A Light from St.
Agnes* (1925) and *Deep River* (1926) on life in New Orleans.

Critics called *St. Agnes* an "American jazz opera."[32] The score includes
saxophones, banjo, xylophone, and humming, with jazzlike effects introduced into the more colorful parts of the score to enlarge realism and
dramatic characterization. Creole folk tunes run through the score, and
modal chant accentuates the story's somber religious mysticism. Occasional
stage directions ("a la foxtrot") and ragtime melodies rising from the tawdry
saloon in the Louisiana bayou characterize the heroine's "jazz [fast] life"
and her stormy relationship with her drunken, abusive lover.[33] The opera
received the Bispham Medal and played successfully in Paris, New York,
Atlantic City, and Chicago, starring Rosa Raisa, a brilliant American dramatic soprano of Polish birth.

Harling's familiarity with George Gershwin's earliest attempt at opera,

Blue Monday (1922), is unclear. Concerned with everyday African Americans in real-life situations, its libretto is set in Harlem and concerns a woman who shoots her husband on the mistaken assumption that he is about to leave her for another woman. There are popular songs, the blues and, significantly, some jazz in recitatives that undoubtedly formed the model for Gershwin's later *Porgy and Bess.* Wayne Shirley has assesed the difference between the two works, "In *Porgy and Bess,* when the characters stop the action to sing a set piece, they not only reveal their souls—something which never quite happens in *Blue Monday*—they even reveal to us something of our own."[34] And that, of course, is what opera is all about.

No composer of the time melded jazz, drama, symphony, and song quite as successfully as George Gershwin did in *Porgy and Bess.* Yet many tried. Hamilton Forrest, a twenty-eight-year-old composer from Chicago, used jazz to update an old story into a modern veristic opera. In 1930 he saw his *Camille* staged in Chicago with the city's reigning diva Mary Garden

Mary Garden, a legendary American soprano, starred in the premiere of Victor Herbert's *Natoma* and also sang in Hamilton Forrest's *Camille. Astor, Lenox and Tilden Foundations, New York Public Library*

in the title role. Recreating the Paris of 1930, *Camille* was a modernized version of the Dumas play, which also inspired Verdi's *La traviata*. It included a fox-trot, rumba syncopations, and a blues song, "La Parisienne." "If we write music in America with feeling for our present culture," asserted Forrest, "we must write jazz. . . . It can be the highest type of culture."[35] Ironically, Forrest's high American culture was realized in a foreign tongue. To satisfy Mary Garden, who commissioned the opera, Forrest wrote the libretto in French.

Surrealism and Angry Agitprop: Antheil and Blitzstein

If jazz for Hamilton Forrest was a vehicle of high culture, it became a method of satire in the hands of George Antheil and Marc Blitzstein. For them, it served symbolic political ends. During the haunting years of depression and war, jazz became a snarling voice of social protest. Operas of the era were often experimental, even iconoclastic. With their spoken dialogue, new staging techniques, and unconventional scores, they led critics to question whether they were even operas at all.

For George Antheil, both film techniques and jazz idioms shaped the messages of his opera *Transatlantic* (Frankfurt, 1930), a Dadaistic and surrealistic satire about an American presidential election. The opera is played out mainly through Homeric and quasi-allegorical characters: Hector, the heroic candidate of the Demopublican Party; Helen, a thoroughly modern woman; and Ajax, an unscrupulous political boss. Antheil originally wrote *Transatlantic* as *Glare,* a serious romantic work involving a melodramatic love triangle. But when *Glare* finally emerged in its revised form, it was totally different—a burlesque of the modern American temperament and a glorification of the machine age modeled after the *Zeitoper* ("timely opera") of Ernst Krenek, Kurt Weill, and Paul Hindemith. In the zeitoper manner, *Transatlantic* weaves many aspects of the era into its plot: a presidential parade, cocktails, revue dancing, neon signs ("Arrow shirts"), typists, a Salvation Army band, and even a soprano who sings an aria in the bathtub. Antheil worked in Germany during the 1920s and well knew the experimental theater movement of the Weimar Republic—a cultural rage that diminished only when Adolf Hitler's reactionary policies toward society began to take hold in 1934.

Antheil was not yet thirty when he composed *Transatlantic,* the same point in life as two other young jazz aficionados of the 1920s, Hamilton Forrest and George Gershwin. In Germany as well as France, jazz was an art of the young. It symbolized America, a young nation—modern, vital,

George Antheil, the ex-
perimentalist who star-
tled many with esoteric
sounds and instrumenta-
tion, at a "steam piano."
George Antheil Archives

exciting, and emboldened by the exigencies of a frenetic lifestyle. *Transat-lantic* refers to jazz often throughout its three acts. The "Tempo di Tango" of act 1, scene 2, picked up later in vocal lines, is colored by the persistent rhythmic connotations of seduction and male sexual aggression.[36] A "Jazz-Chorus" participates in act 2, and in act 3 rapid, syncopated shimmies accompany a revue dancer who, as narrator, provides continuity throughout the opera.

What is most interesting—and must have been problematic for producers of the time—is not *Transatlantic*'s score but its staging. The last act comprises twenty-eight different, very short scenes—a brilliant feat of original design that required four simultaneous stage settings and a large

central motion picture screen. Antheil felt the film techniques in his opera were important to both his visual and musical conceptions for a work
that is a continuous piece and moves from scene to scene rather than exists as separate numbers. Thus, although the four rooms were on different
parts and planes of the stage, characters could move about freely from one
to the other by means of connecting staircases. The upper rooms were a
bathroom, described in the score as "very chic . . . very modern and brilliant," and Jason and Helen's apartment, later a hospital room. The two lower
sets were Ajax's office, suggesting "big business, steel," and Hector's hotel
room, which becomes his hiding place. As events in the drama dictated,
different sets ("rooms") would be lighted, some simultaneously. At the same
time, newspaper headlines and motion picture clips would be appearing
on the screen, some in the new slow motion.[37] With its rapidly changing
scenes, nervous visuals, and continuous action, *Transatlantic* fascinated audiences. But was it opera? Many wondered.

Like *Transatlantic,* Marc Blitzstein's *The Cradle Will Rock* (1937) is a moral
fable. Both operas, products of the socially conscious 1920s and 1930s, reflect

The innovative set by Ludwig Sievert from the last act of Antheil's *Transatlantic* (1930).
George Antheil Archives

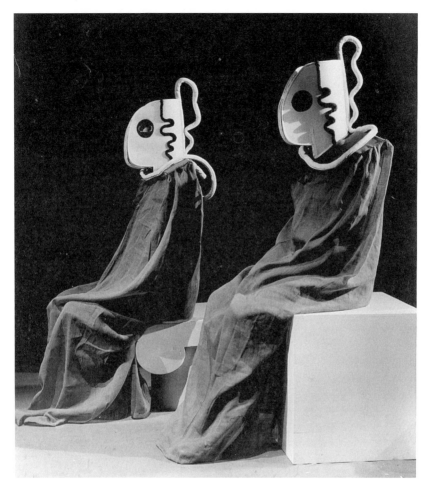

Costumes by Frederick Kiesler for Antheil's *Helen Retires,* which was given its world premiere by the Juilliard School of Music on March 1, 1934. *Photo by Samuel Gottscho, The Juilliard School Archives*

Gebrauchsmusik ("useful" music) and target middle-class audiences. Although parody and satire form the fabric of both works, Antheil's attitudes are expressed in an undertone and Blitzstein's in a shout. Dedicated to Bertolt Brecht, *The Cradle Will Rock* is an angry, non-Aristotelian epic and a product of the agitprop (agitation and propaganda) ideology prevalent in German-speaking workers' theater in New York during the 1930s.[38] Agitprop plays were constructed in several episodes, had satiric cartoon-

like characters, and featured singing actors who spoke directly to the audience—all elements of *The Cradle Will Rock*. Blitzstein's opera, Virgil
Thomson observed, was "the most appealing socialism since *Louise,* and
not without serious power."[39]

Through popular, vaudevillelike songs, clever dialogue, and nonoper-
atic vocal styles, Blitzstein manages to reach out to his audience even
though characters seem oddly detached from each other and the story. The
protagonists are a prostitute, a young organizer, and a "Mr. Mister" whose
Liberty Committee of upright citizens supposedly has "prostituted itself."
The "cradle," of course, is the cradle of liberty, dangerously jeopardized
by the repressive forces of wealth and the status quo. Brecht believed the
performance demanded virtuosity and "couldn't be played by amateurs."
But, he added, it should have "the virtuosity of the cabaret."[40]

Set in Steeltown, U.S.A., *The Cradle Will Rock* is in one act of ten scenes
or episodes that represent various segments of American life—a street
corner, night court, drugstore, hotel lobby, faculty room, "Dr. Specialist's"
office, and the like. "What I really wanted to talk about," Blitzstein emphasized, "was the middle class—the way the intellectual, the professional
and the small shop-keeper were treated by 'big business.'"[41] Thus each scene
challenges some kind of social injustice and the way in which Mr. Mister
corrupts those around him—generally through money. "Of course it's
peace we're for," Dr. Salvation preaches in the mission scene. "This is war
to end the war." "I can see the market rising like a beautiful bird," Mrs.
Mister adds. To which Dr. Salvation calls out in singsong, "Co—llection!"

What ties the opera together is the cumulative effect of its scenes. There
is a certain force of passion that carries the audience along, and the powerful imagery throughout the opera escalates in unrelenting defiance until the final chorus thunders jubilant protest:

> No wonder those stormbirds
> Seem to circle around you!
> Well, you can't climb down and you can't sit still
> That's a storm that's going to last until
> The final wind blows . . . and when the wind blows . . .
> The cradle will rock!

Film techniques in the opera come not only from flashbacks and
montages but also from the imagery of the music itself. Blizstein's concepts of composition illustrate the strong ties between the musical dramaturgy in film and opera:

In *The Cradle Will Rock* I wrote a song called "The Nickel Under the Foot." It was supposed to have a kind of tender cynicism, stating without rancor that in this our world, everything depends on the "nickel under your foot." At one point in the action I introduced the song sung down front as an accompaniment to what was ostensibly a friendly conversation. Actually a scene of venal and unsavory corruption was going on. You got that finally from the conversation itself; but you got it first from the juxtaposition of the song with the conversation. This can be called counterpoint-fore-ground.[42]

Blitzstein's *Cradle* was only one of the many artworks of the time that sought to portray social justice, works ranging from WPA murals to plays such as Clifford Odets's *Waiting for Lefty* (1936). The Federal Theater Project, an arm of Franklin Delano Roosevelt's liberal New Deal, sponsored many projects, including *The Cradle Will Rock*. *Cradle* was produced by John Houseman and directed by Orson Welles, the team that created the popular *Macbeth* the year before. Although reputedly fourteen thousand seats had already been sold for the premiere, the Federal Theater withdrew support at the last minute, fearing political repercussions, and the theater was closed. Undaunted, Blitzstein and company collected a truck and a piano, found another theater (the Venice, twenty blocks uptown), and led the audience up Sixth Avenue and into the new venue. Blitzstein and his piano were placed onstage, but the performers had to skirmish around union legalities by sitting in the house and, as their cues came, walking to the edge of the stage.[43] There they sang their scenes. It was the most unusual opera premiere since *Parsifal* came to the Metropolitan Opera in 1903 amid Cosima Wagner's lawsuit and the wrath of the Child Protection League forcing the boys' chorus to enter the house through a secret back entrance.

The Cradle Will Rock received nineteen more performances following its premiere. When it was revived in 1960 at the New York City Opera, one critic complained that it was "not by any stretch of the aesthetic definition an opera, and therefore ought to have been left to Broadway (if Broadway wants it)."[44] Still, it underlines Blitzstein's premise that "music in the theatre can be a powerful, an almost immorally potent weapon."[45] It also shows that the messages of the opera—like the human traits in *Porgy and Bess*—are timeless. In mirroring the times as he saw them, Blitzstein succeeded in gleaning the essential elements of "avarice and principle, of courage and cowardice, of honor and duplicity," observed Aaron Copland. He also gave a new tone to American opera. "He was the first American composer to invent a vernacular musical idiom that sounded convincing when heard from the lips of the man-in-the-street. This is no small accomplishment, for without it no truly indigenous opera is conceivable."[46]

Copland's profound comment can be augmented. Like the harlequinade, in which popular dance music drives gesture and action, Blitzstein's realization of music's inherent powers to motivate the messages of opera brought fresh new identity to the theatrical arts of the nation at a critical time in its history.

⤝⤞

The era between 1925 and 1940 was one of the most extraordinary in American opera because of its broad range of styles and diversity of subjects. From the Indianist *Winona* in Minnesota to the Wagnerian *King's Henchman* at the Metropolitan, from *Four Saints* in Hartford to *Porgy and Bess* on Broadway, and from *Transatlantic* in Frankfurt to *The Cradle Will Rock* in New York—all had richness and power and an American imprint that defined the nation's culture and spirit. As Ethan Mordden observes, "The praiseworthy American works respond less to tradition and continuity than to the one moment that they themselves create. . . . How unlike are the great American operas—unlike anything at all, including each other."[47] For all their diversity, one vital element—jazz—not only united many of these works but also gave them their most daring and endearing attribute. For it was America's indigenous music—the kaleidoscopic sounds and colors of jazz and its related popular forms—that brought realism to its librettos, depth to its characters, and joy to its musical scores. American opera would never be the same.

12

The Impact of Mass Media

If I find myself tending in composition largely towards writing music for voices, for the theater, for films, for radio and television, it is because I am a product of my time—and my time is one of urgency and direct communication.
   —Marc Blitzstein, January 18, 1948

LEOPOLD STOKOWSKI, grandiloquent conductor and showman, may have had the audacity to present the first American staging of Alban Berg's *Wozzeck* in 1931, but his innovations in opera were not only artistic but technological as well. He planned to revolutionize grand opera by means of a new scientific process. As Wagner banished his orchestra from sight, Stokowski would hide his singers. Only mimes would be seen onstage. How would that be achieved? "The visual and oral parts, or music drama, will be synchronized by means of a new process on which Mr. Stokowski has been collaborating with two groups of scientists," reported the *New York Times* on October 4, 1932. "Thus, in an exacting and exhausting opera, such as *Tristan and Isolde,* it would be a simple matter to have a fresh Tristan to sing each act, because science could alter the sound of their voices to such an extent that an audience would not know the difference."

But science and opera worked together to achieve far more positive ends than Stokowski's obtuse dabblings. Through radio, recordings, and television, opera found an exciting new theatrical venue—the home audience. Advances in technology and mass media provided new avenues of dissemination for opera and new artistic challenges that would change the way opera in America was shaped, transformed, perceived, and accepted. As DuBose Heyward argued: "It is the fashion in America to lament the prostitution of art by the big magazine, the radio, the moving pictures. With this I have little patience. Properly utilized, the radio and the pictures may be to the present-day writer what his prince was to Villon, the king of Bavaria was to Wagner."[1]

In 1920, when station KDKA of Pittsburgh began the first regular broadcasting service, there were not more than five thousand receiving sets in the United States. By 1924 that figure had increased to 2,500,000. A listener could bring distant events into the living room now, as a poem in *The New Yorker* attested:

> He was a distance fiend,
>   A loather of anything near.
> Though WOOF had a singer of opera fame,
> And WOW a soprano of national name,
> He passed them both up for a Kansas quartet
> A thousand miles off and hence "harder to get."
>   New York was too easy to hear.
>   He was a distance fiend . . .[2]

Entertainment, particularly comedy and drama, played an important role in radio's golden age during the 1930s and 1940s. It was the era of Fibber McGee and Molly, Charlie McCarthy, Eddie Cantor, and the new vaudeville radio—all made even more "golden" by networks and broadcast advertising, a form of commercialization known as "sponsoritis." For American opera composers, radio provided a new, broad-ranging opportunity for work and recognition. It is significant that among the first operas to be broadcast were those by American composers. Coming live from the Metropolitan Opera was Deems Taylor's *The King's Henchman,* aired in 1927 on the newly begun CBS radio network. Others followed between 1929 and 1934 during the entrepreneurial Gatti-Casazza period: *Cleopatra's Night, Peter Ibbetson, Emperor Jones,* and *Merry Mount.*[3] These were important years for opera on the radio. In 1931 the Metropolitan Opera broadcasts were inaugurated; still enjoying support by Texaco, they reflect an enduring business-arts friendship.

The most interesting early radio-opera phenomenon, however, was that new works were written specifically for radio transmission—"blind operas" or "nonvisual operas" as they were called during the early days. The first of these, Charles Sanford Skilton's *The Sun Bride,* inspired by a Native American legend, was aired by NBC on April 17, 1930. Two years later, on October 3, 1932, Charles Wakefield Cadman's *The Willow Tree* was broadcast.[4] Although details of *The Willow Tree* are no longer extant, the opera appears to have been like most radio operas, shorter than staged productions and with a simple plot, small cast, and chamber orchestra.[5] Although many of these early works were viewed as curiosities, others, such as the three CBS commissions of Vittorio Giannini (1903–66)—*Flora* (1937), *Beauty and the Beast* (1938), and *Blennerhasset* (1939)—are well-structured small musical dramas that brought national recognition to one of the era's

Deems Taylor (center) with cast from the Metropolitan Opera world premiere of *The King's Henchman* (1927), the first opera aired by the new CBS radio network. *Metropolitan Opera Archives*

most exacting, dynamic composers. Giannini's lyrical *Taming of the Shrew* (1953, after Shakespeare), although not originally composed for radio, won the New York Critics Circle Award in 1955 for both its radio and its television presentations. In three acts, it was the first full-length opera by an American to be televised.[6]

Because it relied heavily upon the audience's imagination and abilities to visualize, the dramatic potential of radio opera was limited. Narrators often had to explain the action, or composers would sometimes write resumes before each scene to avoid confusing listeners with long, incomprehensible skeins of singing. One approach to such challenges was Gian Carlo Menotti's *The Old Maid and the Thief,* commissioned by NBC and aired on April 22, 1939. In this "Grotesque Opera in Fourteen Scenes'" as Menotti called it, each scene is prefaced with a brief description of the action "For Radio Presentation Only." Before scene 3, for example, listeners learn that "Bob's breakfast is ready and Laetitia proudly carries the heaping tray into the guest room where Bob lies drowsily in bed."[7] The opera is an airy little drama embellished with commedia dell'arte characters and a touch of the phantasmal harlequinade—although not without its own brand of misogyny. "The devil couldn't do what a woman can, make a thief of an honest man" sings Bob in what is an early, although superficial, manifestation of Menottian moralizing. That questioning of faith would develop and darken in the later, mature operas of this most distinguished dean of American opera.

Gian Carlo Menotti and His Followers

Radio opened a vast new market for opera—a market that accented short, lyrical, dramatic operas that had small casts and orchestras, were easy to produce, and would appeal to adults and children alike. But if radio encouraged new audiences, television captured them. It not only emphasized opera's visual elements but also enlarged and heightened them. Audiences were drawn into the heart of the action with new intimacy and immediacy. Small details, the count in *Figaro* pricking his finger on a pin or Pamina's portrait in *Magic Flute,* can be effective. Yet too much emphasis on sensation, which is tempting because of advances in technology (soldiers crushing Salome under their shields, supernatural images, electronic wizardry, glitzy stage effects, and arcane camera angles) can be distracting, overpowering the music and the ultimate dramatic message. As Menotti once said, "Opera is not a theater of action, but a theater of contemplation."[8]

Contemplation, the ability of opera to make people more human when they leave the theater than when they walked in, is at the heart of Menotti's operas. When NBC commissioned him to compose the first opera for American television, *Amahl and the Night Visitors* (1951), he had already achieved wide recognition for his darker-hued *The Medium* (1946) and *The Consul* (1950), the first two of only five full-length (or three-act) works among Menotti's twenty-five operas. *Amahl and the Night Visitors* set the stage for numerous short operas that would follow over the decades and gave new visibility and dramatic viability to the growing genre of children's opera— or, in a broader sense, family opera. Yet no opera commissioned for television achieved anywhere near the fame of *Amahl,* and its widespread influence was felt far into the 1950s and beyond. Menotti composed at least eight of the engaging works after *Amahl,* among them *Help, Help, the Globolinks!* (1968), *The Egg* (1976), *Chip and His Dog* (1979), and *The Boy Who Grew Too Fast* (1982). In these operas, Menotti displayed more than mere humor and imagery. His dramatic moodiness, subtle imagination, and deft characterization contributed significantly to U.S. presence as a world leader in operas written expressly for children.

Gian Carlo Menotti was born in Cadegliano on Lake Lugano, Italy, on July 7, 1911, the sixth of ten children. He was eleven when he wrote his first opera, *The Death of Pierrot,* in which, as he says, everyone was a musician and everyone died. Although he came to the United States at age eighteen to study at the Curtis Institute of Music in Philadelphia, his earliest training was in Italy. While still in his teens at the Milan Conservatory, he watched and absorbed all the great formative figures of his time—Mahler, Ravel, Stravinsky, Debussy, and especially Puccini. As with Puccini—and indeed the Italian tradition from Claudio Monteverdi onward—warm, singable melody was always at the core of Menotti's thinking. "When prose cannot say a thing, you turn to poetry," he said. "When poetry cannot say it, you must sing it out. The aim is to reach deep into

Gian Carlo Menotti.
*Astor, Lenox and Tilden
Foundations, New York
Public Library*

the human heart. Melody does that."[9] Yet melodies "that sing themselves" were only part of the picture. Menotti was also a master in creating wonder, suspense, and action through musical imagery.

In *Amahl and the Night Visitors,* almost every aspect of Menotti's dramatic style, both earlier and later, is evident. To understand the nature of grand opera, one need not look much further than this small, bright jewel. It contains fantasy, humor, desperation, self-sacrifice, compassion, joy, and love—a love far more universal than merely the romantic melodramatic kind. There are relationships between mother and son, king and pauper, and man and God. And a ubiquitous element of human frailty, both emotional and physical, brings the audience close to the characters. They question their faith and existence. They argue, they dance, and they share—all in the span of an hour.

Amahl was inspired by *The Adoration of the Magi,* a painting by Hieronymus Bosch that brought back memories of Menotti's childhood Christmases in Italy. He composed the opera in only a few weeks, writing both score and libretto, as he preferred to do for all his operas. Menotti also staged the opera himself, allowing the audience to experience its imagery in the sets and costumes. "The stage is divided into two areas," he outlines in his notes in the score. "One is the interior of the shepherd's hut where Amahl and his mother live. . . . The wood and the stone of the hut have aged and weathered into the hues of grey, brown, and green which bespeak poverty. . . . Snow lies softly on the ground. The night sky is pierced by many stars, but the Star of the East with its flaming tail flood both sky and earth with a glowing radiance."[10] The plain homespun garments that Amahl, his mother, and the shepherds wear, moreover, are a distinct visual contrast with the rich, colorful robes of the Three Kings.

The story takes place on Christmas Eve and concerns a poor crippled boy and his mother who are visited by the Three Kings on their long journey to see the Christ Child. When the half-starved mother tries to steal the gold intended for the Christ Child ("for my child . . . for my child"), King Kaspar tells her compassionately, "Oh, woman, you may keep the gold. The child we seek doesn't need our gold. On love alone he will build his kingdom." In gratitude, Amahl offers the kings his crutch for the Christ Child, and in so doing he miraculously begins to walk. Amazed and overjoyed, he joins the kings on their journey, to the opening music of the opera and the plaintive tune of his shepherd's pipe.

Because the opera is short, its unifying metaphors are especially clear—the generosity of the poor, the compassion of the rich, and the universal joy of giving. One of the loveliest moments in the opera is an ensemble

Menotti's *Amahl and the Night Visitors* (1951), with the original mother and son, Rosemary Kuhlman and Chet Allen. *Astor, Lenox and Tilden Foundations, New York Public Library*

sung by the kings and the mother as they describe a child who has great meaning in their lives. Each sings the same melody, a haunting descending line with modal, oriental–like hues, but "the child" in each case is different. Or is he? To the characters, and to humanity, he is the same. The music tells that, and voices soar together in affirmation on the final words of the ensemble. "Guide" refers to the king's eastern star, and "Amahl" to a mother's only child:

> *The Kings:*
> Have you seen a child the color of wheat the color of dawn?
> His eyes are mild, His hands are those of a King, as King He was born.
> Incense, myrrh, and gold we bring to His side,
> and the Eastern Star is our guide. . . .

The Mother:
Yes, I know a child the color of wheat, the color of dawn.
His eyes are mild, his hands are those of a King, as King he was born.
But no one will bring him incense or gold, though sick and poor and
     hungry and cold.
He's my child, my son, my darling, my own.[11]

It is impossible to pinpoint an American "school" of opera composition. If there were one, it would no doubt be that of Menotti and his fol-
lowers. In 1955 Lukas Foss (b. 1922) wrote a children's opera, also commissioned by NBC television, called *Griffelkin,* a small gem infused with
dark messages illuminated by a witty and graceful score. Menotti's influence
was most direct, however, in the operas of his pupils Lee Hoiby (b. 1926)
and Stanley Hollingsworth (b. 1924). Chilling, moody, and macabre, their
early operas conjure up images of their teacher's *The Medium* and *The Consul*
along with Alfred Hitchcock films of the 1950s.

Hollingsworth's *La grande Bretèche* (1957), commissioned by NBC-TV,
represents a special period in American television opera and brought new
and serious dimensions to the genre. In only a forty-five-minute dramatic episode, a countess hastily hides her lover in a closet just as her husband
returns home. After hearing her swear on a crucifix that no one is in the
closet, her husband orders a servant to wall up the door with bricks. By
morning the distraught countess has gone insane.

But for drama, mysticism, and murder none of the one-act works equals
Lee Hoiby's eerie first opera *The Scarf* (1955). Based on Chekhov's *The Witch*
(the opera's first title), *The Scarf* tells the story of Miriam, a lovely young
woman whose occult powers are symbolized by a red scarf she has woven
at her spinning wheel. Like the weaving of the Norns in Wagner's *Ring*
and the scarf in Ernest Carter's *White Bird,* Hoiby's symbol suggests the
twists and turns of fate. The beautiful scarf intended for the young woman's lover ultimately becomes the satanic weapon she uses to strangle her
betrayed husband.

Menotti's hand in shaping the dramatic imagery of *The Scarf* can be seen
in several aspects of the work, especially its final scene. Before the world
premiere of *The Scarf* at Menotti's Festival of Two Worlds at Spoleto, Italy,
he suggested a more passionate and rapid denouement. The original story by Chekhov portrays Russian peasant life and the miseries of prear-
ranged marriages. Hoiby and his librettist Harry Duncan decided to make
Miriam's nature and motivations more satanic and bring the opera closer
to Menotti's compelling characterization of Madame Flora in *The Medi-*

um. In Chekhov, the heroine is a victim of society's outmoded customs and her jealous husband's cruel insinuations. In the opera, she becomes a practitioner of witchcraft, and her scarf is a unifying visual symbol throughout the opera. How important a visual symbol can become in staged drama is apparent in the opera's final moments. As Miriam cries out for her lover in her lonely little hovel on a snowy night, one end of the scarf is in her hand. The other end is clutched by her husband, who lies dead on the floor. What was to be Miriam's freedom is now her prison.

Hoiby assisted his mentor with the orchestration of *The Consul,* which Menotti composed in 1949, and later with *The Saint of Bleecker Street* and *Maria Golovin.* He also created his own very personal and expressive operatic style. The three characters of *The Scarf* are given inner life through the libretto—strengthened by alliteration and poetic imagery ("I know that when your *b*lood is *b*urning we're *b*ound to have *b*ad weather")—and the music.[12] Orchestral colors often illuminate character and theatrical moments such as the opera's centerpiece, Miriam's aria, which employs a flute obbligato to suggest her detachment from reality (à la Lucia). The celeste and the piano are prominent in Hoiby's operas, from *The Scarf* to *Summer and Smoke* and *The Tempest.* The husband's motif in *The Scarf,* for example, is often given to the celeste.[13] Menotti's influence is apparent in Hoiby's sonorous, transparent orchestration (twenty-six players for the Spoleto premiere) and in the intensification of orchestral colors at key climactic points, sometimes doubled at the unison or octave in the Italian verismo tradition. In 1959 *The Scarf* was given its American premiere by the New York City Opera with Patricia Neway. It has since been performed in Japan, Australia, Italy, Germany, and the Netherlands as well as in many parts of the United States.[14]

Despite the extraordinary success of *Amahl and the Night Visitors,* Menotti wrote only one other television opera, *The Labyrinth,* which NBC produced on March 3, 1963. It was not especially successful. In one act, it is a symbolic journey through life, and its allegory was lost in a maze of video trickery and electronic sounds—the elements Menotti disparaged when he conceived *Amahl:*

Cinema, television, and radio seem rather pale substitutes for the magic of the stage. This is the reason why, in writing *Amahl and the Night Visitors,* I intentionally disregarded the mobility of the screen and limited myself to the symbolic simplicity of the stage. The spectator who takes no journey and has no appointed time or seat but, carelessly clad, sits casually on the first available chair in his living room, and who, knitting or perhaps

playing with the kitten, turns on what he takes to be a theatrical performance, will never know the emotion of a real theatrical experience. The
theater must be a choice—a carefully made appointment. Machiavelli, even
after he retired to the country, used to don his most elaborate and richest
clothes before setting to work on his books. Symbolically, at least, every
artist does the same. He addresses you in utter dignity, whether his message be comic or tragic—and to partake in his experience you must share
this seriousness and receive his message wearing your "Sunday clothes."[15]

Chamber Opera

Menotti's "Sunday" operas, however carefully appointed, became part of
the American theatrical experience in their more accessible, "week-day"
guise. Short television operas, simple to stage and with appealing stories,
instigated opera workshops on college and university campuses that reached
far across the nation. Many of these academic workshops were established
by enterprising émigrés who had fled Europe during or shortly after World
War II. By the early 1950s, the ratio of college workshops to professional
organizations had jumped from one in five to two out of three. The training
they provided for young singers and composers, as well as the development of a new, grass-roots audience, proved invaluable for the course of
opera in the United States.

Short operas with small casts and orchestras were sometimes called
"chamber operas," and their appeal to the mass media and college workshops extended in various ways to community theater as well. Two important women wrote creatively for small-theater audiences during the
1920s and 1940s: Eleanor Everest Freer (1864–1942) from Chicago and Amy
Marcy Beach (1867–1944) from New England. While Freer has been largely
forgotten, Beach, whose reputation continues to grow, was one of America's earliest woman composers to gain widespread recognition for her
large-scale works. Eleanor Freer, however, deserves more attention than
she has received, both as a composer and as an early champion of American music, especially opera.

In the early years of the century, Chicago was especially attuned to
opera and the dissonant bustle of the performing arts. Music was everywhere. One could hear King Oliver's Jazz Band at the Royal Gardens, John
Alden Carpenter at the Chicago Symphony, and Mary Garden at the opera.
"Come and show me another city with lifted head singing so proud to
be alive and coarse and strong and cunning," wrote Carl Sandburg. In its
own special way, one quite different from New York's, Chicago carried

opera on its "big shoulders." Within this cultural mélange, Eleanor Everest Freer stands out as a composer and philanthropist who brought more than one hundred American operas representing in excess of sixty composers to the community's attention. "She has waged 'war,'" asserted Agnes Greene Foster, "a bloodless revolution in their behalf, sacrificing her own work, her time, energy and money."[16]

How Freer waged her "bloodless revolution" is a story worth retelling. After the American baritone David Bispham died, Freer established the Opera in Our Language Foundation to promote American opera, a cause Bispham had also championed throughout his life. In 1924 the foundation became the American Opera Society of Chicago, and Freer was its first president. Before she died in 1942, the society had awarded the David Bispham Memorial Medal to more than fifty composers of operas in English. They included Charles Wakefield Cadman, Frank Patterson, Victor Herbert, Jane van Etten, William Lester, Deems Taylor, Mary Carr Moore, Otto Luening, Clarence Cameron White, Virgil Thomson, George Antheil, George Gershwin, Ernst Bacon, Douglas Moore, and many others.[17] Several Bispham Medal scores were Chicago's—and the nation's—finest, most forward-looking, early verismo works: Harling's jazz-oriented *A Light from St. Agnes* and Forrest's *Camille;* Carter's disturbing *The White Bird* set in an Adirondack hunting camp; and Cadman's brooding *Witch of Salem.* Twelve of the operas Gatti-Casazza staged at the Metropolitan Opera received Bispham Medals. Smiliar to the ideals of John F. Kennedy four decades later, Freer's words seem prophetic: "As art is the expression of the life and thoughts of a people, it must be developed, or a Nation passes, leaving no trace behind. Do we wish such a fate for our country?"[18]

The operas Freer composed are a form all their own—a type of staged song cycle that seems to expand on the colorful sense of prosody and dramatic imagery in many of her songs. Among her compositions are more than 150 songs, the best of which are the cycles *Five Songs to Spring, Six Songs to Nature,* and *Sonnets from the Portuguese,* which she reworked in her operas. The arpeggios and various pianistic figurations in the vocal scores of the operas define character and changing dramatic action, reflecting the accompaniment style of her songs. In *The Brownings Go to Italy* (1936), based on the couple's love during the period of Italy's unification, Freer associates Robert Browning with a repeated triplet figure and Elizabeth Browning with flowing arpeggios, textures that shift and meld in harmonic coloring throughout the opera.

All of Freer's chamber operas are in one act and have up to four scenes. She wrote her own librettos for several of the operas, but not all were orchestrated.[19] Her musical style remains much the same for all the operas, basically tonal and embellished with chromaticism and seventh-chords, although their subjects, locales, and plots are varied. Many, such as *Massimilliano, the Court Jester,* (1925), *A Legend of Spain* (1931), *Joan of Arc* (1929), and *A Christmas Tale* (1928), deal with fantasy and legend or some of the darker, more tragic aspects of human existence.[20] They were performed in modest venues—community arts clubs and similar organizations from Chicago to Lincoln, Nebraska, and from Charleston, West Virginia, to Philadelphia. And in this regard, they make their primary mark within the history of opera as fresh, novel contributions to American society—among the earliest examples of the form.

Like Eleanor Freer, Amy Marcy Beach (1867–1944), often known as Mrs. H. H. A. Beach, was a late arrival within the sphere of opera. Freer was fifty-seven when she wrote her first opera, and Beach was sixty-five. Beach wrote an especially fine piano concerto in 1899 and the notable

Amy Marcy Beach. *Astor, Lenox and Tilden Foundations, New York Public Library*

Gaelic Symphony (1894) but only one opera. *Cabildo* is a semihistorical account of the imprisonment and escape of the pirate Pierre Lafitte from the Cabildo in New Orleans during the War of 1812. It contains an abundance of traditional Creole tunes, and several recurring motival associations identify its main characters.[21] The opera was first performed on December 27, 1945, by students and faculty at the University of Georgia at Athens and remains an excellent dramatic vehicle for young singers and directors.

The Devil and Daniel Webster *and* The Medium

From Arnold Franchetti in Hartford to Carl Venth in Texas, the college and community opera movement afforded careers in music theater to many composers in various regions of the nation. For others, it represented their earliest forays into opera. But the short opera was often more than mere *Gebrauchsmusik* (music to serve society). It had an inner life of its own, and its special form attracted some of the nation's most prominent composers. Kurt Weill's lyrical *Down in the Valley* (1948) abounds in folk tunes, barndance rhythms, and church music that make it accessible to audiences young and old. Aaron Copland claimed he wrote his well-crafted one-act *Second Hurricane* (1937) to provide repertoire for school music organizations, which he noticed were showing remarkable growth throughout the country. These short operas, and also operas by many others, tell much about American composers and their interest in the nation's talented youth.

Short operas also have the added advantage of being able to pair with another work of modest length to form a full and varied evening's entertainment. At the New York City Opera in 1958, for example, Leonard Bernstein's *Trouble in Tahiti* formed an interesting double bill with Mark Bucci's *Tale for a Deaf Ear,* both being about marital difficulties. Pairing Douglas Moore's *Devil and Daniel Webster* and Gian Carlo Menotti's *The Medium* opens a special world of symbolism, irony, and spiritual searching—one from a folksy American field of vision and the other from the dramatic depth of the Italian melodrama. Both are staples in modern operatic repertory and are among the most widely performed of all American operas. Although their approach to pitting fantasy against reality differs considerably, they are notable examples of the shorter operatic genre and its enduring significance in American theatrical life.

Douglas Moore (1893–1969), who was chair of Columbia University's music department from 1940 to 1962, composed twelve operas. Most were concerned in some way or another with rural or pioneer American

life, notably the popular *Ballad of Baby Doe,* which some call the quintes-
sential American opera. Moore's one-act *Devil and Daniel Webster* is based
on Stephen Vincent Benet's popular short story about a New Hampshire
farmer, Jabez Stone, who makes a Faustian pact with the devil because he
wants "clothes from a city store, and a big, white house with a big front
door."[22] He also wants to be a state senator. The devil comes to his wedding to the lovely Mary. Accompanied by a discordant violinist (hence the
devil's name, "Mr. Scratch") whose tuning and fiddling à la "Danse Macabre" (and *L'histoire du soldat*) become a characteristic symbol throughout the opera, the devil seeks to collect his due.

Scratch then summons a jury of "American ghosts": "There's Blackbeard Teach, the pirate Fell, Smeet the strangler, hot from hell. Dale, who
broke men on the wheel, Morton of the tarnished steel." His mundane
lines contrast with the eloquent ones of Daniel Webster, who comes to
plead for Stone: "Freedom is the bread and the morning and the risen sun.
It was for freedom that we came in the boats and in the ships. . . . . Have
you forgotten this? Have you forgotten the forest, the rustle of the forest,
the free forest?" As the ghosts vanish and the devil is driven out of New
Hampshire, the chorus sings in celebration: "We'll drive old Scratch
away. . . . He can't come here for his codfish balls! . . . . Pie for breakfast,
pie! Apple, pumpkin, mince and raisin. . . . New England's pride."

The American flavor of *The Devil and Daniel Webster* harks back to such
early American sentimental operas as *The Saw Mill* and *The Forest Rose,*
which have lovers, a hero, a villain, and happy endings. The phantasmal
transformation scenes relate once again to the harlequinade. The music is
lyrical, modern, and cleverly woven through arioso, recitative, and spoken
dialogue with and without orchestral accompaniment. The changing forms
and textures of the score go hand in hand with the many variations of
dialogue. There are no set pieces, but the opening suggests a joyous barn
dance, and the duet between Jabez and Mary is a stunning, soaring ballad.
The opera demands a cast of sixteen principals and a sizable chorus and
orchestra. The American Lyric Theater at the Martin Beck Theater in New
York first produced it in 1939, and in June 1953 it was televised by CBS.
Although it is in a single act, *The Devil and Daniel Webster* is not a chamber
work but a special form of American opera that has lived and flourished
by virtue of an excellent libretto and imaginative musical score.

Perhaps the most famous pairing in American opera is Gian Carlo
Menotti's *The Telephone* and *The Medium.* The latter was first produced alone
on May 8, 1946, at the Brander Matthews Theatre of Columbia University. Revised and restaged by Menotti, it was then performed with a frothy,

twenty-two-minute opener, *The Telephone,* on February 18, 1947, at New York's Heckscher Theatre. Recorded by Columbia, they were the first American operas to be recorded in entirety. After their Heckscher Theatre run, the two operas were honored with six months on Broadway at the Ethel Barrymore Theatre, beginning May 1.

The reviews were extraordinary. *"The Medium,* an eerie musical melodrama, is both spine-tingling thriller and genuine opera," wrote Winthrop Sargeant. And the quixotic and rather eccentric Marie Powers was just right for the role of Madame Flora, possessing a voice of brilliant colors and dramatic sheen. In London and throughout Europe the operas continued to draw raves. Jean Cocteau observed, "Menotti has made out of plays, operas, and out of opera, plays. He has been able to find, in his admirable 'Medium,' a vocal style which elevates the ordinary and every-day into lyric drama." To Paris's *La Bataille, The Medium* was a "veritable revelation. There was an atmosphere absolutely magical, and a psychological sense of dramatic intensity rarely encountered. It was a very important moment in the contemporary lyric theatre."[23] Two years after their Broadway premiere, the operas were staged at the New York City Opera as well as by numerous smaller companies and amateur groups throughout the United States. In two years alone, *The Medium* had been performed six hundred times.[24]

Why all the fuss over a two-act chamber opera with a cast of six and orchestra of between twelve and twenty-five? The opera contains no spectacle, no showy aria, no novel instrumental sound, and no chorus. Critics called it a "melodrama," and it did contain a traditional melodramatic triangle—a pair of lovers and a villain—but with a unique twist. The controlling father was now a phony spiritualist, Madame Flora ("Baba"), and her childlike daughter, Monica, has a deaf-mute named Toby for a lover. There are no heroes in the story, but there is heroism, excitement, irony, and suspense. What sets *The Medium* apart from other operas of the time—and frees it from common melodrama—is Menotti's genius in portraying character. Within the mysticism and symbolism in the story, the powerful human elements of love, frustration, compassion, and guilt shine through, not only in the actions of the characters but also in what these actions symbolize.

Most of the narrative takes place at a séance, during which Madame Flora thinks she hears voices and feels a ghostly hand. She accuses her assistant, the deaf-mute Toby, whom she has repeatedly abused. A terrified victim of her own fraud, she ultimately kills Toby as he hides behind the curtain of the puppet theater. As his bloody hand clutches the curtain, she leans over his body. "Was it you? Was it you?" she questions in a breathless whisper. If the opera ends with a question, with Madame Flora's probing and searching for answers, it reflects Menotti's personal crisis of faith—a theme that would appear in *Amahl and the Night Visitors, The Saint of Bleecker Street,* and many of his other operas. "I am a would-be Voltaire yearning to be Tolstoy," he said, "and it is this very duality in my character, this inner conflict, that I have tried to express in some of my operas, first with *The Medium.*"[25]

Menotti does not merely present his characters, he develops them through contrasts—intense, stark, and chilling—that in their constant juxtaposition make the characters seem real and believable. Throughout the opera, the simple, even spirits of Monica and Toby move in vivid counterpoint to the violent, mercurial disposition of Madame Flora. Toby, in turn, is the Pierrot of Menotti's childhood, the Harlequin of old who mimes, gestures, and dances. His imagination is linked to the phantasmal puppet theater, but he lives in the real world and has real feelings of love and tenderness for Monica.

Menotti gives Monica (soprano) arias and ariosos that are lyrical and tuneful, as "Mummy, Mummy dear, you must not cry for me" (as she imitates the Gobineaus' dead daughter) and the modal, oriental-flavored "O black swan." Madame Flora (mezzo-soprano) has passages that are more in the spirit of free ariosos, declamatory and intensely dramatic. "I'll make you talk," she sings to Toby as she whips him unmercifully. The orchestra follows along with equivocal tonal inflections, momentary dissonance, and an effective use of solo instruments, sometimes the celeste, sometimes xylophone. The high, screeching violins in Flora's monologue at the end of the opera ("Afraid, am I afraid?") create an effect Bernard Herrmann must have recalled when he composed the music for the shower murder scene in Alfred Hitchcock's *Psycho* (1960). Even Flora's lines at this point reflect the film: "In my young days I have seen many terrible things! / Women screaming as they were murdered."[26] For Toby's pantomimed segments, Menotti uses rapid, jagged pianistic figures that suggest the half-human puppet world of Igor Stravinsky's ballet *Petrushka.*

The tenderest, most human display of character in the *The Medium* is Monica's lovely scene with Toby that opens act 2. Kneeling behind him as if the words were coming from him, she sings "Monica, Monica, can't you see / That my heart is bleeding, bleeding for you? / I loved you, Monica, all my life." She then caresses Toby's head and tenderly lifts his tear-stained face so she can see his eyes. "Toby," she sings, "I want you to know that you have the most beautiful voice in the world!" Menotti gives the most lyrical moments in the opera to Monica. When the opera closes with Flora's brutal murder of Toby, it is the reaction of Monica, pathetically running for help, that reinforces the tragedy when her cries rise above the orchestra.

✍

The Medium illustrates that English is every bit as adaptable to the requirements of realistic operatic tragedy as Italian, French, or German and that American opera can be just as exciting and fast-moving as any Broadway show. Gian Carlo Menotti channeled the contemporary opera movement in America into a new world of dramatic realism and, more important, a new world of theater. Creatively, he opened television to families and gave new stature to the genre of the children's opera and chamber opera.

Menotti's operas are also extremely singable, and their vocal lines carry the crux of the drama. "After the success of *The Medium*," observed the composer Ned Rorem, "every composer in America said, 'If Menotti can hit the jackpot, so can I.' Everyone in the middle 1940s was writing operas like mad. And yet nobody made it the way Menotti has made it. . . . Charm and grace, the very essence of that which is Italian, and which pervades Menotti's music, are villainous qualities in America. You can, nevertheless, get away with it in opera—and Menotti did."[27] At a time when many opera composers favored American idioms and innovative sonorities, Menotti remained rooted in the romantic Italian tradition. More than mere "charm and grace," he found in that heritage a way to communicate, a challenge every modern composer of opera faces but often cannot solve.

The powerful impact of mass media on American opera composers extended beyond allowing their work fresh visibility and outreach. Radio and television managed to rescue opera from large and imposing opera houses and bring it into American homes. Like the simple theaters and democratic spirit of early American opera, mass media drew audiences into the action and characterization of the works with a new intimacy and power. That, in turn, inspired shorter, more dramatically and musically compact operatic forms that reached young and old alike. Simple to stage and having small casts and orchestras, such works played a major role in furthering the college and university opera workshop movement of the 1950s that still produces and gives premieres of important American operas.

PART 3

The Discoveries, 1945 to the Turn of the Century

We know the characters of an opera from their words, but we believe them because of what they sing. The music will appear to reflect them, as in an enlarging mirror; rather, as though the music were a magic mirror, it will appear to create them.
—Jack Beeson, 1976

I came to realize that writing a libretto is in the end like working inside someone else. The words have to make the bird sing, or they're of no use.
—Jack Larson, from *The Virgil Thomson Centenary*, 1996

Why then do some of us continue to make the awesome investment of time and energy required to write an opera? For me, it is for the simple reason that, when all the elements of drama, music, singing, design, and stagecraft are successfully fused in a theater, there is nothing in the entire realm of the arts that can surpass the kind of purely visceral, as well as aesthetic, excitement that results.
—Carlisle Floyd, in *Perspectives*, 1984

13

The New American Verismo

Verismo is to naturalism what the "shocker" is to the realistic novel, and the music corresponds to this conception.
  —Donald Grout, *A Short History of Opera*

VIOLENT PASSIONS, melodramatic plots, intense emotional contrasts, and moments of excitement in swift climactic succession—these are the ingredients of the Italian operatic style known as verismo. Everyday characters are caught up in powerful, often tragic, dramatic crises, following those ubiquitous icons of verismo, Ruggiero Leoncavallo's *I Pagliacci* (1892) and Pietro Mascagni's *Cavalleria rusticana* (1890). There was plenty of veristic precedent in Gaetano Donizetti and Giuseppe Verdi, notes Donald Grout, but in verismo "the nitrogen has been withdrawn, so that everything burns with a fierce, unnatural flame, and moreover, quickly burns out"—like the verismo movement itself.[1]

Had Grout looked in his own backyard, he would have found verismo alive and well, for verismo (realism) brought new life to American opera in the 1940s, 1950s, and beyond. American verismo composers centered action around plausible, everyday characters and brought them into focus through richly expressive melodic and orchestral means in a form of music drama that has enlarged the repertoire of opera houses across the nation.

Because of the sweeping, graphic role that music plays in reflecting the passions of common people in critical situations, the early operas of Gian Carlo Menotti are often cited as models of American verismo. It is true that Menotti's great popularity gave fresh focus to the term and a uniquely personal adaptation through his accent on the supernatural and the anguish it often generated in his characters. Before Menotti, though, elements of American verismo could be seen as early as 1911 in works about Native Americans, such as Victor Herbert's *Natoma* (1911) or Charles Wakefield Cadman's *Shanewis* (1918), or in those dealing with new Italian Americans, as Frederick Converse's *The Immigrants* (1914) or George Whitefield Chadwick's *The Padrone* (1912), a passionate story of impoverished Italian immigrants whose lives are crushed by the Mafia.

In verismo, local settings provide backdrops for intense actions and feelings—murder, lust, and greed—one step away from those of nineteenth-century melodrama. Characters manage to relate to one another just as tempestuously in the Adirondacks (Ernest Carter's somber *The White Bird,* 1924) as on the streets of Charleston (*Porgy and Bess*). Gods, the nobility, Byronic heroes, and ancient legends have little place in verismo. The focus is on the here and now—elements with which an audience can strongly sympathize. As a stagehand at the New York City Opera said about his favorite opera, Anthony Davis's *X: The Life and Times of Malcolm X* (1986): "I like operas about things I can identify with—people being disenfranchised, people robbed of their rights."[2]

As in Italy, verismo in America has roots in nineteenth-century literature and plays—dramatic effusions by Bartley Campbell, William Dean Howells, William Gillette, and others that forever seemed tied to the romantic melodrama no matter how reality-bound their aspirations. In his popular play *Margaret Fleming* (1890), James A. Herne took a giant step toward realism by creating plausible characters who had conviction. Herne had to stage the play with his own resources, however. No New York producer would touch it because its themes included infidelity and illegitimate pregnancy.

Some writers were more successful than others in reshaping their plays so the melodramatic elements remained effective within their new, more realistic environment. David Belasco's *The Girl of the Golden West* (1905), which inspired Giacomo Puccini, brings to the melodrama a new type of hero and heroine: an admitted thief and a rough-and-ready woman able to hold her own against any man. Steele MacKaye's greatest box office success *Hazel Kirke* (1880) contains such melodramatic trappings as asides and the clichéd plot of "spoiled" female honor and potential loss of a family home. But its characters are working class and speak with natural dialogue rather than the high-blown rhetoric of a usual melodrama. In fact, "the alienation of the melodramatic material from its traditional formal universe forces the viewer not only to recognize the existence of these elements but also to realize that emotional intensity is not the sole property of melodrama."[3]

Emotional intensity is indeed not the "sole property of melodrama." It became a driving force in early-twentieth-century realism, especially in film, music theater, and opera. America's addiction to the melodrama, as some writers claimed, carried well into the twentieth century and transformed into some of the nation's finest dramatic works. The plays of Lillian Hellman, for example, have been called "melodramas without the traditional melodramatic ending. Rather than showing virtue rewarded and villainy punished, they depict goodness so weak that it is trodden underfoot by evil."[4] What was often missing in modern melodrama (of 1930, for example)—music—became the life's blood of opera and motion pictures. It was not only the emotional intensity of romantic melodrama that gave these forms special American identity but also the role music played in them. As reshaped melodrama, verismo became a characteristic American phenomenon with its own enduring vigor.

To many composers of the time, motion pictures were a new, American form of opera. Most of Hollywood's finest film scores of the period were composed by European musicians such as Max Steiner, Dimitri Tiomkin, Franz Waxman, and Erich Korngold. Numerous young American-born symphonic and opera composers also went to Hollywood during the 1930s to try their hands at the thriving new dramatic art. Their work in films played a role in their creative process within opera. "I have tried *a new kind of opera*," wrote George Antheil about his fast-moving, farcical *Volpone*, "an opera style influenced by the pacing which the public in general has wanted since its taste has been educated or corrupted by . . . the movies and, now, television. In short, opera which is less static on stage."[5] The British composer Constant Lambert also noted parallels between opera and film: "Films have the emotional impact for the twentieth century that operas had for the nineteenth . . . D. W. Griffith is our Puccini, Cecil B. DeMille our Meyerbeer."[6] And Alfred Newman is our Wagner. Hollywood's abundant use of the leitmotif technique paralleled that of Wagner's musical psychodrama *Der Ring des Nibelungen*. After all, where else could opera go after *The Ring* except into film?

The vital commonality of music's role in film and opera is perhaps best expressed by Bernard Herrmann, the dean of American film composers. When Erich Leinsdorf commented that music in films had to be "subordinate," Herrmann replied:

> If film music is subordinate, so is music in the theatre and the opera house. . . . Music on the screen can seek out and intensify the inner thoughts of the characters. It can invest a scene with terror, grandeur, gaiety, or misery. It can propel narrative swiftly forward, or slow it down. . . . If this is "subordination" then so is the role of music in opera, which, no matter how extended, is governed finally by the needs of the drama. So it is with the best film music. It identifies itself with the action, and becomes a living part of the whole.[7]

Music in opera, as Herrmann attests, is governed by the needs of drama. But opera is also sung. Its arias and certain styles of recitative not only serve the drama but also define characters by allowing them to express in song their innermost thought and emotions. As composers well know, song must be more than a showpiece for a singer. Perhaps no other operatic period or style illustrates that as acutely as verismo, in which characters are not only transcriptions of life but also embodiments of it. Ultimately, it is the mission of American verismo composers and librettists to set the maximum desires of a character at maximum intensity and against maximum opposition to create maximum drama.

Menotti's Verismo Operas

During the 1940s and early 1950s, three important composers—Gian Carlo Menotti, Kurt Weill, and Marc Blitzstein—wrote operas that reflected different aspects of the new realism that was also infusing film and music theater at the time. Although the characters in both Weill and Blitzstein develop and deepen in their interaction with one another, it is the steady, stately character of Magda Sorel that we follow most closely to her tragic end in Menotti's *The Consul* (1950). A harbinger of later great American heroines such as Vanessa, Lizzie Borden, and Emmeline, Magda reflects a realism more intense, more tragic, and closer to the Italian verismo style, than that of Weill or Blitzstein.

Menotti, moreover, worked in a different direction. He avoided both spoken dialogue and the extended use of American traditional or popular music. He well knew how to handle melodramatic, cinematic, and vocal techniques, however, and *The Consul* dazzles like few American operas ever have. Robert Sabin once described Menotti as "a diverse musical personality—a skillful and witty comedian who nonetheless writes grim and horrible tragedies . . . a realistic social commentator, who bursts out into the most fantastic impossibilities."[8] Menotti claimed he never considered himself a verismo composer in the vein of Ermanno Wolf-Ferrari or Giacomo Puccini because he explored the deeper, symbolic elements in life rather than the merely "photographic." That seems true of *The Medium, The Saint of Bleecker Street,* and *Maria Golovin,* but *The Consul* presents its messages up front. Almost half a century later, it is just as somber and shocking as it was to audiences at its spectacular Broadway premiere on March 15, 1950.

The subject of immigration had interested earlier American composers, notably Converse and Chadwick, but Menotti found an even deeper

Lyric Opera of Chicago's staging of Menotti's *The Consul* with Emily Golden as The Secretary and Barbara Daniels as Magda Sorel. *Photo by Dan Rest.* © *1996 Lyric Opera of Chicago*

message in the plight of individuals seeking a new land, and he penetrated more deeply into human feeling. He focuses on a single obscure woman, Magda Sorel, as she tries to escape from an unidentified savage and hostile police state into the free world. Anguished and desperate, she cries out for help, but the cool indifference of the bureaucracy fails to recognize her needs. "Papers! Papers! Papers!" she cries. "But don't you understand? What shall I tell you to make you understand? My child is dead. John's mother is dying. My own life is in danger. I ask for your help." The Secretary replies, "Your name is a number . . . your hopes will be filed. Come back next week." When she realizes that her husband has been taken by the police and she has lost all whom she loves, she turns on the gas in her oven and kills herself. Pure melodrama. But the horror lies in a villain far more frightening because he is faceless and amorphous—a villain called "bureaucracy" that no dagger can strike down. The frustrations of the poor woman become all the more real.

Like the role of Regina in Marc Blitzstein's opera of the same name, Magda Sorel must be played with forceful integrity. It requires an exceptional singing actress, and twenty-seven-year-old Patricia Neway was praised as a find of real magnitude. Her voice had glitter and warmth, and she moved onstage with grace and conviction. Neway sang the role in the New York City Opera's premiere in 1952 and continued to make it her own for many years. In *The Consul,* which Menotti called a "musical drama," singers benefited from a composer who lavished great care on the union of prose, poetry, and music in defining his character.

Within a framework of biting dissonance, *The Consul's* score is highly pictorial and closely tied to the action, and its characteristic and transparent orchestral textures bring special clarity and impact to the drama. Fragmentary use of solo instruments—piano, muted trumpet, oboe, and clarinet—echo a word or phrase of the text. Strings reflect passion, and the harp a fleeting dream. As Magda starts to hallucinate before she dies ("Oh, God, forgive me. I never meant to do this"), tremolo strings combine with a single repeated tone struck on the barren xylophone, creating an eerie, hypnotic commentary on her act of desolation. Menotti also offers moments of levity throughout the opera. An Italian woman who speaks no English sings in Puccini-like style, and a magician who must prove his identity in the consulate waiting room hypnotizes the other occupants, making them dance. The mood is never lightened for long, however, and there is always a dramatic rationale for doing so. The Italian woman becomes pathetic because no one understands her; the magician, in turn, becomes the tragic motivating voice of Magda's suicide. "You want to sleep," he says. "Breathe deeply." The opera ends in one of the most hair-raising scenarios in all theater.

The most famous scene in the opera—and likely American opera's most tortured verismo expression—is Magda's long cry of pain, rage, and despair closing act 2. "To this we come: that men withhold the world from men," she sings. Weakened by anxiety, her patience eventually gives way to an impassioned lyrical outburst:

> Oh, the day will come I know,
> when our hearts aflame
> will burn your paper chains!
> Warn the Consul, Secretary, warn him!
> That day neither ink nor sea
> shall cage our souls.[9]

She stumbles back to the benches of the waiting room and collapses. The powerful orchestral theme associated with Magda's protest returns at the end of the opera as her body falls lifeless across the chair.

The Consul received two distinguished theater awards for 1949–50: the New York Drama Critics' Circle Award and the Pulitzer Prize. After 269 performances in New York, it was staged in London, Paris, Berlin, Zurich, and at Milan's La Scala.[10] In 1961 *The Consul* became the first Broadway production to be prepared exclusively for pay-per-view television. "Its eloquence, beauty and sheer excitement are realized on the small screen with consummate skill," Jack Gould wrote, "and the use of the camera for purposes of emphasis and clarity truly inspired. . . . Her [Patricia Neway's] aria, 'To This We've Come,' will rank as a treasured moment in TV's library of performance."[11] In 1996 the Lyric Opera of Chicago presented a provocative new staging of *The Consul* directed by Robert Falls. The opera had been set in the present, underscoring its classic theme of bureaucratic indifference to human rights.

Menotti's eighth opera, *The Saint of Bleecker Street,* is considered his most successful monument to realism. Critics called it "first-rate theater that gives one the feeling of a masterfully integrated whole" and "verismo opera, with a dash of modern psychology."[12] Although the opera was an artistic success, it was a commercial failure following its premiere at New York's Broadway Theater on December 27, 1954. Its large cast, orchestra, and chorus strained resources, and it ran for only four short months—long for a new

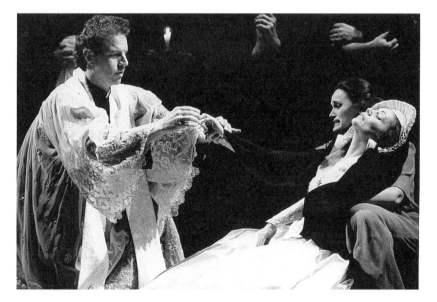

In the Washington Opera's performance of *The Saint of Bleecker Street* by Menotti, John Stephens played the priest; Gail Dobish, Carmela; and Maryanne Telese (reclining), the saintly Annina. *Photo by Art Stein*

American opera but brief for Broadway theater. Opera houses worldwide welcomed it, however, and it was produced by BBC television in 1957 and at the New York City Opera in the 1964–65 season. Like *The Consul, The Saint of Bleecker Street* won for Menotti a Pulitzer Prize for music and the Drama Critics' Circle Award for best play. With *The Saint of Bleecker Street,* Menotti could also count among his accolades the New York Music Critics' Circle Award for the best opera.

One of the most outstanding features of *The Saint of Bleecker Street* is its strength of characterization. Its clarity of delineation transcends any of Menotti's earlier operas. Much of that strength derives from the contrast he sets up within the story: religious faith pitted against harsh disbelief; an abusive, controlling male against a frail, saintly female; Italian folk tunes against liturgical chant; large processional scenes against simple duets; and the ways of the Old World against the climate of the new. All provide contrasts that Menotti used with dramatic integrity and musical power.

Both orchestral motifs and expressive arias within the opera define characters' actions and feelings. Annina's long narrative or scena in act 1, "Oh, Sweet Jesus," is one of Menotti's most exciting theatrical moments. "I see now," she sings as she is about to experience the stigmata. "Oh blinding sight! Oh, pain! Oh love!"[13] Her emotions are captured by the orchestra, which reiterates the ethereal chordal motif associated with her spirituality from the opening of the opera. Ascending majestically like the Holy Grail motif in Wagner's *Parsifal,* Annina's motif reappears many times throughout the opera in response to the actions and emotions of the moment. Another extended scena takes place in act 2 when Michele's pent-up rage explodes. "Since I was a child you've always hated me, because I never asked for love, only understanding," he sings to a shocked group of neighbors in a local restaurant. The outburst exposes Michele's fiery disposition and resentful attitude through a moving piece of Italian lyricism for the tenor voice, rising to a high C at the end. It is the chorus, however, that heightens and motivates the story. Not only does it further delineate and fine-tune the characters but it also takes an active part in the action. In addition, it brings important pageantry, mystical imagery, and local color to many scenes.

Maria Golovin, Menotti's third and final large-scale verismo masterpiece, focuses on a highly theatrical subject: the unfulfilled passion of a blind youth for an older married woman, Maria Golovin, that results in his tragic attempt to kill her. Like *The Consul* and *The Saint of Bleecker Street, Maria Golovin* was produced on Broadway but closed after only five performances. The opera did enjoy a successful world premiere at the Brussels World's

Fair on August 20, 1958, and was televised by NBC, which had commissioned it. New York critics, however, thought the opera either combined "sleazy, old-fashioned melodrama with muddy and often all-too-obvious symbolism" or portrayed characters that were "caught in an emotional trap" and did not grow in stature.[14] Was the novelty of Menotti's dramatic style wearing thin, perhaps? Were newer operatic currents in the air?

To Menotti, *Maria Golovin*'s lukewarm reception was a sad finale to a brilliant and successful creative period. He turned to other avenues of composition, primarily theater works for children, church, and dance and to the opening of the Spoleto Festival of Two Worlds, which he founded and directed. *Maria Golovin* remains one of Menotti's most important works, however, with a score of lush, melodic contour and beauty.

Street Scene *and* Regina

Characterization in the verismo operas of Kurt Weill and Marc Blitzstein is less graphic than in Menotti, perhaps because it is often mollified through the use of spoken dialogue and popular tunes. *Street Scene* (1947) was composed after Weill (1900–1950) had come to America from Germany in 1935 following a six-year collaboration with Bertolt Brecht. During those years, Weill had produced some of his best-known theatrical achievements, among them *Mahagonny* (1927) and *Die Dreigroschenoper* (1928), a jazzy, sardonic version of *The Beggar's Opera*. With book by Elmer Rice and graceful, poetic lyrics by Langston Hughes, *Street Scene* is based on Rice's Pulitzer Prize–winning play of the same name, first staged in 1929 and made into a motion picture two years later. The play, or "realistic tragedy," wrote John Anderson in the *Evening Journal,* "builds engrossing trivialities into a drama that is rich and compelling and catches in the wide reaches of its curbside panorama the heartbreaks that lie a few steps up from the sidewalks of New York."[15]

Like the play, the opera revolves around the truculent Frank Maurrant, his neglected wife Anna, and their distraught daughter Rose, whose lives cross with others in the hot and faded tenement district of Manhattan. When Frank discovers that Anna is having an affair with the local milk carrier, he kills the couple in the heat of drunken jealousy. Left alone to care for her small brother, Rose gives up her own emotional involvement with a young law student because "loving and belonging are not the same." If her mother had "belonged to herself," she sings, the murder would never have happened. And so she chooses to live a life of her own rather than follow the tormented path of her parents.

New York City Opera's production of *Street Scene* by Kurt Weill. The opera displays a verismo style some called "Manhattan melodrama." *Astor, Lenox and Tilden Foundations, New York Public Library*

Critics were not at all sure what to call *Street Scene*. Drawing analogies with Gershwin's *Porgy and Bess,* some used the term *folk opera*. Others preferred its original billing as a "dramatic musical." And then there were those who questioned the way the opera "rides the uncomfortable line between musical comedy and serious musical drama." But no one questioned the work's unique dramatic power. For all its "musical embellishments," it was a work of "savage realism," a "Manhattan melodrama" that seemed timeless.[16]

Street Scene's integration of jazz and popular styles within a large symphonic score is less successful than *Porgy and Bess*'s. Weill appears to shift between operatic and pop techniques rather than assimilate them as Gershwin does so successfully. The work is cast as an old-fashioned "number opera" of set pieces in the Italian manner. The two acts are divided into segments with such labels as "Scene," "Duet," "Arioso," "Cavatina," "Blues," "Scene and Song," and the like. The "Ice Cream Sextet" in act I is an obvious take-off on Donizetti's *Lucia*. In a fractured Italian dialect, Lippo sings, "When I go into the drug-store, ah, eet is da wonderful spot. . . . There doctor, sailor or worker can sit on a little round seat-a and buy from the soda jerker a million good things to eat-a." "Ah, spumoni!" Mrs. Fiorentino adds in diva-like, overblown fioriture.

Even within the number-opera framework, solos, scenes, and ensembles flow beautifully—and powerfully—one into the other. Moments of humor move easily into outbursts of tragedy, and many fine tunes and delicate lyricism relieve the cinematic scoring that Weill called "mood music." Perhaps this cinematic approach gives the work special sophistication and complexity. Weill had written scores for four films between 1937 and 1944, but the operatic form was far more challenging. With effective ease, though, he moves back and forth from spoken dialogue to dialogue underscored by music, to recitative, to aria, to ensemble, to patterned speech, and to duet so that the drama is constantly propelled forward with great momentum and a variety of means.

The large cast of *Street Scene* includes thirty-six individual roles and an array of "street types" (neighbors, vendors, police officers, a grocery boy, an ambulance driver, a violin pupil, furniture movers, and Salvation Army members). From that mélange, the opera's tragic heroine, Anna Maurrant, stands out in bold relief. In a long, impassioned aria in act 1 she sings of her disillusionment: "Folks should try to find a way to get along together, a way to make the world a friendly, happy place":

I don't know—it looks like something awful happens
in the kitchens where women wash their dishes.
Days turn to months, months turn to years,
the greasy soap-suds drown our wishes.[17]

"I never could believe that life was meant to be all dull and grey," she continues. "I always will believe there'll be a brighter day," and on the word *day* she soars in brilliant Puccini style to a resplendent high A.

Weill's use of satiric imagery, spoken theater, and popular musical idioms played a formative role in the theater works of Marc Blitzstein. A great admirer of Weill, Blitzstein during the 1950s translated Weill's *Die Dreigroschenoper,* thus contributing to its long, successful American run.

Blitzstein's *Regina* (1949) is more ambitious and has a wider, fuller dramatic range than the earlier *Cradle Will Rock.* It resembles Weill's *Street Scene* in its imaginative dialogue techniques but does not always share Weill's gift for memorable tunes. Like Weill, Blitzstein employs the number-opera approach, with the various scenes and solos tied together in a continuous musical and dramatic fabric. What is most impressive and distinctive about *Regina,* however, is how Blitzstein uses spirituals, Victorian parlor music, dance forms, ragtime, aria, operatic scenes, varied techniques of dialogue, and a large, symphonic score to tell the story and paint the characters. He created a unique form of opera rather than a mere combination of opera and Broadway as critics have observed. "I remember certain things I was looking for" Blitzstein recalled about choosing the subject for *Regina:*

> I know I wanted to do a strong piece, rather than a predominantly lyrical one. It was to have a big role for a woman. . . . It was to stress some primary human passion, and some aspect of comedy. At the time I was not much caught by the love-jealousy or love-religiosity axes, so often used in libretto-land; nor by the comic possibilities of mistaken identity or the wrong bedroom. I hit upon human greed. . . . And I wanted a sharp climax which might even resolve in a violent death. Then I recalled Lillian Hellman's *The Little Foxes,* a play I admired enormously; and I realized my plan and story had already been done for me.[18]

When Blitzstein approached Hellman, the feisty playwright looked at him in astonishment. "Of course you may do it if you really wish to," she said, "but I don't know how you can add anything to the Hubbards that will make them any more unpleasant than they are already."[19]

Although Hellman's story about corruption and greed in the Deep South provided a superb springboard for an opera, fashioning the libretto was not easy. Blitzstein followed the original play closely, eschewing the romantic interludes between Alexandra and David in William Wyler's brilliant film version (1941). When he did want to make important changes for the opera, fiery clashes with Hellman came hard and fast. Blitzstein added, for example, additional scenes using African American characters and their music, yielding additional material for musical imagery and characterization. Hellman was not pleased. "I feel that the whole approach to the Negro in the play, whether it is the jazz band, or Jabez's singing to Birdie, or the Negroes at the party, is sentimental," she argued. Ultimately, however, she confessed, *"Regina* is, to me, the most original of American operas, the most daring. The theme of *The Little Foxes* did not seem the proper subject for opera—although God knows what *is* a proper subject. And yet the bite and power of the music comments on the people in a wonderfully witty way, and the sad sweetness of the music for the 'good characters' makes them better."[20]

As in both play and opera, Blitzstein's characters are real, imperfect human beings. The opera's themes of greed, money-grubbing, and hate-filled family conflicts place the rapacious Regina as a key player—a kind of "Alabamian Clytemnestra." "Money means things, and the things I can do with things," she sings. "For the half-poor are poorer than poor. Unhappy, unloved, unsure." The characters who form the greedy part of the Hubbard clan are Regina, her brothers Ben and Oscar, and Oscar's son

Leo. Oscar's wife Birdie, Regina's husband Horace, their daughter Alexandra ("Zan"), and the black housekeeper Addie add moral counterbalance. During the progress of the story—as part of a manipulative scheme—Regina allows her ill husband to die. Although she wins the deal, however, she loses her daughter. Zan leaves her mother because, as she says, "I want to. Because I know Papa would want me to."

Certain aspects of both play and film made their way into Blitzstein's opera. The characters in Hellman's *The Little Foxes* use a taut, tough dialogue, often when discussing money, that hardly lends itself to musical underpinning. In the film, music is rare and is reserved for transitions between scenes and for the melodramatic closing. In the opera, Blitzstein handles such dialogue by inventing his own special kind of dialogue that skillfully moves from speech to recitative to song in smooth, expressive transitions. Sometimes one character speaks an answer to a sung question, or a musical phrase may be interrupted in the middle for a conversational interpolation. Like the musical score itself, the way in which Blitzstein handles speech in the opera is yet another vital dramatic tool.

Joan Diener-Marre and George Gaynes in Marc Blitzstein's *Regina* as staged by Michigan Opera in 1977. *Michigan Opera Archives*

Changing or rearranging the lines from one art form to another often enlarges a character and reinforces a drama's primary message. In Hellman's play, Addie says wistfully, "Well, there are people who eat the earth and eat all the people on it like in the Bible with the locusts. Then there are people who stand around and watch them eat it."[21] In the motion picture, Addie's moody observation forms an introduction to Horace's relevant lines that immediately follow. He quotes from Song of Solomon 2:15, lines that, significantly, appear in neither play nor opera: "Take us the foxes / The Little Foxes that spoil the vines / For our vines have tender grapes."

In the opera, Blitzstein uses Addie's lines from the play as part of the gentle "rain ensemble" sung by Horace, Addie, Alex, and Birdie. In doing so, he not only enlarges the moralizing metaphor of the play but also the characters themselves, who sing:

> The falling of friendly rain.
> It serves the earth,
> then moves on again.
> The nourishing rain.
> Some people eat all the earth
> Some people stand around and watch while they eat.
> And watch while they eat the earth.
> Now rain. Consider the rain. Rain. Rain.[22]

In all three art forms—play, motion picture, and opera—Alexandra reiterates Addie's "eat the earth" lines at the end of the work. This not only accentuates Alexandra's newly found independence and moral conviction but also reinforces the drama's powerful message.

Just as additional dialogue is added to Hellman's text for the film, Blitzstein often adds his own poetic lines as well. By adding lines, or interpolating and rearranging them, he fashions a more expansive vocal number and reveals further dimensions of a character. One of the opera's loveliest moments is Birdie's long arioso from act 3, "Mama Used to Say." The piece is drawn from Birdie's introspective monologue in both play and film and reflects her pathetic loneliness, longing for the life she knew at her gracious plantation Lionnet, and attempts to escape through alcohol. By consolidating other lines from the play and film into the aria, Blitzstein reveals Birdie's disappointment in Leo and warning to Alexandra: "Don't love me / Because in twenty years you'll be just like me / Trailing after them like me." The lines allow for a wonderfully transparent musical score that surges and holds back to support changing levels of intensity in the melody.

The spirituals that form the title music of the motion picture and brief interludes within it may have given Blitzstein the idea of opening and closing the opera with expanded spiritual scenes. The warmth they provide stands out against the icy materialism of the Hubbards. They also provide an upbeat, Broadway-like, closing for the opera. "Certainly, Lord . . . a new day is coming" sings the chorus as Alexandra asks "What's the matter, Mama? Are you afraid, Mama?" At this point the film surpasses both play and opera in dramatic interest because it accents the broken spirit of its protagonist, Regina. Against somber, desolate background music, Horace dies and Alexandra discovers the truth. As Regina looks out into the rain, watching her young daughter drive away, the camera closes in on her bitter face. The effect is chilling.

The film version of *The Little Foxes*—brilliantly acted with Bette Davis as Regina, Herbert Marshall as Horace, and Dan Duryea as the spineless Leo—places powerful emphasis on Regina. Even the addition of a new character (absent in the play and opera), Alexandra's boyfriend David, draws attention to Regina's barren love life. To reinforce his image of Regina, Blitzstein also uses irony and contrast. A graceful, romantic waltz to her line "to want and to take is the best thing of all" has the effect, as Leonard Bernstein said, "of coating the wormwood with sugar." One of the opera's most effective scenes is the ball episode closing act 2. How highly charged Regina's words to her husband become when she sings them as guests whirl around the dance floor in a spirited galop. "I hope you die!" she cries, and—climbing to a high C—"I'll be waiting."

As a rule, American verismo heroines do not resemble Wagner's noble women. They are usually beaten down and abused, and life is rarely kind. For all her callousness, Regina is crafty, intelligent, and in control of herself and those around her. Hellman, as America's first important female playwright, was a courageous innovator in many areas. Her first Broadway play, *The Children's Hour,* deals with lesbianism and suspected child abuse. *The Little Foxes,* which opened in 1939 and starred Tallulah Bankhead, was a natural for Blitzstein. But there was more in his mind. "I wanted to write something as real musically to Americans as Italian opera is to the Italians," he said.[23] Through a wide-ranging vision of humanity Blitzstein achieved his aims.

Bernard Herrmann's Wuthering Heights

In Bernard Herrmann's extraordinary opera *Wuthering Heights* (1947–51), based on Emily Brontë's strange, haunting tale of the Yorkshire moors, the impact of the action is structured closely around the tortured passion of its two protagonists, Cathy and Heathcliff. Before he began work on the opera, Brontë's somber story had already been adapted for a motion picture (1939) directed by William Wyler and starring Merle Oberon, Laurence Olivier, and David Nevin, with a musical score by Alfred Newman. It may have been the competition from that award-winning film or the opera's three-and-one-half-hour length, which Herrmann refused to cut, but his only grand opera did not see a staging until its world premiere in a shortened version by the Portland Opera in 1982.[24] It is a remarkable work and a landmark in the study of character portrayal and realization of music's dramatic potential.

Bernard Herrmann (1911–75) is best known as the composer of more than fifty notable Hollywood film scores. Trained at the Juilliard School of Music, he was one of the earliest champions of the music of that legendary American iconoclast Charles Ives. Although he composed choral and instrumental music, he has become identified mainly with the suspense thrillers of Alfred Hitchcock: *Psycho, Vertigo, North by Northwest, The Man Who Knew Too Much,* and many others. For Herrmann, Hitchcock's films allowed great scope for sensual musical treatment. Indeed, who can forget the murder scene in *Psycho* (1960) in which flashes of butcher-knife blade and splashing jets of water (becoming spurts of blood) meld with short violin swoops of "screaming, marrow-scraping intensity"?[25]

Film and opera for Herrmann seemed to have much in common. Like Richard Wagner, he used instrumental color in new ways to enlarge the drama. In *Psycho* he used only strings, and for *Torn Curtain* only brass. For the grotesque moan of the monster in *A Journey to the Center of the Earth* (1959) he chose the serpent, a nineteenth-century predecessor of the valved bass brass instruments that was shaped like its namesake. To reflect the shimmering sea in *The Ghost and Mrs. Muir* (1947), he used not one or two harps but nine, outdoing even the six in Wagner's *Das Rheingold.* Herrmann even went so far as to call his motion picture score for Charlotte Brontë's *Jane Eyre* (1944)—replete with leitmotifs and full symphony orchestra— his first "screen opera."[26] The most significant use of color in *Wuthering Heights,* however, is found not only in the orchestra but also in the characteristic use of the lower, darker registers of the voices, including the soprano's. Through the singers' vocal ranges, Herrmann paints the mercurial moods of his characters and clothes those moods in the grey and gloomy colors of Brontë's moors.

The librettist for *Wuthering Heights* was the noted suspense author Lucille Fletcher (who was married to Herrmann). Like the 1939 film,

Fletcher uses only about half of the Brontë novel, the period up to Cathy's death. Eliminating the story's continuation with Heathcliff's and Cathy's heirs places all impact on the agonized relationship of the protagonists. The story is set in the mid–1850s, about fifty years later than the novel, and revolves around the Earnshaw family of Wuthering Heights, a rambling mansion on the bleak, wind-swept moors. When Earnshaw adopts a street waif named Heathcliff, Cathy Earnshaw, his daughter, finds in the poor, wild boy a life-long soulmate. Although their lives move in different directions and are torn apart by bitterness and betrayal, Cathy and Heathcliff never forget their love. Rushing to Cathy's bedside as she dies, Heathcliff cries out the novel's legendary lines: "Be with me always—take any form—drive me mad! Only do not leave me in this abyss, where I cannot find you! Oh God! I cannot live without my life! I cannot live without my soul!" Those impassioned lines compliment Cathy's earlier outburst at the end of act 2: "I am Heathcliff," thus reinforcing the oneness of both their bodies and their spirits.[27]

A great deal of lush musicality exists in the Brontë novel itself. Literary scholars have noted a force of metaphor in the text and that the "relentless life of the elements—fire, wind, water—inform many of Emily Brontë's analogies." Human actions, responses, and states of being, Schorer found, are "captured in the novel in a rhetoric suggesting the activities of the landscape, a language of wind, cloud and water, of floods, deluges, torrents and clouds, articulated in and by verbs of violent movement."[28]

But if *Wuthering Heights* stands out in its "violent movement" and metaphorical handling of the orchestra, it perhaps falls short in the wide, melodic dimensions needed for a long four-act opera. The extensive use of parlando, or heightened lyrical speech as Herrmann called it, rises and falls with the drama, but seems to need more melodic moments for contrast. The few arias that Herrmann does introduce into the fabric, however, are warm and lovely.

For many of these arias, Herrmann and Fletcher borrowed the texts from Emily Brontë's separate collection of poems, and their meter and imagery add welcome luminosity to the opaque darkness of the surrounding score. Among the loveliest are Edgar's ode to Cathy ("Now, art thou, dear, my golden June") and Isabel's charming "Love is like the wild rosebriar," both from act 3. With its text taken directly from the novel, Cathy's beautiful reminiscences to her housekeeper Nelly in act 2 are dramatically enlarged by orchestral text painting. "I have dreamt in my life dreams that have stayed with me forever," she sings. And on her words "the angels flung me back to earth and Wuthering Heights, where I awoke sobbing for joy," the motif associated with her appears in the orchestra, and with it a sudden burst of brilliant harmonic colors as her voice rises.[29]

Herrmann once commented that in his opera, "Each act is a landscape tone poem which envelops the performers."[30] Much of the score owes debts to Wagner, Strauss, and Mahler, but there are areas that sound French and even English (like Frederick Delius, who also attempted an opera on the Brontë subject). In the duet between Cathy and Heathcliff that opens act 1, the lovers express their feelings for each other through reference to their wild and natural surroundings ("The crags are gleaming, the moor is arched with stars"). The orchestral Nocturne closing this scene, one of Herrmann's most lyrical expressions, is colored by a passionate horn theme and delicate harp and woodwind arpeggios as Cathy and Heathcliff look out across the fading horizon. Herrmann had used the beautiful passage again as title music for *The Ghost and Mrs. Muir.*

Some critics of *Wuthering Heights* regretted Herrmann's frequent attention to action rather than the feelings of the characters. But what is important in opera is not only what characters feel but also what they are. In the novel, the adult Heathcliff is portrayed as fierce, cruel, and even a "savage beast." Brontë offers a clue to his behavior in the early pages: "He seemed a sullen, patient child; hardened, perhaps, to ill-treatment: he would stand Hindley's blows without winking or shedding a tear."[31] Thus, Heathcliff's introspective aria in act 1, with text from Brontë's poetry, allows him to speak for himself and tells more about him than did Laurence Olivier's rather colorless portrayal in the motion picture. "I am the only being, whose doom / No tongue would ask," he sings. "No eye would mourn. / I never caused a thought of gloom / A smile of joy, since I was born."[32] It is not the events of the action that draw sympathy but the intrinsic nature of the characters.

To intensify the mystical love between the two characters, Herrmann makes one important change from both the novel and film (missing also in Carlisle Floyd's *Wuthering Heights* of 1958), a change found in the opera's eerie, cinematic ending. Brontë and Wyler open their stories with Lockwood's description of Cathy's ghostly hand appearing at the icy, snow-covered window as she cries out "Let me in. Let me in." In the opera, that scene becomes the prologue. The flashback to twenty years earlier begins act 1. To end the opera, Herrmann brings back Cathy's pitiful cries and Heathcliff's anguish ("Oh, Cathy at last!") as an epilogue to her death scene. Instead of searching into the storm, as in the prologue, Heathcliff sinks broken and desperate beside the windows. That allows Herrmann to close the opera with the same musical material that he used in the opening, creating a cyclic effect and unity both musically and dramatically. Like the message of spiritual rebirth in the *Ring,* the immortality of a strange, intense passion implied in Brontë is made explicit in Herrmann. With its sweeping musical gestures, brilliant scoring, and moody protagonists, Herrmann's *Wuthering Heights* captures a rare, sublime moment in the history of American opera.

✂

After the experimentation in the styles and subjects of opera between the two world wars, verismo of the 1940s and 1950s brought a new, finely tuned dramatic truth to American opera, especially in the portrayal and development of characters. These qualities would ensure opera's growth in the decades to come and become especially prominent later in the century with works based on realistic plays such as Andre Previn's *A Streetcar Named Desire* (1998) after Tennessee Williams and William Bolcom's *A View from the Bridge* (1999) based on Arthur Miller.

Whether composers were conservative or innovative, eclectic or individual, there was always something fresh about the American operatic sound and the special way Americans combined music and drama. College and university opera workshops across the country, less dependent on box-office receipts and full houses, recognized that and tended to program more and more new works. One pioneer program was Columbia University's Opera Workshop, which staged at least fifteen American works between 1941 and 1958, including the premieres of Menotti's *The Medium,* Thomson's *The Mother of Us All,* and Douglas Moore's Pulitzer Prize–winning *Giants in the Earth.*

Several hundred American and world premieres took place because of academic institutions. Many were composed by prominent American composers in the early stages of their careers, such as Dominick Argento, Leonard Bernstein, Carlisle Floyd, and Jack Beeson. That felicitous phenomenon, in turn, brought about a new kind of democratization of opera. From north to south and east to west, small companies sprang up and gave new life to American theater: Kentucky Opera (1952), Tulsa Opera (1953), Santa Fe Opera (1956), Seattle Opera (1962), Minnesota Opera (1964), and others. Larger companies, too, opened their doors during this period. The Dallas Opera was inaugurated in 1957 with a gala concert by Maria Callas, and with verve and daring, the Lyric Opera of Chicago (1954) and Houston Grand Opera (1955) eventually established traditions of featuring contemporary American repertoire. Of all the nation's opera companies, however, none has "championed the home team" quite like the New York City Opera. On the national opera field, it is one of America's key players.

14

New York City Opera's "American Plan"

I love to be versatile, love to try to extract the essence of what makes one composer different from another.
   —Julius Rudel, *Opera News*

IT WAS A VERY STRANGE structure—this ornate, Moorish edifice—a bit too garish, a bit too reminiscent of a left-over Arabian Nights movie set. But as the first home of City Center Opera Company, it worked. "I have long cherished a dream of a center of cultural activity to be enjoyed by all the people of our city," claimed Mayor Fiorello La Guardia. "The old Mecca Temple, which is now owned by the people of New York, can in my opinion be put to no more useful purpose. . . . If New York leads the way, our example will be followed in our sister cities and American life will become spiritually enriched in the post-war years to come."[1] Founded in 1943 "to meet a demand for cultural entertainment at popular prices," the young company moved to the New York State Theater at Lincoln Center in 1966. By then it bore the designation "New York City Opera," a prestigious rival to the time-honored Metropolitan Opera that had dominated the city's operatic scene for almost a century.

Although the threat of communism continued to trouble the world after the war, Americans enjoyed unprecedented prosperity during the 1950s. The arts were beginning to develop and thrive as never before, with increased sources of patronage, both public and private, and ever-expanding audiences. Arts centers such as Lincoln Center were being planned and built across the nation, providing a fresh focus on music theater and dance, and cultural exchange programs proved that the arts could also be a vital bridge between nations. With the new, long-playing microgroove recordings, moreover, the music industry was booming.

The war brought about several changes, however. Thousands of immigrants, many poor but accustomed to culture in their homelands, made up a large potential audience base for inexpensive, varied music theater. The war also encouraged the hiring of fine American singers, well educated in their native environment and less expensive than foreign artists. The accent on American singers, composers, and designers became a vital mandate of the New York City Opera, which expanded the horizons of operatic experience not only for New Yorkers but also for the nation at large. As Beverly Sills put it, "We were risk takers, not only in repertoire, but in looking for new and different ways to entertain our audience. . . . We were young Americans who didn't feel opera belonged to the Europeans. We didn't feel we were better than other singers. But we knew we were just as good."[2] Because of such energy, more black singers were cast in wider roles, women appeared on the roster of conductors, new works were commissioned on a large-scale basis, several American works were recorded or telecast, and entire seasons were devoted to operas by American composers.

From its very earliest years, the New York City Opera exhibited the rich and varied repertoire that would become its signature. From *The Pirates of Penzance* to *Ariadne auf Naxos,* from Bartok's *Bluebeard's Castle* to Walton's *Troilus and Cressida,* from *Aida* to *Die Meistersinger, Showboat* to *Wozzeck*—the 1940s and 1950s were exciting and daring years. Most significant of all, however, were the American works. During this period alone, twenty-five different American operas were performed. Throughout its history, moreover, the New York City Opera has staged more than sixty American operas, twenty-three as world premieres. The first was William Grant Still's *Troubled Island* (1949), also the first major premiere by a black opera composer. Other premieres include Aaron Copland's *The Tender Land* (1954), Douglas Moore's *The Wings of the Dove* (1961), Robert Ward's *The Crucible* (1961), Carlisle Floyd's *The Passion of Jonathan Wade* (1962), Ned Rorem's *Miss Julie* (1965), Gian Carlo Menotti's *The Most Important Man* (1971), Dominick Argento's *Miss Havisham's Fire* (1979), and Anthony Davis's *The Life and Times of Malcolm X* (1986). Between October 6 and 12, 1993, the first World Premiere Festival took place, showcasing three American operas: Eric Laderman's *Marilyn,* Lukas Foss's *Griffelkin,* and Hugo Weisgall's *Esther.* In addition, many American works have had repeated performances. *Street Scene* productions number more than fifty. Whether premieres or revivals, all vividly reflect City Opera's views that American operas and musicals are national treasures to be cherished and enjoyed.

Probably no one individual influenced the course of American opera more than the New York City Opera's Julius Rudel (b. 1921). Within his unusually long tenure as artistic director (from 1957 to 1979), Rudel developed the company into one of the best and most enterprising in America. These were years of dramatic growth, of exploring, reaching out, and doggedly persevering. Born in Vienna, Rudel came to America when he was seventeen and joined City Opera's music staff in 1943, the year of the company's founding. A brilliant and versatile conductor, he boasts a repertoire of 144 works and remains in demand at the Paris Opera, Vienna Staatsoper, Covent Garden, and other leading houses. When Rudel obtained Ford Foundation grants for two series of American operas, his creative efforts were considered unprecedented in American musical life. "I shall be surprised if musical history does not record that American opera, as a movement, had its beginnings at the New York City Center in the spring seasons of 1958 and 1959," wrote Lester Trimble of *The Nation*.[3]

After examining nearly two hundred scores of both older American works and new operas sent to him by composers across the nation, Rudel selected ten works for the first series and twelve for the next year's series. He scheduled performances for practically every night, alternating and repeating them during the single month of April of each year. He conducted several operas himself: *Regina,* Floyd's *Wuthering Heights,* and Robert Kurka's *The Good Soldier Schweik.* It was a bold and noble experiment but successful, and the ongoing collaboration it established meant that the Ford Foundation would be identified with American opera for other companies as well. Ford grants also allowed several New York City Opera productions to go on tour, such as *The Ballad of Baby Doe, Susannah, Street Scene,* and *Six Characters in Search of an Author.*[4] Most important was the profound effect the Rudel years would have on the acceptance and enjoyment of American opera. Within the vital seasons of 1958 and 1959 were many operas that continue to be among the most popular American repertoire.[5]

First Ford Foundation American Series, April 1958

Douglas Moore	*The Ballad of Baby Doe* (New York premiere)
Mark Bucci	*Tale for a Deaf Ear* (New York premiere) and
Leonard Bernstein	*Trouble in Tahiti*
Kurt Weill	*Lost in the Stars*
Vittorio Giannini	*The Taming of the Shrew* (New York premiere)
Gian Carlo Menotti	*The Old Maid and the Thief* and *The Medium*
Robert Kurka	*The Good Soldier Schweik* (world premiere)
Carlisle Floyd	*Susannah*
Marc Blitzstein	*Regina*

Second Ford Foundation American Series, April 1959

Kurt Weill	*Street Scene*
Lee Hoiby	*The Scarf* (American premiere) and
Douglas Moore	*The Devil and Daniel Webster*
Carlisle Floyd	*Wuthering Heights* (New York premiere)
Gian Carlo Menotti	*Maria Golovin*
Douglas Moore	*The Ballad of Baby Doe*

Marc Blitzstein	*Regina*
Robert Ward	*He Who Gets Slapped*
Gian Carlo Menotti	*The Medium* and
Norman Dello Joio	*The Triumph of St. Joan* (New York stage premiere)
Carlisle Floyd	*Susannah*
Hugo Weisgall	*Six Characters in Search of an Author* (world premiere)

Aaron Copland at City Opera

In planning his Ford Foundation series, Julius Rudel at one point considered bringing back the lyrical folk opera *The Tender Land,* which had received its world premiere at City Opera on April 1, 1954. The opera was written by Aaron Copland, the distinguished American composer who several years earlier had completed the three ballets that became his signature—*Billy the Kid* (1938), *Rodeo* (1942), and *Appalachian Spring* (1944). Commissioned by Richard Rodgers and Oscar Hammerstein, Copland's charming pastoral was inspired by two pictures in James Agee's *Let Us Now Praise Famous Men.* The libretto by Horace Everett (whose earlier pen name was Erik Johns) revolves around a farm family in the Midwest during the 1930s and the attraction of young Laurie to a drifter who arrives on the scene.[6] The opera closed after only two performances, and Rudel later scheduled a far more dramatic treatment of American country life—Carlisle Floyd's compelling *Susannah. The Tender Land,* however, occupies a special place in American opera. It brought a highly visible rural folk idiom to the postwar lyric theater and was a harbinger of the more dramatic folk operas of Floyd, Moore, Giannini, and others.

Copland tried his hand at opera only twice. In 1936 he composed a little school opera, *The Second Hurricane,* and nearly twenty years later the more ambitious *The Tender Land.* He was frank in admitting that opera for him was "a very problematical form—*la forme fatale.* . . .The basic difficulty of the lyric stage, comes from the fact that there are so many imponderables."[7] As for the singers, "I don't like to feel that I'm being personally involved in a performer's private emotions. A voice that is deeply emotional makes me cringe!" Copland also felt that it was hard to find a professional librettist. "We don't have people in this country who do nothing but write librettos for operas!" he lamented. "Librettists usually don't know much about music, unfortunately. I think they would write better librettos if they could imagine what the music is going to do to their words." Fashioning a libretto from a play is not easy because the requisites are different, Copland maintained. Thornton Wilder once told him, "I'm convinced I write *a-musical* plays: that my texts 'swear' at music."

Aaron Copland (1900–
1990). *Van Vechten Collection, Library of Congress*

Although Copland's score is a work of fine lyrical sense, sonorous vocal
lines and brilliant orchestration characteristic of the composer, Everett's libretto is less than dramatically persuasive. The total effect of the opera is
that of a landscape with painted figurines rather than a drama of vivid,
moving human beings. We are told things about them but rarely share their
feelings. Copland, however, does often color characters instrumentally.
Oboes, bassoons, and clarinet augment the humor and gruff attitudes of the
drifters, and the magical glockenspiel underpins their enticement of Laurie ("We've been everywhere, would you like to go there?"). But these techniques create atmosphere rather than drama. Still, as Will Crutchfield observed after a Long Wharf Theater production in 1987, "The music has a
melancholy, wide-plains melodiousness that evokes the feel of rural America. The quintet finale to Act I brings atmosphere and characterization together successfully and builds to a strong climax. When to those virtues are
added the fact that it is a work full of resonance for our own American singers, it is easy to agree that 'The Tender Land' merits revival."[8]

For its New York City Opera world premiere, *The Tender Land* in original two-act format was paired with Menotti's *Amahl and the Night Visitors.* Several debuts were made in the former, such as Rosemary Carlos, who played Laurie; Jean Handzlik, her mother; and Adele Newton, her younger sister Beth. In addition, Jerome Robbins made his debut as stage director and Oliver Smith as scenic designer.[9] Four months later, Copland and his librettist revised the opera, adding new material and dividing the work into three acts. Further revisions were made in 1955. The American bicentennial encouraged several performances, notably by the Bronx Opera Company at Hunter College in 1976. In 1990 Virgin Classics recorded the complete opera. Staged performances though, have been relatively rare and then mainly on college campuses. But that, of course, was the venue Copland cherished.

The Early Stagings of American Staples

Three premieres by the New York City Opera deserve special attention because, after *Porgy and Bess,* they are the earliest American operas to appear regularly in season repertoires of major companies. If one were to ask who are the "Three Bs" of postwar American opera, the answer would undoubtedly be Douglas Moore (1893–1969), Robert Ward (b. 1917), and Carlisle Floyd (b. 1926) by virtue of their wide popularity and the strong Americana of their works. Born in New York, Ohio, and South Carolina, respectively, each wrote several operas. Only one of each composer's full-length works, however, continues to dominate American repertoire: Moore's *The Ballad of Baby Doe,* Ward's *The Crucible,* and Floyd's *Susannah.* They vividly represent the saga and spirit of America's people—the leathery legends of the West, the stark tales of New England, and the somber stories of the South. Not only are the three operas favorites with the New York City Opera and other companies, but they have also become emissaries of American culture overseas. Lyrical, intense, and eminently accessible, they are valid American classics of the 1950s and early 1960s—offering a bit of verismo, a touch of melodrama, a whiff of Broadway, and, always, a plethora of pure joy.

Within Douglas Moore's large output of chamber music, songs, and choral works are eleven operas. In addition to *The Ballad of Baby Doe,* three others have been performed by the New York City Opera. The popular one-act *The Devil and Daniel Webster* was staged in 1954, and *The Wings of the Dove,* after Henry James, received its commission from the City Opera in 1961. First performed by City Opera in 1968, *Carrie Nation* is Moore's last opera. It is based on incidents in the life of the woman who roused the passions that led to Prohibition and is an effective work that deserves more performance visibility.

For all of his accomplishments, however, none has added to Moore's career quite like his magnum opus *The Ballad of Baby Doe*. After its premiere by the Central City Opera Association in Colorado on July 7, 1956, the opera became immediately and resoundingly popular. The original cast included Walter Cassel (baritone) as Horace Tabor, Martha Lipton (mezzo-soprano) as Augusta, and Dolores Wilson (soprano) as Baby Doe. Emerson Buckley conducted, and the set designer, Donald Oenslager, ingeniously captured the tale with projections of old photographs of Tabor homes and buildings in Leadville and Denver. For the New York City Opera's production on April 3, 1958, Beverly Sills sang the role of Baby Doe with great charm and brilliance.

Beverly Sills as Baby Doe in New York City Opera's *The Ballad of Baby Doe* by Douglas Moore. *Astor, Lenox and Tilden Foundations, New York Public Library*

By the end of Julius Rudel's tenure as director in 1979, *The Ballad of Baby Doe* had achieved thirty-five performances at City Opera in eleven seasons, with well-filled houses every time. ABC televised it in 1957, although in a drastically cut version. During 1976, the American bicentennial year, the opera was accorded at least five separate productions in the United States alone. Two years later, Dallas Opera staged it with Ruth Welting as Baby Doe. More recent performances include those of the Central City Opera during Denver's 1996 summer festival and Washington Opera in 1997.

Why the great popularity of *Baby Doe?* It is a true tale of America's open frontier life, of rugged individualism and unlimited horizons. Too, Americans have always loved gossip and intrigue, scandals and love triangles right out of afternoon soap operas and melodramas. The powerful Horace Tabor and the women who loved him have become romanticized American folk heroes. But there is far more to the story. Horace, Augusta, and Baby Doe are compelling human beings, struggling with their feelings and the crises in their lives like everyone else. That fact, and the ability of the composer and librettist to make the audience believe it, is what makes the work timeless.

The story of Baby Doe had fascinated Douglas Moore for many years. "When I first read the newspaper accounts of the death of Baby Doe in 1935," he said, "I began to think of writing an opera about her. Here was a woman once famous for her beauty, who had been married to the richest man in Colorado, whose wedding had been attended by the President of the United States, and who had been found frozen to death in a miserable shack beside an abandoned silver mine. . . . I found myself always returning to the theme and wondering how it could be realized in an opera."[10] Moore reacted favorably when Central City Opera approached him in 1953 about writing an opera on the Baby Doe story. He worked diligently with his librettist John Latouche, lyricist for such musical shows as *Beggar's Holiday* by Duke Ellington, *The Golden Apple* by Jerome Moross, and Leonard Bernstein's *Candide*. After the opera's premiere, they planned several revisions, but Latouche died tragically at the age of thirty-five before all could be realized. For the New York City Opera production in 1958, however, two additions had been made in act 2: the poker game scenario of scene 2 and Baby Doe's aria in scene 1, "The fine ladies walk with their heads held high."

The libretto retains most of the events and characters of the actual story, changed and rearranged to accommodate the conventional demands of music theater. To understand the characters of both real life and the opera, however, the tale is worth recounting.[11] Baby Doe was born Eliza-beth (Lizzie) McCourt in 1854 in Oshkosh, Wisconsin. She was one of fourteen children, strong-willed and beautiful and with large blue eyes and curly blond hair that drew men to her in droves. At twenty-three she married Harvey Doe, whose father, a prosperous lumber merchant, gave his son charge of the family goldmine. Harvey, however, had neither en-ergy nor initiative to run the mine, so Lizzie donned men's clothing, took up pick and shovel, and set to work on the mine herself—rare activities for women in those days. After her divorce from Doe, she went to Lead-ville, Colorado, to find a new life in a region where the silver boom was in high gear and great opportunities were at hand. It was here she met Horace Tabor, twenty-four years her senior and married to the sturdy Augusta. A New England woman with a practical, no-nonsense aura about her, Augusta had worked alongside her husband in various business pur-suits before he made his fortune in mining. Unlike Baby Doe who craved wealth and fashion, Augusta had little use for luxury and Tabor's lavish spending habits.

Several strokes of fortune enabled Tabor to build his empire. Among them were the millions he made from a $64.75 investment in the mining business and the $11 million earned from the legendary Matchless Mine. He bribed a judge in Durango to grant him a secret divorce, and he and Baby Doe were married illegally, making Horace a bigamist. Humiliated, Augusta finally granted her husband the divorce he sought, and the de-lighted couple celebrated with a large wedding in Washington, D.C., where Horace had a thirty-day interim term in the senate. Although President Chester Arthur and a bevy of Washington politicians attended the wed-ding, their wives stayed home. Baby Doe was never accepted in the social circles of the elite.

For all his vast wealth, Tabor had built a fragile empire, weakened by swindlers, extravagant living, and, finally, the great crash of 1893 as the strug-gle concerning free gold and silver coinage nearly split the nation asunder. The Tabors lost everything. Baby Doe remained at her husband's side while he worked as a common laborer for $3 a day. When Horace died in 1899, all he had to leave his wife was the useless Matchless Mine. Her older daugh-ters had deserted her, and the younger one, known as Silver Dollar, became a prostitute and an alcoholic. The end came on a cold night in 1935. In the midst of a fierce blizzard, Baby Doe was found lying on the floor of her shack next to the abandoned mine, frozen to death. She was eighty-one.

How does one make all of this into an opera? Historical figures and events are not always the most pliable clay from which to shape musical theater—witness *Valentino* and *Marilyn* in the 1990s. Latouche realized that when he wrote, "How to make human beings out of characters is usually the chief difficulty in writing an opera on a historical subject. Once they get into the history books, they seem to want to stay there. The more famous they are the less likely they are to come to life on the stage."[12] But he was totally successful in bringing his characters to life. He was equally adept at handling a broad setting that ranged across almost a century, from Tabor's early life to Baby Doe's death. What Latouche undoubtedly discovered, too, is that any characters—real or imaginary—must have an innate robust passion to make a story work for opera.

Moore and Latouche begin the opera in 1880 when Tabor and Baby Doe first meet. To recount their earlier and later lives, they use a closing dream fantasy, a wonderfully effective technique no doubt borrowed from Broadway and Hollywood. The opera is in two acts, with multiple scenes in each. If *The Ballad of Baby Doe* gives voice to America's romantic and rowdy frontier, it also allows the three main characters to develop and grow within a viable, effective framework. The three protagonists are introduced in the opening scene, each identified and colored by their individual lines, music, and surroundings. "What's the matter, Fogarty, ain't my money good enough?" sings a slightly woozy old miner as the curtain rises on a lively scene of cowboys, barroom girls, and townspeople. "Found a peerless, matchless mine," he sings. "I call it the Matchless Mine—got a right to raise some hell. Silver oozing from the soil! Yippee!"[13]

When Horace Tabor emerges from the Opera House, he has four cronies with him. According to the libretto, he is "a tall, bold-looking man in his forties, vigorous and impulsive, with a bright eye and heavy mustache which masks a somewhat weak mouth." "It's a bang-up job," Horace sings, "smart as any opry house you're likely to see. Chandeliers a-glitter, real imported velvet, brass and mahogany, tapestries from Europe." There is no doubt about Horace Tabor's lifestyle and leanings. As a rowdy western dance ensues, the doors of the opera house open and Augusta and her women friends stand aghast. "Horace," she admonishes angrily. "What is this? Just one evening can't you act with a bit of dignity?" While Tabor and Augusta are highlighted by dramatic arioso, Baby Doe is given a graceful waltz. As she goes up to Tabor to ask directions to the Clarendon Hotel, she indicates the beautiful, prismatic arias that will later define her youth and charm. "I'm sure we'll meet again, Horace Tabor," she sings as the curtain falls. Indeed she will. In just one short opening scene an entire opera has been outlined.

As the story develops and progresses, so do the characters. Moore and

Latouche bring out these changes through the musical realization of individual lines. The opera is sung throughout via arioso, dramatic scenes, and arias cast sometimes in the style of popular period songs, as Baby Doe's "Willow Song" in act 1, scene 2. Embellished with colorature brilliance, the song climbs to the D above high C on the word *returning:*

> Oh, willow, where we met together
> Willow, when our love was new
> Willow, if he once should be returning
> Pray tell him I am weeping too.

As Baby Doe's first aria, these bittersweet tones seem prophetic. The imagery and irony in the text is revealed in the lyrical "Silver Song," which she sings at her wedding: "Gold is the sun, but silver lies hidden in the core of dreams." If her tough and resolute nature is not clearly defined by Moore and Latouche, Baby Doe's steadfast love for Tabor is. "Unusual men all have unusual ways. All we can do is to try to be worthy—that is our duty," she sings to the enraged Augusta.

In many ways, Augusta Tabor is the most interesting character of the threesome. Given many of the most dramatic moments in the opera, she emerges a noble and tragic figure through Moore's sensitivity to her inner emotional conflicts. In her long, expressive aria in act 2, scene 4, she realizes that she still loves Tabor and wants to help him in his time of great need but cannot. I must "die in the prison of myself, alone," she had sung earlier. But now she wrestles further with her conscience: "Augusta, Augusta! This is your failure too. You bear his name. Although he has grieved you, he is still part of you. . . . Oh, my beloved! Why, why did you ever leave me? . . . Once again I hear him calling. Calling on Augusta, Augusta, but I cannot go." Moore's lush, symphonic score flows along with her anguish, melodramatically, as in the scores of Puccini and the films of Max Steiner. Her vocal lines grow increasingly intense as well, and there is no doubt that she must come to grips with her identity.

Horace Tabor's most effective scene comes at the end of the opera. Like the tableaux of the early melodrama, figures reappear onstage in a kind of apotheosis.[14] In this case they reflect and prophetize in song. As in a dream, Tabor returns to the Opera House in Leadville, now an old man in work clothes. He sees before him his early life along with images of Augusta, various miners, politicians, and his two daughters. A chorus of phantoms sings motet-style the inscription printed on the curtain of the Opera House (which still stands):

So fleet the works of man,
Back to the earth again,
Ancient and holy things
Fade like a dream.

Horace Tabor's final vision is that of Baby Doe as she sings gently:

Always through the changing
Of sun and shadow, time and space,
I will walk beside my love
In a green and quiet place
. . . .
As our earthly eyes grow dim,
Still the old song will be sung.
I shall change along with him
So that both are ever young,
Ever young.

As she pushes back her hood and reveals her white hair, the rear stage becomes transparent and the Matchless Mine comes into view. She sits by the mineshaft, waiting, while a delicate drift of white snow falls gently upon her. And the curtain closes.

Robert Ward's The Crucible

The New York City Opera triumphed once again when Robert Ward's *The Crucible* was given its world premiere on October 26, 1961. Douglas Watt wrote, "'The Crucible' is one more impressive example of the coming of age of American opera." "If a finer opera has been written since the days of Strauss and Puccini," Winthrop Sargeant reported, "I have not heard it."[15] Critics also observed the work's powerful yet conservative neoromantic score. That, they felt, was characteristic of American composers of the time, a characteristic Harold Schonberg called "an American phenomenon." "Certainly none of the young composers in Europe," he said, "would think of setting a libretto with the conventional harmonies that Mr. Ward has used. Generally speaking, European operatic composers, with the sole exception of Poulenc, are wedded to dodecaphony and its derivations."[16]

True, a Wagnerian-Straussian influence runs throughout *The Crucible,* largely in the way voices weave in and out of the lush, romantic orchestral fabric in a kind of relentless quasi-recitative or parlando. What results is exciting theater. Ward's style, unlike Douglas Moore's, allows few *aba* or strophic arias with poetic texts or even extended lyrical moments where dialogue gives way to reflection. Reflection, however, is not what the opera is about. It is about demonic ritual, pierced, doll-like images, and satanic possession—the stuff of *The Exorcist*. It is also about passionate emotions: fear, frustration, and anguish. John's aria at the end of act 2 is vehement. "I'll tear your tongue from your head," he sings to Mary Warren, one of the so-called devil-worshipers. Grabbing her by the throat and hurling her to the ground, he lashes out, "Now Hell and Heaven grapple on our very backs, and all pretense is ripped away. . . . And the wind will blow, God's icy wind."[17] A melismatic heightening on the word *blow* and a high baritone G-sharp on *wind,* and the audience is sitting on the edge of its seats, waiting to see what happens next. As one critic said, "Ward uses melody as a dramatic weapon."[18]

The story of *The Crucible* derives from Arthur Miller's play of the same title about the Salem witchcraft trials of the 1690s. Tales of religious fanaticism in New England were the subjects of earlier American operas, such as *Merry Mount* by Howard Hanson and Charles Wakefield Cadman's *The Witch of Salem*. *The Crucible,* however, surpasses them all in its compelling, lurid tale of animosity and greed. It is a world devoid of reason or compassion, and it must deal with the conscience of a community stirred to a storm of hatred. Modern society might find its "devils" in McCarthyism or the Ku Klux Klan. *The Crucible,* both play and opera, is about mass hysteria set against common reason. It argues the senseless morality that allows those who confess to demon worship to be spared and those who protest their innocence to be hanged. More specifically, it tells of the lascivious desires of young Abigail Williams for the dissenting farmer John Proctor. Because he refuses to compromise his personal integrity, Proctor and his wife Elizabeth are ultimately led out to be executed.

For his first four operas, Ward chose as his librettist Bernard Stambler, a colleague at Juilliard who was a fine violist and scholar of both Italian and English literature. Ward comments, "A play is ordinarily made up of comparatively short lines, though you do sometimes have soliloquies and longer segments. Because ordinarily a libretto is about two-thirds the length of a play, a major cutting job has to be done. Working with contemporary playwrights can be a problem, because they're not excited about having one-third of their masterpiece cut away. Arthur Miller was extremely understanding and unusual in this regard. When he first looked at the subject of the Salem witchcraft, he even thought it would lend itself better to an opera than a play."[19]

Cutting a play can create problems in the sense of the drama, however. Miller established Abigail's invidious nature early in one of the play's best scenes. By omitting that scene in the opera, the rationale for Abigail's initial vindictive behavior becomes somewhat mollified. Ward adds:

> In determining the cuts within the play, the first thing is to get rid of repetition. The next thing is to determine whether there are some characters that can be combined. In the original play, there were several judges, and we wanted to embody that whole quality and spirit in one role [Judge Danforth], so that we could build him up to be a bigger character. There was also a sheriff and a bailiff that we could combine and a number of the young women, who then became a vocal sextet in the opera, an important small chorus that one was very much aware of in the big trial scene. Then, the next thing one does is to look for those places in the play that can become a real ensemble, trio, or aria—whatever seems to be called for by the drama at that point. Sometimes the librettist gets into a different kind of writing here, more in the style of lyric poetry. After the libretto is by and large completed, the composer can then shape his musical score.[20]

Ward deplores the tendency—exemplified in Alban Berg's *Wozzeck*—to shift dramatic emphasis from singers to orchestra. Thus he places most of the responsibility for unity in the opera in the melody or vocal lines. The initial melodic idea of Reverend Hale's first aria, "For much in the world seems Devil's work," returns at the end of the act as all rejoice in Tituba's "confession," creating musical unity and heightened dramatic irony. With the exception of one blues aria sung by Tituba, the demon-conjuring Trinidadian slave in act 4, there is little hint of Broadway or popular American styles in the opera. In several superb ensembles such as that in the scene at the end of act 1, Abigail's voice soars in gloriously acerbic counterpoint above the town elders' infectious psalm, pulsating in a hemiola-like, seven-eighths meter.

Ward's command of prosody is always secure. He dwells lovingly on some words ("house") and snaps off sharply on others ("poppet"). Inner passion comes not only from characters and their vocal lines but also from the melodramatic treatment of the orchestra. Paul Henry Lang called it "suspense music." Although Ward emphasizes his use of voice for dramatic impact, he relies also on the evocative propulsion of the orchestra. Where Strauss and Mahler do not shine through, film composers Alex North and Bernard Herrmann often do.

The Crucible was commissioned by the New York City Opera, and the year after its premiere it won both a Pulitzer Prize and the New York Music Critic's Circle Award. The original cast included Patricia Brooks as Abigail, Chester Ludgrin as John, Frances Bible as Elizabeth, and Norman Treigle as the Reverend Hale. The opera has also been performed in German in Wiesbaden and in Korean as part of the fortieth anniversary celebration of the liberation of that country from Japan. In Osaka, it was staged in Japanese, a language Ward finds interesting to sing ("It contains beautiful vowels, like Italian") and is also being translated into Swedish.

Susannah, *a Biblical Tale Americanized*

When Erich Leinsdorf, conductor of the Cleveland Symphony Orchestra, assumed his new post as general manager of the New York City Opera in 1955, he brought with him a whirlwind of ideas about ways to revitalize the ailing company—or so he thought. One was to build a revolving stage that would minimize production costs. The experiment failed, however, and the company's grim financial situation continued to escalate.[21]

One bright spot under Leinsdorf was the New York premiere of Carlisle Floyd's *Susannah* on September 27, 1956, which Leinsdorf himself conducted. It turned out to be the major event of the season, with Phyllis Curtin as the tragic, victimized Susannah and Norman Treigle in a compelling interpretation of the itinerant preacher Olin Blitch. "Some of the most powerful pages in American opera were heard at the City Center last night," wrote Louis Biancolli. "To my mind," observed Winthrop Sargeant, "'Susannah' is probably the most moving and impressive opera to have been written in America—or anywhere else, as far as I am aware—since Gershwin's 'Porgy and Bess.'" "For those who believe in the future of American music," added Miles Kastendieck, "'Susannah' should be a tonic. It brought distinction both to the new regime and the history of opera at City Center."[22]

Susannah received its world premiere at Florida State University on February 24, 1955, with Phyllis Curtin, whose glorious nuances from pianissimo to fortissimo in the lead role rapidly became a tradition at City Opera and elsewhere. Julius Rudel brought the opera back once again to New York in 1958 for the first Ford Foundation series, and in the summer the production traveled overseas, where it was staged at the Brussels World's Fair. Since its premiere, *Susannah* has been performed more than seven hundred times, both professionally and by college opera theaters worldwide. According to one report, it has seen more performances in the United States than

Phyllis Curtin, Norman Treigle, and Eb Thomas in New York City Opera's production of *Susannah* by Carlisle Floyd in 1958. *Astor, Lenox and Tilden Foundations, New York Public Library*

any other opera including *Carmen, La Bohème,* and *Porgy and Bess*.[23] Among the opera's most successful and widely acclaimed revivals have been those at the Lyric Opera of Chicago in 1993, L'Opera de Nantes in 1997 (its French premiere), and the Metropolitan Opera (with Renée Fleming) in 1998. *Susannah* also won several honors for its composer, among them a Music Critics' Circle Award and a Guggenheim Fellowship. Paradoxically, although Carlisle Floyd has composed twelve operas and his work has been more frequently performed on American stages than that of any other living composer except perhaps Menotti, he receives scant mention in surveys of opera, twentieth-century music, or even American music.[24]

In many ways, *Susannah,* like *The Crucible,* is cast in the shadow of the political witch-hunts of the McCarthy era. The innocent individual versus the bigotry of the masses was a familiar theme during the 1950s. But Floyd expresses it quite differently from Ward, both musically and dramatically.

Running throughout are set pieces resembling the many moods of American culture: folk songs, revival hymns, and Appalachian square dances. Only a single character, Susannah herself, is the focal point of Floyd's story.

The inspiration for *Susannah* comes from the apocryphal tale of Susannah and the Elders. Drawing on his background in the rural South, Floyd set the opera in an isolated community without electricity or running water in the mountains of Tennessee, like other rural communities in America after World War II. Only twenty-eight and teaching at Florida State University when he wrote the opera, Floyd knew from his childhood the type of revival meetings he portrayed. They provided "these rural, remote people their meagre allotment of excitement for one week of each year," he said, "almost always in the stifling heat of midsummer."[25] Yet heat may not explain abhorrent behavior. As Sam, Susannah's brother, sings:

> It's about the way people is made, I rekon.
> An' how they like to believe what's bad.
> How short they are on lovin' kindness.
> It must make the good Lord sad.

In Floyd's reinterpretation of the biblical tale, the lovely young Susannah becomes the victim of malicious gossip ("that pretty face must hide some evil"). When she is found bathing nude in the baptismal creek, the town elders ostracize her. Even a simple-minded lad, Little Bat, is badgered into falsely admitting that Susannah had tried to "love him up." The itinerant preacher Olin Blitch first tries to persuade Susannah to repent a sin she feels she did not commit, and then he seduces her. Caught up in a war between flesh and spirit, Blitch attempts to convince the villagers that she is innocent, but to no avail. The townspeople are too enmeshed in bigotry and hatred. When Susannah's alcoholic brother Sam learns of Blitch's behavior, he shoots and kills the preacher at the very creek in which his sister was found bathing. Enraged, mobs come after Susannah, but she picks up a gun and points it at them menacingly, laughing wildly and derisively as they move away. She calls Little Bat over to her seductively and then slaps him viciously across the face. Susannah stands alone in the doorway, physically strong but defeated in spirit and destroyed by the hypocrisy of her people.

If Copland's Laurie does not grow and develop, Susannah does. She moves from being a simple mountain girl singing about nature and birds to an "inexorably lonely prisoner of self-imposed exile," as the final stage directions spell out.[26] Those changes are seen not only in the course of the drama but also in Susannah's two arias from acts 1 and 2, her only arias in the opera. Floyd even provides a suggestion of these changes before the opera starts. Themes from each aria are heard in the short opening orchestral prelude but in reverse order. "Ain't it a pretty night?" Susannah sings in the first act as her voice whispers and soars in longing.

> The sky's so dark and velvet-like
> And it's all lit up with stars.
> It's like a great big mirror
> Reflectin' fire-flies over a pond.

Then, like Laurie in *The Tender Land,* she reflects, as her voice builds in volume and intensity: "Someday I'll leave an' then I'll come back / When I've seen what's beyond them mountains." But unlike Laurie, Susannah provides a glimpse into the dark shadows that inhabit her psyche and soul. By act 2, scene 3, "The trees on the mountains are cold and bare," she sings in a plaintive, folk-like strophic aria colored by a lowered leading tone and other modal inflections, "There's darkness around me an' not even a star to show me the way to lighten my heart."

Susannah's melodies contain moments of great beauty and poignancy, but Floyd can also write powerful, harrowingly dramatic scenes. A fine example is the orgiastic revival meeting featuring Blitch's hell-fire preaching in act 2. While Susannah sits huddled on the last bench, the choir sings a lusty revival tune. Over their invitation for salvation, Blitch shouts his cause for taking up the collection ("Don't shortchange the Lord!"). As he begins the sermon, his words are at first spoken, but as his exhortation becomes ever more frenzied his message evolves into a kind of speech-song. At the height of the scene he is singing in full voice. With the choir's hymn "Come, Sinner, Salvation Is Free," couples come forward one by one until finally Susannah rises and begins to move toward Blitch, "a confusion of fear, bewilderment and protest on her face." "No! No!" she suddenly screams and, "shattering the hypnotic power of the meeting," she runs down the aisle and out into the night.

The scene is remarkable in its projection of "the tension, effrontery and, above all, the terror implicit in the revival meeting of this nature," Floyd writes in the stage directions. The piano-vocal score for *Susannah* looks and reads like the early-nineteenth-century melodrama scores of John Bray and others, linking the practices of early and modern music theater. Floyd is so attuned to the dramaturgical aspects of *Susannah* that he describes every detail of action, facial expression, and emotion. He also expects them to be realized in the staging: "Her face is flushed with high spirits and excitement"; "it should be immediately apparent that the bond between brother and sister is one of loyalty, warmth and tenderness"; and "his hands are clasped tightly together, and they from time to time emphasize his desperate sincerity . . . here is Blitch for the first time stripped of his bravado and evangelical trappings: a man terrified by his own image of a vengeful god."[27]

Like Menotti and others—Wagner, Berlioz, Leoncavallo, and Berg—Floyd prefers to write his own librettos. He has been a skilled creative writer since his youth and asserts that to know his subjects he must remain in contact with the public. Because it furnishes precisely such contact, music for theater, films, and ballet interests Floyd as much as that of opera. "A libretto should make some comment on contemporary life and timeless human problems," he maintains. It should also meet "all the stipulations of competent playwriting—for instance, careful, logical structure, thorough motivation both in plot and in character development . . . and a well-defined conflict with at least partial resolution."[28] Floyd prefers to adapt plots in which "the characters are trapped as frequently as possible in near-crisis, or in provocative situations which force them into an exposure of intense feelings." In addition, "A good librettist must insure that a margin of time be allowed the composer for what he terms 'an emotional expansion.'"[29] Floyd also thinks that a librettist should not be preoccupied with "telling the listener everything about the characters through the text, but rather should be concerned with creating situations within the plot that permit the characters to reveal themselves to the audience through their own dramatic actions."[30]

In addition to *Susannah,* the New York City Opera has staged three other operas by Carlisle Floyd: the world premiere of *The Passion of Jonathan Wade* (1962) and the New York premieres of *Wuthering Heights* in 1959 and *Of Mice and Men* in 1983. Of Floyd's twelve operas, *Wuthering Heights* (1958) and *Markheim* (1966, after Robert Louis Stevenson) are the only ones that do not have American settings. In some of his later operas, *Of Mice and Men* (1970), *Bilby's Doll* (1976), and *Willie Stark* (1981), for example, Floyd uses more chromaticism and plunges deeper into human emotions than in his earlier, less pretentious verismo works. But in his stunning and highly successful *Cold Sassy Tree* (Houston 2000), he returns to what has given *Susannah* its lasting power—a wealth of melody, an accessible tonal palette, and strong propulsion toward a compelling conclusion. Clearly, Floyd knows how to give audiences a memorable dramatic experience.

✍

The New York City Opera was the first to bring the American folk opera style of the 1950s—that of Copland, Moore, and Floyd—into the sphere of professional production. Later in the decade, however, City Opera's American repertoire began to move away from that rural, homespun idiom to a more international and grander operatic expression. Simple, folklike American concert music was, of course, an outgrowth of the period from 1936 to 1942, the years of the Great Depression's Federal Music Project that encouraged reaching to the far corners of America "in the simplest possible terms," as Aaron Copland once said.

That concept extended into the postwar 1950s. But times were changing. The spaces for opera were expanding. To the bountiful stage of the Metropolitan Opera House came *Vanessa* by Samuel Barber, and then the new Met at Lincoln Center staged his *Antony and Cleopatra*. Other works by different composers—*Six Characters in Search of an Author, The Golem, Natalia Petrovna,* and *Mourning Becomes Elektra*—became new expressions of a confident age. Regional Americanism was beginning to give way to more sophisticated international libretto sources—Strindberg, Pirandello, Turgenev, Dinesen, Hasek, Kafka, and Wedekind. America could now be assured, as Carlisle Floyd noted, that it had developed "a type of lyric theater that could stand without apology, yet in graceful acknowledgment of its predecessors in Europe."[31] Through the long skein of brilliant American works featured at the New York City Opera, Floyd's words have been rightfully realized.

15

Dreamers of Decadence

Please do not be so surprised when a reality is born, formed and invoked by the magic of the stage itself.
  —Hugo Weisgall, *Six Characters in Search of an Author*

IF SAMUEL BARBER was considered lushly conservative in the manner of Richard Strauss and Giacomo Puccini, other American composers— Marvin Levy, Hugo Weisgall, Robert Kurka, Ned Rorem, and Jack Beeson—moved more readily into the bold new dimensions of modern music and dramatic form. Emphasis on craft, on the compositional techniques of Alban Berg, Leoš Janáček, Darius Milhaud, Arnold Schonberg, and Igor Stravinsky, allowed them to move away from neoromanticism and into more pronounced dissonance, dodecaphony, polytonality, and free chromaticism. Many of the advanced ideas in William Bolcom's *Greatshot* (1966) drew from Charles Ives. And Gunther Schuller's *The Visitation* (1966) used a combination of serialism and jazz ("Third Stream Music") to transfer the nightmare symbolism of Kafka's *The Trial* to the realistic world of the American racial problem.[1]

Themes for the librettos of the period were often more philosophical than they had been earlier, probing the inner workings of the heart and mind. Verismo was not merely action, dialogue, and violence, but—as Jack Beeson's *Lizzie Borden* attests—it could project strong psychological images as well. Expressionist symbolism and the investigation of illusion versus reality were valid issues of operatic concern. Samuel Lippmann's view of Hugo Weisgall as "the thinking man's Menotti" was well on mark.

The folklike influences of Americana that had left their mark on the operas of the 1940s and 1950s had little place in the creative minds of many composers in the decade following. That is especially evident in three premieres of American works at the Metropolitan Opera between 1958 and 1967: Samuel Barber's *Vanessa* (1958), his *Antony and Cleopatra* (1966), and Marvin David Levy's *Mourning Becomes Electra* (1967). It would be twenty-five years before the Met would commission another work by an

American, John Corigliano's brilliant *Ghosts of Versailles,* which was staged in 1991.

Three Important Premieres

Perhaps it was Julius Rudel's visionary American series at City Opera in 1958 that prompted Rudolph Bing, then in his eighth year as general manager of the Metropolitan Opera, to come to grips with the dilemma of American opera. The Met's staging of Bernard Rogers's short-lived *The Warrior* a decade earlier offered little encouragement, but when the Met unveiled Samuel Barber's *Vanessa* on January 14, 1958, the arts world took notice. Both its composer and librettist were well known, and one of the world's greatest opera houses was providing the showcase. The most gifted and popular American composer of mid-century, Samuel Barber (1910–81) received a Pulitzer Prize for *Vanessa.* In addition to *Vanessa,* Barber had one other opera performed at the Metropolitan Opera: *Antony and Cleopatra* opened the new opera house at Lincoln Center. Among other American composers, only Walter Damrosch and Deems Taylor have had more than one opera staged at the Met.

A good part of the success of *Vanessa* lies in Barber's collaboration with Gian Carlo Menotti, his lifelong friend from the Curtis Institute of Music. Before asking Menotti to be his librettist, Barber had approached several authors, including Thornton Wilder, Stephen Spender, and James Agee, but with no success. At one point he even thought of making an opera out of Tennessee Williams's *Streetcar Named Desire,* but he felt the texture of Williams's poetic language allowed "no room for music. . . . Writers must get the feel of the lyric stage," he said, "the real smell of the stage. One must be a habitue of the opera, like Stendhal at La Scala."[2]

Barber and Menotti eventually settled on Isak Dinesen's *Seven Gothic Tales* as the source for *Vanessa,* although more for atmosphere than specific plot. "An opera need not have an American setting to be an American opera," Barber admitted. "Besides, art is international, and if an idea is inspired, it needs no boundaries."[3] *Vanessa* is a melodramatic tale of dark passion and somber irony. As Menotti tells it:

> This is the story of two women, Vanessa and Erika, caught in the central dilemma which faces every human being: whether to fight for one's ideals to the point of shutting oneself off from reality, or compromise with what life has to offer, even lying to oneself for the mere sake of living. Like a sullen Greek chorus, a third woman (the old Grandmother) con-

demns by her very silence the refusal first of Vanessa, then of Erika, to accept the bitter truth that life offers no solution except its own inherent struggle. When Vanessa, in her final eagerness to embrace life, realizes this truth, it is perhaps too late.[4]

Vanessa was originally written in four acts, but in 1964 Barber combined the first two, and that three-act version is usually performed today. The newer edition also eliminates Vanessa's glittering "skating aria," which has difficult coloratura passages. The action takes place in a "northern country" about 1905 and opens in Vanessa's luxurious country home. "A lady of great beauty," she has waited more than twenty years for the return of her only love, Anatol ("I have scarcely breathed so that Life should not leave its trace"). She, her lovely young niece Erika, and her mother the baroness (Erika's grandmother) live in a home in which mirrors and portraits are covered with cloth. When a stranger named Anatol comes to visit, Vanessa discovers that it is not the Anatol she knew but his son. The scoundrel first seduces Erika and then manages to become engaged to Vanessa. At a New Year's ball, when the couple announce their plans for marriage Erika, stunned and carrying Anatol's child, runs out into the freezing night, causing a miscarriage. Although she confides her anguish to the baroness, Erika hides the truth from Vanessa, who blindly marries Anatol. After the couple leaves for Paris, Erika covers the pictures once again. "From now on I shall receive no visitors," she tells the housekeeper. "Now it is my turn to wait."

In Menotti's explanation, *Vanessa* tells us that "love only exists as a compromise. . . . Whomever we love, it's not the image of the one we expected."[5] But *Vanessa* offers a still wider-ranging message. Waiting, in effect, is a kind of yearning, a longing for that which is unattainable. "You do not love him, then?" asks the baroness. "Oh, yes," answers Erika, "I love someone like him!" Vanessa, too, is able to love only a mere image—a false Anatol not the real one. Critics have found Erika to be the more central character of the opera; she also completes Vanessa's persona. "Sometimes I am her niece but mostly her shadow," Erika sings in answer to Anatol's question about who she is.

It is Erika who completes the dark and cyclic boundaries of the opera. Menotti and Barber also emphasize the desolation of the characters through their bleak, sunless environment. Chilling, snow-laden landscapes shape the text and provide the music with vibrant lyrical potential. The first aria in the opera, Erika's, sets the scene with poetic yearning. "Must the winter come so soon?" she sings gently:

Night after night I hear the hungry deer
wander weeping in the woods,
and from his house of brittle bark
hoots the frozen owl.[6]

The true magic of the opera lies in its music. *Vanessa*'s score moves from dialogue to reflection to action seamlessly and sensitively. Arioso-like passages expand into the sweeping, impassioned melody characteristic of Barber's arias and love duets. In serving the drama, Barber leaves no stone unturned. Special effects advance the action and emphasize the symbolic message, whether sleigh bells, the tower bell tolling ever faster, comic relief in the antics of the old doctor, the grotesque polytonal inflections in the New Year's ball scene, or the canonic structure of the quintet at the close of the opera. After its premiere, Paul Henry Lang observed that "a broad and unified mood, an all-encompassing musical picture seizes the listener. Mr. Barber's mastery of the operatic language is remarkable and second to none now active on the Salzburg-Milan axis . . . His vocal writing is impeccable and his handling of the orchestra virtuoso to a Straussian degree."[7]

In *Vanessa,* the orchestra becomes another character, colored by a lush, dramatic instrumental fabric calling for the power of doubled winds and the sensitivity of solo oboe and English horn. Sharp, biting fragmentary punctuations, recalling Stravinsky, often comment on the dialogue, a style of dramatic writing seen later in the works of Lee Hoiby and Jack Beeson. At times the orchestra matches the text, as in the humorous fumbling of the doctor ("Good Heavens where is my speech?"), at which the orchestra shivers in rapid tremolo and piccolo runs. With sudden, intense dissonance Vanessa cries out concern for Anatol's safe arrival ("Oh, I shall die if anything happens to him!"). Much more interesting, however, are less explicit passages in which the orchestra, in the manner of Bernard Herrmann and Richard Wagner, tells more than the characters themselves say or know. In the first scene of act 1, Anatol tells Erika that Vanessa will let him stay the night. The orchestra grasps his remarks with violence and intensity, warning of Erika's impending seduction.

The orchestra also provides continuity throughout the opera in its persistent use of leitmotifs associated with characters and their plight. Barber often uses the leitmotif technique contrapuntally to give some of his most intense scenes a sense of dramatic confusion. After Anatol's impassioned aria "Outside this house the world has changed," the orchestra bursts forth with biting Stravinskian accentuations as the distraught Erica realizes the truth about Anatol. As the family prepares for chapel, the chorus sings a simple hymn offstage. Simultaneously, the leitmotif associated with Erika's anguished, distorted mind expands into a violent countermelody shrouding the simple diatonic tonality with grotesque chromaticism. Finally, Erika cries out her answer, "No, Anatol, my answer is no. Let Vanessa have you, she who for so little had to wait so long!" And she falls, sobbing hysterically, onto a sofa as the curtain descends.

Barber's fine sense of counterpoint as a means of enhancing the drama is also apparent in the brilliant New Year's ball scene closing act 2. He pits joy against tragedy by superimposing contrasting instrumental textures, meters, and melodic phrases. Three musical vehicles enlarge the conflict: the full and impassioned orchestra, a smaller offstage dance orchestra, and a solo violinist and accordion player onstage. This striking instrumental layering underlines Erika's despair and near-madness as she leaves the party and stumbles out into the snowstorm. The mildly modal peasant dance becomes increasingly distorted and contaminated by polytonal and bimetrical intrusion until only the lone accordion player is heard as a somber reminder of Erika's loss.

The Metropolitan Opera premiere of *Vanessa* spared no expense in staging, costumes, and performers. Cecil Beaton made certain that Vanessa was lavishly clad in velvet, fur, or gold brocade, and she wore million-dollar diamond jewelry on loan from Harry Winston Jewelers. The production, conducted by Dimitri Mitropoulos, comprised some of the finest internationally known singers of the time. For the demanding role of Vanessa, with its wide vocal range and extended phrases, Barber at first tried to interest Maria Callas. When that failed, he engaged the Yugoslavian soprano Sena Jurinac, but she had to cancel only weeks before the premiere. Fortunately, Eleanor Steber stepped in and learned the role in six weeks, having become familiar with Barber's music when she sang in the premiere of his *Knoxville: Summer of 1915*. Other stellar cast members included the mezzo-sopranos Rosalind Elias (Erika) and Regina Resnik (the baroness); the Swedish tenor Nicolai Gedda (Anatol); and the noted bass Giorgio Tozzi as the bibulous old family doctor. The audience, which included Artur Rubinstein, Fritz Reiner, Katherine Cornell, and many other luminaries, thundered approbation, and Barber was greeted by "deafening delirium."

Vanessa was staged in Baltimore, Boston, Philadelphia, and in major cities overseas. It was the first American opera to be produced in Salzburg, and in 1961 it was performed in Italian at the Spoleto Festival, receiving thirty curtain calls. In 1965 the revised three-act version was produced by the

Samuel Barber, Gian Carlo Menotti, and Eleanor Steber in one of her elegant costumes for the Metropolitan Opera's world premiere of Barber's *Vanessa. Metropolitan Opera Archives*

Metropolitan Opera, with Mary Costa as Vanessa and John Alexander as Anatol. The opera was televised in 1979 as part of the PBS *Great Performances* series, and companies such as Opera Theatre of St. Louis and the Washington Opera directed by Michael Kahn have staged it. Perhaps *Vanessa* will make its way once again to the Metropolitan.

Barber's next full-length opera, *Antony and Cleopatra,* had little of the panache and success of *Vanessa.* Commissioned by the Metropolitan Opera for the opening of its new $50 million house at Lincoln Center, *Antony* received more publicity worldwide than any other American opera in history. Its glittering premiere on September 16, 1966, was attended by Ladybird Johnson, and the cast included Leontyne Price as Cleopatra; Justino Diaz, Antony; Rosalind Elias, Charmian; and Jess Thomas, Caesar. Thomas Schippers conducted. On a stage twice the size of the old Met, the production was described as a kind of "latter-day *Aida,*" with tons of tulle, Roman armies, live camels, and a cast of hundreds. It was a grandiose spectacle "situated on the cosmic scale somewhere above the primeval atom that caused the original Big Bang, and somewhere below the creation of the Milky Way."[8]

It also was beset with mechanical problems. One week before opening night, the new revolving stage broke down and had to be moved manually by stage crew dressed in costume. Even the lighting cues misfired, and Cleopatra had to make her entrance on a pitch-black stage. "I was locked in the pyramid at the first aria because something mechanical didn't open up at the right time," Price recalls. "There was no way in the world I could make that cue. I was to be dressed in the pyramid for the next scene, and I simply said 'Zip this one back up, whether it fits or not, I'll keep singing, and just go out.'"[9]

The tragedy of *Antony and Cleopatra* lay not so much in Franco Zeffirelli's over-effulgent staging or in numerous technical mishaps (the production proceeded "with the enthusiasm of a group of children around a big, new Erector set") but in the way it was perceived by the press.[10] The social occasion and visual elements overshadowed the music, and the blame for *Antony*'s failure fell unjustly on the composer. Barber, devastated, returned to Italy. "As far as I'm concerned," he admitted, "the production had nothing to do with what I had imagined. . . . The Met overproduced it. . . . What I wrote and what I envisioned had nothing to do with what one saw on that stage. Zeffirelli wanted horses and goats and two hundred soldiers, which he got, and he wanted elephants, which fortunately he didn't get. The point is, I had very little control—practically none. . . . On the other hand, management supported every idea of Zeffirelli's."[11]

How Zeffirelli came into the picture as Barber's librettist and the Met's stage director for *Antony and Cleopatra* was likely due to the success he had in directing Shakespearean plays for film, theater, and opera. His brilliant production of Verdi's *Falstaff* at the old Metropolitan in 1964 is legend. But while Zeffirelli was directing *The Taming of the Shrew* in Italy with Elizabeth Taylor and Richard Burton, another Taylor-Burton film was released, the ill-starred cinematic fiasco *Cleopatra* (1963). Twentieth-Century Fox's $32 million motion picture extravaganza ran for four interminable hours and was so unsuccessful that the studio's stock plummeted overnight and its president was fired. Boring dialogue and unrealistic characters were not its only problems. The film version of *Cleopatra* (perhaps like the opera) came a year or two too late. The 1950s boom in postwar spectacle—*Samson and Delilah* (1949), *The Ten Commandments* (1956), *Quo Vadis* (1951), *Helen of Troy* (1955), and *Spartacus* (1960)—was over. Audiences of the 1960s were no longer mesmerized by historical romance. Cleopatra had had her moment of mid-twentieth-century popularity.[12] Barber, Zeffirelli, and the Metropolitan apparently did not see things that way.

In providing the libretto with scenes in both Rome and Egypt, Zeffirelli created a collage of images through which Barber could shape his score.[13] Among his "Roman" musical forces are military fanfares, formal designs (a two-part invention and a passacaglia), and angular, energetic declamations. His "Egyptian music," by contrast, is sensuous and exotic, with delicate woodwind and percussion effects and opulent harmonies. By repeating certain key lines of Shakespeare's text, Zeffirelli gave Barber an opportunity to develop musical motifs through repetition, transformation, and association with the unfolding drama. One of the most striking of these motifs accompanies the image of Antony as Cleopatra sings "My Man of Men." Soaring initially through a minor ninth to the word *man,* the motif returns in the revised 1975 ending of the opera as Cleopatra dies ("Now I feed myself with most delicious poison / That I might sleep out this great gap of time / My man of men!"). Many motifs throughout the opera are so lyrical that they become integrated into the vocal line. In so doing, they become extended themes and give the opera a more mellifluous unity than the cinematic orchestral motifs found in *Vanessa.*

The orchestration in *Antony* is especially rich and varied. The score calls for a huge, romantic sound. It is also more sensuous and flowing than *Vanessa's*, and fewer Herrmannesque punctuation marks emphasize action and dialogue. Barber, however, could also say a great deal with the least possible means. Antony's long suicide scenario is scored effectively for only kettledrum ostinato and lone, mournful flute. And the ghostly visions outside Antony's tent with the eerie "music i'th'air" is imaginatively rendered by the ondes martenot (i.e., electronic instrumentation).

One problem that seemed to haunt Barber as he wrote *Antony and Cleopatra* was how to deal with a love story that had no true love scenes. For the 1975 revision of the opera, produced successfully—and simply—

by the Juilliard American Opera Center with Menotti as stage director, Barber asked Menotti to rewrite the libretto. Together they shortened the opera by one hour, pared down the size of the huge cast, and extended Cleopatra's final, magnificent death scene, making her, in Dyer's words, "a most triumphant lady."[14] Stripped of its "camelflage," the opera was now stronger in continuity and dramatic thrust, and the lovers were more clearly focused. Cleopatra's short aria in act 2, "If This Be Love," was more fully realized. Perhaps the most important and satisfactory addition to the opera was the love duet in act 2, "Take, O Take Those Lips Away," a set piece with a hint of Puccini's *Turandot* and an abundance of Barber's lyricism.[15]

In 1983, two years after Barber's death, the Juilliard revision of *Antony and Cleopatra* was produced at the Spoleto Festival in Charleston, South Carolina, and recorded for New World Records. In the first revival by a major company, the Lyric Opera of Chicago staged it in 1991 in two acts as part of the "Toward the Twenty-first Century" series of revivals and commissions. The performance appeared on PBS television later the same year. Catherine Malfitano as Cleopatra brilliantly handled the wide leaps and drops of Barber's difficult vocal lines, and Richard Cowan was a powerfully moving Antony.

Barber's opera is also a taut, riveting piece of music theater. "With Barber's lush, sinuous melodies contributing to the steamy atmosphere," wrote Wynne Delacoma in the *Chicago Sun-Times,* "Shakespeare's tale of sex and violence becomes as compelling as a finely crafted R-rated action flick."[16] The allusion to an R-rated film was not far off mark. Although the score called for a Roman banquet, the Lyric Opera provided instead a dimly lit room where men, stripped to the waist, sat on the floor and caressed each other. "This is not music you whistle as you leave the theater," added Delacoma, "but its heat lingers long after the final curtain." Certainly as much as various Janáček revivals, *Antony and Cleopatra* deserves to stay in the repertoire, hopefully with much of the original uncut version retained. It is a rare American opera in the grand tradition.[17]

With *Antony and Cleopatra* and Blitzstein's opera on the Sacco-Vanetti case (left unfinished with the composer's untimely death), *Mourning Becomes Electra* was the third Ford Foundation work commissioned by the Metropolitan Opera and the last American work to be commissioned by the Met for a quarter of a century. The opera is based on Eugene O'Neill's somber trilogy after the *Oresteia* but is set in a New England seaport at the end of the Civil War. The libretto by Henry Butler, the Metropolitan's long-time stage director, cuts O'Neill's original six-hour epic to operatic dimensions and uses the titles of individual plays—*Homecoming, The Hunted,*

Michael Yeargan's set for *Antony and Cleopatra* by Samuel Barber staged by Lyric Opera of Chicago in 1991. *Photo by Dan Rest*

and *The Haunted*—for each of the opera's three acts. This "cozy Aeschylean tangle" focuses almost exclusively on the psychological currents that churn relentlessly beneath the surface of each of the main characters, as does the play. As *Time* observed, tongue in cheek, "The daughter loves the father, hates mother, The mother loves another man, hates the father and daughter. The son loves the mother and the daughter. The mother kills the father. The son kills the mother's lover. The mother commits suicide. The son commits suicide."[18] And the daughter goes mad and entombs herself in the family home. Great fodder for opera, but was Levy up to the task?

Mourning Becomes Electra was Marvin David Levy's first full-length opera and is his best-known work. His one-act *The Tower*, set in biblical antiquity, had its world premiere on August 2, 1957, at the Santa Fe Opera Festival on the composer's twenty-fifth birthday. Born in Passaic, New Jersey, Levy has composed numerous orchestral, choral, and chamber works and won several prestigious awards. In addition to *Mourning*, he received another Metropolitan commission, *The Balcony* (1978), but the opera was never performed, reputedly because of a change of administration at the Met.

Levy's dramatic talent is apparent. Admitting that he viewed the original play version of *Mourning Becomes Electra* as a "verbal opera," he tried musically to approach the dramatic cycle forms that O'Neill used.[19] Although the score is dissonant and expressionistic, its rhythmic drive and instrumental colors often provide a bracing American quality. Significantly, the intensely cinematic orchestral score at times resembles that of Bernard Herrmann's film thriller *Psycho,* which was produced only the year before Levy began work on his opera.

The Metropolitan Opera premiere of *Mourning Becomes Electra* on March 17, 1967, included one of the company's finest casts: Evelyn Lear, Marie Collier, Sherill Milnes, John Reardon, and John Macurdy, with Zubin Mehta conducting. Both sopranos, Lear and the Australian-born Collier, were making their debuts, and it was the Greek director Michael Cacoyannis's first position with the Met. Reviews were exceptionally good. *Mourning Becomes Electra* was "the finest American opera yet to come to the Met's stage. . . . The sounds he [Levy] creates are of a beauty rare in the American opera." Levy was said to have "created a chilling atmosphere that whips through [Henry] Butler's lean, taut, effective libretto, like a raw wind." And the opera was called "a much finer work" than Benjamin Britten's *Peter Grimes,* "partly because it has one of the truly great librettos of modern times."[20]

Not all agreed. Donal Henahan thought the score was "'moderne' in the manner of luxury-motel furniture that copies Scandinavian originals." And Harold Schonberg questioned whether the subject was "too strong for any composer except one of the level of Wagner or Berg."[21] All did concur, however, that the strength of the production lay in its singers and in the bitter war between Lavinia (Evelyn Lear) and Christine (Marie Collier) that motivates the lurid drama. "Like a lynx and a bobcat," they spit "psychic hate at each other," wrote Schoenberg, and were hailed as two of the most dynamic singing actresses the Met has ever had.[22]

Levy maintains that he looks for great moments rather than a complete story when writing an opera. A line from O'Neill's play, "How death becomes the Mannons," attracted him and thus became the springboard for recurring thematic associations that are powerfully realized, especially at the end of scene 1, act 2 as John Reardon sings "may the soul of Adam Brand rest in peace, and burn in hell."[23] Several big moments are also given to Lavinia, who achieves greater prominence in the opera than the play. Her greatest scene comes at the close, when she sings a beautifully sustained G-sharp within a highly expressive melodic contour that gives weight to her lines "I am bound forever to you [the ghosts]."

Mourning Becomes Electra ran for eleven performances in two seasons

Evelyn Lear (Lavinia) and Marie Collier (Christine) confront each other with vicious psychic hate in their stunning Metropolitan debuts in *Mourning Becomes Electra* by Marvin David Levy. *Metropolitan Opera Archives*

at the Metropolitan and was not heard from again until the Lyric Opera of Chicago produced it in 1998 with revisions in both vocal lines and orchestration. It deserves further performances. It is a powerful and rewarding vocal showpiece, and its melodic lines are lyrical spotlights that unforgettably delineate each character's raw emotions. If it does not rise above Barber's *Vanessa* in lyricism and grace, *Mourning Becomes Electra* is compelling theater and a first-rate operatic tragedy.

Illusion, Reality, and the Magic of Hugo Weisgall

The late 1950s provided several bold new avenues for the performing arts in America, especially for opera. President Dwight D. Eisenhower broke ground for Lincoln Center in May 1959, and the ceremonial mood was heightened by the singing of Risë Stevens and Leonard Warren. During the 1950s some of the century's finest singers made their debuts at the Metropolitan Opera: Leontyne Price, Joan Sutherland, Sherrill Milnes, Alfredo Kraus, Grace Bumbry, and Luciano Pavarotti to mention only a few.

With the founding of the National Endowment for the Arts and Humanities in 1965 and government's increased role in American cultural life, not only the opera house but also the White House became a centerpiece for the glories of music drama. Although great singers had appeared at the Executive Mansion since the Lincoln administration, it was during the administrations of John F. Kennedy and Lyndon Johnson that operas, replete with costumes, scenery, and a special stage, were performed in the East Room. From Mozart's *Magic Flute* to Offenbach's *Voyage to the Moon* in honor of the Apollo 7 and 8 astronauts, opera enlarged America's dreams, hopes, and faith in the artistic directions of its future.

The New York City Opera produced ten world premieres during the 1960s, all by American composers who represented a broad spectrum of the nation's creative processes. Whether drawing from symbolism, verismo, satire, or neoclassicism, the composers brought individual perspectives to their art that were lucidly informed by twentieth-century modes and American tastes and training. The more innovative American composers of the 1960s followed the expressionist musical idioms of Europe, especially those of Arnold Schoenberg, who taught in California during the war. American composers were also part of a world that paralleled the artistic ambience of the turn of the century. The drug culture of the 1960s, the mind-expanding hallucinations of LSD, the orgiastic rituals of rock, pop art, long-haired hippies, the Beatles' "Sergeant Pepper" and his panoply of kinky friends—all seemed flashbacks to the *Jugendstil* and surrealist gaucherie of the fin de siècle. A place as bizarre as the Electric Circus and a film as poetic as *The Yellow Submarine* were logical continuations of the Decadents' dream. It was a world in which, like the plays of Pirandello, reality became dreams and dreams often became nightmares.

In Europe, the cinema gave life to modern images through works such as Roger Vadim's *Barbarella* or Federico Fellini's *Satyricon,* which imitated Aubrey Beardsley and Gustav Klimt—the former's demonic *Salome* and the latter's exotic *Judith.* The woman of fin-de-siècle art, sensuous and erotic, was at once the Darwinian source of all life and the misogynistic source of all evil. August Strindberg saw the female as the chief obstacle to redemption. And to Friedrich Nietzche, she was voluptuous and cunning, "a dangerous, beautiful cat." "When you go to Woman," he warned, "forget not the whip."[24]

Although romantic European operas often feature heroines who are "undone," to use Catherine Clement's term, they are frail and lovely Victorians. Twentieth-century expressionism takes a more virulent viewpoint. In Alban Berg's powerful *Lulu,* based on plays by Frank Wedekind, the grotesque heroine is the incarnation of the primal woman-spirit, and her fatal attraction to lovers brings her downfall. If the two most important eras for woman's rights—the fin de siècle and the 1960s—seemed to create antifeminist revenge within the arts, the results were often electrifying. As Strindberg admitted, the emergent feminist question often provided a way for artists to consider certain unexplored areas of the human soul.[25]

American operas of the 1960s were also infused with neurotic, abused, or suffering women—the women of Strindberg and Wedekind, whose plays inspired the operas' librettos. Hugo Weisgall's stunning one-act *The Stronger* (after Strindberg) is a monologue for a soprano who addresses a mute character, her husband's mistress, in a cocktail lounge. The wife carries on at great length while her rival sits in controlled silence. Which is the "stronger"? Perhaps it is the husband, who does not appear. In Weisgall's *The Tenor,* which is based on Wedekind, the jilted Helen shoots herself while her lover Gerardo steps over her body on the way out the door. The protagonist of *Miss Julie* by Ned Rorem has a "weak and degenerate mind" said Strindberg, and "her monthly illness" contributes to her suicide.[26] Lizzie Borden, the disturbed heroine of Jack Beeson's opera of the same name, was in actual life accused of killing her abusive father and stepmother with an axe. In these operas it is women's emotions, their fears and dreams rather than their acts, that motivate the drama and provide the scores with some of their finest music.

Stereotypical images of women were not the only formative elements of fin-de-siècle aesthetics that made their way into operas of the 1960s. The Bergsonian concept of the contrast between immutable form and fluid, continuously changing life—characteristic of the ornamental designs of art nouveau and *Jugendstil*—also informed the creative process of Luigi Pirandello. In *Six Characters in Search of an Author* (1921), which made its first New York appearance in 1931, Pirandello pits the colorless, static existence of the production crew with the élan vital of the characters. He provides a play-within-a-play, a family tragedy in which *each* of four adults—father, mother, stepdaughter, and son—is obsessed with his or her own pain. This results in the death of the two children, a little girl by drowning and a little boy by suicide. By rapidly alternating the dialogue among stage personnel and characters, Pirandello extends phantasmagoric gauze over the differentiation of reality and illusion. Are the fluid dreams we create more real than the static exigencies of life itself? he asks.

Hugo Weisgall's (1912–97) *Six Characters in Search of an Author,* based on Pirandello's play, is one of the most adventuresome and fascinating of the postwar operas. As the first composer to set American opera on the firm path to modernism, Weisgall ranks among the nation's most important musical figures. Born in Ivançice, Bohemia, in 1912, he came to the United States as a child, studied at the Peabody Conservatory in Baltimore, and after military service in Europe became a prominent teacher, composer, and conductor in Baltimore and New York. Weisgall is best known for his operas, which number at least ten. Three were given their premieres at the New York City Opera: *Six Characters in Search of an Author* (1959); *Nine Rivers from Jordan* (1968), a large-scale cinematographic work whose complex plot symbolizes the confusion of the World War II years; and the biblical tale *Esther* (1993). Weisgall originally conceived his one-act *Purgatory* as the last in a trilogy with *The Tenor* (1950) and *The Stronger* (1952). It is one of the earliest American operas to use the dodecaphonic (twelve-tone) technique. An eerie tale that employs two characters and two mute ghosts, it was given its premiere at the Library of Congress in 1961. Other Weisgall operas include the "neo-Lulu" *Athaliah* (1963) after Racine; *The Gardens of Adonis* (1959); the non-fable adaptation *Jenny; or, The Hundred Nights* (1976); and the romantic drama *Will You Marry Me?* (1989).

Six Characters in Search of an Author, commissioned by the Ditson Fund of Columbia University, is considered Weisgall's most theatrically successful opera. Yet it remained only two seasons in the repertoire and was not revived by a major company until Chicago's Lyric Opera Center for American Artists staged it in 1990. Several months later it was broadcast by

National Public Radio, and in 1994 it was recorded by New World Records. Critics have praised the opera's extraordinary adaptation of the play and the superb libretto by the Irish playwright Denis Johnston. Johnston managed to strengthen and sharpen the play by eliminating much of its philosophizing dialogue, which allowed the characters to stand out in prismatic colors. Although it is not an easy opera to assimilate, *Six Characters* is a challenging and theatrically exciting work to produce.

For Weisgall, however, the challenge lay in the score and in delineating the many diverse characters, unifying the musical concepts, and providing melodic interest in the vocal lines. "The score," wrote Andrew Porter, "might be likened to a skillful production that does not seek to explain, amplify, or decorate; it is mysterious, poetic, melodramatic, brutal, amusing in Pirandellian proportion. The composer's invention is precise, his craftsmanship sure. The result has a strange—but the right—combination of passion and coldness."[27] The audience experiences that passion and coldness, however, in rapidly moving glimpses. Pirandello's play-within-a-play is now an opera-within-an-opera in which music and drama move forward at a breathless pace. The nine members of the production company include The Accompanist, The Stage Manager, The Prompter, The Director, and the singers—notably The Coloratura (sung by Beverly Sills in the premiere). Drawing upon his command of expressive post-Bergian chromaticism and constantly shifting tonal centers, Weisgall gives the characters more warmth and lyricism than the less human and one-dimensional production members, whose melodic lines are often fragmented and declamatory.

Most of the more arching aria or arioso segments, moreover, are given to the characters. In a passionate aria in act 3, The Father sings, "What a misfortune for a Character / To have been born with limbs and parts and human passion / And then denied existence in a work of art." In act 1, The Stepdaughter sings "A Quiet Room," a truncated da capo aria whose final lines and tonal gravitation are clouded by delicate, equivocal harmonies. In act 3 she sings a portion of the same aria. After The Basso compliments her, she adds, "Yes, but we have heard it before / And I do not like reprises." To which The Father replies, "For us, all life is a reprise."[28]

Although the ensembles given to the soloists resemble at times the jostling polyphony of Verdi's *Falstaff*, the chorus generally sings in a simpler, more homophonic texture. Their a cappella passages provide a pseudo-religious mood that is sometimes satirical and more often chilling. In Weisgall's melodramatic climax, the young boy shoots himself after drowning his little sister as she plays in a fountain. The Director, frightened and puzzled by these grim occurrences, demands, "Close the book. It's all finished." But is it? The Stepdaughter's laughter jolts him further. "What was that?" he asks. "Is there anyone there?" The only answer comes from the chorus, which intones a solemn Latin dirge from the Requiem Mass as the empty stage darkens. In this, the most dramatic scene in the opera, Weisgall's orchestra explodes powerfully in true verismo style. Is he telling us, perhaps, that the art of opera allows us to see ourselves as we really are, to find the passionate emotions within us that are hidden behind the superficial masks of everyday life?

Six Characters in Search of an Author is not without wit and joy, however. It opens with an expressionistic, atonal arioso about St. Anthony's pig. "It's lousy enough with the right notes" sings The Accompanist as he corrects The Mezzo's performance. Throughout the opera the composer shows enormous skill in switching rapidly between comedy and tragedy. For Pirandello, that mixture of tragedy and comedy was the mark of every true work of humor. In presenting a tragedy, he wrote, a farce included its self-parody "like the projections of shadows from its own body, awkward shadows that accompanied every tragic gesture."[29]

Pirandello's "theater of the grotesque" recalls the commedia dell'arte and the fantastic antics of Harlequin, Pulcinella, and Pantalone that amazed and enchanted audiences. Weisgall emphasizes that remnant of the harlequinade, with its trap doors and hero-magician, in *Six Characters*. A startling seventh character, Madame Pace, steps out of a prop door, "apparently from nowhere . . . a sinister and impressive figure," according to the stage directions.[30] "Just a trick, a silly trick," sings The Stage Manager, who is accompanied by a whimsical scherzo in pizzicato strings. This is also black comedy, for Madame Pace, keeper of a brothel, is the centerpiece of the seduction scene, one of the opera's most dramatic moments. Two hundred years earlier, another opera had woven the phantasmal harlequinade into its dramatic fabric—James Ralph's *The Fashionable Lady,* the first opera by an American.

Another venture into new operatic territories was Robert Kurka's *Good Soldier Schweik,* given its premiere at City Opera during the first Ford Foundation series in 1958, the year before *Six Characters* opened. Kurka's clever opera, with irony and biting satire, mirrors the style of Bertolt Brecht and Kurt Weill, and its lovable lead character—an innocent who pretends to be dim-witted in order to frustrate Austro-Hungarian officers during World War I—is a refreshing change from the victimized heroines. Accepting his misfortunes with a welcoming smile, he salutes everything he sees, including the enema equipment in the hospital. He also elects "to take a quiet road" where "I won't need my gun."[31]

Robert Kurka (1921–57) was born in Chicago of Czech parents and died when he was only thirty-six. He never saw his opera staged. In two acts and twenty scenes, it is set to a libretto by Lewis Allan after Jaroslav Hasek's bright and brittle novel. It reels with waltzes, polkas, blues, and jazz in a score of only woodwinds and percussion played by sixteen instrumentalists. Critics called *Schweik* a dilution of Berg and Gershwin with touches of Prokofiev and Copland. There are also unmistakable neoclassical elements that resemble Stravinsky's *Soldier's Tale* and *Rake's Progress*. After its premiere, the opera enjoyed nearly five hundred performances in Europe within the ensuing decade, and it has been staged often in the United States.

Moody Mysteries of the Heart and Mind

Among the operas of the 1960s that have been revived successfully, two stand out by virtue of their intriguing heroines—disturbed women who offer the musical scores full dramatic play within a variety of intense psychological moods. Ned Rorem's *Miss Julie* and Jack Beeson's *Lizzie Borden* were given their premieres at the New York City Opera in 1965, eight months apart. Kenward Elmslie wrote the librettos for both, well-constructed psychological studies of the main characters' sexual inhibitions and neuroses. Rorem and Beeson approached their dramas from different aspects, however. A distinguished Pulitzer Prize-winning composer of songs, instrumental works, and at least seven operas, Rorem is less compelling than Beeson as a musical dramaturge, mainly because of the Strindberg play upon which *Miss Julie* is based.[32]

The heroines in Rorem and Beeson are both "madwomen" but invite different forms of musical illumination. Julie's is more subtle and implicit (as Rorem illustrates), and Lizzie's more intense and explicit. Madwomen, of course, have been favored subjects from opera's earliest history. Claudio Monteverdi's Ninfa, Gaetano Donizetti's Lucia, Richard Strauss's Salome, and Arnold Schoenberg's antiheroine of *Erwartung* are perhaps the most famous examples. Susan McClary has shown how the dementia of these women is delineated by extraordinary musical means, such as excess chromaticism and ornamentation that provide the scores with strikingly innovative idioms.[33] During the nineteenth century, madness came to be regarded as a peculiarly female malady, usually a manifestation of excess sexuality. That belief is reflected not only in literature, art, and music but also in the psychiatric profession, which "became focused on the 'problem' of Women, and so it has remained with substantial help from Darwin and Freud."[34] By the turn of the century, during the suffrage era, the madwoman appeared not only demented but also evil, her Dionysian sexuality a threat to the inherent rational control of the male. Put another way, madwomen of whatever period in history "are first and foremost male fantasies of transgression dressed up as women."[35]

Rorem's *Miss Julie* has a well-structured score suited to its lyric and narrative requisites, but *Lizzie Borden* holds interest from beginning to end in a portrayal of madness that is both passionate and plausible drama. Especially provocative is the way the composer and librettist have molded the story to reflect both Victorian and current attitudes. The opera is based on an incident that took place in Fall River, Massachusetts, in 1892—Lizzie Borden was accused of butchering her parents with an axe. Although she was tried and acquitted, the tantalizing question of her guilt remains. The gruesome crime has inspired books, films, a play starring Lillian Gish (*Nine Pine Street*), and even a ballet, Agnes de Mille's *Fall River Legend*.

Although the real Lizzie was never considered to be insane, Elmslie and Beeson see her in that light, and that viewpoint allows music and drama to take on exciting dimensions. Lizzie's tortured psyche undergoes a dynamic progression. The audience comes to know her well and to believe her, and they gradually learn the reasons for her neuroses: a miserly, abusive father, a flighty, insulting stepmother, a younger sister who has found love, and a sea captain who rejects her advances. It is, as Beeson called it, a "Family Portrait in Three Acts" and could (and does) take place daily in actual life. *Lizzie Borden* is totally riveting theater and has a heroine who is wholly believable.

Jack Beeson (b. 1921), from Muncie, Indiana, has written nine operas, all of which show his capricious individualism, strong feeling for character, and wry sense of humor. Before *Lizzie Borden,* he composed *Hello Out There* (1954) and *The Sweet Bye and Bye* (1957) and a sparkling romantic comedy, *Captain Jinks of the Horse Marines* (1975), that is perhaps the best comic opera of its era. Beeson chose the Lizzie Borden story at the suggestion of Richard Plant, a German professor living in the United States whose parents had committed double suicide during World War II. The action of the opera takes place in the Borden home. Not long after the curtain rises, the characters are effectively delineated as Lizzie's wealthy, miserly father insists she wear a dress from the attic rather than buy a new gown. "In the garden the flowers wither and die," sings Lizzie's younger sister dolefully, as she longs for freedom and life with her sea-captain fiancé—a longing for freedom Lizzie also shares.

Dressed in richly colored finery, Lizzie's stepmother Abigail opens act

2 by singing a parlor ballad at an old harmonium with a broken key. She is a used, shallow figure who has little interest in her stepdaughters' lives or happiness. Andrew, Lizzie's father mocks his daughter, telling her that she is the one who should marry Jason. She is an old maid and unmarriageable, as thirty-two-year-old daughters were thought to be in those days. In one of the opera's most challenging dramatic scenes she sings:

> I'll breathe water,
> swallow earth.
> Lizzie has a body.
> Lizzie has a head.
> Lizzie's cut to pieces.
> Lizzie must be dead.[36]

The murders do not occur onstage, but Lizzie's scarlet-stained gown as she steps from the room upstairs tells enough. So does the opera's chilling final scene. Lizzie sits motionless in her living room while a chorus of children, to whom she had been teaching hymns at the opening of the opera, taunts her in eerie innocence (like "vocal gargoyles") from offstage. Does she secretly share their laughter? After all, she has won.

Beeson's score illuminates vividly from within through powerful lyrical conviction. Violent, impassioned scenes are relieved by moments of humor and parody, such as the parlor game rendered by the quintet for Abigail, the preacher, Margaret, and Jason, with Lizzie off to the side in a world of her own. Even when the music is harmonically simple, odd chromatic colors pull it askew. Like Lizzie's distorted mind, a ballad or a waltz can be momentarily slightly off. If characters are humanized by New England hymns and folk tunes, they are dramatized by clashing dissonance and atonal colors—as in Lizzie's irrational outbursts in speech-song style. The kaleidoscopic orchestral colors highlight voices that weave in and out of a sea of sound enriched by multiple leitmotifs that seem to pile one upon the other as Lizzie's great mad scene reaches its peak of frenzy.

Elmslie's superb libretto often allows Beeson to elongate individual words melismatically for expressive accentuation: *sea, blood, mound, wait.* But the libretto is far more than mere words. It is a beautifully constructed dramatic work. Beeson stresses that a librettist in opera is too often overlooked. "The libretto is like the skeleton in a human being," he says. "You cannot have the flesh without the skeleton."[37] To provide both dramatic and musical balance in the opera (and because Beeson did not want another female voice), he and Elmslie fabricated the role of Jason, Margaret's sea-captain lover, and omitted the Borden's real-life maid. Some ac-

Lizzie Borden in a rage,
as sung by Phyllis
Pancella in Jack Beeson's
graphically intense *Lizzie
Borden* staged by Glim-
merglass Opera in 1996.
*Photo by George Mott/
Glimmerglass Opera, copy-
right 1996*

counts reported a lesbian relationship between Lizzie and the maid. The
stepmother found them in bed together in the nude, said Beeson, an incident that provided motivation for her murder.[38]

Some of the most revealing insights into the opera have come from
the production team for the Glimmerglass revival of *Lizzie Borden* during
the summer of 1996. Viewing the opera from the eyes of the scenic designer, stage director, and singers yields further understanding of the imagery within the elusive art called opera. John Conklin, one of America's
most important stage designers, created the sets for Glimmerglass and
undoubtedly took a cue from Lizzie's lines at the start of her mad scene:
"Walls! Walls! All these many walls!" Conklin designed a square set that
used what could be either the inner or outer walls of a home or a church.
They reflect, as he said, "the confusion in Lizzie's brain. . . . There is the

strange staircase that rises like a gallows, or a stairway to heaven, again the ambiguous image. It is a long climb upward for the characters, so that when Lizzie emerges from that staircase in a soft, flowing white dress, she is like an angel. Instead of being a dried-up creature, she is radiant, powerful. We wanted her to be in a world that the audience could fill. We wanted a landscape, not a location."[39]

Rhoda Levine, the director for Glimmerglass's *Lizzie,* added, "I think this is an opera that is exceedingly contemporary, because it deals with very important issues: how we victimize each other, how we often give double messages, and how we do not listen to each other. When the father caresses Lizzie's shoulders, we don't know why he does this. He is sending her—and us—mixed messages. There is a mystery to the entire Lizzie story, but each character knows he or she is right. When people know they are right, this creates the friction and tension that motivates the story."[40]

The opera also helps the audience understand the role of Victorian women in society. At the time, says Levine, it was inconceivable that a woman of Lizzie's family background and social status could have committed such a heinous crime. A woman in those days was "the angel in the house." Sheri Greenawald, who sang the role of Abigail with brilliance and conviction, sees the stepmother as a shallow figure catering passively to the boisterous demands of her husband. As she reflected, "the opera shows what women had to endure in their male-dominated households."[41]

Brenda Lewis, the Birdie of Blitzstein's first *Regina,* sang the original Lizzie. Ellen Faull was the original Abigail, and Herbert Beatty sang the father. For Glimmerglass, the demanding role of Lizzie was interpreted by Phyllis Pancella, who carried Lizzie's dementia to exciting heights dramatically and vocally. However irrational her behavior, Lizzie is a winner. Unlike Rorem's Miss Julie who was acted upon, she does the acting herself. In that light she is a modern woman, and perhaps that is why she—and the opera—continue to fascinate.

In their focus on the darker side of human relationships and their exploration of new ways to manifest that in operatic form, American composers of the late 1950s and 1960s such as Samuel Barber, Marvin David Levy, Hugo Weisgall, and Jack Beeson met challenges with fresh imagination and dramatic invention. There were no easy answers. No longer could they be found close to home in American settings and traditions like those of *The Tender Land* and *The Ballad of Baby Doe.* Operas of the 1960s moved into more far-reaching territories—the strange world of Pirandello, the eroticism of antiquity, the violence of abuse, and the phantasmal dreams of madness. If the tunefulness and Americana-like charm of the 1950s is missed, audiences have nonetheless gained exciting new characters and insight into interpersonal relationships. Finely drawn through graphically explicit orchestration, such relationships would intensify and define American opera through the turn of the century.

16

Bold Turns on Familiar Paths

True freedom implies the conscious absorption and understanding of the great traditions without the need reflexively to emulate—or, for that matter, reflexively to deny—them.

—Tim Page, *Newsday*

"PACEM! PACEM!! PACEM!!!" cries out a young celebrant with increasing emotional intensity as he violently hurls the sacred monstrance to the floor during the holiest portion of the mass. In shocked silence, the congregation stares while in hushed tones and wild-eyed near-madness the celebrant sings, "Look . . . Isn't that odd. . . . Glass shines—brighter—When it's broken. . . . How easily things get broken."[1] It is an operatic mad scene for the 1970s, a period of antiwar protest and a search for peace. It was also a time of drugs, doubt, and despair, especially among the young. Leonard Bernstein took Christianity's oldest, holiest, and most intensely dramatic musical form—the liturgy of the Roman Catholic mass—and made it relevant within the sphere of a secular ideology. Significantly, the ancient mass form is in itself a kind of opera, expressing humanity's inner desires, fears, and conflicts in varied musical modes. The Last Supper, at the heart of the mass, is a profound drama of faith as intense as any theatrical form.

Leonard Bernstein did not call his *Mass* an opera, but "a Theatre Piece for Singers, Players and Dancers." Yet his disarming piece illustrates how close American music theater can come to being opera—not so much in the style of its music but in the way music is used as drama. *Mass*'s protagonist, the twenty-year-old celebrant, appears at first in blue jeans and a simple shirt. With a strum of his guitar, he wipes out the cacophonous "Kyrie eleison" (Lord, have mercy). "Sing God a simple song, Laude, Laude," he sings in a gentle descending modal line. "For God is the simplest of all. I will sing the Lord a new song."

And so we follow the celebrant and congregation as they move through the various parts of the Latin mass, with its added vernacular texts—like medieval tropes and sequences—composed for modern ears by Bernstein and Stephen Schwartz. Through the power of the score, we are caught up in the young man's excruciating doubts as he reaches the peak of an emotional crisis. Composed for the opening of the John F. Kennedy Center for the Performing Arts in Washington, D.C., in 1971, *Mass* celebrated not only the Kennedy family's Roman Catholic heritage and Bernstein's passion for peace but also the joyous melding of liturgical, musical, and dramatic forms. It was a *Parsifal* for the 1970s—a *Bühnenweihfestspiel* (sacred festival play) for the modern age.

Bernstein's *Mass* was composed the same year as Andrew Lloyd Webber's "rock opera" *Jesus Christ Superstar* and Stephen Schwartz's *Godspell*, which drew upon the parables and life of Jesus in a lively, circuslike setting. The use of serious subjects for Broadway musicals was far from new. Works such as Jerome Kern and Oscar Hammerstein's *Show Boat* and Richard Rodgers and Hammerstein's *South Pacific* and *The King and I* considered timely social themes that ranged from prejudice and class conflict to women's issues and war. But they also retained a characteristically positive spirit and had an aesthetic treatment that was essentially light. From the 1970s onward, what separated opera from Broadway became increasingly blurred. Works (both European and American) such as *Street Scene*, *Lost in the Stars*, *Porgy and Bess*, *Amahl and the Night Visitors*, *Song of Norway*, *Phantom of the Opera*, *Les Miserables*, *The Sound of Music*, *South Pacific*, *The Most Happy Fella*, *Sweeney Todd*, and many others have been performed in both opera houses and commercial theaters.

Cross-overs: Broadway and American Opera

Writing in 1985, Harold Prince noted that since the *Candide* in 1974, "There has been a cross-over movement in musical theater brought about by two curious phenomena. The Broadway musical, racing ahead for so many years, is experiencing a lull primarily because of prohibitive costs but also because of the need for finding new directions. Opera, identified during these same years as a kind of museum art form, is suddenly revitalized—new audiences, new works, a renewed interest in it as theater."[2] Prince also saw truth in modern musical theater, a truth well understood by Verdi, Puccini, and Wagner. "Who says to be entertained means to be tickled?" he admitted. "I think it's more stimulating to be upset. I try to be part of what I want to see. And I go to the theater to see a little blood drawn."[3]

Operas and musicals now share many elements of style. Both can have spoken dialogue or be sung throughout; both can also have full symphonic textures or smaller, pop-style ensembles and either complex musical scenarios or simple tunes.[4] As modern musicals have picked up elements of opera—dramaturgical importance of music, grandiose spectacle, and melodramatic conflicts and contradictions—opera often draws from such popular entertainment as folk, jazz, and vernacular styles. That, of course, has been true throughout theatrical history. *Don Giovanni, The Magic Flute, Fidelio,* and *Carmen* are only a few of many operas interspersed with musical comedy–inspired techniques and traditions.

Grand opera, moreover, borrowed the extended ensemble finale from opera buffa, whereas comic opera drew its more expressive, melodramatic orchestra and virtuoso arias from grand opera. Although the manner of belting out songs serves the untrained voices that form many popular music theater casts, other Broadway singers have classical techniques. Andrew Lloyd Webber's *Phantom of the Opera,* sung throughout like grand opera, requires The Phantom to have a two-octave span and Christine an almost three-octave range that would challenge any singer. Anna Maria Kaufmann and Peter Hofmann are operatically trained singers who have mastered the miked and amplified idioms of popular music theater. Some opera singers, notably Jose Carreras, Dawn Upshaw, and Frederica von Stade, have even become cross-over artists, comfortable in both Broadway shows and opera.

Leonard Bernstein (1918–90) and Stephen Sondheim (b. 1930) are two of America's most beloved composers of a music theater form that reaches into the structure and sweep of opera. The tragic Romeo and Juliet theme that shapes Bernstein's *West Side Story* (1957) is recounted not only in song and symphonic music but also in the kinetic power of modern dance. Like other musicals, *Kiss Me, Kate, Fiddler on the Roof,* and *My Fair Lady,* it has appeared often in the repertoire of opera houses worldwide. Bernstein also wrote *On the Town* (1944), *Trouble in Tahiti* (1952), with its sequel *A Quiet Place* (1983), and *1600 Pennsylvania Avenue* (1976).

Bernstein's most frequently performed stage piece after *West Side Story,* however, is *Candide.* With a libretto by Lillian Hellman, *Candide* opened at the Martin Beck Theatre in 1956. It has gone through numerous revisions since, among them the one-act version of 1973 staged by Harold Prince with a new libretto by Hugh Wheeler and the two-act "Opera House Version" performed at the New York City Opera in 1982 with much of the original 1956 music restored. The last revision Bernstein approved was made in 1989 from a concert performance the composer conducted in London. With its superb lyrics, *Candide* underscores Voltaire's satire with charm, power, and humanity. It is, as Theodore Chapin attests, "one of this century's most alluring and provocative works of musical theater. Or opera, Or both."[5]

Like Candide, Stephen Sondheim's *Passion* (1994) lies somewhere among "musical theater or opera or both." Based on I. U. Tarchetti's novel *Fosca* and through a dramatic, operatic score, *Passion* recounts a dashing young military officer's tragic relationship with two women. Fosca's amorous pursuit of the handsome Giorgio is so obsessive that it eventually contributes to her death—and almost to his. Throughout his score, Sondheim allows the Fosca motif to become a musical obsession as well, and in the final scene even her ghost sings with the devastated Giorgio.

The special way Sondheim melds declamation and lyricism within the story—brief spoken passages woven into vocal lines for dramatic emphasis—allows Tarchetti's poignant tale to flow in intensely emotional waves. As a kind of chamber opera, *Passion* also works well on television. Its intimate personal scenes are given weight through close-ups of the tormented non-lovers (Donna Murphey and Jere Shea) and through contrasting cinematic effects: slow-motion camera techniques, sepia tones for flashbacks, and fade-ins of Giorgio's elegantly attired mistress Clara.

Leonard Bernstein (1918–90) masterfully blended music theater and operatic styles in his stage works. *Van Vechten Collection, Library of Congress*

One area that usually separates opera and music theater composers is the task of orchestration. Due to enormous pressures to produce a full score despite limited time and resources, Broadway composers usually work with professional orchestrators. For *West Side Story,* Bernstein indicated his intentions to his orchestrators Sid Ramin and Irwin Kostal through a kind of shorthand, note by note. Film composers, too, work with orchestrators, although Bernard Herrmann preferred not to.

Sondheim has admitted knowing little about the special art of instrumentation, but he knows the exact "feel" he wants in a work. *A Little Night Music* should be "transparent" and "waft" perfume into the audience he told orchestrator Jonathan Tunick.[6] In *Follies,* Tunick set the song "In Buddy's Eyes" to highlight the heroine's anger at being jilted. Phrases referring to her husband were orchestrated with woodwinds, but when she referred to herself he used the warmer tones of strings. At the climax of the song, Tunick added one of his favorite instrumental images, a combination of muted trumpets and bells that gave the passage "an icy, buzzing sound."[7] For *Sweeney Todd* (1979), the composer told Tunick that he wanted the frightening, unsettling sound of a sepulcher organ.

More than any of Sondheim's works, *Sweeney Todd* has established the composer as a giant of the musical stage. The complex, ambitious show is not only an American classic but also a staple of opera companies worldwide. Under the direction of Harold Prince after his brilliant success with Andrew Lloyd Webber's *Evita, Sweeney Todd* ran for some 550 performances at New York's Uris Theater. In 1984 it was produced at the New York City Opera and Houston Opera and then toured nationally and was videotaped for Home Box Office. Although Angela Lansbury and Len Cariou starred in the original Uris Theater production, Peter Glossop, an opera singer, sang the role of Sweeney for the Manchester Library Theatre's performance in 1989. *Sweeney Todd* won for Sondheim and Prince their fifth consecutive Drama Critic's Circle Award for Best Musical and a plethora of Tony Awards for its outstanding book (by Hugh Wheeler), score, costume, and scenic design, as well as Tonys for best actor, actress, and director.

Unlike Sondheim's other shows, which were called "musicals" or "musical comedies," *Sweeney Todd* is designated a "musical thriller." It is based upon the melodrama by the English playwright Christopher Bond, who drew his story from an older melodrama written in 1847. Sondheim perceived the lurid story of insanity, blood, and horror (bodies are chopped and eaten as meat pie filling) as a metaphor of the industial age and its effect on the human spirit. He humanized the melodramatic form, as Bond had done, and by transforming the original character from a sinister villain to

Rosalind Elias and Timothy Nolen in Stephen Sondheim's *Sweeney Todd* (1979), as produced by New York City Opera in 1984. *Photo by Carol Rosegg*

an impotent victim; Todd reflects (and distorts) the horrors of modern life. *Sweeney Todd*'s use of film score techniques—leitmotivic imagery and continuous music even during the speaking—reflects Sondheim's experience writing music for television and motion pictures. "I thought, 'Bernard Herrmann,'" Sondheim explained, "and out came . . . that kind of music, filled with unresolved dissonances that leave an audience in a state of suspense."[8] Through arias, duets, and choruses, Sondheim also unconsciously grasped the theatrical essence of one of America's oldest operatic forms: romantic melodrama.

Is *Sweeney Todd* opera, musical theater, or Broadway show? Are we merely caught up in a play of terms? Martin Gottfried has one answer: "There is an operatic kind of music, of singing, of staging. There are opera audiences, and there is an opera sensibility. There are opera houses. *Sweeney Todd* has its occasional operatic moments, but its music overall has the chest tones, the harmonic language, the muscularity, and the edge of Broadway theater."[9] But, Howard Kissel argues, if "operatic" means "the highest form of theater, a way of capturing all the energy, all the emotional rhythms of the drama in music, then *Sweeney Todd* is indeed operatic. If popular American theater cannot absorb such serious, provocative musical theater, then the development and evolution of the form are in jeopardy."[10]

Dominick Argento

Stephen Sondheim is to musical comedy what Dominick Argento is to opera. Both are key figures in the kaleidoscopic arena of modern music theater, and through their impressive long skeins of achievements they represent American culture in a special way. At times their artistic planes intersect, but Argento (b. 1927) has achieved fame as a composer of operas, most commissioned and produced by such major houses as the New York City Opera, Minnesota Opera, Dallas Opera, and Washington Opera and by university opera workshops. "Operas are about people, not events or concepts," he maintains. "Through music, the character is no longer a stranger," and he cites the examples of Mimi and Rodolfo, who become real people through Puccini's music. "I want my work to have emotional impact," he continues. "I want it to communicate, not obfuscate. I am always thinking of my audience, how they will hear it, and what it will mean to them." For Argento, "The voice is our representation of humanity. . . . all music begins where speech stops."[11]

Pulitzer Prize–winner Dominick Argento came from an Italian immigrant family. He studied at the Peabody Conservatory in Baltimore, gaining insight and guidance in the operatic form from Hugo Weisgall. With his earliest librettist John Olon-Scrymgeour, Argento founded the Minnesota Opera in 1964, and by the millennium it had produced more than thirty premieres, many by American composers. Argento's fourteen operas range from *Sicilian Limes* (1954) to *Casanova's Homecoming* (1985) and *The Dream of Valentino* (1994). But the first that brought him national recognition was *Postcard from Morocco,* which was commissioned by the Minnesota Opera and given its premiere in Minneapolis on October 4, 1971.

Argento writes so sympathetically for the voice that he has been called the twentieth century's "bel-canto composer." The lyrical thrust of his melodic lines adds special beauty to the modern twists and turns of harmony, texture, and drama in *Postcard from Morocco.* The conceptual plan of *Postcard* bears some resemblance to Sondheim's work of the early 1970s—people disillusioned, trying to relate to one another, and searching for answers in a confused world. Argento, however, casts a phantasmal cloak over his characters. He has fashioned a sublime, surreal harlequinade that allows people to see their anxieties through both real and cardboard characters.

The text of *Postcard from Morocco,* written by John Donahue, offers vir-

Composer Dominick Argento (b. 1927). *Minnesota Opera*

tually no plot. "The scene is like a memory," Donahue notes, "like an old postcard from a foreign land showing the railway station of Morocco or some place, hot and strange, like the interior of a glass-covered pavilion or spa."[12] Seven travelers are stranded in a station and struggle gamely with their inhibitions. Like Weisgall's *Six Characters in Search of an Author,* Argento's opera derives dramatic tension from human foibles and emotions—fear, anger, compassion, loneliness, and humor. The characters try to protect themselves by hiding their dreams and secrets in their suitcases. The "Cake" Lady keeps her "beloved" in a box for safe-keeping. The "Cornet" Man stores his instrument in his case "whenever special music is needed." The "Old Luggage" Man never places anything he loves in his suitcase ("no secrets or old magic formulas") for fear it will be lost or stolen.

Longing for the comfort of communication, the characters confront and cajole each other until the only person who has an actual name, Mr. Owen, is tricked into opening his suitcase, revealing it to be empty—like his life. Cut off from the others, he sets out on a voyage of self-discovery in a ship built by a group of puppets. As Argento explains, *Postcard from Morocco* and Richard Wagner's *The Flying Dutchman* have much in common. *Postcard* suggests "a different but equally possible" origin of the *Dutch-man*'s journey, "not launched by supernatural forces at all, but by very human ones, by people who fail to show charity or pity, love or under-standing for a fellow creature."[13]

Argento uses a small chamber ensemble of eight instrumentalists that gives the opera a transparent, neoclassical feeling. The players often func-tion brilliantly as soloists, as in The "Mirror" Lady's coloratura aria "I Nev-er Travel without One" or the puppets' opening scenario in which the pi-ano shimmers phantasmagorically in the upper registers, as it does for another quasi-human puppet in Igor Stravinsky's *Petrushka*. Instrumental color and motion deepen pantomime scenes and add dramatic emphasis in vocal passages. Mr. Owen's descriptive aria "Once, When I Was a Young Man" begins with unaccompanied singing. The orchestra creeps in, film-style, as the narrative builds vocally and dramatically in a description of a magic sailing vessel carried by the wind ("the ropes danced round the mast").

Throughout the score Argento employs both old and new musical styles that make sense dramatically and also create warm, subtle humor. Unlike Jack Beeson, who often juxtaposes vernacular and cultivated musical styles—or George Gershwin who melds them—Argento layers them polyphonically in a kind of modern-day quodlibet. One delightful pas-sage occurs when the Operetta Singers render a traditional Viennese *ländler*-like tune ("Komm' doch") coincident with the lyrical, atonal meander-ings of The "Cake" Lady and Mr. Owen in "Oh, Somewhere among My Things."

The opera closes with Mr. Owen's haunting aria "We Sail This Sum-mer Morning." "We sail new waters," he sings, "uncharted seas with new stars on high and new sea-beasts at our side. But do not fear! The boat is magical, made out of glass and ice. We'll sail through fire and clouds . . . for this is my ship. My ship! I'm captain of this magic ship." Within the aria's solid tonal assertions are fleeting inflections of atonality. As the cur-tain descends on an empty stage, the audience is left with both assurance and doubt as well as reality and dream—with what they are and what they hope to be.

Argento composed his psychological fantasy *The Voyage of Edgar Allan Poe* (1976) on a bicentenary commission from the University of Minne-sota. The libretto was written by Charles Nolte, an actor and playwright who appeared on Broadway as Billy Budd and was known for *A Summer Remembered* and *Alexander's Death*. Nolte effectively integrates Poe's words into Argento's text. He depicts the somber storyteller at the end of his life, overcome by hallucinations of ghostly vessels and tormenting images of his soul. Like Wozzeck, Poe is crazed by poverty and desperation; he is a hapless character victimized by a misspent life. Victimization of a main character is also found in Argento's *The Dream of Valentino*. Like Poe, Valentino is acted upon, and that type of character is perhaps less interesting than one in control of his own actions and destiny.

The Voyage of Edgar Allan Poe received its first European performance in Gothenburg, Sweden, in 1986, with stage designs by John Conklin. The Lyric Opera of Chicago staged it during the 1990–91 season, and Dallas Opera presented it the next, using expansive cinematic projections to enlarge the inherent symbolism and fantasy of the work. The score mixes tonal and twelve-tone techniques in an accessible work that has been compared with the dreamscapes of Federico Fellini and early Ingmar Bergman. What is most striking about the work is its lyricism. Lush, melodious, and wonderfully suited to voice, it is enriched by numerous fine choral ensembles both offstage and on.

Argento's *The Aspern Papers* and *The Dream of Valentino,* also Conklin stagings, were among the composer's most publicized and lavishly presented works. Both were jointly commissioned with Dallas Opera: *The Aspern Papers* with KERA Public Television and its *Great Performances* series and *The Dream of Valentino* with Washington Opera. *The Aspern Papers* was given its premiere at Dallas's Fair Park on November 19, 1988, and was televised nationwide in the spring of 1989. It was the first time that a complete Dallas Opera production had been televised as well as the company's first full-length world premiere. The Dallas Opera assembled Argento's dream cast: Elisabeth Soederstroem as Juliana and Frederica von Stade as Tina, with Katherine Ciesinski (Sonia), Neil Rosenshein (Aspern), Richard Stilwell (The Lodger), and Eric Halfvarson (Barelli).

The libretto, written by Argento, is based on Henry James's 1888 novella of the same name, but the action takes place at Lake Como rather than Venice. As the composer explained, he wanted the imagery of warmth and the subtropical lake along with the glaciers of the Alps in the distance: "The combination of ice and sun is part of my opening line in the opera."[14] The poetic image "snow and cypress, glacier and leaf" sung by Juliana also bears the plaintive twelve-tone motivic structure that recurs throughout the opera. The primary changes from James's story to Argento's, however, lie in the characters and their motivations. Jeffrey Aspern is no longer a fictional poet but a Bellini-like composer, and the famous papers are not love letters but an opera manuscript suppressed by Aspern's mistress.

The Dream of Valentino reflects changes that took place in American opera from the late 1970s onward—changes influenced by cinematic approaches, seen also on Broadway, that placed challenging new demands on designers. "You seldom find a three-or four-act opera like in the nineteenth century, rather lots and lots of shorter scenes," said *Valentino*'s designer John Conklin. "The musical and dramatic form of opera is changing, therefore so is the method of presentation. I find myself part of the writing team, in a way. Valentino is about movie images and the dichotomy between the person and the image. . . . The character seems trapped in his own stereotype, so I tried to use this as a visual dramatic device."[15]

The Dream of Valentino is molded into a series of episodic flashbacks showing the great silent film icon of romance and male sensuality as a sacrificial victim of greed, lust, and publicity. The atmosphere of Hollywood in the 1920s is echoed in the score laced with ragtime, fox trots, and the piano accompaniments of silent film. Argento gives the opera a striking opening. Valentino's coffin is shown, symbolically underscored by a complex layering of popular song and dirgelike segments from the Requiem Mass. But the staging tells the real story. At various times throughout the opera, Valentino's face is projected onto multiple screens and distorted and surrealistically broken into pieces. Sometimes, for example, all that is seen are his large, hypnotic eyes. All become visual leitmotifs, unifying and enlarging the lost dreams of an actor who reached for greatness that money-mad moguls denied him. As one mogul screams at the end of Part One:

> The hell with "actor!"
> Who gives a damn?
> Give me a face.
> I want that FACE![16]

Lee Hoiby and Thomas Pasatieri

Two important contemporaries of Sondheim and Argento—Lee Hoiby (b. 1926) and Thomas Pasatieri (b. 1945)—brought fresh perspective to a familiar, romantic operatic style, dramatically in progressive narrative structures and musically in long, mellifluous, Italianate lines. Both are conservative composers who have retained their identities within a tonal idiom. Their music is colored by postromantic harmonies, regular rhythmic alliances, and strong lyrical outlines. "I'm a mainstream composer," Hoiby comments, "and my style has never really changed." The 1940s and 1950s were a dogmatic time. "I was told, 'You must invent new sounds.' It was as if I'd been told, 'You can have a garden—but grow only cactuses.'"[17]

Motion picture and camera techniques play important roles in Hoiby's dramatic concepts but more indirectly than in Argento's work. He has written nine operas, but his most provocative and successful are *Summer and Smoke* and *The Tempest*. *Summer and Smoke* (1971) was produced in 1980 by the Chicago Opera Theater, which specializes in works in English, and was televised nationally in 1982. Close-ups of the characters' expressions and details of properties, costumes, and gestures created intimacy and dramatic interest that was missing in the New York City Opera's staging in 1972.

Under the direction of Kirk Browning, the televised production focused almost exclusively on the two principal characters and the tortured facets of their relationship.[18] For television, Hoiby had to reduce the original orchestra from fifty-five to twenty-six; he also had to cut twenty minutes from the staged version to accommodate a two-hour time slot. But he kept many of the cuts in later opera-house performances and came to prefer a smaller, chamber orchestra for the work.

Summer and Smoke is based on a play of the same name by Tennessee Williams. It was originally commissioned by the St. Paul Opera Association and directed by Frank Corsaro. In two acts with six scenes in each, the libretto was written by the prolific dramatist Lanford Wilson, whose *The Rimers of Eldritch* had won the coveted Vernon Rice Award for Best Off-Broadway Play in 1967. *Summer and Smoke* tells the story of Alma Weinmiller, who is the inhibited daughter of a southern minister and his unbalanced wife. Alma, in Williams's words, "suffocated in smoke from something on fire inside her," for she cannot release her love for a young doctor, John Buchanan, until it is too late. The action traces the poignant interior journeys of the two potential lovers as their lives intersect with tragic futility. The dramatic changes that take place in their attitudes are reflected in Alma's line at the close of the opera: "I came here to say you need not be a gentleman, but you're telling me I've got to remain a lady." In anguish and desperation she gives herself casually to a man she meets in the town park, where, as a young girl, she first met John.

Hoiby's original uncut story, which takes place in 1910, closely follows Williams's play, adding some new scenes drawn from his *Eccentricities of a Nightingale* (1964). A good librettist, maintains Hoiby, must know where and how to insert more lines so that the music can "take hold."[19] Some critics thought the play was too subtle for musical treatment. Even Elmer Bernstein, who wrote the score for the movie version of *Summer and Smoke* (1961), admitted that Williams's play posed great problems in composition because of the story's delicate balances. "I tried to write tenuous, shimmering music for the relationship of the two main characters, within the broader framework of the period and the southern locale," he said, "with the overall music tinged with a folk song–like quality."[20]

As an opera composer, Hoiby had other ideas. *Summer and Smoke* illustrates his characteristic conservative, postromantic approach and also his skillful sensitivity to the inner conflict of characters. He gives the character of Alma a haunting, chromatic motif that becomes associated with her throughout the opera. Alma holds her inner pressures in check behind a mask of gentility until they become "her phantom double, her Doppelgänger," says Hoiby.[21] Thus he takes the somber four-note chromatic theme of Franz Schubert's lied "Der Doppelgänger" and presents it backward, or in retrograde, first at the opening of the opera when Alma makes her appearance and then to reflect numerous emotional situations as the opera progresses. Alma's motivic cell colors the score with delicate chromatic inflections, creating almost a French feeling. For John, however, the composer provides a more positive, decisive motif of two rising perfect fourths. Hoiby's innate sense of melody is apparent in long, flowing lines that are lyrical, expressive, and at times deeply melancholic. These skills are apparent especially in the opera's anatomy lesson scene and in act 2, scene 7 with the poignant, revelatory lines "Eternity and Alma have such cool hands."[22]

Lee Hoiby's elegant spectacle *The Tempest* remains the composer's finest work. Commissioned by the Des Moines Metro Opera, where it had its premiere on June 21, 1986, it contains traditional set pieces: preludes, trios, large ensembles, and arias that are haunting and dramatic. John Rockwell wrote of its "lush, beautiful and stratospherically difficult music" for the leading soprano, a coloratura, and Thor Eckert called it "a gracious, effective opera that aims to let singers really sing."[23]

What is most interesting about *The Tempest* is the way Hoiby and his librettist Mark Shulgasser shaped Shakespeare's phantasmagorical play into an opera. Dating to at least 1611, the play has all the spectacle of later harlequinades. It includes a rousing storm scene, segments of magical manipulation of people and things, spirits in the form of a pack of hounds, invisible characters, and a hero who puts on magic shows. The characters are more telling than the story, and the dream is more intense than the reality, although Shakespeare gives his magical island a specific and credible landscape. Like the island, the play abounds in references to music. *The Tempest* contains more indications for songs and instrumental music than any of Shakespeare's plays, and the texts of those songs provide fine opportunity for arias and set pieces in Hoiby's opera.

Unlike *Summer and Smoke,* which flows in a Puccinian manner with long, dialogic scenes and intense lyrical phrases that blossom into arias, *The*

Tempest is more formally poetical. Mark Shulgasser describes it as "a fairy tale with a Renaissance flavor that seems to call for a more formalistic musical style."[24] And yet it was the words rather than the form of the play or even the colorful characters that provided the primary musical inspiration for the opera. "Certain lines were like beacons," said Hoiby. "Even just read or spoken, they would move me to tears." Both composer and librettist were inspired by the "great language" before them. "I think the idea that English is hard to set and to sing is unfounded," Shulgasser adds. "In fact, Shakespeare is beautiful, dramatic poetry. There is no reason that there should be any difficulty in setting him to music. The only problem is intelligibility, where the language becomes obscure, and then the librettist has to know where to cut out the difficult passages and still preserve the dramatic through-lines."[25] Arrigo Boito had the same problem in adapting Shakespeare's *Othello* for Verdi, for he had to compress some 3,500 lines of the play to eight hundred for the opera.

But cutting is not always the answer. "At the end of act 2, where Ariel sings a denunciation of the free men of sin, the language is very convoluted and difficult," Hoiby observes. "Yet we used it all and it was very effective. The confusing syntax is actually part of Ariel's character, a non-human who uses a language that is not quite real. We had to very, very carefully plot out the tactical structure of the scene to make it not only musically coherent but also an exciting presentation that reflected the convolutions that Shakespeare had put into the syntax."[26] For Shulgasser, "The task of subduing Shakespeare's raw, tumultuous dramaturgy, his many scenes, his sometimes whimsical transitions, his frequent entrances and exits was by no means easy."[27] There are times, however, when the play seems to sing itself. Caliban's big aria in act 2, for example, became a favorite with Leontyne Price, who included it in many of her concerts: "Be not afeared," it begins in both Shakespeare's and Hoiby's versions:

> the isle is full of noises,
> Sounds and sweet airs, that give delight and hurt not.
> Sometimes a thousand twangling instruments
> Will hum about mine ears; and sometimes voices,
> That, if I then had wak'd after long sleep,
> Will make me sleep again.[28]

The Tempest has piqued the imagination of poets from Milton to T. S. Eliot and W. H. Auden as well as countless composers. Mozart, Mendelssohn, and Benjamin Britten contemplated the task of adaptation but then decided against it. American composers who composed operas based on various Shakespearean plays include Henry Hadley, Samuel Barber, Vittorio Giannini, Dominick Argento, John Harbison, David Amram, Elie Siegmeister, Louis Gruenberg, and Ernest Bloch, a Swiss composer who became an American citizen in 1924.

The year before Hoiby's *Tempest* was staged, John Eaton produced his version of the play to a libretto by Andrew Porter, and it was given its premiere by the Santa Fe Opera. Although the libretto remained faithful to many aspects of Shakespeare's intricate comings and goings, Eaton's treatment is overtly contemporary, with quarter-tone sonorities, extreme vocal registers, and even aleatoric writing in the orchestra.

Hoiby's setting is far closer to the vision and imagery of Shakespeare than Eaton's. In November 1996 Dallas Opera gave the first staging of Hoiby's *Tempest* by a major company. With the brilliant singing of Constance Hauman as Ariel, designs by Japan's Setsu Asakura, and lighting by Sumio Yoshii, the production was a huge success, replete with seven tons of plexiglass and the modish glow of Vari-lites.

Thomas Pasatieri, like Lee Hoiby, is also an exponent of what has been called the "New Romanticism" in music. He shares with his American compatriots of Italian genetic heritage—Menotti, Giannini, and Argento— an operatic style that is basically conservative and melodic and has dramatic, soaring lines in the manner of Puccini and Strauss. He began his career by composing at least thirteen operas by the time he was thirty, most of them commissioned and produced by major opera companies and colleges throughout the United States. Some of Pasatieri's operas represent various states' first world premieres of a major opera, such as Michigan (*Washington Square,* 1976); Ohio (*Three Sisters,* 1986); and Texas, where *The Seagull* (1974) was also the first work to be commissioned by the Houston Grand Opera in its nineteen-year history. Composed in 1979 and based on Anton Chekhov, *Three Sisters* was also staged in Russian at the Moscow Musical Theater in 1988 and was the first of Pasatieri's operas to be recorded complete.

Pasatieri's career is somewhat enigmatic, although perhaps no more so than many Americans whose operas have been initially well received and then failed to stay in the repertoire. A student of Nadia Boulanger, Vittorio Giannini, and Darius Milhaud, Pasatieri received the first doctorate awarded at the Juilliard School of Music when he was only nineteen. While in his twenties, he saw six of his operas produced in Seattle during the same season, including *Calvary* (1971), which was based on William Butler Yeats, and *Black Widow* (1972), staged by Lotfi Mansouri in the Seattle Opera

Scene from The Dallas
Opera's 1996 production
of *The Tempest* by Lee
Hoiby featuring Jacque
Trussel as Caliban and
Constance Hauman as
Ariel. *Photo by Andy Scott*

House. Written for television with flashbacks, dissolves, and voice-overs, *The Trial of Mary Lincoln* (1972) was broadcast nationally by National Educational Television.

Argento, Hoiby, and other American composers including Pasatieri were drawn to Chekhov, especially during the self-conscious 1970s, and of Pasatieri's long list of operas, *The Seagull* has remained the most popular and is his most solid achievement. In three acts with set pieces and occasional spoken dialogue, it is based on a play by Chekhov, whose work is often difficult to set as operas because they are plays of atmosphere. They de-theatricalize the theater, for the action is less important than the emotional accompaniment of the action. And unlike Chekhov's stories, which center around a single person, his plays give all the characters more or less equal rights onstage.

The Seagull depicts the destructive interaction of five highly wrought individuals, each in love with the wrong person. To make the play more effective as musical theater, Pasatieri and his librettist Kenward Elmslie concentrate the action of the story, thus heightening the personal and dramatic relationships. They have also added an aria to expand the role of Marsha, an overtly incestuous duet between Madam Arkadina and Konstantin, and a dramatic final aria that coincides with Konstantin's offstage suicide. But the complex emotions and relationships of the characters seem to compete with one another in a work that is almost too dense dramatically.

The lyrical, singable nature of Pasatieri's style, however, not only in *The Seagull* but also in most of his other operas, has attracted many leading singers to participate in the premieres of his works, among them Evelyn Mandac, James Morris, Jennie Tourel, Theodore Uppmann, Alan Titus, Joanna Simon, and Lili Chookasian. The impressive cast of *The Seagull* included Evelyn Lear, Frederica von Stade, Richard Stilwell, John Reardon, and Patricia Wells. "Most modern composers write against the singers," noted Lear, "as if our voices were clarinets or something. Tom composes for the voice; he doesn't injure your instrument."[29] That point alone makes Pasatieri's operas significant contributions to the American repertoire.

Lighthearted Opera for Young and Old

The 1970s and 1980s saw a great increase in the commissioning and production of operas for children. These and other lighthearted operas brought fresh levity and joy to repertoires everywhere. Menotti wrote most of his children's operas during the 1970s, and in the 1980s his *Bride from Pluto* was staged at Kennedy Center and *The Boy Who Grew Too Fast* by Opera Delaware. Gunther Schuller's *The Fisherman and His Wife* (1970), John Eaton's *The Lion and Androcles* (1973), Lee Hoiby's *Something New for the Zoo* (1982), and Charles Strouse's *Charlotte's Web* (1988) were only a few of the many fine short works that enlarged the repertoire. During the 1980s alone, Susan Bingham wrote both the music and librettos for more than twenty short operas, many for children. A popular trilogy was formed in 1981 when Stanley Hollingsworth's lyrical, well-paced *Selfish Giant* and *Harrison Loved His Umbrella* were staged along with his *The Mother* at the Spoleto Festival in Charleston, South Carolina.

American comic opera, too, took new turns in the later part of the twentieth century in that it managed to humanize characters in a warm, personal way that was not always apparent earlier. "We know the characters of an opera from their words," says Jack Beeson, "but we believe them because of what they sing. . . . The music will appear to reflect them, as in an enlarging mirror; rather, as though the music were a magic mirror, it will appear to create them."[30]

There are far more serious operas in company repertoires—both European and American—than comic. (Of Donizetti's some seventy operas, only twenty-three are comic.) Why? Is comic opera harder to write than serious, and are opera audiences more eager to cry than laugh? One answer may lie in opera's derivation from melodrama, which played upon dramatic tension and character delineation in a pacing that is generally slower and more suited to the needs of opera than the rapid pulse of comedy. Comic pacing and believable characters who have genuine feelings were problems for Jack Beeson and his librettist Sheldon Harnick (lyricist for *Fiddler on the Roof*) when they wrote a modern comic opera on a turn-of-the-century melodrama, Clyde Fitch's *Captain Jinks of the Horse Marines*. But they solved the problems boldly and creatively.

To shape a modern opera from an outmoded play, Harnick and Beeson eliminated certain topical illusions and segments that poked fun at immigrant accents. They also expanded some characters and cut others. The most essential change came with the heroine. Clyde Fitch's leading lady was a "relentlessly coquettish, eighteen-year-old," but Harnick and Beeson decided that their diva Aurelia should be an older woman of more serious emotional depth and range. What emerged was an opera that retained some of Fitch's humorous lines but allowed the comedy to unfold within *"relationships* among more fully rounded characters."[31]

Captain Jinks tells of an opera singer's on-again-off-again love affair with Jonathan Jinks in a setting that captures the glitz and glitter of the New York operatic culture in the 1870s. Beeson accents the comedy in various ways. The police are represented in strict serial procedures (a twelve-tone row), and there are period waltzes, overstated contrapuntal passages, melodramatic orchestral underpinnings, and military instrumentation (brass and drums). Satie-like sounds color the score and even some polytonal whimsy reminiscent of Milhaud's *Le boeuf sur le toit.* If Aurelia, "a slave to vocalizzi," sings a nineteenth-century coloratura aria, she sings over a biting orchestral fabric that is far from Italian. Yet always there is a human element. The characters have true feelings. For all her formidable public success, Aurelia is, after all, just another woman in love.

Bold Ventures in the 1970s

Composers took many bold turns during the 1970s—whether in opera or music theater, verismo or comedy—but their main paths remained essentially conservative. John Harbison and John Eaton, however, took a somewhat different route, and their originality in subject, musical dramaturgy, and overall sound marks them as two of America's most eloquent and interesting composers. Harbison's *A Full Moon in March* (1979) might be considered one of the last utterances of the 1960s' "dreamers of decadence" phase. In the legendary vein of *Salome* and *Turandot,* the libretto is an abridgement of W. B. Yeats's dance-play of 1935 and tells of a cold and vicious queen who offers to marry the suitor most capable of expressing his passions in song. When a simple swineherd comes to her, she warns in her initial aria, "Remember through what perils you have come; / That I am crueller than solitude. / . . . Cruel as the winter of virginity." Believing The Swineherd has come to insult her rather than to sing, The Queen orders his execution. Bearing his head on a stake (a dancer replaces the original queen, a mezzo-soprano), she begins a seductive dance of adoration before the head, kissing it and holding it to her breast. Her attendants conclude, "What can she lack whose emblem is the moon? / But desecration and the lover's night."[32]

The composer explains that *Full Moon in March* "was written in a nonreflective state, well before any effort to understand the matter beyond the absorption of the images."[33] Yet his brilliantly sensual score tells all one needs to know. *Full Moon* is a chamber opera of four characters, The Queen, The Swineherd, and two attendants, with an eight-piece ensemble comprising strings, winds, percussion, and prepared piano. The music often has an exotic, Asian flavor, delicate and transparent with arabesques from the bass clarinet or a gamelan sound from the prepared piano. Dissonance and expressionist atonality abound but are tempered by the lyrical vocal lines and Stravinskian shifting metrical patterns that color moods and characters. *Full Moon in March* is an oddly compelling opera that is irresistible because of its sonorous beauty and elegant structure.

John Eaton (b. 1935), like Harbison, also moves in exciting and propulsive new dramatic directions through innovative sonorities. Within the seventeen-piece instrumental fabric of his one-act chamber opera *The Cry of Clytemnestra* (1980) are two pianos, one tuned down a quarter tone, and in the vocal parts are quarter-tone accidentals. Both microtonal and just intonation are used for dramatic ends. Eaton associates "the former with states of extreme psychological conflict and the latter with innocence and purity."[34]

A professor of composition at Indiana University, Eaton has written eight operas, many reflecting his background in electronic music and his work in the early designs of the Moog synthesizer. His *Myshkin* (1971), based on Dostoyevsky's *The Idiot,* employs quarter-tone orchestral tuning and electronic music to underpin the title character's fluctuations between rationality and irrationality. "For years," Eaton explains, "I have been fascinated by and devoted to the development of a richer yet simpler music based on notes (pitches) other than those found on the piano keyboard. The possibilities of expressing psychological nuance and dramatic movement are enormously expanded by singing and playing notes that lie between the white and black keys."[35] He cites similar subtle inflections found in jazz, bluegrass, and other forms of vernacular music.

Eaton's *Danton and Robespierre* (1978) is a sweeping heroic epic in the vein of Roger Sessions's *Montezuma* (1964) or Samuel Barber's *Antony and Cleopatra* (1966). Although *Danton* contains especially rich and colorful choral writing and its orchestration is exciting and varied, it is also a demanding score to sing, with quartertones mixed with normal intonation, frequent wide and dissonant leaps, and complex meters. The opera's libretto by Patrick Creagh has all the volcanic action and seething passions of Paris during the Reign of Terror. The final scene, with screaming crowds and horrific shrieks as the guillotine blade falls on Robespierre, is vividly theatrical. In the French Revolution Eaton found "nearly every trait of modern societies in embryo. . . . Certainly in writing *Danton and Robespierre*," he says, "I did not feel that I was creating a morality play or a remote historical piece but rather that I was addressing our own time in terms people of today would understand only too well."[36]

✍

The 1970s and 1980s taught much about the way people approach opera. Bernstein and Sondheim wrote musicals that bordered on operas; Argento, in works such as *The Voyage of Edgar Allan Poe, The Aspern Papers,* and later *The Dream of Valentino,* composed operas that borrowed staging techniques from film and television. Some composers, Hoiby and Pasatieri, for example, remained essentially romantic; others, such as Eaton and Harbison, brought new, acerbic sonorities to their scores. A rare grand epic with a rich, dense orchestration and vocal lines often layered polyphonically, Roger Sessions's stirring *Montezuma* (1964) was given its premier in Boston in 1976, the year of Glass's *Einstein on the Beach,* but failed to attract much attention.[37] By this time, audiences were turning to less complex sonorities, to the more popular, hypnotic sounds of minimalism. The protagonists of opera, too, were changing from Danton and Cortez to Malcolm X and Harvey Milk. These were the heroes of the time, the emblems of both contemporary music drama and modern media.

17

Heroes for Our Time

The opera house is the arena of poetry *par excellence,* where the normal rules of historical research need not be applied and where, in the world of artistic imagination, a different kind of truth can be discovered.
—Philip Glass

AMERICAN OPERA composers at century's end appeared to be searching for larger-than-life images that would provide fresh dramatic springboards for their work. Critics called their musings "CNN Opera" in which newsmakers are elevated to mythic proportions. Significantly, what appears to be often missing in American families, communities, and culture—a hero—has been transferred to the protagonists of opera. These operatic heroes can be noble or self-destructive, macabre or isolated by obsession. They can also be biblical, historical, literary, or sociopolitical. Since the 1970s, however, they have formed both the subjects and the titles of a colorful panoply of American operas. There is *Nixon in China* (John Adams), *Harvey Milk* (Stewart Wallace), *X: The Life and Times of Malcolm X* (Anthony Davis), *The Dream of Valentino* (Dominick Argento), *Goya* (Gian Carlo Menotti), *Willie Stark* (Carlisle Floyd), *The Mighty Casey* (William Schuman), *McTeague* (William Bolcom), *Frankenstein* (Libby Larsen), and *The Death of Klinghoffer* (John Adams). There is even an opera about Frank Lloyd Wright, *Shining Brow* (Daron Auric Hagen), and one on John Ruskin, *Modern Painters* (David Lang). Two black composers, Ulysses Kay and Dorothy Rudd Moore, each chose Frederick Douglass as the protagonist for their operas.

If these operas are composed mainly by men about men, the 1990s saw some changes, with works such as Hugo Weisgall's *Esther,* Ezra Laderman's *Marilyn,* Michael Daugherty's *Jackie-O,* and Anthony Davis's *Tania.* Women composers were also active. Libby Larsen's *Claire de Lune* is about a female aviator, and Thea Musgrave is the composer of *Mary, Queen of Scotts* and *Harriet, the Woman Called Moses* on Harriet Tubman. The heroine of

Meredith Monk's *Atlas* is a female explorer, and there are operas by Margaret Garwood, Vivian Fine, and others.

These are the subjects that have appealed to contemporary composers, but "subject" is not the only point. What matters is how the heroes (or "pedestal personalities") are perceived as characters. That varies from superficial hagiography to a deeper perception of their courage and growth as human beings. In order to work within opera, a protagonist's life must offer a universal message. Protagonists must become myths, allowing composers to reach beyond historic facts and into the inner core of their souls, the source of life's true drama. Richard Wagner knew that. "Myth and History stood before me with opposing claims," he wrote, "forcing me to decide whether it was a musical drama, or a spoken play, that I had to write." Thus, in selecting the mythical hero Siegfried over a "historico-political" character, Wagner saw not just the "figure of conventional history, whose garment claims our interest more than does the actual shape inside: but the real naked Man . . . the true human being."[1] That search for a "true human being" offers formidable challenges to modern American opera composers as well.

Minimalism and Philip Glass

The composer who seems to have set the hero trend in motion is Philip Glass. Each figure in his striking "portrait opera" trilogy, *Einstein on the Beach, Satyagraha,* and *Akhnaten* —changed the world through the power of ideas. In these episodic-symbolic portraits, Glass shows masterful understanding of his protagonists' inner spiritual strengths as they relate to the prismatic messages of today. In *The Voyage,* Christopher Columbus becomes a universal metaphor for discovery, "that impulse, that gene that moves people to leave wherever they are and look for something new," Glass says.[2] His Heroes Symphony (1996), derived from the music of David Bowie and Brian Eno, is another of Glass's explorations of these timeless images in musical form.

With Charles Ives and John Cage, Philip Glass is modern American music's best-known icon of innovation. Through his enthusiastic following, ranging from the soberly dressed business crowd to the trendy young counterculture, Glass has brought a new, diverse audience to modern opera. His operas and concerts are invariably sold out, and he has been heard in venues from discos to symphony halls and from opera houses to sports arenas. His many commercial recordings have reached a wider audience than those of any other American classical composer. *Einstein on the Beach,* for example, has sold at least a hundred thousand copies since its premiere in 1979, and Low Symphony (1993), based on themes by Brian Eno and David Bowie, passed two hundred thousand within three years. Many of Glass's works have been commissioned by countries outside the United States. *The White Raven* (1998), a grand opera, was commissioned by Portugal; *Marriages between Zones Three, Four and Five* (1997) by the Heidelberg Opera; and a ballet, *The Witches of Venice,* by Teatro alla Scala. The Philip Glass Ensemble, moreover—composed primarily of amplified keyboards, voice, saxophones, and flutes—is a vital element in Glass's creative life and concert career. The fact that Glass himself appears, performing his own music, has led to new intimacy and communication between audiences and opera composers.

There is an exhilarating, euphoric quality to the music of Philip Glass, a propulsive energy that has permeated not only serious music but also rock and pop. Motion picture and television psychodramas continue to find inspiration in his mystical, minimalist style, as do classical composers such as John Adams, La Monte Young, Marian Zazeela, Robert Moran (*Desert of Roses, Towers of the Moon*), Conrad Cummings (*Tonkin*), the Russian Alfred Schnittke, and several young English composers. As Robert Jones observes, whether Philip Glass is a "musical messiah or a sonic anti-Christ is a matter of conjecture, but his impact on the world of music cannot be disputed."[3] Decades after the groundbreaking *Einstein on the Beach,* audiences were still enchanted by Glass's cohesive style and the seductive, hallucinatory world he opened for modern American opera.

Philip Glass (b. 1937) grew up in Baltimore and at nineteen graduated from the University of Chicago. He went on to study at the Juilliard School of Music and then with Nadia Boulanger in Paris, where he met Ravi Shankar. Eastern music was a revelation, especially because of its rhythm. Unlike Western music that divides time "like slicing a loaf of bread," Glass explains, non-Western music takes small units and "strings them together to make up larger time values."[4] His fascination with non-Western sonorities led him to research music in India, North Africa, and the Himalayas. When he returned to New York in the late 1960s, he applied what he had learned to his own compositions. Working part-time as a cab driver and plumber, he began to compose music for the experimental Mabou Mines Theater Company, which he had co-founded. It was his first opera, *Einstein on the Beach,* written in 1976 with the dean of the "theater of images" Robert Wilson, however, that brought Philip Glass international fame.

Listening to the music of Philip Glass has been compared to watching a modern painting that initially appears static but metamorphoses slowly

Composer Philip Glass rehearsing his *Einstein on the Beach*. *Photo by John Elbers, 1976*

Robert Wilson, innova-
tive director and design-
er, collaborated with
Glass on some of his ma-
jor operas, notably *Ein-
stein on the Beach* and *the
CIVIL warS*. *Photo by
Ralf Brinkhoff*

as one concentrates. Glass's musical style, often referred to as "minimalism," is based on what he calls the "additive process and cyclic structure." As in Eastern music, rhythm becomes the organizing principle, and cells of notes repeat and grow in additive procedure quite different from Western music, in which contrasting themes provide the tension and release that propel the music forward. According to Glass, "A simple figure can expand and then contract in many different ways, maintaining the same general melodic configuration but, because of the addition (or subtraction) of one note, it takes on a very different rhythmic shape."[5] Contrapuntal complexity comes into play with what Glass calls "rhythmic cycles" (repeating fixed rhythmic patterns of specific lengths) by superimposing two different rhythmic patterns of varying lengths. Depending on the length of each pattern, they eventually arrive, together, back at their starting point. A complete cycle has been made.

The term *minimalism* was used during the 1960s to describe a style of visual art or design that used the fewest and simplest elements to achieve the greatest effect. Sculptors such as Don Judd and Richard Serra created work described as "minimalist." In music, the origins of minimalism can be traced to the music of India, Bali, and African countries. Minimalist-like repetitive patterns can even be found in Western medieval music, in the music of Claudio Monteverdi, and the keyboard works of Johann Sebastian Bach. In America the term was first used during the 1960s and early 1970s to describe music consisting of extended reiterations of a motif or group of motifs, as in the work of Terry Riley (*In C,* 1964), Steve Reich (*Come Out,* 1966), and Glass's *Music in Twelve Parts* (1971). Reich, Glass, and other young minimalists reflected the turbulent moods of the times. Dubbing serialism "ugly and didactic," they rebeled against atonality, aleatoric music, and the idea that music had to be an intellectual enterprise. In *Einstein on the Beach,* Glass created a new form of functional harmony that moved hypnotically in a vastly elongated time-frame.

Glass's style sounds simple at first and even monotonous. Melody is reduced to rocking broken chord or ostinato figures that provide motion but little variety in tonality or timber. The harmonic rhythm is so slow, and chord changes move so relentlessly around a single tonal center, that dissonance sometimes seems a thing of the past. It is not so much dissonance that highlights Glass's dramatic messages but the subtle, small changes that titillate and challenge the ear. Although dynamic levels are not highly contrasted or graduated as in traditional opera, buildup in the laycring of textures, rhythms, and instrumental color often provides sensuous dramatic climaxes. In certain passages the use of solo instruments in obbligato fashion enlarges the imagery of the text—like the trumpet in "Hymn to the Sun" from *Akhnaten* or the saxophone in "Song 7" from "Howl" in *Hydrogen Jukebox*. Within a single large theatrical work, great variety in mood, intensity, and atmosphere is achieved from piece to piece or from scene to scene.

Einstein on the Beach, seen as a landmark of twentieth-century music theater, is an abstract work that combines music, dance, spoken text, and singing in a series of mystical pantomimes.[6] There is no story, but rather various images of Einstein appear as metaphors. At times he is a violinist, or he writes mathematical formulas on a blackboard, or the theories that led to the splitting of the atom are suggested by a "nuclear holocaust" heightened by blasts of amplified instruments and hysterical choral voices. There are also whimsical references to the era: the popular song "Mr. Bojangles," the Beatles, David Cassidy, and the women's liberation movement ("Are women the equal of men? There are those who tell us that they are. . . . You male chauvinist pig! You put that kiss right back where you got it from").[7] The seductive beauty of the music draws one in irre-

Original staging for *Einstein on the Beach. Photo by Johan Elbers*

sistibly, for the unique atmosphere of minimalism in Glass's operas well serves their mystical, tableau-like theatrical style.

Einstein is nearly five hours long, with several scenes and five intervening interludes ("Knee Plays"). The audience is encouraged to imagine what it wants and to leave the theater and return at will during the performance. "The kinds of theater which spin familiar stories, moralizing, sometimes satirizing, occasionally comforting us about our lives, have never meant much to me," writes Glass. "What has always stirred me is theater that challenges one's ideas of society, one's notions of order."[8] Unlike traditional opera that evolves from a libretto, Glass's ideas in *Einstein* are influenced by the drawings of Robert Wilson, who imbues its main scenes—a train, a trial, and a spaceship—with elusive, eerie mysticism. It is a new kind of musical dramaturgy—an aural and visual montage that brilliantly reflects the moody, hyper-stimulated spirit of the 1970s just as Stephen Sondheim's musicals did in a more traditional narrative way.

Glass's work was given its premiere on July 25, 1976, at the Avignon Festival in France and the following November at the Metropolitan Opera House (although not by the Met itself). Performances were sold out. It toured to Paris, Venice, Brussels, and other cities outside the United States and was staged at the Brooklyn Academy of Music in 1984 and 1992, again to packed houses.

Glass intended his next two operas—*Satyagraha* (1980), about Ghandi, and *Akhnaten* (1984), about the pharaoh believed to be history's first monotheist—to form a trilogy with *Einstein,* thus representing heroic figures of science, politics, and religion. The trilogy was performed in June 1990 in Stuttgart, Germany. Although all three works are structured within the sphere of minimalism, each opera has a distinctive overall sound and imagery. For *Einstein on the Beach,* about the great physicist who loved music, Glass uses an amplified ensemble and small chorus that sings a text composed of numbers (actually, the beats of the music) and solfège syllables. *Satyagraha,* about a man who leads his people to independence, is a large choral opera with text in Sanskrit and taken directly from the Bhagavad-Gita. And in *Akhnaten,* Glass emphasizes the orchestra, with choral and solo voices sharing equal importance.[9] The trilogy is linked musically through the "Knee Plays" of *Einstein,* which provide musical material in the other two operas.

Compared to Glass's first opera, the two that followed suggest the sweep and scope of more traditional grand opera. *Satyagraha,* its book by Glass and Constance DeJong, was first performed in Rotterdam in 1980 and shortly thereafter by the New York City Opera and the Lyric Opera of

Chicago. More pageant than narrative, it portrays Gandhi during his early years in South Africa, protesting against the discrimination of Indians.
Satyagraha ("force of truth" in Sanskrit) was the term Gandhi applied to
his nonviolent civil disobedience movement; images within the opera, such
as that of Martin Luther King, Jr., create a timeless feeling as the medita-
tion on nonviolence unfolds. Scored for traditional instruments—strings,
woodwinds, and organ with no brass or percussion—the opera also employs a large chorus. It is a work of ephemeral beauty; voices move dramatically over lush orchestration in broad, arching lines. Gandhi's expressive apostrophe to freedom at the end is one of the most powerfully moving
moments in modern opera. Glass, like Roger Sessions and John Eaton,
created a heroic work. It is an epic form of opera that few modern American composers have attempted.[10]

Akhnaten, the third opera of the trilogy, is based on the life of the pharaoh who ruled Egypt from 1375 B.C. to 1358 B.C. "The main point for me,"
explains Glass, "was that Akhnaten had changed his (and our) world
through the *force of his ideas* and not through the *force of arms.*"[11] Glass
employs more traditional operatic techniques of musical association in
Akhnaten; the pharaoh, for example, is usually heralded by the solo trumpet in the orchestra. "The musical themes and their key relationships form
a changing mosaic throughout the opera," Glass observes, "reaching a
specific musical resolution in the very last moments."[12] The opera's book
is by Glass, with Shalom Goldman, Robert Israel, and Richard Riddell.
Its libretto is written in ancient Egyptian, Akkadian, and biblical Hebrew.
A narration in English provides a rich confluence of drama, imagery, and
atmosphere.

Three of Glass's chamber operas were given their American premieres
by the American Repertory Theater of Cambridge, Massachusetts: *The
Juniper Tree* (1985), composed with Robert Moran on a Grimm fairy tale
(one of Glass's most popular operas); *The Fall of the House of Usher* (1988)
after Edgar Allan Poe; and *Orphée* (1993), the first of a trilogy based on
the films of Jean Cocteau.

In *Usher,* Glass provides a "House" with windows that keep blowing
open, lights that flare up and die, strange noises, and a dinner table set at a
weird and ominous slant. Several other of Glass's operas also rely on the
strange and bizarre. In the popular science-fiction music drama *1000 Airplanes on the Roof* (1988), Freud, Kafka, and Steven Spielberg are melded
in a kind of "hoary melodrama." Featuring an actor and a small ensemble,
the work is scored for synthesizers, amplified winds, and wordless soprano. It also illustrates Glass's daring collaborative effort with the Chinese

American playwright David Henry Hwang and scenic designer Jerome Sirlin. In place of sets, holographic projections are used. Nine projectors create a cinematic illusion that allows an actor to dash up the steps of an "apartment building" and vanish inside or float high above New York. For some, the effect is like putting a live actor into a film.

In the Cocteau trilogy, however, Glass goes one step further and does indeed put live actors "into" a movie. The films of Jean Cocteau form the inspiration for each of the three operas, but Glass realizes each film differently. A retelling of the ancient Orpheus legend, *Orphée* is an opera with a new libretto based on the original screenplay. But *La belle et la bête* (1994), called an "opera for ensemble and film," and *Les enfants terribles* (1996), "a dance-opera spectacle," use original Cocteau scripts to create groundbreaking mixed-media venues—or modern *Gesamtkunstwerke* ("a union of all the arts"). In *La belle et la bête,* Glass created what resembles a silent movie but employs a live symphonic ensemble and singers. The restless energy of the score pulls one into the film in a way that mere background music never could.

Of all Glass's operas, the most ambitious is his large-scale *The Voyage,* commissioned by the Metropolitan Opera to celebrate the five-hundredth anniversary of the arrival of Christopher Columbus in the New World. Under the baton of Bruce Ferden, it was given its premiere on Columbus Day, October 12, 1992, and staged again by the Met during its 1995–96 season, playing again to packed houses. *The Voyage* is scored for larger forces than other Glass operas: a tenor, two sopranos, two mezzo-sopranos, two bass-baritones, a bass, mixed chorus, and full orchestra. "I had the luxury of writing for a gigantic house, with wonderful facilities," said Glass, "and the best opera orchestra in the world."[13]

Significantly, *The Voyage* shows more harmonic complexity and uses chromaticism more than is normally associated with Glass's style. The melodic cells that characteristically dominate his music are often hidden or disappear altogether, and a wonderfully opulent and varied orchestral fabric comes to the fore. Adding color to the music are polytonal passages ("C major cohabitates with E major"), frequent augmented triads, and a mercurial mixture of major and minor tonalities that sometimes sounds like Bernard Herrmann's "voyage" in his score for *Journey to the Center of the Earth.*

In creating *The Voyage,* Glass worked closely with his librettist David Henry Hwang of *M Butterfly* fame, who also wrote the libretto for Glass's *1000 Airplanes on the Roof.* The opera is a science-fiction allegory that eulogizes the process of human discovery. For Glass, Columbus is "a composite character, a stand-in for all who are compelled to question, to ex-

Scene from act 3 of *The Voyage* by Philip Glass, with Patricia Schuman as The Commander, Metropolitan Opera (1992). *Photo by Winnie Klotz*

plore, to search beyond current boundaries."[14] Played by baritone Timothy Noble, Columbus appears only twice, in the second act with Queen Isabella and the Spanish court as he sets out for the Indies in 1492 and when he returns in the Epilogue. Act 1, set during the Ice Age, involves four intergalactic travelers who crash to earth when their spaceship goes out of control. Act 3 features—rather whimsically—twin archeologists, who during the year 2092 have unearthed crystals left behind by the Ice Age astronauts. The Commander, soprano Patricia Schumann, appears in a silver jumpsuit, and a large cast offers spectacular stage images. There are even moments of humor, as a chorus of dignitaries and world rulers gathers to see off the explorers. Directed by David Poutney and with designs by Robert Israel, the opera is a surreal collage of visions, among them a rocket launching and a huge head of the Statue of Liberty. A transparent pyramid containing a tilted platform poised atop an earthlike globe turns out to be Columbus's deathbed.

There is a Baroque feeling to the entire enterprise—the spectacle and metaphorical characterization and in the way its music and staging seem inseparable. The characters generally sing to the audience and do not interact with each other. Glass's tendency to write at the highest ranges requires skillful vocal techniques, like those needed for a Bach aria. There is always a lesson to be learned, moreover. In the Prologue, a scientist (resembling Stephen Hawkings) is seated in a wheelchair that descends from the stars. "The voyage lies where / The vision lies," he sings. According to the synopsis of the libretto, "Despite faulty equipment, inadequate bodies and finite minds, there always have been people who have the courage to follow where their vision leads."[15] In scene 3 of the third act, a quartet of astronauts sings poignantly, each "alone in his or her solitude" and saying farewell on telephone headsets.

The opera's most moving scene comes at its end. Referring to the controversial actions of Columbus, who set in motion mass suicide, murder, and the mutilation of Indians—as well as Queen Isabella's reputation as an anti-Semite who presided over the Inquisition—the opera's final message is powerfully consoling. Isabella, in modern dress, tries to seduce Columbus ("judge yourself, and enter my world"). He refuses. Before his bed is transported to the stars in a deus ex machina–style apotheosis, he sings:

And if our human voyages
Are riddled sometimes with horrors
With pride, with vanity
With the mother's milk of cruelty
Yet finally human evil
Does not deny the good
Of knowledge
Of light
Of revelation
Of the hope that lo one day
Exploration will make obsolete
Even the sins of the explorer.[16]

The Expressive Approaches of John Adams

In the operas of Philip Glass, major heroic figures are usually drawn from history and treated more as metaphors than characters. John Adams and Anthony Davis, however, focus on contemporary American heroes. In so doing they have opened the style of minimalism to a greater variety of dramatic impulses and colors. In their operas, they illustrate that the often mystical, elusive vocabulary of minimalism can serve drama in a clearly defined, persuasive way. If their approach to musical dramaturgy is more traditional than Glass's, their use of minimalism moves beyond the trends of the times, adds other musical styles, and brings valuable new perspectives in characterization to American opera.

When the iconoclastic director Peter Sellars asked John Adams to write an opera about Richard Nixon, Adams at first admitted that he "just couldn't imagine the character Nixon singing." Barely thirty at the time, Sellars had directed more than a hundred plays and operas and was known for his avant-garde approaches to visual and dramatic imagery. His *Così fan tutte,* for example, was set in a neon-lit diner; *Don Giovanni* in Harlem; and Handel's *Orlando* partly on Mars. For Sellars, Richard Nixon's memorable 1972 visit to China had great dramatic potential. It evoked noble, heroic, and almost mythic dimensions and yet involved characters who were complex and even flawed. In the background was the ever-present real-life drama of West meeting East and the polarization of two very different worldviews.

When Adams accepted the idea, Sellars brought in the Minnesota-born poet Alice Goodman to write the libretto and Mark Morris as choreographer. The result was a grand "heroic opera for an unheroic age."[17] After its Houston Opera premiere on October 22, 1987, *Nixon in China* played at the Brooklyn Academy of Music and Kennedy Center for the Performing Arts. Moving on to Los Angeles, Helsinki, the Netherlands, and Australia, it became the most talked-about opera since Glass's *Einstein on the Beach.*

To some, *Nixon in China* created the sensation of a masquerade or charade; it was a spectacle in the grand tradition, embellished with warmth, humor, and a modicum of compassion. The sets by Adrianne Lobel fell somewhere between abstractions and traditional scenography. A gigantic poster of Mao Tse-tung dominates the stage in act 2, and a replica of the Spirit of '76 allows Pat and Richard Nixon to deplane in grandiose contemporary style at the opening of the opera. A rousing agitprop Chinese ballet *The Red Detachment of Women*—like the one the Nixons actually

Act 1, scene 1 of *Nixon in China* by John Adams. The opera was coproduced by the Houston Grand Opera, the Brooklyn Academy of Music, Kennedy Center, and the Netherlands Opera. © *1987 Jim Caldwell*

saw—offers a dazzling dance scenario, and a grand-opera-style chorus adds color and verve in a banquet scene in the Great Hall of the People. "'It's like a dream,'" sings Nixon. "And suddenly, the picture freezes, as if the hold button had been pressed on a VCR."[18]

One of the most impressive aspects of *Nixon in China* is Alice Goodman's superb libretto, a feat of pacing, poetry, and subtle caricature, although Goodman firmly denies any satirical gestures. "I pondered Nixon's love of history and his belief in peace and progress," she has observed. "I became more and more certain that every character in the opera should be made as eloquent as possible. . . . the heroic quality of the work as a whole would be determined by the eloquence of each character in his or her own argument."[19]

In Goodman's libretto, Nixon is "emotionally repressed and socially awkward but acutely aware of his role in history."[20] He speaks or sings in a "combination of crude colloquialism—the sort of thing we didn't even know about until the Watergate tapes—and windy grandiloquence."[21] Pat Nixon in act 2 visits a commune, a pig farm, and an acupuncture clinic and then sings a lyrical aria about her vision of America. Henry Kissinger is cast as a basso buffo with lines such as "I'm lost. . . . Please, where's the toilet?" But Goodman gives Premier Chou En-lai the final words in a text of grace and vision that closes the opera:

> How much of what we did was good?
> Everything seems to move beyond
> Our remedy. Come, heal this wound.
> At this hour nothing can be done.
> Just before dawn the birds begin.
> The warblers, who prefer the dark,
> The cage-birds answering. To work!
> Outside this room the chill of grace
> Lies heavy on the morning grass.[22]

John Adams's score gives life to the characters by reaching beyond the repetitive rhythmic figures and broken chords of minimalism to include other styles, such as American popular music, jazz and swing. Adams (b. 1947) composed his earliest works in a conservative, academic style, but in the 1970s he experimented not only with minimalism but also with combinations of classical, folk, and popular forms. *Nixon in China* draws upon a rich variety of American vernacular music. Adams uses a saxophone quartet, Glenn Miller style, to evoke the Nixons' romantic reverie. Mao, "the great mythic figure," gets a funky Motown harmony, Adams explains, because he is a genius whose "back on the farm" aspect is very much rooted in the people. "The dangerous and vindictive Madame Mao is a shrieking coloratura" like the devilish Queen of the Night.[23]

Although he makes fleeting references to Strauss and even Debussy, Adams explains his *Nixon* style as "intensely American, no *chinoiserie*. If there's a model for its simplicity, I would have to say it's Mozart. . . . But I believe that you can continue to peel the layers back and find beneath the surface a lot of very complex relationships. Complexity can take different courses. A complex emotion, or atmosphere, or ambiguity in tone is to me far more interesting that the abstruse rhythmic and tonal experimentation that's been going on ever since I was a kid."[24]

One of the most effective scenes in the opera comes at its end, when the principal characters—Pat, Richard, Mao, and his wife—lie on their beds, expressing their thoughts and reminiscing. "You won at poker," sings Pat. "I sure did," replies Richard:

> I had a system. Five-card stud
> Taught me a lot about mankind.
> Speak softly and don't show your hand
> Became my motto.

"Tell me more," Pat replies.[25] As the scene moves to a close, Adams shows his mastery of the four characters' innermost feelings. His score reflects the closing lines of each with great poignancy and depth.

John Adams's second opera, *The Death of Klinghoffer,* differs from *Nixon in China* in several aspects. Both deal with important recent events, but the events in the latter are noble and in the former they are tragic. In *Klinghoffer,* there is no comedy or gentle parody as in *Nixon,* and the pacing and visual presentation is also less naturalistic. The music in *Klinghoffer* is generally darker, more passionate, flowing, and contrapuntal, than that of *Nixon.* Both operas, however, shared the same production team; the librettist was Alice Goodman; the director, Peter Sellars; and the choreographer, Robert Morris.

The Death of Klinghoffer received its premiere on March 19, 1991, in Brussels, and the following September it was staged for the first time in America at Brooklyn's Academy of Music. Several of the original *Nixon* cast appeared also in *Klinghoffer,* among them James Maddalena (Nixon) as The Captain, Sanford Sylvan (Chou En-lai) as Leon Klinghoffer, Thomas Hammons (Henry Kissinger) as The First Officer and also "Rambo," and Stephanie Friedman (Mao's secretary) as Omar. Sheila Nadler sang the role of Marilyn Klinghoffer and Eugene Perry that of Mamoud.

The Death of Klinghoffer is based on a tragic incident that took place in 1985—the hijacking of the cruise ship *Achille Lauro* by a group of Palestinian terrorists and the murder of Leon Klinghoffer, an elderly Jewish American passenger confined to a wheelchair. Sellars and his team did not intend to produce a "docu-opera." They wanted instead to create a series of fluid and timeless meditations with no linear narrative and little action. In that regard, the opera proceeds more like a staged oratorio in the tradition of other American composers from Silas Pratt in *Triumph of Columbus* (1892) to Ezra Laderman with *Galileo Galelei* (1979). The non-narrative format works especially well in Adams's opera because it allows the symbolism of the emotionally charged incident full play.

As in Bach's Passions, the chorus plays a primary role in *Klinghoffer.* For the most part, it exists outside the time-frame of the opera. Some of the most beautiful poetry in the opera is given to the choruses, as well as the richest, most expressive music. With the exception of "Hagar and the Angel," which opens act 2, the choruses are paired: Night and Day, Desert and Ocean, and Exiled Palestinians and Exiled Jews. Adams begins the opening chorus quietly, like a baroque lament, with repeated "weeping" orchestral pulsations underneath the plaintive voices. As the textual outcry becomes angrier ("Of that house, not a wall / In which a bird might nest / Was left to stand"), the chorus becomes more violent and explosive. Powerfully, the

Sets for Adams's *The Death of Klinghoffer* featured large steel girders and gangplanks and a screen that showed closeups of the singers. *Photo by Hermann J. Baus*

minimalist figurations in the orchestra seem to cry out an anguish of their own. Choral lines are also minimal at times, as if to provide dramatic accents within certain arias and solo passages. In these instances, short, wordless choral phrases, relentlessly repeated, become poignant exclamations—sighs, moans, and otherworldly colors—as in Omar's "it is as if our earthly life were spent miserably" from act 2, scene 1.[26]

As the choruses comment on universal, often abstract, issues outside the timespan of the opera, the roles of the Klinghoffers and the Palestinian terrorists are placed in the present while The Captain and the other survivors reminisce in the past—a layering of narrative strata similar to that found in the Bach Passions. Adams points out, "You have a constantly shifting scale of closeness and distance. . . . At one moment you feel as though you're right there on the deck under the blistering sun with the rest of the passengers, and a moment later you feel like you're reading about it in some very ancient text."[27] The essence of Bach is also reflected in certain arias. The Captain's long, declamatory narrative in the opening of act 1, for example, is actually a duet for voice and oboe, as Bach's cantatas and Passions often feature solo voice and instrument. In act 2, scene 2, Mamoud, the hijacker, guards his prey to a sinuous bassoon obbligato.

Adams's effulgent musical style, which some call "neosensualism," can often be long-breathed and chromatic, recalling the early style of Arnold Schoenberg. But minimalist figurations in the orchestra, colored at times by pianos and synthesizers and cast within a pantonal or atonal framework, create a sound more characteristic of Adams. Although these figurations (rocking thirds, repeated vertical harmonies, and waving arpeggios) act as orchestral accompaniment patterns, they very often have surging power and a dramatic life of their own. Like the repetitive words of a rosary, they heighten the spirituality of both form and text. One particularly effective example occurs during Marilyn Klinghoffer's impassioned lament for her lost husband at the end of the opera. As she sings out her grief, a heartbeat of repeated tones in the orchestra grows in searing intensity until the strings take over, sustained and consoling, on her final words: "They should have killed me—I wanted to die." Clearly, Adams, in that compelling closing, means to extend the heroic image to her.

Heroic Icons for the Modern Age

Not all viewers have responded favorably to Adams's Nixon and Klinghoffer operas. David Littlejohn prefers the composer's slender, pop-cabaret style *I Was Looking at the Ceiling and Then I Saw the Sky* (1995), which is set in contemporary Los Angeles and is again a collaboration with Sellars. "Both 'Nixon' and 'Klinghoffer,'" Littlejohn notes, are "sunk by the weight and confusion of their socio-political freight and demonstrate the folly of trying to make grand operas for today out of yesterday's news."[28] In opera, however, it is not "the news" that makes news but the human reactions to it.

Other composers also saw contemporary controversial issues and attitudes as the subjects of their operas. In turn, their main characters—a modern black activist and a gay politician—became firsts in operatic history. In these characters, the audience has the opportunity to look beyond the outer man (as Wagner would say) and far into the icon; in doing so, the audience sees itself as it really is. Perhaps, in the words of Malcolm X, they "want the truth" but "don't want to know." Yet *X: The Life and Times of Malcolm X* (1986) by Anthony Davis and *Harvey Milk* (1995) by Stewart Wallace draw audiences into an understanding of the new heroism, the modern legends that inform their age.

In the liner notes to his solo piano album *Lady of the Mirrors* (1979), Anthony Davis wrote, "I feel that I am part of a new revolution in art which turns away from the minimalistic exaltation of the small idea to a concept of a larger, more fertile imaginative universe."[29] Davis then turned to the musical form that embraced poetry, drama, action, and design—opera. Composed a year before Adam's *Nixon in China, X: The Life and Times of Malcolm X* displays a more frenzied, dissonant, and rhythmically complex minimalism than Adams's work and leaves behind the simpler, mystical colorings of Glass and Reich. To recount the despair of blacks in the 1930s to 1960s, Davis zeros in on the plight of Malcolm Little (Malcolm X), whose assssination in 1965 made him a legend and, to some, a hero. This infuses his music with a multiplicity of angry, snarling, bitter, powerful, and heroic sounds. In what could be termed "verismo minimalism," Davis offers a perfect match of music and subject. Along with his drone-like ostinatos, he blends swing, be-bop, scat, rap, and modal jazz along with the styles of Duke Ellington, John Coltrane, Alban Berg, Leonard Bernstein, and even non-Western music. All enlarge the dramatic message with seamless elegance and finesse.

Not all responded favorably to Davis's message, though. John Adams commented that people often told him of their uncomfortable surprise that Anthony Davis and he were using stories from contemporary life as subjects for operas. "It's always asked," Adams said, "with eyebrows slightly raised, as much as to say, 'When are you going to write a *real* opera, about

King Lear or Oedipus?'" "If opera is going to stay alive," Adams responded, "these kinds of issues that Anthony has chosen are what's needed."[30]

No doubt a certain percentage of the public will always have problems with operas about contemporary subjects. History, however, has shown
that operas based on contemporary issues can be both effective and enduring despite criticism. To satisfy Venetian authorities, Verdi had to move
the time of *La traviata* from his era to a century earlier, and Bizet was attacked for showing realistic smoking, sexuality, and violence onstage in
Carmen.

Malcolm X is considerably more compelling as lyric drama than Davis's
Amistad (1997), which delutes audience sympathies by focusing on a large
mass of characters, however tragic their fate.[31] Although a broad, romanticized biography, *Malcolm X* draws immediate attention to the power struggle between Malcolm and his mentor Elijah Muhammad for control of
the Black Muslim movement. Malcolm is caught between fate and self-
determination and is also shown to be a victim of whites, who killed his
father and drove his mother mad when he was a child. Those events shaped

Composer Anthony
Davis. *Photo by Ray Block*

Thomas Young and Ben
Holt in the New York
City Opera's world pre-
miere of *X: The Life and
Times of Malcolm X* in
1986, by Anthony Davis.
Photo by Carol Rosegg

his future as a drug dealer, convict, follower of Elijah, and, finally, as a convert to the Moslem religion. The opera takes place over a broad timespan:
act 1 (three scenes) runs from 1931 to 1945; act 2 (four scenes), from 1946
to 1963; and act 3 (five scenes), from 1963 to 1965. Textual references include everything from zoot suits to the assassination of John F. Kennedy.
With a story treatment by the composer's brother Christopher Davis and
a libretto by Thulani Davis, their cousin, *X* received its world premiere
September 28, 1986, at the New York City Opera. It was directed by Rhoda
Levine, with Ben Holt as Malcolm.

Davis's father was the first black professor at Princeton University and
a descendant of the founders of the Hampton Institute; his mother came
from a long line of physicians, including several connected with Howard
University. Young Anthony, who was born in 1951, wanted to be a classical pianist but was taken aback when a professor at Phillips Exeter Academy said, "I didn't know black people played classical music." "That was
when I stopped," said Davis.[32] He majored in music at Yale University and
then founded the octet Episteme ("knowledge" in Greek), a group that
specialized in his own work as well as pieces integrating jazz, non-Western music, and the classical avant-garde. Episteme also formed the impulses
that gave rise to the musical style of *X*, especially the use of improvisa-

tion. Improvisational passages played mainly by solo instruments are not merely juxtaposed throughout the opera but interact with its more formal elements, creating complex polyrhythmic textures and an equivocal tonal base. In Davis's original holograph, such improvisatory passages are indicated in standard jazz notation.[33]

Unlike *The Death of Klinghoffer,* which is a listener's opera, *X* needs to be seen to be fully appreciated. Although its propulsive, relentless rhythmic patterns shift unmercifully in meter and accent, the restlessness of these drone-like patterns can become monotonous and even cloying. Yet Davis's skill in handling so many elements simultaneously is impressive. The vocal lines are extremely difficult, primarily because of perpetually changing meters. Bernstein-like syncopations and Stravinskian primitivism, as in *Le sacre du printemps,* appear not only in the orchestra but also extend into choral texts, becoming hypnotic rhythmic incantations that promulgate key messages. Under a vocal solo line, they also provide mind-jolting rhythmic ostinatos, as in the opening chorus with Louise and The Preacher: "Africa's time has come, Africa's time has come, Africa's time has come." The choral incantory cells also cloud tonality and heighten the atonal structure of the opera.

Lyricism is not what *X* is about. But there are moments of desolate, bitter beauty in the score, as the duet between Elijah and Malcolm at the end of act 1 that begins with Elijah's "Malcolm, who have you been?" and Elijah's arioso, "An 'X' you must claim." Scene 2 of act 1 contrasts the tenderness of Ella, Malcolm's sister, with the frenzied pop sounds that characterize Street and his friends. The scene is remarkable in its rapidly changing, richly varied, moods and colors. Ella's vocal passages are sinuous and warm ("come with me, child"), while the men of the street sing to the jazzy improvisation of saxophone, vibraharp, piano, and bass ensemble. The street styles break out into swing and rap, and an intermittent scat solo rises over the frenetic incantations of craps players: "The white man takes / while the black man breaks." Ella, a counterbalance to the men, sings gracefully to a sustained string background:

> Some men are strivers
> with dreams of their own;
> and some are believers
> who help a dream along;
> and some speak of prophecy,
> of Garvey, slavery,
> of nations, visions and hope.
> They make the street their church,
> from a soap box perch.[34]

Emotionally charged contemporary subjects appealed to American composers with increasing frequency after *X*. William Harper's *Snow Leopard* (1989) is inspired by the Iran-Contra affair, with a spiritual overlay derived from the Tibetan Book of the Dead. Conrad Cummings, in his minimalist-based *Tonkin* (1993), treats the Vietnam War, and John Duffy's moving *Black Water* (1997) is based on the tragedy at Chappaquiddick.

During the second half of the 1990s, a new subject—homosexuality—became a prime subject within both opera and musical theater. As frontier optimism invaded Broadway during the 1940s (*Oklahoma*), romantic moralism during the 1950s (*Guys and Dolls*), and religious crises during the 1970s (*Jesus Christ Superstar*), so the dark dilemma of AIDS informed the theater of the 1990s. The brazen sexuality of Broadway's *Angels in America* is at once surreal and tragic, elegiac and hilarious, as homosexual yearnings playfully define its characters, which include a Mormon Republican and Joseph McCarthy. Jonathan Larson's ebullient *Rent* is even more telling in its portrayal of young gays, lesbians, and transvestites. Based loosely on Puccini's *La bohème, Rent,* set among artists and street people in New York City, became one of Broadway's greatest hits. It is an audacious "rock opera" (with no spoken dialogue) that enlivened the modern music theater audience with a bevy of enthusiastic young people. Harold Blumenfeld's *Seasons in Hell* (1996), cast within an expressionist musical framework, vividly tells of the homosexual life of the nineteenth-century French poet Arthur Rimbaud.

The opera that deals most successfully with sexual issues, however, is Stewart Wallace's *Harvey Milk*. With libretto by Michael Korie, *Harvey Milk* is the story of the closeted Jewish New Yorker who later became a gay politician in San Francisco. When he was shot and killed in 1978, Milk became a martyr of the homosexual rights movement. The opera received its world premiere by the Houston Grand Opera in January 1995 and then went on to fulfill co-commissioned engagements at the New York City Opera and San Francisco Opera the following year. Christopher Alden staged all productions, which included Robert Orth as Harvey and Raymond Very as Dan White, the right-wing city supervisor who eventually kills both Milk and San Francisco's mayor, George Moscone. For the San Francisco production, Wallace revised the orchestration, reworked the opera's conclusion, and added two arias for Harvey, giving him more heroic weight as he sings defiantly before his assassination:

The lies we told our mothers
Turned to shame,

And shame to rage,
And rage to pride,
And pride to hope,
And hope will never be silent.[35]

Perhaps the most startling aspect of the opera is the way in which it successfully blends disparate elements. Fact and fiction, conversation and effusion all mix and meld with equal ease in a score that is lively and engaging. One of the most effective scenes in the opera is a tender love duet for Harvey and his boyfriend Scott Smith, sung while they lie in bed— "what must surely be an operatic first," wrote *Time*.[36] Harvey himself is less hero than emblem, and the opera sends forth a message that is as vital as its music.

Writing about Anthony Davis's *Tania* (on Patty Hearst) and why such an angry topic should shape an opera, the librettist Michael LaChiusa has provided a rationale that applies to many contemporary operatic heroes: "What's relevant in this story for women, for blacks, for gays, is that iden-

Houston Grand Opera's world premiere of *Harvey Milk*. Left to right: Robert Orth (Harvey), Chuck Winkler, Bradley Williams, and Randall Wong. © *1995 Jim Caldwell*

tity is defined by your experience. But when you negate your experiences, what kind of identity do you have? Either we find a peaceful coexistence with our experiences, or we shove them back into the closet, where they'll become a nightmare that we'll all be dealing with for the rest of our lives."[37] As for *Harvey Milk,* writes Mark Adamo, the opera is an "astounding achievement—lively, artful, tough-minded American music-drama, deeply satisfying to ear, eye and mind. It may or may not be opera for all time. But it is—brilliantly, hearteningly—unequivocally for our own."[38]

⌒

Philip Glass and Robert Wilson's *Einstein on the Beach* was the first truly innovative approach to American opera since Virgil Thomson's *Four Saints in Three Acts* in 1934. For the most part, postwar American operas relied on the Wagner-Strauss-Puccini sense of musical dramaturgy. But in developing a new theatrical approach, a "theater of images" where noble ideals and deeds are visually symbolized and staging and music are intertwined and codependent, Glass and Wilson discovered an inspirational font unparalleled in the history of opera. Unlike *Four Saints,* which anticipated approaches but spawned no immediate successors, *Einstein* inspired other contemporary composers to use minimalism in various ways that would evoke atmosphere, character, and mood and especially define their heroes.

John Adams, Anthony Davis, and Stewart Wallace moved in a different direction from Glass and added jazz, rock, Motown, and other vernacular American sounds that enlarged their minimalistic approaches. Their heroes were the icons of a modern age—heroes whose messages demanded a new musical perspective that would inform, liberate, and empower. Not all modern opera heroes are found within the cast, however. Advances in technology, ever-increasing accents on visual elements brought about by television and motion pictures, and also new conceptual approaches to opera have all placed formidable demands on directors, who have become as important in the production of opera as conductors were in decades past.

18

Toward the New Millennium and Beyond

If ours is a living culture, then there will always be a core of new works that should be performed.
—John von Rhein, *Chicago Tribune*

WHEN THE METROPOLITAN OPERA asked Philip Glass to compose *The Voyage* (1992), he was offered a commission of $325,000, at the time the largest amount ever awarded for an opera. The sum even exceeded what Verdi received for *Aida* (in today's currency, $225,000).[1] What mattered, of course, was Glass, the Met, and the quincentennial of the discovery of America. Companies of all sizes throughout the nation, however, saw audiences increase dramatically during the 1980s and into the 1990s. Although the United States has never enjoyed the same degree of public support for the arts as Europe, visionary leadership and a wide variety of private support did allow opera to move into the twenty-first century with imagination and vigor.

For many years, the National Endowment for the Arts and the Ford Foundation provided major funding for new operas. After cutbacks in those two sources, other granting agencies included the James Irvine Foundation, AT&T, Philip Morris, and the Rockefeller Foundation. Opera America, founded in 1970, also has added to the momentum of the productions. A nonprofit trade organization, Opera America has provided information services and funding sources for new works, primarily through its Lila Wallace–Reader's Digest Opera for a New America program and The Next Stage, a regranting program for the continuation of previously performed North American works. Among Opera America's membership of 132 professional companies, twenty world premieres took place in North America during the 1998–99 season alone, and more than a hundred new works were produced during the 1990s.

To cut costs, many opera companies, notably those of Houston, Dallas, Washington, and San Francisco, share the commissioning and production of new operas. The Houston Grand Opera was the first company to secure a transatlantic triple co-commission with Leonard Bernstein's *A Quiet Place,* staged with La Scala and the John F. Kennedy Center in 1983. In 1987 Gershwin's *Porgy and Bess* was co-produced by thirteen American opera companies, and the following year Philip Glass's *The Making of the Representative for Planet 8* was co-commissioned by Houston Grand Opera, English National Opera, the Muziektheater Foundation of Amsterdam, and Kiel Opera. Another joint staging was that of Stewart Wallace's *Harvey Milk,* produced by the Houston Grand Opera, New York City Opera, and San Francisco Opera between 1995 and 1996. Co-commissioning also ensures that a new work will receive performances in more than one venue.

Several companies are giving focus to contemporary opera in creative marketing and programming strategies. The Opera Company of Philadelphia, for example, has inaugurated "The Experimental Stage," in which new operas are to be presented at three stages: workshop, staged reading, and a full production. The Houston Grand Opera's Opera New World Program is an ongoing effort begun in 1990 to commission and produce works that will develop new audiences for opera. Houston is also the first major American opera house to commission a Spanish-language opera, *Florencia en el Amazonas* by the Mexican composer Daniel Catán. In 1984 Ardis Krainik initiated the Lyric Opera of Chicago's unique Composer-in-Residence Program to nurture talented American opera composers. Among the five world premieres that have taken place is *Between Two Worlds* by Shulamit Ran, a Pulitzer Prize–winner who began her residency in 1994. The Lyric Opera's "Toward the Twenty-First Century Initiative" offers one new American and one new European opera each season. Both Boston Lyric Opera and Washington Opera have also committed to producing an American work within each season's repertoire.

Other companies, such as the Houston Grand Opera, New York City Opera, and Opera Theatre of Saint Louis, have continued their recognized accent on American repertoire. By the year 2000, Houston Grand Opera had presented twenty-five world premieres, twenty-three of them by American composers.[2] In a festival-like setting and to celebrate its fiftieth anniversary, the New York City Opera gave three important world premieres of American operas on consecutive nights in October 1993. College workshops and small regional companies, moreover, continue to produce American chamber operas with excellent talent. Innovative visual and technological effects as well as creative, Broadway–opera styles draw new, often younger, audiences. In addition, the United States is a world leader in the creation of opera for children. As the Houston Opera's general director David Gockley points out, "Opera in America today is far more than merely 'grand.'"

Projections for the future seem bright. After its success with Jack Beeson's *Lizzie Borden* in 1996, the Glimmerglass Opera changed its plans for 1997 from *Curlew River* by the English composer Benjamin Britten to Carlisle Floyd's hauntingly eloquent *Of Mice and Men*. That same summer, the Santa Fe Opera presented Peter Lieberson's *Ashoka's Dream,* the third in a series of operas commissioned from distinguished young American composers. The nation's larger opera companies, too, are producing more American works. The Los Angeles Opera produced the world premiere of *Fantastic Mr. Fox* by Tobias Picker in 1998, and the San Francisco Opera commissioned three new operas, one each by Bobby McFerrin (*St. Cecilia*), Andre Previn (*A Streetcar Named Desire*), and Jake Heggie (*Dead Man Walking*). In April 2000 the Houston Opera gave the premiere of Carlisle Floyd's *Cold Sassy Tree*. Perhaps the most eagerly awaited operatic event of the era was the Metropolitan Opera–commissioned *Great Gatsby* by John Harbison, based on F. Scott Fitzgerald. The Metropolitan has also commissioned two more works, one by Tobias Picker and the other by Chinese-American Tan Dun. Both are part of a plan to commission a new opera every three years.

An interest in American stylistic traditions has brought a wide range of earlier works to the contemporary operatic stage. Between 1991 and 1996 *Postcard from Morocco, Four Saints in Three Acts, Lizzie Borden, The Saint of Bleecker Street, Vanessa, Wuthering Heights, The Crucible, The Consul, Susannah, Maria Golovin, The Postman Always Rings Twice, The Ballad of Baby Doe, The Passion of Jonathan Wade, Miss Julie,* Conrad Susa's *Transformations* and *Black River,* and Lee Hoiby's *The Tempest,* among others, were produced across the United States. In 1996 Charles Wakefield Cadman's *Garden of Mystery,* first performed in concert at Carnegie Hall in 1925, was given its staged premiere by the American Chamber Opera Company. In 1998 the Minnesota Opera produced George Antheil's *Transatlantic* (1928); the Metropolitan Opera, Carlisle Floyd's *Susannah;* and the Lyric Opera of Chicago, Marvin David Levy's *Mourning Becomes Electra,* a revision of the 1967 Metropolitan commission. Many opera company directors are now looking for American works to round out their seasons of old standbys and give audiences a variety from which to choose.

If new works are performed in Europe, they are usually those of a country's own composer. Interest in American works abroad is growing, however. *Porgy and Bess* had been performed in Finland and also in Austria during the outdoor festival at Bregenz. Ernst Toch, an Austrian-born

American, died before he could witness the premiere of his *The Last Tale* (*Scheherezade*), composed in America in 1962. The opera was first staged in what was formerly East Germany thirty years later. Significantly, the 1995 index to volume 46 of *Opera* magazine listed fourteen American works staged in various parts of Europe and Australia during that year. Among these are Leonard Bernstein's *Candide* (staged in Lisbon, Saint-Etienne, and Reggio Emilia), Steve Reich and Beryl Korot's *The Cave* (Turin), Gian Carlo Menotti's *The Consul* (Monte Carlo) and Menotti's *The Medium* (Paris), Thea Musgrave's *Símon Bolívar* (London and Regensburg), Kurt Weill's *Street Scene* (Lisbon), and Stephen Paulus's *The Woodlanders* (Oxford). Still, there is a need for the U.S. government to take a more active part in promoting American arts overseas.

By the century's end, American opera composers were producing works of power, energy, and diversity as never before. John von Rhein has noted a "pluralistic explosion of styles."[3] Indeed, styles and subjects were given a fresh perspective, theatrical images were provocative, and musical dramaturgy took on the unique aura of the age. If some composers chose more futuristic, modern approaches, others preferred the "neo-sensualism" of Puccini. Lee Hoiby noted a path toward more traditional, romantic trends in the 1990s. "Atonality is beginning to crumble. The minimalists are sinking of their own dead weight. I'm not the only one who feels this way. There are others who have stuck to their guns and refused to toe the party line," he said.[4]

The millennium began with several questions: Who in the early twenty-first centry would be among the important composers of new American operas? What new operas would receive the most attention, and what subjects would American composers choose? In addition, what musical styles would draw audiences, and which works would last? Among the staples by Dominick Argento, Carlisle Floyd, Gian Carlo Menotti, Robert Ward, Douglas Moore, Philip Glass, Leonard Bernstein, Aaron Copland, and Samuel Barber are many others. Some are by established artisans: Conrad Susa, John Adams, Dorothy Rudd Moore, Thea Musgrave, Stephen Paulus, Hugo Weisgall, William Bolcom, Libby Larsen, Lee Hoiby, Ulysses Kay, and John Corigliano. Others are the work of younger composers, and those just breaking into the operatic arena: Tobias Picker, David Lang, Deborah Drattell, Michael Torke, David Carlson, Lowell Liebermann, Jake Heggie, Robert Greenleaf, Daron Auric Hagen, and Jorge Martin. All, however, were contributing to American opera as the century turned, whether in premieres or revivals.

Operas by Modern American Women

By the 1970s, operas written by women were gaining attention. Edith Borroff lists more than one hundred women who have written operas and had them produced and published since the postwar years.[5] Many were chamber operas and theater works for children, but the growth of the women's movement in the late 1960s contributed to more large-scale operas by women being successfully staged. Organizations such as American Women Composers (AWC), founded in 1976, began to develop and prosper. By the 1990s AWC maintained a rental archive of more than three thousand scores in every medium. In 1977 Thea Musgrave's powerful *Voice of Ariadne* (1974) after Henry James was staged by the New York City Opera—the first opera by a woman to be performed by a major American house since the Metropolitan Opera's staging of *Der Wald* by the English composer Ethel Smyth in 1902. And when the Frankfurt Opera produced Louise Talma's *The Alcestiad* in Germany in 1962 the occasion marked the first opera by an American woman to be performed by a major European house. It received a twenty-minute ovation, seven subsequent performances, and won for Talma the Waite Award of the American Institute of Arts and Letters.[6]

Some modern women composers remain relatively conservative in dramatic form and musical style, and others seek new directions in sound and imagery. Margaret Garwood (b. 1927) is a skillful orchestrator and librettist whose musical palette has been likened to Debussy, Strauss, and sometimes Stravinsky. She is best known for *The Trojan Women,* first staged in 1967 and revised in 1979, and for *Rappaccini's Daughter* (1983), based on Nathaniel Hawthorne's supernatural love story. Although her overall style is tonal, Julia Smith (1911–89) peppered her scores with dissonance, jazz, and modern French harmonies. The most successful of her six operas are *Daisy* (1973), based on the life of Girl Scouts founder Juliette Gordon Low, and *Cynthia Parker* (1935), a tale of conflicts between white and Native American cultures in the nineteenth century. An internationally recognized conductor, Victoria Bond (b. 1945) has composed numerous vocal and instrumental works. Her *Travels* (1995) is inspired by Jonathan Swift's *Gulliver's Travels* but is perceived as a twentieth-century search for self.

Many of the twentieth century's most adventuresome excursions in opera and music theater came from the pens of women. Vivian Fine's *The Women in the Garden* (1977) added a new dimension to the "plotless opera" concept of the 1970s. The four main characters—Emily Dickinson,

Isadora Duncan, Gertrude Stein, and Virginia Woolf—are drawn to each other through emotional rather than intellectual means, and they reveal themselves to one another in a non-narrative form of expression. Twenty years later Fine employed multimedia techniques in *Memoirs of Uliana Rooney* (1996), a one-act chamber opera with a libretto and video montage by Sonya Friedman, an award-winning documentary film writer. *Memoirs* is a biting, amusing, meditative story about a fictional American woman composer whose feisty feminism and quest for recognition carries her through the turbulent decades of the 1920s and to the present.

Innovative multimedia effects have long fascinated Laurie Anderson (b. 1947), Meredith Monk (b. 1943), and Libby Larsen (b. 1950), who have all broken ground with exciting, angular operas born of the latest technology. Some would argue that Anderson's controversial theater works are not operas at all. She was part of an experimentalist Soho "loft" team that included Philip Glass, Steve Reich, and the choreographer Lucinda Childs during the early 1970s. Her distinctive style combines music, narrative, films, and slides. One of her most interesting works is the six-hour epic *United States, Parts I-IV,* which played first in Amsterdam in 1982 and the following year at the Brooklyn Academy.

Meredith Monk's work has fewer elliptical messages than Anderson's. Her *Atlas,* she says, "illustrates the loss of wonder, mystery, and freshness in our contemporary life and the possibility of rediscovering it." Monk wrote her own libretto for *Atlas,* which is based loosely on the life of the female explorer Alexandra David-Neel. She uses haunting sounds—melismas, ethereal choral tones, lulling triads, and improvisation on vocal sounds or phonemes—along with the lively rhythms of jazz and folk music "to bypass the intellect and speak directly to the soul."[7] There is virtually no text, but the tale unfolds with humor and warmth through pantomime, instrumentalists, synthesizers, film, and a rich, wide-ranging panoply of vocal music. *Atlas* was given its premiere by the Houston Grand Opera on February 22, 1991.

Like Monk's operas, those of Libby Larsen also speak lyrically to the soul, but they do so in a manner quite unlike any other. Larsen, a former singer, perceives the human voice as a lyrical tool for dramatic expression, and she also uses modern technology as a kind of "visual music" to enlarge the subliminal messages of singers. Having studied screen writing, she is acutely aware of the way films and television condition theater audiences. "I think movies have changed our perception of how emotion unfolds in a human being," she says. For Larsen, the posturing over love or hate or nobility found in the conventional theater seems less valid to

Young Alexandra (Dina Emerson) is introduced to her spiritual guides in Meredith Monk's *Atlas* (1991). *Houston Grand Opera Archives, photo by Jim Caldwell*

younger viewers. Television allows emotion to be experienced quickly and intensely, which is why she wants to work in what she calls the "new proscenium," where an eye or a jaw can be framed in such a way as to carry emotional content.[8]

In Larsen's *Frankenstein: The Modern Prometheus,* produced by the Minnesota Opera in 1990, the composer and her creative team positioned two giant television screens on either side of the hall for close-up views and an oversized projection screen at the back of the stage to show what the monster was thinking, seeing, or remembering. The ambiguous environments of the set were created by hung ropes and rope ladders, constructed levels, and multilayered hanging scrims. Most stage designs were black and white, while the screen images were in color, suggesting perhaps that the monster was more real than its creator.

Inspired by Mary Shelley's novel of 1830, the opera is about an ambitious scientist who creates a monster that ultimately destroys all close to him—a monster that cannot love because it was not created in love. As Larsen explains:

> In *Frankenstein,* I focused on the relationship of Dr. Frankenstein and the monster, keeping close to the book. Both characters represented to me

much larger, timeless issues, mainly the dilemma as to how far we can push scientific research without considering the consequences. . . . Dramatically we see what the monster sees on film projections, which is very different from what we see on stage. As to the music, I put the orchestra under the stage, not in the pit. I mixed the entire sound, and all the singers wore microphones. I did this because I wanted to represent the monster with many elements, especially electric guitar and synthesizer, sometimes whisper-soft like the person who guides or comforts himself with small sighs.[9]

Larsen scored the opera for a quartet of woodwind players, two brass players, three percussionists, a string quintet, multiple keyboards, and a backstage chorus. She also used a digital sound system and an Akai AXBO, "an old rock and roll synthesizer." Her sounds are intriguing and lyrical, always closely allied to the imagery of the story. "The vocal lines come from the characters," she observes. "For Dr. Frankenstein, the lines are disjunct. We needed a strong, athletic voice for that role. For Frankenstein's eighteen-year-old fiancée Elizabeth, we needed a classical lyric soprano, because she represented a sort of Victorian caring. I used areas of tonality or twelve-tone as the drama required—but the drama must always control the music."[10]

If the drama controlled the music, commercial timing shaped the overall form of the opera. According to Larsen, the way in which the plot is structured and the characters unfold is closely related to the timing of commercial breaks on television. Frankenstein is in fourteen scenes with no intermission. "I composed the piece in such a way that the scenes themselves are between six or seven, maybe twelve, minutes long, but that every twelve minutes or so something happens, then there is a break. The exposition, in other words, is very different from that of traditional opera."[11]

Some of the opera's most striking visual effects emanate from the monster, a tall, thin, chalk-white figure (a horror-story Harlequin) that dances and mimes with commanding grace. If critics were at times baffled—George Haymont observed that *Frankenstein* was radically different from any opera he had seen in twenty-five years—they had considerable praise for the production as a whole. Larsen's skills as a musical dramatist are everywhere evident in an imaginative work that melds motion picture and opera into an exciting new stage art.

Libby Larsen is co-founder of the American Composers Forum and has served as composer-in-residence with the Minnesota Orchestra. Among her many operas, chamber works, and solo instrumental works are twenty-five commissions and fifteen awards. Such noted conductors as Neville Marriner, Leonard Slatkin, Zubin Mehta, and Catherine Comet have performed her symphonic compositions throughout the United States and Europe. She considers herself, however, primarily an opera composer. She has written nine, including *Eric Hermannson's Soul,* which is based on a story by Willa Cather and was performed by Opera Omaha during the 1998–99 season. As for female characters, Larsen is interested in "finding and enhancing women who are strong and complex. It is difficult to find in opera a women, who is not defined by crises—either her own or someone else's. I like to study characters as they move and grow and become something else."[12]

Several African American women have been recognized for the operas they composed. Among them are Lena McLin (b. 1929) and Julia Perry (1924–79), a winner of the American Academy of Arts and Letters Prize for *The Selfish Giant* in 1964. Dorothy Rudd Moore's ambitious *Frederick Douglass* is based on events in Douglass's life between 1844 and 1863. It was given its premiere by New York's Opera Ebony on June 28, 1985, and

Libby Larsen. *Courtesy Libby Larsen*

drew praise from critics for its vigor, nobility, and lyricism. "She is able to convey the emotions onstage as human rather than merely operatic," wrote Gary Schmidgall. "And her dignified 'less is more' libretto discreetly eschews every invitation to fall back upon a rhinestone phrase. . . . It would not be surprising to see *Frederick Douglass* take a place beside *Lizzie Borden, Baby Doe* and Thomson's *Mother of Us All*. In one respect—its inspiring theme—it outclasses them all."[13]

Of all modern women composers, though, Thea Musgrave, born in Scotland in 1928, is the most widely recognized. Although some consider her a Scottish composer, her role in American opera production has been an important one. Musgrave came to the United States in 1970 as guest professor at the University of California at Santa Barbara. Since 1972 she has resided in the United States with her husband Peter Mark, general director of the Virginia Opera Company. A former student of Nadia Boulanger, she quickly established herself as an active composer and conductor and has worked with major British and American orchestras, often conducting her own work. Many of her compositions have been performed at well-known international venues from the Edinburgh Festival to Carnegie Hall.

It is in her operas, however, that Thea Musgrave reveals her dramatic gifts most fully. They cover a wide range of subjects and expression. Two have American subjects: *Harriet, the Woman Called Moses* on Harriet Tubman and *The Occurrence at Owl Creek Bridge* (1982), a radio opera about a southern planter at the time of the Civil War. Musgrave notes that she could not have written the two operas "without having lived in America and the American South." Because she writes her own librettos, she had to know "what the language sounded like . . . you have to have an ear for that."[14]

Thea Musgrave's approach to drama has visionary theatricality, but each opera comes to life through the imaginative use of expressive devices and materials, whether serial procedures, mime, sound effects, or spirituals. As she explains:

> The story of Harriet Tubman concerns an individual gifted with those rare qualities of courage and imagination which enabled her to overcome seemingly insuperable odds. . . . *Harriet* is every woman who dared to defy injustice and tyranny; she is Joan of Arc, she is Susan B. Anthony, she is Anne Frank, she is Mother Teresa. And to provide depth to the story, I used several spirituals in *Harriet*. Sometimes, they're quoted exactly, but they're always embodied in something else (e.g., other kinds of harmo-

nies), which will lend to the opera as a whole. I felt [that the use of spirituals] was important because these melodies are famous—and justly so; and I felt that their use would give the kind of color to the story that would help to bring the opera off musically.[15]

Teamwork and TV

For many composers, writing operas during the 1980s and 1990s involved close collaboration with a team of specialists: librettist, director, principal singers, set and lighting designers, choreographer, and conductor. Stephen Paulus has described the importance of the early meetings at which a work is played through at the piano. The initial meeting for his *The Postman Always Rings Twice* (1982), he said, "proved very helpful as some of the singers indicated that they could sing some parts higher or lower than I had written and thereby give their character more depth or range."[16] Conrad Susa, too, drew valuable comments from Frederica von Stade, Thomas Hampson, and Renée Fleming before he wrote the score for *The Dangerous Liaisons.*

The visual explosion in the theater and its modern, technological realization have made teamwork imperative and not always easy for a composer. As Libby Larsen admits, "I had researched Mary Shelley's *Frankenstein* for several years and felt her work always at my side. The director came in and wanted to move one of the scenes to a hospital ship. He said, 'I will not direct this scene unless we move it.' I said, 'Then you will not do this opera.' In the end the director won. But it is the composer who has the *ur* vision."[17]

Opera companies hire specialists to do everything from serve as "flying consultants," as for Ariel's airy escapades in the Dallas Opera's *The Tempest,* to monitor intricate computerized lighting. Modern multimedia operas place extraordinary demands on creative teams. Todd Machover's *VALIS* (1989) requires an array of electronic devices, two television monitors, and a playing space that moves beyond conventional theater. A tale of ancient biblical conflict as viewed by modern-day Palestinians, Israelis, and Americans, *The Cave* (1993) by Steve Reich and Beryl Korot is an exciting dramatic hybrid, part MTV, part documentary, and part music theater. It uses computer technology to synchronize live musicians, digitally sampled speech, and a multichannel video.[18]

Even the more conventional American operas, from Thomas Pasatiere's *The Seagull* (1974) to Conrad Susa's *Dangerous Liaisons* (1994), often use projections to enlarge tonal-visual images. As technology has come to opera, so opera has come to technology—and in ways Cadman and the early composers of radio operas could never have dreamed. Telecasts of the initial productions of American operas have become increasingly common, especially through Public Television's *Great Performances* series. *Sweeney Todd, Nixon in China, Einstein on the Beach, The Dangerous Liaisons, Willie Stark, Vanessa, The Ghosts of Versailles, The Aspern Papers, Goya, Summer and Smoke,* and *McTeague* have been some of the series' most important events.

How successful are such videoized operas relative to their real-life counterparts? For someone who has never seen an American opera—and many have not—do they do justice to the art? Most do, although others are less successful. The 1981 PBS broadcast of Hoiby's *Summer and Smoke* suffered from mixtures that altered the composer's original balance of orchestra and voice. The world premiere of Menotti's *Goya* (1986), however, was more effective on television than stage. Under the direction of the composer, *Goya* became the sixth Menotti opera produced by the Washington Opera. It was presented at the Kennedy Center with Placido Domingo in the title role. Menotti's libretto concerning the great Spanish painter's affair with Cayetana, Duchess of Alba, was criticized as trivial. On television, however, the close-ups of Domingo's telling portrayal of Goya as he deals with his impending deafness demonstrates Menotti's effectiveness as a musical dramatist. And the finale, in which Goya's paintings come to life in dance and pantomime to haunt him on his deathbed, is one of Menotti's finest scenes.

That camera perspectives and editorial concepts can be influential in promoting the best in new American works is illustrated especially by three operas: *Willie Stark* (1981) by Carlisle Floyd; *The Dangerous Liaisons* (1994) by Conrad Susa; and *McTeague* (1992) by William Bolcom. These productions also benefited from prominent directors: Harold Prince, Colin Graham, and Robert Altman, respectively.

Willie Stark is based on Robert Penn Warren's Pulitzer Prize–winning novel *All the King's Men* (1946) and relates the tale of Huey Long, the unscrupulous politician and former governor of Louisiana. Floyd's libretto is compressed into ten days of events played out during the effort to impeach Stark. Produced by the Houston Grand Opera in cooperation with the John F. Kennedy Center, the opera was broadcast on PBS's *Great Performances* series and cut from three hours to just over two. In Prince's opinion, the use of six cameras and close-ups improved the pacing and look of the production. "We did a lot of reverse shots," he explains, "which means that we not only shot the production from the point of view of the audience, but we also went behind the set and shot out towards the audience to give it an added cinematic feeling . . . I saw Willie as a tragic hero, so I did the sets from a mythological point of view . . . the sets on stage often swamped the players, the proportion between players and set was in the wrong direction. We redressed that with close-ups that lent an immediate intimacy to the goings-on."[19]

Close-ups of sexual ecstasy and copulation may have shock value in *The Dangerous Liaisons* (and *McTeague*), but at other times close-ups are less effective. Susa's engrossing opera has many ensembles, and the camera cannot always catch the lively interplay among characters that draws the audience into the musical realization of their escapades. Focusing on only two characters at a time in the sextet in act 1 dilutes the brilliant effect of six simultaneous soliloquies, which Susa works out so tellingly.

For the long, fluid solos of the Marquise de Merteuil, sung by Frederica von Stade, the camera can be a masterful mirror. The audience shared every detail of her interpretation, a "mercurial mix of butter and hydrochloric acid." *The Dangerous Liaisons* is fashioned from Choderlos de Lac-

Left to right: Harold Prince and Carlisle Floyd with conductor John Demain and Houston Grand Opera general director David Gockley during rehearsals for the 1981 world premiere of Floyd's *Willie Stark*. *Houston Grand Opera Archives*

los's eighteenth-century novel by librettist Philip Littell, great-grandson of Walter Damrosch, and whether televised or live it is in every way a thrilling piece of music theater. Colin Graham's flexible, cinematic production for the San Francisco Opera transformed the celebrated novel into a finely wrought near-masterpiece that ennobles its characters. It is a work, some said, that hated the sin of licentiousness but loved the sinner "as all good operas do."[20] And there are plenty of sinners. Capping the list is the promiscuous Vicomte de Valmont, brilliantly played by Thomas Hampson, another key player in this elegant "sexual chess match" of prerevolutionary France.

McTeague's director Robert Altman, who was also co-librettist with Arnold Weinstein, tried a different approach in bringing opera to television. Altman did not like the shrinking effect television usually has on opera, an art form whose nature is essentially "grand." *McTeague* is a grimy ver-

San Francisco Opera's *The Dangerous Liaisons* (1994) by Conrad Susa with mezzosoprano Frederica von Stade as the Marquise de Merteuil and baritone Thomas Hampson as Vicomte de Valmont. Television closeups bring out interpersonal relationships with special intimacy. *Photo by Larry Merkle for San Francisco Opera*

ismo melodrama inspired by a murder case that took place in San Francisco. The journalist who covered the story, Frank Norris, turned it into a novel in 1899, and in 1924 it became a ten-hour film epic, *Greed,* directed by Erich von Stroheim, with Gibson Gowland and ZaSu Pitts in the major roles. The plot concerns a hulking dentist and his obsessive wife, Trina, who gradually destroy themselves over $5,000 worth of gold that Trina wins in the lottery. When McTeague loses his dental practice, he murders Trina, steals her gold, and flees into the desert with his invidious friend Marcus Schouler in pursuit. The opera ends with the riveting irony of both novel and film. Although McTeague kills Marcus and keeps the gold, he can only look forward to a slow demise in the rotting sun of Death Valley. Before he dies, Marcus manages to handcuff himself to McTeague. The dentist, unable to break free, is destroyed by his own lust.

Altman's plan in producing the opera on television was to create a synthesis of music, literature, and film. He took taped segments from the opera's 1992 premiere by the Lyric Opera of Chicago (starring Canadian heldentenor Ben Heppner and soprano Catherine Malfitano), and blended them into the corresponding segments of von Stroheim's film, adding a narrator reading from the original novel between segments. The gripping and enlightening result opens the door to similar programs on American opera that will enlarge the story of the nation and its culture. Also revealing—and startling—were the similarities between the old film and the modern opera, from details of facial expression and gesture to overall dramaturgy and action. Whether conscious or deliberate, the links illustrate further the strong interplay within American theater arts.

There are also Wagnerian overtones. If not in its score, then at least in its messages, *McTeague* tells of man's gradual decay and destruction through lust for gold. McTeague himself is a kind of oafish Alberich, and he fights over the gold like Fasolt with Fafner. There is even a common symbol of greed and decay. In Wagner it is the gold ring, and in *McTeague* a huge gold tooth hangs over the dentist's door at the opening of the opera. The sepia-toned sets are allied with other golden images in the opera, such as McTeagues's canary, the intense heat of the desert, and the glimmer of coins. William Bolcom's eclectic score adds a further element to the story by drawing out the tragedy, irony, and rough-hewn temper of the characters beyond both film and novel. Bolcom, a prolific, Pulitzer Prize–winning composer and professor at the University of Michigan, weaves many disparate elements into a colorful whole: blues, rags, passacaglia, cakewalk, barber-shop quartet, and touches of Mascagni and Puccini. But what he does best is underplay melodrama with flashes of comedy and irony. If the

World premiere of *McTeague* by William Bolcom, Lyric Opera of Chicago. Left to right:
Catherine Malfitano (Trina), Timothy Nolan (Marcus), Wilber Pauley (Lottery Agent),
and Ben Heppner (McTeague). *Photo by Tony Romano*

opera opens with the bouncy "Golden Tooth Duet," it closes with a banal
blues number that makes the fate of the characters all the more chilling.
There is no Brünnhilde to save the world from damnation in this opera.
Trina hardly fills the bill, but *McTeague* brings us all much closer to reality.

Heroes and Antiheroes

American composers of the late twentieth century wrote operas that featured strong, evocative characters. Some are antiheroes like Stark, Valmont,
and McTeague—power-hungry, without courage, and invidious without
remorse. Others are noble, for example, Esther, The Woman of Otowi
Crossing, or Frederick Douglass. But it seems to be the base, groveling,
and desperate characters who provide melodrama and draw attention and
outrage. "There is a lust for psychobiography today," observes William
Bolcom, who delighted in composing for the "operatically crazy Trina"
and the "incommunicative, slow-witted McTeague."[21]

  Like Val Xavier in Bruce Saylor's *Orpheus Descending* (1994) after Tennessee Williams, Frank Chambers in *The Postman Always Rings Twice* (1982)
by Steven Paulus (b. 1949) is an antihero. Both operas follow the increas-

ingly common novel to play to film route. Whether the characters are heroes or antiheroes, however, it is their journey from beginning to end, their steamy relationships and longings, that count. In 1946 John M. Cain's novel *The Postman Always Rings Twice* was made into a film starring Lana Turner; another version was made in 1982, the year before the story became an opera. Its characters are cut from the same melodramatic cloth as *Clari; or, The Maid of Milan* and *The Tender Land,* in which young rural women fall in love with strangers and must deal with angry fathers or, as in verismo later, violent husbands. In *Postman,* Cora and Frank are obsessed lovers who kill Cora's husband only to find themselves doomed. Colin Graham, who also directed the premieres of four of Paulus's five operas for Opera Theatre of St. Louis, wrote the libretto. It is brilliant and well structured and has relentless graphic cinematic flow. Paulus's lush symphonic score, tinted with saxophone and barroom piano, adds dramatic intensity and defines the characters with expressive lyricism.

The importance of the libretto in the success of an opera is underscored in Paulus's view. He found in *The Postman* a vital "interplay of opposites." There were "two main features . . . the dramatic, driving tension which runs throughout, and the underlying tenderness which evolves as the two main characters develop."[22] Paulus was able to reflect those features in his score and thus produce a great variety of compelling sounds such as sudden volume changes, outbursts of tones, and wide-ranging orchestral figures. The opera has been staged in Texas, Florida, Washington, D.C., Minnesota, and Massachusetts and in 1983 became the first American opera to be produced at the Edinburgh International Festival. A powerful and riveting work, *The Postman Always Rings Twice* is one of modern opera's most highly profiled works.

The New York City Opera, reaffirming its intent to broaden its audiences and vary its repertoire, continues to program many new works. When the company gave the premiere of Leroy Jenkins's eclectic "dance opera" *Mother of Three Sons* (1991), the performance (and its African American creative team) reinforced general director Christopher Keene's plan to make the opera house accessible to multicultural activities and a wide range of people.[23]

Of the three new operas offered in 1993 by New York City Opera (all in October), *Esther* by Hugo Weisgall was the most successful. Less so was Ezra Laderman's *Marilyn,* cast within the antiheroine mold and with a score that "disguised as high art [and] forced upon the hapless actress . . . becomes one more way to take advantage of her."[24] Lukas Foss's *Griffelkin,* originally commissioned by NBC for television in 1955, is a charming cele-

Nickolas Karousatos (Frank), Donald Kaasch (Nick), and Pamela South (Cora) in *The Postman Always Rings Twice* by Stephen Paulus, produced by the Washington Opera, John F. Kennedy Center for the Performing Arts (1988). *Photo by Joan Marcus*

bration of innocence, a family opera about a little devil who wants to do good.

Weisgall's *Esther,* however, was the high point of the series, and the elegant epic won critical accolades and extended applause for the eighty-one-year-old composer. The libretto for *Esther* is drawn from the Bible by Charles Kondek, and Weisgall's acute sense of musical characterization is particularly evident in the score's richly varied melodic lines: lyrical for Esther, declamatory for Haman, and erratically angular for Zeresh, Haman's wife. The chorus, too, plays an important role, the voice of the people, and urges the noble queen to act. Esther, in her struggles to define herself, brings an ancient message to modern life.

Younger Composers

Weisgall's *Esther* was the last of twelve operas that the eminent veteran composer wrote over a period of sixty years. But also arriving on the operatic scene is a new contingent of composers. Many are young, in their mid-thirties and have been recognized for their prize-winning orchestral scores. Their operas reflected their instrumental skills through romantic textures and evocative colors. Sometimes dubbed "post-minimalists"— although David Lang uses minimalism in *Modern Painters* (1995)—they employ skillful pacing, dramatic shape, and melodic fluency in their work. What is more, they are winning standing ovations and proving that not all the best new opera comes from New York. Younger composers now have "fewer chips on their collective shoulders than any in the century," observes Mark Swed. "They grew up with all kinds of music readily available to them, easily heard on recordings and in concert. They are composers for whom all the big, stylistic battles of the century . . . have already been fought and are irrelevant."[25]

Many current opera composers are interested in real-life protagonists. David Lang's well-crafted *Modern Painters* is the story of the English painter John Ruskin and his strange, unconsummated marriage to his cousin, Effie Gray. Another riveting character is Tobias Picker's Emmeline in the opera of the same name. The libretto by J. D. McClatchy tells of young girl seduced and betrayed in the mills of nineteenth-century Massachusetts.[26] The

Aunt Hanna, sung by Anne Marie Owens, steadies the distraught Emmeline (Patricia Racette) in the Santa Fe Opera's world premiere of *Emmeline* (1996) by Tobias Picker. *Photo by David Stein*

role of Emmeline is that of a true operatic heroine, and her gloriously soaring melodic lines reveal not only her plight but also advance the story with supple movement and suspense. Where in all opera is there such a startling dramatic peroration as the scene in which, to her horror, Emmeline discovers she has unknowingly married her own son? The Santa Fe Opera's premiere in 1996 with Patricia Racette was such a resounding success that the accolades and standing ovations seemed endless, and the New York City Opera production two years later was equally well received.

Contemporary opera companies from Monaco to Utah stage American works. Lowell Liebermann adapted his text for *The Picture of Dorian Gray* (1996) from Oscar Wilde's grotesque story of 1891. Dedicated to Princess Caroline of Monaco, it was the first opera by an American to be given its premiere by Opera de Monte Carlo. Liebermann's score is neoclassical. His aim, he says, is to restore the vocal line to its traditional place in opera. David Carlson's *Dreamkeepers* (1996), based on Native American lore, is not only tonal but also, and unashamedly, neoromantic. Even more impressive than the vocal lines is the evocative orchestration that Carlson manages to build with emotional power and finesse. The Cuban-born composer Jorge Martin chose a less realistic subject and created *Beast and Superbeast,* a fascinating tetrology on the stories of H. H. Munro ("Saki"). Performed in June 1996 by the American Chamber Opera Company of New York, *Beast and Superbeast,* like the original stories, explores the foibles of humanity by comparing human and animal behavior. As so many of his award-winning colleagues, Martin prefers tonal and melodic qualities in his music. "Nowadays," he says, "just about anything you can imagine is being written. It's really a global village."[27]

The Ghosts of Versailles

One work draws viewers into the "global village" of American opera like no other—John Corigliano's *The Ghosts of Versailles.* It is a grand opera buffa that carries us full circle from the first American operas—those zany mixtures of humor, satire, elegance, and fantasy—to the comic opera, harlequinade, and melodrama, all in one magnificent package. Unlike many modern composers, who wrote for smaller theaters and forces, Corigliano (b. 1938) had both the luxury and the challenge of composing for the enormous theatrical venue of the Metropolitan Opera. When *Ghosts of Versailles* received its premiere on December 19, 1991, it was the first opera by an American the Met had commissioned in twenty-five years. It garnered an unprecedented amount of pre- and post-publicity with sold-out houses, deafening standing ovations, and wildly ecstatic reviews. "The Met's biggest hit in many a season," wrote Allan Kozim. "A triumph!" added Susan Elliott, and Bill Zakariasen termed it "a masterpiece." "Opera history was made at the premiere of *Ghosts,*" commented David Patrick Stearns. "It proves that a fine, new contemporary opera can be far more exiting than the most spectacular *Aida.* "[28] More significant, *The Ghosts of Versailles* triggered a new wave of American operas.

The extraordinary success of *Ghosts of Versailles* is all the more impressive when one realizes it was John Corigliano's first opera. A seasoned composer of award-winning works, Corigliano drew inspiration for his Symphony Number 1 from the deaths of several friends from AIDS. It was given its premiere by the Chicago Symphony Orchestra and found to be one of the most compelling and nightmarish symphonies since those of Dimitri Shostakovich.

Ghosts' librettist William Hoffman, one of America's most accomplished playwrights, was also writing his first libretto. Like Wagner's *Ring* with its three mythical realms, *The Ghosts of Versailles* takes place on three planes of reality. They are, as Hoffman explains, "1. The world of eternity, inhabited by ghosts; 2. The world of the stage, peopled by dramatic characters; and 3. The world of history, populated by mortals." The opera represents a "journey from the most fantastic to the most realistic."[29] By the end of the opera the action is occurring on all three planes simultaneously.

The opera opens with a bevy of ghostly figures in tattered, eighteenth-century dress. All are assembled to witness an opera at the Palace of Versailles, which they have been haunting since the French Revolution. The composer of the opera is the ghost of Beaumarchais (Håken Hagegård), author of the plays upon which *The Barber of Seville* and *The Marriage of Figaro* are based. He is in love with another specter, Marie Antoinette (Teresa Stratas). Beaumarchais tries to gain the affections of the ever-grieving queen with a little opera based on his *La mère coupable.* He claims that the plot will change the course of history and prevent her from dying on the scaffold. Instead, she will be able to escape with him. Among the cast are Susanna, Count and Countess Almaviva, Cherubino, and Figaro, whose help Beaumarchais enlists to further his plot.

When Figaro (Gino Quilico) refuses to cooperate, Beaumarchais is obliged to enter the opera world he created and make him comply. As soon as he does, Beaumarchais, Figaro, and all the other buffa (or commedia dell'arte) characters are plunged into the "real" Paris and the throes of revolution. Marie Antionette decides she must hold to her destiny and accept the guillotine, knowing she and Beaumarchais will be together through the power of their love for all eternity ("the sacrifice has set me free"). As they enter the gardens of Aquas Frescas, home of the Almaviva family in *The Barber of Seville* and *The Marriage of Figaro,* it is apparent that their "eternity" is the enduring art of opera.

What is surprising is that throughout the multilayered and ghostly comings and goings the characters feel and react with real human emotion. As they move from one plane of reality to the next, Corigliano magically retains their identities with his music. The ghosts are given eerie, dissonant, and atonal sonorities; the commedia or play-within-a-play characters (Figaro and friends) have a quasi-Mozartean or Rossini-like style that employs arias, recitative, and harpsichord. The revolution scene is imbued with warmth, lyricism, and melodramatic suspense. Yet all these styles are skillfully blended throughout the opera and provide dramatic escapades and moods at every turn.

Melody in Corigliano's vision serves both singer and drama in a variety of ways. Snatches of Cherubino's "Voi che sapete" from Mozart's *The Marriage of Figaro* become a new, romanticized aria. And melody, in fluid ballad style, redefines the art of song in a duet between Susanna and Rosina in act 2 ("Give Me Back My Stolen Years"), elegantly sung by Judith Christin and Renée Fleming. In stark contrast, the villain of old American melodrama (*Pizarro* and *The Brazen Mask*) is conjured up yet again in the ominous and maniacal "Aria of the Worm," sung brilliantly by Graham Clark as Almaviva's treacherous friend Begearss. Wagnerian overtones, too, have special messages, sublime as well as ridiculous. A three-note motif, strongly resembling the "fate motif" in the *Ring,* underpins Marie Antoinette's poignant aria "Once There Was a Golden Bird" and becomes sensitively associated with her throughout the opera. Wagnerian references take a different turn when the "woman with the hat" cries out during the riotous Turkish spoof closing act 1: "This is not opera!! Wagner is opera!!"

Of all the scenes and styles in *The Ghosts of Versailles,* none calls up history quite like the homage to eighteenth- and early-nineteenth-century Turkomania that forms the finale of act 1. Turkish interludes were all the rage at the time, and when Corigliano emphasizes the humor, spectacle, and phantasmagoria of the scene he recalls the spirit of Rossini's *L'Italiana in Algeri* as well as the way in 1730 that James Ralph interpolated the harlequinade into the first opera by an American. There are vestiges of both the English and American harlequinade throughout *Ghosts:* "Giant statues singing, an enormous rose floating in midair, trap doors, flying apparitions, lightning, acrobats, and, of course, ghosts. The Turkish interlude adds

Marilyn Horne as Samira
in Corigliano's *The
Ghosts of Versailles,* Metropolitan Opera (1991).
Photo by Winnie Klotz

a twelve-foot pasha, dancing girls, campy disguises, and Marilyn Horne as
the sultry Egyptian Samira, who sings:

> I am in a valley and you are in a valley.
> I have no she- or he-camel in it.
> In every house there is a cesspool.
> That's life.

Is *The Ghosts of Versailles,* with its European roots and styles, a truly
American opera? "Some parts remind me of a musical," admits Håkan
Hagegård, who sang Beaumarchais. "I would call it American music."
"Ghosts of Versailles is written like a film script," director Colin Graham
adds, "constantly rolling from one world into another. . . . It's not an op-
era buffa in the same way as Rossini. There is also a great sense of sadness.
In that respect, it's very much aligned to the feelings of the 1990s."[30]

Even if Corigliano does draw from eighteenth- and nineteenth-century European forms, so much the better. These are the styles and charac-

ters audiences know. More than an American opera, Corigliano and Hoffman have created a work about how Americans perceive opera, and perhaps that is the most magical achievement of all.

American opera has a long and fulfilling heritage, and many talents and
dreams have created a unique national art form. As Marie Antoinette says
to Beaumarchais:

> You called me.
> Luminous and noble,
>
> . . . .
>
> My pride has kept us far apart.
> Your warmth now melts my frozen heart.[31]

Epilogue: American Opera at the Crossroads

WHEN JOHN HARBISON'S *The Great Gatsby* received its world premiere run at the Metropolitan Opera from December 22, 1999, to January 15, 2000, it became the last major opera of the old millennium and the first of the new. More significantly, it provided a focal point for what was happening in American opera as the century turned.

The Great Gatsby, Andre Previn's *A Streetcar Named Desire* (1998), Stephen Paulus's *Summer* (1998), and William Bolcom's *A View from the Bridge* (1999) are all based on important icons of American literature that infused the operas with a strong thrust of verismo. In these works, human characters—often more flawed than heroic—magnetically draw the audience into their emotional worlds of lust, guilt, and compassion. American locales and popular music may pepper these operas, but it is not their American elements alone that make them part of the nation's cultural legacy. Rather, it is the composer's skills in musically interpreting the elements as drama.

The primary aim of this book has been to show how American opera has reflected the life and times of its people throughout history and offer a broad overview of the musical and dramatic strengths within the operas themselves. Americans have traveled far, in a journey with many twists, turns, and surprises along the way. These diverse social and political inroads have revealed as much about Americans as about their opera. As a nation of explorers, rugged individualists of many national origins and modes of thought, is it any wonder that American operas reflect that diversity as well? Pinpointing an overall "American style" is elusive. It is possible, however, to discern a common creative approach that American composers throughout history have shared.

The nation has enjoyed a rich history of operatic forms—from pantomime to melodrama to Wagnerism to verismo—in which the orchestra has played a key role in defining the drama. In modern times, the most successful American operas have displayed not only strong characterization and rhythmic energy but also vividly colored orchestration that follows and motivates the action, as in a film score. It is perhaps more than coincidental that the United States has long been a world leader in the motion picture field.

Vocal styles in modern American opera also seem to fall under the spell of the motion picture, where directness of communication and the expressive use of words keep the drama in motion. To portray mood and feelings, many American composers use a style of vocal writing that favors more direct lyric declamation rather than traditional, action-stopping arias. A case in point is William Bolcom's *A View from the Bridge,* in which the composer propels the drama forward with great intensity by skillfully matching the music to the sentiment. Whether lyrical vocal lines, recitative, pitched speech, or dialogue, Bolcom uses varied approaches to provide the action, pacing, and passion that are the hallmarks of verismo opera.

But audiences, their tastes shaped by Broadway and popular operas, remember a new opera less by its declamation than by its tunes—arias that remain in the psyche and become a work's enduring trademark. Scientists have observed that people are "wired" for music from birth, and although they readily forget words and speeches, they remember tunes. Composers, then, might reconsider the staying power of the aria and melodious set piece as they search for viable ways to give their works longevity.

The long journey, however, is far from ended. Boldly, brashly, and joyously, its road winds into the future. Where will it lead? There are no ready answers. Television, the Internet, and a vast array of new technology are continually opening new avenues for bringing American opera to a wider public.

Central Park (1999), which aired on PBS-TV in January 2000, illustrates one of the newest and most successful approaches to American verismo. Glimmerglass Opera first commissioned three librettists, all prominent playwrights, and then hired three young composers to collaborate on the creation of a trilogy of short, one-act operas. The result is a strong dramatic work in which individual operas are bound by a common New York setting and by original librettos that deal with contemporary social issues and the people entwined in them: a family during the Jewish New Year, the plight of the elderly, and a homeless mother and baby.

The music of the trilogy is colorful and sensitive and seems to become progressively more vital to the drama through the poignant last opera. More important, these engaging operas are derived not from novels or plays but from real-life situations. Their simple staging and fine vocal writing make them especially attractive to universities and smaller opera companies, and their believable characters portray the "least of the brethren," the true heroes of our times. This indeed is provocative American verismo, not a verismo of action but a verismo of the soul. In the end, this is what opera is all about.

Appendix: Milestones in American Opera

The chronology is according to dates of first performances, or, in the cases of *The Disappointment; or, The Force of Credulity* (1767) and *The Joust; or, The Tournament* (1885), dates of publication.

1730   *The Fashionable Lady; or, Harlequin's Opera* by James Ralph, written and given its premiere in London, is the earliest opera by an American to be both published and produced.

1757   *Alfred,* heroic opera (or masque) by William Smith that was first performed at the College of Philadelphia, is the earliest documented serious opera written and performed in America.

1767   Andrew Barton's [pseud.] *The Disappointment; or, The Force of Credulity* is the first comic opera libretto written and published in America and the first opera with an American plot.

1794   Ann Julia Hatton's *Tammany; or, The Indian Chief,* with music by James Hewitt, is the earliest American opera by a woman librettist; the earliest by one composer (rather than multiple composers); and the first serious opera on an American subject.

1794   The libretto of *Slaves in Algiers; or, A Struggle for Freedom* by Susanna Rowson illustrates a rare feminist approach in early American opera. The opera was given its premiere to celebrate the opening season of the two-thousand-seat Chestnut Street Theatre in Philadelphia.

1800   *Pizarro in Peru* by William Dunlap, with music composed, selected, or arranged James Hewitt, appears to be America's first important operatic melodrama.

1803   William Dunlap and Victor Pelissier's *The Voice of Nature* is the earliest extant orchestral score of an American opera.

1808   James Nelson Barker and John Bray's *The Indian Princess; or, La Belle Sauvage* is the first full piano-vocal score of an opera published in America that has survived and the first opera composed in America to receive a performance in England (London, 1820).

1814   *The Aethiop; or, The Child of the Desert* by Rayner Taylor, an important early example of an American romantic grand opera, was especially long-running—from 1814 to the Civil War.

1824   Micah Hawkins, composer of *The Saw Mill; or, A Yankee Trick,* appears to be the first American-born composer to have written both the music and the libretto for an opera.

1825 John Davies's *The Forest Rose; or, American Farmers,* with text by Samuel Wood-worth, contains a role (probably the first) for an African American woman and places new emphasis on the singing star.

1845 Written in the bel canto tradition, *Leonora* by William Henry Fry is the first grand opera by an American-born composer to receive wide-ranging pub-licity and reviews.

1855 George Frederick Bristow's *Rip van Winkle* is one of the earliest operas to be based on work by an important contemporaneous American author, Washington Irving.

1868 *Virginia's Ball* by John Thomas Douglass is believed to be the earliest opera by a black composer.

1885 *The Joust; or, The Tournament* by G. Estabrook is the first complete opera by an American woman to be published (by the Chicago Music Company).

1889 The earliest operettas by American women to be produced (all in the same year) were: *Dovetta* by Emma Marcy Raymond; *Fleurette* by Emma Rob-erts Steiner; and *Leoni, the Gypsy Queen* by Louisa Delos Mars, the first black woman to have her operas staged.

1896 With its popular march, *El Capitan* by John Philip Sousa is the composer's most successful of his fifteen operettas, enjoying a run of nearly four years.

1896 *The Scarlet Letter,* an important Wagner-influenced music drama based on an American novel, was composed by Walter Damrosch, the first American composer to have two of his operas performed at the Metropolitan Opera: *Cyrano de Bergerac* (1913) and *The Man without a Country* (1937).

1902 *Zenobia, Queen of Palmyra* by Louis Adolphe Coerne is the earliest success-ful American opera to be produced in Germany.

1909 *The American Maid* (formerly *The Glass Blowers*), an operetta by John Philip Sousa, uses motion pictures in its staging, perhaps for the first time in American musical theater.

1910 Arthur Nevin's *Poia,* on a Native American legend, is the first American opera to be staged in Berlin. With Frederick S. Converse's *Iolan; or, The Pipe of Desire* (1908), it is one of the first full scores of an American opera to be published overseas.

1910 *Iolan; or, The Pipe of Desire* by Frederick Converse is the first opera by an American to be staged at the Metropolitan Opera.

1911 and 1912 Victor Herbert's Native American–inspired *Natoma* (1911) and George Chadwick's *The Padrone* (1912), about the tragic plight of Italian im-migrants, appear to be the earliest examples of verismo (realism) in Amer-ican opera.

1915 *Treemonisha* by Scott Joplin received its piano-vocal premiere in 1915, but its first full production was not until 1972. Its heroine is a unique early voice for the advancement of African Americans through education and knowl-edge.

1921 Paul Allen's *Cleopatra* is the first American opera to be commissioned by an Italian publisher.

1927 *The King's Henchman* by Deems Taylor, with libretto by Edna St. Vincent Millay, is the first opera to be broadcast from the Metropolitan Opera on the newly begun CBS radio network. *Henchman* and Taylor's *Peter Ibbetson* (1931) are not only the first American operas to be commissioned by the Met but also the longest-running.

1928 *Voodoo* by the black composer Harry Lawrence Freeman is one of the earliest grand operas composed in America to be embellished with jazz, blues, and spirituals and one of the first American operas to be broadcast on the radio (WGBS, New York).

1930 George Antheil's Dadaistic satire *Transatlantic,* given its premiere in Frankfurt, draws creatively from jazz, Stravinskian neoclassicism, and the visual, mechanical, and aesthetic techniques of the motion picture.

1930 Charles Sanford Skilton's *The Sun Bride,* inspired by a Native American legend, is the first opera by an American to be composed especially for radio.

1934 Virgil Thomson and Gertrude Stein's innovative *Four Saints in Three Acts* illustrates a brilliant collaboration between composer and librettist.

1935 George Gershwin's *Porgy and Bess* is given its premiere at New York's Alvin Theater, but to an initially poor reception. Now, as the most widely performed American opera, it is one of America's most cherished cultural products.

1937 With its explosive social and political themes, *The Cradle Will Rock* by Marc Blitzstein is, according to Aaron Copland, "the first opera to invent a truly vernacular, convincing musical idiom when heard from the lips of the man-in-the-street."

1947 The short-opera pair *The Telephone* and *The Medium* by Gian Carlo Menotti were the first American operas to be recorded in their entirety and among the earliest to achieve a successful Broadway run.

1949 *Troubled Island* by William Grant Still is the first opera by an American composer to be produced at the New York City Opera and the first opera by an African American to receive a world premiere by a major company.

1950 In the character of *The Consul's* Magda Sorel, Gian Carlo Menotti gives opera one of the most intense and tragic heroines of American verismo style.

1951 Menotti's ever-popular one-act *Amahl and the Night Visitors* is the first opera commissioned especially for American television.

1953 *The Taming of the Shrew* by Vittorio Giannini is the first full-length opera by an American to be televised.

1955 and 1956 Carlisle Floyd's *Susannah* and Douglas Moore's *The Ballad of Baby Doe* (1956), both based on folk-like rural subjects, were staged at the New York City Opera during its Ford Foundation American Opera series of 1958 and 1959. They have become among the top American operas to be performed nationally. In 1976 Moore's *Baby Doe* became the first American opera to be telecast on the *Live from Lincoln Center* series.

1958 Commissioned by the Metropolitan Opera, Samuel Barber's elegiac *Vanessa,* with libretto by Gian Carlo Menotti, wins a Pulitzer Prize.

1961 *The Crucible* by Robert Ward, after Arthur Miller, commissioned by the New York City Opera, has become the composer's most widely performed work. Translated into six languages, including Japanese, Swedish, and Serbo-Croatian, it has been staged by more than twenty-seven professional opera companies.

1966 *Antony and Cleopatra* by Samuel Barber, with libretto by Franco Zeffirelli, opened the Metropolitan Opera House at Lincoln Center in New York.

1970 Carlisle Floyd's *Of Mice and Men,* after Steinbeck, remains one of this major American opera composer's most compelling and frequently performed works.

1971 Surreal and non-narrative, *Postcard from Morocco,* commissioned by Minnesota Opera, established national recognition for composer Dominick Argento.

1971 Leonard Bernstein's controversial *Mass* opened the John F. Kennedy Center for the Performing Arts in Washington, D.C., and in 1974 appeared on Public Television's *Great Performances* series.

1977 *The Voice of Ariadne,* after Henry James, by Thea Musgrave is the first opera by a woman to be performed by a major American opera company (New York City Opera) since 1902.

1979 *Einstein on the Beach* by Philip Glass, structured around minimalism and the visual imagery of Robert Wilson, is a landmark abstract opera that brought international fame to its composer.

1979 Stephen Sondheim's *Sweeney Todd,* directed by Harold Prince, illustrates the successful melding of Broadway and opera styles.

1986 *X: The Life and Times of Malcolm X* by Anthony Davis, a black composer, reflects an original dramaturgical style through its dissonant, rhythmically complex score.

1986 Lee Hoiby's *The Tempest* showcases especially brilliant coloratura passages for soprano. With libretto by Mark Shulgasser, Hoiby's opera is one of the most successful American settings of Shakespeare.

1987 The Houston Opera's world premiere of John Adams's ground-breaking *Nixon in China,* to a libretto by Alice Goodman, is a called a "heroic opera for an unheroic age."

1988 *The Aspern Papers* by Dominick Argento, based on a novella of Henry James and jointly commissioned by Dallas Opera and Public Television, was broadcast nationally in 1989.

1990 Libby Larsen's *Frankenstein: The Modern Prometheus* uses techniques from motion picture and television to create strong characterization and moving modern metaphors.

1991 With his highly successful spectacle *The Ghosts of Versailles,* John Corigliano became the first American composer in twenty-five years to receive a commission by the Metropolitan Opera.

1992 *The Voyage* by Philip Glass, commissioned by the Metropolitan Opera, celebrates the five hundredth anniversary of the arrival of Columbus in the New World.

1996 In *Emmeline,* first produced by the Santa Fe Opera, composer Tobias Picker gives American opera one of its most provocative heroines.

1998 Andre Previn's *A Streetcar Named Desire,* based on the play by Tennessee Williams, is one of three operas by American composers commissioned by the San Francisco Opera for the turn-of-the-century period.

1999 Based on Arthur Miller's tragedy of sexual obsession and jealousy, *A View from the Bridge* by the Pulitzer Prize–winning composer William Bolcom, was given its world premiere by the Lyric Opera of Chicago on October 25 in a stunning staging that features projections and photographic images.

1999 John Harbison's *The Great Gatsby,* after F. Scott Fitzgerald, commissioned by the Metropolitan Opera to honor the twenty-fifth anniversary of conductor James Levine's Metropolitan debut, received its world premiere on December 20. Featuring Dawn Upshaw (Daisy), Jerry Hadley (Gatsby), and Victoria Livengood (Myrtle), its sophisticated, sensual score is colored by jazz styles of the 1920s.

2000 *Central Park,* first produced by Glimmerglass Opera, received its television premiere in January 2000. A warm, sensitive treatment in the American verismo style, it is a trilogy of one-act operas based on contemporary social issues: *The Festival of Regrets* by Deborah Drattell and Wendy Wasserstein, *Strawberry Fields* by Michael Torke and A. R. Gurney, and *The Food of Love* by Robert Beaser and Terrance McNally.

2000 *Cold Sassy Tree,* composed by Carlisle Floyd, is given its premiere by Houston Grand Opera on April 14. Based on Olive Ann Burns's best-selling novel (1984), it features Patricia Racette and Dean Peterson in a masterly crafted work with flowing set pieces and tonal harmonic language. With Floyd's extraordinary achievement, raved critics, American opera received its true voice.

Acknowledgments

NUMEROUS BOOKS, articles, reviews, scores, librettos, recordings, and videocassettes were consulted for this project and are documented in the notes for each chapter. Certain reference sources were especially helpful, however, and are important for anyone attempting further research in this area. Opera America <http://www.OperaAmerica.org> is an invaluable resource for information about new works. Its *Season Schedule of Performances,* published annually, lists the current repertoires of more than 160 professional opera companies; its two series, *Works in Progress* and *Encore,* give composer, librettist, length, performance forces, synopsis, and production contacts for each of the new operas, which can number close to two hundred per issue. Other useful sources include Edith Borroff, *American Operas: A Checklist* (Warren, Mich.: Harmonie Park Press, 1992); Rebecca Hodell Kornick, *Recent American Opera: A Production Guide* (New York: Columbia University Press, 1991); Stanley Sadie, editor, *The New Grove Dictionary of Opera,* four volumes (New York: Macmillan, 1992); and Rudolph S. Rauch, editor, *Opera News,* a periodical of the Metropolitan Opera Guild.

The gracious help and warm encouragement of many individuals allowed my research to progress smoothly. I extend warmest and sincerest thanks to my dear friend and colleague Adelaide Whitaker for her good advice, perceptive artistic eye, and invaluable research assistance with the numerous photographs in the book. I also offer special appreciation to my long-time friends Plato Karayanis, former general director of the Dallas Opera, and his wife Dorothy, as well as to Marc Scorca, Elizabeth Cecchetti, and Krista Rimple, Opera America; Joseph McLellan, *Washington Post;* Wayne Shirley, Library of Congress; Joan Dessens, Glimmerglass Opera; Roger Pines, Lyric Opera of Chicago; Robert Tuggle and John Penino, Metropolitan Opera Archives; Lee Pecht, Houston Grand Opera Archives; and Susan Woelzl, New York City Opera. The staffs of the libraries of Catholic University of America, American University, and George Washington University were always extremely helpful, but I would like to single out Maurice Saylor of the Benjamin T. Rome School of Music Library, Catholic University, and James Heintze, Kreeger Music Library of American University, for their seemingly never-ending assistance and knowledge.

Of enormous value to my project were the composers, librettists, directors, designers, and singers whom I interviewed or consulted, especially those composers who sent me scores, videos, and tapes of their works. I am deeply grateful to Lee Hoiby, Stephen Paulus, Libby Larsen, Robert Ward, Jack Beeson, Carlisle Floyd, John Harbison, Robert Greenleaf, and Jake Heggie, as well as to Roman Terleckyj, John Conklin, Michael Daugherty, Philip Glass, Alice Goodman, Evelyn Lear, Rhoda Levine, Peter Mark, Lotfi Mansouri, Thea Musgrave, Sheri Greenawald, Mark Shulgasser, Richard Stilwell, Thomas Hampson, Phyllis Pancella, Michael Kahn, Kathleen Segar, Stanley Hollingsworth, Thomas Pasatieri, Peter Russell, Marguerite Krull, Bruce Beresford, Kimm Julian, and Russell Currie.

In addition to these individuals, I am especially grateful to the Newberry Library, Chicago, for awarding me a resident fellowship to work among its important holdings. The following archives and special collections also provided invaluable primary source materials:

American Antiquarian Society

American Heritage Center, University of Wyoming, Laramie

The American Music Center, New York (for published and self-published full scores of American opera composers)

Bernard Herrmann Archive, Martin Silver Music Library, University of California at Santa Barbara

Boston Lyric Opera Company

Caryl Florio Papers, Lincoln Center Performing Arts Library, New York

Central Opera Service Files, Opera America, Washington, D.C.

Chicago Historical Society

Clarence C. White Collection, Schomburg Center for Research in Black Culture, New York Public Library

Damrosch Family Collection, Performing Arts Division, Library of Congress; also Damrosch Collection, Music Research Division, Lincoln Center Performing Arts Library, New York

David Tamkin Collection, Moldenhauer Archives, Spokane, Washington

Dunvagen Music Publishers, Jim Keller, director

Eleanor Everest Freer Collection, Performing Arts Division, Library of Congress

The Eric Friedheim Library and News Information Center, National Press Club, Washington, D.C.

The Ernst Bacon Society, Roslindale, Massachusetts

Harvard Theatre Collection, Harvard College Library, Cambridge, Massachusetts

Historical Society of Pennsylvania, Philadelphia

Hoblitzelle Theatre Arts Library, University of Texas, Austin

Houston Grand Opera

Howard Hanson Archives, Sibley Music Library, Eastman School of Music, Rochester, New York

International Production Associates, New York

James W. Ellsworth Papers, 1893 World's Columbian Exposition, Chicago Public Library

John Knowles Paine Papers, Houghton Library, Harvard University, Cambridge, Massachusetts

Library Company of Philadelphia

Library of Congress: Performing Arts Division; Rare Books; Recorded Sound Archives; Prints and Photos Division

Louis Gruenberg Papers, Lincoln Center Performing Arts Library, New York

Metropolitan Opera Archives, Lincoln Center, New York

Minnesota Historical Society, St. Paul

National Negro Opera Company Archives, C. C. White Papers, Performing Arts Division, Library of Congress

Newberry Library, Chicago, Illinois: Theodore Thomas Collection; Frederick Grant Gleason Papers; American Opera Society of Chicago Scrapbooks

New England Conservatory of Music Library, Boston, Massachusetts

Opera Theatre of Saint Louis

Papers of Daniel Hertz, Special Collections, University of California at Berkeley

Portland Opera

River Bluffs Regional Library, St. Joseph, Missouri

The Santa Fe Opera

Smith College, William Allan Neilson Library, Northampton, Massachusetts

State Historical Society of Wisconsin, Madison (Blitzstein materials)

Tams-Witmark Collection, Performing Arts Division, Library of Congress

WETA, Public Television Archives, Washington, D.C.

William B. Wood Playbill Collection, Maryland Historical Society, Baltimore

Yale University Oral History Project, American Music Series, New Haven, Connecticut

Finally, I am indebted to certain individuals who kept afloat my work and sanity during the final stages of writing this book. I extend sincerest thanks to MaryJac Reed, director of academic computing services at the Catholic University of America, for literally salvaging the entire manuscript from being swallowed by the ravages of technology, and to my children, Harris Kirk, Colleen Roeschel, and Karen Kirk, who were never too busy to answer computer questions at critical times. I also extend thanks to Tom Schleis for reading my manuscript and sharing his suggestions and to Judith McCulloh, Mary Giles, and the other members of the fine University of Illinois Press staff. To my children, their families, and my many friends, especially Ruth and Burt Knauft, I offer my appreciation for their interest and caring during the long, arduous years of this project.

Notes

Introduction

1. Remarks by Carlisle Floyd at the twenty-seventh annual conference of Opera-America, Philadelphia, April 28, 1997.

2. Tony Thomas, *Music for the Movies* (Cranbury, N.J.: A. S. Barnes, 1973), 133.

3. Author telephone interview with Libby Larsen, Oct. 21, 1996.

4. Author interview with Lotfi Mansouri, San Francisco, Sept. 17, 1998.

5. Edward Ellsworth Hipsher, *American Opera and Its Composers* (1934, repr. New York: Da Capo Press, 1978), 89.

6. Otis Stuart et al., "First Nighters: Sounding Out the Principal Players in *The Ghosts of Versailles,*" *Opera News,* Jan. 4, 1992, 30.

7. Remarks by Michael Daugherty at the forty-second annual conference of the National Opera Association, Washington, D.C., Jan. 16, 1998.

8. Jack Kaminsky, *Hegel on Art: An Interpretation of Hegel's Aesthetics* (New York: SUNY Press, 1962), 129.

Chapter 1: The British Connection

1. Daniel J. Boorstin, *The Americans: The Colonial Experience* (New York: Vintage Books, 1958), 150–51.

2. Quoted in Boorstin, *The Americans: The Colonial Experience,* 188.

3. *The Beggar's Opera* (1728) was not staged in America until its performance in New York in 1750. Soon thereafter, however, its popularity spread rapidly to other cities, such as Philadelphia, Boston, Providence, Newport, Baltimore, Richmond, Williamsburg, Norfolk, and Charleston. Alfred Loewenberg, *Annals of Opera 1597–1940,* 3d ed. (Totowa: Rowman and Littlefield, 1978), 159–60.

4. Louis C. Madeira, comp., *Annals of Music in Philadelphia and History of the Musical Fund Society* (1896, repr. New York: Da Capo Press, 1973), 17.

5. Robert W. Kenny, "Ralph, James," *Dictionary of American Biography* (New York: Charles Scribner's Sons, 1963), 8:331–32. For more on Ralph's possible birthplaces, see Patricia H. Virga, *The American Opera to 1790* (Ann Arbor: UMI Research Press, 1982), 10; and articles on Ralph in *The Dictionary of National Biography* (London: Oxford University Press, 1917), 16:664–67 and *Appleton's Cyclopedia of American Biography,* ed. James Grant and John Fiske, 6 vols. (New York: D. Appleton, 1888), 5:164; see also Robert W. Kenny, "James Ralph, Author by Profession," Ph.D. diss., Brown University, 1934.

6. Leonard W. Larabee et al., eds., *The Autobiography of Benjamin Franklin* (New Haven: Yale University Press, 1964), 90, quoted in David McKay, *"The Fashionable Lady:* The First Opera by an American," *Musical Quarterly* 65 (July 1979): 360–67. McKay's piece must be read with caution, however, for it contains several errors.

7. W. Van Lennep et al., eds., *The London Stage—1660 to 1800,* 12 vols. (Carbondale: Southern Illinois University Press, 1960–68). Volume 1 (1965) provides a daily chronology of the works presented in the various theaters during this period.

8. See Harold G. Moss, "Ballad-Opera Songs: A Record of the Ideas Set to Music, 1728–1733," 4 vols., Ph.D. diss., University of Michigan, 1970. Moss claims a major source for ballad opera songs is Thomas D'Urfey's *Wit and Mirth; or, Pills to Purge Melancholy* (1719–20). Nearly 50 percent of the tunes appear in this popular compilation.

9. James Ralph, The Fashionable Lady; or, Harlequin's Opera, *In the Manner of a Rehearsal as It Is Performed at the Theatre in Goodman's-Fields* (London: Printed for J. Watts, 1730), 94 pp., facsimile reprint in *The Influence of Pantomime and Harlequin,* volume 9 in the Ballad Opera Series edited by Walter H. Rubsamen (New York: Garland Publishing, 1974), 1–94.

10. Rubsamen, ed., *The Influence of Pantomime and Harlequin,* 9:2, 9:35, 9:44, 9:16.

11. Moss, "Ballad-Opera Songs," 1:24.

12. Ibid., 1:25.

13. Ibid., 1:81.

14. Roger Fiske, *English Theatre Music in the Eighteenth Century,* (New York: Oxford University Press, 1986), 125.

15. Fiske, *English Theatre Music,* 117, 108.

16. Ibid., 69.

17. Ibid., 71.

18. Gabriel Odingsell's *Bay's Opera* also employed the Harlequin technique. Staged only a few days before Ralph's *Fashionable Lady,* it failed miserably, and Odingsell committed suicide not long afterward. The influence of the harlequinade is also seen in Theophilus Cibber's *The Harlot's Progress; or, The Ridotto al' Fresco* (1733), which was inspired by the paintings of Hogarth, as was Stravinsky's *The Rake's Progress* (1951).

19. Ralph, *Fashionable Lady,* in *The Influence of Pantomime and Harlequin,* ed. Rubsamen, 9:87.

20. Anne Dhu Shapiro, "Action Music in American Pantomime and Melodrama, 1730–1913," *American Music* 2 (Winter 1984): 51–52; see also Charles Dibdin, *The Touchstone; or, Harlequin Traveller* in *Music for London Entertainment 1660–1800,* series D, vol. 1, ed. John M. Ward (London: Stainer and Bell, 1990), with an introduction by A. D. Shapiro.

21. Ralph, *Fashionable Lady,* in *The Influence of Pantomime and Harlequin,* ed. Rubsamen, 9:53.

22. Ibid., 9:19.

23. Ibid., 9:94.

Chapter 2: The Earliest American Operas

1. Edward Potts Cheyney, *History of the University of Pennsylvania, 1740–1940* (Philadelphia: University of Pennsylvania Press, 1940), 12.

2. Martin Meyerson and Dilys Pegler Winegrad, *Gladly Teach and Gladly Learn: Frank-*

lin and His Heirs at the University of Pennsylvania, 1740–1976 (Philadelphia: University of Pennsylvania Press, 1978), 24.

3. The autograph manuscript of songs composed and collected by Hopkinson is in the Performing Arts Division of the Library of Congress. For more on Hopkinson, see Charles Hamm, *Yesterdays, Popular Song in America* (New York: W. W. Norton, 1979), 90–92; Cheyney, *History of the University of Pennsylvania,* 92–93; Richard Crawford, "Hopkinson, Francis," in *The New Grove Dictionary of American Music,* ed. H. Wiley Hitchcock and Stanley Sadie (New York: Grove's Dictionaries of Music, 1986), 2:421; and Oscar G. T. Sonneck, *Francis Hopkinson and James Lyon* (New York: Da Capo Press, 1967).

4. George Everett Hastings, *The Life and Works of Francis Hopkinson* (New York: Russell and Russell, 1968), 52–54.

5. "Poetical Essays," *The Gentleman's Magazine* 27 (April 1757): 178, in Archives General, folder 1913, University of Pennsylvania Archives.

6. Arthur Hobson Quinn, *A History of the American Drama* (New York: Appleton Century Crofts, 1923), 1:18.

7. Thomas Arne's *Alfred* was first performed at Cliveden, the residence of Frederick, Prince of Wales, on August 1, 1740. It thereafter underwent so many revisions, including a version sung throughout, that scholars have concluded there is no definitive form of the work. Smith, however, most likely used the 1753 libretto revised by David Mallet and James Thompson, which used spoken dialogue and restored the role of the Hermit omitted from some of the earlier versions. See *"Alfred* by Thomas Augustine Arne," in *Musica Britannica,* vol. 47, ed. Alexander Scott (London: Stainer and Bell, 1981). Scott's Introduction provides details of the various revisions. See also Roger Fiske, *English Theatre Music in the Eighteenth Century* (New York: Oxford University Press, 1986), 222–29; and T. J. Walsh, "Arne's *Alfred," Music and Letters* 55 (Oct. 1974): 385–97.

8. *Pennsylvania Gazette,* Jan. 20, 1757. Excerpts from the libretto with Smith's commentaries appear in four consecutive issues of the *Pennsylvania Gazette:* act 1, Jan. 20; act 2, Jan. 27; and act 3, Feb. 3 and 10.

9. *Pennsylvania Gazette,* Feb. 10, 1757.

10. *Pennsylvania Gazette,* Jan. 27, 1757. Borrowing music was just as common in serious operas and masques as it was in comic opera. Handel, for example, arranged at least twelve pastiche operas that contain music by other composers, such as Vinci and Hasse, and frequently borrowed from his own works. Some versions of Arne's *Alfred* also added or substituted the works of other composers.

11. Thomas Arne, Alfred the Great, *an English Opera; Altered from the Play Written by Mr. Mallet and the Late Mr. Thomson* (London: Walsh, 1753), 5. This libretto, the primary source for Scott's edition in *Musica Britannica,* contains twenty-seven songs.

12. Domènech Terradellas was one of the most gifted opera composers of his generation. His music contains strong contrasts created by changes of color, texture, and key, with an absence of heavily ornamented melodic lines. His arias are often marked by a particular "ferocity of expression." Michael F. Robinson, "Terradellas, Domènech,"

in *The New Grove Dictionary of Opera,* ed. Stanley Sadie (New York: Grove's Dictionaries of Music, 1992), 4:699.

13. In Hopkinson's 1759 collection of songs, the aria "Figlio ascolta" has been transposed from the original E-flat to C, thus lowering the original bravura high D on the words "disperata morirà." Hopkinson's designation "l'aria presto" also differs from the original marking, "allegro."

14. Sonneck, *Francis Hopkinson,* 22; *Gentleman's Magazine,* 178; see also *Pennsylvania Gazette,* Feb. 10, 1757.

15. Cheyney, *History of the University of Pennsylvania,* 88.

16. *Gentleman's Magazine,* 178.

17. For an account of the operas produced in Philadelphia at this time, see Oscar Sonneck, *Early Opera in America* (1915, repr. New York: Benjamin Blom, 1963), 29–37; see also Sonneck, *Francis Hopkinson,* 17–21.

18. Sonneck, *Early Opera,* 27.

19. Unsubstantiated possibilities for authorship include Thomas Forrest, Joseph and John Leacock, and James Allen. For more on *The Disappointment,* see Patricia H. Virga, *American Opera to 1790* (Ann Arbor: UMI Research Press, 1982), chs. 2 and 3; and The Disappointment; or, The Force of Credulity *(1767),* in *Recent Researches in American Music,* vol. 3, ed. Jerald C. Graue and Judith Layng (Madison: A-R Editions, 1976), preface and full score with libretto and piano-vocal score included.

20. Virga, *American Opera,* 21.

21. Graue and Layng, eds., *Recent Researches,* 45.

22. "The Author's Preface to the Public," in Carolyn Rabson, *"Disappointment* Revisited: Unweaving the Tangled Web, Part 1," *American Music* 1 (Spring 1983): 26–27. A facsimile edition of the opera appears in volume 28 of the Ballad Opera Series edited by Walter H. Rubsamen.

23. Rabson, *"Disappointment* Revisited," 15–19. Rabson argues convincingly against the previous assumption that Raccoon is black and, in turn, American opera's first black character.

24. Virga, *American Opera,* 22.

25. Ibid., 91–93. "Yankee Doodle" may have been associated with the battle at Cape Breton in 1758. Carolyn Rabson, *"The Disappointment,* Part 2," *American Music* 2 (Spring 1984): 8. Later the tune was associated with what came to be the typical Yankee: Jonathan in Royall Tyler's *The Contrast* (1787).

26. Oscar O. G. Sonneck, "Early American Operas," *Sämmelbände der internationalen Musikgesellschaft* 6 (1904–5): 443.

27. Cheyney, *History of the University of Pennsylvania,* 95.

28. Ibid., 90.

29. Esmond Wright, *Franklin of Philadelphia* (Cambridge: Harvard University Press, 1986), 191. For more on the altercations between Smith and Franklin, see Leonard W. Larabee, ed., *The Papers of Benjamin Franklin* (New Haven: Yale University Press, 1967), 1:486–516.

30. "The Author's Preface to the Public," in Rabson, *"Disappointment* Revisited," 26–27.

31. The 1796 edition interpolates four new scenes, expands the dialogue, and changes the literary style of the epilogue. Although more genteel and sophisticated, the new edition is less interesting and has a slower dramatic pace. Virga, *American Opera,* 59–62.

32. A sound recording of the Eastman School of Music's production of *The Disappointment* was made in March 1976, with musical setting by Samuel Adler.

Chapter 3: National Themes and the American Image

1. Russel Blaine Nye, *The Cultural Life of the New Nation, 1776–1830* (New York: Harper and Row, 1960), 127.

2. Julian Mates, *The American Musical Stage before 1800* (Westport: Greenwood Press, 1962), 4.

3. Nye, *Cultural Life,* 126.

4. Susan Porter, *With an Air Debonair: Music Theatre in America, 1785–1815* (Washington: Smithsonian Institution Press, 1991), Appendix A, 425–500.

5. Mates, *The American Musical Stage,* 223.

6. Julian Mates, *America's Musical Stage* (New York: Praeger Publishers, 1987), 48–49; Mates quotes from Sol Smith, *Theatrical Management in the West and South for Thirty Years* (1868).

7. Oscar G. T. Sonneck, *Early Opera in America* (1915, repr. New York: Benjamin Blom, 1963), 118. For more on Reinagle, see Martha Furman Schliefer, ed., *American Opera and Music for the Stage: Eighteenth and Nineteenth Centuries* (New York: G. K. Hall, 1990), xv–xvii; Robert Hopkins, "Reinagle, Alexander" in *The New Grove Dictionary of American Music,* ed. H. Wiley Hitchcock and Stanley Sadie (New York: Grove's Dictionaries of Music, 1986), 4:26–27; and Anne McClenny Krauss, "Alexander Reinagle: His Family Background and Early Professional Career," *American Music* 4 (Winter 1986): 425–56.

8. For lists of Reinagle's operatic works and those of other composers, see Edith Borroff, *American Operas: A Checklist* (Warren, Mich.: Harmonie Park Press, 1992).

9. For more on Hewitt, see John W. Wagner, "James Hewitt: His Life and Works," Ph.D. diss., University of Indiana, 1969; and John W. Wagner, "James Hewitt, 1770–1827," *Musical Quarterly* 58 (April 1972): 259–76.

10. Ronnie L. Smith, "Benjamin Carr," in *The New Grove Dictionary of American Music,* ed. H. Wiley Hitchcock and Stanley Sadie (New York: Grove's Dictionaries of Music, 1986), 1:360–61; Harold Gleason and Warren Becker, *Early American Music,* volume 3 in the Music Literature Outlines Series (Bloomington, Ind.: Frangipani Press, 1981), 67–68; Mates, *America's Musical Stage,* 204–7.

11. J. R. Parker, "Mr. Bray," [Boston] *The Euterpeiad,* April 15, 1820, 11.

12. Mates, *The American Musical Stage,* 198.

13. J. R. Parker, "Musical Reminiscences: Pelliser [*sic*]," [Boston] *The Euterpeiad* 3, no. 3 (1822): 18, quoted in Anne Dhu Shapiro, "Pelissier," in *The New Grove Dictionary*

of American Music, ed. H. Wiley Hitchcock and Stanley Sadie (New York: Grove's Dictionaries of Music, 1986), 3:496.

14. For more on Pelissier, see Karl Kroeger, ed., *Pelissier's Columbian Melodies* in *Recent Researches in American Music,* gen. ed. H. Wiley Hitchcock (Madison: A-R Editions, 1984), 13–14:ix–xxviii.

15. Karl Kroeger, ed., *The Voice of Nature* (1803) and Victor Fell Yellin, ed., *The Aethiop* (1813), in *Early Melodrama in America,* volume 2 of *Nineteenth-century American Musical Theater,* gen. ed. Deane L. Root (New York: Garland Publishing, 1994). This volume contains excellent orchestral restorations of both operas: *The Voice of Nature* from the manuscript orchestral parts and *The Aethiop* from the souvenir piano-vocal score.

16. The term *English opera* is discussed in Roger Fiske, *English Theatre Music in the Eighteenth Century* (New York: Oxford University Press, 1986), 171–204.

17. Clifford E. Hamar, "Scenery on the Early American Stage," *Theatre Annual* 7 (1948–49): 89.

18. Sometimes actors even found themselves crowded entirely offstage, "the manager relying chiefly on the magic of paint and canvas to pack the house" (Mates, *The American Musical Stage,* 179). Called a "splendid, allegorical, musical drama," Pelissier's *Temple of American Independence,* complete with horses, artillery, and infantry, was produced in Philadelphia in 1799.

19. Daniel Boorstin, *The Americans: The National Experience* (New York: Random House, 1965), 1.

20. Gilbert Chase, *America's Music: From the Pilgrims to the Present,* rev. 3d ed. (Urbana: University of Illinois Press, 1987), 120.

21. "Hatton, Ann Julia (Kemble)," in *The Feminist Companion to Literature in English: Women Writers from the Middle Ages to the Present,* ed. Virginia Blain, Patricia Clements, and Isobel Grundy (New Haven: Yale University Press, 1990), 122.

22. For more on *Tammany,* see Elena Irish Zimmerman, "American Opera Librettos, 1767–1825," Ph.D. diss., University of Tennessee, 1972, 73–87; Oscar O. G. Sonneck, "Early American Operas," *Sämmelbände der internationalen Musikgesellschaft* 6 (1904–5): 458–64; and E. P. Kilroe, "The Opera *Tammany,*" unpublished MS, Special Collections Division, Columbia University Library.

23. Ann Julia Hatton, "The Songs of *Tammany; or, The Indian Chief: A Serious Opera,*" in *The Magazine of History with Notes and Queries,* extra no. 170, 43, no. 2 (1794): 61–69. The songs were originally published as a pamphlet by John Harrison of New York for distribution at the theater.

24. Richard Moody, *America Takes the Stage: Romanticism in American Drama and Theatre, 1750–1900,* Indiana University Publications, number 34 in the Humanities Series edited by Howard D. Seeber (Bloomington: Indiana University Press, 1955).

25. Zimmerman, "American Opera Librettos," 88–92. For an account of Rowson's life and work, see Elias Nason, *A Memoir of Mrs. Susanna Rowson* (Albany: Joel Munsell, 1870); and R. W. G. Vail, "Susanna Haswell Rowson, The Author of *Charlotte Temple*: A Bibliographical Study," *Proceedings of the American Antiquarian Society* 42 (1932): 47–160.

26. A facsimile edition of the songs from *The Volunteers* appears in *American Opera and Music for the Stage: Eighteenth and Nineteenth Centuries,* ed. Martha Furman Schliefer (New York: G. K. Hall, 1990), 5:5–22. Neither the songs by Alexander Reinagle nor Rowson's lyrics are representative of their best works.

27. Judith Tick, *American Women Composers before 1870* (Ann Arbor: UMI Research Press, 1983), 20.

28. Susanna Haswell Rowson, Preface to Slaves in Algiers; or, A Struggle for Freedom: *A Play Interspersed with Songs in Three Acts by Mrs. Rowson as Performed at the New Theatres in Philadelphia and Baltimore* (Philadelphia: Wrigley and Berriman, 1794).

29. Rowson, Preface to *Slaves in Algiers.*

30. [William Cobbett], *A Kick for a Bite* (Philadelphia: Thomas Bradford, 1795), passim; Susanna Haswell Rowson, Preface to *Trials of the Human Heart* (Philadelphia: Wrigley and Berriman, 1795), xiii–xiv, quoted in Zimmerman, "American Opera Librettos," 98–99.

31. For more on Dunlap, see Robert H. Canary, *William Dunlap* (New York: Twayne, 1970); and William Dunlap, *History of the American Theatre,* 3 vols. (1797, repr. New York: Burt Franklin, 1963). For a list of Dunlap's extant theatrical works, see Oral S. Coad, ed., *William Dunlap,* in *America's Lost Plays* (Bloomington: Indiana University Press, 1963–65), 2:xi–xiv. A facsimile of the libretto of *The Archers* (1796) appears in Julian Mates, *The Musical Works of William Dunlap* (Delman, N.Y.: Scholars' Facsimiles and Reprints, 1980), 9–78.

32. David Grimsted, *Melodrama Unveiled: American Theater and Culture, 1800–1850* (Chicago: University of Chicago Press, 1968), 17.

33. William Dunlap, *Virgin of the Sun* (New York: G. F. Hopkins, 1800). See also August von Kotzebue, Pizarro: *A Tragedy in Five Acts, as Performed at the Theatre Royal at Drury-Lane; Taken from the German Drama of Kotzebue and Adapted to the English Stage by Richard Brinsley Sheridan* (London: James Ridgeway, 1799). Sheridan's edition was also published in New York by Thomas Longworth at the Dramatic Repository, Shakespeare Gallery, in November 1800.

34. Between 1799 and 1800 alone there were four different London editions of *Pizarro:* by Richard Brinsley Sheridan, Thomas Dutton, Benjamin Thompson, and Anne Plumptre. Sheridan's appears to have been the preferred version, using music compiled and selected by Michael Kelly, a prominent composer and manager of the King's Theatre in the Haymarket. In America, William Dunlap's edition, called *Pizarro in Peru,* was based primarily on Sheridan but used music by James Hewitt.

35. Joseph W. Donohue, Jr., *Dramatic Character in the English Romantic Age* (Princeton: Princeton University Press, 1970), 130.

36. Donohue, *Dramatic Character,* 128.

37. Cecil Price, ed., *The Dramatic Works of Richard Brinsley Sheridan* (New York: Oxford University Press, 1973), 2:630.

38. Michael Kelly, *The Music of* Pizarro, a Play, *as Now Performing at the Theatre Royal Drury Lane, with Unbounded Applause; the Music Composed and Selected by Michael Kelly, 9 New Lisle Street and to Be Had at All the Music Shops* [London]: Published for Mr.

Kelly [1779?]. This piano-vocal score is reprinted in Michael Kelly, *Music for Two Theatre Pieces* (New York: Da Capo Press, 1979). Only the "March from Pizarro" remains from Hewitt's score. During the first quarter of the century, several editions were published in piano-vocal edition, attesting to its popularity. See Richard J. Wolfe, *Secular Music in America, 1801–1825* (New York: New York Public Library, 1964).

39. Quoted from the London 1799 libretto, reprinted in *Dramatic Works of Richard Brinsley Sheridan,* ed. Price, 2:676–77.

40. Kelly, "Distant Military March and Chorus of Peruvians," in *The Music of* Pizarro, 17–20.

41. The New York staging as described in the *Commercial Advertiser* appears in George C. D. Odell, *Annals of the New York Stage,* 15 vols. (1927–49, repr. New York: AMS Press, 1970), 2:85.

42. Dunlap's promptbook is in the Theater Collection of the Houghton Library, Harvard University.

43. In stage directions of Le forêt noire; or, Maternal Affection, *a Serious Pantomime in Three Acts as Performed at the Boston Theater with Merited Applause* (Boston: John and Joseph N. Russell, 1796).

44. Donohue, *Dramatic Character,* 125.

Chapter 4: Mime, Melodrama, and Song

1. Anne Dhu Shapiro, "Pantomime," in *The New Grove Dictionary of American Music,* ed. H. Wiley Hitchcock and Stanley Sadie (New York: Grove's Dictionaries of Music, 1986), 3:467; Anne Dhu Shapiro, "Action Music in American Pantomime and Melodrama, 1730–1913," *American Music* 2 (Winter 1984): 69.

2. Susan Porter, *With an Air Debonair: Music Theatre in America 1785–1815* (Washington: Smithsonian Institution Press, 1991), 454–59; David Mayer III, *Harlequin in His Element: The English Pantomime, 1806–1836* (Cambridge: Harvard University Press, 1969), 30 (Mayer quotes from the *Times,* Dec. 27, 1821). See also Allardyce Nicoll, *The World of Harlequin: A Critical Study of the Commedia dell'Arte* (New York: Cambridge University Press, 1963).

3. [James Brady], *The Voice of Nature,* ed. Karl Kroeger [1803], in *Early Melodrama in America,* volume 2 of *Nineteenth-century American Musical Theater,* ed. Deane L. Root (New York: Garland Publishing, 1994).

4. James Hewitt, *The Airs, Songs and Chorus's* [sic] *in the Popular Pantomime of* Brazen Mask; *Arranged for the Piano Forte by James Hewitt at His Musical Repository, 15 Chatham Street, New York* [1811]. See also Mr. Fawcett, *Sketch of the Fable, Arrangement of the Scenery with the Songs and Chorusses* [sic] *in the Grand Ballet Called* Brazen Mask; or, Alberto and Rosabella; *as Performed at the Theatre-Royal Covent Garden. Invented by Mr. Fawcett; the Poetry by T. Dibden* (London: Barker, 1802). In the "dramatis personae," dancers or mimers were listed separately from singers. Men's roles were listed first; then women's (a common order in all theatrical works of the time); and, finally, the "principal vocal characters." Last to be listed was the composer: "The orchestra accompaniments by Mr. Hewitt."

5. Noverre is quoted in Roland John Wiley, "Jean Georges Noverre and the Music of *Iphigenia in Aulis* (London 1793)," *Harvard Library Bulletin* 2 (Winter 1991): 34, 53.

6. The Mad Song is printed only in the English synopsis and Hewitt's score. That it is omitted in the Boston synopsis implies that it may not always have been sung.

7. H. Wiley Hitchcock, ed., The Indian Princess; or, La Belle Sauvage; *An Operatic Melo-drame in Three Acts; Text by James Nelson Barker; Music by John Bray* (New York: Da Capo Press, 1972). Reprint of the original libretto and piano-vocal score published by G. E. Blake (Philadelphia, 1808). The opera was recorded by the Federal Music Society Opera Company along with *The Aethiop* and conducted by John Baldon (New World Records NW 232).

8. Paul H. Musser, *James Nelson Barker, 1784–1858, with a Reprint of His Comedy* Tears and Smiles (Philadelphia: University of Pennsylvania Press, 1929), 208. See also Montrose J. Moses, ed., *Representative Plays by American Dramatists* (New York: Benjamin Blom, 1964), 1:567–77; and Gary A. Richardson, *American Drama from the Colonial Period through World War I* (New York: Twayne, 1993), 60–68.

9. Hitchcock, ed., *The Indian Princess,* 41.

10. John Turnbull, *Rudolph; or, The Robbers of Calabria* (New York: B. True, 1807), passim.

11. Constance Rourke, *The Roots of American Culture* (New York: Harcourt, Brace, 1942), 51.

12. Bray's Preface quoted in H. Wiley Hitchcock, "An Early American Melodrama: *The Indian Princess* of J. N. Barker and John Bray," *Notes* 12 (1954–55): 388.

13. The score of *The Aethiop; or, The Child of the Desert* edited by Victor Yellin is in *Nineteenth-century American Musical Theater,* volume 2 of *Early Melodrama in America,* ed. Deane L. Root (New York: Garland Publishing, 1994), xix. The edition also contains a facsimile of the libretto and introductory notes by Yellin. For more on *The Aethiop,* see Victor Yellin, "Rayner Taylor's Music for *The Aethiop,* Part 1: Performance History," *American Music* 4 (Fall 1986): 249–67; and Victor Yellin, "Part 2: The Keyboard Score and Its Orchestral Restoration," *American Music* 5 (Spring 1987): 20–47. The recorded version with period instruments appears with Bray's *The Indian Princess* (New World Records NW 232).

14. Yellin, ed., *The Aethiop,* act 1, scene 5, 107.

15. Ibid., act 1, scene 2, 101.

16. Anonymous, "Thoughts on the Powers of Music," [New York] *Monthly Magazine and American Review,* Feb. 1800, 85.

17. For more on Davies, see Richard J. Wolfe, *Secular Music in America, 1801–1825: A Bibliography* (New York: New York Public Library, 1964), 232. No score is extant, but the lyrics for nine of the songs are printed in Samuel Woodworth, *Melodies: Duets, Trios, Songs and Ballads,* 3d ed. (New York: Elliot and Palmer), 1831. They are: "My Father's Farm," "Sweet Seclusion," "Smile of Affection," "Dancing Gaily," "The Bashful Lover," "A Smile from Thee," "The Miniature," "Peaceful Home," and "Love's Jealousy."

18. Samuel Woodworth, The Forest Rose; or, American Farmers: *A Pastoral Opera in Two Acts; Music by John Davies,* in *Dramas from the American Theatre, 1762–1909,* ed. Richard Moody (Cleveland: World Publishing, 1966), 155.

19. Micah Hawkins, The Saw-Mill; or, A Yankee Trick: *A Comic Opera in Two Acts as Performed at the Theatre, Chatham Garden, with Distinguished Success* (New York: J and J Harper, 1824), libretto.

20. Vera Brodsky Lawrence, "Micah Hawkins: The Pied Piper of Catherine Slip," *New York Historical Society Quarterly* 62 (1978): 150; see also Peter G. Buckley, "'The Place to Make an Artist Work': Micah Hawkins and William Sidney Mount in New York City," in *Catching the Tune: Music and William Sidney Mount* (Stony Brook: Museums at Stony Brook, 1984).

21. Lawrence, "Micah Hawkins," 158. The original playbill provides a lengthy description of the staging, cast, and musical numbers.

22. Hawkins, *The Saw-Mill,* 9–10.

23. The song is reprinted in Patricia H. Virga, *The American Opera to 1790* (Ann Arbor: UMI Research Press, 1982), 237–42.

24. Reprinted in Grenville Vernon, *Yankee Doodle-Do: A Collection of Songs of the Early American Stage* (New York: Payson and Clarke, 1927), 36–39.

25. Facsimile reprint in Martha Furman Schleifer, ed., *American Opera and Music for the Stage, Eighteenth and Nineteenth Centuries* (New York: G. K. Hall, 1990), 61–63.

26. *Rambler's Magazine,* Feb. 2, 1810, 20, quoted in Porter, *With an Air Debonair,* 344.

27. For Elizabeth Billington, see W. Oxberry, *Oxberry's Dramatic Biography and Historic Anecdotes* (London: G. Virtue, 1825–26), 3:59, quoted in Porter, *With an Air Debonair,* 347.

28. *Lady of the Lake* playbill courtesy of the Maryland Historical Society, Baltimore; see also Elise K. Kirk, "'Hail to the Chief': The Origins and Legacies of an American Ceremonial Tune," *American Music* 15 (Summer 1997): 123–36.

29. [Thomas Dibdin], The Lady of the Lake; *a Melo-dramatic Romance in Two Acts, as Performed at the Theatres Royal, London* (London: G. H. Davidson, 1810); see also Thomas Dibdin, The Lady of the Lake: *A Melodramatic Romance in Three Acts* (New York: D. Longworth, 1811).

30. The tune is believed to derive from an old melody from Swiss cowherds.

31. David Grimsted, *Melodrama Unveiled: American Theater and Culture 1800–1850* (Chicago: University of Chicago Press, 1968), 10.

32. Henry Rawley Bishop, Clari; or, The Main of Milan: *An Opera in Three Acts,* piano-vocal edition, 1823, Performing Arts Division of the Library of Congress. See also John Howard Payne, *Clari; or, The Maid of Milan* (New York: Circulating Library and Dramatic Repository, 1823) and the two-act version published in Philadelphia by Frederick Turner (1836). Nine of the original twenty musical numbers are cut from the 1836 edition, including Clari's first "Home, Sweet Home" in act 1.

33. Laurence Berman, "Claude Debussy, Melodramatist," in *Music and Context: Essays for John Ward,* ed. Anne Dhu Shapiro (Cambridge: Harvard University Press, 1985), 147.

34. David Mayer discusses dandyism and the character Dandy Lover in *Harlequin in His Element.* The term *dandyism* was used in the early and mid-nineteenth century to describe bands of "decadent" young men who dressed in skin-tight breeches and

frilled shirts. The Prince of Wales, a homosexual, endorsed dandyism. See also Rhonda K. Garelick, *Rising Star: Dandyism, Gender and Performance in the Fin de Siècle* (Princeton: Princeton University Press, 1998).

35. David Mayer, "Nineteenth Century Theatre Music," *Theatre Notebook* 30, no. 3 (1976): 122.

Chapter 5: Grand Opera—the American Way

1. *American,* Nov. 7, 1825, quoted in Vera Brodsky Lawrence, *Resonances, 1836–1849,* vol. 1 of *Strong on Music: The New York Musical Scene in the Days of George Templeton Strong, 1836–1875* (Chicago: University of Chicago Press, 1988), xliv.

2. For more on Garcia's orchestra, see Molly Nelson, "The First Italian Opera Season in New York City, 1825–1826," Ph.D. diss., University of North Carolina, 1976, ch. 7.

3. James Hardie, *The Description of the City of New York, Containing Its Population, Institutions, Commerce, Manufacturing, Public Buildings, Courts of Justice, Places of Amusement etc.* (New York: Samuel Marks, 1827), 320.

4. Charles Hamm, *Yesterdays: Popular Song in America* (New York: W. W. Norton, 1979), 66; Nelson, "The First Italian Opera Season," 136.

5. Charles Hamm, *Music in the New World* (New York: W. W. Norton, 1983), 198.

6. Alfred Loewenberg, *Annals of Opera, 1597–1940* (Totowa: Roman and Littlefield, 1978); 730, 740.

7. Hamm, *Music in the New World,* 199.

8. Julius Mattfield, *A Hundred Years of Grand Opera in New York, 1825–1925* (New York: New York Public Library, 1927), 14.

9. Letter to Count Pepoli, early 1834, quoted in Friedrich Lippmann, "Bellini, Vincenzo," in *The New Grove Dictionary of Opera,* ed. Stanley Sadie (New York: Grove's Dictionaries of Music, 1992), 1:391.

10. *Leonora* is scored for piccolo flute, two flutes, two oboes, two clarinets in B-flat, two bassoons, trumpets (B-flat, C, and E-flat), horns (E-flat, F, A-flat, and C), trombones (alto, tenor, and bass), timpani, side drum, bass drum, cymbals, castanets, triangle, first and second violins, violas, cellos, and basses. The organ is used in parts of act 2. Edwin Lester Smith, "William Henry Fry's *Leonora,*" DMA diss., University of Kentucky, 1974, 22.

11. William Henry Fry, "Prefatory Remarks," in *Leonora: A Lyrical Drama in Three Acts, Words by J. R. Fry* (New York: E. Ferretti, 1846).

12. The main source for Fry is William Treat Upton, *William Henry Fry, American Journalist and Composer-Critic* (1954, repr. New York: Da Capo Press, 1974). Upton includes an annotated list of Fry's compositions in the Library Company of Philadelphia (Appendix 1, 305–23), including useful information on the manuscripts, editions, and revisions. The Fry Collection is housed at the Historical Society of Pennsylvania. See also Irving Lowens, "William Henry Fry, American Nationalist," in *Music and Musicians in Early America* (New York: W. W. Norton, 1964), 212–22.

13. Upton, *William Henry Fry,* 57, 112, 269.

14. Ibid., 177. Fry's lectures are discussed in Vera Brodsky Lawrence, "William Henry Fry's Messianic Yearnings: The Eleven Lectures, 1852–53," *American Music* 7 (Winter 1989): 382–411.

15. Fry, "Prefatory Remarks."

16. Fry refers to *recitativo accompagnato,* used mainly in the opera for transitional and dramatic passages. His occasional use of *recitativo secco* is more declamatory and hence somewhat less interesting.

17. Quoted in Lawrence, *Resonances,* 339.

18. William Ashbrook, with John Black and Julian Budden, "Donizetti, Gaetano," in *The New Grove Dictionary of Opera,* ed. Stanley Sadie (New York: Grove's Dictionaries of Music, 1992), 1:1209.

19. Quoted in Upton, *William Henry Fry,* 210–12. For New York, Fry had reworked his 1845 version of *Leonora* into four acts.

20. William Henry Fry, *Notre-Dame of Paris: A Lyrical Drama in Four Acts, Words by J. R. Fry* (New York: W. H. Fry, 1864), vocal and Piano-forte score, with English and Italian words. The Library Company of Philadelphia holds the complete piano-vocal score; the New York Public Library for the Performing Arts at Lincoln Center holds only act 1.

21. William Henry Fry, *Notre-Dame of Paris* (Philadelphia: King and Baird, 1864), piano-vocal score; see also the libretto.

22. Upton, *William Henry Fry,* 220.

23. Quoted in Upton, *William Henry Fry,* 228.

24. Each of these impresarios wrote important memoirs: Luigi Arditi, *My Reminiscences* (1896, repr. New York: Da Capo Press, 1977); Maurice Strakosch, *Souvenirs d'un Impresario* (Paris, 1887); and Max Maretzek, *Revelations of an Opera Manager in Nineteenth-century America* (New York: Dover, 1968), a single-volume reprint of *Crotchets and Quavers* (1855) and *Sharps and Flats* (1890).

25. *Message Bird,* Feb. 1, 1851 (quotation); see also the *New York Tribune,* Jan. 8, 1851. For more on Strakosch and the itinerant Italian opera troupes of the period, see Katherine K. Preston, *Opera on the Road: Traveling Opera Troupes in the United States, 1825–60* (Urbana: University of Illinois Press, 1993). Preston includes companies active mainly between 1825 and 1860, such as the Montresor, Rivafinoli, Palmo, and Havana companies.

26. In H. Earle Johnson, *Operas on American Subjects* (New York: Coleman-Ross, 1964), 71–72. The libretto (New York: Theatre Ticket Office, 1887) contains six selections arranged for piano.

27. For more on Lincoln and opera, see Elise K. Kirk, *Musical Highlights from the White House* (Malabar, Fla: Krieger, Publishing, 1992), 38–45; and Elise K. Kirk, *Music at the White House: A History of the American Spirit* (Urbana: University of Illinois Press, 1986), 77–89.

28. Nicolas Slonimsky, *Baker's Biographical Dictionary of Musicians,* 8th ed. (New York: Schirmer Books, 1992), 514; Edward Ellsworth Hipsher, *American Opera and Its Composers* (1934, repr. New York: Da Capo Press, 1978), 170.

29. J. Remington Fairlamb, *Valerie; or, Treasured Tokens: A Romantic Opera in Four Acts* (Washington: Rufus H. Darby, 1878). The score has apparently been lost.

30. John Brougham, Po-Ca-Hon-Tas; or, The Gentle Savage *in Two Acts*. The libretto is reprinted in *Satiric Comedies,* ed. Walter S. Meserve and William R. Reardon (Bloomington: Indiana University Press, 1969), 115–55.

31. Scrici, *Physiology of the Opera* (1852, repr. New York: Brooklyn College, CUNY, 1981, 27–29 [Institute for Studies in American Music, Special Publications 2].

32. Ibid., 54–55.

33. Ibid., 76–79.

34. Lowens, "Fry," 214.

35. Richard Moody, *American Takes the Stage: Romanticism and American Drama and Theatre, 1750–1900* (Bloomington: Indiana University Press, 1955), 10.

36. See also Daniel Boorstin, *The Americans: The National Experience* (New York: Random House, 1965), 331.

37. George Frederick Bristow to the Editor, *Musical World,* March 4, 1854. For more on Bristow, see Delmer Dalzell Rogers, "Nineteenth-Century Music in New York City as Reflected in the Career of George Frederick Bristow," Ph.D. diss., University of Michigan, 1967.

38. *New York Musical Review and Gazette,* Oct. 6, 1855, 335; see also Hipsher, *American Opera,* 83–87.

39. J. H. Wainwright's libretto for *Rip van Winkle,* 1855, with revisions by J. W. Shannon, reprinted in George F. Bristow, Rip van Winkle: *Grand Romantic Opera in Three Acts,* ed. and with a new introduction by Steven Ledbetter (New York: Da Capo Press, 1991), xxvi.

40. George F. Bristow, Rip van Winkle: *Grand Romantic Opera in Three Acts;* libretto reconstructed by J. W. Shannon (New York: G. Schirmer, 1882). The piano–vocal score is reprinted with the libretto in *Rip van Winkle,* ed. Ledbetter.

41. Boorstin, *The Americans: The National Experience,* 332.

42. Waldemer Rieck, "When Bristow's 'Rip' Was Sung at Niblo's Garden," *Musical America,* Nov. 16, 1925, 19.

43. J. S. Dwight, "Musical Correspondence," *Dwight's Journal of Music,* Oct. 6, 1855, 7.

44. Thomas L. Riis, "The Music and Musicians in Nineteenth-Century Productions of *Uncle Tom's Cabin,*" *American Music* 4 (Fall 1986): 268; Bernard Hewitt, *Theatre U.S.A., 1665 to 1957* (New York: McGraw-Hill, 1959), 178.

45. Letter to *The Liberator,* Sept. 9, 1853.

46. Thomas Riis, ed., Uncle Tom's Cabin *(1853)* (New York: Garland Publishing, 1994), xvi. A facsimile of the original libretto or play text is included, as well as seven of the musical numbers.

47. Riis, ed., *Uncle Tom's Cabin,* 14.

48. John Francis Marion, *Within These Walls: A History of the Academy of Music in Philadelphia* (Philadelphia: Academy of Music, 1984), 104.

49. "Uncle Tom's Cabin," article with background on the opera, cast, and composer

in Chestnut Street Opera House playbill, Monday, May 22, 1882. Florio Collection, Special Collections, New York Public Library for the Performing Arts at Lincoln Center.

50. "Biographical Sketch of Caryl Florio," Chestnut Street Opera House playbill; see also Florio's obituary, *Ashville Times,* Nov. 22, 1920; Hipsher, *American Opera,* 181–82; and Barton Cantrell, H. Wiley Hitchcock, and David Kelleher, "Florio, Caryl," in *The New Grove Dictionary of American Music,* ed. H. Wiley Hitchcock and Stanley Sadie (New York: Grove's Dictionaries of Music, 1986), 2:144.

51. Caryl Florio, *Ellis and Florio's Opera of* Uncle Tom, *from Mrs. Harriet Beecher Stowe's Novel of* Uncle Tom's Cabin, libretto. The libretto contains the cast, scenes, and text of the musical numbers but not the spoken dialogue. The manuscript orchestral score, diaries, and correspondence (including letters to Florio from Charles Ives) are in the Florio Collection, Special Collections, New York Public Library for the Performing Arts at Lincoln Center.

Chapter 6: In the Spirit of Comedy

1. Louise Cowan, "The Nature of Comedy," presented to the Dallas Institute of Humanities and Culture, University of Dallas, Irving, Tex., Feb. 1979.

2. Ronald L. Davis, *The Gilded Years, 1865–1920,* vol. 2 of *A History of Music in American Life* (Huntington, Fla.: Krieger, 1980), 139–41; Deane L. Root, *American Popular Stage Music* (Ann Arbor: UMI Research Press, 1981), 79–90.

3. Gerald Bordman, *American Operetta from* H.M.S. Pinafore *to* Sweeny Todd (New York: Oxford University Press, 1981), 11.

4. Charles William Heffernan, "Thomas Whitney Surette: Musician and Teacher," Ph.D. diss., University of Michigan, 1962, 50. Heffernan quotes from the *Brooklyn Daily Eagle,* Dec. 11, 1891.

5. Lists of the operettas of Kerker, Robyn, and Spencer appear in Edith Borroff, *American Operas: A Checklist,* ed. J. Bunker Clark (Warren, Mich.: Harmonie Park Press, 1992). For Robyn, see also Ernst C. Krohn, *Missouri Music* (1924, repr. New York: Da Capo Press, 1971), 64.

6. Sands W. Forman, "Argument," in Captain Cook: *A Romantic Historical Opera in Three Acts, Music by Noah Brandt,* vocal score, rev. ed. (San Francisco: Sherman, Clay, 1893).

7. In 1869, when the Central and Union Pacific Railways joined the East and West Coasts, San Francisco flourished economically and culturally as never before. At the Tivoli Opera House, where Stahl's *Said Pasha* was first performed, almost ten thousand performances of opera are estimated to have been given between 1879 and 1906, including forty-two consecutive nights of Gounod's *Faust.* Robert Commanday, "San Francisco," in *The New Grove Dictionary of Opera,* ed. Stanley Sadie (New York: Grove's Dictionaries of Music, 1992), 4:165; see also Edward Ellsworth Hipsher, *American Opera and Its Composers* (1934, repr. New York: Da Capo Press, 1978), 81.

8. Bernard Hewitt, *Theatre U.S.A.* (New York: McGraw-Hill, 1959), 227–28. In Jan-

uary 1872 *The Galaxy* criticized Charlotte Cushman's acting in "the old, old British legitimate style . . . with its pompous and cumbrous dignity . . . its staginess."

9. "Dramatic and Musical: A New Comic Opera by the Authors of 'Robin Hood' Produced at the Broadway Theatre. 'The Highwayman' Pleasing," *New York Times,* Dec. 14, 1897.

10. Bordman, *American Operetta,* 26.

11. Harry B. Smith, *First Night and First Editions* (Boston: Little, Brown, 1931), 145.

12. Richard Moody, *American Takes the Stage: Romanticism and American Drama and Theatre, 1750–1900* (Bloomington: Indiana University Press, 1955), 238.

13. For more on Sousa's operettas, see Paul E. Bierley, *John Philip Sousa: A Descriptive Catalogue of His Works* (Urbana: University of Illinois Press, 1973). A project to restore and record all of Sousa's operettas is being undertaken by Lyric Theatre International.

14. Harry B. Smith, The Highwayman: *Romantic Comic Opera in Three Acts, Music by Reginald de Koven* (New York: T. B. Harms, 1898), vocal score, 177–229; reprinted in *Later Operetta, Part II:* The Highwayman, volume 15 in the Garland Series edited by Orly Leah Krasner (New York: Garland Publishing, 1994).

15. Martha Furman Schleifer, ed., *American Opera and Music for the Stage: Eighteenth and Nineteenth Centuries* (New York: G. K. Hall, 1990), xxviii. The 1891 piano-vocal score of *Robin Hood* is reprinted on 107–326.

16. Smith, *The Highwayman,* 177–229.

17. Elise K. Kirk, *Musical Highlights from the White House* (Malabar, Fla.: Krieger, 1992), 71.

18. Quoted in Mabel Collins Donnelly, *The American Victorian Woman: The Myth and the Reality* (Westport: Greenwood Press, 1986), 15.

19. Joseph McLellan, "Assault on the Sopranos," *Washington Post,* Nov. 8, 1992.

20. Margaret Gibbons Wilson, *The American Woman in Transition: The Urban Influence, 1870–1920* (Westport: Greenwood Press, 1979), 6.

21. Wilson, *American Woman in Transition,* 8.

22. Frances E. Willard and Mary A. Livermore, eds., *American Women: Fifteen Hundred Biographies with over 1,400 Portraits; a Comprehensive Encyclopedia of the Lives and Achievements of American Women during the Nineteenth Century,* vol. 2 (1897, repr. Detroit: Gale Research, 1973). This volume was originally published, with the same editors, as *A Woman of the Century* (Buffalo: Moulton, 1893). The classified index appears only in the 1897 edition.

23. Jane Bowers and Judith Tick, eds., *Women Making Music: The Western Art Tradition, 1150–1950* (Urbana: University of Illinois Press, 1986), 333.

24. George P. Upton, *Women in Music: An Essay* (Boston: James R. Osgood, 1880), 21–22.

25. Otto Ebel, *Women Composers: A Biographical Handbook of Women's Work in Music* (Brooklyn: Chandler-Ebel Music, 1913), iv.

26. Willard and Livermore, eds., *American Women,* 599.

27. Krohn, *Missouri Music,* 63, 65. None of Whitely's works seem to have survived.

28. Ardennes Foster, ed., *Women in Music and Law* (New York: Authors' Publishing, 1895), 24.

29. "The Prince of Asturia" MS and "Constance Faunt Le Roy Runcie" by Ellinor Dale Runcie (2 pp., typscript), both in the possession of the St. Joseph, Mo., Public Library. See also "Runcie, Mrs. Constance Faunt Le Roy," in *American Women*, ed. Willard and Livermore, 625–26; and Edwin N. C. Barnes, *Tuning in on American Music: American Women in Creative Music* (Washington, D.C.: Music Education Publications, 1936), 1–2.

30. *Indianapolis Freeman*, Dec. 14, 1889.

31. Hipsher, *American Opera*, 279.

32. *San Francisco Examiner*, Feb. 8, 1917; Hipsher, *American Opera*, 278.

33. Nicolas Slonimsky, *Baker's Biographical Dictionary of Musicians*, 8th ed. (New York: Schirmer Books, 1992), 1777 (quotation); see also Christime Ammer, *Unsung: A History of Women in American Music* (Westport: Greenwood Press, 1980), 167–69.

34. Willard and Livermore, eds., *American Women*, 684.

35. The manuscript for *Burra Pundit* is in the Performing Arts Division of the Library of Congress.

36. Stella Prince Stocker, "Song of the Novice" from *Ganymede* (Chicago: Lyon and Healy, 1897).

37. The program is in "Women's Amateur Music Clubs," folder 40, James W. Ellsworth Papers, World Columbian Exposition Collection, Chicago Public Library. For more on Stocker, see *The International Cyclopedia of Music and Musicians*, ed. Oscar Thompson, 11th ed. (New York: Dodd, Mead, 1985); and Barnes, *Tuning in on American Music*, 5–6.

38. The libretto, including fifteen Native American melodies, was published in Duluth in 1916 and is in the Library of Congress; Stocker's annotations are on pages 42 and 43.

Chapter 7: Wagnerism and the American Muse

1. Rupert Hughes, with additional chapters by Arthur Elson, *American Composers, a Study of the Music of This Country and of Its Future, with Biographies of the Leading Composers of the Present Time, Being a New Revised Edition of* Contemporary American Composers (1914, repr. Boston: AMS Press, 1973), 50.

2. For more on Wagner in America, see Joseph Horowitz, *Wagner Nights: An American History* (Berkeley: University of California Press, 1994), 8, 26.

3. Joseph A. Mussulman, *Music in the Cultured Generation: A Social History of Music in America, 1870–1900* (Evanston: Northwestern University Press, 1971), 147, 158.

4. Frederic L. Ritter, *Music in America* (New York: Charles Scribner's Sons, 1883), quoted in Horowitz, *Wagner Nights*, 49.

5. Elise K. Kirk, *Musical Highlights from the White House* (Malabar, Fla: Krieger, 1992), 72–73.

6. Elise K. Kirk, "Ringmaster," *Opera News*, March 27, 1993, 9.

7. Mark McKnight, "Wagner and the New York Press, 1855–76," *American Music* 5 (Summer 1987): 149.

8. Kirk, "Ringmaster," 10.

9. Elise K. Kirk, "The Rape of the Grail: The American Premiere of *Parsifal*," presented to the Wagner Society of New York, March 30, 1991.

10. Gary A. Richardson, *American Drama from the Colonial Period through World War I: A Critical History* (New York: Twayne Publishers, 1993), 115.

11. Allardyce Nicoll, *The Theory of Drama* (New York: Arno Press, 1980), 88–89.

12. Quoted in David Mayer, "The Music of Melodrama," in *Performance and Politics in Popular Drama: Aspects of Popular Entertainment in Theatre, Film and Television, 1800–1976,* ed. David Bradby, Louis James, and Bernard Sharratt (New York: Cambridge University Press, 1980), 50.

13. Mayer, "Music of Melodrama," 49–51.

14. S. G. Pratt, Preface to Zenobia, Queen of Palmyra: *Lyric Opera in Four Acts* (Boston: Oliver Ditson, 1882), piano-vocal score.

15. Parts of *Otho Visconti* were published by W. A. Pond in New York City. For more on Gleason, see *A Hundred Years of Music in America, an Account of Musical Effort in America during the Past Century, Together with Historical and Biographical Sketches of Important Personalities,* ed. W. S. B. Matthews (1889, repr. New York: AMS Press, 1970), 698–700; and Edward Ellsworth Hipsher, *American Opera and Its Composers* (1934, repr. New York: Da Capo Press, 1978), 216–17. *Otho Visconti* was given three performances at the College Theater, but the new theater attracted more attention than the opera, described erroneously as a "twelfth-century Florentine opera" (*Chicago Daily Tribune,* June 5, 1907). See also the composer's piano-vocal autograph manuscript, Frederick Grant Gleason Collection, Newberry Library, Chicago.

16. Martha Furman Schleifer, ed., *American Opera and Music for the Stage: Early Twentieth Century* (New York: G. K. Hall, 1990), xv. This volume contains a facsimile of the piano-vocal score of *Ben Hur* published by Towers and Curran in 1902. For more on Kelley, see M. R. King, "Edgar Sillman Kelley: American Composer, Teacher and Author," Ph.D. diss., Florida State University, 1970; and Leonard Rivenberg, "Edgar Stillman Kelley and the American Musical Theatre," in *Musical Theatre in America: Papers and Proceedings of the Conference on the Musical Theatre in America,* ed. Glenn Loney (Westport: Greenwood Press, 1984).

17. M. A. DeWolfe Howe, "John Knowles Paine," *Musical Quarterly* 25 (July 1939): 264.

18. John C. Smith, *The Life and Works of John Knowles Paine* (Ann Arbor: UMI Research Press, 1980), 561.

19. John Knowles Paine, Azara: *Opera in Three Acts,* autograph manuscript, full score in Houghton Library, Harvard University; manuscript copy of the piano-vocal score published in Leipzig by Breitkopf and Härtel in 1901 is in the Performing Arts Division of the Library of Congress.

20. Smith, *Paine,* 563

21. See also Elise K. Kirk, "Art Nouveau and the Melodic Style of Charles Koechlin," *Miscellanea Musicologica* 13 (1984): 117–29.

22. See also Walter Damrosch, *My Musical Life* (1923, repr. Westport: Greenwood Press, 1972); and George Martin, *The Damrosch Dynasty: America's First Family of Music* (Boston: Houghton Mifflin, 1983).

23. Lathrop's libretto is reproduced in *Grand Opera in America:* The Scarlet Letter, ed. Elise K. Kirk, vol. 16 of *Nineteenth-century American Musical Theater,* ed. Deane L. Root (New York: Garland Publishing, 1994). Volume 16 also contains a facsimile reprint of Damrosch's original piano-vocal score published in Leipzig by Breitkopf and Härtel (1896).

24. Kirk, ed., *Grand Opera in America:* The Scarlet Letter, 342–55.

25. The full orchestral holograph remains unpublished and is at the Americana Division of the New York Public Library for the Performing Arts at Lincoln Center. Instrumental parts are extant for strings; flute (1,2,3 piccolo); clarinet (1,2, and bass clarinet); oboe (1,2); bassoon (1,2); horn (1,2,3,4); trumpet (1,2,3); and trombone (1,2,3), as well as tuba, timpani, bass drum, cymbals, and harp.

26. Henry Edward Krehbiel, *Chapters of Opera* (repr. New York: Da Capo Press, 1980), 262.

27. Seidl quoted in Damrosch, *My Musical Life,* 116.

28. Alfred Remy, "The Scarlet Letter," *The Looker-On* (April 1896): 574. For a Damrosch bibliography, see *Grand Opera in America:* The Scarlet Letter, ed. Kirk, xviii–xix.

29. Victor Fell Yellin, *Chadwick, Yankee Composer* (Washington: Smithsonian Institution Press, 1990), 186. See also Steven Ledbetter, "Two Seductresses: Saint-Saëns *Delilah* and Chadwick's *Judith,*" in *A Celebration of American Music: Words and Music in Honor of H. Wiley Hitchcock,* ed. Richard Crawford, R. Allen Lott, and Carol J. Oja (Ann Arbor: University of Michigan Press, 1990).

30. Holograph full score of *Judith,* Dec. 12, 1900, and piano-vocal score (G. Schirmer, 1901), Performing Arts Division of the Library of Congress.

31. Jane Marcus, "Salome: The Jewish Princess Was a New Woman," in *Art and Anger: Reading Like a Woman* (Columbus: Ohio State University Press, 1988), 19.

32. William K. Kearns, *Horatio Parker, 1863–1919: His Life, Music, and Ideas* (Metuchen: Scarecrow Press, 1990), 147. The libretto for *Mona* was published by Dodd, Mead (New York, 1911), and the orchestral parts and piano-vocal score by G. Schirmer (New York, 1912).

33. Kearns, *Horatio Parker,* 155. For more on the thematic analysis of *Mona,* see J. van Broekhoven, *"Mona:* The American Prize Opera," *Musical Observer* 6 (April 1912): 22–28.

34. Mussulman, *Music in the Cultured Generation,* 167.

35. Ibid., 168.

Chapter 8: Native Americans through Symbolism and Song

1. John Comfort Fillmore, "A Study of Indian Music," *Century Illustrated Monthly Magazine,* Feb. 1894, quoted in Joseph A. Mussulman, *Music in the Cultured Generation: A Social History of Music in America, 1870–1900* (Evanston: Northwestern University Press, 1971), 163.

2. Charles Hamm, *Music in the New World* (New York: W. W. Norton, 1983), 17–18.

3. Richard Erdoes, *Crying for a Dream: The World through Native American Eyes* (Santa Fe: Bear, 1990), 95.

4. Natalie Curtis (Burlin), *The Indians' Book* (1923, repr. New York: Dover, 1968), vii.

5. As early as 1735, Jean-Philippe Rameau composed *Les Indes galantes.* Niccolo Piccini's *L'americano ingentilito* (The civilized Indian) was performed in Vienna in 1770, and Indian operas and ballets were staged by Stephen Storace, Franz Genée, Adolphe Adam, and many others. The Bohemian composer Anton Dvorák had visited America from 1892 to 1895 and heard the music of the Iroquois in Iowa. He wanted to write an opera on Longfellow's *Hiawatha,* but the poem proved to be too static for dramatic treatment. Frank M. Flack, "Dvorák and American Opera," *Opera News,* Jan. 24, 1955, 29. H. Earle Johnson lists eighty-three operas on Indian themes, although not all are Native American. See Johnson, *Operas on American Subjects* (New York: Coleman-Ross, 1964).

6. Edward Ellsworth Hipsher, *American Opera and Its Composers* (1934, repr. New York: Da Capo Press, 1978), 342.

7. Johnson, *Operas on American Subjects,* 80.

8. "Explains Berlin's Attack upon Poia," *Musical America,* May 21, 1910, 25.

9. Hipsher, *American Opera,* 339.

10. Arthur Finley Nevin, Poia: Oper in Drei Akten. *Text von Randolph Hartley. Nach den von Walter McClintok Gesammelten Indianer-Legenden. In Deutsche übertragen von Eugenie von Huhn. Orchester Partitur* (Berlin: Adolph Fürstner, 1910). The work is scored for three flutes (piccolo), two oboes, English horn, two clarinets, bass clarinet, two bassoons, contrabassoon, four horns, three trumpets, three trombones, tuba, timpani, percussion, harp, and strings. The piano-vocal score was also published by Fürstner in 1910, with text in both English and German.

11. "Composer of 'Poia' Undaunted by Merciless Attack of Berlin Critics," *Musical America,* May 14, 1910, 7; see also "New Indian Opera Given in Berlin," *Boston Herald,* April 24, 1910.

12. For various interpretations of the legend of Poia (sometimes called "Scar Face") according to Native American oral tradition, see Clark Wissler and D. C. Duvall, *Mythology of the Blackfoot Indians* (1908, repr. Lincoln: University of Nebraska Press, 1995), 61–66.

13. Erdoes, *Crying,* 20, 63.

14. Linda Hutcheon and Michael Hutcheon, "The Pox and the Prostitute." Presented at "Representations of Gender and Sexuality in Opera," State University of New York at Stony Brook, Sept. 14–17, 1995. See also Linda Hutcheon and Michael Hutcheon, *Opera: Desire, Disease, Death* (Lincoln: University of Nebraska Press, 1996).

15. "Mickey Mousing" usually refers to the technique of using music to mimic the action in graphic detail, as in an animated cartoon. Nevin, *Poia,* piano-vocal score, 48.

16. Richard Aldrich, "'Natoma' Greeted by Great Audience," *New York Times,* March 1, 1911.

17. [Lawrence Gilman], "'Natoma' Endorsed by New York for Its Music, Alone," *Musical America,* March 4, 1911.

18. The arias are available on *Toward an American Opera, 1911–1954* (New World Records NW241), introduction and notes by Patrick J. Smith. The arias were originally recorded by Victor—Barbara's on June 10, 1912, and Paul's on April 3, 1912.

19. Leon Maurice Aufdemberge, "An Analysis of the Dramatic Construction of American Operas on American Themes, 1896–1958," Ph.D. diss., Northwestern University, 1965, 74–78; see also Victor Herbert, Natoma: *An Opera in Three Acts; the Book by Joseph Redding* (New York: G. Schirmer, 1911), piano-vocal score.

20. Louise Llewellyn, "'I Believe in Writing for the Public,' Says Victor Herbert," *Musical America,* Feb. 11, 1911, 3.

21. "Tsianina Redfeather Blackstone," *Youngstown* [Ohio] *Vindicator,* Jan. 20, 1985. Other Native American singers who achieved fame during these years were Yakima Chief Yowlache, who sang Verdi arias and Zuni chants for Herbert Hoover in the White House, and Princess Te Ata, who sang for Eleanor and Franklin Roosevelt.

22. Charles Wakefield Cadman to Nelle Richmond Eberhart, March 1, 1917, quoted in Harry D. Perison, "The 'Indian' Operas of Charles Wakefield Cadman," *College Music Symposium* 22, no. 2 (1982): 38.

23. Cadman to Eberhart, March 1, 1917. Cadman did not consider *Shanewis* to be "Indian opera." "It is not a mythical tale, nor yet an aboriginal story," he said, "and since more than three-fourth of the actual composition of the work lies within the boundaries of original creative effort . . . let it be an opera upon an American subject or if you will—an American opera!" Foreword to Charles Wakefield Cadman, The Robin Woman (Shanewis): An American Opera (in One Act), *Libretto by Nelle Richmond Eberhart* (New York: White-Smith Music Publishing), 1918.

24. The 1927 edition adds twelve pages to the conclusion and includes more dramatic action for the role of Philip Harjo, sung this time by Chief Os-ke-non-ton. "Fifth Summer Season at the Hollywood Bowl," *Musical Courier,* July 1, 1926, 1, 32.

25. For more on *The Sun Bride,* see Lillian White Spencer, "Book of the Sun Bride," typescript, Performing Arts Division, Library of Congress.

26. Catherinne P. Smith, Introduction to Mary Carr Moore, *David Rizzio* (New York: Da Capo Press, 1981), vocal score, v. For more on Moore see Catherine Parsons Smith and Cynthia S. Richardson, *Mary Carr Moore, American Composer* (Ann Arbor: University of Michigan Press, 1987).

27. Mary Carr Moor, Narcissa: *An Opera in Four Acts; the Book by Sarah Pratt Carr* (New York: M. Witmark and Sons, 1912), piano-vocal score.

28. Cyril Player, "'Narcissa' Sung: Well Received," *Seattle Post-Intelligencer,* April 23, 1912.

29. Victor Nilsson, "Audience of Nine Thousand Hail 'Winona' at N.W. Premiere in Auditorium," *Minneapolis Journal,* Jan. 28, 1928.

30. Alberto Bimboni, "Winona: A Romantic Opera in Three Acts," piano-vocal MS, Performing Arts Division, Library of Congress; see also Winona: *An American Opera,* souvenir program, Minnesota Historical Society, Minneapolis.

31. Peter Wynne, "Return of the Native," *Opera News,* Jan. 6, 1996, 28; Scott Cantrell, "In Review: From Around the World," *Opera News* 6 (July 1998): 46–47.

32. Author telephone interview with Stephen Paulus, Feb. 1, 1997.

33. Erdoes, *Crying,* 2.

34. Arthur Farwell, "An Affirmation of American Music," quoted in Daniel Kingman, *American Music: A Panorama* (New York: Schirmer Books, 1990), 445. For a study of American national identity and the definition and limitation of Native American rights and status, see Susan Scheckel, *The Insistence of the Indian: Race and Nationalism in Nineteenth-Century American Culture* (Princeton: Princeton University Press, 1998).

Chapter 9: American Opera at the Met

1. Ralph F. Bogardus, "Urban Cultural Institutions," in *Encyclopedia of American Social History,* ed. Mary Kupiec Cayton, Elliott J. Gorn, and Peter W. Williams (New York: Charles Scribner's Sons, 1993), 3:2482.

2. T. J. Jackson Lears, "Mass Culture and Its Critics," in *Encyclopedia of American Social History,* ed. Mary Kupiec Cayton, Elliott J. Gorn, and Peter W. Williams (New York: Charles Scribner's Sons, 1993), 3:1595.

3. "Big Gains for American Music," *Musical America,* May 14, 1910, 18.

4. De Koven quoted in "America Coming into Its Own Musically," *Musical America,* Oct. 19, 1918, 4–5.

5. Gatti-Casazza quoted in "America Coming into Its Own Musically."

6. Martin Mayer, *The Met: One Hundred Years of Grand Opera* (New York: Simon and Schuster, 1983), 128.

7. Giulio Gatti-Casazza, *Memories of the Opera* (1941, repr. New York: Vienna House, 1973), 236–37.

8. Gatti-Casazza, *Memories of the Opera,* 170–71.

9. Frederick S. Converse, Iolan; or, The Pipe of Desire: *Romantic Opera in One Act, Op. 21. Text by George Edward Barton* (New York: Novello, 1908), reprinted in *American Opera and Music for the Stage, Early Twentieth Century,* ed. Martha Schleifer (New York: G. K. Hall, 1990). The text is in both English and German (translation by Charles Henry Meltzer).

10. Horatio Parker, Mona: *An Opera in Three Acts; the Poem by Brian Hooker* (New York: G. Schirmer, 1911), piano-vocal score; see also William K. Kearns, *Horatio Parker, 1863–1919: His Life, Music, and Ideas* (Metuchen: Scarecrow Press, 1990), 151, 162.

11. "Indian Opera and Negro Ballet Make New American Bill at the Metropolitan," *New York Herald,* March 24, 1918. In a single act, *Shanewis* turned out to be one of the most successful works of Cadman's career. It was performed several times by the Metropolitan Opera and Chicago's American Grand Opera Company, and in 1926 it was revised and expanded for the Hollywood Bowl.

12. Quoted in Edward Ellsworth Hipsher, *American Opera and Its Composers* (1934, repr. New York: Da Capo Press, 1978), 173.

13. Dorothy J. Teall, "Mr. Breil's 'Legend' Embodies His Theories of Practical Democracy," *Musical America,* Sept. 28, 1918, 4–5.

14. Hipsher, *American Opera,* 89.

15. Carleton Smith, *"In the Pasha's Garden," Letters and Art,* Jan. 24, 1935, 26.

16. Lawrence Tibbett, *The Glory Road* (1933, repr. New York: Arno Press, 1977), 26–27.

17. Gerald Fitzgerald, ed., *Annals of the Metropolitan Opera: The Complete Chronicle of Performances and Artists, Chronology, 1883–1985* (Boston: G. K. Hall, 1989), passim.

18. A. J. Liebling, "Taylor, Analyst," unidentified clipping in "Deems Taylor" clipping file, Research Division, New York Public Library for the Performing Arts at Lincoln Center.

19. Ray C. B. Brown, "Taylor Opera in World Reaches New Goal," *Musical America,* Feb. 26, 1927, 1–2, 7.

20. Samuel Chotzinoff, "Great Success for 'The Henchman' at the Metropolitan in New York," *Music News,* Feb. 25, 1927, 8.

21. "Night Lead Opera," press release, typescript, Metropolitan Opera Archives.

22. "'King's Henchman,' American Opera Draws Notable Audience at Metropolitan," *The World,* Feb. 20, 1927.

23. This chorus and the closing scene of act 3 with Lawrence Tibbett are recorded on *Toward an America Opera, 1911–1954* (New World Records NW241), introduction and notes by Patrick J. Smith.

24. Winthrop P. Tryon, "Peter Ibbetson," *Christian Science Monitor,* Feb. 14, 1931.

25. For further details of the story, see the synopsis derived from Deems Taylor's narration for the NBC Metropolitan Opera Broadcast of *Peter Ibbetson,* March 26, 1932, typescript, Metropolitan Opera Archives.

26. Excerpts from *Peter Ibbetson* were recorded on reel-to-reel tape in March 1934 during a performance with Gladys Swarthout in the role of Mrs. Deane. See UORC 143, Special Collections, Oscar Hammerstein Recorded Sound Archives, New York Public Library for the Performing Arts at Lincoln Center. The opera was revived, with Licia Albanese as The Duchess, in 1960 at the Empire State Music Festival near New York City.

27. Olin Downes, *"Merry Mount* Gets a Stirring Ovation," *New York Times,* Feb. 12, 1934.

28. Richard Stokes, Merry Mount: *A Dramatic Poem for Music in Three Acts and Six Scenes* (New York: Farrar and Rinehart, ca. 1932), piano–vocal score.

29. "Merry Mount, New Opera, Described by Dr. Hanson," *Musical Courier,* March 5, 1932, 5. The holograph orchestral score of *Merry Mount* is in the Sibley Music Library of the Eastman School of Music, Rochester, New York; the original stage designs are in the Metropolitan Opera Archives.

30. Lawrence Gilman, "'Merry Mount' World Premiere Is Acclaimed at Metropolitan," *New York Herald Tribune,* Feb. 11, 1934. The opera was staged also in Philadelphia and Brooklyn. In 1955 it was performed at the Eastman School and also aired nationwide. It was produced successfully in 1964 in San Antonio with Beverly Sills and Brian Sullivan in the principal roles and again in 1976 at Chatauqua, New York, with Hanson himself conducting.

31. Eugene O'Neill to Barrett Clark, quoted in Marjorie Mackay Shapiro, "A Strange Case: Louis Gruenberg's Forgotten 'Great American Opera'—*The Emperor Jones*," in *Opera and the Golden West*, ed. John Di Gaetani and Josef Sirefman (Rutherford: Fairleigh Dickinson University Press, 1994), 234.

32. Jo Mielziner, "'The Emperor Jones,' Notes on Production," typescript, 1–2, Metropolitan Opera Archives.

33. Louis Gruenberg, *The Emperor Jones* (New York: Cos Cob Press, 1932), piano-vocal score.

34. Olin Downes, "'The Emperor Jones' Triumphs as Opera," *New York Times,* Jan. 8, 1933.

35. Louis Gruenberg, "For an American Gesture," *Modern Music* 1 (June 1924): 27–28.

36. Hipsher, *American Opera*, 226; Lawrence Gilman, "Some Letters from Opera-goers," *New York Herald-Tribune,* Jan. 22, 1933.

37. W. J. Henderson, "'Emperor Jones' Has Premiere," *New York Sun,* Jan. 9, 1933; Downes, "'The Emperor Jones' Triumphs"; Leonard Liebling, "'Emperor Jones' New American Opera Has World Premiere at Metropolitan Opera," *New York American,* Jan. 8, 1933.

38. Henderson, "'Emperor Jones' Has Premiere"; Downes, "'The Emperor Jones' Triumphs"; Liebling, "'Emperor Jones.'"

39. Richard Stokes to Giulio Gatti-Casazza, New York, March 12, 1934, Metropolitan Opera Archives.

Chapter 10: From the Black Perspective

1. James Weldon Johnson, *Black Manhattan* (1930, repr. New York: Arno Press, 1968), 175.

2. Johnson, *Black Manhattan,* 3–4.

3. Elise K. Kirk, *Musical Highlights from the White House* (Malabar, Fla.: Krieger, 1992), 77.

4. Harold Rosenthal, ed., *The Mapleson Memoirs: The Career of an Operatic Impresario, 1858–1888* (1888, repr. New York: Appleton-Century, 1966), 218.

5. Lawrence Freeman, "The Negro and Grand Opera," *Master Musician* 1 (Feb. 1920): 6–7.

6. For more on Dede and Lambert, see Celia Elizabeth Davidson, "Operas by Afro-American Composers: A Critical Survey and Analysis of Selected Works," Ph.D. diss., Catholic University of America, 1980, 457–59. African Americans were writing plays as early as 1847 (Ira Aldridge, *The Black Doctor*) and 1858 (William Wells Brown, *The Escape; or, The Leap for Freedom*).

7. Davidson, "Operas by Afro-American Composers," 12.

8. Arthur P. Davis, "Growing Up in the New Negro Renaissance," in *Cavalcade: Negro Writing from 1760 to the Present,* ed. Arthur Davis and Saunders Redding (Boston: Houghton Mifflin, 1971), 429.

9. For more on the Harlem Renaissance, see *Black Music in the Harlem Renaissance:*

A Collection of Essays, ed. Samuel A. Floyd (New York: Greenwood Press, 1990), which includes a bibliography of works, scores, manuscripts, and premieres.

10. See Davidson, "Operas by Afro-American Composers," 132–44, for details on Freeman's complete operatic output. The composer's manuscripts are in the Schomberg Center for Research in Black Culture, New York Public Library. See also the souvenir libretto for H. Lawrence Freeman, Vendetta: *Grand Opera in Three Acts* (New York: Negro Grand Opera Company, 1923), Performing Arts Division of the Library of Congress.

11. "'Voodoo,' a Naive Melange Opera by Negro Composer Is Given with All-Negro Cast of Thirty," *New York Times,* Sept. 11, 1928.

12. These and other reviews are quoted in Davidson, "Operas by Afro-American Composers," 74–81.

13. Interview with Valdo Freeman, New York, Dec. 28, 1971, American Music Series, Yale University Oral History Collection, quoted in Davidson, "Opera by Afro-American Composers," 24.

14. *The Ragtime Dance* was published in 1902; the score of *The Guest of Honor* appears to have been lost. See Edward A. Berlin, "On the Trail of *A Guest of Honor:* In Search of Scott Joplin's Lost Opera," in *A Celebration of American Music: Words and Music in Honor of H. Wiley Hitchcock,* ed. Richard Crawford, R. Allen Lott, and Carol J. Oja (Ann Arbor: University of Michigan Press, 1990), 50–65.

15. Vera Brodsky Lawrence, "Scott Joplin and *Treemonisha,*" jacket notes and libretto for *Scott Joplin's* Treemonisha (Deutsche Grammophon, stereo 2707 083), 11, by the Houston Grand Opera conducted by Gunther Schuller with the original cast. The Houston production appeared on PBS television in 1986. For more on the life and work of Joplin, see Rudi Blesh and Harriet Janis, *They All Played Ragtime,* 4th ed. (New York: Oak Publications, 1971); and Addison A. Reed, "Scott Joplin, Pioneer," *The Black Perspective in Music* 1 (Spring 1975): 45–52 and 2 (Fall 1975): 269–77.

16. William J. Shafer and Johannes Riedel, *The Art of Ragtime: Form and Meaning of an Original Black American Artist* (Baton Rouge: Louisiana State University Press, 1973), 218.

17. Lawrence, "Scott Joplin and *Treemonisha,*" jacket notes and libretto, 13.

18. All citations from *Treemonisha* are from Scott Joplin, Treemonisha: *Opera in Three Acts* [performing edition by Vera Brodsky Lawrence and William Bolcom] (Chicago: Dramatic Publishing, 1972).

19. Harold Schonberg, "The Scott Joplin Renaissance Grows," *New York Times,* Feb. 13, 1972.

20. Darwin T. Turner, ed., *Black Drama in America: An Anthology* (Greenwich: Fawcett Publications, 1971), 5.

21. For details of the "Voodoo *Macbeth,*" see Wendy Smith, "The Play That Electrified Harlem," *Civilization* 3 (Jan.–Feb. 1996): 38–43.

22. Hall Johnson, "Run, Little Chillun; or, Across the River: A Play in Two Acts," 1–2–1 [typescript libretto], Federal Theatre Project Records, George Mason University, Library of Congress.

23. Johnson, "Run, Little Chillun," 2–2–12.

24. Doris E. McGinty, "The Washington Conservatory of Music and School of Expression," *The Black Perspective in Music* 7 (Spring 1979): 61. For biographical details on White, see Vernon H. Edwards and Michal L. Marks, "Clarence Cameron White," *The Black Perspective in Music* 9 (Spring 1987): 51–72.

25. Howard Taubman, "Negro Group Presents Work at the Met," *New York Times,* May 28, 1956; see also Clarence Cameron White to Mary Dawson, Feb. 28, May 6, 1958, National Negro Opera Company Collection, Library of Congress. The letters, with notes by Wayne Shirley, have been published; see "In Retrospect: Letters of Clarence Cameron White in the Collections of the Music Division of the Library of Congress," *The Black Perspective in Music* 10 (Fall 1982): 202–4.

26. Howard Taubman, "Opera: 'Ouanga,' Voodoo on Haiti," *New York Times,* May 28, 1956; P. L. Prattis, "National Negro Opera Company," *Pittsburgh Courier,* Feb. 5, 1955; "Chicago Musicians Honor Mary Cardwell Dawson at Reception," *Chicago Defender,* Nov. 10, 1956. Clippings in files of the National Negro Opera Company Collection, Library of Congress.

27. White knew Matheus when both were members of the faculty at West Virginia State College.

28. Clipping in the Moreland Collection, Howard University, Washington, D.C.; see also Davidson, "Operas by Afro-American Composers," 213.

29. Clarence Cameron White, preface to piano-vocal score of *Ouanga* (New York: Sam Fox Publishing, 1955).

30. White, preface to "Ouanga" piano-vocal score, 61–62; see also Clarence Cameron White, "'Ouanga': Music Drama in Three Acts, Based on the Haitian Drama by John F. Matheus" (1939), National Negro Opera Company Collection, Library of Congress. The manuscript shows various revisions from the original 1929 libretto. The Python of Dambala ("Damballah Wedo") is the powerful serpent god of voodoo mythology. Entwined with his wife Ayida, he manifests himself in the sky as a rainbow. The strong Christian influence on voodooism is seen in the iconography of voodoo deities, who often appear as saints. Damballah Wedo, for example, is identified with Saint Patrick, who is said to have driven the serpents of Ireland into the sea. Arthur Cotterell, *A Dictionary of World Mythology* (New York: G. P. Putnam's Sons, 1980), 175–76.

31. John W. Vandercook, *Black Majesty* (New York: Literary Guild of America, 1928), 99.

32. Clarence Cameron White, "'Ouanga: A Musical Drama of Haiti'; Drama by John Frederick Matheus," libretto typescript, 1929, 13, 14, National Negro Opera Company Collection, Library of Congress. Historically, Jean-Jacques Dessalines had no sympathy for voodoo practices. He regarded voodoo chiefs as a threat to military discipline. When he became emperor of Haiti, he prohibited voodoo services and shot its adherents. See Charles Arthur and Michael Dash, eds., *Libète: A Haiti Anthology* (Princeton: Markus Wiener, 1999), 255–60.

33. Turner, ed., *Black Drama,* 49; see also Langston Hughes, *Emperor of Haiti,* in *Black*

Drama in America: An Anthology, ed. Darwin T. Turner (Greenwich: Fawcett Publications, 1971), 51–114.

34. Verna Arvey, *In One Lifetime* (Fayetteville: University of Arkansas Press, 1984), 97.

35. Quoted in Eileen Southern, "William Grant Still—Trailblazer," in *William Grant Still Studies at the University of Arkansas: A 1984 Congress Report,* ed. Claire Detels (Fayetteville: University of Arkansas Press, 1985), 9.

36. For production details on Still's operas see Edith Borroff, *American Operas: A Checklist* (Warren, Mich.: Harmonie Park Press, 1992), 288–89; and Thomas Warburton, "The Operas of William Grant Still," in *William Grant Still Studies at the University of Arkansas: A 1984 Congress Report,* ed. Claire Detels (Fayetteville: University of Arkansas Press, 1985), 18–19. Piano-vocal manuscript copies of the operas are in the Performing Arts Division of the Library of Congress. For availability of full scores and parts see Arvey, *In One Lifetime,* appendix 3, and *William Grant Still Sheet Music Catalogue* (New York: ASCAP, 1997), 7–8. Cassette tape recordings of the premieres of *Troubled Island, Highway No. 1 U.S.A., A Bayou Legend,* and *Minette Fontaine* are available from William Grant Still Music, Flagstaff, Ariz.

37. Warburton, "The Operas of William Grant Still," 23. The piano-vocal score of "Songs of the Desert" is reprinted with the text.

38. William Grant Still, "An Afro-American Composer's Point of View," quoted in Warburton, "The Operas of William Grant Still," 22.

39. John De Mers, review in [Baton Rouge] *Sunday Advocate,* Nov. 24, 1974.

40. Arthur Cunningham, program notes for *Music by Black Composers* (Desto DC7102–7103 [1970]), reprinted by permission.

Chapter 11: Innovators and Iconoclasts; or, Is It Opera?

1. Virgil Thomson, "George Gershwin," *Modern Music* 13 (Nov.–Dec. 1935): 43.

2. Samuel A. Floyd, Jr., ed., *Black Music in the Harlem Renaissance: A Collection of Essays* (New York: Greenwood Press, 1990), 22. Floyd quotes from W. T. Kirkeby, *Ain't Misbehavin': The Story of Fats Waller* (New York: Dodd Mead, 1966), 53.

3. Floyd, ed., *Black Music,* 23.

4. By the time *Porgy and Bess* was staged, Gershwin had composed music for at least twenty-five shows and revues, among them *Strike Up the Band* (1927; rev. 1930), *Girl Crazy* (1930), *Of Thee I Sing* (1931), and *Pardon My English* (1933). A commission in 1929 from the Metropolitan Opera to write a "Jewish opera" (to be called *The Dybbuk*) was never fulfilled.

5. James Weldon Johnson, *Black Manhattan* (New York: Arno Press, 1968), 218.

6. Gershwin's and Heyward's plans were momentarily complicated when they learned that Al Jolson was considering the role of Porgy in blackface in a possible musical version of Heyward's play by Jerome Kern and Oscar Hammerstein. Nothing ever came of the venture, however.

7. Wayne D. Shirley, "Porgy and Bess," *Quarterly Journal of the Library of Congress* 31 (July 1974): 98.

8. Charles Schwartz, *Gershwin: His Life and Music* (Indianapolis: Bobbs-Merrill, 1973), 267.

9. See George Shackley, arr. and ed., *Spiritual Songs from the Theatre Guild Production Porgy* (New York: Bibo, Bloedon and Lang, 1928), 3, 16, 17. The collection contains eleven songs.

10. For a detailed study of the history of *Porgy and Bess,* see Hollis Alpert, Porgy and Bess: *The Story of an American Classic* (New York: Alfred A. Knopf, 1990).

11. Gershwin's manuscript of the full score is in the Performing Arts Division of the Library of Congress, as is his first-draft typscript libretto. The piano-vocal score was published by Chappell in 1935. One CD recording (Angel 49568, 1988) is with the London Philharmonic, conducted by Simon Rattle, with Cynthia Heyman, Williard White, and the Glyndebourne Opera Chorus (also on laser disk 724377754-1).

12. Stravinsky's landmark of modernism *Le sacre du printemps* (1913) was performed on the same program as Gershwin's *An American in Paris* on January 15, 1931, by the Los Angeles Philharmonic. Gershwin admired Stravinsky and wanted to study with him in Paris. "How much money do you make a year?" Stravinsky asked. Gershwin named a six-figure sum. "In that case," said Stravinsky, "I should study with you." Edward Jablonski, *Gershwin* (New York: Doubleday, 1987), 168.

13. In "Rotating Porgy and Bess," Wayne Shirley investigates four of the variants of the Porgy motif and their relationship with the theories of Joseph Schillinger, one of Gershwin's teachers. Typescript, Performing Arts Division, Library of Congress.

14. Thomson, "George Gershwin," *Modern Music* 13 (Nov.–Dec. 1935): 36.

15. Quoted in Schwartz, *Gershwin,* 245.

16. Roger Shattuck, *The Banquet Years: The Origins of the Avant Garde in France, 1885 to World War I: Alfred Jarry, Henri Rousseau, Erik Satie, and Guillaume Apollinaire* (New York: Vintage Books, 1968), 4.

17. See also Alan Howard Levy, "The Search for Identity in American Music, 1890–1920," *American Music* 2 (Summer 1984): 79.

18. Imbs and Thomson are quoted in *The Life and Music of George Antheil, 1900–1959,* ed. Linda Whitesitt (Ann Arbor: UMI Research Press, 1983), 25 and 26.

19. Ernest Hemingway, *A Moveable Feast* (New York: Scribner's Sons, 1964), title page, quoted in *Life and Music of George Antheil,* ed. Whitesitt, 13.

20. Quoted in John Rockwell, "Four Saints in Three Acts," in *The New Grove Dictionary of Opera,* ed. Stanley Sadie (New York: Grove's Dictionaries of Music, 1992), 2:266. For more on Stein, see Florence Stevenson, "A Continuous Present," *Opera News,* April 10, 1971, 8–12.

21. Maurice Grosser, full-score MS copy with composer's addendum for Gertrude Stein and Virgil Thomson, *Four Saints in Three Acts: An Opera to be Sung,* 3 vols., Performing Arts Division, Library of Congress.

22. Quoted in Victor Fell Yellin, "The Operas of Virgil Thomson," in Virgil Thomson, *American Music since 1910* (New York: Holt, Rinehart and Winston, 1971), 94.

23. Yellin, "The Operas of Virgil Thomson," 95.

24. Stevenson, "A Continuous Present," 12.

25. Kathleen Hoover and John Cage, *Virgil Thomson: His Life and Music* (New York: Thomas Yoseloff, 1959), 157. Among other stagings of *Four Saints in Three Acts* is the Houston Grand Opera's production, directed by Robert Wilson, which also played at Lincoln Center and the Edinburgh Festival in 1996.

26. Hoover and Cage, *Virgil Thomson,* 202.

27. Quoted in Robert Marx, "Thomson, Stein and the Mother of Us All," in notes and libretto for the Santa Fe Opera's *The Mother of Us All* (New World Records NW288/89), 11, conducted by Raymond Leppard. Mignon Dunn sang Susan B. Anthony and Philip Booth, Daniel Webster.

28. The list of characters is in Virgil Thomson, *The Mother of Us All* (New York: Music Press, 1947), 14, piano-vocal score.

29. Jack Larson, "Three Operas in Four Productions," in *The Virgil Thomson Centenary, 1896–1996,* ed. Joseph Horowitz (New York: Brooklyn Philharmonic Orchestra, 1996), 57.

30. Quoted in David Ross Baskerville, "Jazz Influence on Art Music to Mid-Century," Ph.D. diss., University of California at Los Angeles, 1965, 1.

31. Frederick Shepherd Converse, "The Immigrants," full-score manuscript, Performing Arts Division, Library of Congress. The stage directions for the opening of act 3 are possibly incomplete. The opera has not been published and appears not to have been performed.

32. Edward Ellsworth Hipsher, *American Opera and Its Composers* (1934, repr. New York: Da Capo Press, 1978), 253.

33. See W. Frank Harling, *A Light from St. Agnes* (New York: R. L. Huntzinger, 1925), piano-vocal score.

34. Wayne Shirley, "Notes on George Gershwin's First Opera," [Institute for Studies in American Music] *Newsletter* 11 (May 1982): 8–10. In 1925, the year before *Deep River*'s premiere, *Blue Monday* was revised and produced at Carnegie Hall by Paul Whiteman under a new title: *135th Street.* Originally only a short melodrama with routine verse-and-chorus revue songs interspersed, *Blue Monday* was included as part of *George White's Scandals of 1922.* Failing miserably, however, it was withdrawn after the first night.

35. Edward Hagelin Pearson, "The Other *Traviata:* Hamilton Forrest's *Camille,"* *Opera Quarterly* 11, no. 2 (1995): 19.

36. See also Susan Cook, "George Antheil's *Transatlantic:* An American in the Weimar Republic," *Journal of Musicology* 9 (Fall 1991): 513.

37. Georges Antheil, Transatlantic (The People's Choice): *Opera in Three Acts. Für die deutsche Bühne bearbeitet von Rudolf Stephan Hoffmann* (Vienna: Universal-Edition A.G., 1929), piano-vocal score. The Minnesota Opera presented the first full-stage realization of the opera on April 18, 1998, in the brilliant staging by John Conklin, with Sherrill Milnes as the tycoon, Ajax. See John W. Freeman, "In Review: From around the World," *Opera News* 63 (Aug. 1998): 40; and Anthony Tommasini, "An Opera of Yesterday with the Cynicism of Today," *New York Times,* May 3, 1998.

38. Robert J. Dietz, "Marc Blitzstein and the 'Agit-Prop' Theatre of the 1930s," *Yearbook for Inter-American Musical Research* 6 (1970): 52.

39. Virgil Thomson, "In the Theatre," *Modern Music* 15 (Jan.–Feb. 1938): 113.

40. Dietz, "Marc Blitzstein," 56.

41. Ibid., 57.

42. Marc Blitzstein, "On Writing Music for the Theatre," *Modern Music* 15 (Jan.–Feb. 1938): 84.

43. Howard Da Silva, notes accompanying the recording of *The Cradle Will Rock*, from the production at Theater Four, November 1964 (MGM E/SE-4289-20c); the recording was rereleased by Composers Recordings, Inc. (CRI SD 266).

44. Winthrop Sargeant, quoted in Andrew H. Drummond, *American Opera Librettos* (Metuchen: Scarecrow Press, 1972), 29.

45. Blitzstein, "On Writing Music for the Theatre," 85.

46. Aaron Copland, "Marc Blitzstein Remembered," *Perspectives of New Music* 2 (Spring–Summer 1964): 61; Blitzstein, "On Writing Music for the Theatre," 85.

47. Ethan Mordden, *Opera in the Twentieth Century: Sacred, Profane, Godot* (New York: Oxford University Press, 1978), 304–5.

Chapter 12: The Impact of Mass Media

1. Charles Schwartz, *Gershwin: His Life and Music* (Indianapolis: Bobbs-Merrill, 1973), 257.

2. "The Distance Fiend," *The New Yorker*, May 1924, 16.

3. Gerald Fitzgerald, ed., *Annals of the Metropolitan Opera; Chronology 1883–1985* (Boston: G. K. Hall, 1989), 185. The practice of recording complete operas began in 1906 in Berlin with *Carmen* and *Faust,* but it would be many years before operas would be broadcast any way other than live. On January 13, 1910, the Metropolitan Opera relayed the complete *Cavalleria Rusticana* and *Pagliacci,* with Caruso as Canio, from a rooftop transmitter erected at the opera house. The sound quality was poor, however, and reached audiences only as far away as New Jersey.

4. Charles Wakefield Cadman, "The Willow Tree," WEAF master script, Monday, Oct. 3, 1932, NBC Collection, Recorded Sound Archive, Library of Congress.

5. Forgotten now, many early works became important models for later composers such as Leslie Kondorossy (1915–89), a Czech who believed so vehemently in radio's outreach potentials that in 1955 he created *Opera on the Air,* a long-running series for Cleveland's WSRS, which gave premieres of several of his short operas. Elise K. Kirk, "Kondorossy, Leslie," in *The New Grove Dictionary of Opera,* ed. Stanley Sadie (New York: Grove's Dictionaries of Music, 1992), 2:1018.

6. Peter Adler conducted both the televised production and the later staging by New York City Opera on April 13, 1958, which starred Phyllis Curtin and Walter Cassel. For more on Giannini and his operas, see Michael L. Mark, "The Life and Works of Vittorio Giannini (1903–1966)," DMA diss., Catholic University of America, 1969.

7. Gian Carlo Menotti, *The Old Maid and the Thief: A Grotesque Opera in Fourteen Scenes* (New York: G. Ricordi, 1943), piano-vocal score. An April 22, 1939, recording of the original production with Margaret Daum, Dorothy Sarnoff, Robert Weede, and others is in the Recorded Sound Archive of the Library of Congress (Tape 8575-54B [WJZ]).

8. Quoted in John Ardoin, *The Stages of Menotti* (New York: Doubleday, 1985), 145.

9. Ardoin, *Stages of Menotti,* 12, 10 (quotation).

10. Gian Carlo Menotti, Amahl and the Night Visitors: *Opera in One Act* (New York: G. Schirmer, 1951), piano-vocal score, vi.

11. Menotti, *Amahl and the Night Visitors,* 28–29, 32. The original production starred Chet Allen as Amahl and Rosemary Kuhlman as the mother.

12. Lee Hoiby, The Scarf; *Libretto by Henry Duncan* (Melville, N.Y.: Belwin Mills, 1959), piano-vocal score, 24.

13. For more on *The Scarf* and its orchestration, see William David Krusemark, "Two Early Operas by Lee Hoiby: A Stylistic Analysis and Commentary," DMA diss., University of Kansas, 1989, 32–69.

14. See also "Critical Responses to the Works of Lee Hoiby," typescript sent by Lee Hoiby to the author, Jan. 1990 [a three-page compendium and synopses of various published reviews of Hoiby's compositions].

15. Quoted in Ardoin, *Stages of Menotti,* 144–45.

16. Agnes Greene Foster, *Eleanor Everest Freer, Patriot, and Her Colleagues* (Chicago: Musical Art Publishing, 1927), 147–48; see also "Chicago" in *The Complete Poems of Carl Sandburg* (New York: Harcourt Brace Jovanovich, 1970), 3.

17. For a complete list of Bispham Medal recipients and their operas, see Sylvia Miller Eversole, "Eleanor Everest Freer: Her Life and Music," Ph.D. diss., City University of New York, 1992, 413–14.

18. "Eleanor E. Freer," in American Opera Society Scrapbooks, Newberry Library, Chicago.

19. For reviews of Freer's works, see Glen Dillard Gunn, 'Legend of Piper' Enchants Throng at Enchanted Isle," *Chicago Herald and Examiner,* July 20, 1933; and Cecil Smith, "Opera's in English," unidentified newspaper clipping, 1938, both in American Opera Society Scrapbooks, Newberry Library, Chicago.

20. Freer's manuscripts and the published piano-vocal scores of her operas are in the Performing Arts Division of the Library of Congress. She discusses her operas in *Recollections and Reflections of an American Composer* (Chicago, 1929).

21. Leslie Petteys, *"Cabildo* by Amy Marcy Beach," *Opera Journal* 22 (March 1989): 17–18. For more on Amy Beach, see Adrienne Fried Block, *Amy Beach, Passionate Victorian* (New York: Oxford University Press, 1998).

22. Douglas Moore, *The Devil and Daniel Webster,* libretto accompanying recording by the Festival Choir and Orchestra conducted by Armando Aliberti (PHCD 103 stereo, 1988). The cast includes Joe Blankenship, bass; Lawrence Winters, baritone; Doris Young, soprano; and Frederick Weidner, tenor.

23. Undated review in "The Medium" clipping file, Research Division, New York Public Library for the Performing Arts at Lincoln Center. Cocteau is quoted in John Gruen, *Menotti: A Biography* (New York: Macmillan, 1978), 72; see also Winthrop Sargeant, "American Opera on Broadway" in "The Medium" clipping file.

24. In 1959 the New York City Opera staged *The Medium* with Norman Dello Joio's award-winning *The Triumph of St. Joan,* a revision of his earlier *Triumph of Rouen* pro-

duced in 1956 on NBC television. In 1950 *The Medium* was made into a motion picture filmed in Rome at Scalera Studios, with Marie Powers and Anna-Maria Alberghetti. The film version is available on videocassette (VAI-OP-4 [1984]) and conducted by Thomas Schippers.

25. Quoted in Ardoin, *Stages of Menotti,* 41.

26. Gian Carlo Menotti, *The Medium* (New York: G. Schirmer, 1947), libretto and piano-vocal score.

27. Quoted in Gruen, *Menotti,* 79–80.

Chapter 13: The New American Verismo

1. Donald Jay Grout, *A Short History of Opera,* 3d ed. (New York: Columbia University Press, 1988), 510.

2. Unidentified article from the *New York Times,* July 12, 1998, clipping files, Research Division, New York Public Library for the Performing Arts at Lincoln Center.

3. Gary A. Richardson, *American Drama from the Colonial Period through World War I: A Critical History* (New York: Twayne Publishers, 1993), 171.

4. Oscar G. Brockett and Robert Findlay, *Century of Innovation: A History of European and American Theatre and Drama since the Late Nineteenth Century* (Boston: Allyn and Bacon, 1991), 300.

5. Quoted in Linda Whitesitt, ed., *The Life and Music of George Antheil, 1900–1959* (Ann Arbor: UMI Research Press, 1983), 184; see also Howard Klein, "The Man Who Composed 'Citizen Kane,'" *New York Times,* June 27, 1971.

6. Clifford McCarty, ed., *Film Music I* (New York: Garland Publishing, 1989), 89.

7. Quoted in Steven C. Smith, *A Heart at Fire's Center: The Life and Music of Bernard Herrmann* (Berkeley: University of California Press, 1991), 122.

8. Quoted in John Ardoin, *The Stages of Menotti* (New York: Doubleday, 1985), 10.

9. Gian Carlo Menotti, *The Consul,* libretto, 4, 8, from the Decca recording (Decca LP DX-101 [1950]), conducted by Lehman Engel, with Patricia Neway, Marie Powers, Cornell MacNeil, and others of original cast. See also Menotti, *The Consul: Musical Drama in Three Acts* (New York: G. Schirmer, 1950), 44–53, 198–211. A CD from the Spoleto Festival is also available.

10. Viennese critics thought the production was "strictly American" even though it demonstrated the "spirit of Prokofiev, Puccini's caresses and Mascagni's grandiose climaxes." Staging in Vienna included barbed wire surrounding the stage and interlude visions of marching soldiers and a firing squad. See "Vienna," unidentified newspaper clipping, 1951, in "The Consul" clipping file, Research Division, New York Public Library for the Performing Arts at Lincoln Center.

11. Jack Gould, "TV: 'The Consul' for Cash Customers," *New York Times,* March 17, 1961.

12. Olin Downes, "Opera: *The Saint of Bleecker Street,*" *New York Times,* Dec. 28, 1954; Ardoin, *Stages of Menotti,* 71.

13. Gian Carlo Menotti, *The Saint of Bleecker Street* (New York: G. Schirmer, 1955), libretto. See also RCA Victor LM 6032 (1955), conducted by Thomas Schippers, with Gabrielle Ruggiero, David Poleri, and Gloria Lane.

14. Walter Kerr in the *New York Herald-Tribune,* Nov. 6, 1958; Donald Mintz in the *New York Times,* Jan. 25, 1965.

15. Quoted in Gerald Boardman, *The Concise Oxford Companion to American Theatre* (New York: Oxford University Press, 1987), 396.

16. See Howard Barnes, "The Theater: Broadway's Bull Market in Musicals," *New York Herald-Tribune,* Nov. 9, 1947; Douglas Watt, "An Opera with Champion Form Hits Comeback Trail," *New York Daily News,* July 26, 1949; John Gruen, "Street Scene— Fish, Fowl, Cobwebs," *New York Herald-Tribune,* Feb. 25, 1966.

17. Kurt Weill, *Street Scene,* libretto, 9–30 (London CD 433 371–2 [1991]), with the Scottish Opera Orchestra and Chorus conducted by John Mauceri, with Josephine Barstow as Anna Maurrant, Samuel Ramey as Frank, and Angelina Reaux as Rose,

18. Quoted in Andrew Porter, "Musical Events," *The New Yorker,* Oct. 24, 1977, 162. In his notes, Porter quotes Blitzstein on the 1959 Santa Fe production of *Regina.*

19. Eric Gordon, "The Roots of *Regina,*" *Performing Arts: The Houston Music, Dance and Theater Magazine* 3 (April 1980): 2.

20. From the liner notes of a recording following the 1958 production, quoted in Leon Maurice Aufdemberge, "An Analysis of the Dramatic Construction of American Operas on American Themes," Ph.D. diss., Northwestern University, 1965, 254.

21. Quoted in Porter, "Musical Events, 162.

22. Marc Blitzstein, *Regina,* libretto, 76 (London CD 433 812–2 [1992]), with the Scottish Opera Orchestra and Chorus conducted by John Mauceri, with Katherine Ciesinski, Samuel Ramey, and Sheri Greenawald. Based on manuscripts at the State Historical Society of Wisconsin, John Mauceri's recording of *Regina* restored many of the composer's original intentions. The original cast included Jane Pickens, William Warfield, and William Wilderman, with Brenda Lewis (who would later sing the role of Regina).

23. Gordon, "The Roots of *Regina,*" 3.

24. According to a libretto supplied courtesy of the Portland Opera, its production cut nearly forty-five minutes of the score, compressing the four acts into three. Doing so appears to have altered dramatic pacing in spots. Herrmann also wrote *A Child Is Born* (1955), a half-hour television opera for CBS based on the Christmas story. Like *Wuthering Heights,* it is continuously scored and uses orchestral color for imagery and dramatic effect.

25. See also Howard Klein, "The Man Who Composed 'Citizen Kane,'" *New York Times,* June 27, 1971.

26. Steven C. Smith, *A Heart at Fire's Center: The Life and Music of Bernard Herrmann* (Berkeley: University of California Press, 1991), 107. One melody that Herrmann created for the film returns as Cathy's dramatic aria, "Oh—I'm Burning," in act 3 of his opera.

27. Bernard Herrmann, Wuthering Heights: *Opera in Four Acts,* libretto, 34, 26 (UKCD/2050 [1966, reissued 1972]), with the Pro Arte Orchestra conducted by the composer, with Morag Beaton, soprano; Donald Bell, baritone; Joseph Ward, tenor; and Pamela Bowden, mezzo-soprano. Herrmann underwrote the recording himself using British singers and orchestra.

28. Peter Miles, *Wuthering Heights,* Critics Debate Series (New York: Macmillan, 1990), 45.

29. Herrmann, *Wuthering Heights,* libretto, 25.

30. Bernard Herrmann, "The Music of Wuthering Heights," jacket notes with libretto and recording, 9.

31. Emily Brontë, *Wuthering Heights* (New York: Macmillan, 1963), 37.

32. Herrmann, *Wuthering Heights,* libretto, 20.

Chapter 14: New York City Opera's "American Plan"

1. Martin L. Sokol, *The New York City Opera: An American Adventure* (New York: Macmillan, 1981), 11.

2. Beverly Sills, quoted in Cori Ellison, comp., "Of Thee We Sing," *New York City Opera, Fiftieth Anniversary: 1943–1993, Stagebill* (New York: B and B Enterprises, 1993), 54.

3. Sokol, *New York City Opera,* 162. See also Martin Bernheimer, "Altmeister," *Opera News,* March 2, 1996, 17–19, which is an interview with Julius Rudel.

4. Sokol, *New York City Opera,* 154–65; Wriston Locklair, "American Opera Comes of Age," *Playbill,* March 31, 1958, 22.

5. For more on the New York City Opera's repertoire, see *New York City Opera, Fiftieth Anniversary,* 48–49.

6. Aaron Copland, The Tender Land: *Opera in Three Acts; Libretto by Horace Everett* (New York: Boosey and Hawkes, 1956), 194.

7. Aaron Copland and Vivian Perlis, *Copland since 1943* (New York: St. Martin's Press, 1989), 211–15 passim.

8. Will Crutchfield, "Opera: Copland's 'Tender Land,'" *New York Times,* May 3, 1987.

9. New York City Opera Guild Archives Committee, *New York City Opera Sings: Stories and Productions of the New York City Opera, 1944–79,* ed. Harold J. McKenna (New York: Richards Rosen Press, 1981), 342.

10. Douglas Moore, "How the 'Ballad of Baby Doe' Was Written," notes with long-playing recording *The Ballad of Baby Doe* (Deutsche Grammophon 2709-061), with the New York City Opera Orchestra and Chorus conducted by Emerson Buckley, with Beverly Sills, Walter Cassel, and Frances Bible.

11. Olin Chism, "The Ballad of Baby Doe," *Dallas Civic Opera Magazine* 1, no. 4 (1978): 29–31. Not all events in the life of Baby Doe Tabor can be authenticated. See also R. L. Blooding, "Douglas Moore's 'The Ballad of Baby Doe': An Investigation of Its Historical Accuracy and the Feasibility of a Historical Production in the Tabor Opera House," Ph.D. diss., Ohio State University, 1979.

12. John Latouche, "About the *Ballad of Baby Doe,*" *Theatre Arts,* July 1956, 83.

13. Douglas Moore, *The Ballad of Baby Doe* (Deutsche Grammophon 2709-061), libretto, 7; see also *The Ballad of Baby Doe,* original 1959 recording reissued by Polydor on CD in 1998, with Beverly Sills, Frances Bible, and Walter Cassel.

14. Douglas Moore, *The Ballad of Baby Doe; Libretto by John Latouche* (New York: Chappell Music, 1956), piano–vocal score, 218–50. The work was commissioned in honor of the Columbia University Bicentennial by the Koussevitzky Foundation of

the Library of Congress and dedicated to the memory of Serge and Natalie Koussevitsky.

15. Douglas Watt, "'Crucible' Flames as an Opera," *New York Times,* Oct. 27, 1961; Winthrop Sargeant quoted in Andrew H. Drummond, *American Opera Librettos* (Metuchen: Scarecrow Press, 1973), 114.

16. Harold Schonberg, "Opera: Robert Ward's 'The Crucible,'" *New York Times,* Oct. 27, 1961.

17. Robert Ward, The Crucible: *An Opera in Four Acts; Libretto by Bernard Stambler* (CRI 168 [1961]), libretto, the New York City Opera Orchestra and Chorus conducted by Emerson Buckley, with Patricia Brooks, Chester Ludgin, and John McCurdy. See also Ward, *The Crucible* (New York: Highgate Press, 1962), piano-vocal score, 162–67. The score is in English and German; *The Crucible* is translated as "Die Hexenjagd" (the witch hunt).

18. *Time,* November 3, 1961, in "Robert Ward" clipping file, Research Division, New York Public Library for the Performing Arts at Lincoln Center.

19. Author telehpone interview with Robert Ward, July 17, 1996.

20. Ibid.

21. Sokol, *New York City Opera,* 135.

22. Reviews from *New York Journal American, The New Yorker,* and *New York World Telegram and Sun,* respectively, quoted in *Susannah* promotional brochure (Boosey and Hawkes, n.d.) in *"Susannah"* clipping file, Research Division, New York Public Library for the Performing Arts at Lincoln Center.

23. Nick Kimberly, "Floyd and His *Susannah,*" *Opera* (Aug. 1994): 911.

24. Andrew Stiller, "Floyd, Carlisle," in *The New Grove Dictionary of Opera,* ed. Stanley Sadie (New York: Grove's Dictionaries of Music, 1992), 3:247.

25. Carlisle Floyd, "Recalling *Susannah's* Beginnings," in libretto and notes for *Susannah: A Musical Drama in Two Acts* (Virgin Classics 5 45039 2 [1994]), Lyon Opera Orchestra with Cheryl Studer and Samuel Ramy.

26. Carlisle Floyd, *Susannah: A Musical Drama in Two Acts* (New York: Boosey and Hawkes, 1956), 130.

27. Floyd, *Susannah,* act 1, scene 1, 4; act 1, scene 2, 29: act 2, scene 4, 105.

28. "Carlisle Floyd, Biographical Notes," in "Boosey and Hawkes News," publicity department typescript, 4–5, May 1956.

29. Carlisle Floyd, "On the Librettist's Art," *American Music Teacher* 16 (April–May 1967): 36.

30. Floyd, "On the Librettist's Art," 37; see also Carlisle Floyd, "Playwriting in the Opera House," *Theatre Arts* 42 (Jan. 1958): 32–33.

31. Floyd is quoted in Andrew Porter, "Musical Events," *The New Yorker,* Feb. 4, 1991, 78.

Chapter 15: Dreamers of Decadence

1. Gunther Schuller, "Concerning My Opera, *The Visitation,*" in *Musings: The Musical Worlds of Gunther Schuller* (New York: Oxford University Press, 1986), 228.

2. Emily Coleman, "Samuel Barber and *Vanessa*," quoted in Barbara B. Heyman, *Samuel Barber: The Composer and His Music* (New York: Oxford University Press, 1992), 377.

3. Coleman, "Samuel Barber," 379.

4. Preface to Gian Carlo Menotti, Vanessa: *Opera in Three Acts; Music by Samuel Barber* (New York: G. Schirmer, 1964), vocal score, iv.

5. Frank Merkling, "Two Worlds," *Opera News,* Jan. 27, 1958, 9.

6. Samuel Barber, *Vanessa,* with the original Metropolitan Opera cast, including Eleanor Steber, Nicolai Gedda, Giorgio Tozzi, Regina Resnik, and Rosalind Elias, conducted by Dimitri Mitropoulos. The CD (7899–2–RG) is a reissue of the original RCA recording of 1958, four-act edition, libretto, 24, 29, 33–34, 86.

7. Paul Henry Lang, "New American Opera Is Hailed at the Met," *New York Herald-Tribune,* Jan. 16, 1958.

8. Harold C. Schonberg, "Onstage, It was 'Antony and Cleopatra,'" *New York Times,* Sept. 17, 1966.

9. Leontyne Price, interview with Peter Dickinson for "Samuel Barber Retrospective," BBC broadcast, Jan. 23, 1982, quoted in Heyman, *Samuel Barber,* 446.

10. Schonberg, "Onstage."

11. John Gruen, "And Where Has Samuel Barber Been . . . ?" *New York Times,* Oct. 3, 1971.

12. Jon Solomon, "The Spectacle of Samuel Barber's *Antony and Cleopatra,*" in *Opera and the Golden West: The Past, Present and Future of Opera in the U.S.A.,* ed. John L. DiGaetani and Josef P. Sirefman (Rutherford: Fairleigh Dickinson University Press, 1994), 253.

13. Like Britten's *Midsummer Night's Dream* and Giannini's *Taming of the Shrew,* Barber and Zeffirelli used only Shakespeare's words in the opera. In doing so they departed from Verdi, whose *Otello* and *Falstaff* are adapted translations. They also reduced Shakespeare's original five acts and forty-one scenes to three acts and sixteen scenes.

14. Richard Dyer, "Barber's *Antony and Cleopatra,*" *Antony and Cleopatra,* notes accompanying the libretto. Recorded live (New World Records NW 322/323/324) at the Festival of Two Worlds, Spoleto, Italy, 1983, conducted by Christian Badea, with Esther Hinds and Jeffrey Wells.

15. In two stanzas, the text of the duet is taken from Beaumont and Fletcher's *The Bloody Brother.*

16. Wynne Delacoma, "Lyric Whittles 'Cleopatra' into Slim, Sexy Style," *Chicago Sun-Times,* Sept. 27, 1991. In the *New York Times,* Sept. 29, 1991, Edward Rothstein asked why the audience should care about characters that Barber had made "thoroughly unlikable."

17. See also Ned Rorem, "A Note on Barber's *Antony and Cleopatra,*" in *Settling the Score: Essays on Music* (New York: Harcourt Brace Jovanovich, 1988), 50.

18. "Ripples Instead of Waves," *Time,* March 31, 1967, 74.

19. "Act of Opera Based on 'Electra' of O'Neill Is Given a Reading," *New York Times,* Jan. 13, 1964.

20. Paul Hume, "'Electra' Becomes the Met . . . Hits Magnificient Height," *Washington Post,* March 26, 1967; Harriet Johnson, "World Premiere of Levy's 'Electra,'" *New York Post,* March 18, 1967; Alfred Frankenstein, "Levy's 'Electra'—Tremendous Opera," *San Francisco Chronicle,* March 22, 1967.

21. Donal Henahan, "Levy's *Electra* Offered at Met," *New York Times,* Dec. 1, 1967; Harold C. Schonberg, "Opera: 'Mourning Becomes Electra,'" *New York Times,* March 18, 1967.

22. Schonberg, "Opera"; see also Miles Kastendieck, "New American Opera, 'Electra' Sparks," *World Journal Tribune,* March 18, 1967; and Hume, "'Electra.'"

23. Marvin David Levy, *Mourning Becomes Elektra,* Metropolitan Opera Broadcast, April 1, 1967, WQXR-FM, tape 201 in Rodgers and Hammerstein Archives, New York Public Library for the Performing Arts at Lincoln Center. See also Lyric Opera of Chicago, *Stagebill,* 1998–99 season.

24. S. Tschudi Madsen, *Art Nouveau* (New York: World University Library, 1967), 37.

25. Evert Sprinchorn, trans., *Selected Plays: August Strindberg* (Minneapolis: University of Minnesota Press, 1986), xii. See also Catherine Clément, *Opera; or, The Undoing of Women,* trans. Betsy Wing (Minneapolis: University of Minnesota Press, 1988).

26. Harry G. Carlson, *Strindberg and the Poetry of Myth* (Berkeley: University of California Press, 1982), 64.

27. Andrew Porter, "Musical Events," *The New Yorker,* July 16, 1990, 78.

28. Hugo Weisgall, Six Characters in Search of an Author: *Opera in Three Acts; Libretto by Denis Johnston* (New World Records NW 80454-2 [1994]), libretto. Lyric Opera Center for American Artists, Chicago, conducted by Lee Schaenen, with Robert Orth, Elizabeth Byrne, Kevin Anderson, and Elizabeth Futral.

29. Ranate Matthaei, *Luigi Pirandello,* trans. Simon Young and Erika Young (New York: Frederick Ungar, 1973), 22.

30. Weisgall, *Six Characters in Search of an Author,* libretto, 49.

31. Howard Taubman, "Opera: Kurka's 'Schweik,'" *New York Times,* April 24, 1958; see also Raymond Ericson, "Opera: 'The Good Soldier Schweik' in Minneapolis," *New York Times,* Feb. 12, 1966.

32. Ned Rorem, "Recalling *Miss Julie,*" *Miss Julie* (Newport Classic 48:52 and 39:14 [1994]), notes accompanying libretto. Revised version recorded live at the Manhattan School of Music Opera Theatre, conducted by David Gilbert, with Theodora Fried, Philip Torre, and Heather Sarris. The piano-vocal score (New York: Boosey and Hawkes, 1968) is the original New York City Opera edition.

33. Susan McClary, *Feminine Endings: Music, Gender, and Sexuality* (Minneapolis: University of Minnesota Press, 1991), ch. 4, 80–111.

34. Elaine Showalter, *The Female Malady: Women, Madness and English Culture 1830–1980* (New York: Pantheon, 1985), quoted in McClary, *Feminine Endings,* 84.

35. McClary, *Feminine Endings,* 110.

36. Jack Beeson, *Lizzie Borden: A Family Portrait in Three Acts* (CRI CD 694 [1979, 1982, 1995]), libretto, 32. New York City Opera Orchestra conducted by Anton Cop-

pola, with the original cast, Brenda Lewis, Ellen Faull, Herbert Beatty, Ann Elgar, Richard Fredricks, and Richard Krause.

37. Author interview with Jack Beeson, Glimmerglass Opera, Cooperstown, N.Y., July 7, 1996. Jenny Kallick has commented on the libretto's symbolic use of textual references that recur like leitmotifs. Flowers and leaves, for example, become distorted and surreal, and there are many references in the opera to keys, locks, and secrets. Symposium on *Lizzie Borden,* Amherst College, July 30–31, 1997.

38. Jack Beeson, panel discussion on *Lizzie Borden,* New York State Historical Society, July 7, 1996.

39. John Conklin, panel discussion on *Lizzie Borden.*

40. Rhoda Levine, panel discussion on *Lizzie Borden.*

41. Author interview with Sheri Greenawald, Glimmerglass Opera, Cooperstown, N.Y., July 7, 1996.

Chapter 16: Bold Turns on Familiar Paths

1. Leonard Bernstein, *Mass,* conducted by the composer and sung by Alan Titus (Columbia M231008), libretto; piano-vocal score published by Boosey and Hawkes (New York, 1971).

2. Harold Prince, *Candide,* jacket notes (New World Records NW340/341 [1982]). New York City Opera with Erie Mills, David Eisler, and John Lankston, conducted by John Mauceri; book adapted from Voltaire by Hugh Wheeler and lyrics by Richard Wilbur. The 1956 and 1989 versions have also been recorded by Sony, New World, and Deutsche Grammophon.

3. Quoted in Joanne Gordon, *Art Isn't Easy: The Achievement of Stephen Sondheim* (Carbondale: Southern Illinois University Press, 1990), 5.

4. For more on this subject, see Maria Verdino-Süllwold, "Opera, Operetta, or Musical? Vanishing Distinctions in Twentieth-Century Music Drama," *Opera Journal* 23 (Dec. 1990): 31–43; and Eric Salzman, "Notes for an American Musical Theater," in *Perspectives: Creating and Producing Contemporary Opera and Musical Theater* (Washington: Opera America, 1983), 7–18.

5. Theodore S. Chapin, *Candide,* jacket notes.

6. Stephen Banfield, *Sondheim's Broadway Musicals* (Ann Arbor: University of Michigan Press, 1993), 80.

7. Craig Zadan, *Sondheim & Co.* (New York: Harper and Row, 1986), 157.

8. Martin Gottfried, *Sondheim* (New York: Harry N. Abrams, 1993), 125.

9. Gottfried, *Sondheim,* 125.

10. Gordon, *Art Isn't Easy,* 253. The original production of *Sweeney Todd* was recorded for RCA in 1979 and is available on CD (3379–2).

11. Richard E. Rhoda, "Notes on the Composer and the Program," *Stagebill,* Nov. 1992; program notes for *A Water Bird Talk* and *Miss Havisham's Wedding Night* performed at Kennedy Center. Argento emphasizes that his music is lyrical and traditional and not especially dissonant. Author interview with Dominick Argento, Nov. 1992, Kennedy Center.

12. John Donahue, "Author's Notes," libretto accompanying *Postcard from Morocco* (CRI CD 614 [1972, 1992]), conducted by Philip Brunelle, with Sarita Roche, Barbara Brandt, Janis Hardy, and others from the original Minnesota Opera cast.

13. Dominick Argento, "Authors' Notes," libretto accompanying *Postcard from Morocco.*

14. Roger Pines, "Dominick Argento: Writing American Bel Canto," *Opera Monthly* 1 (Dec. 1988): 22.

15. Ellen Lampert-Graux, "Projections," *Opera News,* Jan. 8, 1994, 23–25.

16. Dominick Argento, The Dream of Valentino, *an Opera in Two Parts; Libretto by Charles Nolte* (Washington, D.C.: Washington Opera, 1993).

17. Quoted in Gary Schmidgall, "A Long Voyage," *Opera News* 50 (June 1986): 13.

18. For reviews, see "Lee Hoiby" clipping file, Research Division, New York Public Library for the Performing Arts at Lincoln Center.

19. Barbara Fischer-Williams, "'Summer and Smoke'—On the Wings of Music with Lee Hoiby," *City Center Arts* 2 (Winter 1971–72): 3.

20. Tony Thomas, *Music for the Movies* (New York: A. S. Barnes, 1973), 191.

21. Lee Hoiby, "Making Tennessee Williams Sing," *New York Times,* June 13, 1971.

22. The anatomy lesson scene has been recorded by New World Records (New World Records NW 80475–2); Belwin Mills (New York) published the libretto (1972) as well as the piano-vocal score (1976).

23. John Rockwell, in the *New York Times,* July 9, 1986; Thor Eckert, Jr., in the *Christian Science Monitor,* July 10, 1986.

24. Author telephone interview with Lee Hoiby and Mark Shulgasser, Nov. 3, 1996.

25. Ibid.

26. Ibid.

27. Quoted in Schmidgall, "A Long Voyage," 12.

28. Lee Hoiby, The Tempest: *Opera in Three Acts;* libretto adapted from the play of William Shakespeare by Mark Shulgasser; composer's piano-vocal manuscript courtesy of Lee Hoiby, 205–8.

29. Hubert Saal, "Chekhov from the Heart," *Newsweek,* March 18, 1974, 75.

30. Jack Beeson, "And What, If Not Who, Is Captain Jinks of the Horse Marines?" Preface to libretto, *Captain Jinks of the Horse Marines,* RCA Red Seal (ARL2–1727 Stereo [1976]). Kansas City Lyric Theater conducted by Russell Patterson.

31. Beeson, "And What, If Not Who?"

32. John Harbison, *Full Moon in March,* libretto with LP recording (CRI SD 454 [1983]). Boston Musica Viva conducted by Richard Pittman, with the original cast, D'Anna Fortunato, David Arnold, Cheryl Cobb, and Kim Scown.

33. Harbison, *Full Moon in March,* composer's notes with libretto (CRI SD 454).

34. Robert P. Morgan, "Cry of Clytaemnestra, The," in *The New Grove Dictionary of Opera,* ed. Stanley Sadie (New York: Grove's Dictionaries of Music, 1992), 1:1022.

35. John Eaton, *Danton and Robespierre* (CRI IUS 421 [1980]), notes, original Indiana University production conducted by Thomas Baldner.

36. Eaton, *Danton and Robespierre,* notes.

37. Roger Sessions, *Montezuma* (New York: E. B. Marks Music Corp., 1965), vocal score; tape recording from Robert Orchard Collection, Indiana University, Blooming-ton.

Chapter 17: Heroes for Our Time

1. Richard Wagner, "A Communication to My Friends," in *Richard Wagner's Prose Works,* trans. William Ashton Ellis (New York: Broude Brothers, 1966), 1:361, 1:366, 1:358.

2. Quoted in Tim Page, "Return Trip," *Opera News,* March 30, 1996, 9.

3. Robert T. Jones, "Philip Glass, Musician of the Year," *High Fidelity/Musical America* 35 (April 1985): MA9.

4. Philip Glass, *Music by Philip Glass,* ed. Robert T. Jones (New York: Harper and Row, 1987), 17. Glass devotes nearly a third of his book to the music and dramatic concepts of his trilogy *Einstein on the Beach, Satyagraha,* and *Akhnaten.*

5. Glass, *Music by Philip Glass,* 58, 59.

6. Tim Page, notes to libretto, Philip Glass and Robert Wilson, Einstein on the Beach: *Opera in Four Acts* (Elektra Nonesuch 79323–2 [1993]), the Philip Glass Ensemble conducted by Michael Riesman, with Patricia Schuman, Gregory Fulkerson, Lucin-da Childs, and Sheryl Sutton (CD based on the 1990 production and not shortened, as is the 1979 release). See also *Songs from the Trilogy* (CBS Records MK45580) and *"Einstein on the Beach:* Changing Images of Opera," PBS-TV, Jan. 1986.

7. Samuel M. Johnson, "Old Judge—All Men Are Equal," *Einstein on the Beach,* li-bretto; alternate speech from the 1984 revival of the opera.

8. Glass, *Music by Philip Glass,* 4.

9. Philip Glass, "Preface," *Akhnaten,* notes to libretto, 11–12 (CBS Records 42457), the Stuttgart State Opera Orchestra and Chorus conducted by Dennis Russell Davis, with Paul Esswood and Milagro Vargas.

10. *Satyagraha* has been recorded on CD by Sony Masterworks (M3K39672), con-ducted by Christopher Keene and performed by the New York City Opera Chorus and Orchestra (1985).

11. Glass, *Music by Philip Glass,* 138.

12. Ibid., 172.

13. Quoted in Page, "Return Trip," 9.

14. Ibid.; see also Anthony Tommasini, "Notes on *The Voyage,*" Metropolitan Opera *Stagebill,* April 1996 (n.p.).

15. Philip Glass, *The Voyage,* synopsis from the libretto (New York: Dunvagen Mu-sic Publishers for the Metropolitan Opera Guild, 1992), 5.

16. Glass, *The Voyage,* libretto, 25.

17. Michael Walsh, "Stagecraft as Soulcraft," *Time,* Nov. 9, 1987, 110.

18. Walsh, "Stagecraft as Soulcraft."

19. Quoted in Andrew Porter, "Nixon in Houston," *The New Yorker,* Nov. 30, 1987, 128.

20. Walsh, "Stagecraft as Soulcraft."

21. Joan Acocella, "A Hero for Our Time?" *Art in America* 76 (April 1988): 53.

22. Goodman's text quoted in Porter, "Nixon in Houston," 128.

23. Nancy Malitz, "John Adams' Revolutionary New Opera, *Nixon in China,*" *Opera News* 52 (Oct. 1987): 18.

24. Malitz, "John Adams' Revolutionary New Opera."

25. For the Elektra Nonesuch recording of the opera (79177 [1978]) conducted by Edo de Waart, James Maddalena as Nixon and Sanford Sylvan as Chou En-lai give particularly moving performances, as they did in the original Houston production.

26. John Adams, *The Death of Klinghoffer* (Elektra Nonesuch 7559–79281–2 [1992]), with the Orchestra of the Opera de Lyon conducted by Kent Nagano, several members of the original *Nixon in China* cast, and the London Opera Chorus. Piano-vocal score published by Boosey and Hawkes (New York, 1991).

27. Adams, *The Death of Klinghoffer,* notes to libretto, 12.

28. David Littlejohn, "Onstage: The United Colors of Los Angeles," *Wall Street Journal,* May 25, 1995.

29. Anthony Davis, *X (The Life and Times of Malcom X),* notes to the libretto by Francis Davis (Gramavision, 1992), conducted by William Henry Curry, with Eugene Perry, Thomas Young, and Priscilla Baskerville.

30. Quoted in K. Robert Schwarz, "A Composer between Two Worlds," *New York Times,* June 7, 1992.

31. *Amistad* was given its world premiere by the Lyric Opera of Chicago on November 29, 1997.

32. Schwarz, "Composer between Two Worlds," 30; see also Donald Henahan, "Anthony Davis's 'X (The Life and Times of Malcolm X),'" *New York Times,* Sept. 29, 1986.

33. A holograph copy (G. Schirmer, 1987) of the final version as staged by the New York City Opera of Davis's, *X (The Life and Times of Malcom X)* is in the Performing Arts Division of the Library of Congress.

34. Davis, *X (The Life and Times of Malcolm X),* libretto with Gramavision recording, 7.

35. Quoted in Kip Cranna, "Harvey Milk: From Man to Myth to Opera," *San Francisco Opera Magazine* 74 (1996–97): 28. *Harvey Milk* has been recorded on CD by Teldec (0630–15852–2), conducted by David Runnicles.

36. Michael Walsh, "Moses in San Francisco," *Time,* Feb. 13, 1995, 79. Leonard Bernstein included the gay character, Junior, in his opera *A Quiet Place* (1983). See David J. Baker, "Song at Twilight," *Opera News* 65 (July 2000): 32–36, 70.

37. Quoted in Schwarz, "Composer between Two Worlds."

38. Mark Adamo, "A Brave and Brilliant 'Harvey Milk,'" *Washington Post,* Jan. 23, 1995.

Chapter 18: Toward the New Millennium and Beyond

1. John Duffy's comments in James R. Oestreich, "A Persistent Voyager Lands at the Met," *New York Times,* Oct. 15, 1992.

2. See Alan Rich, *An American Voice: Houston's Grand Opera Celebrates Twenty-five World Premieres* (Houston: Houston Grand Opera, 2000).

3. Author interview with John von Rhein, Chicago, July 15, 1994.

4. Quoted in Brian Kellow, "Double Recipe," *Opera News* 56 (Sept. 1991): 24.

5. Edith Borroff, *American Operas: A Checklist* (Warren, Mich.: Harmonie Park Press, 1992).

6. Marjorie Mackay Shapiro, "Talma, Louise," in *The New Grove Dictionary of Opera*, ed. Stanley Sadie (New York: Grove's Dictionaries of Music, 1992), 4:639. See also Sophie Fuller, *The Pandora Guide to Women Composers* (San Francisco: Harper Collins, 1994), 300–303; and Sophie Fuller, *Women Composers, Conductors, and Musicians of the Twentieth Century,* (Metuchen: Scarecrow Press, 1980), 1:226–40.

7. Meredith Monk, *"Atlas:* An Opera in Three Parts," *Encore* 1 (Sept. 1996): 8. See also Patrick Stearns, *"Atlas* Shows Monk's Way to Mainstream Opera Success," *USA Today,* Feb. 25, 1991; and William Albright, "In Review: From around the World," *Opera News* 55 (June 1991): 47.

8. George Heymont, "Minnesota Opera's 'Frankenstein': Breaking New Ground," [San Francisco] *Bay Area Reporter,* July 12, 1990; see also Nancy Malitz, "Song of the Monster," *Opera News* 54 (May 1990): 44–45.

9. Author telephone interview with Libby Larsen, Oct. 21, 1996.

10. Ibid. In the composer's videotape of the production (courtesy of Libby Larsen), Steven Tharp sang the role of Dr. Victor Frankenstein; Elizabeth Comeaux, Elisabeth; and Christian Swenson, the monster.

11. Ibid.

12. Ibid.

13. Gary Schmidgall, "In Review: From around the World (New York City)," *Opera News* 50 (Oct. 1985): 54; Opera Ebony possesses a videocassette recording of the opera. *Frederick Douglass* is in three acts, eight scenes with a ballet and chorus.

14. Vivian Perlis, in an interview with Thea Musgrave, May 12, 1983, Santa Barbara, Calif., Yale Oral History Project, tape C, transcript, 56–57. Musgrave's operas have been published by Novello, Chester Music Limited, and G. Schirmer.

15. Georgia A. Ryder, "Thea Musgrave and the Production of Her Opera *Harriet, the Woman Called Moses,"* in "An Interview with the Composer" in *New Perspectives on Music: Essays in Honor of Eileen Southern,* ed. Josephine Wright with Samuel A. Floyd, Jr. (Warren, Mich.: Harmonie Park Press, 1992), 467, 470. See also Andrew Porter, "There Is a River," *The New Yorker,* March 25, 1985, 99–103.

16. Stephen Paulus, "Creating Opera: The Composer as Collaborator," in *Perspectives: Creating and Producing Contemporary Opera and Musical Theatre* (Washington, D. C.: Opera America, 1984), 35.

17. Libby Larsen, with Suzanne Cusik and Elizabeth Wood, "Round Table: The Compositional Voice," presented at a symposium on "Representations of Gender and Sexuality in Opera," State University of New York, Sept. 14–17, 1995.

18. K. Robert Schwarz, "'The Cave' Walks, but Doesn't Quack, Like an Opera," *New York Times,* Oct. 10, 1993.

19. John Durka, "'Willie Stark'—From Opera House to Home Screen," *New York Times,* Sept. 27, 1981.

20. Michael Walsh, "The Mating Game," *Time,* Sept. 26, 1994, 74.

21. John Woodford, "His Night at the Opera," *Michigan Today* 24 (Dec. 1992): 1, 2.

22. Quoted in Gary Schmidgall, "Some Observations on the Libretto," *Perspectives: Creating and Producing Contemporary Opera and Musical Theater* (Washington, D.C.: Opera America, 1984), 73.

23. Robert Sandla, "Terra Nova: *The Mother of Three Sons* Due at New York City Opera This Month," *Opera News* 56 (Oct. 1991): 33.

24. Mark Swed, "In Review: From around The World (New York City)," *Opera News,* Dec. 25, 1993, 34.

25. Mark Swed, "Six Strange Years," *Opera News* 59 (June 1995): 19.

26. *Emmeline* was telecast by PBS-TV and has been recorded by Albany Records (CD 284/5 [1998]), with Patricia Racette, Anne Marie Owens, and Michelle Bradley in the Santa Fe Opera production.

27. Andy Kirkaldy, "Composer Finds His Inspiration in Addison," *Addison Independent,* June 24, 1996.

28. The quotations are from among more than twenty reviews excerpted in *Opera News* 57 (Sept. 1992): 47. The opera was telecast on September 14, 1992, and is available on videocassette (Deutsche Grammophon). It was also staged by Lyric Opera of Chicago and again at the Metropolitan during the 1994–95 season.

29. William M. Hoffman, "Production Notes," *The Ghosts of Versailles* (New York: G. Schirmer, 1991), libretto, v.

30. Otis Stuart et al., "First Nighters: Sounding Out the Principal Players in *The Ghosts of Versailles,*" *Opera News,* Jan. 4, 1992, 30–31.

31. Hoffman, *The Ghosts of Versailles,* libretto, 81.

Index

Academy of Music (New York City), 79–80, 88, 133

Academy of Music (Philadelphia), 85, 95, 133

Adamo, Mark, 358

Adams, John, 337, 346–51, 352–53, 358, 362; *The Death of Klinghoffer,* 335, 349–51, 355; *Nixon in China,* 335, 346–49, 388

Adventures of Harlequin and Scaramouch, The, 21–22, 59

Aethiop, The; or, The Child of the Desert (Rayner Taylor), 40–41, 42, 60, 66–68, 73, 77, 385, 403n13

African Americans, 184–205; all-black companies, 184, 186, 197–98, 217–18, 367–68; as composers of opera, 110, 111, 184, 185–205, 335, 352–56, 367–68, 386, 387; *The Emperor Jones,* 4, 166, 174, 177, 179–82, 184, 195, 196, 198, 207, 234; Haiti and, 197–204, 419n32; Harlem Renaissance, 184–85, 187, 206; as librettists, 199, 200; music styles, 114, 158, 182, 184, 188, 190, 194, 196, 223, 267; New Day Pilgrims, 196–97; as performers, 111, 185, 187, 188, 194, 197–98, 200, 207, 217–19; *Porgy and Bess,* 4, 193, 206–14, 223, 225, 231, 254, 262, 277, 286, 360, 361, 387; *Run, Little Chillun,* 196–97, 207; *Treemonisha,* 5, 189–95, 386; *Voodoo,* 184, 187–88, 191, 207, 387; voodoo mythology, 184, 187–88, 191, 195–97, 419n30

afterpiece, 12, 59

Agee, James, 275, 293

agitprop, 229–30

Ahmed al Kamel (Charles Edward Horne), 91

Aida (Giuseppe Verdi), 132, 359

Aiken, George: *Uncle Tom's Cabin,* 94–95

Akhnaten (Philip Glass), 336, 340, 341, 342

Alboni, Marietta, 88

Alden, Christopher, 356

Aldrich, Richard, 124

Alexander, John, 296–97

Alfred (William Smith), 1, 3, 25, 26–29, 33–34, 35, 44, 385

Alfred the Great, 26–29

Alglala (Francesco de Leone), 141, 146

Alice M. Ditson Fund, 222

Allan, Lewis, 309

Allen, Paul, 162, 387

Althouse, Paul, 166

Altman, Robert, 370

Alvin Theatre (New York City), 213, 387

Amahl and the Night Visitors (Gian Carlo Menotti), 236–37, 238–40, 241–42, 248, 277, 387

America Independent (Francis Hopkinson), 44

American Chamber Opera Company of New York, 361, 378

American Company, 24

American Composers Forum, 366

American Guild of Organists, 89

Americania and Elutheria; or, A New Tale of the Genii, 44

American Indians. *See* Native American motifs

American Institute of Arts and Letters, 363

American Lyric Theater (New York City), 246

American Maid, The (John Philip Sousa), 5, 105, 386

American opera: audience for, 7; British influence on, 11–22; for children, 101, 112, 179, 236–37, 238–40, 331–32, 387; crossover of styles in, 12; as democratic music form, 7; diversity of, 2, 7, 12, 43–44; as elitist, 7; European opera versus, 1, 2, 11, 12, 78–80, 87–91; motion picture influence on, 4–6; nature of, 3; oeratic melodrama, *see* operatic melodrama; origins of, 1–2; realism of, *see* American verismo; romanticism of, *see* American Romanticism; spread across nation, 2; staged in Europe, 162, 177; television influence on, 6; unique qualities of, 2; Wagner craze and, 121–38

American Opera Society of Chicago, 243

American Philosophical Society, 25

American Repertory Theater, 342

American Romanticism, 3, 35, 43–44; comedy and, 102–8; opera in, 66–68; Yankee roles and characterization, 68–72

American Society of Composers, Authors and Publishers (ASCAP), 171

American verismo, 253–71; composers influenced by, 2, 147–51; early waves of, 147–51; in light opera, 102–5; motion pictures and, 5–6; nature of, 2–3

American Women (Willard and Livermore), 109

American Women Composers (AWC), 363

Amistad (Anthony Davis), 353

Amram, David, 329

Anderson, Hans Christian, 112

Anderson, John, 261

Anderson, Laurie, 364

Anderson, Marian, 198

Antheil, George, 5, 119, 215, 226–28, 243, 255, 361, 387

Anthony, Susan Brownwell, 108, 217, 220–22

Antony and Cleopatra (Samuel Barber), 291, 292, 293, 298–300, 334, 388

Apotheosis of Franklin; or, His Reception in the Elysian Fields, 44

Appalachian Spring (Aaron Copland), 275

Archers, The (Benjamin Carr/William Dunlap), 40, 51

Arditi, Luigi: *La Spia,* 88

Argento, Dominick, 6, 170, 271, 273, 321–25, 326, 329, 362; *The Aspern Papers,* 324, 334, 388; *The Dream of Valentino,* 280–81, 324–25, 334, 335; *Postcard from Morocco,* 321–23, 388; *The Voyage of Edgar Allan Poe,* 323–24, 334

Ariadne Abandoned by Theseus in the Isle of Naxos (Victor Pelissier), 41

Aristophanes, 130

Arne, Thomas, 24, 32, 44, 62; libretto for *Alfred,* 26–29; *Love in a Village,* 23

Arnold, Samuel, 40

Arthur, Chester, 280

Arthur and Emmeline; or, The Prospect of Columbia's Future Glory, 58

art nouveau, 132–33, 306

Arvey, Verna, 200

Asakura, Setsu, 329

Ashton, Frederick, 218

Aspern Papers, The (Dominick Argento), 324, 334, 388

Astor Place Opera House (New York City), 79

Atlas (Meredith Monk), 364

atonality, 362

AT&T, 359

Attwood, Thomas, 24

Auber, Daniel François Esprit, 60, 80, 81, 85

Auden, W. H., 221

Audin, Monsieur, 44

Auditorium Theater (Chicago), 126–27

Aurelia the Vestal (William Henry Fry), 83

Avignon Festival, 341

awards and prizes: American Academy of Arts and Letters, 367; Benjamin Award, 197; David Bispham Memorial Medal for American Opera, 165, 197, 224, 243; Guggenheim Fellowship, 287; Harmon Award, 198; Naumberg Award, 198; New York Drama Critics' Circle Award, 235, 258–59, 260, 319; New York Music Critics' Circle Award, 260, 285–86, 287; Pulitzer Prize, 172, 189–90, 207, 258–59, 260, 261, 271, 285–86, 293, 321, 360, 370, 373, 388, 389; Tony Award, 319; Vernon Rice Award, 326; Waite Award, 363

Azara (John Knowles Paine), 130–32, 135

Bach, Johann Sebastian, 339, 349, 351

Bacon, Ernst, 243

Balfe, William, 87–88

Ballad of Baby Doe (Douglas Moore), 245–46, 274, 277–83, 313, 368, 387–88

ballad opera, 43; audience behavior during, 29; *The Beggar's Opera,* 12, 13, 14, 16, 30; defined, 12; evolution into pastiche, 23; *The Fashionable Lady,* 3–4, 11, 13–22, 32–33, 59, 308, 385; first recorded performance of, 13; *Flora; or, Hob in the Well* (Colley Cibber/John Hippesley), 13, 21; harlequinade (English pantomime) in, 14–16, 18, 20–22, 59; main centers for, 12–13; masque compared with, 26; popularity of, 14

ballet, 43

ballet d'action, 58

ballet-pantomime, 60, 61–62

Balthrop, Carmen, 194

Bankhead, Tallulah, 267

Barber, Samuel, 313, 329, 362; *Antony and*

Cleopatra, 291, 292, 293, 298–300, 334, 388; *Vanessa,* 5, 291, 292, 293–97, 304, 388

Il barbiere di Siviglia (Gioacchino Rossini), 78–79, 89, 379, 380

Barker, James Nelson: *The Indian Princess,* 40, 42, 43, 46, 60, 61, 62–65, 66, 67, 73, 76, 385

Baroque opera, 19–20

Barras, Charles M.: *The Black Crook,* 100

Barre, Isaac, 33

Barrymore brothers, 175

Barton, Andrew (pseudonym), 29–35, 385

Bashe, Em Jo, 195

Baum, L. Frank, 113

Bayou Legend, A (William Grant Still), 202–3, 204

Bayreuth, 123–24

Beach, Amy Marcy, 109, 242, 244–45

Beach, John, 162

Bearden, Romare, 194

Beaser, Robert, 389

Beast and Superbeast (Jorge Martin), 378

Beatles, 304–5, 340

Beaton, Cecil, 296

Beatty, Herbert, 313

Beeson, Jack, 251, 271, 292, 295, 313, 323, 331, 332; English language and, 7; *Lizzie Borden,* 292, 305, 309, 310–13, 361, 368, 431n37

Beethoven, Ludwig van: *Fidelio,* 53, 61, 89, 317

Beggar's Opera, The (John Gay/Johann Pepusch), 12, 13, 14, 16, 30

Beggar's Opera, The (Kurt Weill/Bertolt Brecht), 261

Belasco, David, 139, 207, 254

bel canto style, 88, 321, 386

Bel Geddes, Norman, 167

Belle of New York, The (Gustav Kerker), 101–2

Bellini, Vincenzo, 61, 80, 83, 85, 87, 106; *Norma,* 79, 81, 89, 90; *La sonnambula,* 79, 90, 126–27

Benet, Stephen Vincent, 246

Ben-Hur (Edgar Stillman Kelley), 130

Beresford, Bruce, 6

Berg, Alban, 4, 182, 233, 285, 290, 292, 305, 352

Bergman, Ingmar, 324

Bergmann, Carl, 122

Berlin, Irving, 117

Berlioz, Hector, 290

Berman, Lawrence, 77

Bernstein, Elmer, 326

Bernstein, Leonard, 83, 171, 267, 271, 274, 352, 359–60; *Candide,* 279, 316, 317, 362; *Mass,* 315–16, 388; *Trouble in Tahiti,* 245, 274, 317; *West Side Story,* 317, 319

"Bess, You Is My Woman Now" (from *Porgy and Bess*), 208, 211, 213

Between Two Worlds (Shulamit Ran), 360

Biancolli, Louis, 286

Bible, Frances, 286

Billington, Elizabeth, 73

Bimboni, Alberto, 141, 154–55

binary design, 73

Bingham, Susan, 331

Bing, Rudolph, 293

Birth of a Nation (film), 169

Bishop, Henry Rowley, 74; *Clari; or, The Maid of Milan,* 66, 74–77, 375

Bispham, David, 135, 243

Bizet, Georges: *Carmen,* 86, 317, 353

Black Crook, The (Charles M. Barras), 100

Blackstone, Tsianina Redfeather, 140, 150–51, 152, 414n21

Blakeslee, Charles Earle, 152

Blitzstein, Marc, 4, 5–6, 205, 226, 233, 256, 257, 261, 313; *The Cradle Will Rock,* 228–32, 263, 387; *Regina,* 263–65, 274, 275

Bloch, Ernest, 329

blues, 188, 190, 213, 215, 223, 225

Blumenfeld, Harold, 356

Boaden, James, 61

Boatner, Adelaide, 198

Boatright, McHenry, 198

body-language approach, 6–7, 18–19

Bogardus, Ralph, 160

Boito, Arrigo, 328

Bolcom, William, 6, 194, 292, 362; *McTeague,* 335, 370, 372–74; *A View from the Bridge,* 271, 383, 384, 389

Bond, Christopher, 319

Bond, Victoria, 363

Boorstin, Daniel, 11–12, 44–45, 93

Borden, Lizzie, 292, 305, 309, 310–13

Bori, Lucretia, 175–77

Boris Godounov (Modest Mussorgsky), 178

Borroff, Edith, 363

Bosch, Hieronymus, 238

Boston Lyric Opera, 360

Boston Opera, 224

Boston Theatre, 61–62, 65

Boulanger, Nadia, 214–15, 329, 337, 368

Bowie, David, 336, 337

Boyce, William, 32

Braham, John, 100

Brandt, Noah, 102

Braslau, Sophie, 166

Bray, John, 289; *The Indian Princess; or, La Belle Sauvage,* 40, 42, 43, 46, 60, 61, 62–65, 66, 67, 73, 76, 385

Brazen Mask, The (John Fawcett/James Hewitt), 42, 61–62, 380

Brecht, Bertolt, 229, 230, 261, 308

Breil, Joseph, 5, 168–69; *The Legend,* 165, 166, 169, 170

Brice, Carol, 198

Bridal of Dunure (William Henry Fry), 83

Bristow, George Frederick: *Rip Van Winkle,* 91–93, 386

Britten, Benjamin, 302, 361

broadsides, 42

Broadway musicals, 180, 213–14, 217, 231, 256, 259–60, 316–21, 356. *See also names of specific musicals*

Brontë, Charlotte, 268

Brontë, Emily, 267–71

Bronx Opera Company, 277

Brook, The (Nate Salisbury), 99

Brooklyn Academy of Music, 341, 346, 349

Brooks, Patricia, 286

Brougham, John: *Po-Ca-Hon-Tas;, or, The Gentle Savage,* 89

Brown, Anne Wiggins, 213

Browning, Kirk, 326

Browning, Robert, 162

Brownings Go to Italy, The (Eleanor Everest Freer), 243

Brussels World's Fair (1958), 260–61, 286

Bryant, William Cullen, 36–38

Bubbles, John W., 213

Bucci, Mark, 245, 274

Buckley, Emerson, 278

Bühnenweihfestspiel, 316

Bumbry, Grace, 304

burlesque, 89–91

Burns, Olive Ann, 389

Burra Pundit (Emma Roberts Steiner), 113–14

Burton, Richard, 298–99

Bush Street Theater (San Francisco), 102

Busoni, Ferruccio, 139–40

Butler, Henry, 300, 302

cabaletta, 84

Cabildo (Amy Marcy Beach), 245

Caccini, Giulio: *Il rapimento de Cefalo,* 1

Cacoyannis, Michael, 6, 302

Cadman, Charles Wakefield, 116, 140, 141, 147–51, 187, 234, 243, 284, 361; *Shanewis, the Robin Woman,* 149–51, 152, 164–65, 166–68, 174, 224, 253, 415n11

Cage, John, 220

Caignez, L. C.: *Le Jugement de Salomon,* 61

Cain, John M., 375

call-and-response, 194, 223

Callas, Maria, 271, 296

Campbell, Bartley, 254

Candide (Leonard Bernstein), 279, 316, 317, 362

The Canterbury Pilgrims (Reginald De Koven), 165, 166

Captain Cook (Noah Brandt), 102

Captain Jinks of the Horse Marines (Jack Beeson), 332

caricature: in ballad opera, 16

Cariou, Len, 319

Carlos, Rosemary, 277

Carlson, David, 155–56, 158, 362, 378

Carmen (Georges Bizet), 86, 317, 353

Carnegie, Andrew, 160–61

Carnegie Hall (New York City), 133, 135, 161, 198, 361

Carpenter, John Alden, 131, 223, 242

Carr, Benjamin: *The Archers,* 40, 51

Carreras, Jose, 317

Carroll, Lewis, 171

Carr, Sarah Pratt, 152–54

Carr's Musical Repository, 40

Carrie Nation (Douglas Moore), 277–78

Carter, Ernest, 207, 240, 243, 254

Caruso, Enrico, 87, 161, 165

Cassel, Walter, 278

Cassidy, David, 340

Castle, William, 86

Catán, Daniel, 360

Cather, Willa, 367

Cave, The (Steve Reich/Beryl Korot), 362, 369

Cavelleria Rusticana (Pietro Mascagni), 138, 253

CBS: radio broadcasts, 172, 234–35, 387; television broadcasts, 246

Central City Opera (Colorado), 278, 279

Central Park, 384, 389

Cervantes Saavedra, Miguel de, 49

Chadwick, George Whitefield, 126, 129, 130, 200, 224, 256–57, 386; *Judith,* 132, 136; *The Padrone,* 253–54, 386 chamber opera, 242–49, 364

Chapin, Theodore, 317

Chaplin, Charlie, 18

Chase and Sanborn, 171

Chatham Garden Theatre (New York City), 70

Chaucer, Geoffrey, 174

Checklist (Borroff), 363

Chekhov, Anton, 240–41, 329, 330

Cherubini, Luigi, 53, 60

Chestnut Street Theatre (Philadelphia), 36, 40, 48, 62, 66, 80–81, 95–96, 385

Cheyney, Edward Potts, 28–29, 33

Chicago Civic Opera House, 198

Chicago Opera House, 106

Chicago Opera Theater, 326

children's opera, 101, 112, 179, 236–37, 238–40, 331–32, 387

Children's Theater (San Francisco), 112

Childs, Lucinda, 364

Chilson-Ohrman, Luella, 154

Chookasian, Lili, 331

Chou En-lai, 348

Chris and the Wonderful Lamp (John Philip Sousa), 105

Christin, Judith, 380

Cibber, Colley: *Flora; or, Hob in the Well,* 13, 21

Cibber, Theophilus: *The Harlot's Progress,* 17

Ciceri, Charles, 46, 56

Ciesinski, Katherine, 324

City Center Opera Company, 272. *See also* New York City Opera

Civil War, 66, 85, 88–89, 91, 100, 188, 368

Clari; or, The Maid of Milan (Henry Rowley Bishop/John Howard Payne), 66, 74–77, 375

Clarke, John, 74

Clark, Graham, 380

Clark, Hilda, 103

Clement, Catherine, 305

Cleopatra (Paul Allen), 162, 387

Cleopatra's Night (Henry Hadley), 165, 166, 167, 168, 234

Cleveland, Grover, 106, 122

Clifton, Arthur: *The Enterprise,* 73

Cobbett, William, 50

Cocteau, Jean, 214–15, 247, 342, 343

Coeline; ou, L'enfant mystère (Guilbert de Pixèrécourt), 60

Coerne, Louis Adolphe, 162, 386

Colavecchia, Frank, 194

Cold Sassy Tree (Carlisle Floyd), 290, 361, 389

College of Philadelphia (University of Pennsylvania), 24–26, 29, 33–34, 385

Collier, Constance, 175

Collier, John, 145

Collier, Marie, 302

Colored Opera Company (Washington, D.C.), 186

Coloured Players, 184

Coltrane, John, 352

Columbian Exposition of 1893 (Chicago), 129

Columbia University, 222, 245–47, 271, 306

Columbus, Christopher, 110, 336, 343–45, 389

comédie en vaudevilles, 14

Comet, Catherine, 366–67

comic opera, 12, 99–117, 332; *The Disappointment,* 3, 29–35, 385; in early America, 1–2, 24, 29, 43; *The Reconcilliation,* 38, 73; *The Saw-Mill,* 66, 70, 77, 385. *See also* ballad opera; operatic melodrama; pastiche

comic superman, 93

commedia dell'arte, 3–4, 18, 60, 67, 236, 308

Compte Borchard, Mme., 86

Congress, U.S.: antitheater law (1778), 38

Conklin, John, 312, 324, 325

Connelly, Marc, 207

Conried, Heinrich, 112–13, 124

Consul, The (Gian Carlo Menotti), 2, 236, 240, 241, 256–59, 260, 362, 387

Contrast, The (Tyler), 36, 42, 68

Converse, Frederick Shepherd, 131, 168, 256–57; *The Immigrants,* 223–24, 253–54; *Iolan; or, The Pipe of Desire,* 143–44, 161–62, 164, 166, 386

Cooper, James Fenimore, 88

Copland, Aaron, 5, 206, 231–32, 245, 273, 275–77, 291, 362, 387

Coq d'Or, Le (Nikolai Rimsky Korsakov), 165

Corigliano, John, 362; *Ghosts of Versailles,* 6, 15, 292–93, 378–82, 389

Cornell, Katherine, 296

Corsaro, Frank, 194, 326

Così fan tutte (Wolfgang Amadeus Mozart), 34

Costa, Mary, 296–97

Costaso (William Grant Still), 203–4

Covent Garden (London), 56–57, 66, 76, 88, 274

Cowan, Louise, 99

Cowan, Richard, 300

Cowell, Henry, 179

Cowles, Eugene, 103

Cradle Will Rock, The (Marc Blitzstein), 228–32, 263, 387

Creagh, Patrick, 334

Creole folk tunes, 224, 245

Crèvecoeur, Michel Guillaume Jean de, 12

Crimean War, 92

I Cristiani e Pagani (William Henry Fry), 83

Crockett, Davy, 105

Crow Dog, Henry, 139

Crucible, The (Robert Ward), 4, 6, 277, 283–86, 287, 388

Crutchfield, Will, 276

Cry of Clytemnestra, The (John Eaton), 333

Cummings, Conrad, 337, 356

Cunningham, Arthur, 204

Curtin, Phyllis, 286

Curtis, George William, 138

Curtis Institute of Music, 237, 293

Curtis, Natalie, 140

Cyrano de Bergerac (Walter Damrosch), 133, 166, 386

da capo aria form, 73, 203

Dafne (Jacopo Peri), 1

Dallas, George M., 85

Dallas Opera, 271, 279, 321, 324, 329, 369, 388

Daly, Augustin, 124

Damrosch, Leopold, 133

Damrosch Opera Company, 133

Damrosch, Walter, 2, 125, 129, 130, 293, 372; *Cyrano de Bergerac,* 133, 166, 386; *The Man without a Country,* 133, 386; *The Scarlet Letter,* 132, 133–36, 166, 386

dance opera, 375

Dance in Place Congo (Henry Gilbert), 164–65, 167–68

dandyism, 77, 404n34

Dangerous Liaisons, The (Conrad Susa), 369, 370, 371–72

Danton and Robespierre (John Eaton), 334

Da Ponte, Lorenzo, 41, 79

Darnley, F. O., 92

Daugherty, Michael, 7, 335

Daughter of the Regiment (Gaetano Donizetti), 89

David Bispham Memorial Medal for American Opera, 165, 197, 224, 243

David-Neel, Alexandra, 364

Davies, John, 386; *The Forest Rose; or, American Farmers,* 68–70, 78, 386

Davis, Anthony, 254, 273, 335, 346, 352–56, 357–58, 358, 388

Davis, Arthur P., 187

Davis, Bette, 267

Davis, Christopher, 354

Davis, Jessie Bartlett, 103, 106

Davis, Thulani, 354

Dawson, Mary Cardwell, 198

Death of Klinghoffer, The (John Adams), 335, 349–51, 355

Debussy, Claude, 172, 215, 237, 348, 363

declamatory style, 179

Declaration of Independence (1776), 24, 36

Dede, Edmund, 186

de Jaffa, Kathleen, 179

DeJong, Constance, 341

De Koven, Reginald, 117, 121, 162; *The Canterbury Pilgrims,* 165, 166; *The Highwayman,* 103, 105, 106, 107; *Robin Hood,* 103, 105, 106

Delacoma, Wynne, 300

Delius, Frederick, 270

Dello Joio, Norman, 275

De Mers, John, 204

de Mille, Agnes, 310

de Mille, Cecil B., 255

Densmore, Frances, 150

De Reszke, Jean, 127

Désirée (John Philip Sousa), 105, 106

Des Moines Metro Opera, 327

Dessalines, Jean-Jacques, 197–204, 419n32

Destinn, Emmy, 161

deus ex machina, 19–20

Devil and Daniel Webster, The (Douglas Moore), 245–46, 274, 277

dialogue: recitative versus, 4, 179, 211, 214

Diaz, Justino, 298

Dibdin, Charles, 24; *The Touchstone; or, Harlequin Traveller,* 20

Dimond, William, 66

Dinesen, Isak, 293

Dippel, Andreas, 147, 163

Disappointment; or, The Force of Credulity (Andrew Barton, pseud.), 3, 29–35, 385

Doctor of Alcantara, The (Julius Eichberg), 99–100

dodecaphonic (twelve-tone) technique, 306

Domingo, Placido, 370

Donahue, John, 321–22

Don Carlos (Giuseppe Verdi), 88
Don Giovanni (Wolfgang Amadeus Mozart), 79, 317
Donizetti, Gaetano, 43, 60, 80, 87, 253, 332; *Anna Bolena,* 83; *Daughter of the Regiment,* 89; *Lucia di Lammermoor,* 61, 262, 309
Donohue, Joseph, 56
Don Quixote (Cervantes), 49
Dostoyevski, Fyodor, 333
Douglass, David, 29
Douglass, Frederick, 335, 367–68
Douglass, John Thomas, 110, 186, 386
Dovetta (Emma Marcy Raymond), 110, 386
Dow, Dorothy, 222
Downes, Olin, 177, 180, 182
drama lyrique, 136
Drattell, Deborah, 362, 389
Dreamkeepers (David Carlson), 155–56, 378
Dream of Valentino, The (Dominick Argento), 280–81, 324–25, 334, 335
Drury Lane (London), 52–53
Duché, Elizabeth Hopkinson, 27
Duché, Jacob, 27, 30
Duffy, John, 356
Duncan, Harry, 240
Duncan, Todd, 213
Dunlap, William, 76; *The Archers,* 40, 51; *Pizarro in Peru,* 43, 51–56, 61, 380, 385, 401n34; *Virgin of the Sun,* 43, 51–52, 56; *The Voice of Nature,* 42, 61, 385
Dun, Tan, 361
Durang, Charles, 39, 47
Duryea, Dan, 267
Dvořák, Anton, 413n5
Dwight, John Sullivan, 88, 93
Dyer, Richard, 300

Eames, Emma, 127
Eastman School of Music, 177–78
Easton, Florence, 143, 174
Eaton, John, 329, 331, 333–34, 342
Ebel, Otto, 109–10
Eberhart, Nelle Richmond, 149–51
Eckert, Thor, 327
Edinburgh International Festival, 375
Edwards, Julian, 114
Edwin and Angelina (Victor Pelissier), 42, 73
Eichberg, Julius: *The Doctor of Alcantara,* 99–100
Einstein, Albert, 44
Einstein on the Beach (Philip Glass), 334, 336–37, 339, 340–41, 358, 388

Eisenhower, Dwight D., 304
El Capitan (John Philip Sousa), 105, 106–7, 386
Electric Circus, 305
Elektra (Richard Strauss), 143
Elias, Rosalind, 296, 298
Ellington, Duke, 214, 279, 352
Elliott, Susan, 379
Ellis, Wayne, 96
Elmslie, Kenward, 309, 310, 311, 331
Emerson, Ralph Waldo, 91
Emmeline (Tobias Picker), 377–78, 389
Emperor Jones, The (Louis Gruenberg), 4, 166, 174, 177, 179–82, 184, 195, 196, 198, 207, 234
English language: *Alfred* and, 26–27, 33–34; David Bispham Memorial Medal for American Opera, 165, 197, 224, 243; use in opera, 6–7
English National Opera, 360
English opera. *See* masque
English pantomime. *See* harlequinade
Eno, Brian, 336, 337
Enterprise, The (Arthur Clifton), 73
Erie Canal, 70, 79
Estabrook, G., 110, 386
Estes, Simon, 194
Esther (Hugo Weisgall), 273, 306, 335, 375–76
Ethel Barrymore Theatre (New York City), 247
Euridice (Jacopo Peri), 1
Everett, Horace, 275, 276
Exorcist, The (film), 284
experimental theater, 226
expressionism, 292, 305
Eyre, John Edmund, 74

Fairlamb, James Remington: *Valerie; or, Treasured Tokens,* 89
Fair Park (Dallas), 324
Fall of the House of Usher, The (Philip Glass), 342–43
Falls, Robert, 259
Fanning, Cecil, 141
Farner, Eugene Adrian, 168
Farwell, Arthur, 140–41, 158, 160, 415n34
Fashionable Lady, The; or, Harlequin's Opera (James Ralph), 3–4, 11, 13–22, 32–33, 59, 308, 385
Faull, Ellen, 313
Faust (Charles François Gounod), 89, 100

Faust legend, 18, 89, 100

Fawcett, John: *The Brazen Mask,* 61–62, 380

Fax, Mark, 204

Federal Music Project, 291

Federal Theater Project, 35, 231

Fellini, Federico, 324

feminism, 49, 108, 136, 217, 220–22, 305–6, 309–10, 340

Ferden, Bruce, 343

Ferrar, Geraldine, 161, 162

Festival of Two Worlds (Spoleto, Italy), 240, 261, 296

fiaba, 139–40

Fidelio (Ludwig van Beethoven), 53, 61, 89, 317

Fielding, Henry, 14

Fillmore, John Comfort, 139

film. *See* motion pictures

Fine, Vivian, 336, 363–64

Fiske, John, 131

Fitch, Clyde, 332

Fitzgerald, F. Scott, 361, 389

Fleming, Renée, 6, 287, 369, 380

Fletcher, Alice Cunningham, 140, 150

Fletcher, Lucille, 268–69

Fleurette (Emma Roberts Steiner), 110, 113, 386

Flora; or, Hob in the Well (Colley Cibber/ John Hippesley), 13, 21

Florida State University, 286

Florio, Caryl: *Uncle Tom's Cabin,* 94, 95–98

Flotow, Friedrich von: *Martha,* 88–89

Floyd, Alpha, 194

Floyd, Carlisle, 2, 3, 251, 271, 273, 291, 362, 388, 389; *Of Mice and Men,* 290, 361, 388; *Susannah,* 4, 274, 275, 277, 286–90, 361, 387–88; *Willie Stark,* 335, 370–71; *Wuthering Heights,* 270, 274, 290

Floyd, Samuel, 206

Flying Dutchman, The (Richard Wagner), 155, 322–23

folk music, 2

folk opera, 210, 262

Foote, Arthur, 131

Ford Foundation, 274–75, 286, 300, 308–9, 359, 387–88

Forest Rose, The; or, American Farmers (Samuel Woodworth), 68–70, 77, 78, 386

Forrest, Hamilton, 225–26, 243

Foss, Lukas, 240, 273, 375–76

Foster, Agnes Green, 243

Foster, Stephen, 158

Four Saints in Three Acts (Gertrude Stein/ Virgil Thomson), 206, 216–20, 221, 222, 358, 387

Franchetti, Arnold, 245

Frankenstein: The Modern Prometheus (Libby Larsen), 335, 365–66, 369, 388

Frankfurt Opera, 363

Franklin, Benjamin, 13–14, 25, 34, 44

Frazer, John, 83–84

Freeman, Carlotta, 187–88

Freeman, Harry Lawrence, 185–88, 189, 191, 197, 200, 205, 224; *Voodoo,* 184, 187–88, 207, 387

Freeman, Valdo, 187–88, 189

Freer, Eleanor Everest, 242–44

Der Freischütz (Karl Maria von Weber), 89

French pantomime, 58, 60, 62

French Revolution, 46, 334, 379

Freneau, Philip, 46

Freud, Sigmund, 135, 179, 309–10, 342

Friedman, Sonya, 364

Friedman, Stephanie, 349

Friends and Enemies of Modern Music, 217

"From the Land of the Sky Blue Water" (from *Shanewis*), 149

Frost, Thomas, 107

Fry, Joseph Reese, 83, 85

Fry, William Henry, 2, 80–87, 92; *Leonora,* 4, 80–81, 83–85, 386; *Notre-Dame of Paris,* 83, 85–87

Full Moon in March, A (John Harbison), 333

Fürstner, Adolph, 144

Gadski, Johanna, 135

Galli, Rosina, 168, 178

Ganymede (Stella Prince Stocker), 114–16

Garcia, Manuel, 78–79

Garcia, Manuel Patricio, 78

Garcia, Maria (Madame Malibran), 78

Garden, Mary, 147–48, 161, 225–26, 242

Garden Theater (New York City), 184

Garland, Robert, 188

Garwood, Margaret, 336, 363

Gatti-Casazza, Giulio: background, 163–64; as director of Metropolitan Opera, 6, 162–83, 234, 243; return to Italy, 183

Gay, John: *The Beggar's Opera,* 12, 14, 15, 16, 30

La gazza ladra (Gioacchino Rossini), 79

Gebrauchsmusik, 228–29, 245

Gedda, Nicolai, 296

George R. Smith College for Negroes (Sedalia, Missouri), 190
Germania Orchestra (New York City), 122
Gerrish-Jones, Abbie, 57, 111–12
Gershwin, George, 2, 117, 133, 205, 224–25, 226, 243, 323; *Porgy and Bess,* 4, 193, 206–14, 223, 225, 231, 254, 262, 277, 286, 360, 361, 387
Gershwin, Ira, 213, 214
Gesamtkunstwerke, 343
Ghandi, Mahatma, 341, 342
Ghosts of Versailles (John Corigliano), 6, 15, 292–93, 378–82, 389
Giannini, Vittorio, 234–35, 274, 329, 387
Giants in the Earth (Douglas Moore), 271
Gibson Girl, 108
Gilbert, Henry, 164–65, 167–68
Gilbert, William S.: *H.M.S. Pinafore,* 100; *The Mikado,* 100, 106
Gillette, William, 254
Gilman, Lawrence, 178
Giovanna prima de Napoli (Maurice Strakosch), 88
Girl of the Golden West (Giacomo Puccini), 139, 155, 164, 254
Girl of the Golden West, The (David Belasco), 254
Gish, Lillian, 310
Glass, Philip, 2, 6, 44, 170, 336–45, 360, 362, 364; *Akhnaten,* 336, 340, 341, 342; *Einstein on the Beach,* 334, 336–37, 339, 340–41, 358, 388; *Satyagraha,* 336, 341–42; *The Voyage,* 336, 343–45, 359, 389
Glass Blowers, The. See American Maid, The (John Philip Sousa)
Gleason, Frederick Grant, 125, 127–29
Glimmerglass Opera, 312, 313, 361, 384, 389
Glossop, Peter, 319
Gluck, Christoph Willibald, 53; *Orfeo,* 63, 67
Gockley, David, 360–61
Godfrey, Thomas, 30
Goldman, Shalom, 342
Goodman, Alice, 346, 347, 349, 388
Goodman's Fields (Philadelphia), 13, 17
Goodrich, Arthur, 162
Good Soldier Schweik, The (Robert Kurka), 274, 308–9
Gottfried, Martin, 320
Gottschalk, Louis Moreau, 110
Gould, Jack, 259
Gounod, Charles François, 106, 185; *Faust,* 89, 100

Gowland, Gibson, 373
Goya (Gian Carlo Menotti), 335, 370
gracing, 73
Graham, Colin, 6, 370, 372, 381
Graham, Shirley, 196, 204
Graham, Susan, 6
La grande Bretèche (Stanley Hollingsworth), 240
La Grande Duchesse de Gérolstein (Jacques Offenbach), 100
grand opera: in American literature, 88, 91–98; European, in the U.S., 78–80, 87–91; of William Henry Fry, 80–87; nature of, 238; parodies of, 89–91; as term, 80; Wagner craze in, 121–38
Graupner, Gottlieb, 49
Great Britain: end of Revolutionary War, 36; influence on American opera, 13–22; opera professionals from, 39–41
Great Depression, 35, 163, 184, 231, 291
Great Gatsby, The (John Harbison), 361, 383, 389
Greed (film), 373
Greek mythology, 114–16, 195–96
Greenawald, Sheri, 313
Greenleaf, Robert, 362
Green Pastures (Marc Connelly), 207
Green, Paul, 207
Griffelkin (Lukas Foss), 240, 273, 375–76
Griffith, D. W., 169, 255
Griffith Stadium (Washington, D.C.), 198
Griswold, Putnam, 143
Grosser, Maurice, 218–19, 220
grotesque: as term, 18
Grout, Donald, 253
Gruenberg, Louis, 168, 170, 200, 223, 329; *The Emperor Jones,* 4, 166, 174, 177, 179–82, 184, 195, 196, 198, 207, 234
Gurney, A. R., 389

Hadley, Henry, 161, 162, 166, 167, 329; *Cleopatra's Night,* 165, 166, 167, 168, 234
Hadley, Jerry, 6, 389
Hagegård, Håken, 379, 380, 381
Hageman, Richard, 162
Hagen, Daron Auric, 335, 362
Haggard, Henry Rider, 186
"Hail to the Chief" (from *The Lady of the Lake*), 73–75, 77
Haiti, 197–204, 419n32
Halfvarson, Eric, 324
Hallam, Lewis, 29

Hall Johnson Choir, 207

Hamm, Charles, 139

Hammerstein, Oscar, 275, 316

Hammons, Thomas, 349

Hampson, Thomas, 6, 369, 372

Handel, George Frideric, 3, 27, 40, 44, 79

Handzlik, Jean, 277

Hanson, Howard, 166, 170, 177–78, 200–
202, 284

Hanson, William, 141–42

Harbison, John, 329, 333, 334, 361, 383, 389

Hardie, James, 79

Hargreaves, Charles, 154

Harlem Renaissance, 184–85, 187, 206

Harlem Symphony Orchestra, 187

harlequinade (English pantomime), 43, 58;
in ballad opera, 14–16, 18, 20–22, 59; *The
Fashionable Lady* as, 3–4, 11, 14–16, 18–21,
59, 308, 385; nature of, 3–4, 6, 18, 20;
stock characters of, 18, 20

Harling, W. Frank, 195, 224–25, 243

Harlot's Progress, The (Theophilus Cibber),
17

Harnick, Sheldon, 332

Harper, William, 356

Harrigan, Ned, 100

Hartley, Randolph, 143

Harvard University, 130–31

Harvey Milk (Stewart Wallace), 335, 352,
356–57, 358, 360

Hasek, Jaroslav, 309

Hatton, Ann Julia, 42; libretto for *Tammany,*
40, 45–48, 51, 56, 62, 141, 385; *Needs
Must; or, The Ballad Singers,* 45–46

Hatton, William, 45

Hauman, Constance, 329

Havana Italian Opera Company, 88

Hawkins, Micah: *The Saw-Mill,* 66, 70, 77,
385

Hawthorne, Nathaniel, 91, 134–36, 178, 363

Hayes, Roland, 187

Haymont, George, 366

Hazel Kirke (Steele MacKaye), 254

Hearst, Patty, 357–58

Heckscher Theatre (New York City), 246–
47

Hegel, G. W. F., 7

Heggie, Jake, 5, 361, 362

Heidelberg Opera, 337

Hellman, Lillian, 255, 264–66, 317

Hemingway, Ernest, 215

Henahan, Donal, 302

Henderson, William J., 138, 182

Henry IV, 1

Heppner, Ben, 373

Herbert, Victor, 117, 121, 125, 243; *Madeleine,*
147, 165, 166; *Natoma,* 126, 142, 147–49,
253, 386

Herne, James A., 254

heroic opera: *Alfred,* 1, 3, 25, 26–29, 33–34,
35, 44, 385

Herrmann, Bernard, 5–6, 119, 248, 255–56,
285, 295, 302, 319, 320, 343; *Wuthering
Heights,* 4, 267–71, 426n24

Hertz, Alfred, 124, 163

He Who Gets Slapped (Robert Ward), 275

Hewitt, James, 53, 60, 70, 77; *The Brazen
Mask,* 42, 61–62, 380; *Tammany; or, The
Indian Chief,* 40, 45–48, 51, 56, 62, 141,
385; *The Volunteers,* 42, 48

Heyward, Dorothy, 207–8, 210, 211

Heyward, Dubose, 207–8, 210, 211, 233

Highwayman, The (Reginald De Koven),
103, 105, 106, 107

Highway No. 1 (William Grant Still), 202,
204

Hill, Edward Burlingame, 131

Hindemith, Paul, 226

Hippesley, John: *Flora; or, Hob in the Well,* 13

Hipsher, Edward Ellsworth, 141, 182

Hitchcock, Alfred, 240, 248, 268

Hitler, Adolf, 226

H.M.S. Pinafore (William S. Gilbert/Arthur
Sullivan), 100

Hodgkinson, Frances Brett, 47

Hodgkinson, John, 47

Hoffmansthal, Hugo von, 208

Hoffman, William, 379

Hofmann, Gerda Wismer, 112

Hofmann, Peter, 317

Hogarth, William, 14

Hoiby, Lee, 2, 5–6, 240–42, 295, 325–29, 331,
334, 362; *The Labyrinth,* 241–42; *The Scarf,*
240–41, 274; *Summer and Smoke,* 241,
326–27, 370; *The Tempest,* 241, 326, 327–
29, 361, 388

Holcroft, Thomas: *A Tale of Mystery,* 60

Hollingsworth, Stanley, 240, 331

Holt, Ben, 354

Homer, Louise, 166

"Home Sweet Home" (from *Clari*), 74–77

homosexuality, 356–57

Hone, Philip, 80

Hopkinson, Francis, 23–25, 30, 33, 44, 45

Hopkinson, Thomas, 33
Hopper, De Wolf, 103
Horne, Charles Edward: *Ahmed al Kamel,* 91
Horne, Marilyn, 381
Houseman, John, 195, 218, 231
Houston Grand Opera, 194, 271, 319, 329,
   346, 356, 359–61, 364, 370, 388, 389
Howard, George C.: *Uncle Tom's Cabin,* 94–
   95
Howard, Samuel, 32
Howard University, 354
Howells, William Dean, 254
Hughes, Langston, 199, 200, 261
Hughes, Rupert, 121
Hugo, John Adams: *The Temple Dancer,* 165,
   166, 168
Hugo, Victor, 85
Hwang, David Henry, 342–43

Ibsen, Henrik, 125, 146
"I Got Plenty o' Nuttin'" (from *Porgy and
   Bess*), 211, 213
Imbs, Bravig, 215, 220
Immigrants, The (Frederick S. Converse),
   223–24, 253–54
Indiana University, 333–34
Indian Princess, The; or, La Belle Sauvage
   (James Nelson Barker/John Bray), 40, 42,
   43, 46, 60, 61, 62–65, 66, 67, 73, 76, 385
industrialization, 108–9
In the Pasha's Garden (John Laurence Sey-
   mour), 165, 166, 170
Iolan; or, The Pipe of Desire (Frederick S.
   Converse), 143–44, 161–62, 164, 166, 386
Irving, Washington, 88, 91–93, 386
Isaacson, Charles, 210
Israel, Robert, 342, 345
"It Ain't Necessarily So" (from *Porgy and
   Bess*), 210, 212
Italian Opera House (New York City), 79,
   80
Italy: origins of opera in, 1
Ives, Charles, 179, 221, 268, 292
*I Was Looking at the Ceiling and Then I Saw
   the Sky* (David Littlejohn), 351–52

Jackie-O (Michael Daugherty), 335
Jackson, Andrew, 221
Jackson, Clarence, 204
Jackson State University, 202–3
James, Henry, 108, 277, 324, 363, 388
James Irvine Foundation, 359

Janáček, Leoš, 292, 300
jazz, 2, 179, 188, 206–7, 215, 223–32, 262
Jefferson, Thomas, 36
Jenkins, Leroy, 375
"jig-piano," 190
John F. Kennedy Center for the Performing
   Arts (Washington, D.C.), 194, 316, 331,
   346, 360, 370, 388
Johns, Erik, 275
Johnson, Edward, 174, 175–77
Johnson, Hall, 196–97, 207
Johnson, James Weldon, 182, 184, 207
Johnson, Ladybird, 298
Johnson, Louis, 194
Johnson, Lyndon, 304
Johnson, Samuel, 14
Johnston, Denis, 307
John Street Theatre (New York City), 45
Jones, John Paul, 49
Jones, Robert T., 337
Jones, Sissieretta, 111, 185
Joplin, Scott, 188, 197, 224; *Treemonisha,* 5,
   189–95, 386
Joust, The; or, The Tournament (G. Estabrook),
   110, 386
Judith (George Whitefield Chadwick), 132,
   136
Jugendstil movement, 126, 132–33, 305, 306–
   7
Juilliard School of Music, 179, 196, 222, 268,
   299–300, 329, 337
Jung, Carl Gustav, 179
Jurinac, Sena, 296

Kafka, Franz, 292, 342
Kahn, Michael, 297
Kahn, Otto, 163
Kastendieck, Miles, 286
Kaufmann, Anna Maria, 317
Kay, Ulysses, 204, 335, 362
Kean and Murray Company (Philadelphia),
   29
Keene, Christopher, 375
Keisler, Frederick, 5
Kelley, Edgar Stillman, 125–26, 129–30
Kellogg, Clara Louise, 108
Kelly, Michael, 53
Kemble, Sarah and Roger, 45
Kempton, Jenny, 86
Kennedy Center for the Performing Arts
   (Washington, D.C.), 194, 316, 331, 346,
   360, 370, 388

Kennedy, John F., 243, 304, 354
Kentucky Opera, 271
Kerker, Gustav, 101–2
Kern, Jerome, 117, 174, 207, 316
Kiel Opera, 360
Kiesler, Frederick, 170
King, Juanita, 198
King, Martin Luther, Jr., 342
King's Henchman, The (Deems Taylor), 166, 172–75, 234, 387
King's Theatre (London), 28
Kirchhoff, Walter, 143
Kissel, Howard, 320–21
Klein, Charles, 106
Klinghoffer, Leon, 349–51
Kondek, Charles, 376
Korie, Michael, 356
Korngold, Erich, 5
Korot, Beryl, 362, 369
Kostal, Irwin, 319
Kotzebue, August von, 51, 52, 53, 76
Kozim, Allan, 379
Krainik, Ardis, 360
Kraus, Alfredo, 304
Křenek, Ernst, 143, 226
Kurka, Robert, 274, 292, 308–9

La bohème (Giacomo Puccini), 165, 356
Labyrinth, The (Lee Hoiby), 241–42
LaChiusa, Michael, 357
Laclos, Choderlos de, 371–72
Laderman, Ezra, 273, 335, 349, 375
Lafayette Theater (New York City), 187
La Guardia, Fiorello, 272
Lambert, Constant, 255
Lambert, Lucien, 186
Lame Deer, 145
Lang, David, 335, 362, 377
Langdon, William Chauncy, 136
Lang, Margaret Ruthven, 109
Lang, Paul Henry, 285, 295
Lansbury, Angela, 319
Larsen, Libby, 5, 6, 57, 170, 335, 362, 364–67, 369, 388
Larson, Jack, 222, 251
Larson, Jonathan, 356
La Scala (Milan), 177, 259, 293, 360
Last Tale of Scheherezade, The (Ernst Toch), 361–62
Lathrop, George Parsons, 134–35
Latouche, John, 279, 281, 282
Law, Andrew, 70

Lawrence, Vera Brodsky, 191, 194
Lear, Evelyn, 302, 331
Lears, T. Jackson, 161
Leaves of Grass (Whitman), 9, 91
Legend, The (Joseph Breil), 165, 166, 169, 170
Legend of Sleepy Hollow, The (Max Maretzek), 91
Lehar, Franz: *Merry Widow,* 100–101
Leinsdorf, Erich, 255, 286
leitmotifs: in *Azara,* 132; defined, 125; in *Mona,* 137; in *Vanessa,* 295–96; in Wagnerian opera, 125, 255
Leoncavallo, Ruggiero, 253, 290
Leone, Francesco de: *Alglala,* 141, 146
Leoni, Franco, 168
Leoni, the Gypsy Queen (Louisa Delos Mars), 110, 386
Leonora (William Henry Fry), 4, 80–81, 83–85, 386
Lester, William, 243
Levine, James, 389
Levine, Rhoda, 313, 354
Levy, Marvin David, 313; *Mourning Becomes Electra,* 6, 291, 292, 300–304, 361
Lewis, Brenda, 313
Lexington Opera House (New York City), 186
Lhut, Daniel de Gresollon du, 116
Library of Congress, 306
Liebermann, Lowell, 5, 362, 378
Lieberson, Peter, 361
Liebling, Leonard, 182
light opera, 99–117
Lili'oukalani, Queen, 102
Lincoln, Abraham, 88–89, 304
Lincoln Center (New York City), 217, 272, 291, 293, 298, 304, 388. *See also* Metropolitan Opera (New York City); New York City Opera
Lincoln's Inn Fields (London), 14, 18
Lippmann, Samuel, 292
Lipton, Martha, 278
Littell, Philip, 371–72
Little, Malcolm (Malcolm X), 352–56
Little Foxes, The (film), 264–66
Littlejohn, David, 351–52
Livengood, Victoria, 389
Livermore, Mary, 109
Lizzie Borden (Jack Beeson), 292, 305, 309, 310–13, 361, 368, 431n37
Lobel, Adrianne, 346
Lohengrin (Richard Wagner), 122

Longfellow, Henry Wadsworth, 101

Long, Huey, 370–71

Long Wharf Theater, 276

Loomis, Henry Worthington, 140

Lord Byron (Virgil Thomson), 222

Los Angeles Opera, 361

Lost in the Stars (Kurt Weill), 274

Love in a Village (Thomas Arne), 23

Low, Juliet Gordon, 363

Lucas, Carrie Melvin, 111

Lucia di Lammermoor (Gaetano Donizetti), 61, 262, 309

Ludgrin, Chester, 286

Luening, Otto, 243

Lyon, James, 24

lyric opera, 127, 178

Lyric Opera of Chicago, 259, 271, 287, 300, 304, 306, 324, 341–42, 360, 361, 373, 389

Lytton, Edward Bulwer, 83

Mabou Mines Theater Company (New York City), 337

Macbeth (John Houseman), 195, 231

MacDonald, Margaret I., 113

Machover, Todd, 369

MacKaye, Steele, 254

Macurdy, John, 302

Madama Butterfly (Giacomo Puccini), 141

Maddalena, James, 349

Madeleine (Victor Herbert), 147, 165, 166

Madison Square Garden (New York City), 161, 184, 198

Maeder, James Gaspard, 89; *The Peri; or, The Enchanted Fountain,* 91

Magic Flute, The (Wolfgang Amadeus Mozart), 17, 89, 236, 317

Mahler, Gustav, 163, 237, 270

Making of the Representative Planet 8, The (Philip Glass), 360

Malfitano, Catherine, 300, 373

Mandac, Evelyn, 331

Mansouri, Lotfi, 5, 329–30

Man without a Country, The (Walter Damrosch), 133, 386

Mao Tse-tung, 346, 348

Mapleson, James Henry, 185

Marcus, Jane, 136

Maretzek, Max, 88; *The Legend of Sleepy Hollow,* 91

Maria Golovin (Gian Carlo Menotti), 241, 256, 260–61, 274

Marilyn (Ezra Laderman), 273, 280–81, 335, 375

Marine Band, 106, 122

Marines' Hymn: origin of, 100

Markoe, Peter: *The Reconcilliation,* 38, 73

Mark, Peter, 368

Marriage of Figaro (Wolfgang Amadeus Mozart), 67, 236, 379, 380

Marriner, Neville, 366–67

Marshall, Herbert, 267

Mars, Louisa Delos, 57, 110, 111, 186, 386

Martha (Friedrich von Flotow), 88–89

Martin Beck Theater (New York City), 246, 317

Martin, Jorge, 362, 378

Mascagni, Pietro, 253

Masked Ball, A (Giuseppe Verdi), 43, 129

Mason, Lowell, 70

masque: in *Alfred,* 3, 26–29, 35; all-sung (English opera), 44; *America Independent,* 44; defined, 26; patriotic, 44

Mass (Leonard Bernstein), 315–16, 388

Massenet, Jules, 172, 198

Mates, Julian, 41

Matheus, John F., 198, 199, 200

Maurier, George du, 175

May Day in Town; or, New York in an Uproar (Royall Tyler), 42

Mayer, David, 77, 125

Mazzucato, Alberto, 110

McClary, Susan, 309

McClatchy, J. D., 377

McClintock, Walter, 144

McCormack, John, 147

McCoy, Seth, 194

McFerrin, Bobby, 361

McFerrin, Robert, 198

McLellan, Joseph, 108

McLin, Lena, 204, 367

McNally, Terrance, 389

McTeague (William Bolcom), 335, 370, 372–74

McVicker's Theater (Chicago), 127

Medici, Marie de, 1

Medium, The (Gian Carlo Menotti), 2, 236, 240–41, 245, 246–49, 256, 271, 274, 275, 362, 387

Mehta, Zubin, 302, 366–67

Meignen, Leopold, 81

melodrama, 12; examples of operatic, 43, 63–65; growth in popularity, 43; influences on, 58–65; leitmotifs in, 125;

music in, 4; opera versus, 43; popularity of, 124–25; structure of, 60; techniques of, 4; as term, 98, 124–25, 254–55; Wagner craze and, 121, 124–25. *See also* operatic melodrama

Melville, Herman, 91

Memoirs of Uliana Rooney (Vivian Fine), 364

Memorial Arts Center (Atlanta, Georgia), 194

Mendelssohn, Felix, 132

Menotti, Gian Carlo, 235–42, 253, 256–61, 273, 299–300, 329; *Amahl and the Night Visitors* (Gian Carlo Menotti), 236–37, 238–40, 241–42, 248, 277, 387; *The Consul,* 2, 236, 240, 241, 256–59, 260, 362, 387; *Goya,* 335, 370; as leader in American opera, 2; *Maria Golovin,* 241, 256, 260–61, 274; *The Medium,* 2, 236, 240–41, 245, 246–49, 256, 271, 274, 275, 362, 387; *The Old Maid and the Thief,* 235–36; *The Saint of Bleecker Street,* 241, 248, 256, 259–60; *The Telephone,* 246–47, 387; *Vanessa,* 291, 292, 293–97, 304, 388

Merope (Domènech Terradellas), 28

Merry Mount (Howard Hanson), 166, 174, 177–78, 180, 183, 234, 284

Merry Widow (Franz Lehar), 100–101

Mesmer, Friedrich, 34

Metropolitan Opera (New York City), 80, 103, 112–13, 160–83, 224, 231, 272; African American performers, 197, 198, 214; audition requirements for, 7; Heinrich Conried as manager, 112–13, 124; Giulio Gatti-Casazza as director, 6, 162–83, 234, 243; opening, 100, 117, 122, 161; premieres of American operas, 6, 165–83, 287, 291, 292, 293–304, 341, 359, 361, 378–82, 383; radio broadcasts, 172, 234; stage designs, 5, 167, 168–70; tours, 127, 161

Meyerbeer, Giacomo, 56, 60, 80, 129

Mielziner, Jo, 180

Mighty Casey, The (William Schuman), 335

Mikado, The (William S. Gilbert/Arthur Sullivan), 100, 106

Milan Conservatory, 237

Milhaud, Darius, 215, 223, 292, 329, 332

Millay, Edna St. Vincent, 172–73, 174, 387

Miller, Arthur, 271, 284, 285, 388, 389

Miller, Glenn, 348

Milnes, Sherrill, 302, 304

mime, 20, 233; in *The Brazen Mask,* 61–62

minimalism, 2, 220, 362, 377; of John Adams, 346–51; of Philip Glass, 336–45

Minnesota Opera, 271, 321, 361, 365–66, 388

minstrels, 114, 158, 184

Miss Julie (Ned Rorem), 309, 310, 430n32

Mitropoulos, Dimitri, 296

Mona (Horatio Parker), 136–38, 165, 166

Monk, Meredith, 57, 335–36, 364

Monroe, George, 17

Monteverdi, Claudio, 237, 309, 339

Montezuma (Roger Sessions), 334, 342

Moody, Richard, 103

Moore, Dorothy Rudd, 335, 362, 367–68

Moore, Douglas, 2, 243, 271, 273, 284, 291, 362; *Ballad of Baby Doe,* 245–46, 274, 277–83, 313, 368, 387–88; *Carrie Nation,* 277–78; *The Devil and Daniel Webster,* 245–46, 274, 277

Moore, Grace, 164

Moore, Mary Carr, 57, 110, 152, 158, 243

Moore Theater (Seattle), 154

Moran, Robert, 337, 342

Mordden, Ethan, 232

moresca (Moor's dance), 17

Moross, Jerome, 279

Morris, James, 331

Morris, Mark, 346

Morris, Robert, 349

morris dance, 17

Moscow Musical Theater, 329

Mother of Three Sons (Leroy Jenkins), 375

Mother of Us All, The (Gertrude Stein/Virgil Thomson), 217, 220–22, 271, 368

motion pictures: American verismo and, 5–6; cinematic techniques and, 2, 230–31; influence on American opera, 4–6, 168–70, 305, 324; music for, 130, 255–56, 263, 267, 268; as opera scenery, 105, 227–28; silent films, 5, 191, 193; special effects, 204

Mount, William Sidney, 70

Mourning Becomes Electra (Marvin David Levy), 6, 291, 292, 300–304, 361

movies. *See* motion pictures

Mozart, Wolfgang Amadeus, 5, 11, 41, 149, 348; *Così fan tutte,* 34; *Don Giovanni,* 79, 317; *The Magic Flute,* 17, 89, 236, 317; *Marriage of Figaro,* 67, 236, 379, 380

Muck, Karl, 143, 147

Muhammad, Elijah, 353–55

Munro, H. H., 378

Murphey, Donna, 318

Musgrave, Thea, 335, 362, 363, 368–69, 388
music: expressive powers of, 3; increasing alignment with text, 3; motion pictures and, 5–6, 130, 255–56, 263, 267, 268; in operatic melodrama, 51–57; orchestra as character and, 5
music under dialogue, 4
Musselman, Joseph, 121–22
Muziektheater Foundation of America, 360
Myshkin (John Eaton), 333–34

Nadler, Sheila, 349
Napoleon Bonaparte, 200
Narcissa (Mary Carr Moore), 152–54
Nassau Street Theatre (New York City), 12–13
Natalia Petrovna, 291
National Endowment for the Arts and Humanities, 304, 359
National Federation of Music Clubs, 110
nationalism, 43–44
National Negro Opera Company, 197, 198
Native American motifs, 2, 139–59; *Alglala,* 141, 146; *Dreamkeepers,* 155–56, 378; *The Indian Princess; or, La Belle Sauvage,* 40, 42, 43, 46, 60, 61, 62–65, 66, 67, 73, 76, 385; *The Legend of Wiwaste,* 152; *Narcissa,* 152–54; *Natoma,* 126, 142, 147–49, 253, 386; *Po-Ca-Hon-Tas; or, The Gentle Savage,* 89; *Poia,* 141, 142–47, 161–62, 386, 413n10; *Shanewis, the Robin Woman,* 149–51, 152, 164–65, 166–68, 174, 224, 253, 415n11; *Sieur de Lhut,* 116; *Tammany; or, The Indian Chief* (James Hewitt), 40, 45–48, 51, 56, 62, 141, 385; *Winona* (Alberto Bimboni), 141, 142, 154–55; *The Woman at Otowi Crossing,* 156–57
Natoma (Victor Herbert), 126, 142, 147–49, 253, 386
NBC: radio broadcasts, 149, 151, 171, 234, 235; television broadcasts, 236, 240, 241–42, 261
Needs Must; or, The Ballad Singers (Mary Ann Pownell/Ann Julia Hatton), 45–46
Negro Grand Opera Company, 187
neoromanticism, 186, 283, 292
neosensualism, 351, 362
Neuendorff, Adolf, 122
Nevin, Arthur Finlay, 116, 158; *Poia,* 141, 142–47, 161–62, 386, 413n10
Nevin, David, 268
Neway, Patricia, 241, 257–58, 259

New Company (Philadelphia), 39
New Day Pilgrims, 196–97
New Deal, 35, 231
Newman, Alfred, 255, 268
Newton, Adele, 277
New York City: as cultural capital, 23, 78–80, 160–61; as financial center, 161; Harlem Renaissance, 184–85, 187, 206; rise of, 36–38, 78–80. *See also names of specific theaters and institutions*
New York City Opera, 247, 271, 272–91, 356, 378; Ford Foundation series, 274–75, 286, 308–9, 387–88; Julius Rudel as manager, 273–75, 279, 286, 293; premieres of American operas, 200, 214, 241, 245, 254, 257–58, 273–75, 290, 304, 306–13, 317, 319, 321, 326, 341–42, 354, 360, 363, 375–76; revivals, 231; tours, 274–75
New York Philharmonic, 79, 81–83, 85–86, 92, 133
Niblo's Garden (New York City), 92
Nicoll, Allardyce, 124
Nielsen, Alice, 103
Nietzsche, Friedrich, 305
Nixon in China (John Adams), 335, 346–49, 388
Noble, Timothy, 343–44
Nolte, Charles, 323–24
Nordica, Lillian, 135, 149
Norma (Vincenzo Bellini), 79, 81, 89, 90
Norris, Frank, 373
North, Alex, 285
Notre-Dame of Paris (William Henry Fry), 83, 85–87
Noverre, Jean Georges, 62
number-opera framework, 127
Nye, Frederick, 110

Oakland Conservatory of Music, 110
Oberlin Conservatory of Music, 197, 200
Oberon, Merle, 268
Odets, Clifford, 231
Oenslager, Donald, 278
Offenbach, Jacques, 99, 106; *La Grande Duchesse de Gérolstein,* 100
Of Mice and Men (Carlisle Floyd), 290, 361, 388
"Old Folks at Home" (from *Uncle Tom's Cabin*), 96–97
Old Maid and the Thief (Gian Carlo Menotti), 235–36, 274
Olivier, Laurence, 268, 270

Olon-Scrymgeour, John, 321

O'Neill, Eugene, 179, 180, 195, 200, 207, 300, 302

1000 Airplanes on the Roof (Philip Glass), 342, 343

opera: American, *see* American opera; components of, 1; defined, 1; earliest works, 1, 12; imported from Europe to America, 38, 39; melodrama versus, 43; origins in Italy, 1; as term, 43; traditional repertoire, 4, 43; as ultimate musical tale, 1

Opera America, 359

opera buffa, 6, 100–107, 317

Opera Company of Philadelphia, 360

Opera Delaware, 331

Opera de Monte Carlo, 378

L'Opera de Nantes, 287

Opera Ebony (New York City), 367–68

Opera in Our Language Foundation, 243

Opera Omaha, 367

opera seria, 14, 27

Opera Theatre of St. Louis, 297, 360, 375

operatic melodrama: *The Aethiop,* 40–41, 42, 60, 66–68, 73, 77; *Clari,* 66, 74–77; examples of, 43; *The Forest Rose,* 68–70, 77, 78, 386; role of music in, 51–57; *The Saw-Mill,* 66, 70, 77

operetta, 100–107, 110

oratorial entertainment, 29, 44

Oratorio Society, 133

Orfeo (Christoph Willibald Gluck), 63, 67

ornamentation, vocal, 84

Orphan, The (Thomas Otway), 59

Orth, Robert, 356

Os-ke-non-ton, Chief, 152

Otello (Giuseppe Verdi), 127

Otho Visconti (Frederick Grant Gleason), 129

Otway, Thomas: *The Orphan,* 59

Ouanga (Clarence Cameron White), 197–99, 419n30, 419n32

Owen, Robert, 111

Pacini, Giovanni, 85, 87

Padrone, The (George Whitefield Chadwick), 253–54, 386

pageant, 116, 221

Page, Tim, 315

I Pagliacci (Ruggiero Leoncavallo), 138, 165, 253

Paine, John Knowles, 121, 125, 129, 130; *Azara,* 130–32, 135

Palestrina Choir (New York City), 97

Palma, John, 28, 29

Palmer, T. and G., 40

Palm Garden Theater (New York City), 184, 188

Palmo (New York City), 79

Pancella, Phyllis, 313

panorama, 221

pantomime, 12, 125–26; cues for, 58–59; English, *see* harlequinade (English pantomime); growth in popularity, 43. *See also* French pantomime; harlequinade (English pantomime)

Paris Academy, 87

Paris Opera, 274

Parker, Horatio, 129, 130; *Mona,* 136–38, 165, 166

Parker, Louise, 194

Park Street Theater (New York City), 36, 40

Park Theatre (New York City), 51, 76, 78

parlando: defined, 4; in *Wuthering Heights,* 4, 269

parody, 14; in ballad opera, 16–17; burlesque, 89–91; in heroic opera, 27

Parsifal (Richard Wagner), 123–24, 126, 133, 146, 231, 260

Pasatieri, Thomas, 325, 329–31, 334, 369

Passion (Stephen Sondheim), 318

pastiche, 23, 26, 43

Paterson, William, 30, 33

Patterson, Frank, 224, 243

Patterson, Sam, 191

Patti, Adelina, 88

Paulus, Stephen, 2, 5–6, 155, 158, 362, 383; *The Postman Always Rings Twice,* 369, 374–75; *The Woman at Otowi Crossing,* 156–57

Pavarotti, Luciano, 304

Payne, John Howard: *Clari; or, The Maid of Milan,* 66, 74–77, 375

Peabody Conservatory of Music, 110, 306, 321

Pelissier, Victor, 60, 74, 77; *Ariadne Abandoned by Theseus in the Isle of Naxos,* 41; *Edwin and Angelina,* 73; *The Voice of Nature,* 42, 61, 385

Penn, William, 23–24

pentatonic scale, 149

Pepusch, Johann: *The Beggar's Opera,* 12, 14

Peri, Jacopo: *Dafne,* 1; *Euridice,* 1

Peri, The; or, The Enchanted Fountain (James Gaspard Maeder), 91

Perry, Eugene, 349

Perry, Julia, 367

Peter Ibbetson (Deems Taylor), 166, 172, 174, 175–77, 234, 387

Peterson, Dean, 389

Petrushka (Igor Stravinsky), 213, 248, 323

Phantom of the Opera (Andrew Lloyd Webber), 316, 317

Philadelphia, Pennsylvania, 23–36; as birthplace of Declaration of Independence, 24, 36; as cultural capital of America, 13, 23–24, 39–41; as national capital, 36

Philadelphia and Chicago Opera Company, 147

Philharmonic Society of New York, 79

Philip Glass Ensemble, 337

Philip Morris, 359

Physiology of the Opera ("Scrici"), 90

Picker, Tobias, 5, 361, 362, 377–78, 389

Picture of Dorian Gray, The (Lowell Lieberman), 378

Pierrot Lunaire (Schoenberg), 179

Pinero, Arthur, 125

Pipe of Desire, The (Frederick S. Converse), 143–44, 161–62, 164, 166, 386

Pirandello, Luigi, 306, 308

Pitts, ZaSu, 373

Pixèrécourt, Guilbert de, 60

Pizarro in Peru (William Dunlap), 43, 51–56, 61, 380, 385, 401n34

Plant, Richard, 310

Player, Cyril, 154

Po-Ca-Hon-Tas;, or, The Gentle Savage (John Brougham), 89

Poe, Edgar Allan, 91, 342–43

Poia (Arthur Nevin), 141, 142–47, 161–62, 386, 413n10

Pommer, William Henry, 101

Ponselle, Rosa, 164, 169

Pope, Alexander, 14

Porgy and Bess (George Gershwin), 4, 193, 206–14, 223, 225, 231, 254, 262, 277, 286, 360, 361, 387

Porter, Andrew, 307, 329

Porter, Susan, 59

Portland Opera, 268

Postcard from Morocco (Dominick Argento), 321–23, 388

Postman Always Rings Twice, The (film), 375

Postman Always Rings Twice, The (Stephen Paulus), 369, 374–75

post-minimalism, 377

potential song, 211

Poutney, David, 345

Powers, Marie, 247

Pownell, Mary Ann: *Needs Must; or, The Ballad Singers,* 45–46

Pratt Institute of Music and Art (Pittsburgh), 127

Pratt, Silas G., 121, 126–29, 349; *Zenobia,* 126, 127, 128–29

Previn, Andre: *A Streetcar Named Desire,* 5, 271, 361, 383, 389

Price, Leontyne, 298, 304, 328

Prince, Harold, 316, 317, 319, 370–71, 388

Prince of Asturias (Constance Faunt de Roy Runcie), 111

Priscilla (Abbie Gerrish-Jones), 112

Priscilla; or, The Pilgrim's Proxy (Thomas Whitney Surette), 101

prizes. *See* awards and prizes

Psycho (film), 248, 268, 302

Puccini, Giacomo, 4, 148, 172, 237, 256, 282, 292, 316, 329, 362; *La bohème,* 165, 356; *Girl of the Golden West,* 139, 155, 164, 254; *Madama Butterfly,* 141; *Manon Lescaut,* 161; *Turandot,* 130–40, 141, 300, 333

Quiet Place, A (Leonard Bernstein), 359–60

Quilico, Gino, 379

Quinn, Arthur, 26

Racette, Patricia, 378, 389

radio, 233–36; CBS opera broadcasts, 172, 234–35, 387; Chase and Sanborn opera program, 171; Metropolitan Opera broadcasts, 171, 234; National Public Radio broadcasts, 306–7; NBC opera broadcasts, 149, 151, 171, 234, 235; origins of broadcasting, 233–34; radio opera, 149, 179, 234–36, 368; vaudeville, 234; WGBS opera broadcasts, 187, 387

ragtime, 117, 190–94, 215, 223, 224

Raisa, Rosa, 224

Ralph, James, 3, 13–14, 23, 27, 380; *The Fashionable Lady,* 3–4, 11, 13–22, 32–33, 59, 308, 385

Rameau, Jean-Philippe, 413n5

Ramey, Samuel, 6

Ramin, Sid, 319

Ran, Shulamit, 360

Rapee, Erno, 174

Il rapimento de Cefalo (Giulio Caccini), 1

Ravel, Maurice, 215, 237

Raymond, Emma Marcy, 110, 386

realism. *See* American verismo

Reardon, John, 302, 331

recitative: accompanied by orchestra, 84; dialogue versus, 4, 179, 211, 214; innovative approaches to, 4

Reconcilliation, The (Peter Markoe), 38, 73

Redding, Joseph D., 148–49

Redfeather, Tsianina, 140, 150–51, 152, 414n21

Regina (Marc Blitzstein), 263–65, 274, 275, 313

Reich, Steve, 339, 362, 364, 369

Reinagle, Alexander, 39–40, 70, 77; *Slaves in Algiers; or, A Struggle for Freedom* (Susanna Rowson/Alexander Reinagle), 48, 49–51, 385

Reinagle, Hugh, 70

Reiner, Fritz, 296

Remy, Alfred, 136

Resnik, Regina, 296

Revolutionary War, 36, 92

Rice, Edward Everett, 112, 114

Rice, Elmer, 261

Richards, Lulu, 111

Rich, John, 18

Riddell, Richard, 342

Rieck, Waldemer, 93

Riley, Terry, 339

Rimbaud, Arthur, 356

Rimsky-Korsakov, Nikolai, 165

Der Ring des Nibelungen (Richard Wagner), 19, 47, 122–23, 127, 146, 158, 174, 186, 255, 268, 270–71, 379

ring plays, 190

Rip Van Winkle (George Bristow), 91–93, 386

Ritter, Frederic, 122

Robbins, Jerome, 277

Robeson, Paul, 207

Robin Hood (Reginald De Koven), 103, 105, 106

Robyn, Alfred, 102

Rockefeller Foundation, 359

rock opera, 316, 356

Rockwell, John, 327

Rodgers, Richard, 275, 316

Rogers, Bernard, 293

Rogers, Clara Kathleen, 109

Rogers, Robert, 46

Ronconi, George, 110

Roosevelt, Franklin Delano, 231

Roosevelt, Theodore, 140, 143, 160

Rorem, Ned, 249, 273, 292, 305, 309, 310, 430n32

Rosenshein, Neil, 324

Rossini, Gioacchino Antonio, 43, 81, 85, 99, 106; *La gazza ladra,* 79; *Il barbiere di Siviglia,* 78–79, 89, 379, 380

Rourke, Constance, 65

Rowson, Susanna Haswell, 45, 48–51; *Slaves in Algiers; or, A Struggle for Freedom,* 48, 49–51, 56–57, 385; *The Volunteers,* 42, 48

Royal Academy of Music (London), 84

Royal Opera House (Berlin), 143, 161–62

Royal York Theatre (London), 40

Rubinstein, Artur, 296

Rudel, Julius, 272, 273–75, 279, 286, 293

Rudolph; or, The Robbers of Calabria (John Turnbull), 65

Runcie, Constance Faunt le Roy: *Prince of Asturias,* 111

Run, Little Chillun (Hall Johnson), 196–97, 207

Ruskin, John, 335, 377

Russell, Lillian, 221

Sabin, Robert, 256

Sacchini, Antonio, 53

Le sacre du printemps (Igor Stravinsky), 213, 355

Sadler's Wells (London), 40

Saint of Bleecker Street, The (Gian Carlo Menotti), 241, 248, 256, 259–60

Saint-Saëns, Camille, 133, 136

Salisbury, Nate: *The Brook,* 99

Salome (Richard Strauss), 136, 137, 236, 309, 333

Sandburg, Carl, 242

Sanderson, James, 73–75

San Francisco Opera, 5, 356, 360, 361, 372, 389

Santa Fe Opera, 271, 301, 329, 361, 378, 389

Sargeant, Winthrop, 247, 283, 286

Satie, Erik, 215–16, 332

Satyagraha (Philip Glass), 336, 341–42

savage realism, 262

Saw-Mill, The; or, A Yankee Trick (Micah Hawkins), 66, 70, 77, 385

Saylor, Bruce, 374

Scarf, The (Lee Hoiby), 240–41, 274

Scarlet Letter, The (Walter Damrosch), 132, 133–36, 166, 386

scena-ed-aria structure, 84

Schickle, Peter, 89

Schippers, Thomas, 298
Schmidgall, Gary, 368
Schmidt, Adolph, 80
Schnittke, Alfred, 337
Schoenberg, Arnold, 179, 292, 304, 309, 351
Schoenefeld, Henry, 141
Schonberg, Harold, 194, 283, 302
Schopenhauer, Arthur, 122, 146
Schubert, Franz, 327
Schuller, Gunther, 194, 292, 331
Schuman, Patricia, 345
Schuman, William, 335
Schwartz, Stephen, 316
Scott, Walter, 74
Scribe, Eugene, 60
"Scrici," 90
Seagull, The (Thomas Pasatieri), 329–31
Seattle Opera, 271, 329–30
Sedgwick, Alfred B., 100
Seguin, Anne, 83–84
Seguin, Edward, 83–84, 86
Seguin English Opera Company, 84
Seidl, Anton, 122, 136
Selika, Marie, 111, 185
Sellars, Peter, 346, 349, 351–52
Serafin, Tullio, 174
serialism, 339
Sessions, Roger, 334, 342
Seymour, John Laurence, 165, 166, 170
Shakespeare, William, 65, 67, 298–300, 327, 328–29, 388
Shanewis, the Robin Woman (Charles Wakefield Cadman), 149–51, 152, 164–65, 166–68, 174, 224, 253, 415n11
Shankar, Ravi, 337
Shapiro, Anne, 58–59
Shattuck, Roger, 215
Shaw, Anne Howard, 221
Shaw, Artie, 200
Shaw, George Bernard, 119
Shaw, Robert, 194
Shea, Jere, 318
Shelley, Mary, 365, 369
Sheridan, Richard Brinsley, 52–53
Shield, William, 24
Shirley, Wayne, 225
Shostakovich, Dmitri, 379
shouts and hollers, 190
Show Boat (Jerome Kern/Oscar Hammerstein), 174, 207, 316
Shulgasser, Mark, 327–28, 388
Siddons, Sarah, 45

Siegmeister, Elie, 329
Sieur de Lhut (Stella Prince Stocker), 116
Sills, Beverly, 273, 278, 307
Simon, Joanna, 331
singspiel, 139–40
Sirlin, Jerome, 342–43
Sitches, Joaquina, 78
Six Characters in Search of an Author (Hugo Weisgall), 274, 275, 291, 292, 306–8, 322
Skilton, Charles Sanford, 140, 146, 151, 234, 387
Slatkin, Leonard, 366–67
Slaves in Algiers; or, A Struggle for Freedom (Susanna Rowson/Alexander Reinagle), 48, 49–51, 56–57, 385
Sleepy Hollow; or, The Headless Horseman (Giuseppe Verdi), 88
Smalls, Samuel, 207, 208
Smith, Carleton, 170
Smith, Elihu Hubbard: *Edwin and Angelina; or, The Banditti,* 42
Smith, Harry B., 103, 107
Smith, Julia, 363
Smith, Marion Couthouy, 121
Smith, Oliver, 277
Smith, Sol, 39
Smithsonian Institution, 141
Smith, William, 30; *Alfred,* 1, 3, 25, 26–29, 33–34, 35, 44, 385
Smyth, Ethel, 363
Snow Queen, The (Abbie Gerrish-Jones), 112
Soederstroem, Elisabeth, 324
Sondheim, Stephen, 317, 318–21, 341; *A Little Night Music,* 319; *Passion,* 318; *Sweeney Todd,* 319–21, 388
La sonnambula (Vincenzo Bellini), 79, 90, 126–27
Sonneck, Oscar, 29, 33
sound recordings, 277, 300; African American opera, 194; Native American music and, 141; New World Records, 306–7; origins of, 140
Sousa, John Philip, 117; *The American Maid,* 5, 105, 386; *El Capitan,* 105, 106–7, 386; *Désirée,* 105, 106; Marine Band and, 106, 122
Southwark Theatre (Philadelphia), 24, 30
Spaeth, Sigmund, 223
spectacle, 18, 19, 43, 100
speculum vitae, 38
Spender, Stephen, 293
Spenser, William, 102

Spia, La (Luigi Arditti), 88

Spielberg, Stephen, 342

spirituals, 182, 188, 190, 196, 267

Spoleto Festival (Charleston, South Carolina), 300, 331

Spoleto Festival of Two Worlds, 240, 261, 296

sprechgesang, 4, 179

Sprotte, Anna Ruzena, 154

Stadt Theater (New York City), 122

Stadttheater of Frieburg-in-Breisgau (Germany), 162

Stage Yankee, 32, 68–72, 77, 105

Stahl, Richard, 102

Stambler, Bernard, 284–85

Stamp Act, 33, 34

Stark, John, 190

Stearns, David Patrick, 379

Steber, Eleanor, 296

Steinbeck, John, 388

Steiner, Emma Roberts, 110, 111, 112–14, 386; *Burra Pundit,* 113–14

Steiner, Max, 282

Stein, Gertrude, 49, 57, 206, 214–22, 387

Steinway Hall, 96

Stettheimer, Florine, 218

Stevenson, Robert Louis, 290

Stevens, Risë, 304

Stevens, Thaddeus, 221

Still, William Grant, 5, 197–99, 205; *A Bayou Legend,* 202–3, 204; *Costaso,* 203–4; *Highway No. 1,* 202, 204; *Troubled Island,* 4, 197, 199–204, 273, 387

Stilwell, Richard, 324, 331

Sting, The (film), 194

Stocker, Stella Prince, 57, 111, 141; *Ganymede,* 114–16; Native American influence on, 116; *Sieur de Lhut,* 116

Stokes, Richard, 178, 183

Stokowski, Leopold, 171, 200, 233

Storace, Stephen, 24

Stowe, Harriet Beecher, 91, 93–98

St. Paul Opera Association, 326

Strakosch, Maurice: *Giovanna prima de Napoli,* 88

Stratas, Teresa, 379

Stratton, George W., 101

Strauss, Richard, 4, 133, 208, 270, 285, 292, 329, 348, 363; *Elektra,* 143; *Salome,* 136, 137, 236, 309, 333

Stravinsky, Igor, 179, 206, 213, 215, 221, 223, 237, 248, 292, 309, 323, 355, 363

Streetcar Named Desire, A (Andre Previn), 5, 271, 361, 383, 389

Street Scene (Kurt Weill), 200, 261–63, 273, 274, 362

Strindberg, August, 305, 309

Strouse, Charles, 331

Stuart, Gilbert, 23

Sullivan, Arthur S.: *H.M.S. Pinafore,* 100; *The Mikado,* 100, 106

Summer and Smoke (Lee Hoiby), 241, 326–27, 370

"Summertime" (from *Porgy and Bess*), 210, 212

Sun Bride, The (Charles Sanford Skilton), 146, 151, 234, 387

Sun Dance, 145–46, 158

Sun Dance (William Hanson), 141–42

Surette, Thomas Whitney, 131; *Priscilla; or, The Pilgrim's Proxy,* 101

Surrey Theatre, 74

Susa, Conrad, 361, 362, 369, 370, 371–72

Susannah (Carlisle Floyd), 4, 274, 275, 277, 286–90, 361, 387–88

Sutherland, Joan, 304

Swarthout, Gladys, 164

Swedish Theatre and Lithuanian Opera Company (Chicago), 160

Swed, Mark, 377

Sweeney Todd (Stephen Sondheim), 319–21, 388

Swift, Jonathan, 363

Sylvan, Sanford, 349

Tabor, Augusta, 280, 281, 282

Tabor, Elizabeth ("Baby Doe"), 277–83

Tabor, Horace, 279, 280, 281

Tale for a Deaf Ear (Mark Bucci), 274

Tale of Mystery, A (Thomas Holcroft), 60

Talley, Marion, 164

Talma, Louise, 363

Taming of the Shrew, The (Vittorio Giannini), 235, 274, 387

Tammany; or, The Indian Chief (James Hewitt), 40, 45–48, 51, 56, 62, 141, 385

Tania (Anthony Davis), 335, 357–58

Tannhäuser (Richard Wagner), 122

Tarchetta, I. U., 318

Taylor, Deems, 2, 170, 171–77, 187, 243, 293; *The King's Henchman,* 166, 172–75, 234, 387; *Peter Ibbetson,* 166, 172, 174, 175–77, 387

Taylor, Elizabeth, 298–99

Taylor, Emory, 204

Taylor, Rayner: *The Aethiop; or, The Child of the Desert,* 40–41, 42, 60, 66–68, 73, 77, 385, 403n13

Teatro alla Scala (Milan, Italy), 110, 337

Teatro Reale (Rome), 174

Tecumseh, 140

Telephone, The (Gian Carlo Menotti), 246–47, 387

television, 369–74; ABC broadcasts, 279; BBC productions, 260; cable productions, 319; CBS broadcasts, 246; influence on American opera, 6; NBC broadcasts, 236, 240, 241–42, 261, 375–76; operas commissioned for, 236–37, 238–40, 241–42, 329–30, 387; pay-per-view, 259; PBS opera productions, 203, 297, 300, 324, 370, 384, 388

Tell, William, 40, 51

Telva, Marian, 177

Tempest, The (Lee Hoiby), 241, 326, 327–29, 361, 388

Temple Dancer, The (John Hugo), 165, 166, 168

Tender Land, The (Aaron Copland), 273, 275, 277, 289, 313, 375

Terradellas, Domènech, 3, 397–98n12; *Merope,* 28

Texaco, 234

theater of the grotesque, 308

Theodore Drury Opera Company, 186

Thomas, Jess, 298

Thomas, John Charles, 103, 164

Thomas, Rose Fay, 123

Thomas, Theodore, 85–86, 96, 123, 129

Thomson, Virgil, 2, 195, 206, 214–22, 230, 243, 271, 358, 368, 387

Thoreau, Henry David, 91

Tibbett, Lawrence, 135, 164, 170, 174, 175–77, 178, 182

Tick, Judith, 109

Tilghman, Amelia, 111

Titus, Alan, 331

Toch, Ernst, 361–62

Toklas, Alice B., 221

Torke, Michael, 362, 389

Toscanini, Arturo, 161, 163

Touchstone, The; or, Harlequin Traveller (Charles Dibdin), 20

Tourel, Jennie, 331

Townsend, Marie Mansfield, 111

Tozzi, Giorgio, 296

Transatlantic (George Antheil), 5, 226–28, 361, 387

La traviata (Giuseppe Verdi), 88, 226, 353

Treemonisha (Scott Joplin), 5, 189–95, 386

Treigle, Norman, 286

Trimble, Lester, 274

Tristan und Isolde (Richard Wagner), 122, 135, 172

tri-tone, 84

Triumph of St. Joan, The (Norman Dello Joio), 275

Troubled Island (William Grant Still), 4, 197, 199–204, 273, 387

Trouble in Tahiti (Leonard Bernstein), 245, 274, 317

Il trovatore (Giuseppe Verdi), 87

Tubman, Harriet, 335, 368–69

Tucker, Sophie, 200

Tulsa Opera, 271

Tunick, Jonathan, 319

Turandot (Giacomo Puccini), 139–40, 141, 300, 333

Turnbull, John: *Rudolph; or, The Robbers of Calabria,* 65

Turner, Darwin T., 195

Turner, Lana, 375

Twain, Mark, 158

Tyler, Royall, 46; *The Contrast,* 36, 42, 68; *May Day in Town; or, New York in an Uproar,* 42

Uncle Tom's Cabin (Caryl Florio), 94, 95–98

Uncle Tom's Cabin (George Aiken/George C. Howard), 94–95

University of California at Santa Barbara, 368

University of Chicago, 337

University of Georgia at Athens, 245

University of Michigan, 373

University of Pennsylvania, 24, 81. *See also* College of Philadelphia

University of Southern California, 196

Uppmann, Theodore, 331

Upshaw, Dawn, 6, 317, 389

Upton, George P., 109

Upton, William Treat, 87

urbanization, 108–9

Urban, Josef, 174

Uris Theater (New York City), 319

Utah Opera, 155–56

Valdo (Henry Lawrence Freeman), 186

Valerie; or, Treasured Tokens (James Remington Fairlamb), 89

Vanessa (Samuel Barber/Gian Carlo Menotti), 5, 291, 292, 293–97, 304, 388

van Etten, Jane, 243

van Hagen, Peter, 49

Varèse, Edgard, 179, 200

vaudeville radio, 234

Venth, Carl, 245

Verdi, Giuseppe, 5, 11, 41, 43, 56, 60, 79, 99, 106, 148, 253, 316; *Aida,* 132, 359; *Don Carlos,* 88; *A Masked Ball,* 43, 129; *Otello,* 127, 328; *La traviata,* 88, 226, 353; *Il trovatore,* 87

Very, Raymond, 356

Vienna Staatsoper, 274

View from the Bridge, A (William Bolcom), 271, 383, 384, 389

Virginia Opera Company, 368

Virginia's Ball (John Thomas Douglass), 110, 386

Virgin of the Sun (William Dunlap), 43, 51–52, 56

Voice of Ariadne (Thea Musgrave), 363, 388

Voice of Nature, The (William Dunlap/Victor Pelissier), 42, 61, 385

Volpone (George Antheil), 255

Voltaire, 317

Volunteers, The (Susanna Rowson/James Hewitt), 42, 48

von Rhein, John, 359, 362

von Stade, Frederica, 6, 317, 324, 331, 369, 371

von Stroheim, Erich, 373

Voodoo (Harry Lawrence Freeman), 184, 187–88, 207, 387

voodoo mythology, 184, 187–88, 191, 195–97, 419n30

Voyage, The (Philip Glass), 336, 343–45, 359, 389

Voyage of Edgar Allan Poe, The (Dominick Argento), 323–24, 334

Wagner, Cosima, 124, 231

Wagner craze, 121–38; American opera composers and, 125–26; reasons for, 121–22

Wagner, Richard, 4, 11, 84, 99, 106, 121, 139, 148, 172, 267, 270, 290, 295, 316, 336; *The Flying Dutchman,* 155, 322–23; *Lohengrin,* 122; *Parsifal,* 123–24, 126, 133, 146, 231, 260; *Der Ring des Nibelungen,* 19, 47, 122–23, 127, 146, 158, 174, 186, 255, 268, 270–71, 379; *Tannhäuser,* 122; *Tristan und Isolde,* 122, 135, 172

Wainwright, Jonathan Howard, 92

Wallace, Lew, 130

Wallace, Stewart, 335, 352, 356–57, 358, 360

Ward, Robert, 2, 7, 273, 275, 287, 362; *The Crucible,* 4, 6, 277, 283–86, 388

War of 1812, 66, 245

Warren, Leonard, 304

Warren, Robert Penn, 370

Washington Conservatory of Music, 197

Washington, George, 91

Washington Opera, 6, 279, 297, 321, 324, 360, 370

Wasserstein, Wendy, 389

Watt, Douglas, 283

Weaver, John, 18

Webber, Andrew Lloyd, 316, 317, 319

Weber, Karl Maria von: *Der Freischütz,* 89

Wedekind, Frank, 305

Weill, Kurt, 4, 5–6, 226, 245, 256, 308; *Street Scene,* 200, 261–63, 273, 274, 362

Weimar Republic, 226

Weinstein, Arnold, 372

Weisgall, Hugo, 305, 313, 321, 362; *Esther,* 273, 306, 335, 375–76; *Six Characters in Search of an Author,* 274, 275, 291, 292, 306–8, 322

Weiss, Julius, 190

Welles, Orson, 195, 231

Wells, Patricia, 331

Welting, Ruth, 279

West, Benjamin, 30

West Side Story (Leonard Bernstein), 317, 319

Wexley, John, 207

Wharton, Edith, 78

Wheeler, Hugh, 317, 319

White Bird, The (Ernest Carter), 207, 240, 243, 254

White, Clarence Cameron, 200, 243; *Ouanga,* 197–99, 419n30, 419n32

White House, 304

Whitely, Bessie Marshall, 110–11

Whiteman, Paul, 200, 206

Whitman, Marcus, 152–54

Whitman, Narcissa, 152–54

Whitman, Walt, 9, 91

Wiborg, Mary, 195

Wignell, Thomas, 39, 48

Wilde, Oscar, 125, 378

Wilder, Thornton, 275, 293
Willard, Frances, 109
Williamsburg Theater, 12
Williams, Margaret, 110
Williams, Tennessee, 271, 293, 326, 374, 389
Willie Stark (Carlisle Floyd), 335, 370–71
Willow Tree, The (Charles Wakefield Cadman), 149, 234
Wilson, Addie Anderson, 110
Wilson, Dolores, 278
Wilson, Lanford, 326
Wilson, Robert, 44, 217, 337, 341, 358, 388
Windsor, Frank, 113
Winona (Alberto Bimboni), 141, 142, 154–55
Winter, Charles, 112
Witch of Salem, The (Charles Wakefield Cadman), 284
Wolf-Ferrari, Ermanno, 256
Wolf Trap Park (near Washington, D.C.), 194
Wollstonecraft, Mary, 49
Woman at Otowi Crossing, The (Stephen Paulus), 156–57
women: as conductors, 112–13, 152, 154; feminism and, 49, 108, 136, 217, 220–22, 305–6, 309–10, 340; as instrumentalists, 109; as librettists, 40, 45–51, 56, 62, 111, 113, 141, 149–51, 152, 179, 268–69, 385, 387; Native American studies of, 140, 141, 150; as opera composers, 44–51, 108–17, 152, 242–45, 335–36, 363–69, 386; as performers, 109, 111; as protagonists, 126, 132–38, 142, 150–54, 267–71, 309–13, 335–36, 363–64, 367, 387–89; sexuality of, 132–38; and Wagner craze, 121
Women in the Garden, The (Vivian Fine), 363–64

Woodlanders, The (Stephen Paulus), 362
Woodworth, Samuel, 68–70, 78, 386
Works Progress Administration (WPA), 35, 231
World War I, 162–63, 308
World War II, 109, 242, 288, 310
Wozzeck (Alban Berg), 182, 233, 285, 323–24
Wright, Frank Lloyd, 335
Wuthering Heights (Bernard Herrmann), 4, 267–71, 426n24
Wuthering Heights (Carlisle Floyd), 270, 274, 290
Wyler, William, 130, 264, 268, 270

X: The Life and Times of Malcolm X (Anthony Davis), 254, 273, 335, 352–56, 388

Yale University, 354
"Yankee Doodle": in *The Contrast*, 68; in *The Disappointment*, 32
Yeats, William Butler, 329, 333
Yellin, Victor, 219, 403n13
Yiddish Theater (New York City), 160
Yoshii, Sumio, 329
Young, Eliza Mazzucato, 110
Young, La Monte, 337

Zakariasen, Bill, 379
Zazeela, Marian, 337
Zeffirelli, Franco, 298–99, 388
Zeitoper, 226
Zenobia (Louis Adolphe Coerne), 162, 386
Zenobia (Silas G. Pratt), 126, 127, 128–29
Ziegfield Theater (New York City), 161
Zululand (Henry Lawrence Freeman), 186

ELISE K. KIRK, an author, lecturer, and musicologist, is founding editor of *Dallas Opera Magazine* and coeditor of *Opera and Vivaldi*. Her articles have appeared in *Opera News, The New Grove Dictionary of Opera, American Music,* the Library of Congress *Performing Arts Annual,* and numerous other publications. Her book *Music at the White House: A History of the American Spirit* (reissued as *Musical Highlights from the White House*) received the ASCAP/Deems Taylor Award. Both books became the subject of a documentary film produced by John Goberman for PBS. She studied at the University of Michigan, Catholic University of America, and the University of Zurich and has taught at Bernard Baruch College of the City University of New York and Southern Methodist University. She has been, as a presidential appointee, a member of the National Advisory Board of the John F. Kennedy Center for the Performing Arts. Currently she teaches at Catholic University and is a member of the board of directors of the White House Historical Association.

Music in American Life

Only a Miner: Studies in Recorded Coal-Mining Songs   *Archie Green*
Great Day Coming: Folk Music and the American Left   *R. Serge Denisoff*
John Philip Sousa: A Descriptive Catalog of His Works   *Paul E. Bierley*
The Hell-Bound Train: A Cowboy Songbook   *Glenn Ohrlin*
Oh, Didn't He Ramble: The Life Story of Lee Collins, as Told to Mary
    Collins   *Edited by Frank J. Gillis and John W. Miner*
American Labor Songs of the Nineteenth Century   *Philip S. Foner*
Stars of Country Music: Uncle Dave Macon to Johnny Rodriguez   *Edited by
    Bill C. Malone and Judith McCulloh*
Git Along, Little Dogies: Songs and Songmakers of the American West
    John I. White
A Texas-Mexican *Cancionero:* Folksongs of the Lower Border   *Américo Paredes*
San Antonio Rose: The Life and Music of Bob Wills   *Charles R. Townsend*
Early Downhome Blues: A Musical and Cultural Analysis   *Jeff Todd Titon*
An Ives Celebration: Papers and Panels of the Charles Ives Centennial
    Festival-Conference   *Edited by H. Wiley Hitchcock and Vivian Perlis*
Sinful Tunes and Spirituals: Black Folk Music to the Civil War   *Dena J. Epstein*
Joe Scott, the Woodsman-Songmaker   *Edward D. Ives*
Jimmie Rodgers: The Life and Times of America's Blue Yodeler   *Nolan Porterfield*
Early American Music Engraving and Printing: A History of Music Publishing
    in America from 1787 to 1825, with Commentary on Earlier and Later
    Practices   *Richard J. Wolfe*
Sing a Sad Song: The Life of Hank Williams   *Roger M. Williams*
Long Steel Rail: The Railroad in American Folksong   *Norm Cohen*
Resources of American Music History: A Directory of Source Materials from
    Colonial Times to World War II   *D. W. Krummel, Jean Geil, Doris J. Dyen, and
    Deane L. Root*
Tenement Songs: The Popular Music of the Jewish Immigrants   *Mark Slobin*
Ozark Folksongs   *Vance Randolph; edited and abridged by Norm Cohen*
Oscar Sonneck and American Music   *Edited by William Lichtenwanger*
Bluegrass Breakdown: The Making of the Old Southern Sound   *Robert Cantwell*
Bluegrass: A History   *Neil V. Rosenberg*
Music at the White House: A History of the American Spirit   *Elise K. Kirk*
Red River Blues: The Blues Tradition in the Southeast   *Bruce Bastin*
Good Friends and Bad Enemies: Robert Winslow Gordon and the Study of
    American Folksong   *Debora Kodish*
Fiddlin' Georgia Crazy: Fiddlin' John Carson, His Real World, and the World of
    His Songs   *Gene Wiggins*

America's Music: From the Pilgrims to the Present (rev. 3d ed.)   *Gilbert Chase*

Secular Music in Colonial Annapolis: The Tuesday Club, 1745–56   *John Barry Talley*

Bibliographical Handbook of American Music   *D. W. Krummel*

Goin' to Kansas City   *Nathan W. Pearson, Jr.*

"Susanna," "Jeanie," and "The Old Folks at Home": The Songs of Stephen C.
  Foster from His Time to Ours (2d ed.)   *William W. Austin*

Songprints: The Musical Experience of Five Shoshone Women   *Judith Vander*

"Happy in the Service of the Lord": Afro-American Gospel Quartets
  in Memphis   *Kip Lornell*

Paul Hindemith in the United States   *Luther Noss*

"My Song Is My Weapon": People's Songs, American Communism, and the
  Politics of Culture, 1930–50   *Robbie Lieberman*

Chosen Voices: The Story of the American Cantorate   *Mark Slobin*

Theodore Thomas: America's Conductor and Builder of Orchestras,
  1835–1905   *Ezra Schabas*

"The Whorehouse Bells Were Ringing" and Other Songs Cowboys Sing
  Guy Logsdon

Crazeology: The Autobiography of a Chicago Jazzman   *Bud Freeman, as Told to
  Robert Wolf*

Discoursing Sweet Music: Brass Bands and Community Life in Turn-of-the-
  Century Pennsylvania   *Kenneth Kreitner*

Mormonism and Music: A History   *Michael Hicks*

Voices of the Jazz Age: Profiles of Eight Vintage Jazzmen   *Chip Deffaa*

Pickin' on Peachtree: A History of Country Music in Atlanta, Georgia
  Wayne W. Daniel

Bitter Music: Collected Journals, Essays, Introductions, and Librettos   *Harry Partch;
  edited by Thomas McGeary*

Ethnic Music on Records: A Discography of Ethnic Recordings Produced in the
  United States, 1893 to 1942   *Richard K. Spottswood*

Downhome Blues Lyrics: An Anthology from the Post-World War II Era
  Jeff Todd Titon

Ellington: The Early Years   *Mark Tucker*

Chicago Soul   *Robert Pruter*

That Half-Barbaric Twang: The Banjo in American Popular Culture   *Karen Linn*

Hot Man: The Life of Art Hodes   *Art Hodes and Chadwick Hansen*

The Erotic Muse: American Bawdy Songs (2d ed.)   *Ed Cray*

Barrio Rhythm: Mexican American Music in Los Angeles   *Steven Loza*

The Creation of Jazz: Music, Race, and Culture in Urban America
  Burton W. Peretti

Charles Martin Loeffler: A Life Apart in Music   *Ellen Knight*

Club Date Musicians: Playing the New York Party Circuit   *Bruce A. MacLeod*

Opera on the Road: Traveling Opera Troupes in the United States,
  1825–60   *Katherine K. Preston*

The Stonemans: An Appalachian Family and the Music That Shaped
  Their Lives   *Ivan M. Tribe*
Transforming Tradition: Folk Music Revivals Examined   *Edited by*
  Neil V. Rosenberg
The Crooked Stovepipe: Athapaskan Fiddle Music and Square Dancing in
  Northeast Alaska and Northwest Canada   *Craig Mishler*
Traveling the High Way Home: Ralph Stanley and the World of Traditional
  Bluegrass Music   *John Wright*
Carl Ruggles: Composer, Painter, and Storyteller   *Marilyn Ziffrin*
Never without a Song: The Years and Songs of Jennie Devlin,
  1865–1952   *Katharine D. Newman*
The Hank Snow Story   *Hank Snow, with Jack Ownbey and Bob Burris*
Milton Brown and the Founding of Western Swing   *Cary Ginell, with special*
  assistance from Roy Lee Brown
Santiago de Murcia's "Códice Saldívar No. 4": A Treasury of Secular Guitar Music
  from Baroque Mexico   *Craig H. Russell*
The Sound of the Dove: Singing in Appalachian Primitive
  Baptist Churches   *Beverly Bush Patterson*
Heartland Excursions: Ethnomusicological Reflections on Schools
  of Music   *Bruno Nettl*
Doowop: The Chicago Scene   *Robert Pruter*
Blue Rhythms: Six Lives in Rhythm and Blues   *Chip Deffaa*
Shoshone Ghost Dance Religion: Poetry Songs and Great Basin Context
  Judith Vander
Go Cat Go! Rockabilly Music and Its Makers   *Craig Morrison*
'Twas Only an Irishman's Dream: The Image of Ireland and the Irish in American
  Popular Song Lyrics, 1800–1920   *William H. A. Williams*
Democracy at the Opera: Music, Theater, and Culture in New York City,
  1815–60   *Karen Ahlquist*
Fred Waring and the Pennsylvanians   *Virginia Waring*
Woody, Cisco, and Me: Seamen Three in the Merchant Marine   *Jim Longhi*
Behind the Burnt Cork Mask: Early Blackface Minstrelsy and Antebellum
  American Popular Culture   *William J. Mahar*
Going to Cincinnati: A History of the Blues in the Queen City   *Steven C. Tracy*
Pistol Packin' Mama: Aunt Molly Jackson and the Politics of Folksong
  Shelly Romalis
Sixties Rock: Garage, Psychedelic, and Other Satisfactions   *Michael Hicks*
The Late Great Johnny Ace and the Transition from R&B to Rock 'n' Roll
  James M. Salem
Tito Puente and the Making of Latin Music   *Steven Loza*
Juilliard: A History   *Andrea Olmstead*
Understanding Charles Seeger, Pioneer in American Musicology   *Edited by*
  Bell Yung and Helen Rees

Mountains of Music: West Virginia Traditional Music from *Goldenseal*   *Edited by John Lilly*

Alice Tully: An Intimate Portrait   *Albert Fuller*

A Blues Life   *Henry Townsend, as told to Bill Greensmith*

Long Steel Rail: The Railroad in American Folksong (2d ed.)   *Norm Cohen*

The Golden Age of Gospel   *Text by Horace Clarence Boyer; photography by Lloyd Yearwood*

Aaron Copland: The Life and Work of an Uncommon Man   *Howard Pollack*

Louis Moreau Gottschalk   *S. Frederick Starr*

Race, Rock, and Elvis   *Michael T. Bertrand*

Theremin: Ether Music and Espionage   *Albert Glinsky*

Poetry and Violence: The Ballad Tradition of Mexico's Costa Chica   *John H. McDowell*

The Bill Monroe Reader   *Edited by Tom Ewing*

Music in Lubavitcher Life   *Ellen Koskoff*

Zarzuela: Spanish Operetta, American Stage   *Janet L. Sturman*

Bluegrass Odyssey: A Documentary in Pictures and Words, 1966–86   *Carl Fleischhauer and Neil V. Rosenberg*

That Old-Time Rock & Roll: A Chronicle of an Era, 1954–63   *Richard Aquila*

Labor's Troubadour   *Joe Glazer*

American Opera   *Elise K. Kirk*

Typeset in 11/13 Bembo
with Bembo display
Designed by Paula Newcomb
Composed by Jim Proefrock
at the University of Illinois Press
Manufactured by Cushing-Malloy, Inc.

University of Illinois Press
1325 South Oak Street
Champaign, IL 61820-6903
www.press.uillinois.edu